THE NEW INFORMATION
INFRASTRUCTURE

A Twentieth Century Fund Book

The New Information Infrastructure

Strategies for U.S. Policy

William J. Drake
editor

The Twentieth Century Fund Press ◆ New York ◆ 1995

The Twentieth Century Fund sponsors and supervises timely analyses of economic policy, foreign affairs, and domestic political issues. Not-for-profit and nonpartisan, the Fund was founded in 1919 and endowed by Edward A. Filene.

Library of Congress Cataloging-in-Publication Data

The new information infrastructure: strategies for U.S. policy/
    edited by William J. Drake
        p. cm.
    "A Twentieth Century Fund Book."
    Includes index.
    ISBN 0-87078-366-1
    1. Information technology–Government policy–United States.
    2. Information technology–Economic aspects–United States.
    3. Information services industry–Government policy–United States.
    4. Telecommunication policy–United States.   I. Drake, William J.
    HC110. I55N49   1995
    303.48'33–dc20   94–23937
                                                                  CIP

Cover Design and Illustration: Claude Goodwin
Manufactured in the United States of America.
Copyright © 1995 by the Twentieth Century Fund, Inc.

▌▌ FOREWORD

O ne of the distinguishing characteristics of democratic capitalism is the need for a free and reliable flow of information. Self-government is all but impossible without strong and independent sources of news; and effective markets depend on a ready supply of facts about a host of economic matters. For more than seventy-five years, the Twentieth Century Fund, an institution engaged in the study of public policy, regulation, and politics, has been interested in communications policy.

Given the media-drenched character of modern politics and government, the way journalists and their employers choose to report public issues is a matter of obvious interest to anyone seeking to comprehend the formulation of policy. Thus, during the 1990s, the Fund has sponsored a number of inquiries exploring the current and prospective circumstances of American media. They range from speculations about the future of newspapers by Howard Kurtz to discussion of the quality of presidential campaign coverage by Ken Auletta. In 1991, we asked Anthony Smith to look at some of the implications of increasing concentration of media ownership. More recently, Lewis Friedland and Richard Parker have examined the changes in international television news reporting. In addition, a Fund task force has explored the debate over the financing of public television and Lawrence Grossman has explored the electronic media in the recently released *The Electronic Republic*.

This volume, originally conceived in 1990, was actually one of the first ideas developed for the Fund's communications program. Right at the start, as we attempted to construct an agenda for new projects relating to media, politics, and governance, it became obvious that the revolution under way in communications and information technology not only generated questions of public communications policy but also would alter many of the familiar patterns of media and political interaction. We also found considerable differences in the level of understanding among policymakers and journalists regarding the potential issues raised by these changes.

Thinking of communications in this expansive sense, the Fund, led by Michelle Miller, a vice president for programs, cast a wide net, seeking advice about what the emerging issues were and, to the extent possible, what policy ought to be in this area. *The New Information Infrastructure: Strategies for U.S. Policy* is one major result of that effort. The volume represents more than the product of a series of writing assignments, for the participants met on several occasions under Fund sponsorship. They discussed the developing set of issues in this area, and monitored the ongoing intense legislative struggle in Washington. The increasing saliency of the subject created one of the major difficulties for those attempting to organize their thoughts and recommendations on paper. After all, in the course of the project, the political environment changed and then changed again.

In 1993, the Clinton administration introduced its national information infrastructure and global information infrastructure initiatives. In 1994, the 103d Congress took up but ultimately failed to enact new communications legislation. And in 1995, a newly elected Republican majority shifted the parameters of the debate, moving quickly to pass legislation.

These events underscored the importance of this investigation. Because partisan tactics and shifting alliances among interest groups dominated both the action and the press coverage, the need for accessible information about the policy issues has grown. At the same time, the sheer technical complexity of these matters has left large segments of the public in the dark about how their lives might be affected. We believe that bringing together in one volume explanations of some of the technical matters and clear descriptions of most of the policy issues serves an important public purpose. While perhaps nothing can make these discussions simple, every day we find new evidence of their potential importance to virtually all Americans. The proposed combinations of the Walt Disney Company and Capital Cities/ABC, Inc. and of Westinghouse Electric Corporation and CBS Inc. are only the most recent and sensational examples of the relentless concentration of media ownership. They also are an expression of the drive to marry companies that control the content of entertainment programs with those that control the "carriage" or delivery mechanism—a drive with implications discussed in the pages that follow.

The essays in this volume take the reader well beyond the current legislative debate. They provide essential information for understanding issues as diverse as telecommunications deregulation, privacy protection, ownership concentration, and the struggle over content. The debate over the future of the nation's information infrastructure will not end with passage of a law in 1995. The public interest coalition that formed around that legislative battle will remain intact and will continue to work for a national information infrastructure that takes into account the needs of noncommercial users. Further, the global policy issues remain largely unaddressed by current legislation.

For most of the nation's history, newspapers were a key element connecting citizens to the actions of their government. Radio and television sharply increased the timeliness of news reporting (although it is far from clear exactly what they have added to public understanding of the complexity of national issues). Today, in an era of especially swift advances in communications technology, we are in the early stages of another extraordinary change in the way many Americans transmit and receive information. In this case, as with the advent of electronic media, it is not certain how the process of governance will be affected by the spread of these new technologies. Given how much is at stake, in both money and power, it is not surprising how vigorous the debate is about what sort of policy framework should be put in place to govern the use of these systems. We hope that this volume will help Americans understand that debate.

On behalf of the Trustees of the Twentieth Century Fund, I thank these fourteen dedicated authors of these essays for their efforts.

Richard C. Leone, PRESIDENT
The Twentieth Century Fund
August 1995

▌▌ Contents

PART IV: OUTLOOK AND CONCLUSION

❙❙ Executive Summary

*T*he communications and information industries in the United States and abroad are undergoing rapid and far-reaching change. For the past several years, the Clinton administration and Congress have been engaged in efforts to forge a new national strategy for the information age. The administration's initiatives on the development of national and global information infrastructures are part of this effort, as is the sweeping communications legislation approved by the 104th Congress in mid-1995. In this volume, the Twentieth Century Fund brings together experts in communications and information to address both the current national strategy and the broader questions facing the United States. For example,

▼ Will the National Information Infrastructure (NII) be designed primarily to serve the demands of its major suppliers and corporate customers? Or will it be flexibly configured so that small businesses, nonprofit organizations, and individual users can draw on network capabilities without restrictions on access?

▼ What kinds of new policy approaches to communications regulation are needed in today's world? Should the Internet model of a decentralized and open system serve as the backbone of the NII? Is it possible to develop a mixed model of access and control—one that accommodates the aspirations of all types of users?

▼ Other countries—developing and industrialized alike—face the challenge of constructing and governing broadband information infrastructure. Does the U.S. experience or approach hold any lessons for them?

▼ As the boundaries between national economies erode with the spread of global networks, trade, and investment relations, how can countries move beyond separately and potentially incompatible NIIs to the development of a publicly accessible and fully interoperable global information infrastructure?

Questions like these are too important to be left to special interest groups, because the way communications and information industries are structured in the years ahead will affect all Americans directly. Thus, it is essential that policymakers, the press, and the interested public gain a broader awareness of the historical transformation under way and its policy implications. This volume provides the background and analysis necessary to understand the issues at stake and their future significance.

▌ ACKNOWLEDGMENTS

Michelle Miller-Adams of the Twentieth Century Fund provided extensive intellectual input, editorial guidance, and operational support at every stage of this project. Her expertise and patient management of the group's work (a task one participant likened to "herding cats") were essential to the completion of this book; we are much indebted to her. Our thanks also to Beverly Goldberg of the Fund for her careful and insightful editing of the manuscript which, among other things, forced us to scale back on industry jargon and make the discussion as accessible as possible. Finally, we gratefully acknowledge the Fund's Board of Trustees and its President, Richard C. Leone, for supporting this project.

INTRODUCTION

THE TURNING POINT

WILLIAM J. DRAKE

The good news from Washington is that every single person in Congress supports the concept of an information superhighway. The bad news is that no one has any idea what that means.
—Congressman Edward Markey[1]

We have reached a turning point in the history of communications and information. Over the next few years, the public and private sectors will make choices that will lead us rapidly down one of several possible paths to the future. Along the way, a new matrix of government policies, market structures, and technological practices will be created that will, in turn, shape the development of the industry into the next millennium. At the same time, other paths that might have been feasible may be left behind and disappear from view.

It has happened before. Since the invention of the telegraph, there have been several similar moments in the development of electronic media where the fundamental parameters of industry structure and government policy were up for grabs by competing societal interests—and where different visions of the future were in contention. In response, the federal government made decisions that effectively institutionalized new status quos in telecommunications and broadcasting that lasted for decades and that just happened to follow the paths favored by the larger and more well organized interests. Now we again have the opportunity to choose a direction for a new set of media that will have far-reaching implications for American society. But which road should we take? And how do we evaluate the options?

THE NEW INFORMATION INFRASTRUCTURE

At issue is the development and governance of a new information infrastructure. The computerized telecommunications networks, customer interfaces, services, and applications that make up the national information infrastructure (NII) of

1

today are the heart of an increasingly integrated communications and information business, which is one of the largest, most dynamic, and rapidly growing sectors in the world economy, valued domestically at $718 billion in 1993.[2] Not surprisingly, with this kind of money at stake, the emerging technologies that will define the NII of tomorrow, such as high capacity or "broadband" networks, have become the subject of much discussion and many grand schemes in the private sector. At the same time, these technologies seem to undermine the traditional rationales for the legal and regulatory separation of local and long-distance telecommunications industries on the one hand, and of the telecommunications and cable television industries on the other. Hence, with the federal government expected to liberalize its restrictions on market entry in the near future, major players like the Regional Bell Operating Companies (RBOCs), long distance telephone companies like AT&T, and the big cable systems operators are all repositioning themselves for head-on competition in an age of "media convergence." These network operators are hoping to reap a financial bonanza by providing cyberspaced couch potatoes with a multitude of movies, on-line games, and shopping services. They and other players also expect to generate significant revenues by developing new wireless personal communications systems (PCS), which will allow customers to send and receive voice and data messages wherever they are.

Manufacturers also hope to reap big profits from the new information infrastructure by building equipment for network operators and service suppliers, as well as the diverse terminals customers will need to use the anticipated explosion of on-line information resources. Software suppliers hope to thrive by providing the operating systems and applications for this hardware. Content providers like Hollywood studios and information services firms expect to be major beneficiaries—some would argue, *the* major beneficiaries—as distributors seek to fill their expanding digital pipes with product. And seemingly everyone wants to stake a claim on the Internet. The major telecommunications and cable television companies, commercial information services like America Online, software houses like Microsoft, and a host of other players want to provide access services, while thousands of large and small firms from every sector of the economy are advertising—and with the advent of digital cash,[3] will be selling directly—their products and services there as well.

But suppliers are not the only ones anticipating big benefits from the new information infrastructure. Users also hope to increase their productivity and quality of life through the application of technologies and services in a wide variety of contexts. For example, librarians want to make digitized texts, pictures, video, and sound freely available to patrons without regard to their geographical locations. Educators want to use advanced networks to provide distance education[4] to underprivileged localities and to use new multimedia systems for classroom instruction and student assignments. Health-care professionals hope to provide telemedicine services over advanced networks to far-off patients. Artists, musicians, and other creative people want to share their visions with one another and with audiences directly from their desktop computers, rather than having to go through intermediaries like studio owners. Civic activists want to foster widespread access to government information, create more immediate links between voters and their elected representatives, and develop a vital and diverse electronic public sphere in which citizens can meet to swap information and debate the issues of the day. Corporate users, such as automobile manufacturers, financial institutions, advertising agencies, and so on, want to connect their internal enterprise networks to public systems to create better linkages with suppliers, customers, and other relevant contacts. On both the supply and demand sides of the market, the list of players and plans goes on and on.

But despite all the great expectations of industry insiders and technology users, the general public remains largely unaware of exactly what is taking place. Several opinion polls conducted over the past two years indicate that a majority of the people who have heard of it think the new information infrastructure will be a "good thing," but also that they do not really know what it is. This seemingly paradoxical attitude is entirely understandable if one considers how this infrastructure has been presented in the sphere of mass communication. Television viewers are bombarded with advertisements from major firms promising that "you will" have access to dazzling multimedia services at some unspecified future date, but aren't told much more than that. Corporate hype and unexplained buzzwords may help establish brand-name recognition for new services when they finally arrive, but they do not provide citizens with an understanding of what the NII is, who will provide it on what terms, how it will be used, or what it really means for the American people.

Of course, advertisements are not public service announcements; ideally, the responsibility to provide a fuller picture of the transformation under way would fall to the press. But the television news media is too preoccupied with more sensational matters to seriously explore the issues involved in the NII. What little television coverage there is usually makes brief reference to "the much ballyhooed information superhighway" and then illustrates some new product or service under development with the same sort of eye-catching video supplied by corporate marketing departments seen in advertisements. In essence, the underlying message being conveyed is simply that new and wonderful things are on the horizon; a sense of marvel and wonderment are encouraged, but the details are presumably too complex for ordinary citizens to understand. The print media have done somewhat better. A handful of comparatively elite general-interest publications like the *New York Times*, the *Wall Street Journal*, *Business Week*, and the *Economist* have devoted serious and frequent coverage to the NII. But since this is not where most Americans get their news, it is no surprise that the general public is broadly enthusiastic yet largely uninformed. And as the quote above from one of its leading experts in the field suggests, much of Congress—which will be called upon to make critical decisions about the NII in the coming years—may be in the same boat.

Arguably, the dominant metaphor used for the NII contributes to this lack of clarity. Vice President Al Gore and other proponents have invoked the image of an "information superhighway" to fire the public's imagination, and corporate marketing departments and the press have picked up and popularized the term indiscriminately. In advertisements and news reports, seemingly every new communication product or service is presented as a being part of the super-highway, regardless of how advanced its capabilities are—or are not. Similarly, almost every news report about the NII, whether in print or on television, relies on the metaphoric highway—speed bumps, danger signs, traffic jams, road-kill, and so on—to frame the issues involved. To the average person, the men-tal image of a superhighway connotes a high-capacity system capable of carrying all kinds of traffic, be it sound, images, video, text, or a multimedia combination thereof. In this sense, the metaphor is useful. But in another sense, it may also be misleading if it leads the public to expect a single, integrated, nation-wide, and universally accessible system of wires that will take us virtually any-where we want to go. Indeed, even policymakers and industry leaders have at times found their thinking and discussions misdirected by the mental image of a superhighway.[5] One of the oddest instances occurred last year, when pre-emptive complaints from the chairman of AT&T effectively forced Vice President Gore to declare publicly that, unlike the interstate highway system, the govern-ment would not attempt to build the information superhighway—as if that had ever been on the table.[6]

THE NATURE OF INFORMATION INFRASTRUCTURE

How, then, should we think about the NII? An obvious starting point is that, from an organizational perspective, the NII is not, nor will it be, a single, integrated superhighway—rather, it is and will remain a vast collection of net-works, most of them privately owned and operated. Many of these are publicly accessible, such as the public switched telephone networks (wired and wireless), the cable and direct-broadcast satellite television networks, the Internet, and commercial computer networks like America Online, Prodigy, and CompuServe. Many others are internal enterprise networks used by large corporations and organizations, which vary in their degree of accessibility to and from public net-works. Some networks are physically interconnected and functionally interop-erable so that information can flow seamlessly from one to the next, but others are not. And a great many services are provided not by the owners of the under-lying facilities, but by separate firms that lease capacity on them or act as sys-tems integrators to draw together and customize network functionalities from different sources.[7]

In short, from a network standpoint, the NII is an extremely heterogeneous collection of local and regional information infrastructures and long-haul networks rather than one big superhighway; moreover, its component parts will be developed at different rates and organized in different ways. But what else does the NII encompass besides networks, and what technological capabilities distinguish it from the electronic media of the past?

In its September 1993 vision statement, which has played an important role in framing the debate, the Clinton administration defines the NII this way:

> The NII includes more than just the physical facilities used to transmit, store, process, and display voice, data, and images. It encompasses:

▼ A wide . . . and ever-expanding range of equipment including cameras, scanners, keyboards, telephones, fax machines, computers, switches, compact disks, video and audio tape, cable wire, satellites, optical fiber transmission lines, microwave nets, switches, televisions, monitors, printers, and much more. . . .

▼ The information itself, which may be in the form of video programming, scientific or business databases, images, sound recordings, library archives, and other media. . . .

▼ Applications and software that allow users to access, manipulate, organize, and digest the proliferating mass of information that the NII's facilities will put at their fingertips.

▼ The network standards and transmission codes that facilitate interconnection and interoperation between networks, and ensure the privacy of persons and the security of the information carried, as well as the security and reliability of the networks.

▼ The people—largely in the private sector—who create the information, develop applications and services, construct the facilities, and train others to tap its potential. Many of these people will be vendors, operators, and service providers working for private industry.[8]

The administration's definition is expansive, covering much more than a superhighway of telecommunications networks.[9] Too expansive, in fact: to return to the metaphor, it includes not only the highway, but everyone's driveways and vehicles, regardless of their technical capabilities, and the drivers as well. By this definition, my television and compact disc collection are part of the NII, and so, it seems, am I and my text.

This volume adopts a less all-encompassing definition that comes closer to the conventional understanding of an infrastructure. By information infrastructure, we mean the computerized networks, intelligent terminals, and accompanying applications and services people use to access, create, disseminate, and utilize digital information. Why digital? Because, as Brian Kahin notes, "it makes little sense to talk of an [information] infrastructure for analog information. Analog information is passively carried by a telecommunications infrastructure; digital information . . . can be logically linked and perfectly replicated and . . . (in the form of a computer program) it can organize and manipulate other digital information."[10] *Manipulate* is the key word here: From an operational standpoint, what distinguishes digital information infrastructure from the telecommunications systems of old is that computers and microelectronics in the networks and customer terminals allow us to actively (re)configure the content, representational format, and technical management of information.

This definition may still seem rather broad insofar as it includes millions of networked customer terminals. However, in using these intelligent information appliances, people are able to instruct networks to behave in different ways, thereby flexibly redefining what the networks "are" at any given time. The boundary line between networks and terminals blurs when the latter actively customizes the former to perform user-defined functions—a reality captured by Sun Microsystems' often quoted slogan, "The computer is the network." The intelligent televisions of the future (not an oxymoron, at least in terms of technical capability) will be part of the NII, but the dumb analog televisions of today, which can only passively receive signals defined by someone else, are not. Nor is a compact disc player, which, while digital, is not connected to electronic networks and does not allow the user to manipulate information beyond moving around the CD. What about the information itself, which the administration includes in its definition? While the applications and software that operate networked devices are integral components of the NII, the content generated with them is not. It is not that information content is unimportant; it is, of course, why the infrastructure matters in the first place. But from a definitional standpoint, the case for considering a videotape of *Seinfeld*, a recording by the Rolling Stones, or an image of Bill Gates on the Internet's World Wide Web as essential parts of the NII is no more obvious than the case for treating as infrastructure the people who create them.

Hence, the NII is an array of computerized networks, intelligent appliances, applications, and services that people use to interact with digital information. We already have in place today the foundation of a robust and powerful NII. But what is generating all the excitement and debate are the emerging technological capabilities that will be incorporated into that infrastructure in the near future. To varying degrees in different parts of the NII, these will include the following:[11]

▼   *Broadband Capacity.* Probably the most important and distinguishing feature of the new information infrastructure is a radical increase in the speed and carrying capacity of telecommunications networks, both wired and wireless. Fiber optics and other innovations facilitate the deployment of megabit- and gigabit-per-second networks, with terabit networking a future possibility in some connections (such as linking supercomputers). Today, broadband capacity is found primarily in certain long-distance lines; corporate enterprise networks; and specialized local-, metropolitan-, and wide-area networks (known, respectively, as LANs, MANs, and WANs) used by large organizations. Industry economics and government policy permitting, telecommunications carriers will soon deploy broadband more widely in the public switched networks we all use. Cable television networks, which already deliver analog broadband capacity to the home, could be reconfigured to relay more than video signals, ideally on a fully interactive and switched basis. These develpments would make it possible to carry all forms of information—voice, data, graphics, video—through the same pipes and to facilitate the growth of interactive multimedia services.

▼ *Data Compression.* For years it was believed that bringing broadband telecommunications networks to the home would require hundreds of billions of dollars of fiber-optic cables in the local extensions of the public networks (the "local loop"). Recent developments in compression technology, which in effect squeeze more digital information into a smaller space, may obviate that problem and allow local broadband delivery over hybrid networks scaled up from the existing physical plant.

▼ *Network Intelligence and Flexibility.* Computerization has turned telecommunications networks into software-defined information processing systems, the various functions of which can be unbundled, combined, and reconfigured to facilitate different technical operations. In the coming years, the increasing intelligence and flexibility of networks and terminals will increase the ability of service suppliers and end users alike to customize the management of on-line information resources.

▼ *Networked Computer Servers.* Data communications networks, such as those comprising the global Internet, maintain files on a variety of workstations and larger computers. Network users can upload or download the files, thereby greatly enhancing free speech and access to information on an infinite range of topics. Technical advances will allow all forms of information, including video, to be stored and made available in the same fashion. This will mean that a vast array of news, opinion, and entertainment could be retrieved on demand via personal computers, intelligent televisions, public kiosks, and other terminals.

▼ *Interactive Capabilities.* The broadband networks of tomorrow may allow users to interact with and customize information of all types, whether for educational, entertainment, or other purposes. A major outstanding question is just what level of interactivity the major network operators will build into their systems; for example, will users be able to originate as well as retrieve video and other information forms, whether for direct communication with each other or to be stored on publicly accessible servers?

▼ *Multimedia Services and Applications.* Information infrastructure adds value to existing single media transmissions such as telephone calls through special features (such as call forwarding, conference calling, and 900-number blocking) and new modes of message delivery (such as wireless PCSs that transfer calls to mobile users wherever they roam). But it also can allow the mixing of different information formats—sound, video, text, graphics—in the same transmission to be accessed on the same customer terminal. For example, users conceivably could participate in video-telephone conversations while viewing separate video images or working on a text in other windows on their screens.

▼ *Intelligent Information Appliances.* Users will access advanced networks through a variety of intelligent terminals that can be customized for different services and applications. In the home or office, this will mean increasingly powerful personal (super)computers, multimedia "telephones," and intelligent televisions with computerized set-top boxes serving as the network interface and, some believe, high definition displays. On the road, it will mean pocket-sized PCS telephones and multimedia personal digital assistants (PDAs), perhaps even with an 8 1/2 x 11 inch flat panel display.

▼ *Navigational Tools.* A major focus in the years ahead will be on the development of the software tools people need to access and manage information, such as interface applications and network directories. In the data communications world, much effort is being devoted to developing "intelligent agents" that can search the Internet and retrieve files (using customer-defined parameters, such as keywords) from anywhere in the world, presenting them to the user in a format of his or her choice. In the future, people may use personal agents to search for other types of files like digitized films or television shows (or perhaps even for portions thereof), which can be combined into customized personal programs.

THE PROMISE AND THE PROBLEM

Cumulatively, the deployment of these technological capabilities will sharply distinguish the new information infrastructure from traditional forms of electronic media. Plain old telephone service provides two-way interactive sound, but not multiple information formats, information retrieval, or one-to-many or many-to-many transmission. Broadcasting and cable television involve a one-way flow of information to mass audiences from programmers who serve as the gatekeepers to the public sphere and the arbiters of what to think about and, often, how to think about it. They decide which events are newsworthy, which ideas merit dissemination, and what constitutes entertainment. The public has no right to free speech in broadcast television and no ability to control the content or format of the information it receives; changing the channel and refusing to watch or buy are the only options. And while cable operators often provide a channel or two for public access programming, these are not well supported in terms of financing and facilities. In contrast, the new information infrastructure potentially can give users throughout society unprecedented opportunities for free expression and control over information resources. To see the possibilities, one need only look at the global Internet—the principal publicly accessible "information superhighway" of today and a central component of the broader NII of tomorrow.

One feature that distinguishes "the net" is an unprecedented degree of distributed user empowerment. Never before in the history of communication has anyone possessing relatively inexpensive household appliances—a personal computer and a modem—had such access to and control over information. Nuclear physicists, teachers and graduate students, environmental activists, florists, rock and roll bands, the gay community, Christian fundamentalists, public interest activists—*anyone* who can afford a computer and the service fees (an important caveat)—can go on-line and disseminate his or her ideas to one, thousands, or even millions of people. They can create "virtual communities" of like-minded folks around the world to debate and share information on any subject of their choosing in accordance with norms of interaction defined by the group, rather than by some outside arbiter.[12] They can venture out into cyberspace and retrieve thousands of files on an infinite range of subjects from computers located around the world, in some cases without even having to know where those computers are located physically. They can alter and combine these documents as they like, adding customized text and graphics, and share them with others for further circulation and discussion. They can advertise their products and services by creating a multimedia home page on the net's World Wide Web, which potential customers may choose to view without any broadcast-style intrusions.[13] And as more sound and video capabilities come on-line, they will be able to create and disseminate even more forms of information via the net; this could represent a growing challenge to the tariffs and revenues of the traditional telecommunications network operators.

In short, the Internet provides a glimpse of what is possible in the broader NII—a shift from the technological limitations and hierarchical corporate control of traditional media, toward a world in which, in principle, anyone can be an electronic publisher and have access to whatever information she or he desires from an infinite range of suppliers. In practice, of course, this depends on one's technical knowledge, level of interest, and ability to pay—three critical caveats. Despite its phenomenal growth in recent years of 10–15 percent per month and a rapidly expanding global population of approximately 25 million users, the net remains overwhelmingly the province of educated, reasonably well off, white males. Indeed, as Lewis Branscomb points out, the "Internet is egalitarian for those who are on it; it is elitist for those who cannot use it or do not have access to it."[14] But if, over time, the sorts of capabilities found in the Internet could be made available to a substantially wider public at affordable costs, the consequences for our culture, economy, and politics would be enormous.

Although the possibilities have been the subject of a good deal of preliminary discussion within the net community in recent years, serious thinking about their implications is really just beginning. Some analysts, however, already have been inspired to draw rather sweepingly optimistic conclusions from recent developments. For example, George Gilder, one of House Speaker Newt Gingrich's "cyber gurus," has suggested that the new technology

> will blow apart all the monopolies, hierarchies, pyramids, and power grids of established industrial society. It will undermine all totalitarian regimes. Police states cannot endure under the advance of the computer because it increases the power of the people far faster than the powers of surveillance. All hierarchies will tend to become "heterarchies"—systems in which each individual rules his own domain. In contrast to a hierarchy ruled from the top, a heterarchy is a society of equals under the law.[15]

This may sound good, but there is no innate logic to the new systems and services that will lead automatically to their widespread diffusion and adoption and then transform society. Indeed, the predicted "effects of technology," good or bad, are not even effects of the technology per se, but rather of human practices influenced by the capabilities and incentive structures existing in different contexts. Moreover, the technology itself does not point unmistakably to a single best way to configure information infrastructures and on-line resources. Distinctly different ways of organizing and using technologies are not only feasible, but have long been adopted both in the United States and abroad.[16] Technology alone will not point the way or fulfill the dreams of deliverance frequently served up in the popular press, any more than it did a decade ago when the talk was of paperless offices, cashless societies, and a supposed widespread movement of workers into high-quality knowledge jobs. Technology is socially constructed; its character and implications depend on how it is organized, supplied, accessed, and utilized in the context of corporate strategies, market structures, and public policies.

Public policy is necessarily a central part of this mix. Everywhere in the world, governments have adopted policy models that shape the overarching architecture of communications and information industries and, by extension, how their systems and services are supplied and used. Policy models comprise a nexus of interrelated principles, rules, and decision-making procedures applicable to a wide variety of issues, such as the terms of market entry, tariffs, technical standardization, property rights, content rules, and consumer protections. They are implemented through a range of different measures, including regulatory, antitrust, tax, libel, and trade policies. Historically, distinct models were applied to each media system based on its specific technological and economic properties, as well on as the configuration of political power among the stakeholders involved.

In the United States, the print model was the most permissive in terms of supply, in that anyone with the necessary funds could be a publisher, subject to some loose antitrust restrictions and content rules on copyright, obscenity, and the like. The model for public telecommunications enshrined in the Communications Act of 1934 was based on the supposed presence of natural monopoly conditions and led the government to support and protect a few dominant carriers in the hope of achieving universally accessible, nationwide networks for voice and record messages. As a trade-off, the government imposed regulations on prices and other aspects of the business and required switched network operators to act as common carriers serving all customers on a nondiscriminatory basis. Further, carriage and content were separated so that operators could provide transmission but not on-line information services. The broadcast model of the Communications Act was predicated in part on a technological bottleneck—the scarcity of frequency spectrum—with the Federal Communications Commission (FCC) acting to divide and allocate the resource among radio and television stations it licensed. This approach encouraged a complex but concentrated market structure comprising large national networks and affiliated but independently owned local stations, and imposed a selectively loose system of content regulations. Here the separation of carriage and content was not fully applied, and broadcasters, like publishers, controlled both the product and its distribution. Finally, cable television was subject to a hybrid model of rate regulations, local licensing requirements, and related measures, and network operators were left free to decide what programming feeds to carry.

The above are extremely schematic overviews of complex models that evolved and changed over time, but they are sufficient to raise two key points: First, each of the models erected at previous turning points determined how the relevant industry was structured and how its technology could be used, and each gave some stakeholders and their visions of the future advantages over others. For example, the telecommunications model allowed AT&T to acquire or force out of the market the thousands of independent telephone companies that had been launched by farmers, mutual systems, and commercial competitors between 1894 and the early 1920s. These players eventually might have succeeded in constructing a viable alternative national network of networks, perhaps with greater public accountability, but this pathway was closed off. AT&T reigned supreme for decades to follow, suppressing potential competitive entry on the supply side, while constraining customer choice on the demand side until the onset of deregulation in the late 1950s and the divestiture of 1984.[17] Similarly, the broadcast model gave away the radio spectrum—a public resource—for free to the major networks and commercial independent stations, which operated on an advertiser-supported basis, in return for only minimal and poorly enforced public service obligations. At the same time, it pushed aside an array of educational institutions, unions, churches, nonprofit organizations, and public interest groups that wanted to allocate a significant portion of the spectrum for noncommercial programming.[18] The government sided with the big money and established a commercial model that was only marginally affected by the subsequent development of public broadcasting. This model was later extended to the television industry, resulting in a vacuous domain of public information and expression that former FCC chairman Newton Minow described as a "vast wasteland." In neither case did the chosen model absolutely need to be configured as it was—the technology and markets could have been organized in other ways—but power and money talked.

Second, the models are now in the process of breaking down. Over a decade ago, Ithiel de Sola Pool predicted that the computerization of telecommunications and digitization of information would undermine their internal logics and external boundary lines.[19] This is precisely what is happening today. When broadband telecommunications networks can carry audiovisual programming, cable television networks can carry voice and data traffic with the addition of switches, and anyone with access to the Internet and related data networks can "publish" or "broadcast" messages to millions of other people, there is a growing gulf between the transactions under way and the old conceptual and regulatory approaches we have available. Similarly, the technological bottlenecks of the past like spectrum scarcity and natural monopoly conditions in local telephony and cable television are rapidly disappearing, taking with them the rationales for protecting dominant firms in order to maintain broadly accessible systems. Networks of independently operated networks tied together by transparent technical standards and providing open access for separate service suppliers could achieve the same social objectives.

In this environment of rapid and radical change, the challenge is to determine what sort of overarching policy model should be erected for the new information infrastructure. Which of our existing legal, economic, and regulatory concepts apply to its unique properties and the issues it raises; which do not; and, in these latter cases, what new concepts are necessary? Moreover, what is the proper role of government under a new model? Tele-Communications Inc. head John Malone suggests that "the government should be mainly a cheerleader,"[20] Vice President Al Gore sees it as a "Referee. Facilitator. Envisioner. Definer,"[21] while others advocate a more active role. If government—at the federal, state, and local levels—gets the answers right and finds a workable balance between market incentives and corporate accountability, the result could be an extraordinary explosion of new opportunities for wealth creation and personal empowerment across many sectors of society. If it gets it wrong, the result could be a stunted or distorted pattern of development in which the major benefits are concentrated in relatively few hands. The design of a new model for the NII thus has become the subject of an intense debate during the past few years, a debate that itself reflects the changing social organization and capabilities of communications and information technology.

THE REVOLUTION IN THE REVOLUTION

One of the most important technological developments of the twentieth century is the pervasive societal diffusion of digital information processing. Nobody could have foreseen that this would be the case when the first mainframe computers were built fifty years ago. Initially, it was believed that these room-sized monsters packed with vacuum tubes would be used for a narrow range of activities, primarily military cryptography and large-scale calculations in scientific and mathematical experiments. There was little commercial demand for "giant electronic brains," as they were often referred to, and many companies like IBM were reluctant to invest massively in their development. In what must be considered one of the most successful technology policy programs of all time, it was the federal government, and particularly the Department of Defense, that provided the cash necessary to support continuing research and development (R&D) until commercial applications were identified and demand took off.[22]

In the 1950s, the increasing power and shrinking size and cost of computers were accompanied by an expanding conception of how they could be used. Government bureaucracies and large corporations came to see that processing power could be applied to the automation of many routine functions like handling Social Security checks and employee payrolls. The horizons expanded rapidly in the 1960s and 1970s, as advances in memory capacity and digital transmission facilitated the explosive growth of file storage and retrieval and of distributed data processing within large organizations. With the rise of the personal computer and publicly accessible data communications networks in the 1980s, these capabilities became widely distributed and customized to provide an infinite range of user applications.

What this process of technological learning revealed is that the computer's true significance lies in its infinite malleability. Most technologies are fairly task specific: They are designed to perform one or a limited range of functions. In contrast, computers can be applied to literally any task that involves the electronic manipulation of information. Write some computer code, and essentially the same hardware and software functions used to manage global electronic networks in the banking or automobile industries can be drawn on to produce video games, virtual realities, multimedia services, and political advertisements with morphing candidate faces. And they can be incorporated into other complex technical systems—such as satellites, military command-and-control networks and weapons, automated offices and factories, electrical power generators, medical technologies, and so on ad infinitum—in ways that radically expand these systems' capabilities and lead to synergistic cycles of further innovation.

The phenomenal advances that have taken place in microelectronics over recent years is an essential part of this story. Moore's Law states that the processing power of the microchip doubles at least every eighteen months; as more and more sophisticated circuits are densely packed into their silicon, chips themselves have become tiny but incredibly powerful computers that vastly outperform the room-sized mainframes of years past. Indeed, as Richard Solomon notes:

> The personal computer is *not* the computer—the computer is a small chip inside, along with its memory, and the hardware to get signals in and out of these chips. The rest is ancillary. The physical manifestation of computation is bound to change dramatically in the future as it has in the past—from gigantic Rube Goldberg-looking machines with less power than a digital wristwatch of today, to a wide variety of computational appliances of which the personal computer is only one familiar element.[23]

Digital information processing of varying scales and complexity is built into not only large-scale technical systems and production processes, but also an enormous range of smaller machines like microwave ovens, banks' automated teller machines, cash registers, consumer electronics, credit cards, and so on. This widespread diffusion of information processing normally goes unnoticed in daily life—few people stop to think about what is happening when they use an automated teller machine or order a pay-per-view program, much less where their data go and who can access it—but this is a pervasive aspect of contemporary society.

Advances in digital processing not only have facilitated a proliferation of intelligent appliances, but also have profoundly transformed the networks to which they are often connected. To simplify, telecommunications networks historically employed mechanical and later electromechanical and electronic switches to route calls between destinations, carried the low-speed analog transmission of a limited range of basic services through copper wires and microwave relays, and provided customer access through a few specialized terminals such as telephones or telegraph and telex machines. But beginning in the late 1950s, computerization swept progressively across these and other network elements, radically increasing their capacity, speed, accuracy, and flexibility. The big central office switches of the major network operators became advanced computers capable of managing and routing huge quantities of differentiated service traffic with varying bandwidth requirements. New transmission media like satellites, fiber-optic cables, and cellular telephony became available. The range of user terminals exploded, with fax machines, wireless telephones, pagers, and computers (to give just a few examples) becoming woven into the information fabric. And with the incorporation of information processing into all their components, networks were able to carry a vastly increased range of services, from facsimile and video-conferencing to high-speed data communications and beyond.

What does this mean for the NII debate? First, digital processing is obviously the foundation of the new technological capabilities mentioned above—expanding bandwidth, interactivity, multimedia services, and so on—and it will make possible many further advances in the years to come. Indeed, for all the headline-grabbing developments of late, we are really just on the cusp of another wave of tremendous technological change. Second, one reason for this is that, together with the liberalization of the telecommunications industry, the spread of data processing is diversifying the social organization of electronic information resources. James Beniger has noted that the postwar information revolution must be viewed as a control revolution, in that the expansion of computerization was driven by the desire of large organizations to exercise greater control over their internal operations and external environments.[24] What must be added to this observation is that the locus of control has shifted somewhat in recent years.

Computers and advanced telecommunications used to be the sole province of a relatively small number of large organizations. On the supply side of the markets, there were AT&T, IBM, and a handful of lesser firms. On the demand side, there were government agencies like the Department of Defense and the big corporate users like major banks, oil companies, and airlines, all of which had the money, technical expertise, and need to run enterprise-wide management information systems and automated production processes. However, the interests of these suppliers and users were not fully compatible. In the late 1950s, as corporate users began to buy computers and link them together via leased circuits to create advanced private networks and services, they found that restrictive AT&T practices and FCC policies limited their freedom to configure these as they pleased. In consequence, corporate users formed a potent political alliance with the computer industry and telecommunications upstarts seeking market entry to push successfully for liberalization of the United States' domestic and international markets.[25]

The erosion of AT&T's absolute dominance over the next few decades progressively opened up more and more niches for a multitude of new system and service suppliers, while greatly expanding the competitive incentive to innovate in emerging markets. In the 1980s, this process of relative decentralization broadened and deepened enormously with continuing economic and institutional changes, such as the breakup of AT&T and the comparative decline of IBM. At the same time, technological trends like the spread of personal desktop computing and the mass popularization of the Internet meant that millions of people now had both the technical capabilities and the incentive to experiment with information resources, to learn by doing, and to create commercial and noncommercial products, services, and applications that had not been conceived of by the big firms. As a result, the United States developed the most dynamic, heterogeneous, multivendor, and user-driven communications and information industries in the world. (It should be noted that these changes were a mixed blessing: Massive layoffs by big corporations as workers were replaced with technology, the increasing marginalization of unskilled labor, the invasion of personal privacy, and a host of other problems accompanied the shift to a more competitive and market-driven communications and information environment.)

To describe this transformation, Peter Cowhey has distinguished between what he calls the oligopoly revolution and the distributed revolution.[26] The terms capture the character of the shift, but could be misinterpreted to mean that the forces of oligopoly have dissipated in the current era. Instead, one could say that the information economy now has an oligopoly sector and a distributed sector, with neither fully characterizing the entire digital landscape. The oligopoly sector is the land of the giants: on the supply side, firms like AT&T, MCI, Sprint, the RBOCs, the broadcast networks and big cable television companies, IBM, Apple, Intel, Microsoft, Time Warner, Gannett, and the Hollywood studios; on the demand side, big users like Citicorp, American Express, General Motors, American Airlines, Cargill, Boeing, and so on. In each of their respective industries, these firms have the power to set the broad trends to which everyone else must respond. Their changing strategies of competition and cooperation in the convergent world of electronic media will be central to the development of the NII. The distributed sector, in contrast, is a land populated by thousands of small- and medium-sized firms providing customized telecommunications and information services and equipment, systems integration, software, independent films, multimedia products, and the like. It is also the land of millions of individual users and small organizations, in both the private and nonprofit sectors, who have discovered how to employ powerful but increasingly inexpensive technologies, services, and applications to do their jobs better, expand their intellectual horizons, and participate in the digital age.

This growth and differentiation of stakeholders has many consequences, three of which are important here. First, the oligopoly and distributed sectors coexist in a relationship that is alternately mutually fruitful and uneasy, depending on the circumstances. Small users and suppliers may at times benefit from the plans and products of the RBOCs, Microsoft, and other giants, but they are not always happy with the pressures and constraints these impose on them. Conversely, the big players may at times benefit from the smaller ones' actions, but these can also present a challenge to their dominance, as the experience of IBM suggests. Second, denizens of the two sectors often have different visions of how the NII should be organized and governed. Major players like the RBOCs and cable television companies believe that if they are going to spend huge sums of money—billions of dollars, in some cases—to develop the new information infrastructure, they ought to be able to configure it as they see fit in order to maximize their own revenue streams. But many in the distributed sector fear that without adequate safeguards, this could result in concentrated market power, inflexible networks, limited choices, and no public interest protections. Third, and as a consequence, government is faced with the daunting task of finding an equitable and effective balance between the two sides, not just because it is the right thing to do, but because it is the distributed sector that has been the main source of dynamism and innovation in recent years—a vitalizing role it could continue to play in the information economy of tomorrow. The problem is that, thus far, government has failed to find that balance.

THE NII DEBATE

The NII debate actually consists of two separate but interrelated dialogues.[27] The first is an often heated argument and struggle for position among the big suppliers in the oligopoly sector. This is the debate that has attracted most of the press coverage and attention on Capitol Hill. The second is an equally lively discussion within the distributed sector about how to build an open and participatory NII. This debate has found friendly ears in the Clinton administration and among a few leading members of Congress.

The oligopoly debate is, above all, about how to develop a fully commercialized NII that will generate big money while eliminating "government interference." Most of the major suppliers agree in principle that accelerating liberalization and increasing competition should be the major focus of a new policy framework and they have promoted that view in innumerable conferences, meetings with government officials, press releases, position papers, and the like.[28] However, in practice, they often disagree—sometimes sharply—on precisely how and when this should be achieved.

Some market participants worry that when the barriers between industries erected by the old policy models are removed, their new competitors will have an unfair advantage on an unlevel playing field. Hence, they file endless lawsuits to challenge each other's market entry plans and are seeking support through the legislative and regulatory processes by intensive lobbying and public relations campaigns. The principal fault lines have been between the RBOCs, the long-distance carriers, and the cable television networks. However, these may be just the tip of the iceberg, below which lie a host of other divisions associated with the convergence of once separate industries into an integrated digital marketplace. For example, broadcasters and information service providers could be threatened by the entry of telecommunications carriers into content markets or by the construction of closed networks, while small software vendors and manufacturers could similarly lose out if the set-top box connecting televisions to broadband pipes has a closed architecture.[29] These natural competitive tensions often translate into preferences regarding NII rules. Beyond such wars of position, a number of other, usually less divisive, issues also have been important parts of the corporate debate, such as the need for tax incentives for investments, new intellectual property protections, enhanced network security, and so on.

The distributed debate, as its name implies, is substantially broader and more diverse. Its participants are exceedingly heterogeneous, including the research and education communities, librarians, religious institutions, advocates for minorities and the disabled, consumer groups, civil libertarians, labor unions, community activists, public interest groups, artists, foundations, and small businesses. They have technical expertise, direct stakes in the NII, and strong ideas about how it should be organized and governed. One need only log onto the Internet and visit some of the many relevant discussion groups to see this and to realize how unusual it is in historical perspective. Frequently arcane issues that once were debated only among specialists in narrow industry, government, and academic circles—from the costs and benefits of different tariff schemes, network configurations, technical standards, data encryption systems, and software applications, to the implications for consumers, personal privacy, and popular culture—have become the daily fare of freewheeling public discussions as the lines between telecommunications policy and personal computing blur. Like the oligopoly sector, these players hold conferences and issue position papers (both of which are generally ignored by the mainstream press), and they go out and beat the bushes of government agencies and legislatures at all levels in the hope of getting a fair hearing.

Like the coalition that fought unsuccessfully for some noncommercial broadcast spaces in the radio spectrum sixty years ago, they support private sector development of the NII. Most favor varying degrees of liberalization and enhanced competition on the presumption that this could lower prices and increase consumer choice. However, many worry that adopting a purely commercial model in which corporate giants do entirely as they please without any accompanying obligations could distort the NII's development and stifle creativity and innovation. For example, they are concerned that the big network operators will not provide universal access to advanced services at affordable rates; will construct closed networks that do not allow any customer to access any service supplier or to communicate seamlessly with customers on other networks; will not provide for the sort of public, educational, and government services that contribute to a vital civic sector; or will limit the amount of interactivity in their systems to the minimum required for home shopping, electronic games, and purchasing video on demand—in short, a new vast (cyber) wasteland of pay-per-view drivel—rather than the fully interactive broadband multimedia capabilities needed for users to originate and distribute information on a switched basis.

These and many other concerns go well beyond those of traditional consumer activism in telecommunications, which largely involved pushing for affordable telephone rates. What distributed sector participants are variously advocating (not everyone agrees on every point) is some type of mixed model that gives firms sufficient incentives to build networks and provide new services, but that also allows other stakeholders to use the technology creatively. In considering this question, many in the distributed sector are heavily influenced by the Internet model. Beyond empowering users to seamlessly access and communicate all kinds of information without artificial restrictions, as discussed above, the Internet's organization also presents some interesting lessons for the broader NII. For example, the Internet is not centrally controlled, but instead comprises thousands of separate networks that have adopted transparent computer protocols to ensure their interoperability; the networks do not engage in the sort of costly and cumbersome revenue division practices found in the mainstream telecommunications world; the access market is reasonably competitive; the Internet's usually flat rates (that is, not usage sensitive) encourage rapid growth, experimentation, and the vigorous development of new services and applications; and its organizational structure means that decisions on issues like technical standardization are made through democratic and participatory procedures.[30] (However, the Internet's total lack of regulation, which has been essential to its dynamism and culture, would be disastrous if applied to the entire NII.)

What is especially noteworthy about the distributed debate is that it transcends the typical categories and battle lines of public policy fights. It is not about liberals versus conservatives; a broad spectrum of ideological views are involved. Nor is it about whether government is intrinsically good or evil; the focus is more pragmatic and involves defining flexible rules and incentives that will accommodate the broadest possible range of interests, while eliminating those regulations and restrictions that are now plainly outdated. And, as François Bar has suggested, it is not about charity and hand outs. The point of creating an open, flexible, and participatory infrastructure is that it can encourage learning, innovation, and productivity by small businesses, teachers and students, artists, and other segments of society.[31] Hence, many denizens of the distributed sector find it difficult to see how the libertarian vision of "demassified" individual empowerment and community development advanced by George Gilder and others can be achieved simply by adopting a libertarian, free-market model for the NII.[32]

The debate has now been joined in the halls of government. Many municipal and state governments are struggling—often with inadequate resources—to define approaches to information infrastructure suited to their local conditions and constituent needs. Some, in fact, have managed to launch rather promising initiatives. But the big unknown remains federal policy, which will strongly affect their plans. Having come to power stressing the importance of infrastructures to national economic competitiveness and social objectives, the Clinton administration launched an ambitious NII initiative in 1993. Under the leadership of Vice President Gore, it has moved on the multiple fronts of technology, telecommunications, education, training, and other policies in an attempt to establish a comprehensive yet flexible national strategy. It has attenuated the executive branch bureaucratic rivalries and turf battles that have marred telecommunications policy in the past by creating an interagency Information Infrastructure Task Force (IITF); created an advisory council to the IITF comprising representatives of the oligopoly and distributed sectors; held conferences and informal meetings with a broad cross-section of stakeholders;

generated numerous studies and documents on a wide variety of key NII issues; and made these documents, as well as the reports of IITF meetings and much else, freely available over the Internet. From a procedural standpoint, this is undoubtedly the most open and participatory federal telecommunications policy process in history, for which the administration deserves much credit. But from a substantive policy standpoint, it has thus far failed to balance fully the competing interests at stake or to address adequately many of the more difficult issues associated with the NII.

These problems have been even more evident in the Congress. While there is much the administration can do through the FCC and other executive branch agencies under existing statutes, establishing an overarching policy model for the NII requires major legislative reform. The fundamental framework of federal policy remains the Communications Act of 1934, the concepts and rules of which are now wildly outdated. In 1994, Congress took up the challenge, holding hearings and considering multiple pieces of legislation on everything from technology and competitiveness policies to telecommunications and information policies.

The main action surrounded three bills, two in the House and one in the Senate, which would have, inter alia, removed the legal barriers between local and long-distance telecommunications markets on the one hand, and between telecommunications and cable television markets on the other.[33] In both cases, the sponsors and their fellow committee members solicited the views of representatives of both the major corporations and the nonprofit and public interest groups, and some of the latter's concerns were actually translated into legislative provisions. However, as the process unfolded, corporate lobbying and the usual politics of money took over and many of these provisions were watered down or deleted entirely.[34] At the same time, network operators failed to find a mutually satisfactory compromise on the terms of competition and some were troubled by the micromanagement that legislators built into the bills when searching for one. In the end, the House managed to pass its version during the summer, but the more controversial Senate counterpart was killed in the fall amid opposition from the RBOCs and pre-election partisan politics.

The whole process has begun again in the 104th Congress. The pressure to pass legislation is intense, as key segments of the private sector are hesitant or unable to take their investment plans from the drawing board to the market until the rules of the game have been clarified. In line with the positions staked out at the end of the last session, the new Republican majority is pushing for more rapid and thorough deregulation, while deleting the remaining public interest provisions. An oligopoly-oriented policy model for an increasingly distributed era appears to be in the offing. In the process, the more difficult and complicated issues associated with the transition to a new NII could go unattended. The 1995–96 congressional session is therefore witnessing a major struggle that will continue in subsequent policy debates, and lobbyists for the business community, the nonprofit sector, and public interest groups are all involved in the fight.

STRATEGIES FOR U.S. POLICY

Although we are at a turning point in the history of communications and information, it would be overly dramatic to characterize it as a single moment of
reckoning. But if the history of previous turning points is any indication, the
decisions made over the next year or two will lay the foundation of a new policy architecture that will, in turn, shape the way information infrastructure is
supplied and used in the years to come. Although some tinkering around the
edges will be possible down the road to correct small missteps and unanticipated consequences, this fundamental architecture will not be easy to change
once major plans and investments are put into place by the private sector. It is
therefore imperative to decide now the direction in which we want to move—
down the path toward a commercialized NII that is geared largely to the interests
of the oligopoly sector alone, or toward a mixed model that disperses the benefits across a wider range of stakeholders in the interest of a broad-based,
dynamic, and equitable information economy.

The NII debate clearly needs to be broadened. Procedurally, a wider range
of stakeholders should be at the table. How the new information infrastructure
will be structured, and to what ends, are issues that ultimately will affect all
Americans—whether as workers, consumers, or citizens—either directly or indirectly. As with health-care reform, these issues are too important to be left to
industry insiders and must be discussed and decided democratically. Moreover,
the debate should be broadened substantively as well. There are many important issues that have not received serious enough attention in the policy process
and that must be addressed if we are to devise a comprehensive yet flexible
national strategy.

The purpose of this volume is to shed some light on these issues. Given the
state of flux in the relevant technologies and markets, it was not possible to
trace the minutiae of corporate deals being made and unmade on a nearly daily
basis, or to explore the ins and outs of each piece of legislation that has failed
to pass Congress. Indeed, during the time it took to move this large project
from beginning to end, the media business and the legislative process went
through so many convulsions that any such book would have risked being outdated upon publication. What we have tried to do instead is step back from
the trees and consider the forest—that is, to focus on the broad contours of the
historical transformation under way and its implications for U.S. domestic and
foreign policies regarding information infrastructure. And rather than presenting
a technical report accessible primarily to beltway insiders and industry specialists, we have attempted to frame the issues in a manner accessible to general readers in the belief that it is important to help expand public awareness of
these critical issues.

As will be evident, the participants in this project generally agreed on the
main analytical points. There was a strong consensus that, despite all the current innovations making headlines, we are really only at the beginning of further

waves of radical change in communication and information technology. Further, the group agreed that the application of networks and information resources is having major effects on the behavior of firms and markets in user industries and, by extension, on the character of the economy as a whole. The group also agreed that in many ways we are just beginning to understand the implications of these trends and that something on the order of a paradigm shift will be necessary to grasp the magnitude of the transformation to a global information economy. There also was consensus that this conceptual lag plays a role in sustaining important policy lags and that, in some respects, government institutions and programs inevitably will remain somewhat behind the curve. Finally, there was strong support for the sort of broad design principles that the Clinton administration has set forth—including the importance of open networks and flexible customer interfaces, ensuring a pluralistic multinet-work architecture, establishing fair competition between major suppliers, creating privacy protection, and empowering small users and suppliers—mixed with some disappointment in the lack of specifics and follow-through. However, like the participants in the broader national debate, the group disagreed at times on the precise role of government in attempting to realize these goals.

THE NEW POLICY ENVIRONMENT

A national strategy must correspond to the new policy environment, so we begin here by considering the forces unleashed by the information revolution and institutional change. Communications and information are important and lucrative industries in their own right, but their real significance derives from their pervasive roles in other sectors of the economy and society. Telecommunications is a key infrastructure underlying and tying together virtually all domains of economic activity. Every company and industry across the agricultural, manufacturing, and services sectors is dependent on networks, so much so that these frequently are described as the "nervous system" of the national and global economies. In parallel, information is the essential building block of human decision making and activity and a key factor of production in every process, product, and service. Changes in the technology, strategic management, and institutional organization of telecommunications and information therefore have direct multiplier effects across user industries and, cumulatively, on the economy as a whole. It is precisely because of such intensive and extensive effects that we may speak of an "information revolution" that, like the agricultural and industrial revolutions before it, involves large-scale economic and social transformation. This is not to suggest that we have entered a "postindustrial" era in which the manufacturing of physical products no longer matters, nor that we have entered an age of blissful enlightenment that will be free from social divisions, as some pop futurologists seem to suggest. But it does mean that we are living in an information-intensive economy that is dynamic, privately controlled, and increasingly global.

In Chapter 1, Eli Noam of Columbia University assesses the process of telecommunications liberalization that has been a driving force in the transition to an information economy. To set the context for readers new to this field, Noam surveys the history of liberalization in the United States and argues that, on the whole, its proponents turned out to be more accurate in predicting its consequences for the industry than were its critics. The unleashing of market forces lowered prices and increased productivity, research and development, network flexibility, and customer choice without undermining universal service—although it also resulted in massive layoffs of workers by the formerly protected carriers. To place this experience in a larger context, he assesses the uneven pace of liberalization in other industrialized countries and finds that, despite the changes of the past decade, public operators retain near monopoly powers in many key markets, which will in turn translate into rather different NIIs abroad. As for the United States, Noam argues that the continuing process of decentralization and devolution will undermine the power of some dominant operators and throw into question the traditional common carrier policy model. In the future NII, power will shift increasingly to agile "systems integrators" that draw on and add value to unbundled network functionalities to meet the specialized requirements of customers. The movement from a network of networks to a "system of systems," he suggests, will require new thinking about how to preserve universal service, interconnection, and the free flow of information.

In Chapter 2, François Bar of the University of California at San Diego underscores that just as the industrial revolution did not do away with the agricultural sector, the information revolution has not done away with the manufacturing sector. Contrary to the popular concept of "postindustrialism," manufacturing industries remain centrally important in the global information economy, but their mode of organization has changed radically. Large firms have moved from the old Fordist model of mass producing homogeneous products from a fixed technological base to a post-Fordist model of mass producing customized products from a flexible, software-defined technological base. The use of private information infrastructure has been central to the renewed competitiveness of major manufacturers, and smaller firms should have access to the same sorts of capabilities. Bar warns that a closed, inflexible, and inequitable infrastructure would deny small businesses the applications and services they need to remain a vital source of employment and economic growth in the future.

In Chapter 3, Linda Garcia of the Office of Technology Assessment of the U.S. Congress offers her personal view on another key aspect of the information economy—its increasingly worldwide scope. Over the past few years, globalization has become a favorite buzzword in policy circles and a managerial rallying cry in the business community. Nonetheless, precisely what the concept means and how it can be demonstrated empirically are not always clear. Garcia examines two types of globalization—the geographical scope of systems and services and the domain of people who have access to them—and argues that these are often in conflict. The globalization of firms, markets, and technologies imposes a variety of new constraints on governments and national sovereignty and does not necessarily promote broader public access to information infra-structure. Like Bar, Garcia cautions against the risks of fragmentation and argues for a policy approach that balances commercial and social objectives.

Beyond the economic and institutional issues covered above, the new policy environment is also characterized by rather remarkable, if sometimes complicated, technological changes. In his challenging appendix to Part I, Richard Solomon of the Massachusetts Institute of Technology rounds out the first section of the book with an overview of the main trends in intelligent digital networks and information appliances. He argues that the dynamism of information processing and the logic of broadband networks may undermine somewhat the power of the major network operators—a view that echoes the institutional analysis provided by Noam. Moreover, Solomon maintains that these forces will inevitably make it difficult for government to formulate coherent regulatory policies that are up to speed with the pace of change.

POLICIES FOR THE NATIONAL INFORMATION INFRASTRUCTURE

Against this backdrop, the second section of the book examines more specific policy issues involved in the NII. In Chapter 4, Henry Geller of the Markle Foundation surveys the fragmented American telecommunications policymaking apparatus that divides authority over the issues among a wide variety of institutions with sometimes disparate interests and internal dynamics. A former general counsel at the FCC who has experienced the process from the inside, Geller argues that this longstanding pattern of (dis)organization is increasingly antiquated and inadequate to the task of formulating comprehensive and coherent national strategies for the NII. The federal government must move quickly to rationalize the lines of authority, preferably by consolidating functions in a new executive branch agency.

In Chapter 5, Lee McKnight of the Massachusetts Institute of Technology and W. Russell Neuman of Tufts University turn our attention to the technology policy aspects of the NII. The authors begin by arguing that the long-running debate about whether to adopt technology policies is besides the point, as the U.S. government has in fact had them for some time. Moreover, the American model is uniquely well suited to the development of a pluralistic and flexible NII—a thesis they support via case studies of high-definition technology and the Internet. In contrast, they show how the more centralized technology policies employed by our major trade competitors in Japan and Europe may be less appropriate for information infrastructure. They conclude that it is essential for the United States to maintain and expand its flexible technology policy approach if we are to foster dynamic innovation and a diverse NII.

In Chapter 6, Herbert Dordick, a visiting professor at the University of California, San Diego, surveys some of the difficult and conflictual issues that are rarely broached in press coverage of the NII debate. Dordick believes that the liberalization and growing corporate control of communication and information has raised serious social problems that the Clinton administration and Congress must address. Competitive market forces alone will not promote universal access to the NII; new and flexible forms of regulation and financing are required. Similarly, the corporate control and commodification of personal information poses a huge threat to citizens' rights; to address this, the government should create an independent national privacy protection commission. Finally, the transition to an information economy has been accompanied by massive job losses as firms substitute technology for labor; the government must develop a new Technology Extension Service for worker retraining if it wishes to make up some of the lost ground.

POLICIES FOR THE GLOBAL INFORMATION INFRASTRUCTURE

The third section of the book turns from the domestic to the international arena, which has received woefully inadequate attention in the U.S. policy debate thus far. At issue here is the development of a global information infrastructure (GII) in cooperation with governments, corporations, and user communities around the world. Thus far, U.S. foreign policymakers have concentrated largely on the oligopoly sector's concerns with winning access to markets and securing intellectual property rights abroad, rather than on some of the larger issues and possibilities involved in developing a publicly accessible GII. The section addresses these issues in both the bilateral and multilateral policy contexts.

In Chapter 7, Peter Cowhey of the University of California at San Diego (currently a senior counsellor at the FCC) provides an extensive and detailed assessment of U.S. trade relations with the other industrialized countries and their implications for the future of the global marketplace. Cowhey begins by elaborating his distinction between the oligopoly and distributed revolutions mentioned above, then goes on to argue that U.S. policymakers have not caught up with the dynamics of the latter. Our bilateral and multilateral trade postures vis-a-vis Europe and Asia in particular are steeped in outdated assumptions and geared toward supporting the market access demands of a small number of transnational corporations. Cowhey urges a range of specific reforms in trade strategy and tactics and suggests that while the government should continue to promote liberalization abroad, it must do so with an eye toward the interests of the nexus of smaller players that has energized our domestic market.

In Chapter 8, we shift from U.S. relations with the industrialized world to relations with the developing world. Bruno Lanvin of the United Nations Conference on Trade and Development (UNCTAD) addresses the growing division of the international community into the "information rich" and "information poor." He argues that the globalization of the information economy has been highly fragmented. Moreover, allowing the Third World to fall further and further behind will have dangerous economic, social, and political effects that are in the industrialized world's interest to avoid. But rather than reiterating the

traditional prescription that the North should transfer massive amounts of financial aid to the South, Lanvin offers a range of more pragmatic, targeted, and
workable suggestions. In particular, he stresses the importance of providing
technical assistance to governments in reforming their domestic communication and information institutions and promoting "trade efficiency" through the
development of electronic data interchange, which will enhance Third World
competitiveness.

The next three chapters turn from U.S. relations with particular countries
and regions to its approach to international institutions. In Chapter 9, Anthony
Rutkowski of the Internet Society presents a provocative and controversial examination of the traditional multilateral policy apparatus centered in the
International Telecommunication Union (ITU) and the International Telecommunications Satellite Organization (INTELSAT). Rutkowski maps the historical
development therein of the international regimes for telecommunications, spectrum management, and satellite services, arguing that these intergovernmental
arrangements are essentially atrophied, anticompetitive, and counterproductive cartels that impede rather than promote the development of global networks and services. In a dynamic and market-oriented GII, the U.S. government
and its counterparts must reexamine fundamentally their approaches to multilateral coordination and rely more on flexible private sector arrangements in
which users, rather than entrenched dominant suppliers, set the direction. He
concludes that U.S. participation in codifying international rules with foreign
governments should concentrate primarily on the radio regime for spectrum
management and the emerging trade in services regime.

In Chapter 10, Joel Reidenberg of Fordham University shifts the focus from
global networks to the information that flows through them. He maintains that
there is a huge and growing gap in the mechanisms of international cooperation
that, Rutkowski's argument to the contrary, requires greater government involvement. He shows how in two specific areas—the transborder flow of personal
information and the protection of intellectual property rights—the United States
frequently has been on the wrong side of the issue. Over the past decade, the
U.S. government has worked hard to kill all multilateral efforts to develop international privacy protection because of strenuous and self-interested lobbying by
large corporations. In the process, the interests of ordinary citizens here and
abroad were ignored. Similarly, the United States has complicated several
efforts to develop consensual international rules for intellectual property
because they did not serve the maximum agendas of American firms.
Reidenberg sees the U.S. approach as conceptually outmoded and insufficient
in a GII environment. Finally, echoing Henry Geller's chapter, Reidenberg argues
that responsibility for these issues is too fragmented among different government agencies and that institutional consolidation is a necessary first step
toward a more balanced approach to global information flows.

In Chapter 11, Kalypso Nicolaïdis of Harvard University shifts from the sectoral organization of carriage and content to an analysis of the broader trade

framework into which they increasingly will be incorporated in the years to come. She begins by providing a detailed overview of the General Agreement on Trade in Services (GATS) concluded in April 1994 as part the Uruguay Round accords, then assesses its implications for telecommunications, information, and the GII. The GATS, she maintains, is only a first step in a long-term process of bringing the over $1 trillion market for international services transactions under the discipline of trade mechanisms. In the years to come, the trade in services process will have to move into some far more complicated and divisive areas than it has in the past, addressing questions of domestic regulation and global competition policies. However, such efforts will generate substantial controversy, particularly where cultural issues are concerned.

OUTLOOK AND CONCLUSION

The last section of the book provides an overview of where we are today in the information infrastructure policy process and suggests some general directions for U.S. strategy. In Chapter 12, I discuss the major issues, interests, and congressional legislation involved in the NII debate between 1993 and early 1995. The chapter begins with an overview of the Clinton administration's initiative, which constitutes a substantial improvement in executive branch policy on electronic media in several important respects. The second part of the chapter outlines the positions of powerful corporate stakeholders regarding the design of a new policy model for the NII, emphasizing the disagreements over the terms of convergence between once separate lines of business that have defined much of the debate. The third part covers the new public interest coalition's efforts to promote an alternative, mixed policy model that would facilitate both commercial and noncommercial uses of the NII. The fourth part of the chapter walks through the principal legislative reforms taken up in the 103d and 104th Congresses. It suggests that, whereas the Democratic majority of 1993–94 was generally on the right track, the new Republican majority is moving the nation sharply in the wrong direction on many of the key issues.

The volume's Conclusion synthesizes the principal policy recommendations suggested by the participants in the project. A "top forty" list of recommendations lays out a progressive approach to some of the most pressing issues. For the NII, priorities include the promotion of open broadband networks, media diversity, real competition in all major market segments, and the accommodation of both commercial and noncommercial stakeholders and uses. For the GII, priorities include a balance between global liberalization and diverse national interests, greater flexibility in the major international communications regimes, the reform of multilateral institutions, and the removal of artificial barriers to the expansion of today's GII—the Internet.

PART I

THE NEW POLICY ENVIRONMENT

1

Beyond Telecommunications Liberalization: Past Performance, Present Hype, and Future Direction

Eli M. Noam

*T*he first American telegraph message, sent from Baltimore to Washington in 1844, was "What hath God wrought?" The same question was being asked a century and a half later about the effects of liberalization on telecommunications. Finding the answer requires looking at three issues: (1) What is the empirical record of liberalization policy in telecommunications? In the United States, it has been generally positive while in many other countries, where liberalization is only a fairly modest reality, it is too early to tell. (2) What is the record of *prognostication* of the impacts of liberalization? Here the answer is mixed, and predictions were frequently at odds with the unfolding reality. The best predictive record is held by those in favor of deregulation but willing to intervene structurally to reduce monopoly power. (3) What is the future likely to hold? How will the trend of liberalization work itself out?

I argue that the central institutions of future telecommunications will not be carriers but systems integrators that mix and match transmission segments, services, and equipment, using various carriers. What will be the policy agenda in such a telecommunications environment? Liberalization of telecommunications will not mean libertarianism. There will be no "end of history" in telecommunications policy. The new issues will be those of integrating the emerging "network of networks," and the postderegulatory policy agenda will be conceptually and politically complex. Liberalization, in fact, may prove to have been the easy part. Fashioning new tools to deal with its consequences, while protecting traditional policy goals in the new environment, will be the next and more difficult challenge.

WHAT IS LIBERALIZATION?

In the recent past, telecommunications policy debates have tried to answer such questions as: Is competition sustainable? Is it advisable? Who wins? Who loses? These questions all center on the effects of liberalization, that is, the entry into previously monopolized markets and the lowering of restrictions. In the area of telecommunications equipment, this involves the adoption of standards that do not favor any single firm or group of suppliers, simple approval procedures, non-discriminatory procurement, and the absence of protective quotas. In the area of infrastructure, liberalization includes the opening, to new service providers, of already established markets such as long-distance telephony and of new services such as cellular telephony. In the realm of computer-based value-added service, it means access by these new services to main network and central office functions.

Liberalization should not be confused with deregulation. Deregulation is a reduction in government-imposed constraints on the behavior of firms. The term is also used to mean a reduction in red tape and government involvement. Deregulation does not necessarily lead to a diverse market. The result can be a deregulated monopoly or, conversely, a tightly regulated multicarrier system. The experiences in the United States and the United Kingdom, two of the most liberalized markets, reveal that more rather than less regulation emerged, at least initially, after markets were opened. The process of partial liberalization tends to complicate matters and can lead to a more extensive set of rules to address new problems. Partial liberalization requires that interconnection arrangements be set, access charges determined, and a level playing field secured. In some cases, cross-subsidization from monopolistic to competitive services must be prevented. Under liberalization, competitors may receive preferential treatment in order to protect competition in its infancy. All of this leads to considerable regulatory complexity; no system is more lawyer intensive than partial liberalization.

Liberalization should also be distinguished from corporatization and privatization. Corporatization is the transformation of a state monopoly organization into an entity that is partially autonomous; such an entity may still be state owned, but it controls its own managerial and administrative functions. A company's monopoly status is not affected by corporatization as such, although once the close link to the government is severed, a process is set in motion that makes further changes more likely. Sometimes the corporatized entity is described as a "private" firm in the sense that it may be organized under private law provisions, which determine its status in, for example, contract and labor law. But that description often confuses legal detail with the reality of control, which may still be in the hands of the government. In other instances, a minority of shares in a company may be issued to the public, although control is retained by the state. Because corporatization loosens direct administrative controls, it is usually accompanied by the creation or strengthening of a government regulatory mechanism.

Privatization involves the sale by the government of shares in the telecommunications organization to private investors. However, even a complete change in ownership may leave a company's monopoly status untouched and may therefore not achieve the gains of efficiency of a competitive system. In the United States, AT&T was both privately owned and a near monopoly for a very long time. In Canada, private regional monopolies exist, and competition over long-distance telephone rates has emerged only recently. Most of the privatizations of European telecommunications monopolies have been only partial. Privatization may encourage efficiencies of operation. But quality of service may fall if an unconstrained private monopolist seeks to reduce costs without regard to the needs of its captive customers. Privatization can also have the unintended effect of strengthening a monopoly and slowing liberalization as shareholders become a political constituency in favor of preserving a monopoly.

THE HISTORY OF LIBERALIZATION IN THE UNITED STATES

The historical experience in the United States has followed the path from relatively unbridled laissez-faire capitalism to a regulatory system that expanded steadily in the decades following the Great Depression and World War II. In the 1970s, telecommunications policy in the United States began to shift in the opposite direction toward a lessening of restrictions.

This change in policy direction was due partly to a general political and economic philosophy of limiting the role of the state, which made the public more receptive to allowing new entrants into telecommunications markets as a way of offsetting corporate power and as a substitute for direct governmental intervention. The shift back toward laissez-faire policies far antedates the conservative Reagan and Bush administrations. Inspired by Lockean principles of natural law, the classic American ideology of government seeks individualism, fragmentation of private power, limitation of government (with the major exception of its role in national security), and protection of property rights and contracts. As applied to telecommunications policy, this philosophy justified a governmental role that is far narrower than in most other countries: it centered on permitting competitive markets to limit the exercise of dominance by any single firm and in permitting users to choose among service providers. This view was shared by many across the political spectrum, bringing together those Democrats who were distrustful of concentration of private economic power with those Republicans opposed to government interference.

The driving force for restructuring telecommunications in the United States and the other industrialized countries has been the phenomenal growth of user demand for telecommunications, which has been based on the shift toward service- and information-based economies. Electronic information transmission—that is, telecommunications—is of ever-increasing importance to the service sector. Price, control, security, and reliability became variables requiring organized managerial attention within service-sector firms. This, in turn, creates pressure from large and specialized users for services from outside the traditional, slow-moving, and redistributive monopoly network system.

To understand today's move to a liberalized environment in the United States, it is necessary first to understand the instability of the old monopoly. Telecommunications in the United States began in 1836 with Samuel Morse and his electromagnetic telegraph. In 1876, Alexander Graham Bell introduced a workable telephone. From the beginning, the U.S. telecommunications system was never the centralized state monopoly system (or PTT, for postal, telephone, and telegraph) prevalent in other nations. While the Bell firm grew and prospered, its dominance was the outcome of a highly effective strategy developed by Bell's early guiding spirit, Theodore Vail. That strategy centered on Bell's control of interconnection: of rival equipment to its own network, of rival local networks to Bell local networks, and of rival networks to the Bell long-distance system.

Once the basic Bell patents expired in the 1890s, independent competitors entered those areas not serviced by Bell concessionaires, especially in rural districts and in areas facing high prices. In 1895 alone, 199 new firms entered the market; and in 1900, 508.[1] Rival manufacturing firms provided these local carriers with equipment. In several major cities, systems competed side by side.[2] After a few years, the independents were nearly equal in customer size to Bell, and covered a much larger geographic area. The main difference between the two, however, was interconnection. While the Bell telephone system was fully interconnected on a national level through its own long-distance network, AT&T, the independents operated on a fairly limited regional scale.

Several independent companies brought antitrust complaints against AT&T in the early years of the century. As the number of lawsuits mounted, and as they were joined by Justice Department actions, AT&T entered into interconnection agreements with some independents and chose in 1913 to negotiate an agreement with the U.S. government known as the Kingsbury Commitment. The company guaranteed existing independent telephone companies interconnection to its long-distance network and agreed not to expand further geographically. It also promised to limit its activities to communications. This governmental action to constrain AT&T from total market dominance was part of a general trend of antitrust policy. Americans had become concerned about the enormous growth in the size of many businesses in the decades following the Civil War. There has always been a strong populist current in the United States opposing domination by big firms and, in this period, the distrust of big business was shared by the political Left, farmers, small businesses, and Westerners.

This political constellation soon led to the establishment of a regulatory system of utility commissions on the state level that supervised privately owned utilities, including telephone companies. The private utilities were required to interconnect by state law. This regulatory arrangement contrasts sharply with—and is far weaker than—the system of centralized state monopoly telephone administrations prevalent in most countries.

AT&T welcomed the new and weak regulatory structures and, within this environment, its market dominance grew. By 1934, the year in which the Communications Act codified the various federal regulatory powers, AT&T had built and owned 80 percent of all telephones and access lines in the United States and operated the only national long-distance network. Even so, the competing local services took a long time to disappear. In 1945, the last major competitive local loop service in the United States, the Keystone Telephone Company in Philadelphia, was shut down.

But AT&T's dominance remained under attack. In particular, the so-called Walker report, authored by one of the members of the new Federal Communications Commission (FCC), challenged AT&T's vertical integration with equipment manufacturing. World War II delayed any follow-up to the Walker recommendations, but once the war was over, the Justice Department filed an antitrust suit against AT&T in 1949. In 1956, under a more supportive Justice Department, AT&T achieved a favorable settlement of the case. It was not forced to divest itself of its Western Electric manufacturing arm, but its activities were limited to telephony. AT&T succeeded in avoiding a possibly disastrous antitrust judgment, though it also, once again, lost its routes of expansion.

By the early 1950s, universal service provision (the extension of telephone service to all parts of the United States) had been largely completed. The telephone reached most households, and an increasingly elaborate system of transfers from business users kept residential telephone rates low. This soon led to pressures for change by those large-business users whose contributions supported low residential charges, and from manufacturers of equipment other than AT&T. In response, the United States hesitantly began a policy of liberalization of entry and interconnection. The FCC had already been authorized in the Communications Act of 1934 to mandate carrier interconnection when in the public interest. Under pressure from the electronics industry—whose importance grew in World War II, the Korean War, and in the consumer prosperity of the 1950s—the interconnection of other terminal equipment, originally more restrictive than in Europe and Japan, was permitted. The two key decisions were *Hush-a-Phone* (1956) and *Carterfone* (1968), which allowed customer-owned and non-AT&T equipment to be connected to the network.

This interconnection policy was also extended to transmission. Military research, especially in the radar field, had opened the microwave spectrum to communications. In 1959, the FCC's *Above 890* decision permitted large users to operate in-house microwave long-distance service. These users felt that they were increasingly subsidizing local service and small customers, and they sought to move at least part of their traffic off the common-carrier system. By 1969, one microwave delivery company, MCI, won a court ruling against a reluctant FCC and an adamant AT&T to permit "specialized common carriers" to provide private line service for *other* than large users. From there it was an inevitable step to interconnection. MCI soon wanted to expand beyond private line services into general public switched service. To do so successfully, it had to be able to interconnect with AT&T's local networks in order to reach customers and be reached by them. This was permitted by the FCC in its *Execunet* decision (1978), which held in essence that a common carrier such as AT&T has to provide access to all users, whether they are small residential households or AT&T's own competitors. Thus, by 1975, AT&T found itself, after a long-protected period, once again facing facilities-based competition for telephone service.

In 1974, the FCC accepted applications for "enhanced service providers," which leased transmission and switching services from common carriers and added value with computer-based features. Following this decision, the FCC in 1976 went one step further and deregulated the resale and shared use of interstate private lines, even if they did not add value. Before, the approval of resale of lines had been left to AT&T's own judgment. It prohibited the resale and shared use by some private companies, but it leased lines to others, such as the telegraph company Western Union, for resale.[3] Through the FCC's actions allowing the reselling of domestic local and long-distance transmission, such practices became widespread.

The process of liberalization eventually led to the breakup of AT&T. This momentous event—the most massive reorganization in business history—was brought about by a 1974 Justice Department antitrust suit (as well as a private antitrust action by MCI) based on unfair business practices AT&T allegedly employed to suppress its competitors. The result was a consent decree in 1982, requiring that AT&T's monopoly be broken up. The government's main argument for the breakup of AT&T was that the company was inherently incapable of reconciling the liberalized and monopolistic parts of its business. Since regulatory requirements did not work, it was necessary, the government argued and the court agreed, to split off the company's local operations, the source of its monopoly power. The divestiture agreement put AT&T's local Bell Operating Companies—approximately two-thirds of the company's assets and employees—into seven Regional Bell Holding Companies. These provided mostly traditional local exchange telephone service, but began increasingly and aggressively to seek other opportunities inside and outside the communications field and their service territories. Today, the Regional Holding Companies are becoming global and diversified communications companies.

Liberalization in the United States did not stop with domestic services. The FCC, in its 1974 *Domestic Satellite* decision, set an "open-sky policy," which prevented AT&T from owning satellites, while encouraging other companies to enter this market. In the spirit of initiating increased international competition, the FCC in 1983 began to approve the entry of other companies into international satellite communications, and soon thereafter into submarine cables. In the 1990s, the FCC's focus shifted from a liberalization within sectors to a removal of barriers among the sectors of the communications field. Together with several states, the FCC also promoted rivalry in the provision of telecommunications services. Following the lead of the New York Public Service Commission in 1989, establishing interconnected local competition, the FCC in 1992 extended these principles nationally for those services under its jurisdiction, although its efforts were slowed by an unfavorable court decision in 1994. Other decisions, including those by federal courts, lowered the barriers between the telephone sector and cable television carriers, setting the stage for competitive entry and leading to a series of corporate mergers in the telecommunications field.

In 1993, the Clinton administration took office. Vice President Albert Gore, in particular, took the lead in advocating a national information infrastructure (NII). However, despite much excitement and an extension of the concept to the global information infrastructure, little concrete change has actually taken place. Congress, in the meantime, has been working on fashioning a compromise liberalization bill satisfactory to the various parties with interests at stake. For example, in the 103d Congress, the House of Representatives passed bills sponsored by Representatives Markey and Fields, and by Reprsentatives Brooks and Dingell, which further opened local competition in those states that had not yet liberalized. They also opened cable television service to local exchange companies, and long-distance service to the Bell companies under some safeguards. A 1995 senate bill by Senator Pressler proceeded in the same direction. (For details, see Chaper 12.)

PROGNOSTICATING THE IMPACT OF LIBERALIZATION: REVIEWING THE RECORD

That liberalization would have an overall positive impact was not a foregone conclusion, as reflected in the vigorous political and academic disagreements that accompanied it. Who was right in predicting the impact of liberalization? To analyze this question, it is helpful to organize the perspectives on telecommunications along two dimensions—market structure and regulation.

Along the market structure dimension, classic economic analysis suggested that a telecommunications monopoly would lead to incentives to set prices above marginal costs (unless constrained by regulation), and a failure to offer service and equipment options that met user needs. Others argued, however, that in certain situations a natural monopoly was efficient, and that as long as a market was *contestable* (that is, if new entrants could appear if the monopolist became inefficient), a monopolist would behave *as if* competition existed in order to protect its position. As a result, a monopoly was not inefficient per se. Yet even such contestability could be less than optimal under certain circumstances described by economists as "nonsustainability" in a multiproduct setting.

The second dimension along which economists differed was that of regulation versus deregulation, with the advocates of regulation arguing that the public interest needs to be protected, and advocates of free markets pointing to the efficiency costs of unconstrained regulation and to the anticompetitive entry barriers that protected AT&T.

These two dimensions can be mapped into four distinct positions (Figure 1.1). Figure 1.1 includes several names representing academics or policymakers associated with these positions.

Category 1: Proregulation, Antimonopoly. This category includes, in the United States, traditional "good government" advocates and populists in the style of Justice Louis Brandeis or Judge Harold Greene (who presided over the AT&T case), as well as those economists who believe that market forces may need to be curbed by both structural and regulatory intervention. In their view, while the power of AT&T was reduced, its successor companies would be free to operate either with or against the public interest. Those in this category predicted large residential rate increases, reductions in service quality, attempts to create new monopolies horizontally and vertically, and continued control of the equipment market by AT&T through its technical dominance and traditional ties to operating companies.

FIGURE 1.1
POSITIONS ON MARKET STRUCTURE AND REGULATION

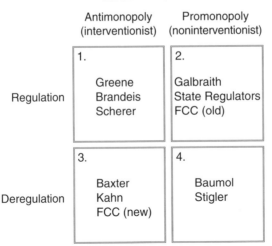

MARKET STRUCTURE

	Antimonopoly (interventionist)	Promonopoly (noninterventionist)
Regulation	1. Greene Brandeis Scherer	2. Galbraith State Regulators FCC (old)
Deregulation	3. Baxter Kahn FCC (new)	4. Baumol Stigler

Category 2: Proregulation, Promonopoly. This category includes traditional state regulators and those economists who believe in the necessity of large firms and who dismiss structural antitrust policy in favor of regulation, such as John Kenneth Galbraith. In their view, the efficient and socially redistributive AT&T system was dismantled by zealots, who are now letting its successor companies run wild. This group expected cost increases, price increases, technical incompatibilities, a reduction in the universality of service, and a reduction in research and development. They also predicted that competition in long-distance rates and equipment provision would be unlikely due to AT&T's continued predominance.

Category 3: Proderegulation, Antimonopoly. This group includes pro-competition centrists (such as Alfred Kahn) and free-market advocates who believe that competition requires intervention (such as William Baxter, the government's chief advocate of the AT&T divestiture). This group's expectation was that once the monopoly—and its attendant inefficiency—was broken, market forces and competition would assert themselves. The results would be falling costs, cost-based pricing, innovation, higher productivity, and faster modernization.

Category 4: Proderegulation, Promonopoly. This category includes many, but not all, members of the Chicago and Princeton schools of economic thought. The former believe that competition rather than bureaucrats should have served to reduce AT&T's power if it was failing to meet demand efficiently. The latter opposed any attack on a natural monopoly, if it was operating efficiently. Both views expected government policy to lead to a reconcentration of the industry, a loss of productivity, and a drop in research and development funds.

Which of these four assessments of the likely impact of liberalization has proved correct? Answering this question requires looking at the empirical record regarding universality of service, prices, equity, service quality and reliability, productivity, research and development, competition, equipment prices and trade, and employment.

UNIVERSALITY OF SERVICE

Overall telephone penetration did not decline with liberalization but actually increased, from a national average of 91.4 percent in 1983 to 93.6 percent in 1991.[4] This was due partly to subsidized "lifeline" service for needy individuals and other safeguards, and partly to the low-demand elasticity for telephone service with respect to price. Although the rate of change has slowed, one would expect this to occur as the 100 percent level of penetration is approached.[5] For the middle class ($30,000 annual household income), penetration was 98 percent and higher.[6] For the poor (those with incomes of $5,000 to $7,500), it rose from 82.7 percent to 84.9 percent in 1989, before sliding back to 82.8 percent in 1991.[7] For poor blacks and Hispanics (incomes of $5,000 to $7,500), telephone penetration has historically been lower than that of the population as a whole or for whites with the same income. For blacks in this income bracket, penetration rose from 74.7 percent in 1983, to 80.0 percent in 1988, and then slid back to 74.3 percent in 1991. For Hispanics at the same income level over the same period, it rose from 71.1 to 72.6 percent in 1989, before falling to 70.2 percent in 1991.[8] Senior citizens are actually, in terms of telephone penetration, above the national average. Penetration among those aged sixty-five to sixty-nine was at 96.9 percent in 1991, and an even higher 97.3 percent for those over age seventy.

Nor do rural telephone subscribers seem to have been forced off the network as a result of liberalization. Rural states such as Iowa, Nebraska, and North Dakota have telephone penetration well above the national average (95.6 percent, 96.0 percent, and 96.6 percent, respectively, in 1991, compared to the 93.6 percent national average). On average, 95.0 percent of all farms have telephones, according to the Rural Electrification Administration. Telephone rates for rural areas are often (but not always) lower than in urban areas because flat rate service is cheaper for small exchanges due to various subsidy mechanisms and lower overheads.

PRICES

One of the major questions raised by liberalization was its likely impact on residential subscribers, with a tripling of rates frequently predicted. But the reality has been different. Nationwide since the AT&T divestiture, the consumer price index (CPI) for all telephone service rose just over half as fast as the CPI for all goods and services in the same period. Telephone service climbed from 99.8 in 1983 to 119.5 in 1991 (based on an index of 100), a rise of 19.7 percent, while the CPI for all goods and services during that time rose about 34.0 percent.[9] Local telephone service increased from 98.3 in 1983 to 153.6 in 1991, an increase of 56.2 percent. During the same period, interstate toll service fell from 101.3 to 67.5, a decline of 33.8 percent. Reversing the trend, between 1991 and 1994, the CPI rose 10 percent, local rates were flat (up 2 percent), while toll rates rose 12 percent.

In absolute terms, the nationwide average for local monthly residential rates for unlimited local calling increased from $11.58 in 1983 to $17.78 in 1990, a change of $6.20, or 53.5 percent, over seven years. When the lowest available rates are considered (not including lifeline low-income assistance rates), monthly rates rose $4.42 in the same period, from $5.93 to $10.35, a rise of 74.5 percent.[10]

If, however, we examine trends in real consumer price indices over a longer period (1964–89), it is clear that costs had been declining through most of that period and thus were not purely a function of liberalization. Between 1977 and 1983, the index for residential telephone services declined at an average rate of 3.7 percent, whereas after divestiture, from 1983 through 1989, it declined at only 0.9 percent. The index for local service, which had a negative 2.5 percent average annual percent change from 1977 through 1983, reversed itself and began to climb at an annual rate of 3.1 percent through 1989. The index for intrastate tolls continued to decline, although slightly more slowly (-5.6 percent compared to -4.2 percent), while the CPI for interstate tolls, which had been dropping between 1983 and 1989 at an average annual rate of -5.0 percent, accelerated to -9.8 percent in the years from 1983 to 1989.[11]

Throughout the period 1980–89, an average household's annual expenditures on telephone service as a percentage of its total expenditures remained remarkably constant at 2.0 percent.[12]

EQUITY

The benefits of liberalization and the AT&T divestiture were not shared equally. Among residential subscribers, the extent of benefits enjoyed as a result of telephone repricing was correlated positively with income. Robert Crandall, calculating both the direct and indirect effects of these shifting patterns in telephone prices, concluded that the overall effect has been "mildly regressive."[13] By assigning values to the indirect benefits when business users enjoy lower telecommunications costs, he finds that the lowest-income households paid approximately $16.00 more per year due to telephone service repricing, while the wealthiest saved close to $15.00 per year.

SERVICE QUALITY AND RELIABILITY

Another projected impact of competition was a decline in service quality. The FCC's measures for national quality trends show that dial-tone delay has been kept reasonably constant; that technical transmission quality has generally risen; that the on-time service performance for residential orders has suffered a steady if minor decay since 1987; and that regional ("intra-LATA") calls have maintained an admirably high level of call completions (over 99.5 percent), while inter-LATA completion rates have climbed steadily since 1986.[14] As for customer satisfaction, large businesses seem to have benefited the most, with 93.5 percent of these customers reporting satisfaction in mid-1989, up from 91.5 percent in 1985. During the same period, customer satisfaction among small businesses rose from 92.3 percent to 93.5 percent, and among residential consumers from 93.5 percent to 94.0 percent.[15]

The above measures of quality address regular, ongoing performance, but the question of reliability in the face of shocks to the system are another issue. Here we find that the vulnerability of the network has grown in recent years.

There have been a series of major service outages that have affected millions of users. Furthermore, with most financial and other transactions conducted electronically, society's vulnerability to outages has grown. (For example, when a fire gutted a central office in Hindale, Illinois, it brought down a national florists' network—on Mother's Day.)

PRODUCTIVITY

Productivity measures for the U.S. telecommunications sector throughout the 1980s show steady improvement. For example, labor productivity for the seven Baby Bells, when measured in terms of lines per employee, show a cumulative gain from 1983 to 1988 of 34.9 percent.[16] The number of access lines per telco employee grew from 66.0 telephone employees per 10,000 access lines in 1984 to 44.4 in 1991.[17] At the same time, revenue per employee grew from $115 in 1985 to $144 in 1990, a gain of 25.2 percent. Annual average total factor productivity (TFP) growth between 1971 and 1983 in U.S. telecommunications, using total deflated real revenues for output, was estimated as 3.8 percent. Following divestiture (1984–88), the Bell system's TFP growth slowed to 3.13 percent, while the TFP growth for the total sector grew at 3.94 percent.[18] A Morgan Stanley report measured annual productivity gains among the Regional Bell Operating Companies in terms of annual growth in expense per line, adjusted for inflation. It found an average of 2.4 percent compound annual growth for the Regional Bells in the years 1984–88, and a jump to 4.7 percent productivity growth for 1989.[19]

RESEARCH AND DEVELOPMENT

Liberalization also raised the specter of a technological decline, based on fears that AT&T's research arm, Bell Labs, might be curtailed by profit-minded corporate management. In fact, the opposite has occurred. Total research and development (R&D) employment rose from 24,100 in 1981 to 33,500 in 1985 (for AT&T and the Regional Bells' joint R&D firm, Bellcore, combined).[20] By 1988, the regional companies were adding their own laboratories, and total R&D employment rose to an estimated 35,600. According to a 1991 *Business Week* survey, the telecommunications industry's average R&D spending per employee for the years 1986–90 ($9,858), or when figured as a percentage of 1990 sales (3.6 percent), outpaced the all-industry figures in those categories ($7,053 and 3.4 percent, respectively). Bell Lab's R&D budget increased from $2 billion to $2.7 billion, of which about 10 percent went to basic research.[21]

LONG-DISTANCE COMPETITION

Between 1984 and 1991, AT&T's long-distance rates were reduced about 45 percent in real terms.[22] AT&T's share of inter-LATA long-distance service (all minutes) dropped from 84.2 percent in late 1984 to 62.9 percent by 1990.[23] As a percentage of all users, however, AT&T's share is higher because it has more small subscribers. If short-haul interexchange service is included in the market definition (by including the local exchange companies' regional [intra-LATA] service), AT&T's share is about 60 percent.

Interstate switched access minutes grew from 37.5 billion minutes in 1984 to 79.1 in 1991, a very substantial increase of 111 percent. AT&T's volume increased 57.9 percent, but that of its competitors rose almost 400 percent from their much smaller base. Americans make substantially more telephone calls per capita than users in other countries—for example, 1,700 in 1988, two or three times as many as the British (800), Japanese (550), Germans (500), and French (400).

The number of competitors to AT&T (long-distance service providers with an FCC identification code) increased from 42 in 1982 to 451 in 1987 to 611 in 1990, before subsiding to 597 in 1991.[24] Of these, most are only resellers rather than facilities-based carriers, and many concentrate on business customers. By 1993, MCI, the strongest of AT&T's rivals, had grown to a $12 billion company offering an ever-increasing line of services. (After divestiture, its revenues had grown at an initial rate of 27 percent a year.) Since divestiture, US Sprint has successfully completed the construction of a $3 billion network, and was granted 40 percent of the large contract for the federal network, FTS-2000. Carrier profits looked healthy, and prices increased slightly in 1993, leading to complaints about a long-distance oligopoly.

LOCAL COMPETITION

Local competition for business customers is emerging principally through fiber-optic-based metropolitan area networks (MANs), also known as alternative local telecommunications systems (ALTS) or competitive access providers (CAPs). CAPs' revenues have been growing at a rate of about 22 percent per year. Residential competition in the local loop is likely to emerge from access based on cable television infrastructure, from cellular and microcellular telephony, and from other local telephone companies.

EQUIPMENT PRICES

Rates for telephone equipment declined between 1984 and 1991, by an average of 8.2 percent annually in real terms, whereas between 1972 and 1983, the decline averaged only 2.7 percent annually.[25] In the past, the U.S. market for network equipment had been fairly closed. The vast Bell system and its customers—comprising 80 percent of the total market—were effectively closed to other suppliers because of the existence of AT&T's manufacturing subsidiary, Western Electric. As a result of the divestiture, the Bell Operating Companies no longer have any incentive to increase AT&T's profits, since none of those profits are returned to Bell. Equipment prices fell as the Bell Operating

Companies and end users gained the freedom to shop around. AT&T's national market share for central office switches dropped from 70 percent in 1983 to 51 percent in 1990, with Northern Telecom reaching 40 percent. While comparisons are always difficult, central exchange equipment costs declined from approximately $325 per digital line in 1984, on an industrywide basis, to $244 in 1990, and to less than $100 in 1992, with the steepest declines after 1989.[26]

EQUIPMENT TRADE

Liberalization has led to lower equipment prices; however, it has also meant the loss of market share for U.S. firms. The U.S. trade balance for telecommunications equipment, which had been positive although shrinking in 1981 and 1982, became a $1.15 billion deficit in 1984. By 1989, this had grown to a $2.3 billion deficit. The deficit improved slightly to $2.1 billion in 1991, and official trade statistics suggest a small improvement to $2.0 billion in 1992. Imports increased from $1.6 billion in 1983 to $4.7 billion in 1991, while exports grew markedly from $0.8 billion to over $3.3 billion, a fourfold increase.[27] The amount of foreign equipment imported, particularly from Asian suppliers, continued to be a dominant factor in this equation; in 1992, 52 percent of total telecommunications imports were from Asian suppliers, with Japan accounting for about a third.[28] With the trade deficit in communications equipment, liberalization has created an unanticipated problem that may become a major political issue for U.S. policymakers.

EMPLOYMENT

The number of employees at AT&T and its successor companies fell as a result of liberalization. By 1990, AT&T had reduced its workforce by 90,000 jobs, 25,000 of which were eliminated in 1989 alone, from a predivestiture total of about 370,000. The Regional Holding Companies fell from 583,332 employees at divestiture to 542,170 by 1991, a loss of 41,162 jobs, or about 7 percent. The most dramatic Regional Holding Company cuts were made in 1984 and 1985 (2.8 percent and 3.1 percent, respectively). In 1990 and 1991, Regional Holding Company cutbacks continued,[29] and the trend toward a shrinking workforce is likely to persist.

Many of these employment losses have been in manufacturing and are part of a more general decline of U.S.-based electronics manufacturing. But if equipment is defined more broadly to include computers, "smart" office equipment, and so on, the number of jobs has increased as the total pie becomes larger. Many of these new jobs, however, are in the area of marketing and similar nonmanufacturing activities, and are often not unionized. Thus, traditional telecommunications job categories, as well as labor unions, suffered as a result of liberalization.

How can the predictive record of the four categories introduced in Figure 1.1 regarding the impact of deregulation and market structure policies be assessed? One way is to assign "box scores" to the quality of predictions of the four categories for the eleven dimensions just discussed and aggregate these dimensions into an overall score of prediction. To do so, the following rather simplistic assumption must be made: first, the predictions are ranked from +2 (substantially correct) to -2 (substantially incorrect); second, each dimension has been given equal weight. This results in the summary score given in Figure 1.2 below.

As Figure 1.2 shows, the predictions of those holding a promonopoly, noninterventionist position were basically incorrect. The lost benefits of the monopoly seem to have been small. And the extent of lowered barriers of entry due to AT&T's restructuring was larger than predicted by those pure free-market advocates that expected eventual entry. While they might be right in the long-term, the divestiture gave entry a jump start.

Along the regulation-deregulation axis, deregulators were more often correct in their predictions than the regulators. However, the latter were also correct in a number of instances, such as service quality or the protection of the safety net. Their alarm often led to policies, such as lifeline service for the poor, which provided some of the safeguards that made deregulation successful.

LIBERALIZATION IN OTHER COUNTRIES

While much of the developed world embraced liberalization in the 1980s, such change had its limits. A monopoly in infrastructure still exists almost everywhere in both the developed and developing world. Only the United States, Japan, the

FIGURE 1.2
SUMMARY OF PREDICTION QUALITY

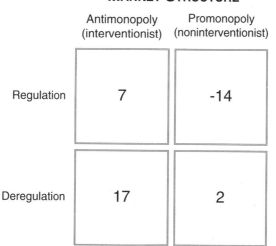

MARKET STRUCTURE

	Antimonopoly (interventionist)	Promonopoly (noninterventionist)
Regulation	7	-14
Deregulation	17	2

United Kingdom, Sweden, and New Zealand permit alternative domestic fixed infrastructure of any consequence. In almost every other country, the monopoly in voice service remains strong, and even resale is rarely available.

Often, the extent to which monopoly has been reduced tends to be exaggerated. An official Danish political agreement on liberalization illustrates the doublespeak: "There will be competition within all spheres of telecommunications in the next few years, apart from telex, ordinary telephony, radio-based mobile services, satellite services, the infrastructure and the use of the telecommunications network for broadcasting radio and television programmes."[30] Similarly, although the European Union instituted the right in principle to offer value-added services in any member country, the detailed legislation in many countries continues to be restrictive. Similar restrictions are likely to weaken the European Union's directive of opening some of the infrastructure to competition by 1998.

Another check on liberalization is the slow pace of its implementation. After eight years of participation in the U.K. market, Mercury still has less than 3 percent of total market share and its core activity remains serving firms in London's financial center as a secondary source for data transmission capacity and as a carrier of trunk calls for businesses. Mercury's residential service has failed to gain even 1 percent of the national market.[31] Where no entrenched incumbent exists, competition is more fully developed. For example, BT's competitor in the cellular service duopoly, Racal Vodafone, holds over 50 percent of market share.

To secure a head start for their national monopolies, the launch of second cellular carriers in competition with the national PTTs (renamed PTOs or TOs, for [public] telecommunications organizations) has been delayed in Germany, Italy, and Spain. The European Union has likewise suffered numerous delays in its efforts to implement liberalized rules for service provision. Thus, where competition against a monopoly exists, it is often a contest between David and Goliath.[32] In some situations, deregulation has actually strengthened the PTOs because restrictions on them were lifted at a time when competition remained embryonic.

For the most part, PTOs have not been divided up. Several countries, such as Denmark, Italy, and Portugal, have even increased barriers to competition by consolidating carriers.

In the equipment market, the liberalization of procurement sources also enhanced the power of the monopoly PTOs. By opening the public procurement process to additional vendors, PTOs are less tied to the technology developed by national champion equipment firms and thus are in a better bargaining position to obtain favorable contract terms and dictate technical specifications.

Only in the liberalization of terminal equipment have powers of PTOs been reduced, but such liberalization was largely an accommodation to reality. This market had already effectively liberalized itself, as numerous consumers—

simply but illegally—bought cheaper and more varied equipment outside the official PTO distribution networks.

Where liberalization has taken place, what has been the impact of changes in ownership and control? Here, too, reforms have increased the power of the PTOs. Corporatization substituted managerial and financial autonomy for direct governmental control of PTOs' operations and the political accountability that came with it. At the same time, the government ministries that assumed regulatory power have tended to be ineffective. These ministries have only a handful of experts with which to confront the huge telephone organizations. In Sweden, for example, after liberalization, Televerket had forty-two thousand employees, while the ministry charged with regulating it had a telecom staff of only six, most of whom perished in a single plane crash in 1989.

Privatization, too, has strengthened the PTOs. The existence of shareholders to whom the PTO must answer has added new incentives for improved performance that were largely absent in the past. Privatization also curbed some efforts at market liberalization by creating a large constituency of shareholders who oppose sweeping reforms. In the past, this was the case only with AT&T; now it is also true for Spain's Telefonica and Britain's BT. Similarly, the remaining shares of Japan's Nippon Telegraph and Telephone (NTT) have not been sold by the government in order to avoid depressing the share price and hurting millions of investors.

The international strategies of PTOs, such as the pursuit of trans-nationalization and building of alliances, have further strengthened their position. Several of the PTOs are becoming far-reaching global organizations, involved in numerous activities that cease to be transparent to governments. Competitors assert that these activities often are supported by the monopoly profits from basic service. At the same time, many PTOs have also formed alliances among themselves, often as a market-sharing arrangement.

Such cooperation is also found among governments in harmonization of their policies, contributing to a continuation of the traditional stability of the telecommunications sphere. While harmonization may eliminate restrictive national rules, it is just as likely to be used to prevent competitive behavior by establishing a policy cartel.

Thus, the modest liberalization that has taken place in most countries has not harmed the traditional telecommunications organizations; indeed, it has even worked to the benefit of many of them. PTOs have been energized and modernized by the recent changes, but continue to enjoy a dominant position in the market. Their competitors are still tiny, their regulatory authorities are frequently underperforming, and their role has been enhanced by national industrial policies. (This is not to say that some users and competitors have not also benefited. Telecommunications is a growth field rather than a zero-sum game.)[33]

But, given the dynamic forces of a liberalized telecommunications market, it is unlikely that the present dominance of the national near-monopolies will last.

In time, PTO market share will decline as competitors grow in size and gain interconnection rights; presently unprepared regulators will become more effective; the PTO's national role in industrial development policies will be shared with other firms; and PTO cartel collaboration will evolve into more head-to-head competition, sometimes prodded by antimonopoly agencies. New domestic entrants, including cellular companies, cable television providers, and value-added networks, will seek opportunities in specialized and general markets, as will foreign entrants, some of them PTOs themselves. Liberalization at home will become critical to PTOs seeking reciprocal market access abroad.

The concept of the single territorially defined carrier for an entire country's electronic information flows is not sustainable in the long run. The strategies followed in the 1980s and 1990s have set forces in motion that will assert themselves over time. What we are witnessing today in these nations is the golden age of the traditional telecommunications organizations, but it will not last, as it did not in the United States or in Japan.

THE FUTURE OF LIBERALIZATION: THE SHAPE OF THE NEW MARKET STRUCTURE

What will be the forces of change in the coming decade? The conventional scenario for the evolution of telecommunications, offered by traditional state monopoly carriers around the world as their vision of the future, was the *integrated single superpipe* that would merge all communications links into a single conduit that they controlled and that was interconnected internationally with similar territorially exclusive superpipes. This scenario of technological integration did not take into account ongoing liberalization, which was accompanied by considerable organizational centrifugalism. Instead of consolidating, the network environment is growing ever more diversified.

The various physical network elements are being linked with one another through various interconnection arrangements, forming what can be described as a "network of networks." Yet this is not the end of the story. Competition begets diversity; diversity begets complexity; and complexity leads to efforts at simplification. In order for the user of telecommunications to handle this fragmented environment—so at odds with the technologists' model of the single superpipe—the numerous network pieces must be integrated into a usable whole. There are several ways to do this, but the most promising relies on the emergence of a new category of "systems integrators," which provide the end user (whether corporate, governmental, or otherwise) with access to a variety of services in one place.

Systems integrators assemble packages of various types of services and equipment and customize these packages to the specific requirements of their customers. The characteristics of "pure" systems integrators—for there will be various hybrids—is that they do not own or operate the various subproduction activities; rather, they select optimal elements in terms of price and performance, package them together, manage the bundles, and offer them to customers on a one-stop basis. This relieves customers of the responsibility of integration, which requires a great deal of expertise.

Today, systems integrators exist only for large customers and customer groups. The next step is for systems integrators to emerge that assemble individualized networks for personal use and offer them directly to end users. One can envision a future of individually tailored "virtual" network arrangements that serve individualized communications needs, providing access to frequent personal and business contacts, data sources, transaction programs, video and audio publishers, data processing and storage, bulletin boards, and personal information screening. As these networks develop, they will access and interconnect with one another and form a complex, interconnected whole that sprawls across carriers, service providers, and national frontiers. The telecommunications environment will evolve from the "network of networks," in which carriers interconnect, to a "system of systems," in which systems integrators link up with one another.[34]

In such an environment, the structure of telecommunications, as far as end users are concerned, will change significantly. Instead of dealing with *carriers*, users will transact with *systems integrators*. In this world, what will happen to traditional regulation? How will consumer protection and universal service be affected? What regulatory safeguards will be necessary?

In telecommunications, government regulation existed in part to affect the balance of power between huge monopoly suppliers on the one hand and small and technically ignorant users on the other hand. Regulation relied on the political and administrative process to alter unconstrained market outcomes that might negatively affect consumers and competitors. In return, the dominant carriers received protection from competition. Even where competition emerged in the form of rival carriers, customers still had no expertise in dealing with a complex set of services and products.

In a system of systems, however, this balance will change dramatically. Systems integrators, competing with one another for customers, will act as users' agents vis-a-vis carriers. They can protect users against carriers' underperformance and power, and secure for them the best deal available. The emergence of systems integrators should resolve many of the problems of price, quality, market power, security, even privacy, that have traditionally plagued the telecommunications field. Business communications will become more effective than ever. Technological innovation is likely to be accelerated by knowledgeable buyers and marketers of services. Assuming (1) that users will have a choice among systems integrators, (2) that systems integrators will have a choice among noncolluding suppliers of underlying services, and (3) that market power by carriers and systems integrators is checked by competition, the need for government intervention can be expected to decline substantially.

On the other hand, not all traditional policy goals will be fully resolved in a system of systems. Special attention must be paid to the following:

1.   *Universal service.* The emerging systems of systems will exert competitive pressures on cost and therefore on many prices, making telecommunications more affordable. But it will be impossible to maintain the traditional redistributive system of generating subsidies and transferring them internally within the same carrier from one category of users to another. Several factors will disrupt this arrangement. In a network of competing carriers, internal redistribution from some customers to other customers is not sustainable once other carriers target those profit-generating users. Furthermore, residential users may end up paying a proportionally higher share than large users because cost shares may end up allocated to an economic "Ramsey" pricing rule, inverse to demand elasticity. Large users have more options and hence greater elasticity and would therefore pay less than residential customers. Thus, the trend that at present is described as a "rebalancing" of prices toward cost would go much further than that, burdening the more inelastic customers. Nor can one expect to continue to rely on a system of access charges to provide the source of subsidies, since these charges imply access into "the network." Access to the network will be a meaningless concept once alternative transmission is easily available.

     Yet these changes need not spell the end of support schemes. If policymakers choose to support some categories of users, such as rural Americans or the poor, either for reasons of social and regional policy or for the benefits their participation offers to others who can reach them, it is still possible to do so; only it must be done in different ways from what is done now.[35] One alternative is to eliminate the present invisible tax system and replace it with a visible charge system, drawing on general government revenue or specialized communications charges, such as communications sales tax or value-added fees. The funds raised could go to a "universal service fund" that would be used to support certain network providers, as well as categories of users, providing them with a choice among carriers. This charge would replace the present opaque system, making it transparent and accountable. It would also decouple discussions of optimal industry structure from those addressing optimal social policy.

     The advantage of systems integrators is that they pay competing carriers a price based only on the latter's short-term marginal costs and can pass this low cost on to their customers. Yet a significant part of cost in a capital-intensive industry such as telecommunications networks is fixed and would not be adequately compensated under such an arrangement. The long-term result might be either a gradual disinvestment in networks or the reestablishment of monopoly, price cartels, and oligopolistic pricing. None of these scenarios would be desirable; all of them will prove to be a challenge to future regulators.

2. *The free flow of information.* In the traditional network environment, the granting of access, nondiscrimination, and content neutrality is required of the public networks by common carriage regulation and by law. The institution of common carriage, historically the foundation of how telecommunications are delivered, will not survive in a system of systems. "Common carriers"—that is, telephone companies—will continue to exist, but the status under which they operate—offering service on a non-discriminatory basis, neutral as to use and user—will not.[36]

The blows to traditional common carriage do not come from rival telecommunications carriers such as MCI, but from two new directions. The first is the increasing overlap between the common-carrier system and well-developed mass media, private contract carriers. The most important of these are cable television networks, which in a remarkably short period have wired the nation with a second and powerful network system, and which are on the verge of entering point-to-point, switched, and mobile telecommunications services. The other challenge to common carriage are systems integrators. Common carriage requirements providing for the free flow of information do not apply to systems integrators. Systems integrators will be able to institute restrictions on their systems and exclude certain types of information, subjects, speakers, or destinations.

In head-to-head competition between a common carrier and a private contract carrier or systems integrator, the former is at a disadvantage:

▼ A common carrier cannot use differentiated pricing due to its nondiscrimination obligation and because it cannot prevent arbitrage. Common carriers' rivals can offer services to some customers at a low enough price to induce them to sign up, and can use this contribution to their revenues to underprice a common carrier for low-elasticity customers.

▼ A common carrier must serve a contract carrier or systems integrator, but not vice versa. There is no reciprocity; competitors can use valuable parts of a common carriers' operations, but need not share their own unique features.

▼ A common carrier cannot choose its customers.

▼ A common carrier cannot manage the competition among its customers and benefit from it.

▼ In assembling a service package, the systems integrator can pick and choose among the lowest-price component providers, while the common carrier is likely to offer only its own.

▼   Competition for transmission and other services will lower their price for
    systems integrators to marginal cost, which is likely to be lower than the
    average cost for both common and contract carriers of providing it.

As a result of these factors, a systems integrator may be able to provide
services more cheaply than a common carrier, even though the systems
integrator is using the carriers' underlying transmission facilities.
It is unlikely that the common carriers will simply tolerate such a
situation. They will operate their own systems integrators and move to
contract carriage themselves, including price differentiation of customers.
And that is, indeed, what is starting to happen. If it continues, the "de-
averaging" of prices will become standard and negotiated rates will spread
to many noncommodity services.
What are the implications? The system of systems may have the
capacity for a large number of voices, yet it may result in a narrower
spectrum of information because systems integrators and carriers may
not want to be identified with certain types of uses and users. The need for
the various systems to have access to one another, and for information to
travel over numerous interconnected carriers, means that the
restrictiveness of any one of the participants would require everyone else
to institute content and usage tests before they can hand over or accept
traffic—alternatively, they could agree to the most restrictive principles.
Information travels across numerous subnetworks until it reaches its
destination, and nobody can tell one bit from another bit. If each of these
networks and systems integrators sets its own rules about which
information can be carried and which cannot, information will not flow
easily. Common carriage can be substituted for by an alternative system—
such as third-party-neutral interconnection—but this, too, is not self-
enforcing.[37]

3.   *Interconnection and compatibility.* The economic reasons for the tension
     between integrative and pluralistic forces is most pronounced on the front
     where they intersect: the rules of interconnection of the multiple hardware
     and software subnetworks and their access into the integrated whole. As
     various discrete networks grow, they must interoperate in terms of technical
     standards, protocols, and boundaries. Yet interconnectivity is not normally
     granted by incumbent firms. That is the lesson of decades of experience in
     the United States. Regulatory requirements of the late 1980s and early
     1990s, such as open network architecture, comparably efficient inter-
     connection, or collocation were part of the evolution toward competition. In
     effect, these provisions regulated in order to deregulate.[38]

4.   *International asymmetry.* The system of systems works as long as it is
     competitive in each of its stages, or as long as regulation establishes

nondiscrimination. However, in an international setting, neither of these conditions is likely to be met. Most countries lag behind the United States and Japan in the evolution of their networks. The traditional monopoly carrier is still almost always firmly entrenched and active in all stages of communications. As a result, systems integrators cannot truly compete against these PTOs in terms of systems integration. This might be considered an internal issue for these countries, except that it has an anticompetitive impact globally. This is because some of these PTOs are aggressively pursuing international systems integration themselves, while at the same time holding gatekeeper powers over entry into their own home markets. For example, the PTO of an important European country could restrict the effectiveness of a U.S. systems integrator to offer global services, while at the same time entering the more liberalized environment in the United States.

Of course, other countries' PTOs can play the same game, and, as a result, a new trend of international carrier collaboration has emerged in which major PTOs enter into joint ventures of systems integration. Potentially at least, these alliances of dominant national carriers could create international cartels and barriers to competitive entry of other systems integrators, whether in their home countries or internationally. This has the anticompetitive potential of "whipsawing" in which a one-sided liberalization across frontiers permits the remaining monopolist to appropriate fully the previously shared monopoly profits. To prevent this, it is essential to reach international nondiscriminatory access, lease, and interconnection arrangements that are neutral as to the nature or the nationality of the systems integrator. The United States, being the largest and most interesting market for systems integrators, can exercise leadership in pressing for such reciprocity.

POLICY IMPLICATIONS

The preceding analysis leads to the conclusion that liberalization will not be the "end of history" as far as telecommunications regulation is concerned and that government is not likely to disappear from this arena. In the 1980s, telecommunications policy was centered on liberalizing entry. This was correct, then and now. The empirical evidence provided above demonstrates the generally positive trends in telecommunications during the phase of liberalization. But throughout the 1990s, second-generation liberalization and issues involving the integration of the various partial networks and services will be at the forefront. Liberalization leads to network pluralism, which in turn generates the incentives for systems integration. Systems integration resolves many of the traditional regulatory issues of traditional telecommunications market structure. But it leaves others unresolved, and it creates new ones. Thus, a new set of regulatory questions may be upon us, many of them requiring new approaches.

Although some of the developments anticipated in this chapter are already under way, none will take place overnight. But this should not lead us to ignore them. The present policy efforts in Washington and Brussels still deal largely with liberalization. The Markey-Fields and Brooks-Dingell legislative initiatives in the House and their counterparts by Senators Pressler and Hollings were efforts at dismantling some barriers to entry and competition. As useful as these changes were, several main issues for the future still need to be tackled. The FCC's (and the New York Public Service Commission's) open network rules were one such effort. The White House's "Title VII" proposal for switched digital broadband services was another. But this is only the beginning. Technical convergence leads to business and global overlap, and both require legal integration. The 104th Congress is now dealing with two major bills that take the deregulatory agenda much further—although it is not yet clear that they will really serve liberalization by fostering true competition.

Liberalizing telecommunications competition will prove to have been the easy part. Developing the tools to deal with its consequences, while protecting traditional policy goals in the new environment, will be the next and more difficult challenge. To paraphrase Thomas Jefferson, "The price of liberalization is eternal vigilance."

2

INFORMATION INFRASTRUCTURE AND THE TRANSFORMATION OF MANUFACTURING

FRANÇOIS BAR

C hanges sweeping information networking in the United States promise a profound transformation of the national information infrastructure (NII) and an equally deep transformation in the economic processes this infrastructure supports. Many of these changes will affect the service sector: bankers, insurers, and educators will obviously benefit from an infrastructure that makes it easier, cheaper, and faster to move and manipulate information—their raw material. But talk about the coming of a postindustrial society[1] should not obscure the tremendous potential of the NII to transform manufacturing. Services are not about to supplant manufacturing as the prime generator of wealth and power. On the contrary, just as the industrial revolution didn't do away with agriculture but instead transformed it through mechanization, the information revolution is redefining and rejuvenating traditional manufacturing activities.[2]

Information has always been central to manufacturing. Information about customer tastes or the possibilities inherent in new production technologies inspire the design of new products. Information serves to translate new design ideas into actual products, allowing the creation of new production processes along the way. Information is the glue that binds shop-floor machines into a production system and links production process designers with production workers. Information about new machines and their operations provides manufacturing employees with the knowledge they need to perform their jobs. Information about demand volume and market characteristics helps manufacturers to determine factory output levels and product mixes and to set distribution logistics. The difference today is that, with the introduction of electronic information technology, manufacturers can process unprecedented amounts of information in ways that are enormously powerful and versatile.

The changes that the introduction of computer and networking technology have made in the manufacturing process reversed the trend toward increased mechanization that prevailed from 1800 to 1950. Ramchandran Jaikumar describes what happened:[3]

> Capital increasingly replaced labor, and economies of scale insured progress. The engineering focus was on machines, and labor was required to adapt to machines and, ultimately, to become yet another machine. Concurrently, machines themselves grew more elaborate and proficient. The governing principle was greater and greater mechanical control. With the introduction of information technology since the 1950s: previous trends in mechanization have reversed themselves. Now, the emphasis is on versatility and intelligence, the substitution of intelligence for capital, and economies of scope. . . . This shift, based on the versatility of information technology and freedom from mechanical constraint, suggests new managerial imperatives: build small, cohesive teams; manage process improvement, not just output; broaden the role of engineering management to include manufacturing; and treat manufacturing as a service.

This reversal, from Fordism to mass variety, constitutes the central theme of this chapter. The emergence of the NII is key to its unfolding and, conversely, it will profoundly shape its character. Policymakers have a critical role to play, to ensure that U.S. manufacturing industries have access to an information infrastructure that is flexible, advanced, seamless, and universal enough to support the current manufacturing transition. As part of this transition, policymakers must also support broad-based training of highly skilled, multidisciplinary workers that will be needed in this new workplace, and assist the smaller manufacturing firms that must remain vital components of the industrial fabric.

The current manufacturing transformation is multifaceted. It is accompanied by profound changes in organizational morphology and industrial structure. Analysts have contrasted the traditional, vertically integrated firms with emerging cooperative small-firm networks and debated how the various organizational forms create and capture value.[4] It provokes a reexamination of social relations,[5] as team-based work organization replaces the traditional Fordist division of labor. It also corresponds to an intensifying world-scale battle among the industrial giants from the developed countries, prompting an active debate about the domestic benefits derived from foreign investment.[6]

These changes are directly related to the new manufacturing and networking technologies, which make possible new organizational structures, force a new social organization of production, and permit the coordination of far-flung corporate empires. The transformation is, of course, more than a consequence of the emergence of new information networking technologies. Rather, specific technology developments are part of broader attempts at tackling profound changes in manufacturers' competitive environment. Information technologies are an essential instrument in manufacturing companies' attempts to adjust to these changes, and information networks have often become the foundation upon which manufacturing activities are being reorganized. Network applications related to the manufacturing process, from design and production engineering to assembly and distribution, generate major needs for advanced network intelligence and broadband capabilities. As a result, manufacturing companies increasingly find themselves at the forefront of the drive to deploy advanced networks.

FROM FORDISM TO MASS VARIETY

The first step to gaining an understanding of the role information networking plays in the current transformation of manufacturing activities requires understanding the changes in the competitive environment within which manufacturing firms operate. Since the heyday of Fordism, several trends have converged to transform the competitive environment of manufacturing firms, pressing them to adapt, to reengineer their production processes, and to transform their organizations.

THE RAILROADS, TELEGRAPH, AND FORDISM

The United States dominated global manufacturing competition through the first three-quarters of the twentieth century as a result of the development of mass production and multidivisional management in the latter part of the nineteenth century. This system was built on an organization of production and management best exemplified by the way Henry Ford transformed his company to produce the 1908 Model T. Fordism, as it came to be known, was geared to the mass production of standardized products at low unit prices. It quickly spread beyond the automobile industry to become the dominant form of manufacturing organization in the United States.

Fordism rested, first and foremost, on innovations in the organization of production, which distinguish it from the former craft production system. With Fordism, products were highly standardized, designed of interchangeable parts, and simple to assemble. At the heart of the manufacturing process were factories organized along a continuous assembly line, in which each worker was responsible for one simple, repetitive task. Similarly, the machines on the assembly line were highly specialized and able to produce mass quantities of the parts needed for the final product. In this era, manufacturing companies became vertically integrated, with single ownership of the entire chain from raw materials to finished products, and were managed through a hierarchical, multidivisional organization.[7]

These organizational innovations were possible only because of the new infrastructure provided by railroads and the telegraph. As Alfred Chandler puts it:

> [This] revolution in the processes of distribution and production rested in large part on the new transportation and communication infrastructure. Modern mass production and mass distribution depend on the speed, volume and regularity in the movement of goods and messages made possible by the coming of the railroad, telegraph and steamship. . . . [A]s the basic infrastructure came into being between the 1850s and 1880s, modern methods of mass production and distribution . . . made their appearance.[8]

Indeed cheap, reliable, regular, and high-volume transportation was essential to guarantee a large and steady flow of raw materials into, and finished products out of, the factories. It was indispensable in order to reach the large markets that justified the production of massive quantities of products. Similarly, the communication networks, first the telegraph and then the telephone, were vital to the coordination of large and far-flung operations.

Just as the railroad and telegraph infrastructure was a key enabler for the transition from craft manufacture to the Fordist system of mass production, the new information infrastructure today is the central enabler of the shift to "intelligent manufacturing," with its themes of globalization, shortened product cycles, flexible production and distribution, and corporate reorganization.

GLOBALIZATION

There is much talk about the impending global competition among global companies, but few clear definitions of "globalization," beyond the general sense that, thanks to better communications, companies have easier access to the far-flung parts of the world and are less constrained by territorial boundaries.[9]

For the manufacturing sector, "globalization" refers to specific developments: U.S. companies are simultaneously facing increasing competition from foreign firms in their home markets and conducting a growing share of their business abroad. They also draw on widespread resources. For example, design, production, marketing, or service facilities involved in the making and selling of each product are often scattered nationally and internationally. This approach has been adopted partly to use corporate resources better (involve the best design teams in each area), partly for closeness to local conditions (design products where they will be manufactured or sold), and partly to address local content requirements. To control and coordinate these far-flung operations, corporations need effective information networks.

The meaning of "globalization" can be clarified by contrasting it with "internationalization," the code word of the earlier era.[10] Internationalization was the spread across borders of a dominant style of production organization— American Fordist methods of mass production—with marginal adaptations to local conditions. Globalization, by contrast, can be characterized by the emergence of multiple innovative methods originating in various places around the world.

Internationalization referred to one basic innovator and a set of followers. It followed traditional technology diffusion models rather well. Therefore, internationalization didn't generate much uncertainty for the followers. For Japan and the nations of Europe, the task was to catch up with the future, not to invent it. By contrast, globalization today is characterized by high uncertainty and intense new competitive pressures from rival innovators in all parts of the world.

Under Fordism, manufacturing firms competed primarily on price. Today's global competition is multidimensional. Price, quality, speed, and product differentiation are new axes along which to compare the merits of alternative models for productive organizations. For the organization of production, economies of scale, scope, and proximity no longer encompass the whole game. Worldwide sourcing, productive arrangements that attempt to take advantage of economies of scope, and different forms of flexible organization have become key. Many of these new dimensions of competition are explored in the following sections.[11]

SHORTENED CYCLES

Competitive success increasingly rests on a firm's ability to differentiate and adapt its products, and to do so rapidly in response to demand changes, or to anticipate such changes in order to identify and occupy lucrative niches. Product cycles have shrunk drastically, for instance, from ten years to four in the automobile industry. At the same time, new products constantly emerge and compete with established ones.

As a result, manufacturing companies are working to shorten the various cycles underlying their activities: concept to product, order to delivery, trouble report to repair. A major motive behind the deployment of corporate networks is to support new functions and applications that allow companies to adjust quickly to their new and changing competitive environments.

A critical part of the reorganization process is advanced information networking, which will enable firms to achieve shortened cycle times in the face of increased geographical dispersion. For example, interconnected use of computer-aided design and manufacturing networks aims at shortening the time from concept to product, and electronic data interchange speeds up part orders and their delivery.

NEW MARKETING AND MANUFACTURING METHODS

One important consequence of these changes is that firms have had to modernize and revitalize their commercial operations and marketing methods substantially. Greater proximity to the market, to clients' needs and demands, has become essential. Except for a few market segments where mass production of undifferentiated products remains viable, firms must react to constantly changing demand for products with shorter design lives. Moreover, the internationalization of markets fostered by greater freedom of trade did not result, despite certain expectations, in the need simply to produce longer series of existing products. On the contrary, market internationalization required firms to adapt to a wide variety of technical or cultural norms.

Commercial organizations and practices must be able to identify demand shifts rapidly, in order to steer their designers and production employees toward product choices that address existing and potential demand from a variety of customers in highly differentiated markets. They must use information networks to gather accurate information on demand and its variations and to send this information quickly to the firm's design and manufacturing decision centers.

On the production side, the new market environment also requires substantial changes. To remain competitive, companies must introduce enough organizational or technological flexibility within their mass production operations to differentiate products. At stake in current reorganizations and equipment choices is the successful transition from large volumes of standardized products to differentiated batches, without losing the benefits of traditional mass production. Thus, telecommunications networks enter the very heart of the production process as they transmit the information needed to program equipment and match production to orders received.

ORGANIZATIONAL INNOVATIONS AND CORPORATE FORM

To navigate the transition successfully, manufacturers can draw on a variety of new information technology tools, including numerically controlled machines, process controllers, and information networks. In addition to these technologies, however, they can build their adjustment around a new generation of organizational innovations. New manufacturing arrangements (such as the various forms of just-in-time supplies of components and raw materials), new logistics know-how (such as autonomous production islands linked through new parts circulation schemes or group technology), and stock management methods (such as materials management planning) together provide a company with an enriched collection of methods for organizing work and production. Effective information networks are vital to their deployment.

The relationships between headquarters and subsidiaries, and with partners and subcontractors, have been similarly transformed. The basic principle behind the new forms of interaction is to keep the economic advantages of integration while decentralizing to reduce fixed costs and specialize production without sacrificing flexibility. Thus, the combination of innovations in internal organization with new kinds of external links leads a company to new and varied forms. They become "network firms" and "virtual corporations," forms that are integral to their competitive drive and adaptation to the transformed environment.

These changes require denser, more flexible information networks within companies to support projects carried out by problem-centered, companywide work groups that cross functional and divisional lines and may involve people who seldom all work in the same location. Equally essential are better links with the outside, through publicly accessible networks, to support increased collaboration with outsiders. For product design and development or marketing and distribution, external partners increasingly need the same access to corporate information networks as the company's own employees. Finally, advanced public networks are becoming important for employees to access information from noncompany locations, whether traveling, working at home, or on customer premises.

MIXING PRODUCTIVITY AND FLEXIBILITY: TOWARD MASS VARIETY

In the end, this boils down to one essential challenge: a company's ability to create relative advantage upon which to establish long-term competitiveness. That ability depends on its capacity to combine economies of scale and economies of scope, to reconcile mass production with rapidly changing, differentiated products. This calls for a new art of manufacturing, in which the search for static flexibility through adaptation to short-term market and demand variations must not compromise the more essential benefits stemming from dynamic flexibility.[12] The result is a new regime of "mass variety."[13]

Meeting this challenge obviously calls, first and foremost, for smart choices of equipment and work organization methods. Here again, the production systems developed around telecommunications applications and network configurations often play an essential role in promoting better integration of production sequences, the only way to improve overall productivity, and greater flexibility in programming and reprogramming production processes. Network uses conceived around application and configuration flexibility can thus speed up the circulation of information essential to a firm's life, and simultaneously permit the firm's adaptation to its constantly changing environment.

However, networking technologies do not take on a preestablished and stable role within the firm. Rather, they come to suggest, supplement, and support sweeping organizational changes that affect virtually all corporate domains, from product design to production methods and marketing techniques. It is precisely in this sense that information technology networks have become "strategic." Indeed, combined with the organizational transformations that preceded them or that they made possible, they constitute a key to renewing the foundations of corporate and national competitiveness.

Individual manufacturers' paths through this transformation are as varied as the companies themselves. The next section examines a specific example: General Motors's deployment of information networking throughout its production process. While the GM approach merely represents one particular answer to the manufacturing transition, the example of the automaker is instructive. As the largest and most complex of manufacturing organizations, automakers have provided the images and the vocabulary that shaped our understanding of traditional manufacturing. Today, as the automakers of the world face common pressures and explore a range of alternative responses, the automobile industry often constitutes the proving ground for the application of information technologies.[14] Furthermore, the challenges faced by GM are not unique to the auto industry, and the dilemmas it faces mirror the broader challenges the nation now confronts in the deployment of the NII.

"From Art to Part": GM's Intelligent Factory

Recent efforts by the General Motors Corporation to transform its manufacturing approach illustrate a specific response to the competitive changes affecting the automobile industry and manufacturing in general. GM has chosen a path emphasizing extensive deployment of information technology to automate, integrate, and speed up its production operations. That choice contrasts with the approach of other car companies, such as Toyota, which has chosen to start from a reorganization of its production process and only to use information technology to support and augment this reorganization.[15] While it is too early to tell which of the two holds greater promise, GM's choices underscore a broader challenge facing U.S. manufacturers and the U.S. economy: should the deployment of the NII's technologies drive the automation of traditional activities or, on the contrary, should it be conceived as a complement to a broader economic reorganization?

General Motors' C4 Program

In 1989, General Motors embarked on a corporation-wide, five-year effort to transform the way it designs and produces automobiles.[16] Under the title "C4 Project"—the four C's stand for CAD (computer-aided design), CAM (computer-aided manufacturing), CAE (computer-aided engineering), and CIM (computer-integrated manufacturing)—the effort aimed at making the best use of existing information processing and networking technologies to speed up car development and manufacturing.

GM's ultimate goal is to deploy a coherent information infrastructure that will integrate design, manufacturing, and business processes throughout GM around a core of three-dimensional CAD data. The new C4 environment, articulated around companywide standards and open systems concepts, will let GM engineers run most software on any of the company's computers and share information among facilities, divisions, and contractors. Driving GM's C4 plans is the company's strategic thrust over the next five years to reduce by 60 percent the time it takes to bring a car from "art to part"—from the artist's rendering of a concept to a car ready for sale. From sixty-five months at the project's start, this cycle should take only eighteen to twenty months in the late 1990s.

Such a drastic reduction requires more than mere automation of traditional design, manufacturing, and business functions. It calls for a thorough re-organization of the car-making process. However, GM chose to drive the reorganization process by deploying advanced information networks. It believes that the key to this kind of production reorganization is a unified information processing infrastructure, able to support consistent methods throughout the company.

Indeed, GM traced its competitive troubles to the ways computer systems and information networks had been used (or not used) throughout the company. In the late 1980s, three-quarters of design and engineering work within GM was still done "manually," with pencils and blueprints rather than computer workstations. Moreover, when automation was used, its deployment was fragmented. Typically at GM, each division chose its own applications software and workstations, and as many as forty different hardware platforms, running twenty-seven incompatible CAD packages, were used throughout the company. Different divisions often used the same car components, but had to re-create CAD files representing these same components to work on their incompatible systems.

This fragmentation made it very difficult for engineers and product designers to share ideas and concepts at the early stages of the vehicle development process and inhibited exchanges throughout the life of a car project. Communicating a design idea or a set of specifications required painstaking translation from one CAD standard to another. Inevitably, data were lost during the translation and had to be reentered manually.

Together, the relative lack of computer tools and the nonstandardization of the existing ones slowed the sequential development process considerably. Most important, information systems fragmentation becomes increasingly troublesome as GM tries to become "fast-to-market." Quick and seamless information exchange becomes indispensable in order to move toward simultaneous engineering, to integrate various aspects of vehicle development right from the start of a project, and to foster interaction among the engineering teams involved.

The reorganization is no small undertaking. GM makes over a hundred different car models, and an average car consists of some ten thousand parts. Many of those parts are designed with the aid of computers, which represent and store them as mathematical models. To take an example, an average fender is represented by a ten-megabyte file. The shapes, dimensions, and material specifications stored in this model are used repeatedly by various GM employees. Stylists and structural and aerodynamic engineers modify and refine the shape as they work on the overall line and structure of the car. Manufacturing engineers use this information to design the stamping dies used to make the part and add to it representations of the complementary surfaces (the shapes of the leftover steel around the part itself) that will prevent wrinkles and tears during the stamping. The tool and measuring instrument makers incorporate this information in the machines they put together to make the parts and check the accuracy of the finished product. Information such as the part reference number, how it is assembled and fastened to other parts in the car, must be attached to the part's representation if they are to be used throughout the manufacturing process. User manuals and service bulletins for maintenance must include drawings of the part along with additional information such as reference numbers and assembly sketches.

Under current processes, when a component's CAD file leaves the design department (and the design automation "island") to be used by production and manufacturing engineers, the data are transformed into a new format—suited to the next "island" of production automation but now inaccessible to the designers. Subsequent changes in design can then take months, as the data need to be reformatted (sometimes reentered) at each iteration.

The problem is not simply to pass computer files from one team to the next in sequential order, but to allow continuous interaction between various teams involved in the design, production, and assembly of a part or system. To continue with our fender example, production engineers and toolmakers must work concurrently on designing the fender and the tools that will be used to produce it, provide continuous feedback to the stylists about the manufacturability of the fender they have designed, and suggest minor shape changes that could make stamping easier.

A networked CAD system supporting such interaction is the basis of simultaneous engineering. Creating shapes and styling, designing the tools that will produce the parts, and organizing the manufacturing and assembly process can then progress simultaneously, no longer sequentially. This is, according to the C4 strategy, how the "art to part" cycle can be cut by 60 percent. The information backbone behind such a strategy must be able to transfer large files among decentralized engineering workstations and let engineering teams work together on-line. It must support an enormous database of multimedia files (containing graphics, math models, text) representing parts, dies, tools, measuring instruments, assembly processes, and service documents.

FROM SOPHISTICATED ISLANDS TO ENABLING INFRASTRUCTURE

In choosing the C4 approach, GM had to tackle two distinct tensions. The first pits performance against standardization: Is it better to seek the most advanced system for each application (and thereby inhibit information sharing) or to favor consistent solutions throughout a company (and accept less-than-maximum performance at some points)? The second tension opposes two visions of information technology's role within the broader process of corporate change: Should information technology be used to overcome the limitations of the existing production and commercialization systems or, on the contrary, be regarded only as one element—not necessarily the most important one—of a broader, but slower, corporate transformation?

Past information technology choices at GM have favored the first term in each of these two tensions. GM had preferred to view and use information technology applications as sophisticated solutions to individual competitive problems rather than as standardized enablers of a broader organizational transformation. By and large, GM had chosen to use advanced technological solutions tailored to each area of application and to use information technology fixes to substitute for broader organizational transformation.

GM's traditional management approach explains many of these choices. By favoring decentralization, it placed decisions in the hands of its divisions or even within divisions of each functional group. By promoting arm's length relationships among its allied suppliers and automotive divisions, and by encouraging outright competition between various divisions, it created incentives for each of them to choose the technological solution best adapted to its individual problems. By declining to enforce corporate-wide standards, it allowed proliferation of incompatible solutions. In some cases, it encouraged individual groups to adopt different approaches in their efforts to gain competitive advantages over each other.

In the mid-1980s, however, GM began a profound shift in its approach and is now attempting to deploy information technologies as part of a standardized enabling infrastructure for the company. The purchase of the Electronic Data Systems Corporation and the corporate-wide C4 program both reflect this choice.

The dominant dimension of this change so far has been the move toward standardized information technology solutions. While C4 is the prominent manifestation of the change, it is not an isolated example. For example, GM is now moving closer to standard electronic data interchange solutions with its subcontractors and partners, and it has deployed a new satellite network for its dealers. Most information technology purchasing and development decisions are now coordinated by Electronic Data Systems. Overall standardization now takes precedence over technological sophistication throughout the deployment of GM's information network systems.

The broader dimension of the transition appears more problematic. While GM's policy documents claim that information technology deployment represents only a small portion of the reorganization effort needed for the company "to get fast," the company has great difficulty stepping back from its traditional technology-fix approach to competitive problems. The C4 Program in particular, which some had hoped would spark a deeper reorganization of GM's production processes, remains largely a technology-driven program.

GM's dilemmas mirror the broader challenges facing the nation as it develops the national information infrastructure. First, should the NII promote individual sophisticated applications rather than universal access and interconnection? The former approach risks leaving behind less innovative segments of the economy for the sake of providing the most advanced corporate users with the means to pursue leading-edge competitive strategies. Second, should the NII provide focus on technology as agent of change or aim to supplement and support broad economic reorganization? The answers to these questions about information networking technology's role in the current transition imply distinct policy choices.

A NETWORK INFRASTRUCTURE
FOR MANUFACTURING

The ways that manufacturing companies use technologies have important implications for the emerging information infrastructure. First, manufacturing applications engender enormous growth in data traffic, with dramatically new communications patterns. Second, they require substantial improvements not only in private networks but, perhaps more surprisingly, in the public networks needed for interaction between various firms involved in common manufacturing processes. Finally, because the best network-based manufacturing practices remain to be invented, they demand networks flexible enough to support wide-ranging experimentation and inclusive enough to foster broad-based cumulative learning. This will succeed only if manufacturing workers are provided with sufficient training and ability to participate in this discovery process.

THE TRAFFIC EXPLOSION[17]

In the past, network suppliers generated most network transformations. Network users now take the lead as they explore the potential of networking technology. Manufacturing companies often find themselves in the forefront of this drive.

Until now, the networks in place had no trouble accommodating data traffic. While data traffic grew faster than voice traffic, overall data volume remained comparatively small, and the predominant types of data applications (for example, file transfer, electronic mail) did not by and large conflict with the dominant network configuration. This is changing rapidly. First, data networking is growing so quickly that it no longer fits quietly within the existing networks. Manufacturing users in particular are reporting data traffic growth commensurate with that of the Internet, on the order of 10 to 20 percent per month. Such growth builds up quickly to require a complete network overhaul. Second, this traffic growth increasingly corresponds to new kinds of networking applications and places very different demands on the networks.

Comprehensive statistics are difficult to come by, but indications of the shift can be found in individual companies. Within Hewlett-Packard for example, wide-area data traffic has skyrocketed from one hundred megabytes per month in 1980 to over one terabyte (one million megabytes) per month in 1993, a ten-thousand-fold increase. This explosion is almost entirely driven by manufacturing and engineering applications, which today account for over 70 percent of total traffic, up from only 7 percent in 1980, dwarfing commercial and administrative uses.

In predicting what this traffic explosion will mean for the networks, extrapolations of current network use can be misleading. Expecting broadband applications to emerge as straightforward extensions of current narrow-band services, we envision making "broadband telephone calls" in which the greater bandwidth simply serves to carry video as well as voice, or to transmit a large file very quickly. We think of applications requiring the transmission of much more information, but we picture communication patterns similar to those of a standard telephone call.

In fact, the actual applications of broadband networking emerging today— those responsible for explosive growth—follow a variety of new patterns, each fundamentally different from that of a telephone call. At one end of the range, real-time interactive applications based on client-server architectures such as GM's distributed CAD library, are growing much faster than traditional file transfers. They require a network capable of switching very large bursts of data very rapidly. The key demands on the underlying network are quick response times and high interactivity. By contrast with a telephone call, they hold the line for only fractions of seconds at a time but need large capacity to guarantee instant response rather than to handle large amounts of data.

At the other end of the range are applications such as GM's video broadcasts to its dealerships. For these, the time required to set up a connection or the transmission delays are less important than for a telephone call, but once the "broadcast call" is established, the broadband conduit is continuously used at its maximum capacity. Applications with similarly unconventional requirements spread along the continuum between these two extremes. Many involve computer-to-computer communications such as CAD interconnection for concurrent engineering or interconnected machine tools. Most of these emerging applications impose requirements on the underlying network that differ drastically from those of traditional telephony.

The shift in usage patterns is fueled by new ways to use computers and by their increasing ubiquity, power, and diverse applications. At the leading edge of the business world, and primarily for manufacturing and engineering applications, a new computing "paradigm" is emerging, one that replaces simple information transfers with "cooperative" computing. The move toward open systems in client-server architectures represents a fundamental change in how computers operate and communicate. Once limited to file transfers and terminal emulation, demands now shift to interoperability and real-time interaction. Cooperative computing is the key to intelligent manufacturing.

WIDE AND OPEN LINKS: THE LIMITS OF PRIVATE NETWORKING

The simultaneous need for better internal networks and better public extensions of these private networks parallels changing patterns of network use, based on client-server environments, and changing patterns of economic organization, emphasizing richer relationships among clients, suppliers, and partners.

Initially confined to local-area networks (LANs), the new computing architecture will soon extend to private wide-area networks (WANs), and require better connections between private and public networks. It also enables new applications, such as cross-functional information systems (supporting variable-geometry "virtual work groups" collaborating on a product design), image storage and retrieval systems, and software distribution mechanisms (for example, the downloading of instructions to numerically controlled machine tools, or on-line access to assembly manuals from the shop floor). These uses are driving the need for low-delay, high-throughput networks.

As telecommunications became deregulated, many U.S. companies deployed private networks to handle their growing networking needs. They were motivated by the shortcomings of public networks unable to handle corporate requirements, as well as their own strategic need to control their telecommunications. Often, however, they would have preferred to use a public network if one that could satisfy their requirements for capability and control were available.[18] Indeed, many companies returned to the public network when Virtual Private Networks (VPN) services became available (VPN gives them significant control over the portion of the public network they use, making it seem "virtually private"). For their data networking needs, however, corporate users remain unsatisfied with the public networking options available, and many continue to maintain and use private networks.

However, emerging corporate uses are straining the limits of purely private networking. As production reorganization reaches beyond the borders of individual companies to involve their suppliers, clients, partners, or subcontractors, it creates a need (and a demand) for public networks able to match the capabilities of the private networks the corporations have built. Frustrated by the limitations of the public network, yet unwilling to remain trapped within private networks, corporate users would be willing to play an active part in helping with the modernization of public networks, provided an adequate policy framework is devised. In addition, an advanced public network is needed to support tight links among a dense fabric of individual firms, to allow them to form manufacturing partnerships with others, in a flexible, changeable pattern of "network firms." Together, these developments suggest new ways to leverage private interests for the good of the public network infrastructure.

NETWORK-SUPPORTED LEARNING CYCLES

As business activities, ranging from design and engineering to manu-facturing and sales, make increasing use of telecommunications to convey information or permit collaboration, a firm's information network comes to mirror its business practices. The shape and characteristics of the network embody the company's business linkages, both internal (the interaction among the firm's units) and external (the firm's interaction with its partners, suppliers, and clients). Corporate information networks evolve jointly with the transformation of business processes. Ultimately, the flexibility of a firm's corporate network infrastructure underpins its ability to automate and reorganize its operations.[19]

A company's organization and the information network that supports it evolve jointly through a "learning cycle."[20] Each cycle consists of three distinct phases: automation, experimentation, and reorganization. During the automation phase, companies apply networking technology to existing activities in a straightforward attempt to reduce costs and speed up operations. Automation allows them to experiment, explore information technology possibilities, and test their limits. Eventually, firms reach the limits of the existing network and need to engage in a next phase: reconfiguring the network to articulate new work processes. They end up with a new network, upon which they can begin to automate new functions, starting another cycle. In succession, the cycles constitute a technology trajectory.

For our purpose here, three characteristics of these phases matter. First, the relationship between the network and the manufacturing processes it supports varies. During automation, the process comes first and the network technologies serve to enhance it, not to transform it. By contrast, during the reorganization phase, network and process evolve jointly: Available technologies suggest possible changes to the process, process evolution forces network reconfiguration. While automation proceeds sequentially (from the definition of a manufacturing process to the application of networking technology to that process), reorganization requires iterative adjustments between process and network.

Second, the firm needs different kinds of control over its network during each phase: While automation simply focuses on network applications, reorganization requires deeper access to network control and management in order to carry out the iterative reconfiguration of the network that accompanies work reorganization.

Third, different kinds of learning take place at each stage of the cycle, accruing to different participants. Network users typically learn "by using" (they determine how they can harness available technology to serve their business objectives), while network providers learn "by doing" (the art of deploying networking technology to serve what they perceive as their clients' demands).[21] In the first, daily practice generates knowledge about networking applications, their possibilities and limits, as well as a clearer vision of the work processes being automated. By contrast, reorganization yields direct knowledge about network management and configuration.

The types of benefits a company seeks through the deployment of network technology vary through the phases of the learning cycle. In addition, corporate ability to obtain the corresponding gains is affected by the way it envisions the relationship between process and network support, by the degree to which it controls various aspects of its network, and by its ability to derive cumulative learning from its use of network technology.

AUTOMATION

Benefits deriving from automation are straightforward. First, companies automate to reduce costs. They seek lower transmission costs and lower transaction costs, and they expect higher reliability from more precise communication. Second, they want to speed up existing processes. Examples range from the deployment of CAD/CAM technologies (to accelerate design and production processes), to the implementation of electronic data interchange (to expedite transactions with suppliers and subcontractors). Third, they turn to automation because it allows increasingly complex processes. For example, the increasing number of parts for the growing number of variants being offered on a basic car model increase the sheer quantity of information that describes design, assembly, and logistics. Managing the resulting complexity requires automation of the processing and transmission of that information.

REORGANIZATION

The benefits of reorganization are more complex: they involve interactive transformation of both information networks and industrial processes. The network simultaneously enables process reorganization and suggests possible ways to transform operations. First, reorganization transforms individual business processes. For example, after the initial experience gained from automating through electronic data interchange, companies may push the technology farther to reorganize their logistics. They can interconnect CAD workstations to permit collaborative work among a team of engineers, articulating a new design process around high-speed networks. They can use information networks to reorganize production to introduce flexibility and variety within traditional mass production operations.

Second, reorganization can involve a variety of formerly independent processes. Networks serve not simply to transform individual business activities, but to integrate separate activities. One of the most ambitious examples is the implementation of simultaneous engineering to replace more traditional sequential processes. At stake there is not only the transformation of isolated design, engineering, or manufacturing processes, but their joint reorganization into a new process that allows wide-ranging collaboration from the start. Sophisticated networking technologies are absolutely critical, not only to make the new organization possible, but also to suggest how it can be carried out.

EXPERIMENTATION

A company's ability to progress through the successive phases of the learning cycle rests on its ability to experiment with the different networks and processes it puts in place and from its skill at learning from that experimentation.

Successful long-term implementation of networking technology is not measured by a single success in one round of automation or reorganization but in cumulative learning through a succession of cycles. This rests upon the balance a firm is able to strike between customizing its network to a specific phase and ensuring its future flexibility for later phases, as well as upon the firm's ability cumulatively to combine what it learns "by using" during automation phases with what it learns "by doing" during the reorganization phases.

When understood as a learning cycle, successful development of a telecommunications infrastructure requires network providers and network users to combine their distinct skills and knowledge. Neither provider nor user possesses the full breadth of knowledge and hands-on experience needed to develop alone a successful infrastructure or to take full advantage of its possibilities. They must build upon each other's insights and cumulatively improve the information infrastructure.

What is true of the relationship between corporate users and their network suppliers becomes absolutely critical within companies: tight collaboration between shop-floor workers (the internal "users") and those responsible for corporate technology deployment (the internal "providers") is key to the transformation of manufacturing. What shop-floor workers know about the production process must be combined with what the technologists know about the technology's potential.[22] This suggests that strategies simply aimed at eliminating labor costs through automation are shortsighted and foreclose further competitive gains through experimentation and reorganization. This in turn demands continuous training to provide workers with the skills they need to participate in this learning cycle.

POLICY RECOMMENDATIONS

Dramatic change, rather than incremental evolution, characterizes the current transformation of the network infrastructure in the United States. Multiple networks and networking applications are emerging, representing different technological trajectories in the face of discontinuous change. They are driven by actual users and real applications, ranging from navigation tools on the Internet to concurrent engineering tools on the private networks of manufacturing firms.

The pluralistic "network of networks" is now a reality. It is fast becoming even more so as new networks (CATV, Internet, and so forth) join the traditional ones (the Bell companies, AT&T, MCI, and so forth) within the national information infrastructure. What is needed are policies that put in place mechanisms to make sure that the various pieces work well together and provide universal opportunities. This imperative applies to all parts of the emerging information infrastructure, but it has specific meaning for manufacturing.

While a pluralistic network makes it possible to serve individual users' needs, it also tends to make advanced capabilities available only to those firms rich enough to afford them and aware enough of the potential benefits to demand them. Others risk being left behind. In the past, when "Ma Bell" deployed new technologies in its network, responding to its most demanding clients, all those connected to the public network benefited. Within a pluralistic network, the challenge is to ensure broad diffusion of innovations and broad access to new services.

Failing that, the United States would end up with a bifurcated infrastructure. Those denied access to advanced information services (for example, small manufacturing companies) would be unable to develop the skills they need to take advantage of the emerging infrastructure. In the short term, fragmentation and unequal access thwart efficient use of the infrastructure, making it harder for assemblers to interconnect seamlessly with their suppliers, partners, or customers.

The long-term consequences could be even more damaging, because fragmentation and uneven access prevent broad-based exploration of telecommunications technologies and services. Nobody can predict with certainty which specific network technologies and applications will be most useful or what their economic benefits will be. The promising applications will be discovered, and their benefits understood, only through sustained experimentation with the network. Network fragmentation runs the risk of preventing exploration of entire classes of applications that rely on interconnection between diverse network resources. Unequal access risks excluding large segments of the economy from contributing to the discovery process.

This is true for every economic activity, but becomes especially relevant for manufacturing. As firms move toward network forms, their survival depends on the accessibility of a wide base of technically sophisticated suppliers and subcontractors. Government policy decisions can play a critical role in fostering a networking environment that promotes experimentation with new patterns of interfirm linkage. The overarching need is for policies that ensure that the appropriate technologies reach the appropriate users in a timely fashion, coupled with help to users throughout the economy in understanding and taking advantage of the technology's possibilities.

These are policy recommendations that would serve the overall goal:[23]

1. Let market competition drive the development of a network portfolio while government policy focuses on reviewing the portfolio for gaps in service to major constituencies, encouraging the development of missing elements and fostering interconnection.

    Network evolution is unpredictable, and few of us can today imagine what will be tomorrow's successful applications. As a result, there is no guarantee that any single category of network providers will offer an optimal infrastructure. Only market competition is likely to provide a broad network portfolio by stimulating development of the variety of networks that embody alternative technological approaches.

    But competition alone cannot fulfill all needs. It will not guarantee access or interconnection among the portfolio constituents. For example, value-added networks could play an important role in the diffusion of electronic data interchange throughout the manufacturing sector but often will do so only when there is a clear market demand. Because many small auto-parts suppliers in the United States have never had a chance to experiment with standardized electronic data interchange with their larger clients, they perceive it simply as an extra cost pushed onto them by the automakers. Failing to see its benefits, they fail to create the interconnection markets value-added network providers would serve.

Wherever there are major constituencies not being served by a given network portfolio (this is particularly the case of many small companies in the manufacturing sector), public policy must explicitly foster universality. Such actions could take a variety of forms, such as direct public funding of development, the imposition of common-carrier requirements upon certain network providers, or old-fashioned cross-subsidies.

Similarly, ensuring access and interconnection between the elements of the network portfolio should remain an essential obligation of the U.S. government. In particular, policy should explicitly pursue real-life trials for interconnection between the portfolio's networks, just as it now licenses field tests for new technologies and services within individual networks. As once-dominant carriers become exposed to increasing competition, interconnection obligations will increasingly need to be reciprocal.

2. To ensure the necessary experimentation and learning, government policy should encourage exploratory use among targeted user populations of special economic significance to the manufacturing sector (such as small businesses or worker training organizations), while conducting fundamentally different field trials for others.

Corporate networking experience suggests that experimentation and learning play an essential role in network development. Some elements of the network portfolio, such as the private networks of large manufacturing corporations, will support that experimentation on their own. Other user populations, including small and medium-sized businesses, may not. Their experimentation and learning will have to be publicly encouraged.

Network providers and other user populations will have to develop initial experimentation and learning the old-fashioned way—through field trials. But current trials, with their emphasis on the provision and development of advanced network technology, are inadequate. Field trials will thus have to be rethought. They will have to be extended in scope and participation (involving more end users, network providers, and third-party service providers) and financed differently (for example, through a royalty on eventual service provision).

In addition to making the network itself available to potential manufacturing users, it would be necessary to demonstrate its possibilities and to provide assistance to targeted users, in particular smaller companies. Such programs should include the provision of training to potential users, particularly within small manufacturing firms, so they can develop sufficient skill to participate in network experimentation. This could be one of the functions of an "industrial extension service," which would provide focused training for information network applications and assistance in their implementation. Field trials specifically aimed at manufacturing applications could also be fostered, with a special emphasis on exploring the support of interfirm linkages (for example, among assemblers and parts suppliers, among partners and subcontractors).

3.   Where possible, U.S. government policy must encourage major network users to finance large pieces of the emerging portfolio while finding other means to reduce the costs to poorer and initially nonparticipating businesses. (This, clearly, will require a great deal of political will.)

Lead users will pay for what they need and consequently can finance a substantial part of the network portfolio. Corporate experience also suggest that where permitted, lead users would also pay to embed the new features they need in public infrastructures. This would probably remain true even if a premium was initially demanded of major users, so long as long-term cost reductions, or enhanced network access, were guaranteed. A variety of incentives could help to encourage major users to finance infrastructure development, from tax breaks to a temporary royalty stream on services they helped to initiate. However, extending the advanced network portfolio universally to smaller manufacturing firms is likely to require other novel financing schemes. Overall, what should be sought is the creation of broader constituencies of network users, to pool their individual resources and expertise into mutually beneficial network arrangements. Unfortunately, legislation in the 104th Congress does not take on this crucial task.

3

THE GLOBALIZATION OF TELECOMMUNICATIONS AND INFORMATION

LINDA GARCIA

I n September 1993, the Clinton administration laid out a vision of a national information infrastructure that would "help unleash an information revolution [so as] to change forever the way people live, work, and interact with one another."[1] In keeping with the global reach of advanced communication and information technologies, the administration did not constrain its vision by national geographic boundaries. Speaking in March 1994 at the World Tele-communication Development Conference held in Buenos Aires, Vice President Al Gore called on world leaders to adopt a global vision of the information highway. A global information infrastructure (GII), said Gore, will not only serve to foster economic growth and development; equally important, it will help to generate political stability, social improvement, and the spread of democracy.[2]

Although new technologies have considerable potential to improve social, economic, and political conditions on a global scale, such an outcome is far from certain. How these technologies will be developed, and to what purposes they will be deployed, will depend not only on the capability of the technology; it will depend as much, if not more, on the social, economic, and political forces driving their evolution.

As in the case of the national information infrastructure (NII), the ad-ministration looks to technology advances and market forces to drive the development of the GII. In keeping with this perspective, the administration has argued that the most important steps the U.S. government can take to realize this vision is to promote the privatization and liberalization of foreign telecommunication regimes.

This paper suggests that this assumption is far too simplistic. Examining the trend toward globalization from two distinct, but related, perspectives, it argues that advances in technology and market forces alone will not suffice to achieve all of the lofty goals associated with the vision of a global information highway. In fact, if these forces are left simply to run their courses, they will likely give rise to a number of conflicts and trade-offs that will require very difficult political choices as well as compromises on the part of all nation-states. Making decisions in the marketplace is appropriate when there is agreement on the measure of exchange. The political arena is far more appropriate, however, when it is necessary to choose among competing values. Thus, sooner or later, political leaders from all countries will need to reach a consensus about the basic "rules of the road."

GLOBALIZATION DEFINED

Samuel Morse was perhaps the first to anticipate the idea of a "global village." Petitioning Congress to support the development and deployment of the telegraph, he wrote: "It will not be long ere the whole surface of this country will be channeled for those nerves to diffuse with the speed of thought, a knowledge of all that is occurring throughout the land; making, in fact, one neighborhood of the country."[3] Morse's vision of linking disparate peoples and cultures from across the globe was revived with each new communication technology that came along. Not surprisingly, therefore, recent advances in communication and information technologies still conjure up, if not a global community, at least a global economy.

Even today, however, notwithstanding major advances in technology, global communications can be spoken of only in a limited sense; for although a number of sophisticated communication systems now span the globe, penetration rates, interconnection, levels of use, and access provisions continue to diverge considerably, in accordance with economic and political geography. The present situation can, however, be distinguished from those of the past. Whereas, in the past, technology advances served as the major impetus for global deployment and diffusion, today a number of other economic and social forces are also pushing in the same direction.

Globalization is related to two distinct but interconnected phenomena that help determine the socioeconomic changes associated with it. The first involves the concepts of comprehensiveness and universality. Global communications, as embodied in these notions, entail the distribution of communication networks and information flows on a worldwide, equally accessible basis. The value, or goal, incorporated in this notion of "globalization" is availability and access, while the forces driving it are technology advance and technology diffusion. From this perspective, globalization—as an ultimate goal—can be said to exist only when any person or communication device can communicate effectively with another person or device, or acquire and process information, regardless of its physical location. Measures of this type of globalization might include, therefore, the ubiquity of technology and its applications, the cost of access, as well as the connectivity of technology.

The second meaning attached to the term *globalization* relates not to geographic scope but to territorial boundaries.[4] In this sense, globalization can be said to occur when social interactions and transactions transcend territorial, state boundaries, and thereby supersede both national and inter-governmental decision-making processes. Market forces drive this type of globalization, which results in a shift in the provisioning of communication and information from the public to the private sector and from the national to the international marketplace. The value associated with this shift is efficiency. Communication resources are assumed to be allocated more efficiently if they are a response to supply and demand signals from a global market. Evidence and measures of this type of globalization might take the form of the growth and development of a world market for communication and information products and services; the proliferation in the number and variety of private-sector communication providers; and the emergence of new, transnational, nongovernmental centers of decisionmaking.

These two types of globalization are interrelated, one often driving the other. For example, the global deployment of communication technology facilitates the development of transnational organizations. In turn, these organizations, through their demand for communications, help drive the diffusion of technology and the development of a global marketplace.

This interrelationship may not always be mutually reinforcing, however. The values of universality and efficiency sometimes conflict. As the history of technology deployment makes clear, national governments have often found it necessary to promote universal access and the deployment of a communication infrastructure because of the failure of the marketplace to support universal service and other related social goals.[5] The economic incentives provided in the international marketplace may similarly inhibit the deployment of technology to all corners of the earth, to rich and poor alike. Nor is the international marketplace, on its own, likely to give rise to communication networks that are interconnected on a global, that is to say, universal, basis.[6]

Such conflicts in values are likely because communication is not simply a commodity—like cars, food, and apparel—that can be bought and sold in the marketplace. More important, communication and the technologies that facilitate and mediate it serve as a basic social infrastructure that supports all forms of human activities. Communication, as Lucian Pye has described it, "is the web of human society, [and] the flow of communication determines the direction and pace of dynamic social development."[7] Thus, how communication technologies evolve, and the way in which they are interconnected and made available, will have major social consequences.[8]

It is in recognition of the importance of this relationship that many governments have fought so tenaciously to promote and channel the development of their communication networks.[9] As many communication policy decisions are shifted to the global marketplace, the criteria on the basis of which they are decided may be at odds with other national policy agendas. Moreover, because markets tend to reduce values to a common measure, the shift of decision making to the global market makes it more difficult to recognize and take into account the need to make difficult social choices and trade-offs.[10] A characterization and discussion of global communications, viewed from both the perspectives identified here may help to elucidate the areas where conflicts in values might arise, and thus where national and international policymakers need to focus their attention.

GLOBALIZATION AS A FUNCTION OF ADVANCES IN AND DIFFUSION OF TECHNOLOGY

Just as the birth of the telegraph, telephone, and television gave rise to communication systems and networks that stretched across the globe, many of the technology advances taking place today will facilitate worldwide access. Major improvements continue to be made with respect to all aspects of communication networking.[11] These advances are fostering both the supply and demand of global communication systems and services. Reduced cost and improved performance support the extension of communication systems and services over wider geographic areas. Global demand is stimulated by reductions in the cost of service, improvements in networking capability, and the development of new and more flexible communication systems and services.

RECENT TECHNOLOGY ADVANCES

One major step toward global service capacity was the development of fiber-optic technology. This technology has greatly reduced cost and increased capacity, and it has facilitated digital connectivity among nations.[12] Thus, today there are more than twenty-five thousand kilometers of optical fiber laid across the Atlantic and the Pacific.[13] Moreover, in the past few years an unprecedented number of new transoceanic fiber-cable projects have been undertaken. Included among these are two in the Atlantic and three more in the Pacific.[14]

Advances in wireless technology also hold promise for global communications, making it possible to extend service to countries and regions where the high costs of communication systems and/or unsuitable geographic terrain have historically stifled development. High-power satellites used with very small aperture terminals (VSATs), for example, can not only deliver one-way video services but also enable high-speed data transfer, imaging, computer-aided design (CAD), computer-integrated manufacturing (CIM), facsimile, digitized video, and audio.[15]

Satellites have proved especially useful for providing service to areas such as Eastern Europe and the former Soviet Union, where demand is much greater than the existing infrastructure can handle. Thus, in Russia today, satellite links carry most of the republic's eight hundred telephone circuits to the West.[16] Latin American countries are also looking to satellite technology to meet their growing global and regional communication needs.[17] There are already a number of earth stations in place in Central and South America that take advantage of INTELSAT's digital links to provide international voice, data, and imaging services for business.[18]

Satellite technology has also allowed the newly industrialized nations of the Pacific Rim to provide communication services at a pace commensurate with the vigorous growth of their economies. International high-speed digital, private-line service, provided through Intelsat Business Service, was introduced in 1987 to link Japan and the United States. Carriers from Hong Kong, Japan, Malaysia, and Singapore quickly followed suit. In fact, with growth rates exceeding 50 percent, demand soon exceeded INTELSAT's capacity, and domestic and regional satellites were required to fill the gap.[19] Japan has already launched a second domestic satellite, while South Korea, Malaysia, Thailand, and the Philippines have either committed to, or are planning, their own systems. As competition among carriers becomes more intense, users benefit from specialized service offerings and discounted prices.[20]

In Europe, satellites (along with cable technology) have been used primarily to support commercial broadcasting. From 1988 to 1990, the number of European satellites increased from 9 to 17, while the number of satellite channels increased from 67 to 138.[21] The Europeans have been much less inclined, however, to foster satellite usage for data and voice services. Satellite services are themselves still somewhat restricted.[22] The European Telecommunications Standards Institute (ETSI) has been accused of delaying the development of a VSAT market as a means of protecting state telecommunications providers. In 1993, there were about sixteen hundred two-way interactive VSAT terminals operating in Europe, with about three thousand more on order; in contrast, in the United States more than fifty thousand such dishes had been installed by Hughes Network Systems alone.[23]

Looking further into the future, global networks based on the development of low earth orbiting satellites (LEOS) offer great promise, allowing communication services to be relayed anywhere throughout the world. LEOS fall into two categories. Those generally referred to as "little LEOS" use very small satellites and operate in frequencies below one gigahertz (in the very high frequency/ultra high frequency bands). Little LEOS can be used to provide two-way data, messaging, and position determination services worldwide. These systems are expected to cost $6 million to $10 million per satellite.[24] In contrast, "big LEOS," which can provide voice as well as data services, are planned to operate in frequencies above one gigahertz. Because these systems are larger and more complex, they are also likely to be twice as expensive, costing on average $10 million to $20 million per satellite.[25]

Although LEOS can greatly extend the geographic scope of communication, they may not necessarily improve access. Some fear that, given the high cost of developing these systems, the services they offer will be prohibitively expensive for many.[26]

For example, even when mass-produced, Motorola's Iridium telephone, which would be necessary for access to these services, is expected to cost about $1,500. At this price, a person living in the Central African Republic, earning on average $376 a year, would have to work four years to buy a telephone. With service expected to cost about $3 a minute, the customer would have to work seventeen hours to pay for a one-minute telephone call.[27]

On a more modest scale, microwave transmission can also be used to enhance global communication. Microwave already provides about one-third of all worldwide transmission capacity, and it is relatively inexpensive to install and upgrade. Recently, firms such as Alcatel and Northern Telecom have adapted microwave for use in high-speed networks. Although there may be limited prospects for this technology in advanced industrial countries where technology options abound, a growing market is predicted in developing countries where costs are high and the alternatives few.[28]

THE ROLE OF INTERCONNECTION

Although some technologies, such as satellites, are inherently global in scope, other technologies can be used to provide global service if interconnected on a worldwide basis. Cellular communication is a particularly promising technology in this regard, given its low cost in relation to wire-line technologies and its rapid growth in markets throughout the world.[29] By 1996, worldwide demand is expected to exceed twenty-three million subscribers.[30] There are already approximately twelve million subscribers alone in the countries of the Organization for Economic Cooperation and Development (OECD). Growth has also been rapid in the Asia-Pacific region, where twelve countries have established cellular systems that together serve more than 1.5 million subscribers.[31]

If cellular is to support global service, however, there will likely need to be greater consensus on international standards. Although Europe has settled on the Global System for Mobile Communication (GSM) standard, U.S. providers are divided between two competing standards.[32] The situation might improve in the future, however, given considerable momentum in support of the European standard. Europe itself will have a sizable market for cellular, increasing from $6.07 billion in 1991 to $14.44 billion in 1996. Countries outside Europe committed to GSM include Australia, Hong Kong, Hungary, India, Russia, Singapore, and the United Arab Emirates. Also favoring the European standard are Brazil, Colombia, Iran, and New Zealand.[33] Agreement on standards not only will facilitate global interconnection; it also may lead to reduced prices due to economies of scale. To this end, European equipment and component manufacturers are also negotiating common standards.[34]

With the evolution of more advanced terrestrially based services such as personal communication systems (PCS) and future public land mobile telecommunications systems (FPLMTS), care will be needed to assure that the interoperability problems that have been associated with GSM are not replayed.[35] Interoperability is still possible, but by no means certain.[36]

Nowhere have the benefits of interconnection been more vividly demonstrated than in the case of the Internet. The Internet is a global computer network that provides technical compatibility and transparent connectivity based on a widely used suite of protocols, Transmission Control Protocol/Internet Protocol (TCP/IP). This network was originally developed by the Defense Advanced Research Projects Agency (DARPA) in 1969, with funds from both the Department of Defense and the National Science Foundation, to support education and research. Commercial demand for Internet services blossomed in the late 1980s, at a time when there were a number of firms available and eager to provide it.[37]

Responding to a large, rising demand for connectivity, Internet usage has been growing exponentially, with traffic increasing at a rate of 12 percent monthly.[38] As of April 1993, there were 40,807 registered IP networks (networks based on the IP protocol). Of these networks, 11,252—themselves connected to 1,486 million computer hosts—were linked to comprise the Internet.[39]

IP internets are increasingly global in scope.[40] Today, there are IP internets in 91 nations. In 53 nations, these internets are linked to the Internet, which provides electronic mail and other gateways to 127 countries. The number of foreign IP internets connected to the Internet is, moreover, growing at an average monthly rate of 8.7 percent. The growth rate in the United States, by comparison, is 7 percent.[41]

Its success notwithstanding, in terms of global connectivity the Internet should be viewed as the exception rather than the rule. Other technologies and applications have been slow to take off on a global basis because of inconsistencies in standards and technology deployment. Thus, although demand for electronic data interchange (EDI)[42] is growing rapidly, an international EDI market barely exists.[43] This lag is due in part to the fact that the United States and Europe have adopted incompatible standards for EDI. Even within Europe, problems of compatible standards have yet to be solved; firms are still using proprietary standards specific to different industries.[44]

THE NEED FOR A CONSISTENT TECHNOLOGY BASE

The worldwide deployment of integrated services digital networks (ISDN) has suffered not only from a lack of interoperability but also from the lack of a ubiquitous and consistent technology base. To understand the problem, one need only consider the situation in Europe, where, despite a common communication policy calling for harmonization, ISDN deployment varies greatly. In France deployment has reached almost 100 percent, while in other countries, such as Greece, it is virtually nonexistent.[45] Spotty interconnection discourages usage, and hence further deployment.[46]

Nor are the prospects for broad-band interconnection much better.[47] A European broadband interconnection trial (EBIT) was undertaken in 1989. This project was designed to support the European Commission Research for Advanced Communications in Europe (RACE) project, by setting up two-megabyte-per-second (Mbps) switched connections among sixteen countries. EBIT soon ran into difficulty, however, because participants sought to implement the program on a national, rather than a Europe-wide basis. Switching incompatibilities and tariff inconsistencies made high-speed pan-European communication networks impossible.[48]

More recent efforts notwithstanding, interconnected broadband is still in the future. The availability of leased two Mbps circuits in Europe continues to be uneven, ranging from forty thousand in Great Britain to seventeen in Ireland as of 1991.[49]

Even if global businesses are increasingly able to interconnect, significant geographic disparities in technology deployment will likely persist, given the rapid pace of technology change, the enormous amounts of money required for infrastructure investments, and major national discrepancies in standards of living and ability to generate the capital and human resources needed. As some countries struggle just to keep up, others are deploying yet more advanced technologies. For example, it is estimated that it will cost $120 billion between now and 2005 just to bring the Central and Eastern European communication networks up to date. During the same period, the European Community will spend approximately $24.8 billion a year to develop a broadband telecommunications infrastructure.[50]

The role that national resources play in determining levels of technology deployment becomes clear when one considers the geographic distribution of very basic technologies such as telephony and facsimile. In countries such as Sweden, Switzerland, Japan, the United States, Germany, and Canada, where per capita income is $20,000 a year or more, the number of telephone lines per person ranges around fifty or more. In contrast, in countries where per capita income is under $5,000, the number of telephone lines per person is likely to be ten or fewer.[51]

Per capita income and technology deployment are similarly related in the case of facsimile. While there are 4.4 million fax machines in the United States, 4.3 million in Japan, and 920,000 in Germany, there are only 90,000 in Brazil, 40,000 in Greece, 30,000 in Portugal, and 30,000 in Turkey.[52]

INSTITUTIONAL BARRIERS TO GLOBAL DEPLOYMENT

Achieving interconnection was relatively easy in the past when there were fewer types of service and when providers were modeled on one another, assuming for the most part the form of the classic postal, telegraph, and telephone (PTT) monopoly. Such uniformity no longer exists. National communication systems now differ significantly, depending on the extent to which they are government owned or operated, monopoly based or liberalized, regulated or not.[53]

At one end of the spectrum are countries like the United States, New Zealand, Great Britain, Japan, Singapore, Malaysia, and Mexico, which are striving to minimize government involvement. At the other end are countries like China, Brazil, Venezuela, and Uruguay, where the legacy of the traditional PTT is very strong.[54] Discrepancies in rules for interconnection reflect these basic organizational and, at bottom, philosophical differences.

Thus, interconnection problems are not rooted in technology alone; institutional arrangements are also a critical part of the problem. To be truly seamless, global communication systems require not only common standards and interfaces but also common rules of access and pricing. Achieving such commonality can be difficult, however, because the rules of interconnection reflect the social and economic goals of nations as well as their communication policies. For example, rules of interconnection establish the basis on which public network operators—from different countries and of different kinds within each country—allow other providers access to their networks and determine the prices that are charged for such access. If communication systems are to be truly global, compatible rules of interconnection need to be consistently and transparently applied; in other words, there will need to be rules governing the relationship between public and private networks, between value-added data services and public networks, and between providers of public voice telephone services, whether they are fixed or mobile.[55]

GLOBALIZATION AS A FUNCTION OF WORLD TRADE AND THE WORLDWIDE PROVISIONING OF SERVICES

Viewing global communications in terms of ubiquity and universality, globalization appears a long way off, with many barriers to be overcome. On the other hand, if global communication refers to the transcending of national boundaries, then the evidence points in the other direction. There are a number of developments driving the trend toward this concept of globalization, among them an increase in the demand for worldwide services, the growth in worldwide trade and the development of a worldwide market, the privatization and commercialization of the telecommunication sector, and the emergence of global service providers.

THE DEMAND FOR WORLDWIDE SERVICES

The provisioning of communication products and services on a worldwide basis both mirrors and drives the broader trend toward development of a global economy. This global economy is characterized by the emergence of economic actors who buy and sell their products and services worldwide. Perhaps even more important, they establish their bases of operations on a transnational basis, allocating their activities among a number of countries to gain optimum advantage.[56] When not fully integrated into multinational corporations, these firms network their activities across national boundaries through a variety of arrangements such as cross-licensing of technology, joint ventures, orderly marketing agreements, off-shore production of components, secondary sourcing, and cross-cutting equity ownership.[57]

As companies spread their corporate boundaries, they must have access to advanced telecommunication products and services that can span the globe. Transnational corporations, for example, must operate on a real-time basis in response to their rapidly changing environments. Moreover, they must be able to balance their global operations with the requirements of local markets—such as the need to establish special marketing channels, service contracts, and work relationships. To function as single units, they must be able to apply information and knowledge to an ever-growing number of complex business problems, as well as to share and leverage these resources both within and across organizational and national boundaries. For these purposes, seamless worldwide networking technologies, which can support applications such as electronic data interchange, computer-integrated manufacturing, databases for information management, video conferencing, and other kinds of groupware, will be critical.

In developing such global strategies, businesses have benefited from major reductions in the cost of buying international communication services. In 1970, for example, a company had to pay about $8,000 to $9,000 a month to lease a single voice-grade channel. Today, it is possible to lease a sixty-four-kilobyte-per-second line that provides eight times the transmission capacity for about $6,000 a month. Declining prices stem not only from advances in technology, such as fiber optics, but also from the growth of international competition. With the pressures toward liberalization (described below) and the privatization of many telecommunication regimes, this competition will become even more intense in the future, continuing to force prices down and demand up.[58]

Increased competition and growth in worldwide demand are also driven by the emergence of new suppliers and the development of new kinds of products and services that are based on the convergence of communication technologies. Included among these, for example, are systems integration, twenty-four-hour commodity trading, credit authorization, and computerized reservation systems.[59] Greater competition and many more such services can be expected in the future because the barriers to entry are relatively low. Often all that is required is software and a computer network link.

Consider, for instance, price-cutting companies like International Discount Telecommunications (IDT). Capitalizing on the gap between U.S. telecommunication prices and prices in other less deregulated countries, IDT uses computerized switches in the United States to reroute calls from foreign subscribers. These companies undercut their competitors' rates by as much as one-third.[60] Similarly, the small but rapidly growing telecommunication services company Viatel sells software-based value-added services to small and medium-sized businesses in Latin America and Western Europe.[61]

The demand for global networking services has also been spurred by the growing complexity of the worldwide marketplace. Today, there are a multitude of available services and providers, divergent standards and levels of technology deployment, as well as differing national languages, rules, and regulations. As a result, many businesses are finding it more cost-effective to "outsource" the management of their international networks on a contract basis.[62] Thus, J.P. Morgan and Company has contracted with BT North America to handle its overseas, terminal-to-host networks. Similarly, BT North America has contracted with Gillette Company to manage its telecommunications operations in 180 countries. AT&T also provides virtual private network services on a global basis. For example, it is providing the network linkages for General Electric in sixteen different countries.

GROWTH IN WORLDWIDE TRADE IN COMMUNICATIONS

The growth in worldwide trade in telecommunications and information-based networking services attests to the demand for more versatile products and seamless worldwide services.[63] Communications is one of the fastest-growing sectors in the international marketplace, with expansion over the past decade outstripping growth in gross national product.[64] In 1990, the market for international telephone calls totaled $50 billion.[65] The world market in telecommunications equipment and services that year was estimated at $370 billion, growing to $400 billion in 1991 and 1992, despite the world recession. Estimated annual growth rates in the telecommunications market ranged between 10 and 15 percent.[66]

Spending on information technologies has remained closely aligned with spending on communication technologies—testimony to the growing convergence of these technologies. Excluding telecommunication hardware and services as well as information services, worldwide spending on information technology totaled $305 billion in 1990. Growth in this sector was about 12 percent from 1989 to 1990; software led the way with a growth rate of 17 percent.[67]

Globalization is also reflected in the growing percentage of national revenue that is derived from the sale of international services. According to one account, for example, 16.3 percent of worldwide value-added services revenue stemmed from international offerings in 1990. Estimates are that this figure will increase to 28 percent by 1996.[68]

This international growth potential is especially important for countries like the United States, where the domestic market for many products and services is becoming saturated. According to a recent report by the Office of Technology Assessment, for example, the European markets for value-added services is projected to grow much faster than the U.S. market.[69] Moreover, the export of services to Europe is expected to foster the sale of U.S. telecommunications equipment and strengthen the competitiveness of U.S. service industries such as airlines, hotels, and banks.[70]

CONVERGENCE OF PRICES AND PRODUCT OFFERINGS

The development of a global market depends on more than increased trade in communication and information-related products and services across national boundaries. For a unified market to exist, there must also be widespread access to market information and a convergence of prices and product offerings. The expansion of trade, such as we are witnessing in telecommunications, will help to drive this convergence. As markets become more global, so will competition and the availability of market-related information.[71] At the same time, however, to the extent that price differentials are artificially maintained, the cost and complexity of doing business will be increased, global trade will be inhibited, and global trading patterns distorted.

Telecommunications pricing is reflected in public tariffs, which lay out all of the telecommunication options, together with price and conditions of service.[72] These tariffs have always been subject to political as well as economic factors because governments have traditionally been the providers of most services. Thus, rates have been set not only to reflect costs but also to promote universal service through cross-subsidization or—as is happening in many developing countries today—to generate revenues for unrelated government operations. Not surprisingly under these circumstances, prices and services have varied widely from country to country.[73]

Significant price distortions were tenable in a national regulatory environment in which most of the trade that took place was internal to the firm. Some services could be used to subsidize others, as long as overall costs were covered. Where transactions occurred across national boundaries, as in the case of international telephone calls, pricing arrangements were negotiated through the appropriate state authorities.

In today's global economy, such pricing strategies will have much greater consequences, serving to inhibit and distort international trade. Without standardized services and a relatively common scheme of pricing, businesses will find it extremely difficult to manage global networks. Special efforts will be required to identify and negotiate the appropriate services and terms. Where there are significant price and service disparities, traffic will probably be routed in roundabout ways through countries, such as Great Britain or Singapore, that serve as low-cost hubs. Given the complexities involved, many businesses will outsource their network management to system integrators that cater to multinational clients. In other cases, however, the search costs entailed in setting up a network may simply outweigh any benefits to be gained from their use.[74]

The impact that pricing disparities can have on trade is particularly apparent when trying to reconcile international accounts. Because international calls entail the use of facilities in two countries, revenues and costs need to be shared between them. To settle accounts, the provider in the country in which a call originates pays the facility owner in the country where the call is completed a sum based on a bilaterally negotiated "accounting rate" (the agreed-upon cost of the call) and "settlement rate" (the agreed-upon percentage split of the revenues, customarily 50–50).

If there is a large gap between the prices charged in each country, problems are likely to arise, as is happening in the United States today. When possible, users initiate calls in the United States because the rates, which are subject to competitive pressures, are lower here. This is not necessarily beneficial, however. Because U.S. providers initiate more calls than they receive, they must pay out an excess of funds, which creates a trade deficit.[75] Moreover, because international accounting rates do not reflect true costs, it may be difficult for U.S. service providers to cover their total costs. In fact, depending on the accounting and settlement rates, they may actually subsidize a foreign vendor's service.[76]

The most formidable obstacle to the development of a worldwide market is, of course, the existence of formal trade barriers. Despite a clear shift toward liberalization, barriers to trade in telecommunications persist. According to a recent U.S. government report, in most European countries state-owned public telephone companies still have monopolies on basic telephone service, with the result that only about 15 percent of the total European telecommunications market is open to competition—primarily in cellular communication, cable television, and some enhanced services.[77]

However, pressures for liberalization continue to swell. These include, for example, the incorporation of telecommunication services within the framework of the General Agreement on Tariffs and Trade (GATT), competition from multinational providers, and advances in networking technology that permit bypass of the public switched networks, the European Community Open Network Directive, and persistent demands from large business users.[78] Given these forces for change, it is not surprising that even in the case of state-oriented stalwarts such as Ireland, Spain, Portugal, and Italy, steps are being taken to move toward international cost-based tariffs.[79]

PRIVATIZATION AND THE SHIFT TO THE MARKETPLACE

Globalization is also being furthered through the movement to privatize the provision of communication products and services.[80] This trend toward privatization reflects the growing economic value of communication and information in society. Although communication has always served a critical function, its economic value looms ever larger in a global, knowledge-based society. To capitalize on this development, PTTs throughout the world are selling either all or part of their telecommunication facilities to private-sector providers and investors who have expertise and capital to spare.[81]

In Europe, privatization is aimed primarily at enhancing the competitiveness of national telecommunication providers.[82] One by one, the nations of Europe are coming to realize that state-owned PTTs will be at a great disadvantage in an intensely competitive and rapidly expanding global market.[83] In fact, they may not even be able to join the fray if they lack the freedom and flexibility necessary to enter new markets and establish new alliances.[84] Most striking in this regard is, perhaps, the recent conversion of the French and German governments. Although long a proponent of centralized state control, the French government recently announced plans to transform France Telecom into a joint stock company with the state retaining majority control. Similarly, the German parliament has agreed to a plan for privatizing Deutsche Telekom.[85]

Similar motives are driving privatization in Asia—at least among the most economically advanced countries—with Japan, Australia, and New Zealand leading the way. Change is also taking place in the less well off regions of Southeast Asia. Singapore Telecom, for example, recently established a joint public-private telecom venture, which many view as a first step toward total privatization.[86] Indonesia already has such a corporate arrangement. In Malaysia, the PTT is privatized, with its stock now floated in the marketplace.[87]

Fully aware of the growing importance of communication for economic growth, many developing countries hope that privatization will help them gain access to the foreign capital and expertise needed to develop their national communication infrastructures. In Latin America, Mexico serves as a model for this kind of industry restructuring, having privatized its state PTT, TELMEX, with record speed.[88] The government plans to sell its remaining stake in TELMEX this year for about $600 million. Foreign capital has also been invested in Telefonos de Venezuela and Telefonica de Argentina.

Similar infrastructure modernization strategies are being pursued in other parts of the world. India, for example, is developing a plan to open its telecommunication sector to private investment, as are countries in Eastern Europe.[89] Even China, which has long opposed foreign investment, is now considering foreign bids to support its goal of providing forty million new lines by the year 2000. Such privatization strategies have also received a boost from the World Bank, which recently decided to make the promotion of competition a condition for receiving financial aid for infrastructure development.[90]

It has not been difficult to find the investors needed to fund such national privatization efforts. Global telecommunication investors view emerging economies as a bargain, if not a potential gold mine.[91] Purchase prices and interest rates are low, and the cost of technology is declining. At the same time, dividends are rising and annual per-share earning growth rates have ranged between 15 and 20 percent.[92] Investors also benefit from preferred access to a new and rapidly expanding market sector.[93] Regulatory restrictions in the United States provide the Bell Operating Companies with an additional incentive for foreign investment; indeed, they have been among the most active in this regard.[94]

Privatization efforts, moreover, need not be limited to national tele-communications systems. Proposals are now under development to privatize INMARSAT, an international treaty organization established in 1979 to provide communication services to ships—especially those from poor countries. As INMARSAT has expanded into more and more lucrative activities, pressure has grown to transform it into a private organization. To this end, a proposal has been made that would allow its members to trade their holdings. The stakes are considerable. Providing services such as portable satellite communications for emergency services, the media, and the airlines, INMARSAT has accumulated assets totaling $4 billion and has been growing at a rate of 20 percent a year over the past decade.[95] INMARSAT's success in these rapidly growing markets has led many of its competitors—among them state-owned, nonprofit organizations and private companies—to call for limitations on its activities. They argue that INMARSAT has an unfair advantage, given its intergovernmental treaty status.[96]

GLOBAL PROVIDERS EMERGE

Global providers of telecommunication and information-based products and services, free of many domestic constraints, are now preparing to meet worldwide demand.[97] To stake out new markets, share the high risks and costs of technology development, and provide their services more effectively on a worldwide basis, these carriers are aggressively setting up global partnerships, consortia, and joint ventures.[98]

However, despite the rapid growth in worldwide demand and the present high rates of investment, many suspect that over the long term there will not be enough money or markets to go around.[99] Some estimate that when the inevitable shakeout occurs, only five to seven global conglomerates can survive.[100] So time is short and the competition for partners fierce. As one participant-observer aptly describes the situation:

> We're at the stage of [the game of] Monopoly where you buy everything that is available. The next stage is to form consortia with other players as the initial opportunities become limited. The last phase, yet to come, could be some form of cash-flow race for the finish line.[101]

The top contenders are focusing on the lucrative "outsourcing" market, striving to become the major provider of seamless global communication to the world's five hundred largest multinationals. This market is estimated at $10 billion a year and is growing rapidly.[102] AT&T, for example, has established WorldPartners, a one-stop shopping consortium and joint venture, in conjunction with Japan's largest international provider, Kousai Denshin Denwa (KDD), and Singapore Telecom.[103] To be truly global, however, AT&T must find itself a European partner. It has had serious discussions with France Telecom and

Deutsche Telekom, but they have foundered on the issue of the scope and extent of a joint arrangement.[104]

Soon after the announcement of WorldPartners's creation, British Telecommunications (BT) and MCI struck a $4.3 billion deal that provides for both a new outsourcing venture to provide global voice and data services and for BT's purchase of a 20 percent stake in MCI. BT will own 75 percent of the joint venture, NewCo, with MCI holding the remaining share. More partners are being sought, most notably Japan's Nippon Telephone and Telegraph Corporation. MCI will market services in the Western Hemisphere while BT will concentrate on sales in Europe and the Far East.[105]

The Swedish, Dutch, and Swiss telecommunications carriers have created a partnership called Unisource. In order to compete on a level playing field with the other major outsourcers, Unisource has recently concluded a nonexclusive alliance with KDD of Japan. It has also entered into an agreement with Telefonica, the Spanish telecommunications operator. This agreement will help to provide Unisource access to markets in southern Europe as well as to markets in Latin America, where Telefonica has holdings in Chile, Argentina, and Puerto Rico.[106]

Alarmed at the prospect of competition from global outsourcers, France Telecom and Deutsche Telekom have also established a joint venture called Eunetcom. This group has had difficulty getting off the ground, especially in terms of finding partners.[107] Its first choice, MCI, defected to establish the joint venture with British Telecom. And talks with AT&T also proved difficult. Most recently, Deutsche Telekom and France Telecom have been pursuing an alliance with Sprint.[108]

FUTURE ISSUES AND PROSPECTS

The shift toward a global communications environment affords a number of opportunities for the United States. The prospects for increased trade in equipment and services are particularly great, given technology convergence and the development of a wide array of new products and services, the growth in worldwide demand, the provisions for telecom services within the GATT, and the liberalization and privatization of many telecommunication regimes. Foreign investment opportunities will also abound, as nations turn to new technologies to modernize and upgrade their communication networks. Global communication networks may also serve to promote worldwide economic growth and development, by allowing businesses to reconfigure and redistribute their research and development, production, and marketing activities to their best advantage regardless of their geographic location.

But the globalization of communication systems may cause new problems as well. These problems stem not only from the unique role that communication plays in a nation's society and economy, but also from the inherent tensions between the political value of universality and the market value of efficiency, both of which are associated with globalization.

To the extent that national communication systems are increasingly integrated in global networks, national governments will have less control over a critical infrastructure that serves to sustain their societies as well as determine their economic fates. In addition, regulatory decisions made in one country may do more than simply undermine regulatory schemes in another. Equally important, because most telecom administrations have generally been linked to national governments, regulatory changes imposed from abroad can serve to unravel fragile domestic alliances, creating political instability.[109] Moreover, given a growing preoccupation throughout the world with national and ethnic identity, efforts to promote trade in content-related products and services that threaten national and ethnic identity will likely encounter increasing resistance.[110] Conflicts may also arise if some countries, which are unable to keep pace with technology advances, fail to integrate their communication systems into global networks and are thus further excluded from an increasingly electronically based world economic system.

Such problems will be especially acute in developing countries. In some cases, the privatization of national communication systems may attract enough foreign investment to finance needed infrastructure deployment. However, foreign acquisition of national communication systems may not serve the broader, long-term goals of economic development. If the developing countries' infrastructures are shaped by the incentives that drive multinational investors, they may be unable to apply modern communication technologies to social programs—such as education, nation building, and health care—upon which economic development ultimately depends. Difficult trade-offs will be required.

Given these dynamic interactions, it can be expected that, as communication networks become more global, so too will many policy issues relating to their deployment, regulation, and use. Already, for example, it is clear that, in an unprotected global market where communication services can be provided from anywhere in the world, regulatory policies must be harmonized if only to prevent arbitrage across national boundaries. In like fashion, national communication and information policies—such as those relating to intellectual property rights, privacy rights, and data protection—will need to be addressed on a worldwide basis. It is these policies that will provide the basic ground rules for what is becoming an increasingly information- and knowledge-based global economy.

New actors will also need to be accommodated. With technologies and markets converging, a broad array of new multinational equipment vendors and service providers will appear on the scene, many of whom will have a major stake in foreign and global communication and information policies. Similarly, many global business users, who are increasingly dependent for their competitiveness on the availability and accessibility of low-cost, interconnected, and flexible worldwide networking, will seek to influence foreign, as well as their own domestic, telecommunication policies. In this context, policy issues will likely emerge not only among competing domestic interests and among nation-states, but also—and increasingly—among domestic, national, and multinational actors.

Resolving these global communication issues will be problematic because there are few institutional arrangements for dealing with them in place. In the United States, for example, the task of reconciling national, foreign, and communication policy goals is compounded by the fragmented nature of the policymaking process. At the international level, many traditional organizations are struggling to keep up with technological advances and the structural changes taking place in the world economy. Slow to act and increasingly less relevant, these organizations are, however, gradually being bypassed in favor of regional and/or nongovernmental bodies.

Absent national and international political leadership, multinational corporations—accountable solely to the global marketplace—will emerge to fill the policy void. Many of the social and political benefits that are potentially associated with global communications will, therefore, be neglected as a result. Over the long term, however, broader social and cultural values, especially those associated with the notion of universality, will need to be addressed. All markets—even global markets—require some form of social consensus and government legitimization if they are to be sustained.

If the global information infrastructure is to promote economic growth and development, social improvement, political stability, and the spread of democracy throughout the world, the present U.S. administration must look beyond the market as the driving force of efficiency. While encouraging the development of a free and open global marketplace in telecommunication and information products and services, the administration will also need to provide leadership in developing truly global decision-making processes where the value conflicts associated with communication technologies can be adequately and fairly addressed.

TELECOMMUNICATIONS TECHNOLOGY FOR THE TWENTY-FIRST CENTURY

RICHARD JAY SOLOMON

E ver since the first electrical telegraphs were introduced a century and a half ago, new telecommunications technologies have continually reduced transmission costs, increased network capacity, and added capability. Until recently, evolution was relatively linear and reasonably easy to plot and predict; this was particularly true of the increase in intercity transmission capacity, the decrease in switching costs, and the growth of telephone demand.

Today, telecommunications planners face a strange dilemma: New technology no longer has a linear effect. Transmission costs are dropping precipitously, while telecom capabilities and demand profiles depend more on customer investments than on carrier strategies. Telecommunications networking no longer involves merely circuits and switches; in such an environment, defining an infrastructure becomes extremely difficult. Just when public policy has begun to focus on the need for a national information infrastructure (NII), forecasting and conceptualizing the future of telecommunications have become murkier than ever. There are five major reasons why this is the case:

▼ Technological choices for telecommunications systems have proliferated due to the application of microelectronics-based computing devices.

▼ This has yielded all-digital networks that are very different from older analog networks in conception.

▼   Digital networks make possible for the first time the competitive provision
     of services and telecom carriage.

▼   In this environment, users are demanding that the NII be based on inter-
     operability, diversity, and technologically very complex open systems rather
     than uniform universality.

▼   Technological stability is not yet in sight.

THE DIGITAL PARADOX

Computerized telecommunications is radically changing the nature of telecom
provision, usage, users, cash flows, and investments. In this environment, the
stored-program digital computer lies at the crux of a paradox. While demand is
apparently increasing for all types of telecom services and applications, provision
of basic carriage may become a risky venture due to commoditization and the
nature of network control dictated by computers interfacing with the network.

The computer has made cost-effective interconnection technically feasible,
facilitating competitive entry into what once was assumed to be a natural
monopoly. Yet computerized, customer-controlled terminal equipment makes
nonsense of traditional centralized network control strategies, intended for
operating efficiency but that served also to maintain operating hegemonies.
Furthermore, with digital processing, radio spectrum no longer needs to be
treated as scarce real estate requiring legally sanctioned access controls to
prevent interference; indeed, spectrum may no longer be a scarce resource
per se, if future allocation is treated less as an analogy to Riparian water rights
and more like the way digital bits are shared on packet networks today, in
microslices of time rather than space.

The telecommunications paradox results from four characteristics inherent
in digital technology. First, computers and computation power have fallen
dramatically in price in a relatively short time period. Second, computers
communicate. A stored-program digital machine cannot work any other way:
Communications is not something added to computers; it is a natural extension
of them. Third, computation devices double in processing speed every two or
three years. But telecom speed (a measure of traffic capacity) has increased by
orders of *magnitude*.[1] This has resulted in a significant reversal in the traditional
communications/computer model with far-reaching implications for infrastructure:
For the first time in forty years, transmission is faster than computation. Telecom
technology no longer acts as a bottleneck, provided we can extend the circuit to
the ultimate user (the "last mile" or, more accurately, the "last hundred feet"
problem)—a large caveat. Finally, while appliances, system components, and
carriage may be approaching the point where they are virtually cost free, systems
implementation, marketing, software, amortization of sunk plant, and investment
capital all remain dear. With equipment and carriage now readily accessible,

customers become competitors to carriers for value-added services. With accessible, open networks, it is not clear whether the network provider is more or less handicapped in offering services; the converse, a *closed* network, is an oxymoron.

Policy options are more complex than ever, conflict resolution is unpredictable, and political gridlock institutionalized. And, despite forty years of technological experience, operating and corporate cultures in the telecom and computer industries (not to mention broadcasting and other media) are still widely divergent. Until recently, carriers have based their core business strategy on reacting to real and potential government regulatory policy, while the computer industry has avoided regulation like the plague.

Both sectors have benefited greatly in the past from government initiatives in research and development, from public subsidies (direct and indirect), and even from regulation stabilizing their respective niches. Like a moving backdrop in a confusing computer game, government directions are changing as a result of technology, but not necessarily in concert with any other shifts.

Proposals in Congress to change the legal framework suggest that we will be taking one step backward before technology inexorably pushes us forward. For example, the bills introduced in the 103d Congress were so convoluted that they might have discouraged convergence of media by overregulation in the guise of defining uses and users of the evolving digital wire-line and radio networks in advance in order to satisfy various political constituencies for censorship, access, and new entries. The Current bills are less detailed, but still problematic. This definitional game has been played now for some thirty years, since computers first began communicating—and to no avail. Next we examine why.

THE TECHNOLOGY OF ABUNDANCE: COMPUTERS AND MICROPROCESSORS

Computer power has evolved from three interrelated technological developments during the past half century:

▼   Miniaturization of electrical and optical components, which increased the ability to switch, store, and process numbers at extremely high speeds and extremely low costs (in extremely small spaces);

▼   The natural extension of stand-alone computing devices into telecommunications transmission, routing, and control (a corollary of the first development, since how they work internally is by communicating); and

▼   The ability of cheap, digital logical devices to capture and convert analog information (sound, vision, tactile and mechanical motion, and even smell and taste) into numerical processes that can be manipulated by computer instructions: a subtle, but critical iteration of both computational theory and component development for telecommunicating.

New processor and memory chips jump a generation every six to eighteen months. One result has been massive write-offs of telecom and computer equipment in the past decade. Most of what is already in place—from telephones and television sets, to central office switching and transmission circuits—will be functionally obsolescent in a decade.[3] Laws, regulations, and directives cannot keep pace with such massive technological change. It is difficult to plan investments, schedule depreciation, and understand windows of opportunity without being blindsided by new devices, new business arrangements, or just plain regulatory lag.

The digital computer unlocks a multitude of new and powerful ways to communicate, yet offers little competitive advantage to entities that provide the basic communications channels. Information infrastructure is not like a highway system; with communications, the added value is found in content, not in the infrastructure itself. Commodity carriage alone will not be able to amortize its investment. To make the paradox complete, specialty networks; isolated networks; closed, one-way systems (such as conventional broadcasting); and incompatible devices also have little chance of surviving a competitive environment where the enabling mechanism—the digital computer—homogenizes all.

This sweeping statement requires some explanation, for most of the literature on telecommunications has ignored the essence of the revolution: what a digital computer is, and what it does when it communicates.

ALL-DIGITAL NETWORKS AND STORED-PROGRAM COMPUTERS

The computer is unlike any other device in the annals of mechanization. Its utility and import are not intuitive for most human beings as, for example, are automobiles, the applications of steel, or a washing machine. Computers do more than calculate, but for most people it is not obvious how or why.

For many years, the computer's effect on electrical communications seemed benign and positive (and generally unnoticed by any but the technically oriented). Computers gave us more efficient billing, faster and more cost-effective telephone switching, airline reservation systems, cheaper communicating appliances (such as facsimile and answering machines), and some minor service variations (useful things such as three-way calling, and maddening offerings in the guise of automatic touch-tone voice response).

The next stage—the oft-heralded *convergence* of telecom and computers—may have only marginal consequences in the form of interactive television game shows or home shopping; alternatively, with some entrepreneurial talent and imagination, it may usher in more powerful societal improvements, such as more efficient delivery mechanisms for quality health care, energy-conserving telecommuting, improved distribution management, and services we can barely imagine today.

The "silver bullet" or "killer" application for future networks is yet to be discovered, but applications like the *Mosaic* interface, developed for the Internet by the National Center for Supercomputing Applications, appears to come close.

Mosaic runs on a workstation or personal computer, is able to pull data and information transparently from other computers all over the world, is easy to use, since all it requires for data retrieval is clicking on words and phrases (and sometimes pictures), and most importantly, has the programming capability to format and present these data to the user without any further effort on the user's part—up to and including sound and high-resolution moving images. Whether or not Mosaic represents the "killer" multimedia application, it consumes a huge amount of bandwidth and has been known to bring down systems not prepared for the demand. Its most popular (and surprising) single application was the retrieval in 1994 of the Dead Sea Scrolls from various worldwide sites, with fine-grained color images of the scroll on one side of the screen, and translations on the other—a good example of the inability of planners to anticipate both levels of demand and what people may want to use their systems for.

The linkage of telecommunications to computers is much more than just intriguing applications like Mosaic (although these applications are the driving force behind it). The evolving all-digital networks are changing the logistics and the structure of society itself because neither time nor space can be regarded as it was in the past. We see this in the expressions of the computer age: real time as opposed to delayed time, and "virtual" or "logical" networks, as opposed to physical networks with defined routes, wires, and cables.

The digital computer itself is a disarmingly simple device, but computers do not necessarily make things simple. *A stored-program device is a machine that may change its own instructions*, and, in effect, become a new machine without leaving a trace of its old self. And it does all this merely by manipulating arithmetic in a set of electrical adders and memory devices.

Any stored-program digital computer—a device that compares logical states ("true or false" or "yes and no") and then makes a binary decision—is capable of imitating any other such appliance without knowing any more than the form of the input information and expected output. In plain terms, this means that a digital computer can be programmed to emulate or control any other machine or process; except for the limitations of the speed of light, it makes no technical difference whether that machine is a millimeter away or on the other side of the planet. For all-digital telecom networks, this fundamental stored-program machine property means that control must be shared on the network; there no longer can be a sole centralizing "gatekeeper" function that the network operator can use as a barrier to entry. As we move toward all-digital networks, with open interfaces, this has profound implications, requiring the decentralization of critical roles in the NII.

The computer's power comes from the fact that it does its adding and comparing tens of millions of times per second, on a chip of silicon the size of a coin, which costs comparatively little to produce in huge quantities. To reach this level of sophistication has taken a half-century of intensive development. We are approaching the time when silicon will be effectively free (hence computation will be free), and the adding and comparing will take place hundreds of million, even billions of times per second.[4] With such power, robotics, software that replicates expert knowledge (expert systems), detection of critical information in a mass of noise, and automation of quite complex processes will become pedestrian. Judging from prototype systems today, the impact on health care, manufacturing, distribution management, environmental monitoring, natural resource recovery, and education will be phenomenal. However, interconnectivity of these high-performance processors is the key to their implementation, especially in a competitive environment.

For a stored-program machine to do more than simple arithmetic, it needs rapid access to very large memory space. The incredible drop in cost of memory with the development of solid-state integrated circuitry in the late 1960s changed the path both of computation and telecommunications. Data processing is now more efficient when it is distributed *and* interconnected—and the more interconnections the better. Memory space is generic; it is not necessarily contiguous in space or time to the computer's processing unit. Memory can at one moment be just a few bits on a processing chip, and the next fraction of a second extend across a continent accessing trillions of bits or more, calling information from various sources, machines, and networks. Interconnection is what makes this virtual memory space—"cyberspace" to the initiated—work. But interconnection is not straightforward.

For telecommunications operations and operators, the stored-program paradigm, which allows digital computers to modify their own instructions,[5] and which mixes instructions with information (or data),[6] thereby creating both the conditions and necessity for virtual networking, is the key to its paradox: The more capability that is built into a digital communications network, the more the carrier loses control of its operation to its customers or to other carriers. Thus, competitive entry into carriage (and services) is another outgrowth of the digital revolution; even if monopoly were not outlawed, it would be difficult to resist the introduction of competition into networking. This is clear in countries that still support monopoly PTTs, but find large portions of their data traffic flowing onto bypass operations, such as the Internet. Even international voice traffic is being diverted with call-back and other such offerings almost impossible to police in a digital world.

Such is the essence of distributed data processing and the underlying technology behind the paradox. All-digital, computer-controlled networks, by definition, cannot completely segregate their signaling, control, or instruction function from the information or data function; *in telecom terms, distributed power blurs the identity of carriers and customers.* We will return to this theme later when we discuss the implementation of broadband networks.

DIGITIZATION AND INTEROPERABILITY

It is now possible to replicate virtually any human sensory input and store the information in machine code, termed "digitization."[7] Digitization of information means that information can be cost-effectively replicated and transmitted *ad infinitum* without *any* degradation or loss—hence the attraction of all-digital appliances for transmission, switching, and information storage. Moreover, digitization is essential to machine manipulation, such as image enhancement, information search, and data matching. Not only can text be treated as a computer "file," but pictures, video and sound clips, abstract relationships between objects, and computer instructions themselves can similarly be manipulated as objects and files.[8]

Digital signal processing (a derivative of digital computer processing technology) can compress data into a fraction of the space or the channel that an uncompressed signal requires. Compression eliminates redundant and unnecessary information—such as blank or repetitive space in an image, or silence in a conversation—further dropping storage and transmission costs and other process requirements. With such technology, it is now possible to send acceptable-quality video telephone images on ordinary digital telephone circuits using the public network, or even a television picture on a specially modified telephone wire pair, although the image quality in several respects is not comparable to conventional television (especially cable) transmission, even though it might be acceptable to the general public.[9]

But signal-processing technology is not confined just to telephone wires. Multiple digitized, full-resolution television programs can now be transmitted on one conventional television channel (six Megahertz in frequency width), via terrestrial broadcasting, satellite, or on cable; hence the ability to carry five hundred channels on cables originally designed for fifty, although quality levels may vary depending on content and the compression techniques used to eliminate unnecessary signals.

Combining compression techniques and computer processing with sophisticated forms of radio modulation such as cellular techniques can dramatically increase the ability of the spectrum to carry information. Essentially, if resources are rearranged for optimum manipulation, spectrum is no longer a scarce resource; the trick is to use inexpensive microprocessor technology for controlling spectrum *temporally*, as well as spatially and by frequency.

The model for spectrum for the past seventy years has been to allocate the spectrum for specified uses—radio or television broadcasting, fixed or mobile applications, paging, cellular telephones, and so forth—and in relatively fixed chunks of frequency space; power levels; propagation characteristics; and physical space for antennas, receivers, and propagation direction. Computers and digital signal processing change that relationship. Spectrum can be reallocated in microseconds from one user to another, and from one use to another, depending on demand. Telephone companies do this all the time on shared trunk lines; it is more complicated for frequencies, but it is also more flexible and offers greater opportunities than those found on wire-line circuits.

Finally, spectrum can be optimized for terrain, multipath reflections, and a host of other characteristics. Cellular techniques similar to those used for cellular telephones can be applied to reuse frequencies over select geographical areas. But our laws and regulations are not ready for such a model, and the economics of different parts of the spectrum applied to this different temporal/spatial relationship will not reflect existing market values. We see a glimmer of the problems to come in the recent effort by television broadcasters to change the laws so they can use their valuable part of the spectrum for purposes other than conventional television broadcasting. The UHF band (channels 14–70 on a television set), in particular, has some of the best characteristics for penetrating walls and minimizing spectrum barriers. Recent research indicates that cellular digital or hybrid techniques alone could free up some 70 percent of UHF spectrum without reducing the number of television channels people typically receive today.[10]

However, compression and link capacity expansion are only the beginning. Signal-processing technology can also enhance an X-ray image to see a tumor where an unaided human eye cannot; enable a search of picture or video files for specific patterns, images, or parameters; and be used to modify, merge, change, and alter images (moving or still) without leaving any tracks. Subjects can be placed in movies where they never appeared; backgrounds can be created from adjacent frames, making a movie scene wider than when it was originally shot; scenes can be rotated, with missing objects created out of seemingly nothing; colors can be changed, added, even derived from mono-chrome originals; and facial features can be distorted, improved, or moved to another individual. In short, *seeing will never be believing ever again*. And if this is already being done with complex moving pictures, the implications for documentation, authentication, copyright, and verification are ominous. The paper trail may soon be meaningless; protection of intellectual property is well-nigh impossible with all-digital media that can be replicated without end, modified, and recombined into different and novel creations.[11]

NETWORK MODELS AND THE SHIFT TO DISTRIBUTED CONTROL

The assumptions of the old telecom network providers (and their regulators, customers, and suppliers) have included fixed overhead, fixed bandwidth, physical analog connections, and hierarchical network architecture. The new public (and private) networks that are being built are increasingly all-digital from end to end (although with mixed analog/digital interfaces during the transition). Intensive digitization took place first in two areas: intercity circuits where high-capacity fiber optics and coaxial cable make possible greater efficiency through resource sharing, and central-office telephone switches, which are essentially large computers optimized for carrying digitized voice signals. With roughly two-thirds of the plant digital, it made economic and technical sense to avoid as much analog/digital conversion as possible, so the next step was to push digital circuits out into the local distribution plant to the "curbside" in telephone networks, or into the private branch exchange (PBX). Few non-PBX telephones are yet digital, but digital terminations in the home and small office are within sight; this will further change the way customers and customer equipment interact with the network.

Radio-based systems, too, are moving toward all-digital, though somewhat slower than wire-line, systems; this is because of the large sunk plant and peculiar problems of spectrum in terrestrial environments where all-digital transmission may not be as efficient as on wire-line or fiber systems. Nevertheless, even with hybrid systems proposed for terrestrial radio, some kernel of information will be digital—enough to change the way networks are controlled and telecom appliances are used.

The new computer-based technologies carry with them a new set of assumptions, including variable bandwidth allocations with logical, instead of physical, connections and a nonhierarchical network architecture with distributed processing nodes and terminals (see Table A.1).

TABLE A.1

EFFECT OF TECHNOLOGY TRENDS ON FUTURE TELECOM MODELS

TECHNOLOGY

Faster and cheaper computer processors ("free" silicon)

- ▼ Intelligent customer equipment
- ▼ Shift from circuit switching to packet switching
- ▼ Shift from fixed to variable speed channels

Virtual end-to-end, digital process connectivity

- ▼ User-to-machine
- ▼ Machine-to-machine
- ▼ User-to-user communications

Shared process and network control

- ▼ Blurred carrier and customer demarcation boundaries
- ▼ Logical networking
- ▼ Virtual memory space ("cyberspace")

POLICY IMPLICATIONS

- ▼ Increased competition for value-added offerings
- ▼ Massive, accelerated write-offs of sunk plant
- ▼ De facto interconnection of public/private networks
- ▼ Network design depends on process definitions
- ▼ Tariffs cannot be based on traffic flow or time of use

SOME RESULTS

- ▼ Flexible and fungible choices among technologies: carriers, rates, tariff and service arbitrage, and standards
- ▼ Decline of network integrity and security
- ▼ Increased network robustness
- ▼ Increased political gridlock

INTEGRATED, DIGITAL NETWORKING

On fully integrated, all-digital networks, switching (which is for all practical purposes just another form of computer processing) and transmission work in conjunction. There is no way physically to separate the switch process from the transmission process—both are a matter of electronic timing circuits internalized by the network sendinsg out pulses that are repeated ad infinitum, constrained only by the speed of light. However, the physical connections can become so complex that network control is structured to work in layers and modules, creating what is known as "virtual networks" with no simple mapping to the physical network. The physical connection itself is the lowest, least important layer in terms of operations, unlike in analog networks, where a great deal of effort goes into optimizing architectural designs for physical connections.

A digital link is merely an extension—a virtual extension—of the switch or node's electrical (or optical) bus, just like on a computer motherboard. This model depends on acceptance of logical, Boolean "states" representing a telecom reality, instead of circuits—but from a customer's viewpoint it is all the same. In an integrated network, signaling and control are all-important, and control can get extremely complicated.

As with the stored-program machine, an end-to-end digital telecom system is totally different from today's analog or hybrid network. On an analog network, digital signals (in the form of binary digits, or bits) are merely carried in analog forms (tones) for later reconversion back to bits; not much can be done with such signals on or by the network. But in an all-digital system, the bits are buffered and manipulated by computers (using timing pulses and very rapid machine arithmetic) until the data reach their "destination"—this can be another computer, another digital network, or a digital device that translates these signals into a form a human (or another machine) can understand.

System timing is critical to the understanding of control, for at any one moment, control of the signal may extend halfway across the world, or just down to the end of your coiled telephone cord.[12] Control becomes vitally important in integrated network designs, but the form of control is different from past telephone systems.[13] Network administrations will have to change their model of carriage to be able to cope with users having access to their formerly rigidly controlled networks. The alternative may be new models of networking, such as user-community derived operations like the Internet.[14]

MULTIPLEXING

One of the fundamental telecom principles established by early computer and data transmission standards was that of multiplexing the bit streams from different sources to economize on (then) very expensive circuit costs. A collateral principle was that the signaling protocol should be designed to handle a variety of noisy channels (and all channels are very noisy).[15]

Multiplexed models and the novel telecommunications concept of moving bitstreams of data in synchronized chunks or "packets"—both to lower costs and to eliminate errors—came together in the Defense Department's Advanced Research Projects Agency Network (ARPANET) in 1969. All future telecom networks will, of necessity, follow this model; such networks require stored-program computers for operation, and machines requiring the packet networks for service—a true symbiosis.

PROTOCOLS AND OPEN NETWORKS

Synchronous transmission as a new link "metaphor" eventually evolved into the *layered* approach for a total network system architecture: Each lower layer nests into the layer directly above it, and within each layer the controlling software is only cognizant of the layer below and the layer above it. Everything else is "baggage" or "payload" to be delivered.[16]

Actual physical connection takes place at the lowest layer; "upper" layers are conceptual. This means that the application software can avoid most, but not all, of the problems of dealing with the physical media and devices, and it permits upgrading (extensibility) as technology changes and improves. Networks have to be "technology neutral" to accomplish this—not an easy requirement. For one thing, different media have different inherent latency, or delay times; synchronous satellites add a short but potentially destructive delay for interactivity; optical disks are much less efficient than magnetic media for access times; and even fiber optics shows speed-of-light problems over transcontinental distances.

In several different, but related standardized layered models for telecom, it is generally understood that above the physical layer, communication takes place only between "peers"—functions that are the same in applications separate from each other—and between adjacent layers via the actual physical layer. Standards define functions and services performed by each layer, and the identical protocols between peer layers. In computer communications terminology, a protocol is "a format and a set of procedures that are commonly agreed to for the purpose of achieving communications. Layering of protocols is the result of a *stratification of function* among parts of the system."[17]

In general, standards attempt only to define these functions, *not* to control how the layers are to perform the functions.[18] Derivative of the stored-program digital computer concept, only the inputs and outputs of a layer need be defined, or "standardized." This permits manufacturers to use any technique to make the layers work, including proprietary techniques; any "black box" or component defining a function, application, or service should be able to connect to any other black box in a layer above or below. This is the basic definition of an open network—that the interconnections are transparent and obvious rather than secret or proprietary; what goes on inside the black box is irrelevant to the interface as long as the interface is understood.

PACKET NETWORK MODELS

The new network paradigm of layered segmentation is quite different from that of hierarchical telephone, telegraph, or even analog radio and television networks, where signal control passed directly from one end to the other, to the point of directly controlling a beam on a cathode ray terminal (CRT) or a vibration in a diaphragm. With the introduction of store-and-forward packet networking techniques in the early 1970s, new and critical issues were raised for handling these data frames.[19] Control of traffic flows, as in conventional telephone systems, was not enough; *congestion* control had to be added to the protocol to prevent resources from becoming overtaxed. Congestion control and its closely affiliated process, *frame routing*, have become major research topics in packet network design for derivative local-area networks and, especially, for future digital broadband networks. There are many solutions, and hence many protocols, leading to differing network architectures, incompatible hardware and software, and widely divergent standards.[20]

Judging from the rapid expansion of packet networks for data (and now also for experimental voice and video links), and the application of these layered and packetized techniques even to transitional hybrid telephony like the integrated services digital network (ISDN), it is likely that all networks will converge on this model. But convergence does not guarantee either interoperability or open access to these networks; digital technologies can just as easily close options as open them—it all depends on how the networks are designed.

Current broadband, packetized standards apply sophisticated relational database software across a high-speed digital link for *both transmission and routing.*[21] Data carriage and network signaling systems are combined, permitting the packets to be self-routing.[22] Broadband network design uses large bandwidths for signaling overhead, made economically possible with inexpensive fiber circuitry. Current international standards call for a broadband payload some ten thousand times greater than the basic rate for local telephone circuits. In the next few years, circuits about ten to twenty times larger than that will be in place. However, the designs are still very controversial, since routing, switching, and terminal devices may not economically tolerate such large overheads, even if they have little impact on transmission per se. It may be several years before all the details of broadband standards can be ironed out.

The most efficient network designs for broadband digital communications may not resemble the telephone plant of the past. Network usage will be both more dynamic and less predictable. To maximize overall system efficiency for the user, customers will demand direct access to network resources, including operations, administration, and maintenance (this is the primary reason customers build their own, so-called private networks). It will become increasingly difficult to pinpoint whether the customer or carrier is conducting a digital transaction in such networks.[23] At any node, the "customer" may be another network or even a competing carrier. Clearly, carriers will resist such access, for no other reason than that it shifts all the value added to their customers and reduces carriage to mere marginal-cost operations. Some political mechanism will be required to balance firms' economic interests with proper technological solutions.

AN ECOLOGY OF LAYERED, OPEN SYSTEMS

The efforts over the past decade to respond with open network models to the potentially anticompetitive networking products of large computer firms and monopoly based carriers imply a reallocation of resources between public and private networks and among users and vendors. Although end-to-end digital architectures will ultimately emerge (with virtual, logical connections defining communications channels, as the various open and integrated systems networking standards already make clear), there are many options and it is not certain how this evolution will take place. A great deal of study, based on practical applications (essentially "trial and error") will have to take place before we understand all of the implications.

Though convergence of technologies may have illustrated the need for radical new models of telecommunications based on layered approaches, open interfaces are not as radical an idea as one might suppose. Their origins and parallel can be found in biophysics and chemical electrodynamics.[24] Ludwig Von Bertalanffy notes: "From the viewpoint of thermodynamics, open systems can maintain themselves in a state of high statistical improbability, of order and organization."[25]

The ability of different system segments, or "layers," to interface without disordering the total system is the general goal of an open telecom system, though structuring such a model is not as easy as observing it in nature. Bertalanffy describes how open living systems may approach a steady state that

> remains constant in its composition, in spite of continuous irreversible processes, import, and export, building up and breaking down, taking place. If a steady state is reached in an open system, it is independent of the initial conditions, and determined only by the system parameters. . . . This is called *equifinality* as found in many organismic processes. . . . In contrast for closed physicochemical systems, the same final state can therefore be reached equifinally from different initial conditions and after disturbances of the process.[26]

As a model of complex systems, this biochemical model is closer to the goals of the layered model than the more rigid, closed, and controlled models of conventional telephony. Nature allows for change in each element of the system, with a "steady-state" interface between the layers. This permits growth and evolution with minimum disturbance of the total environment.

Older networking models called for standards that are dimensional in scope—track gauge, Baudot start and stop bits, voltage and current levels, synchronization signals—and interconnections that are rigid and controlled by the carrier or operator. A minor change can make system elements collapse, or move out of synch. In nature, minor changes may be regressive and an organism may fail to survive or evolve further, but species that *do* survive appear to overcome entropy—that is, they contain negative entropy, which is "information" as defined in communications theory. Herein lies a more useful model for predicting and guiding future telecommunications evolution.

For open interconnection, we need to subsume dimensionality within layers; this implies compatibility and the need to create typologies that permit the disappearance of species (that is, specific hardware or application software) without disturbing the system equilibrium, and to encourage the implementation of new technologies for increased efficiency and increased diversity (to aid in survivability) rather than enshrine vested industries. The parallels to ecology are apparent.

WAVES OF INNOVATION

In assessing where we are going in telecommunications technology, it is useful to review where we have been. There have been four intensive waves of technology development that have brought about today's computer/communications revolution. The first wave began in earnest just before World War II and was pivotal for cryptology and computation for armaments. Some historians give these early stored-program computers credit for the successful Normandy invasion because of their ability to break the German ciphers so that enemy troop locations and movements could be revealed. At the same time, primitive digital logic devices were being used to encipher global Allied voice communications. These wartime efforts provided the basis for the next fifty years of technological development, culminating in digital communications as we know it today: digitization of analog waveforms, computerized control and switching for telecom channels, application of spread spectrum techniques for radio, and, most important, an underlying set of theories about digital computation, information flows, and transmission of electrical communications.

The second wave, coinciding with the origins of the Cold War, created the computer industry. The amount of resources expended by the United States and the former Soviet Union on computation and computers during the Cold War was enormous; the total has yet to be assessed, but a clue can be found in an obscure memo the National Security Agency (NSA) released some years ago. NSA stated that in the decade following 1950, over $1 billion per year (in 1950 dollars) was spent for computer-related R&D alone—a total of $10 billion by 1960.[27] The NSA's very secret financing of generally public research in that decade (disbursed primarily via the National Science Foundation and the Atomic Energy Commission) produced, among other developments, cheap magnetic tape and tape recorders, solid-state memories, high-level computer languages and software techniques, and cost-effective data transmission interfaces.[28]

The third wave of innovation (1960–70) was an accelerated outgrowth of continued Cold War expenditures. Microminiaturization of electronic circuits for civilian and military space activities, and defense requirements for remote computing created the first all-digital telecommunications networks. Computer technology advances made it feasible to build the first digital telecom-switching devices during this era, though computer-controlled electromechanical switching dated to the late 1950s.

We are now in the midst of a fourth wave. Although, to the layperson, the changes taking place may appear wildly innovative, this is more a time of consolidation than of invention. In the past two decades, consumer electronics technology has tended to outpace military and industrial electronics. Much more so than its mainframe and minicomputer predecessors, the personal computer resembles a consumer and commodity item in terms of sales, marketing, and pricing. The shift to consumer marketing has created a new industry, with firms that did not even exist fifteen years ago as market leaders; and it has devastated the old-line computer firms, many of which did not exist thirty years ago. Such is the pace of change that predictions about which firms will dominate—or even survive—into the next century can be nothing more than wild guesses. Traditionally, consumer electronics firms have not been very sophisticated in developing radically new innovations (rather, they have excelled at packaging and marketing inexpensive devices); neither the computer, satellite, fiber optics, nor any of the powerful software found on data networks today has come from the consumer industry. Where future innovations will come from and just how the convergence of media, telecom, and computation will come about are still open questions.

Personal Computers

All of the technical ingredients of the personal computer had been understood and demonstrated in the early 1960s. But production had to await low-cost components and manufacturing techniques and, most important, useful applications. The spread sheet was the first to accelerate sales of personal computers, with word processing a close second "killer" application. Both were obvious applications, but neither had occurred to the vendors of mainframes and minicomputers. Stand-alone word processors, which had been around for a decade, were wiped out by the low-cost and more utilitarian personal computer. Mainframe manufacturers had toyed with the concept of real-time data analysis with timesharing and similar features, but the incentive to give power to users on their own machines was missing from the economic equations of large computer manufacturers and their systems affiliates.

Despite the apparent revolution, it is important to recognize that the personal computer, with its large glass display tube, keyboard, disk drives, and perhaps modems, scanners, laser printers, local-area network wires, and other accessories is only a temporary manifestation of computer technology. The personal computer is *not* the computer—the computer is a small chip inside, along with its memory, and the hardware to get signals in and out of these chips. The rest is ancillary. The physical manifestation of computation is bound to change as dramatically in the future as it has in the past—from gigantic Rube Goldberg-looking machines with less power than a digital wristwatch of today, to a wide variety of computational appliances of which the personal computer is only one familiar element. The next generation is already with us— less visible, but more prevalent than is commonly suspected.

Computers—true, stored-program, digital computers—are found in devices ranging from microwave ovens and toasters to laser printers. Indeed, the latter often have more processing power than the personal computers to which they are connected. In a laser printer, for example, a high-level computer language (a "page description language") interprets the textual and graphic data from the personal computer and rapidly creates a perfectly typeset page. This language is so easy to transmit that a growing body of users today send just the instructions to remote machines (via ordinary telephone lines) to create perfect pages, instead of scanning the pages and sending a facsimile. This trivial step uses roughly a hundred to a thousand times *less* telecommunications capacity than a fax.[29] The implications for telephone carriers are obvious: A significant segment of growth in telephone traffic in recent years has been due to fax machines; suddenly that rate of growth may drop to a trickle through the application of not very new technology. Moreover, telephone company offerings of new, broader band digital services in the local exchange will exacerbate the problem, since these services will make it even easier and cheaper to transmit compressed digital files.

Only new forms of traffic that consume large amounts of data (even with compression), such as full-motion video, may be able to make up for the losses that new compression technology will engender. And it is still too early to determine if, when, and where such video technology will become the next "killer" application—perhaps for education, perhaps for videophone, perhaps for new ways of distributing entertainment, or for all of the above. It is also too early to determine how it will be priced, and which firms and economic sectors will share in the profits (or subsidies).

ARBITRAGE

Shifting traffic is only part of the technology conundrum. Arbitrage of traffic using the telephone company's own facilities is much more serious and is a precursor of many logistical changes to come as a result of computerization.

Any computer can imitate any other computer; proprietary application software is rarely enough to keep hardware market share. The microcomputer is about to enter a new phase as telecom carriers—telephone companies, cable carriers, and satellite providers—plan to put full-fledged computers replete with personal computer-type software in television set-top converters in order to offer interactive consumer services (and make it easier to find programs among the hundreds that will be available). Incompatible standards are rampant, with an eye to creating proprietary devices to divide market share.

But the applications are likely to be liberating. Computers have a way of writing new chapters in the history of unintended consequences. If set-top appliances with built-in microprocessors truly allow interactivity and encourage two-way communication, a closed, constraining system will be difficult to enforce and will not be in a carrier's long-range financial interest. Regulatory influences will surely prevent the set-top device from becoming a bottleneck constraint, either as a carrier-only offering, or as a gateway. Safer predictions are that business applications will take control of the network, and that broadband switching will follow the Internet model, rather than the older hierarchical model of the circuit-switched telephone system.[30] At this point, the carrier will lose control over traffic, and only its involvement in content will be of economic interest. Again, a conundrum is in the making, since the carrier is not technically (or perhaps even legally) able to steer users only to that content which it provides.

POLICY RECOMMENDATIONS

As usual, policy and regulation lag far behind technology, despite the lip service given to change—from the naming of the national information infrastructure, to talk of convergence, open standards, and analogies to "information highways," as if the road system carrying goods and passengers can help us understand invisible electrons and incredibly fast and arcane computational devices.

What we need on a political level is a shift in approaching telecommunications as radical as the one we have had in technology. Given human behavior and vested financial interests, this is a difficult, if not impossible, task, but it is worth examining its consequences.

First, the local access problem—the "last mile"—must be overcome if we are to have widespread connections to the broadband network already in place between cities and even between most urban central offices. This could be done by overbuilding the telephone wire pairs; by rebuilding cable television plants for two-way, interactive digital circuits; or by using spectrum more efficiently. It is likely that pursuing more than one way would offer some competition in the local arena, and would be valuable in keeping the carriers on their toes.

Overbuilding or rebuilding is not a trivial task, for it is necessary to do more than just increase the capacity of the circuits; new architectures for handling digital traffic, for scaling up to thousands of simultaneous users of so-far unknown future services, for billing and revenue sharing, and for distributing information must be invented and tested in the field. All we have heard of so far are the ubiquitous five hundred channels, broadcast essentially one way, with interactivity reduced to ordering up movies, games, or pizza. The last mile deserves better than that. In offices and on university campuses today we already have such an interactive broadband system, called local-area networks. We need to deliver similar service to the home, small businesses, and rural areas so that people can use multimedia video services; establish their own servers for new businesses and distribution of information resources; and improve interconnectivity for education, health care, and things of which we have not yet even thought. One of the more difficult issues will be how to serve the vast majority of the world's population who will never be able to afford or justify economically fiber-optic connections, but will rely primarily on satellites, with their inherent delays that are not conducive to much of the interactive switching technology currently being developed.

Second, to provide the most flexible and potentially most omnipresent NII platform, we need to rethink how we allocate spectrum. The traditional analogy to water rights no longer makes sense in an era of high-speed, cheap microprocessors that can divide spectrum by time as well as space. But reallocating pieces of spectrum little by little will take too long and will have only a minimal impact on local access and competitiveness. A bold statement could be made by reallocating large amounts of spectrum all at once. It is perfectly conceivable that *all* of the UHF television spectrum could be converted to a digital, cellular broadband, radio infrastructure overnight—say, on January 1, 2000—to herald the coming new millennium.

All television users in the United States could be given microprocessor-based boxes before then (essentially providing every home with a supercomputer, since by then that is what the typical chip will be). At midnight on December 31, 1999, these boxes would be connected to the back of the set, just as cable television boxes are today. The boxes would receive channels 2–69 transparently to the user, but in actuality each box would be converting some digitally compressed, dynamic, spread spectrum, cellular signal to these television channels, just as a videocassette recorder converts signals to channel 3 or 4 today (making every VCR a television broadcast station, albeit a tiny one). Meanwhile, the rest of the UHF spectrum (about 70 percent of it), plus all of the VHF television spectrum, would be freed for new services, including digitally compressed video and high-definition television.

Innovative regulatory schemes would have to be invented to accompany such a system—a much harder task than designing the boxes described above, which are not too different from today's technology. However, the benefits would clearly outweigh the cost of the boxes (which would be free to the users and would connect to the cable and telephone networks as well), paid for by the new users of the spectrum. It has been estimated that if the spectrum for a single television station in Los Angeles were converted to telephony, the station would be worth over $1 billion.[31] In this light, a massive conversion might not seem as absurd as it first appears. And there is a precedent: on June 1, 1886, all of the southern railroads and some other railroad lines, over one very long weekend, converted most of their narrow- and broad-gauge lines in the United States to a single, standard gauge.[32] The railroads had been ordered to do this after the Civil War, but approached the task in such a piecemeal fashion that it appeared as if it would never be completed. With one stroke, the U.S. government finished the job for the railroads, and the country entered the new century with a transport infrastructure that posed one less barrier for interchanging traffic. The next century deserves as much for information infrastructure.

Finally, the U.S. government must take the lead in guiding policies for open interconnection between systems and in encouraging competition—both sides of the same coin. As we have seen in the past decades of computerization, digital infrastructure can imply either a more open or a more closed system. We have developed the tools in layered architectures, in understanding how interfaces work, and in cooperative standards-making as on the Internet to make systems interconnect. However, the incentives for closing systems have not gone away, so the role of government will have to be the same as it was in the past: to guarantee a level playing field.

But we must find better ways to do this than a regulatory procedure via proscription, which consistently lags behind technology and user needs. The Internet model, whereby the user community can test new ideas and then propose them as new standards, appears to work better than the older methods. Yet we may kill the goose to get the golden eggs with proposals to regulate the Internet as if it were a conventional common carrier. Since the Internet is nothing more than a group of protocols internetworking tens of thousands of computers, conventional regulation means regulating each and every microprocessor and software kernel that interconnects. A more absurd way to stop the growth and convergence of networking infrastructure could not be devised.

PART II

POLICIES FOR THE NATIONAL INFORMATION INFRASTRUCTURE

4

REFORMING THE U.S. TELECOMMUNICATIONS POLICYMAKING PROCESS

HENRY GELLER

"*H*ere comes mystery land." The chairman of the Federal Communications Commission (FCC) a generation ago used these words to introduce the section of the commission's weekly meetings that dealt with common carriers. To the commissioners, generalists, and lawyers whose main policy focus was television, the field of telecommunications was arcane. Their membership included no economists versed in telecommunications, no spectrum engineers, no computer scientists, no user specialists. The field was wholly dominated by the giant monopoly AT&T and was regulated as a slow-moving administrative minuet between the company and the FCC staff or state utility commissions. Jurisdiction was fragmented among a scattering of government agencies each carrying out a portion of the Communications Act derived from a 1910 Interstate Commerce Commission (ICC) law. Users responded to services offered by AT&T instead of AT&T tailoring its services to the needs and desires of its users.

Today, we have crossed into a digital world driven by extraordinary and continuing advances in the power of the microprocessor.[1] The computer, fiber-optic cable, satellites, and other new technologies have wrought a sea change, which has led to a convergence of previously separate industries. Companies in such industries as telephones (telcos), cable television, broadcasting, newspaper publishing, data processing, and others now seek alliances with one another, even on a global basis, to meet the challenges posed by the emergence of the multimedia computer, the advanced digital television terminal, and personal communications services that give access to anyone, anytime, anywhere. The user is now in control; services must be tailored to his or her needs. The Internet computer network is fast becoming the template for user dominance in a new environment of a network of networks.[2] We begin to see a rapid erosion of some long-established, socially significant policies, such as protected local franchise areas granted in return for providing "carrier-of-last-resort" service.

Most important, as has been described in previous chapters, all our industries must compete in a global economy. To do so successfully, they must equal or exceed the productivity of their rivals or must differentiate their services in ways that attract consumers. Information movement and management are critical to those efforts. Telecommunications is thus a vital tool. With the microprocessor, it is the base of the global information infrastructure.

It is also of critical importance to the quality of life in the emerging information society. To endure, a representative democracy must have an educated citizenry. To flourish, a nation will need a well-educated workforce. Again, telecommunications, although no panacea, can and must contribute greatly to the educational process through such means as shared learning from a distant central location, to make up for the shortage of science or language teachers. A nation without a sound health-care structure fails both its citizens and its industries; again, telecommunications can and must make its important contribution. As a final example, telecommuting can have large benefits for the environment, energy conservation, and efficiencies in operation.

The two goals of telecommunications policy are thus to enable telecommunications to make a maximum contribution to productivity and to the quality of life. The latter goal must extend equitably and fairly to all persons; thus, effective and evolving universal concepts are needed to avoid a nation of have and have-nots.

The great shifts in technology and the market brought on by the emergence of the global information economy are well recognized. What is not recognized is our failure to make corresponding changes in our telecommunications policy process. The defects of a generation ago—the antiquated law, the fragmented policy process, the absence of FCC commissioners with deep expertise and experience in telecommunications—are all still true (although there is now a good chance for progress, especially as to the antiquated law, as will be seen later in this chapter). But the costs today to the national interest are much greater and will continue to increase as the global information economy accelerates in the multimedia, highly mobile world of tomorrow. There is a clear and compelling need for substantial reform.

HISTORICAL BACKGROUND

For most of the twentieth century, U.S. telecommunications policy revolved about the giant monopoly telephone company, AT&T.[3] AT&T and other, smaller telcos were regulated by the ICC under a 1910 law. When radio became a significant technology in the 1920s, a new agency, the Federal Radio Commission, was given regulatory authority over all aspects of radio, including common-carrier radio operations. In 1934, the FCC was created in order to centralize regulatory authority over all interstate common-carrier activities and all radio operations, including broadcasting.

The president of the United States can influence FCC actions only through his appointment powers. Unlike other executive branch agencies, such as the Environmental Protection Agency (EPA), the five FCC commissioners serve for fixed terms and can be removed only for malfeasance. The FCC is thus an independent agency. Its actions are not subject to control of, or review by, the president. They are reviewable only by the courts for lawfulness (that is, that a decision adheres to the provisions of the Communications Act and is not arbitrary or capricious) and by Congress for any and all aspects, including whether they constitute sound policy.

There are limits on the FCC's jurisdiction. For example, its authority to regulate common-carrier rates and practices is restricted to interstate activities. The states retain the authority to regulate such matters in intrastate commerce. The FCC also has jurisdiction only over the nongovernmental portion of the radio spectrum. The president (or his delegatee) has the authority to assign parts of the spectrum to government users, thus necessitating close coordination with the FCC to avoid conflicts. The spectrum is split between government and nongovernment use, with roughly 40 percent shared.

Several entities were created to manage the spectrum and develop executive branch policies in the telecommunications field over the years: first came the director of telecommunications management in the 1960s, then the Office of Telecommunications Policy (OTP) in the Executive Office of the President in 1969, and finally in 1978 the National Telecommunications and Information Administration (NTIA) in the Commerce Department when the Carter administration decided to reduce the size of the Executive Office of the President.

NTIA vies with the State Department in international communications policymaking under a deliberately vague law and executive order, and both must interact with the FCC in this field. In trade affairs, these agencies must mesh with the United States trade representative (USTR), which is part of the Executive Office of the President and has the primary responsibility for developing and implementing U.S. international trade policy. It is therefore the focal point for efforts to remove trade barriers for manufacturers or providers of U.S. telecommunications equipment and services.

The Defense Department is responsible for national security and is by far the largest user of telecommunications services and facilities. It takes part in tariff matters before the FCC, in spectrum allocation issues, and in telecommunications policy deliberations affecting national security.

The Department of Justice, through its antitrust division, has played a critical role in telecommunications policymaking as a result of its antitrust actions against AT&T. Its first action culminated in a 1956 consent decree that confined AT&T to common-carrier communications activities subject to regulation to protect the public interest. In the 1970s, the FCC opened customer-premises equipment and long-distance service to competition. The department brought a second antitrust suit against AT&T because of alleged predatory actions against the new competitors, and this suit ended in 1982 with a consent decree resulting in the breakup of AT&T, leaving it with the long-distance service, manufacturing, and Bell Labs—and divesting it of local Bell operating companies.[4]

CURRENT POWER CENTERS

CONGRESS

Congress stands at the top of the process because it sets both the procedural and substantive guidelines in the governing law. No one would argue for a law that tries to deal with every detail of the regulatory process. That would be folly in this fast-changing field. There is an advantage in having a broad mandate such as protecting the public interest, since it permits executive agencies to adjust to changing conditions. But over time, change can build a need for both procedural and substantive revision of the law.

Congress knows that time has certainly arrived in light of the drastically changed competitive milieu, the convergence and proposed large cross-industry mergers, and the confusion that has resulted from conflicting policy actions of the FCC, the antitrust court, and the state commissions. Congress should not leave basic communications policies to technical and narrow antitrust court decisions. Most important, it should set forth its vision of the directions that all policymakers, federal or state, should take to achieve the goals of the global information economy—greater productivity and an enhanced quality of life.

But after two decades of bills and hearings, Congress has not been able to pass general legislation with new guidelines appropriate to the changed situation. There has, however, been recent specific legislation providing for auctions in the mobile radio field and preemption of state authority to regulate mobile rates.[5] The reason for this gridlock has not been the usual division of government between Congress and the president. The failure lies entirely with Congress. Every proposed law changes the status quo in the telecommunications industries and ignites a fierce clash among established carriers and new competitors. Congress, not wishing to offend any of these powerful industries—some with media clout and all with sizable political action committee contributions—ends up in a legislative stalemate. The stalemate may finally end in the 104th Congress.

While there is legislative gridlock, Congress nevertheless remains a powerful player: It sends "messages" to the FCC that the agency cannot ignore because of Congress's control over the appropriation process. Indeed, that process is sometimes used by adding a rider to the FCC appropriation directing, for example, that no money be spent in a specified docket. A pattern has thus emerged: an industry displeased by an FCC action or proposal runs to the powerful congressional committee chairmen, who then "yank the commission's chain" and force either delay, revision, or a freeze. It can be argued that some such interventions serve a worthy public interest purpose and are part of a de facto system of checks and balances upon which the U.S. system is based. But all too often they give powerful industries an unwarranted club to blunt or delay needed responses to emerging technologies or competition.[6]

FEDERAL COMMUNICATIONS COMMISSION

As a creature of Congress operating under an antiquated law, the FCC has a difficult time responding fully and boldly to fast-driving changes in technology and the market. It is often overwhelmed by its license-processing responsibilities (for example, thousands of applications for some new service or, recently, the need to deal with a great number of new responsibilities in the reregulation of cable television). It thus can be characterized as a reactive agency concerned with manning the barricades, dealing on an ad hoc basis with particular matters but with no guiding vision. Even if the chairman has such a vision, it might not be shared by his or her colleagues in this collegial body, who are often zealous in insisting that all members are equal in setting goals and in voting. The commission at times hangs back in adopting new policies until some state like New York or Illinois has blazed the trail. Despite the Communications Act's intent to centralize authority in one agency, the FCC finds itself sometimes frustrated by the actions of the antitrust court or the state commissions.

Further, no matter how good or bad the governing law may be, what is critical is the quality of appointments to the agency, and they have been disappointing. The problem is that FCC appointments are usually regarded as political plums. Looking over the history of appointments, I can only conclude that with enough political pull, anyone can be appointed to the FCC. That is not true of agencies like the Federal Reserve Board or the Securities and Exchange Commission (SEC). Of course, politics enters into appointments to the agencies, but no person without extensive relevant expertise is nominated to those agencies; if one were, the Senate would be unlikely to confirm the appointment. This is not to say that no good men or women were ever appointed to the FCC; they clearly were. The problem is that while it is helpful to have a savvy generalist or lawyer on the FCC, the telecommunications field is complex, calling for considerable expertise in such diverse disciplines as economics, engineering, or accounting. Today, no one on the commission has such expertise, and no one with such expertise has been with the agency for some time. Now, however, that telecommunications has emerged as far more important than just the regulation of television, appointments to the FCC call for the same treatment as those for the SEC.

This is a crucial problem: "As long as the selection of [people] for key administrative posts is based upon political reward rather than competency, little else that is done will really matter."[7] Presidents tend not to be concerned about the independent agencies, so long as there is no scandal. As has been pointed out, presidents are not helped politically by "even excellent administration of the commissions,"[8] and similarly they are not hurt politically by a poor effort. Unlike the case of executive branch agencies such as EPA, the president is not held accountable for the performance of independent agencies. Therefore, he is under no pressure to appoint the best-qualified people to them; he can give in to political pressures with impunity.

The nature of the appointment process leads to another critical problem—the overidentification of FCC members with regulated industries. There are a number of factors contributing to this. First, while the president and the Congress may be largely indifferent to these agency appointments, the regulated industries are not. They watch the appointments closely, and attempt, often successfully, to block the appointment of someone who might cause them problems. This can lead to the selection of a neutral person with little or no track record in telecommunications.

Second, this neutral person is likely to be assiduously courted by the regulated industries. As has been aptly put, the appointee realizes soon after coming to town that "nobody ever heard of him or cares much what he does—except one group of very personable, reasonable, knowledgeable, delightful human beings, who recognize his true worth. Obviously they might turn his head just a bit."[9]

Third, some agency members desire reappointment. They know that if they take positions strongly at odds with the regulated industries, the latter in turn will strongly oppose their reappointment. This may well lead to the selection of some new "neutral" figure.

Finally, a number of agency members may look ahead to the day when they will leave the agency; in most cases they expect to work for the regulated industries. This can either consciously or subconsciously make the agency member overly responsive or sympathetic to the industry position.[10]

NATIONAL TELECOMMUNICATIONS AND INFORMATION ADMINISTRATION

The Office of Telecommunications Policy, as part of the Executive Office of the President, was effective in formulating and implementing executive branch policy. For example, the highly successful "open skies" domestic satellite policy was largely due to Executive Office's intervention. Unfortunately, during the Watergate period, the Executive Office became an instrument of the Nixon administration's effort to suppress perceived anti-administration viewpoints of the television networks.[11] NTIA, as its replacement in the Department of Commerce, a weak, second-tier cabinet department, lacks clout. Its long-range studies and filings in FCC dockets, however worthy, pass largely unnoticed; it is not even a "bully pulpit." It has difficulty in holding its own against powerful entities like the Defense Department. Even where it has greater expertise than a rival agency, the result has often been unseemly turf wars, for instance with the State Department in the international communications field. Finally, as shown by Joel Reidenberg in Chapter 10 of this volume, there is a need for a governmental focal point for important information policy areas such as privacy issues. NTIA is the logical repository for such policymaking, but it has not been seen, or shown to be, effective in this area.

STATE DEPARTMENT

There was a marked improvement in the State Department's organizational structure to handle telecommunications issues in the early 1980s. Until then, one assistant secretary handled both transportation and telecommunications, and most often the staffing for the latter was headed by a foreign service officer with no expertise in the field who would then be rotated to another position after two or three years. This system worked poorly. It failed to provide the focal point and expertise so much needed in this complex area.

As a result of the reorganization in the 1980s, an assistant secretary (with ambassadorial rank) handled telecommunications exclusively, and headed a more expert staff in the (Bureau of International) Communications and Information Policy (CIP). The CIP reported to the under-secretary of state for security assistance, science, and technology. Principal responsibility for telecommunications trade issues rests with the (Bureau of) Economic and Business Affairs (EBA), reporting to the under-secretary for economic and business affairs.

There were problems even with this improvement because of the vague executive order, now codified into law, dividing authority between the State Department and NTIA. Moreover, a new study within the State Department called for another reorganization eliminating CIP (and its assistant secretary head) and simply putting the telecommunications responsibility into the EBA as one of several divisions, with probably at times a rotating foreign service officer again in charge. This proposal, which Congress allowed to be implemented, is an unsound return to the previous unsatisfactory scheme.

UNITED STATES TRADE REPRESENTATIVE

Trade issues have become increasingly important in the telecommunications field as the global information economy accelerates. The United States Trade Representative (USTR) is trying to deal with vexing problems; for example, with the European Union nations, on both a multilateral and bilateral basis.[12] But to make effective use of all the U.S. government's leverage would require a strong telecommunications focal point in the executive branch, close cooperation between government and the affected industries, and deft wheeling and dealing by executive agencies. Here again shortcomings have surfaced in the coordination process, as the *NTIA Telecomm 2000* report has pointed out.[13] In addition, the FCC is inhibited from lending its full weight and expertise to the trade negotiation efforts because of the adjudicatory rules restricting its procedures and because it runs into turf problems as an independent agency trying to work with executive branch agencies.[14]

A 1993 report by the Office of Technology Assessment (OTA) reached the following conclusion:

> The United States lacks a comprehensive international telecommunications policy incorporating a vision of the global networks of the future. The dispersed responsibilities and competing agendas of several executive branch agencies and the Federal Communications Commission (FCC) encourage "forum-shopping" by carriers, services providers, and large users. The Department of State's Bureau of International Communications and Information Policy (CIP) has the legislated responsibility for coordinating agency programs and initiatives, but is largely ineffective in this role for structural, political, and institutional reasons. USTR has filled the gap, but because international telecommunications policy has become overly subordinated to trade policy, other objectives (e.g., standards setting, interoperability, universal service) have been neglected.[15]

JUSTICE DEPARTMENT

The Justice Department plays a critical role because it instigates, litigates, and settles antitrust suits in the telecommunications field. It now finds itself trapped in a regulatory role under the 1982 AT&T consent decree because the antitrust court refuses to let go of the case and is dealing with matters that would be more appropriately handled by the FCC, subject to congressional and appellate review. Thus, former Assistant Attorney General Charles Rule stated:

> Most fundamentally, the [1982 consent decree] has brought to the telecommunications industry a new set of regulatory institutions that inherently lack many of the resources crucial to successful regulation. Administering the decree involves policing adherence to its restrictions, and—even more important—determining when the restrictions are no longer appropriate. These tasks require . . . technical expertise, regulatory experience, and a set of administrative procedures to implement that expertise and experience. Such resources currently reside in the FCC; a law enforcement agency and the court . . . will never be able to amass more than a pale shadow of the regulators' resources.

> Moreover, because of the role assumed by the court and the Department, regulation of the telecommunications industry has become seriously fragmented and at times potentially inconsistent. . . . [A]ttempts by the FCC to set long-range policy to ensure that America

retains its historic technological lead in telecommunications are frustrated by rigid prohibitions in the decree and the inherently cumbersome mechanism by which they are administered. There is simply no way to coordinate the policies of the traditional regulators and the decree administrators.[16]

APPELLATE COURTS

All final FCC actions can be appealed to the U.S. Courts of Appeal (with possible further proceedings in the Supreme Court). Here again a pattern has emerged in the past two decades: just as almost all important FCC actions end up in appeals to the congressional committees (which can review for policy and send "messages"), so also there are now court appeals of these actions. The courts are not suppose to substitute their policy judgments for those of the agency—that is, to determine whether a decision is a wise one. Rather, they are to review for lawfulness: Were the proper procedures followed, was the action consistent with the governing statutory provisions, and was it reasonable or, stated differently, not arbitrary or capricious? It has been argued that the courts have strayed from that standard of lawfulness and have become a "superagency." Certainly court decisions have had a profound impact at times on the course of telecommunications policy.[17] While there have been decisions that reached beyond the courts' proper role, in my view the reason for so many reversals and remands to the agency has been the poor quality of FCC opinions. Congress can adopt a law and need give no reasons at all for its various decisions or its compromises among contending groups. The FCC has no such leeway: it must set forth its reasons, however succinctly, for all actions, and cannot simply compromise among private interests without showing why that reasonably serves the public interest.[18] All too often it has acted as if it were the Congress, with the courts then reminding it of its responsibilities under the applicable law. Improvement in the quality of appointments to the FCC would go a long way toward solving the judicial problems that the agency has encountered.

STATE PUBLIC UTILITY COMMISSIONS

Since state borders are artificial creations and telecommunications really has no respect for borders, it has been argued that the creation of one national and fifty state jurisdictions to regulate telecommunications makes no practical sense. But such regulation is a huge task in a country as large and complex as the United States. The states have the advantage of grass-roots regulation attuned to their regions, and of being laboratories to try new regulatory approaches, without the vast consequences of a national mistake. In fact, the states have fulfilled this role, with some having led in incentive regulation instead of the traditional rate-of-return approach,[19] innovative interconnection actions to give new competitors more effective access to established local exchange carriers, and accelerated deployment by the local carriers of new technology such as broadband fiber-optics replacement of the copper wire access lines to subscribers. Such state actions put pressure on the FCC and neighboring states to follow the leaders.

There are, however, serious problems at the state level. Too many state regulators hang back in introducing competition or dealing with its effects because of a desire to maintain low residential rates during their "watch." Further, state actions can have effects beyond their borders that frustrate or undermine federal policies. The normal rule of law is that if a state action "stands as an obstacle to the accomplishment and execution of the *full* purposes and objectives . . ." of federal policy,[20] the federal agency can preempt that action. But that is not the case in this one field (common-carrier regulation) because of an anachronism in the 1934 Communications Act. A 1986 Supreme Court decision held that even if the state action does run counter to such full effectuation of federal policy, the act specifically provides for a "dual regulatory system" or "two hands on the wheel,"[21] and thus the states can operate in this area unless their action *negates* the federal policy. This policy holds even if what is involved is the allocation of scarce spectrum by the FCC, and the state action would restrict (but not negate) the beneficial use of that spectrum. The Court stated that the FCC had made "a persuasive case in support of its policy objectives, but that case must be made to Congress and not this court."[22]

Clearly, the answer is to adopt the general rule of preemption in this field. However, with one very important recent exception, the states have wielded their considerable political clout with Congress, and gridlock continues here, too.[23] That exception involves the mobile radio field, where Congress recently preempted the state's authority to bar entry or to regulate rates, and centralized those critical matters in the FCC.[24]

THE MAJOR DEFECT OF THE PRESENT REGULATORY PROCESS

I have set out some specific defects in the present regulatory scheme: the fragmented policy process between the FCC and the antitrust court, the flawed FCC appointments process, the lack of a fully effective federal captain in the federal-state relationship, the flawed international communications policy process in the executive branch, and so forth. The next major defect of the process, namely, the absence of any overarching vision that can be effectively implemented, also needs to be examined.

Other large industrialized nations, such as the United Kingdom, Germany, Japan, and France, have such a vision, and it is reflected in major legislation enacted in the past decade precisely because they recognized the importance of sound policy in the global information economy. The approaches can and, of course, do differ. This is such a dynamic field that policies must be reexamined and revised over and over again as changes occur. Even if the United States strongly disagrees with the wisdom of another nation's scheme, that is not the point here. Rather, it is that these visions do exist and that there is a clear central authority that can and does implement the comprehensive scheme adopted by each nation.

That international picture stands in sharp contrast to the one in the United States. One would look in vain at the 1934 Communications Act to find any vision of our telecommunications approach (other than the recent law in the mobile radio field). It is simply ludicrous that in the digital age, our policy is based on a sixty-year-old act that is, in turn, based on an outmoded 1910 ICC approach, which is itself derived from the railroad situation at that time. For much too long, the United States has acted as if it has no vision of what should be done about the far-reaching technology and market changes now fully under way.

But looking at the policy pronouncements of the FCC, NTIA, some progressive states like New York and Illinois, and activities in the recent 103rd Congress, it is possible to discern the outline of a U.S. vision of telecommunications policy along the following general principles:

1. Allow open entry and all-out competition. Competition is the norm in the United States; it spurs innovation and efficiency and drives prices down to marginal costs. The technology now permits and indeed compels competition in the telecommunications area.

2. Promote competition with policies such as removing state barriers and allowing effective interconnection to existing carriers (called "open network architecture"), while preventing those carriers from improperly cross-subsidizing their competitive ventures by misallocating joint costs to the monopolies' ratepayers.

3. Where effective competition does exist in a given area, deregulate so as to avoid "regulated competition"—really cartel management by the government.

4. Use incentive regulation for the monopoly providers, with awareness of the need for depreciation practices that enable these carriers to modernize in order to meet competition. Allow such carriers pricing flexibility in the new competitive environment and over time move prices closer to costs.

5. Maintain the evolving universal service concept but make subsidies for such service explicit, targeted to those in need of them and administered in a way that does not skew competition or thwart the full realization of the goals of telecommunications policy. This means that such subsidies should come from the general treasury, directly or indirectly.[25]

6. Allocate spectrum in large blocks with great flexibility as to its use, subject to "rules of the road" to prevent electronic interference.

The purpose of these principles or strategies, taken together, is to move the telecommunications industry to full and effective competition, the situation that already exists in the allied computer–data processing field. Competition has already been achieved in customer premises equipment, with large benefits to the nation; is well on its way in the toll-call business; and is just getting under way in the local telecommunications sector. There will be a need for residual regulation for such things as interconnection, standardization rules, and targeted subsidies for the universal service concept. Managing the transition may be long and difficult. But surely there needs to be such a vision or goal if there is to be a sensible coherence to government policies in this vital area.

The FCC has not always been faithful to this vision for a number of reasons: its nature as a collegial body, unwise appointment practices, congressional intervention, and so forth. But even if the flaws were eliminated and the FCC strongly desired to act along these principles, it could not do so because of the fragmented process now at work. Its actions to fully implement the first principle, open entry, would be frustrated by countering policies of the antitrust court and many of the states. Even if there were raging competition in some sector or the absence of any market power to control prices or output, it could not deregulate that sector because of antiquated provisions of the 1934 Communications Act requiring the filing of tariffs and adherence thereto.[26] Because of these provisions, telecommunications companies "game the system" by filing objections to one another's tariffs (or absence thereof) or to spectrum proposals and fight with their lawyers before the agency instead of in the competitive marketplace. There are large costs to the nation from such gaming.

The conclusion is clear: there is a need for the U.S. policy process to develop a vision with supporting general principles. That need can be met only by Congress acting itself or by delegating such authority to a single agency, with continuing oversight of that agency's actions. If there is to be a cohesive vision guiding U.S. telecommunications policy, the nation must reform and restructure its processes for dealing with the challenges it faces.

THE ADMINISTRATION'S NII PLAN AND THE LEGISLATIVE PICTURE

THE NATIONAL INFORMATION INFRASTRUCTURE INITIATIVE

The United States may take action in 1995 to cure the above major defect by supplying an overarching substantive scheme for most important segments of the telecommunications sector. The Clinton administration, led by Vice President Al Gore, announced its national information infrastructure (NII) initiative in September 1993, "establishing an agenda for a public-private partnership to construct an advanced NII to benefit all Americans."[27] This initiative has been dubbed the "information superhighway" because of the belief that it will affect the economy in the coming years in a fashion similar to that of the highway initiative of the prior decades. Indeed, the report of the Council of Economic Advisers estimates that with passage of legislation embodying the NII principles, the U.S. gross domestic product (GDP) would increase about $1 billion over the next decade, and there would be $75 billion in new private-sector investment in telecom products and services in that period; the telecom sector would nearly double in size relative to the economy as a whole, accounting for about 17 percent of the GDP by 2003 (as against 9 percent today), with employment increasing from 3.6 million workers today to more than 5 million in 2003.[28]

The reform of telecom policy urged by the Clinton administration is based on the following principles: encouraging private investment; promoting and protecting competition, providing open access to the NII by consumers and service providers, preserving and advancing universal service to avoid creating a society of have and have-nots, and ensuring flexibility so that the new adopted regulatory framework can keep pace with the rapid technological and market changes that pervade the telecommunications and information industries.

The main focus of the reform effort is on local telecommunications. After all, the equipment side is wide open, and competition has worked brilliantly and will continue to do so in light of Moore's law (the number of transistors on a chip doubles every eighteen months, with corresponding cost reduction). Moreover, in the future, the microprocessor will become even more powerful, ushering in the advanced digital terminal or telecomputer. The Internet model has pointed up the importance of such distributive processing power.

Further, competition has led to rapid modernization in the interexchange (IX) long-distance area, with massive investment in fiber optics, satellites, and innovative marketing approaches. The problem lies in the "last mile" when the transmission leaves the IX highway and hits the dirt road of local telecommunications; the administration's goal is a broadband, switched, digital, interactive local highway. There are two critical bottlenecks there: the local loop of the exchange carrier (LEC) and the coaxial drop of the cable television operator.

The House and Senate bills in the 103rd Congress addressed these bottlenecks. As to the LEC, the bills required states to remove barriers to entry, and then promote such entry by mandating effective interconnection with the LEC, unbundling the functions of the LEC (for example, transport, switching, and the local loop to the subscriber), and allowing the new entrant to have access to the function desired at reasonable charges; resale of the LEC services; and calling for local number portability.[29] As to cable, the LEC is allowed to compete fully, with both bills requiring a separate subsidiary for the LEC video content affiliate. The bills required the LEC to afford open, nondiscriminatory access to its video platform (that is, a common-carrier approach reflecting the administration's goal of providing open access to the NII by consumers and service providers).[30]

Both bills soundly moved the locus for resolving the problems stemming from the divestiture of AT&T from the antitrust court to the FCC and the Department of Justice. Both would allow the divested Bell Operating Companies to engage in manufacturing telecom equipment, and both would set new rules for their entering the IX long-distance market. The bills would largely permit such entry, in effect, when the local or intrastate area has become contestable because of the implementation of competitive conditions such as those set forth above. Opponents of this approach, largely long distance carriers, argue that for in-market long distance, there should also be a showing to the FCC that the Bell Company faces actual and demonstrable competition in the geographic market. I believe that the latter test is appropriate for deregulation (that is, no regulation of prices) but not as entry test. This is the largest issue that must still be resolved today. Finally, both bills called for an evolving universal service approach, with all competitors contributing equitably to the sums needed, and with federal-state cooperation to protect the public interest.

The above is, of necessity, a gross oversimplification of very complex legislation. I have discussed the legislation because, while it failed to pass in the last (103rd) Congress (see note 29), in some respects it was the starting point for legislation in the 104th Congress. On the whole, bills along the above lines would have greatly advanced the NII, but in my view, there were flaws:

1. The bills in the 103rd Congress were much too detailed, placing the agency in a straitjacket in many areas. As the administration stresses when it advocates ensuring flexibility, this is a very dynamic area, with rapidly changing technology and market factors. There should be general guidance to the FCC, but it should have full authority to adjust as conditions change. The states have a large role to play, since while the FCC steers pursuant to the legislation, the states must do the heavy rowing in areas like unbundling or assuring cost-based pricing signals over time.

2. There could also be a serious gap in flexibility: the FCC should have the power to forbear from regulating, when the bills achieve their purpose and a sector becomes effectively competitive, and to preempt state or local regulation in that sector. Such regulated competition is nothing more than governmental cartel management and works against the public interest. As to the power to preempt state or local regulation, Congress wisely bestowed such power on the FCC in the mobile radio area in a 1993 amendment, and the same kind of approach is called here as to the wire segment.

3. The legislation did not deal with the important spectrum allocation field described above, nor did it really consider the regulatory scheme that should apply to broadcast, including public broadcasting, as we move into the next century.[31] This may be understandable in order to avoid "biting off too much," but there is a serious danger that, if it passes this massive reform legislation, Congress will not return to the telecom area for a considerable period of time.

4. The legislation did not require that the subsidies for the have-nots be explicitly targeted to those in need and be derived from the general treasuries. Instead, the legislation looked to obtain the subsidies by, in effect, "taxing" telecom consumers (because any subsidy payment imposed on the carrier is simply passed on to the consumer). The result is not only taxation without accountability (because the tax is hidden), but it militates against achieving the goals of telecom policy. It diminishes the use of telecom facilities (since it makes them more expensive); it imposes burdens on new entrants, even if done equitably; and it encourages bypass by large users who can turn to private telecommunications and thus avoid the "tax."

In this connection, there is also a problem with the proposals by the administration, and reflected in the legislation, to link all schools, libraries, and hospitals to the NII by the year 2000. Again, the sums to be obtained for this purpose are to come from the telecom system. The mission is commendable and vital to the nation's future. But precisely because it is so important, it is a mistake to proceed "on the cheap." The initiative must be carefully planned and implemented by the government, federal and state, and the sums obtained must be supplied by the government and be adequate to carry out that planning. Again, there is no "free lunch"; the carriers will shift any subsidies so imposed to the ratepayers. The sole reason why the administration and legislatures choose the flawed and inadequate subsidy scheme is that it represents off-budget taxation. The monies could be obtained from the telecommunications sector, since we have soundly decided upon spectrum auctions that will bring in billions of dollars in the near future; surely, some modest portion of those billions could be allocated to this critically important purpose.

Finally, the NII initiative and the legislation deal with the telecom policy process in only a few significant respects (mainly, removal of the antitrust court as to Modified Final Judgment reform; some division of labor between the FCC and the states). It is understandable that there would be this large focus on substantive policies and the deferral to another day of any process reform. But however good the substance may be, there is a need for sound process in light of the dynamic nature of the field, and some suggestions about such processes are set forth below.

THE GLOBAL INFORMATION INFRASTRUCTURE INITIATIVE

The Clinton administration's focus has not been confined to the United States (the NII); it is global in nature (the global information infrastructure, GII). At an international telecommunications conference in March 1994 in Buenos Aires, Vice President Gore sounded the first call for the GII, a planetary information network connecting large cities and small villages around the globe. He stated that the United States would actively promote the concept, based on the five principles set out for the NII (private investment, competition, open access, universal service, flexible regulation), among all nations, including the developing Third World.[32] This has been dramatically followed by the action of the Group of Seven (Canada, France, Germany, Italy, Japan, United Kingdom, United States), at the request of President Clinton, at the July 1994 Group of Seven summit in Naples, Italy. At that summit, the Group of Seven decided to convene a conference, which was held in February 1995, aimed at opening global markets to spur global economic growth by reducing telecommunications trade barriers and promoting standardization:

> Aides said President Clinton believes the process is important not just to the U.S. economy, but to the world economy. As White House Press Secretary Dee Dee Myers put it, this is the key to creating a global infrastructure for the 21st century. . . .
>
> The administration pitches stronger international regulation as a move that will benefit developed and developing nations. Officials argue that while more uniform standards and open markets will benefit the G-7 nations who have technology to export, other nations will benefit because in the future business will be able to invest only in locations that are connected to the information superhighway.[33]

In addition, it was agreed that there would be Group of Seven committees established to work on such matters as regulation, technology, and security issues. President Clinton also proposed that the Group of Seven countries make research material from libraries available electronically for educational and commercial purposes.

It is, of course, too early to tell, or forecast, whether the administration will be successful in espousing its principles, especially the desirability of vigorous competition, at the conference or in bilateral follow-ups. There could, for example, be serious obstacles to the competitive and related principles in some regions. In any event, the administration certainly deserves great credit for bringing these issues to the fore in the global arena.

REFORM OF THE POLICY PROCESS

PRINCIPLES FOR REFORM

The following principles should govern the organization or structure of the telecommunications policy process at the federal level:

1. Policymaking must address both international and domestic considerations and all forms of technology or services; for example, common carrier, private radio, broadcasting, cable television, and so forth. These areas are all integrally related and are converging.

2. Contrary to the recommendation of the *NTIA Telecomm 2000* report[34] the authority to establish broad policy must be integrated with the authority to implement it. In these dynamic fields, it is difficult if not impossible to anticipate every policy need; many will become necessary in particular cases. Further, the depth of understanding of the industry and issues comes from implementation, which markedly enhances the ability to promulgate sound policies.

3. With the exception of mass-media matters,[35] policymaking should be centralized in one agency, and in a single administrator: that is the most efficient approach. Divided authority creates delay, confusion, and an absence of focused responsibility. Taking this path requires putting in place strong congressional oversight, and, except where inappropriate (for example, national security; foreign or trade relations), judicial review of the administrator's actions.

4. The agency and single administrator should be located in the executive branch. Only that branch can deal effectively with national security, foreign relations, and trade issues in the telecommunications field. Further, this makes the president responsible for the proper functioning of the agency, so that, unlike today, there is political accountability.[36]

RECOMMENDED REFORMS

To carry out these principles, this section sets out several alternative recommended courses of action. The recommendations are in descending order of effectiveness, but ascending order in terms of ease of implementation.

1. *A single executive branch administrator, with comprehensive authority, housing but not controlling an independent agency to deal with electronic mass-media matters.* This would involve creation of an EPA-type agency, called perhaps the Federal Telecommunications and Information Agency (FTIA). Its administrator would serve at the pleasure of the president and, with the exception of the electronic mass media,[37] would have comprehensive authority over all telecommunications and information policy matters like privacy, and thus could preempt antitrust or state actions if they were obstacles to the full effectuation of the FTIA policies. The new agency would absorb the responsibilities and personnel of the FCC and NTIA. The State Department and the USTR would continue to be responsible for foreign policy or trade concerns in the field, but the FTIA, while coordinating with these two entities, would be the lead player in all telecommunications activities.[38]

    This would create a clear focal point for telecommunications policy: an executive branch agency with comprehensive power, able to deal effectively with our foreign partners and to coordinate governmental policy with the

State Department, the USTR, the Defense Department, and so forth. If the agency were failing in its mission, the president would be responsible and would have to act, as the president did to clear up the controversies involving the EPA in the early 1980s. This is by far the preferable option.

2. *Give the FCC more comprehensive powers, and improve the quality of its appointments.* The FCC could be given more comprehensive powers, such as the authority to deregulate when it finds that effective competition exists in some sector or to preempt antitrust or state actions preventing full effectuation of its policies. With these added powers, it would be even more important to improve the caliber of FCC appointments. There are a number of possible approaches.

First, under legislative requirement or on the president's own decision, the president could appoint a bipartisan, prestigious commission to select five possible nominees for each FCC vacancy, with the president then selecting one from the list. It may seem odd to do this for FCC appointments and not for appointments to the SEC or the Federal Trade Commission, but the FCC does deal with mass-communications media, and it is therefore appropriate to shield its appointment process from political considerations as much as possible.

Second, the commissioners should be given longer terms, such as ten years. A ten-year term would create a new attitude both in the president and the Senate toward FCC appointments. To continue the present pattern of using appointments as political plums, it would mean being stuck with such an appointee for a long period. Having enacted the remedial legislation lengthening the term, the Senate might insist upon a higher caliber of appointees as it does for the Federal Reserve Board (where terms run fourteen years).

A further improvement, allied to long tenure, would be to bar employment in the communications field for a five-year period following FCC service. While the Clinton administration has taken action along these lines by executive order, the present restriction in the Communications Act itself on working in or for regulated industry is too weak. The purpose of the five-year restriction would be to eliminate any incentive to use the FCC as a stepping stone to lucrative industry or professional advancement, thus skewing what should be solely public interest judgments.

3. *Put in place a single administrator, combining present executive branch functions, but with narrowly circumscribed power to direct FCC actions.* Another organizational arrangement would be to combine all existing executive branch telecommunications and information policy responsibilities, but not those of the FCC, in an EPA-like agency. This would give the new agency the authority, after coordination with other departments or agencies (for example, State, Defense, Justice, Commerce, USTR) and subject to

presidential override, to develop policies for the executive branch; to be *the* focal point for foreign and trade negotiations (with USTR involved but able to override the agency only with presidential backing); and to handle all executive branch spectrum matters. Further, the agency, after securing a presidential finding that the national security or foreign policy (including trade relations) so required, could direct the FCC to act in any one of three ways:

▼   Take a particular action, whether rule making or adjudicatory; there would then be no judicial review but there would be the check of congressional oversight.

▼   Institute a rule-making proceeding and conclude it within a specified time (similar to the power of the secretary of energy to direct the Federal Energy Regulatory Commission to open and conclude proceedings).[39]

▼   Veto actions taken by the FCC.

Here again there would be considerable improvement in that a locus of responsibility for telecommunications and information policy issues would be created within the executive branch. There would be an end to the present anomalous situation where the president, despite clear national security or foreign policy considerations, cannot direct a result.

4.   *Presidential Assistant for Telecommunications and Information Policy.* Another option would be to create a Presidential Assistant for Telecommunications and Information Policy, with a small staff (no more than three professionals). This person would have the authority to act for the president to ensure proper coordination among the turf combatants, to facilitate the formulation of executive branch policy, to bring to the president those telecommunications and information policy issues warranting presidential consideration, and, if needed, to prepare presidential messages to Congress or the FCC. The *NTIA Telecomm 2000* report correctly points out that the present executive branch apparatus is not working.[40] It is unlikely that simply reworking the vague language in the law or Executive Order or issuing further memoranda of understanding between the Departments of Commerce and State will correct this flawed situation. The Commerce Department will never have the clout to be truly effective, and the State Department will never have the expertise to be the executive branch's telecommunications honcho. It takes solid knowledge not only of foreign policy, but also of the intricacies of international and domestic telecommunications and information policy development. Therefore, at the least, a presidential assistant would ensure proper coordination and, when appropriate, presidential focus on telecommunications and information policy issues.

5. *Blue Ribbon Commission.* Telecommunications and information is a most difficult area in which to make sweeping organizational or substantive changes. As Senator Warren Magnuson aptly stated, "All each industry seeks is a fair advantage over its rival." If the present structure favors one rival, that industry will lobby furiously to retain its advantage. As noted, Congress does not like to choose between these warring powerful industries, and that has caused the gridlock over the past two decades in the substantive area (with, it is hoped, a breakthrough finally in this 104th Congress).

    It has been suggested by Senator John Breaux, a member of the Senate Subcommittee on Communications, that the president should form a blue ribbon panel of "carefully chosen representatives of academia, industry, regulatory authorities and consumers, with a clear charter and limited duration."[41] That charter would be to develop a comprehensive communications policy. In light of the extensive developments that have taken place in the substantive area both in the administration and in Congress, it would be inappropriate to convene such a commission to hammer out substantive policies. But this route might be helpful to develop or bring to the fore process or organizational reform.

    A strong, prestigious commission, similar to the study commissions in such areas as Social Security and privacy, could propose a framework within which Congress might be motivated to adopt new structural or process policies. Such a commission would be particularly valuable if powerful figures in Congress were fully consulted as to the initiation and composition of the commission.

6. *Ad hoc efforts.* What if there is no legislation? Even if that were the case, there could be strong and effective ad hoc actions to break the deadlock and promote the telecommunications policy goals so vital in the global information economy. The president could invite all the state Public Utility commissioners serving on the Communications Section of the National Association of Regulatory Utility Commissioners and the FCC commissioners to a White House meeting. At that meeting, the president and vice president could state why they believe that it is so important to obtain, on a more expedited basis, the infrastructure, both broadband and mobile, needed for the global information economy, and what policies should be considered to make the necessary progress. Clearly, those policies would be those articulated in the NII initiative, most of which can be implemented without federal legislation if the states are so inclined. The states and their utility commissions are, of course, independent, but such an extraordinary meeting would have impact and would create a new mood or sense of urgency as to these important infrastructure issues.

    This meeting would be followed by a petition from the attorney general, submitted with the endorsement and full backing of the president and vice president, to the antitrust court, requesting relief, with appropriate conditions, from provision of IX services or manufacturing by the Bell Operating Companies (that is, no relief would be finalized until the same kind of conditions as in the pending legislation were met on the state and federal levels, as certified to the Court by the state in question, the Department, and the FCC). There would thus be a "letting in" process of fostering local competition to the Bell Operating Companies, and, correspondingly, a "letting out" process of permitting the Bell Operating Companies to engage in IX (long-distance) services. Such a petition, supported by the president and the FCC and in the context of a large congressional consensus (albeit unsuccessful), would be given the most serious consideration in the judicial process. It would not obviate the need for legislative reform, but even in the absence of such reform, it would mean that considerable progress could be made. Indeed, such a step might, in and of itself, promote legislative action, as was the case in airline deregulation.

Conclusion

The nation has drifted along with the present fragmented and patchwork policy structure for too long. The global information economy demands that we put our policy house in order.[42] The Clinton administration campaigned on the need for sound telecommunications policies—an unusual political development—and has kept that promise in its NII (and GII) initiative. Congress should follow suit by enacting the sound NII policies. If, regrettably, it fails to do so, the administration should take ad hoc measures, along the above lines, aimed at substantively closing the policy gap in this decade. Whatever happens with the pending legislation in the 104th Congress, there remains the need for process or organizational reform. The road to such reform will not be easy, but it is critical that it be taken, soon and successfully.

5

TECHNOLOGY POLICY AND THE NATIONAL INFORMATION INFRASTRUCTURE

LEE MCKNIGHT

W. RUSSELL NEUMAN

> *Our current information industries—cable, local telephone, long distance telephone, television, film, computers, and others—seem headed for a ·Big Crunch/Big Bang of their own. The space between these diverse functions is rapidly shrinking—between computers and televisions, for example, or interactive communication and video . . . there may not be cable companies or phone companies or computer companies, as such. Everyone will be in the bit business . . . there will be information conduits, information providers, information appliances and information consumers.*
> —U.S. Vice President Albert Gore, 1994

*T*he growing importance of information technology in the global economy increases the significance of technology policy for economic growth and development.[1] Digital electronics directly affect the economics of broadcasting, consumer electronics, telecommunications, computers, and publishing, and indirectly affect such sectors as manufacturing, defense, education, and health care. As communications systems become fully digitized, they ride the cost curve of semiconductors and software: reduced prices for components and the growing number of functions they perform enable firms to create new products and services, new markets, and even new industries. Although the frequently used metaphors of information highways and electronic infrastructure may test the patience of weary policy wonks, the intellectual origin of these metaphors rests on solid historical ground.[2]

Michael Boskin, President Bush's chief economic adviser, may have found no significant difference between potato chips and computer chips, but governments globally—including our own—recognize the importance of new technical and economic trends and are seeking actively to develop national comparative advantages in the production and use of information and communication technology. Can the market alone create the incentives for a universal or near-universal, interoperable information infrastructure? Which type of technology policy—that of the United States, Europe, or Japan—will most effectively stimulate the development of a self-sustaining information infrastructure?

In this chapter, we review several key technology policy initiatives in Europe, Japan, and the United States, with a focus on the uniquely American style of building relationships between the state and the marketplace. Our central proposition is that although the United States may not have set out consciously to develop a new form of technology policy, it has in fact done so. We illustrate the evolution of U.S. policy with case studies of high-definition television (HDTV) standards and the Internet. Our conclusion is that in the current environment of converging communications technologies and resulting economic combat between adjoining industrial sectors, economic growth is likely to be well served by the American style of technology policy.

BEYOND THE TECHNOLOGY POLICY DEBATE

THE STATE AND THE MARKET

Cyberspace, the hip, new electronic domain for information exchange and experience, may look like the invention of creative young capitalists. In fact, in the United States it was created largely by military-driven government technology policy and research programs. The U.S. military establishment did not set out to invent cyberspace, but the evolution from a research-oriented network set up by the Department of Defense's Advanced Research Projects Agency (ARPA) to a public Internet is characteristic of what we label "agile policy"—a flexible and nonideological approach to relations between the state and market.

Although Americans have a reputation for heavy reliance on market mechanisms and privatized institutions, government intervention in the economy through support of technological development dates from the founding of the nation. With significant government involvement, our communications infrastructure expanded over time from post roads and the press to include canals, railroads, telegraph, and telephone systems. Over the course of the nineteenth century, these infrastructures, along with energy and water utilities, helped weave the nation together economically and socially.

Federal policies supporting the development and diffusion of new technologies gained new prominence in the 1990s with Vice President Gore's special assignment to spur the economy and the polity toward a reinvigorated national information infrastructure (NII). The ensuing policy debate was dramatized even before the

Clinton administration took office when Vice President Gore and AT&T CEO Robert Allen, having agreed that an NII ought to be built, could not avoid an awkward confrontation over the extent of the government's role in building it: Allen accused Gore of proposing that the government should build the infrastructure, while Gore denied having ever suggested such a thing. Despite this misunderstanding, disagreement on the extent (and existence) of a need for government involvement in the development of the NII was a real issue, with Gore having a more expansive view and Allen arguing for minimal government involvement.

Critics who perceive the current enthusiasm for the NII as a dangerously slippery slope cleaving from traditional American reliance on the marketplace like to point to the case of HDTV.[3] They argue that Japan and Europe developed state-dominated programs to invent new technical formats for television that were overpriced, insufficiently differentiated from the current standard, and quickly overtaken by new digital technologies. The United States, by doing nothing in the way of policy, came out ahead by leapfrogging the Japanese and European entries with a creative new concept for advanced digital television. Such arguments, echoing the central tenets of neoclassical economic orthodoxy, may sound convincing but they represent a serious misreading of recent history. Furthermore, like the standoff between Gore and Allen, they distort the policy debate by defining the issue of technological innovation in terms of a balance of power between the state and the market.

Our review of several cases, including HDTV, suggests that the success of technology policy results not from a particular balance of power between the state and the market but rather from the *structure* of their relationship from the outset. The relative level of state power and degree of government intervention in the United States, Japan, and Europe are not as distinct as the usual stereotypes suggest. This argument is best illustrated by an evaluation of recent technology policy decisions, which show that the relative success of U.S. technology policy resulted not from the lack of state power or activity but from its exercise in a flexible and agile manner.

The cases evaluated in this chapter show that the political cultures of Japan and Europe venerate a critical role for the state in coordination and planning. In contrast, U.S. political culture celebrates laissez-faire policy and has a place of honor for smart and entrepreneurial capitalists, and the mysterious invisible hand of the informed marketplace. But these two contrasting cultures are based on what can be considered "founding mythologies." In the practical world of R&D consortia, trade negotiations, and high-level business strategy meetings, these myths recede before the need to make complex, time-bound decisions.

The argument made here about political and administrative agility and flexibility has roots in a broader tradition of political history that runs from Tocqueville to Louis Hartz's classic of comparative political culture, *The Liberal Tradition in America,* and more recently to Nathan Rosenberg and L. E. Birdzell's *How the West Grew Rich*—each of which documents the fact that the relative lack of established hierarchies and powerful priesthoods (political or otherwise) is important to the U.S. experiment.[4] The administrative culture of the United States is by its nature ad hoc and pragmatic. The lack of a divine right of administrative authority and the almost apologetic exercise of state authority in response to practical problems provide a backdrop for agility and flexibility not easily achieved in other contexts. Apologetic power is agile power because it derives its justification from current developments in the marketplace, rather than from the historical authority of its eminent domain.

THE IMPORTANCE OF STANDARDS

Standardization is becoming the focal point of economic cooperation and competition in electronic markets. Standards provide compatibility through the sharing of information. They reduce variety to increase economies of scale and quality.[5] In the first place, compliance with national and international standards may be required to enter an increasingly broad range of markets. In the second place, the competitive advantage gained through control of a dynamically adaptive standard may be enormous. While few businesses enjoy the fruits of such control to the extent that Bill Gates and Microsoft have by leveraging their control of MS-DOS, many have similar ambitions.

Attention to standards affects policy in two ways. First, a nation may employ technology policy measures to develop new technologies for possible standardization, such as in the case of HDTV. Second, industrial policy initiatives may be developed in an attempt to influence specific standardization outcomes, such as in the cases of the European and Japanese attempts to favor specific firms by attempting to have their technologies incorporated into international HDTV standards.

Digital communication and computing systems should allow seamless interconnection of a variety of platforms and applications.[6] The key issue from a technology policy perspective is open interface specifications. While "open" is always a relative concept in the world of information technology, in general more open is better than less open. And, of course, both are better than closed. All three forms may be proprietary or nonproprietary. The cases studied below suggest that despite the perceptive vision of open systems in Europe and Japan, the advantages of the Internet model in the United States—rapid implementation and demonstration of working code, broad participation and networked collaboration on technology development, and easy access to a network testbed (the Internet itself)—provides a more functional open environment than the European or Japanese alternatives.

Knowing when and how to cooperate (and with whom), and when to compete, in the development of standards is a critical skill for the survival of firms in the information industry.[7] Today's accelerated pace of global innovation in computer, telecommunications, and television technologies has also accelerated the pace at which technologies must move through the standardization process.[8] Exacerbating the challenge for policymakers and firms, standardization must be weighed against the equally pressing need for innovation—that is, the development of nonstandard products and services.

Technology Policy and Virtual Governance

Virtual governance relies on the creation of impermanent, publicly sanctioned organizations to develop and implement public policy; cross institutional boundaries; and employ interdisciplinary teams to analyze problems, identify opportunities, and assess outcomes of precompetitive, generic research and development. These principles flow from the nature of the information economy, which constitutes an exploding information base that is beyond the ability of any individual or firm to understand in all its facets. The growing number of business alliances, joint ventures, consortia, and networks are creating impermanent, agile networks of industry, government, and academia throughout the United States, Europe, and Japan. They operate in a sea of public discourse and debate and rely increasingly on the Internet as a communications backbone. Technology policy must be based on a firm understanding of the principles of virtual governance if it is to serve national interests in economic growth and job creation, as well as support democratic discourse and social interaction.

Technology policy in all industrialized nations supports to some degree precompetitive research and development. The goal of such research is to enhance national industries' ability to compete in domestic and world markets.[9] Consortia are popular techniques for accelerating technological development and information dissemination; they can be considered ad hoc technology policy tools because their creation responds to changing technological opportunities, the government role varies, and the consortia are inherently impermanent.[10] The strength of such ad hoc technology policy mechanisms is that they reduce risk and share costs and information, and respond to perceived market opportunities. The principal weakness is that technological development is by its nature a difficult and uncertain process, so the likelihood of failure of any policy measure taken is high.

The risks involved indicate not the hopelessness of the task, but the need to carefully design and implement effective technology policies for information infrastructure development. An ad hoc technology and industrial policy combines the diversity and dynamism of American cultural values with a coordination and planning mechanism that serves to strengthen industry and improve government performance. U.S. technology and industrial policy should recognize the potential of ad hoc corporatist policy processes to improve flexibility, accelerate decision making, reduce risks, and share costs.[11] Only industrial and technology policies that take account of long-term technology trends; that rely on extensive dialogue with industry, government, and academic representatives; and that create ad hoc organizations to undertake development are likely to succeed. It is difficult, nonetheless, to avoid the inevitable role that politics plays in the creation of many technology and industrial policy initiatives, as the Japanese and European programs described below illustrate.

BUILDING THE JAPANESE INFORMATION SOCIETY

The importance of the keiretsu-style linkages of Japanese firms in cross-industry alliances is increasingly recognized, but discussion of Japanese industrial policy practices is still subject to substantial polarization. A review of recent Japanese industrial policy initiatives shows that the policy mechanisms that worked so effectively to dominate consumer electronics in the 1970s, and dynamic random access chip (DRAM) manufacturing in the 1980s, may be less successful in the network of network topologies of the digital information marketplace in the 1990s.

The Japanese Ministry of International Trade and Industry (MITI) has taken on an almost mythical status in popular accounts of Japan's rise from postwar ruin to economic superpower. In fact, while MITI has played a prominent role, its practices are not well understood and its rate of success is not as high as imagined.[12] Other agencies, private industry, and Japanese economic and cultural practices must be credited with significant contributions to the direction and success of the Japanese economy.[13]

Until recently, many telecommunications industry experts expected the next generation of telecommunications networks to be integrated services digital networks (ISDNs). In Japan, commercial ISDN services, introduced in 1984, were among the first in the world. Despite the large investment already made by the Japanese national telephone company, Nippon Telegraph and Telephone (NTT), ISDN usage in Japan is much lower than forecast. ISDN was positioned as an alternative to analog telephony, but ISDN has been used almost exclusively for computer-to-computer communication. In addition to the disappointing level of acceptance of ISDN, CAPTAIN, the Japanese videotext system, and cable and satellite television have also not grown as rapidly as expected. For example, the Hi-Vision project (Japan's equivalent to HDTV) initiated by Japanese public broadcaster Nippon Hoso Kyokai (NHK) in the late 1960s and supported by the Ministry of Posts and Telecommunications (MPT) and MITI was slow to recognize the implications of digitization of media. Demand has been far less than originally forecast, and the capital investment is not likely to be recovered. The U.S. film and broadcast industry and the Federal Communications Commission (FCC) rejected the Japanese HDTV technology in 1990 because of its limitations in comparison to the new proposed digital television systems. Without the U.S. market, large-scale manufacturing of Hi-Vision systems could not be justified on the basis of cost, condemning Hi-Vision systems to remain practically handcrafted, and therefore expensive, for the indefinite future.

Japan's "regional informatization programs" have also contributed to the confusion over future network strategies. One example of such public-private sector joint network trials is the "Teletopia" large-scale broadband pilot projects. These projects, encompassing entire cities, entail cooperation among Japan's municipal governments, equipment manufacturers, service providers, and NTT. The ambitious goals for the establishment of Teletopia, Information Network Systems, and Hi-Vision Cities have not been realized.[14]

Why have there been so many apparent failures of Japanese industrial policy recently? An important reason is that the critical question of service design was not central to many of the projects, which instead have focused on hardware design and manufacturing. (One should note, however, that it may be too soon to dismiss Japanese firms from a dominant position in, for example, HDTV manufacturing and service delivery.) Since the liberalization of the Japanese telecommunications market in 1985, the industry has tended to focus primarily on price competition rather than the development of new services such as multimedia and intelligent networks, thereby ceding lead to U.S. service and software providers.

The growth of the Internet in the 1990s left Japan behind. The Japanese version of Internet was established only recently to link universities and industry research centers. WIDE (for Widely Distributed Environment) has its own trunk network of leased lines, but the capacity of the "backbone" as of spring 1994 was 192 K bit per second, only 1/200th of the U.S. backbone of 45 Megabits per second. It has been argued that the biggest factor explaining the slow growth of networked services in Japan, despite a long-standing industrial policy goal of gaining a leading position in information technology and software markets, is the high cost of leased line service in Japan.[15] The Internet grew in the United States by linking computers and networks directly via leased lines. In Japan, the prohibitively high cost of leased lines created a bottleneck that slowed the growth of computer-to-computer networks. At present, a 1.5-Megabit line costs at least five times more in Japan than the United States.

To overcome these information infrastructure problems, a "new social infrastructure" initiative in telecommunications and information technologies was proposed in 1993. MITI and the MPT will subsidize computer purchases by universities, research institutes, and schools. However, there are no plans to network all the computers purchased in this program. The MPT is also planning a pilot project as a test bed for a nationwide fiber network offering widespread access to multimedia services for private homes and offering such services as video on demand.[16] MITI claimed that during the 1992 U.S. presidential campaign, the Clinton-Gore team had committed to build a national fiber to the home network in the United States, which therefore required that Japan develop a similar project in order not to be left behind. (Japanese government officials and political leaders often use the perception of a foreign threat or pressure to suppress opposition to policy changes.)[17]

If policies and tariffs could be realigned (that is, the below-cost prices on local calls raised, and the above-cost prices on leased lines reduced), many Japanese universities, research institutions, small private companies, and individual consumers could begin to utilize high-speed networks.

Internetworking in Japan could then also grow rapidly, as could the variety of industries employing an advanced information infrastructure to offer new products and services to national and global markets. Japan is hobbled because powerful Japanese government ministries lack mechanisms for cross-institutional dialogue and cooperation, inhibiting coordinated policy development for information infrastructure. Despite these limitations, Japanese government and industry have been able to articulate a vision of a national information infrastructure. But Japanese technology policy alone cannot remove the economic, institutional, and cultural barriers to the realization of that vision.

EUROPEAN INNOVATION POLICY FOR INFORMATION TECHNOLOGIES

The convergence of means of communication is based on the disappearing difference between one-directional and two-directional networks, on the development of data networks, and on the increasing digitalization of signals.
—Simon Nora and Alain Minc, 1978

The fall of the Berlin Wall and the formation of the European Union out of the European Community symbolized the great hopes for European technology policy widespread in the early 1990s. The social, political, and financial turmoil convulsing Europe has increased the difficulties of building the common European home but has not slowed progress in developing the tools and techniques that will be needed in the future.

Innovation policy for telematics, or *telematique*, a term coined by Alain Minc and Simon Nora in their influential report, *The Computerization of Society*, has been a strategic goal for Europe since the early 1980s.[18] Realizing this vision, however, has proven far more challenging than anticipated by Euro-optimists. Europe's strategy for forging an integrated market in telecommuni-cations has relied largely on exploiting information technology standards so that European telematics firms could enjoy large economies of scale.

A number of technology policy programs were launched in the 1980s to help make this vision a reality. However, European Community initiatives including the European Strategic Programme for Research in Information Technologies (ESPRIT), EUREKA, and Research for Advanced Communications in Europe (RACE) produced few demonstrable economic benefits.

ESPRIT is able to point to a few European firms taking hold in niche semiconductor markets. However, U.S. and Japanese firms dominate the market, and there is almost nothing in the way of an independent European computer hardware industry. Moreover, the decline of European information technology firms has continued unabated despite the vast amounts of money spent by ESPRIT to subsidize research and development.

Begun by President Francois Mitterrand as a commercial response to the U.S. Strategic Defense Initiative (Star Wars), the EUREKA project is formally independent of state control and resembles the leaner U.S. ARPA model, with a small staff facilitating the formation of dozens of industry consortia. While EUREKA can point to some successes, HDTV cannot be considered among them. Initially, preventing the adoption of a worldwide HDTV standard based on proprietary Japanese technologies was considered a crowning achievement of the European Commission's staff. Directorate General 13, "Innovation in Communication and Information Technologies," encouraged development of the HD-MAC standard by European industry through research and development subsidies. The subsidies produced a substantial number of commercial HD-MAC products, but none of these has met with success. Despite its relatively strong record, EUREKA suffers from some of the defects of the other European programs, primarily the fact that European policy for HDTV has been dictated by the continent's two dominant consumer electronics manufacturers without regard for consumer preferences.

Europe no longer has any major computer manufacturers to push European countries toward the development of digital technologies, as was the case in the United States. Thus, it was the consumer electronics firms of Thomson (France) and Philips (the Netherlands) that developed the technologies for the European HD-MAC standard.[19] And these firms shortsightedly chose to focus on the same obsolescent analog-interlaced techniques that are employed by all current television systems—techniques that were state of the art fifty years ago but that were abandoned by the computer industry decades ago as inadequate for high-resolution displays.

The third European Commission initiative, RACE, invested huge sums of money in precompetitive technology development to support the emergence across Europe of an integrated broadband network relying on common standards. The new network, it is hoped, will help European firms compete with their U.S. and Asian rivals by opening national markets to European products relying on common standards. The Advanced Communications Technologies and Services (ACTS) project, the renamed continuation of the RACE project announced in 1994, proposes to move beyond research into commercial production of advanced network technologies, applications, and services. European research projects traditionally encouraged interaction between researchers and manufacturers. ACTS projects would attempt to align research to market demand and involve users as contributors to the projects. For example, computer networks for health care would involve hospitals and health authorities to define jointly goals for standards and technology research projects.

The ACTS project is a focal point of the Fourth Framework of European Union support for research and development, which began in 1995. The goals and directions of ACTS are predefined by government; user interaction and public dialogue occur only after the projects are launched, if at all. Nonetheless, this initiative is a step in the right direction, but is far from the agile policy approach of the United States, which is more attuned to the speed-of-light changes in technology, applications, and user demands that are characteristic of the global information economy. Indeed, the dismal record in the commercial marketplace of most European technology policy initiatives can be explained by the failure to provide for sufficient dynamism and flexibility in government programs to adapt to marketplace and user needs.

U.S. TECHNOLOGY POLICY AND NATIONAL INFORMATION INFRASTRUCTURE

U.S. technology policy, which has traditionally been hidden behind and subsumed under other more publicly pronounced policy objectives such as national security, may appear to outsiders as a "stealth" policy. This traditional model of operation may or may not be altered with the end of the Cold War. But the connection between security and technology policy is likely to be strengthened as U.S. competitiveness and international political standing come to be seen as related to the nation's position in information technology markets.

The diffuseness and subtlety of military-industrial linkages has made the clear articulation of technology policy more difficult. Also hindering effective government action is the fact that over twenty federal agencies claim some jurisdiction over national information and communications policy and are on occasion joined by the courts, the Congress, and state regulatory agencies in formulating policy.[20] Each bureaucracy has its own vision of the public interest. The attempt to develop effective coordination among them is always a struggle— and at first glance nearly impossible. The policy process is still dominated by the traditional industrial sectors of the predigital world. The confrontation of established players concerned that the forces of technology will work to their disadvantage challenges the effectiveness and flexibility of the system and may lead to a uniquely American form of political gridlock.[21] But a coherent and wide-ranging technology policy, we argue, can provide guidance to government, industry, and the public on what to expect from the communications revolution and what to ask of advanced information infrastructure.

U.S. TECHNOLOGY AND INDUSTRIAL POLICY AFTER THE COLD WAR

Early on, the Clinton administration promised change to harness technology, with the goal of stimulating economic growth and job creation. In February 1993, President Clinton and Vice President Gore unveiled a broad technology initiative to strengthen the U.S. economy and promote a cleaner environment, more competitive businesses, more effective government, better educational programs, and technological leadership in critical fields. As the president stated, "In order to revitalize our economy, it is time for a dramatically new approach that recognizes the strength and potential of America's scientific and technological resources to change and improve the quality of our lives."[22] The new initiative, *Technology for*

America's Economic Growth: A New Direction to Build Economic Strength, emphasizes three central goals: long-term economic growth that creates jobs and protects the environment; making government more efficient and more responsive; and world leadership in basic science, mathematics, and engineering. According to the administration, these new policies are a response to the economic challenges posed by competitors around the world and to the needs of U.S. citizens. The hope is that technology may offer new opportunities for job creation, a cleaner environment, better schools, improved health care, and other advances.

The strategy of the administration is for new investments in technology to help the private sector create high-wage, high-skill jobs.[23] The administration's technology policy emphasizes development of a national network of manufacturing extension centers to help small and medium-sized businesses gain access to technology; investment in applied R&D in fields such as advanced manufacturing, aerospace, biotechnology, and advanced materials; increased partnerships between industry and the national laboratories; development of a partnership with the U.S. auto industry; and the expansion of the Commerce Department's Advanced Technology Program to provide matching grants for industry-led R&D consortia.

A priority of the administration is the development of a national information infrastructure and the "information superhighways" initiated by legislation introduced by Vice President Gore when he served in the Senate. The roughly $1 billion of federal support from the Clinton administration is twice as high as the amounts appropriated by President Bush for the High-Performance Computing and Communications Initiative charged with developing new technologies for supercomputers and for a national, high-speed network to make high-performance computing more accessible. The Clinton administration's strategy for information infrastructure development includes developing new applications for high-performance computing and networking in health care, lifelong learning, and manufacturing, as well as creating pilot projects to demonstrate these technologies in schools and among other nonprofit entities. The administration established a task force of the National Economic Council, the Information Infrastructure Task Force, to work with Congress and the private sector to develop policies needed to accelerate the deployment of the NII. Complementing the task force is a private-sector Information Infrastructure Advisory Council to provide business and nonprofit organizations with formal input to the planning process for the federal government's information infrastructure development efforts.

All this suggests that the Clinton administration has embraced the traditional ad hoc, agile policy elements identified above, with the intent of using technology policy to help meet other important national goals, such as helping the federal government use technology to cut its costs, improve energy efficiency, and improve the quality and timeliness of government services. As noted above, the government also intends to work with industry to develop technologies (software, computer, and communications equipment) that increase the productivity of learning in schools, homes, and workplaces.

The plan is to improve the environment for private sector investment and innovation in a variety of ways: by making the research and experimentation tax credit permanent, reducing capital gains for long-term investments in small business, and reforming antitrust laws to permit joint production ventures. Despite the greater emphasis on applied research, the administration reiterated its continued commitment to U.S. leadership in basic research and, therefore, proposed increases in funding for the National Science Foundation. Improved management of U.S. technology policy with leadership and coordination by the vice president, the Office of Science and Technology Policy, and the National Economic Council is planned. The administration's plan also urged partnership between the federal government and industry, labor, academia, and the states in order to realize its technology policy goals. Finally, the administration promised regular evaluation of programs to determine whether they should remain part of the national investment in technology.

Through its technology initiative, the Clinton administration reestablished the principles of agile, ad hoc, flexible government and private sector cooperation that had been opposed in an ideologically polarized Bush administration. The Democratic administration's strategy built upon the legacy of President Reagan's initiatives to maintain U.S. competitiveness in semiconductors, as well as on past federal-private sector initiatives dating at least from the construction of the transcontinental railroads more than a century ago. While a detailed historical analysis cannot be provided here, a brief review of the HDTV case illustrates how agile policy can work in practice through virtual governance processes to strengthen U.S. industry and respond to societal needs.

HDTV AND DIGITAL IMAGE ARCHITECTURE

Is no industrial or technology policy the best policy? Prominent analysts argue that the success of the United States in taking the lead in development of an HDTV standard proves that no policy is best. They claim that in Japan and Europe, government industrial policy squandered billions of dollars developing HDTV systems no one wants, while in the United States, government wisely chose to keep its hands off the development of HDTV technologies and standards, leaving the issue exclusively in the hands of private industry. This view distorts the record.[24] It is clear from observing the HDTV process that the lack of a dominant industry group or state-supported firm, coupled with the lack of a single and determining government bureaucracy, provided a climate of intersector cooperation and the incentive for participation. It is difficult to impute cause and effect from these observations, but the cooperative and participatory climate appears to have enabled the planning for this critical component of the information infrastructure to proceed expeditiously in the United States.

A brief review of the development of the key technical concepts underlying U.S. technology policy for high-resolution systems illustrates the benefits of the flexible, informal collaboration of industry, academia, and government that is characteristic of the ad hoc approach to technology policy in the United States.

The feasibility of developing an architecture of standards that is modular, scalable, and capable of extension with new technologies over time was systematically considered in 1992 by a task force of industry and academic experts from the broadcast, cable, computer, and telecommunications industries, with the encouragement of the U.S. government. (The objective of the digital image architecture is to permit the interoperation of digital media across industries such as the motion picture, broadcasting, cable, computer, satellite, telecommunications, and medical imaging industries.)[25] International cooperation was pursued through dialogue and cooperation with multinational firms and participants in international standards bodies such as the Internet Engineering Task Force, International Telecommunication Union, and International Standards Organization. The key to success is probably found in the principles of ad hoc virtual governance and agile policy response described above.

In their haste to rush to market, Japanese and European efforts to design HDTV systems failed to heed the findings of advanced scientific research that could have been made available to them. In the United States, research conducted at the Massachusetts Institute of Technology, Columbia University, and a variety of large and small industrial laboratories was coordinated through cooperative working parties organized by the Advisory Committee on Advanced Television Systems to the FCC. Audience research, for example, revealed that from the normal viewing distance of nine feet from the set most untrained observers could detect hardly any difference between HDTV and the existing National Television Standards Committee (NTSC) system on twenty-eight-inch displays.[26] Since viewers could not see the difference under normal conditions, they were uninterested in paying large sums for this feature alone. This finding suggested there was ample time for further research and for additional technical innovations to be incorporated into the new infrastructure. This was research the Japanese or Europeans could have conducted but did not.

The Bush White House actively opposed government involvement in the HDTV debates for fear of "picking winners" and preempting the marketplace.[27] At the same time, lobbyists working in Washington for European and Japanese firms and governments encouraged the dominant ideology of the free marketeers.[28] But the ad hoc, agile technology policy process and informal networks remained active and influential throughout the Bush administration's tenure. Even when some of its most visible proponents were eliminated from positions of influence (such as ARPA director Craig Fields), the ad hoc technology policy process continued unabated. In the end, the FCC, the Department of Commerce, the Department of Defense's ARPA, as well as the House Space, Science, and Technology Committee and the House Subcommittee on Telecommunications all played critical roles in the technology policy development process for HDTV in the United States.

Congressmen George Brown and Edward Markey provided the executive branch agencies with congressional support for their behind-the-scene efforts during the Bush administration. In particular, the legislators advocated providing ARPA with several hundred million dollars to support innovative U.S. firms developing "high-resolution systems" (HRSs) technologies. It was this sleight of hand, renaming HDTV "HRS," and emphasizing obvious military applications of high-resolution video compression technologies and displays that refocused and reenergized the cooperative effort. FCC chairman Alfred Sikes artfully dodged the administration's "no industrial policy" bullets that had felled Craig Fields and provided guidance and leadership to steer the FCC Advanced Television standard-setting process toward digital and interoperable HDTV systems and away from the obsolete technologies in which Europeans and Japanese continued to invest significant resources. As is typical in agile policy formation, key individuals at U.S. firms and research institutions with high stakes in electronic imaging played prominent roles in this endeavor.

The need to develop the manufacturing capacity to ensure that U.S. workers would benefit from U.S. technology was the principal motivation for federal funding of high-resolution systems in the 1980s. The fear was that even if the technology was developed domestically, manufacturing would likely be done overseas. The federal government felt that it was necessary to assist industry in rebuilding the consumer electronics industrial base of the United States, which had been largely wiped out by foreign predatory pricing and bad management in the 1960s and 1970s.

ARPA began supporting flat-panel display consortia in the late 1980s, with technologies rivaling those found in Europe or Japan. ARPA also supported the development of magnetic recording devices by funding the critical new R&D needed for HDTV storage. Currently, potential U.S. customers like Apple and IBM are dependent on their Japanese flat-panel suppliers; U.S. firms cannot risk having their supplies cut off while waiting for small domestic firms to build the enormous facilities needed to begin large-volume production of flat-panel displays. And the distribution system in the United States for both professional and consumer video equipment is dominated by foreign manufacturers, making it very difficult for U.S. manufacturers—even those with advanced and superior equipment—to compete. This is where government can help most: by leveling the playing field and giving U.S. firms a chance to enter the marketplace.

To conclude the HDTV saga, it has been shown that what worked so well in the United States was not the absence of any policy, but the absence of a formal policy. Rather, the traditional network of relationships between industry, academia, and government helped the United States avoid backing the wrong technological "horse," as Europe and Japan did, while furthering the development of a flexible technical base to support evolving consumer demand for digital video applications in the United States. The HDTV experience suggests that agile, cooperative policy relationships can help government and industry determine where it is worth investing public and private sector resources. In fact, this policy framework has already led to the creation of the Internet and the uncharted, but commercially promising, realm of cyberspace.

THE INTERNET AND INFORMATION INFRASTRUCTURE

> . . . as telecommunications networking became, in fact, computer networking, the connection of new "information pipeline" directly to the digital information source, or sink became more and more tempting to the network provider. . . . The end of the last decade saw the dawn of the technological opportunity for the data gatherer to become a data provider as well as network provider.
> —Lewis Schnurr, 1987

The need to link diverse computer networks to other data communications networks led to the creation of the Internet, a network of networks. By defining and adhering to a common protocol for internetworking, the Internet can expand without central direction. Firms, individuals, and public institutions can choose autonomously to join the network simply by adhering to Internet network interface specifications.

The Internet is built using a technique to interconnect computers known as the Transmission Control Protocol/Internet Protocol (TCP/IP) suite. Agreement to use common protocols for interconnection is the network's essential characteristic. The Internet is layered on top of the telephone infrastructure, while also traversing computer networks and, increasingly, cable networks. Wireless transmission is also possible.[29] The other noteworthy characteristic of the Internet is its phenomenal growth, averaging 10 percent per month for years, according to the Internet Society. There is no central authority over the Internet other than the engineering task force that maintains, updates, and extends Internet protocols. Voluntary agreement on common protocols enables services to be made available to anyone anywhere.

The Internet's origins are found in ARPA's support in the 1960s for research on techniques to build a rugged data network to connect computers. Packet networks were expected to be helpful in this regard because of the dynamic routing of bits that this technique enables. For example, a network outage in one location could be bypassed without disrupting network operations as a whole. It quickly became apparent that interpersonal communication—electronic mail— could be done inexpensively over this network (although such communication was ostensibly dedicated exclusively to network research).[30] ARPA played a benevolent role in ignoring this "abuse" of federally funded research facilities, thus enabling the Internet to emerge. The managers of the ARPA research effort have continued to play a critical role as this small research effort to connect the computer resources of several leading computer science research programs blossomed into a significant global commercial marketplace. The growth of the Internet following the transition from Defense Department to National Science Foundation leadership in the 1980s demonstrates the potential benefits of an agile technology policy. An important factor enabling such expansion is that the

Internet is highly distributed and the network is maintained mostly by volunteers. By 1992, the Internet had begun to have a tangible effect on the operations of commercial enterprises, in addition to the educational and governmental organizations that had had access to it all along.

With the election of President Clinton and Vice President Gore, public discussion and commercial consideration of the "information superhighway" and information infrastructure began in earnest. Gore recognized that the next generation of networked multimedia may lead to a revolutionary change in how people communicate and how business is conducted. The ramifications extend beyond broadcasting to the fields of telecommunications, computers, and publishing, from services to manufacturing, and from the public to private spheres. Broadband networks (including but not limited to wireless technologies), direct broadcast satellite, and optical-fiber technologies promise to provide the user with as many bits as desired, whether those bits represent high-resolution television programs, conversations, or transactions.

Given this broad potential impact, it is understandable that governments worldwide are following the U.S. lead and have adopted technology policies to support the development of information infrastructure. While the efforts vary in their intent and effectiveness, few have had the stunning impact of the agile policymakers at ARPA and the National Science Foundation. Federal program managers, interacting extensively with leading corporate and university researchers, provided deft guidance to the development of Internet technologies and to the creation of the culture of virtual governance characteristic of the Internet.

We stand at the beginning of a decades-long process of innovation and interconnection that will evolve in directions unforeseeable from the vantage point of 1995. Intelligent networks and displays (that is, televisions and computer workstations) already combine television, video, and computer technologies and may be further integrated with "hard copy" (print) technologies such as facsimile (fax)/photocopying systems. The new systems will be able to display and process digital information including images, text, and sounds with equal facility. The applications, which will take advantage of the unprecedented amount of bandwidth and distributed computing power now being installed, are as yet unclear. But networked multimedia services combining video, text, graphics, sound, and print will surely emerge. How exactly they will be configured, and which industries will be the first to seize the competitive advantages made possible by networked multimedia products and services, remain to be seen.

Broadband digital networks will serve as the central nervous system of the global economy in the next century. Japanese and European development of HDTV and broadband networks has been handicapped by the premature standardization of systems inadequate for the needs of the twenty-first century. In the United States, multimedia communications through cable television networks are being explored. It is not clear whether this is a viable long-term path to the home or an interim step on the way to wireless and fiber to the home. In both Europe and Japan, the average distance between subscribers, central telephone offices, and most homes is less than in the United States, due to differing population densities. This suggests that technology policy may be more inclined to support the rapid shift to fiber to the home—a particularly high capacity technology for building information infrastructure—in Japan and Europe than in the United States. However, this does not imply that European and Japanese nations will be slow to develop information infrastructure. The benefits and economics of a global information infrastructure are still unclear. Since the Internet is not defined by national boundaries, the benefits of U.S. investment in information infrastructure also extend beyond national boundaries. The markets and technologies highlighted above can evolve in many directions; an agile policy process is essential if public policy is to keep up with the rapid rate of technical change.

POLICY IMPLICATIONS

The United States benefits from years of accumulated experience with the Internet. The appeal of widespread, inexpensive access to a vast supply of information has led to the Internet's explosive growth.[31] The Clinton administration's emphasis on information infrastructure as a critical aspect of U.S. technology policy is a reflection of this vast increase of internetworking. Rather than pouring funds directly into telecommunications networks, including fiber to the home, the Clinton administration intends to stimulate private sector investment in information infrastructure by telephone companies, cable television, and computer companies. Another reason for the Clinton administration to avoid direct investment in telecommunications facilities is that there is a growing consensus that new digital wireless technology will be far cheaper than laying fiber for many applications, and that an agile policy framework for industrial development is the most critical contribution that government can make.

Speaking in 1993, Vice President Gore challenged industry to make the NII a reality:

[B]y January 11th of the year 2000, you will connect and provide access to the National Information Infrastructure for every classroom, every library and every hospital and clinic in the entire United States of America. . . . To educate, save lives, provide access to health care, and lower medical costs. . . . Just as communications industries are moving to the unified information marketplace of the future, so must we move from the traditional adversarial relationship between business and government to a more productive relationship based on consensus.

The combination and integration of different technologies for information collection and dissemination has long characterized media and communication systems. Digital technology offers new opportunities to create integrated telecommunications services, flexible networks, and multimedia equipment. The question is: Which nations and regions will benefit from this technological transformation? The United States, with its high computer penetration and advanced telecommunications network? Asia, which is preparing to leap immediately to a twenty-first-century infrastructure? Or a Europe of "megaprojects" in a megamarket—a European Economic Space extending from Iceland to Vladivostok?

Japan's strategy to boost the stagnant consumer electronics market by introducing a new generation of television technology proved to be ill timed and ill directed. The European strategy to follow the Japanese lead, in retrospect, turned out to be even more awkward. In each case, once the direction was set, the political culture focused on implementation and administration of the existing policy in the face of mounting evidence that it was unsuccessful. It was not the relative degree of power held by the state or the marketplace that led to bad policy and bad investment. These efforts were doomed by the inflexibility of the policy structure and the inability of either the state or the market to attend to or interpret feedback from the technical community and the marketplace.

Digital information and communication technology offer a fundamental challenge to individuals, firms, industries, and governments in the global information economy. This challenge—affecting antitrust law, trade, security, intellectual property, tax incentives, standards, access, affordability, First Amendment rights, and privacy issues—is likely to remain a powerful force shaping society well into the next century. The adoption of agile, flexible, ad hoc technology policies for information infrastructure development, while not guaranteeing success, can provide the framework for resolving some of these issues. The Internet model of policy development—that is, voluntary cooperation of autonomous agents to achieve goals defined through interaction—is admittedly imperfect. However, the alternatives—fetishizing or embracing bureaucratic models of industrial policy—are both fatally flawed. Technology policy must recognize the critical features of the global information economy and fashion policy instruments suited to networked firms and the principles of agile policy. Continuing to improve technology policy for information infrastructure along these lines, rather than terminating it, as congressional Republicans propose, would be the wisest choice for the United States as we enter the twenty-first century.

6

THE SOCIAL CONSEQUENCES OF LIBERALIZATION AND CORPORATE CONTROL IN TELECOMMUNICATIONS

HERBERT S. DORDICK

*T*here is today, spreading across the land, a feeling of exuberance and great expectation about the arrival of the information age. The expected competition between the major carriers of information—telephone firms and cable television operators—which was perceived as a barrier to progress, is being resolved through mergers and alliances.[1] The mantra is that the national information infrastructure (NII) is well on its way to reality and that the "information superhighway" will, in the not too distant future, extend to every school, university, business, and home.

As a consequence, the press and pseudoscholarly papers are deluging us with two streams of pronouncements about the benefits that this new age will bring—and about what it will take to achieve them. As in the early years of cable television, the dreamers see in the NII solutions to social problems: failing schools, unemployment, poverty, crime, moral decay, inadequate health care, pollution and urban congestion, and more. They are creating a new fable—the superhighway fable. At the same time, the ever-optimistic and surefooted communications firms are urging government to get out of their way so they can get on with the task of serving the public interest as they understand it.

The superhighway fable obscures important issues that must be resolved so that real social progress can be made and the public interest, as defined by the public, be met. The NII, as are all communications media, is a permissive technology allowing us to do what we wish. But these wishes must be supported by institutional commitments and investments often having little to do with telecommunications. The schools will not be "fixed" just because the highway reaches into classrooms. Nor will health care automatically be available on the end of an intelligent video telephone, since use of this new tool will require both patient training and physician education. Finding ways to use the new infrastructure effectively will just begin with its construction and will cost a great deal more than the superhighway connection itself.

The social advantages of the superhighway will not come easily; after all, monopolists, like leopards, do not change their spots. The Baby Bells continue to exhibit their strong tendency toward monopoly with inevitable market weaknesses, if not failures. If it had not been for government intervention, universal telephone service would not exist, for monopolists would have sought only the most profitable markets.[2] The common-carrier model for the telephone emerged only because the public and the government were attuned to the dangers of monopolies as a result of the inequities thrust upon them by the railroads during the Progressive era. Without government action, telephone service quality would have been reserved for large firms and not for household consumers, for there is small profit in residential rates when compared with the return from business. Moreover, the other chief player in the construction of the superhighway, the cable television operator, is not a common carrier and controls both content and conduit.[3] As an unregulated monopoly, cable television has reaped enormous profits from often unreasonable rates, which the Federal Communications Commission (FCC) has only recently sought to correct and with limited success.

There is every reason, then, to stop awaiting the coming of the super-highway miracle and begin a realistic appraisal of how we can achieve the quality of life we desire as the nation enters a global information economy. While the technology of communications has changed radically and a global economy poses new challenges for domestic economy, the goals and values we have developed for our communications infrastructure have not changed; to contribute to the nation's productivity and to enhance the quality of life of its citizens. Three major issues must be resolved satisfactorily if we are to preserve these hard-won goals and values in the face of radical change:

▼   The promise of information abundance, so necessary in a democracy, can be met only by guaranteeing universal and equitable access to uncensored sources of information. To achieve this, we may have to redefine our traditional notion of common carriage and make a commitment to minimizing or even outlawing "communication redlining."

▼   Personal information is becoming increasingly valuable in our market-oriented society and, with today's information technology, relatively easy to gather surreptitiously. In the workplace, computers have made surveillance a management tool, and the "zone of personal privacy" is in danger of being seriously breached. It is necessary for information users and pro-viders to recognize their responsibilities to protect personal privacy. Barring this, more active federal involvement in rationalizing and enforcing the nation's privacy laws will be required.

▼ Increased global competition and reengineering has resulted in un-employment among skilled and managerial workers and the creation of a part-time job economy. The jobs that have been lost will never be found again. Training and retraining are necessary to develop a workforce for the twenty-first century that is capable of performing high-valued jobs. The only way to solve the dilemma may be an industrial policy that includes retraining for skills and the establishment of a Technology Extension Service modeled on the Agriculture Extension Service to enable small businesses to navigate the complexities of information networks and create information products and services.

UNIVERSAL ACCESS AND UNIVERSAL SERVICE

The telephone is the indispensable gateway to the world of information. Without it, information economies could not prosper, and we as consumers, citizens, and workers could not benefit. Other gateways to the information world have emerged as well, such as the personal computer, the intelligent telephone, facsimile, and the television receiver. But these terminals and others that will enter the marketplace are only as valuable as their access to the carriers that transport information. Neither access to information networks or "free TV" are rights inscribed in the Constitution. However, the founding fathers understood the importance of communications and information for commerce and community building among the scattered settlements across the vast distances of the original colonies and spoke to this in several ways. For example, Benjamin Franklin proposed and the Constitution gave Congress the power "to establish Post Offices and Post Roads."[4] In 1820, the Post Office was promoted out of the Treasury Department to a government department with the aim of reaching all parts of the nation as a common carrier. It was understood that a social goal of the postal service was the diffusion of knowledge: Newspapers, books, and magazines were given large subsidies in mail rates. The First Amendment made it clear that speech was to be unregulated by the federal government, and the Fourteenth Amendment extended the concept to the states. Citizens were to be unrestricted in their communications. This established a fundamental belief in the importance of communications and of access to information for all citizens. In *Democracy in America*, Alexis de Tocqueville noted:

in a democratic society, the individual is powerless whereas in aristocratic communities there are a small number of powerful wealthy citizens . . . who undertake and can achieve great undertakings. . . .

In aristocratic societies, men do not need to combine in order to act, because they are strongly held together.[5]

But Americans must develop associations to maintain and grow their civil life. Associations or communities are created and maintained through communications networks, interpersonal and mediated, and by the exchange of information. Without communications, these associations would be weak and short-lived to the detriment of democracy.

Today, a community may be a network of several persons linked by their need for mutual aid and support or by their common interests. Geography is no longer important. Dispersed communities are maintained and strengthened by electronically mediated interpersonal communications and mass communications such as telephone, electronic mail, and computer bulletin boards. The telephone, that most ubiquitous of mediated interpersonal communications instruments, is relied upon for job seeking, information exchange, sociability, and emergency assistance.[6] In the era of the global Internet and the NII, interactive multimedia communications becomes the means for the formation of virtual global communities.

In the case of the telephone, because community building was important to our society, we accepted the social responsibility of making basic communications services by telephone available to all citizens, trading economic efficiency for social benefit.[7] Assuring that the telephone network would be an efficient, interconnectable, and interoperable system required the creation of a regulated monopoly. The nation's telecommunications infrastructure was, for more than one hundred years, the system envisioned by the driving force behind AT&T, Theodore Vail, who pronounced that the nation should be served by "One System, One Policy, Universal Service."[8] To Vail, this meant service "to everywhere" rather than "to everyone." Nevertheless, this model enabled the nation to develop the policy that has become known as "universal service at affordable costs," a commitment that continues to guide the making of the nation's communications policy.[9] Universal telephone service was made possible by the seamless network essentially provided by a single carrier delivering a single service.[10] When the market could not achieve universal service, subsidies and tariff policies were designed to create and maintain universal telephone services.

The consequence of these policies is a nation in which almost 94 percent of all households (and 97 percent in some states) have at least one telephone—the highest percentage, except for Canada and Sweden, in the world.[11] Although many expected that major disconnections from the public network would result from the 1987 AT&T divestiture, telephone penetration has actually increased, despite rate increases that turned out to be not quite as dramatic as expected.[12] Indeed, no major upheavals have occurred, even though benefits and costs have not been shared equally.[13]

Nevertheless, about seven million households do not have access to telephones, and several states and some populations have penetrations far below the national average. For example, in 1991, penetration for households with a yearly income under $5,000 headed by African-Americans between the ages of sixteen and twenty-four stood at 66.4 percent and those of Hispanic origin at 67.8 percent.[14] Young families with incomes below the poverty line have the lowest telephone penetration, contrary to the widely held belief that the elderly have that dubious honor. In low penetration states such as New Mexico, Alaska, Oklahoma, and Mississippi there are areas in which telephone services are not being offered. Telephone companies have failed to interconnect households where they believe there is no suitable market for telephone services or where very low household density would make the cost of extending service too high when compared to expected returns.[15] Clearly, this is unfinished business; if all members of our society are to receive the full benefits of the information revolution, these inequities must be removed.

THE NEW ENVIRONMENT

Many forces are acting to change telecommunications significantly in the United States and, indeed, throughout the industrialized world. First, telecommunications infrastructures are now global information infrastructures that play significant roles in the world economy.[16] Second, the variety of terminals and the uses to which they are put demand flexible and adaptable network configurations leading to the need for competing and often private networks that may not be interconnected or interoperable with the public network. Third, the information market is exploding as consumers and small and medium-sized firms join large firms as participants in the information economy. Fourth, society itself is becoming more comfortable with computers and information networks. Dual-wage-earner households, which represent almost 40 percent of the nation's households, depend on access to information in order to manage their lives. Work-at-home households, in which someone spends at least eight hours a week on job-related or income-producing tasks engaged in independent businesses or corporate activities, currently account for almost 30 percent of the nation's households and their number is growing.[17] For these types of households information technology, from the intelligent telephone to the personal computer and network information services, is a necessity. Fifth, the "National Information Infrastructure: An Agenda for Action" issued by the Clinton administration has stirred the imagination of the computer community, from grade school to the university, in the home and in the office.[18] During one week in August 1993, the New Republic reported 133 mentions of the Internet in the news.[19] The telecommunications industry, which has been threatening to break out of the constraints imposed by the AT&T Modified Final Judgment, is now doing so with vehemence and passion.[20]

As a result of these changes, the characteristics of the nation's telecommunications infrastructure that made possible the social policy of universal service and enabled the nation to achieve the high levels of access to the public network no longer exist. Today, competing carriers, initially long-distance providers but in the very near future local exchange carriers as well as private carriers, are entering the market, making it difficult to identify the boundaries of the public network.[21] Furthermore, the distinction between telecommunications and video carriers such as cable television will soon disappear as both converge in a digital pathway. Convergence, that old buzzword, has been given dramatic new life. These networks will be wired and wireless; copper and fiber; cellular, personal communications networks/systems (PCN/PCS), and digital.[22] Some will provide access to a closed user group; others may provide wider but still limited access.[23] Some will interconnect, others may choose not to. Rather than a single network, the nation's infrastructure will consist of networks of networks on multiple carriers. All will be capable of transporting information and services in multimedia formats to households as well as small and large firms, domestically and internationally.[24]

This conglomeration of networks raises questions about the continued viability of a public network, what that network has to offer, and how it is to be supported. The concept of common carriage is also called into question, as is the canon of universal service.

In the past, universal access equaled universal service. Access meant the ability to obtain a dial tone and voice communications. Not included in the basic access package today is touch-tone dialing, increasingly necessary to reach free information services such as those provided by 800-number services. It makes little sense that, with electronic switching essentially available universally, charges are added for touch-tone dialing.

A more difficult task is to determine just what constitutes universal service in the new environment. What, if any, services including information should be made available to everyone as part of an information safety net? Individual information needs are extremely diverse. What is critical information to one household may be perceived as information overload to another. There are important information services that should be available to all citizens regardless of their ability to pay—information concerning local government, health, education, and emergency services—information and services that contribute to a tolerable quality of life. A basic package of information services may evolve as the public becomes more aware of and at ease with the network experience. Alternatively, state and federal experimentation with various levels and mixtures of services could lead to a national consensus for a universal information service policy.

How are we to pay for universal access and for basic services for those who are now recipients of telephone subsidies?[25] Without a monopoly carrier, the complex scheme of cross-subsidies and geographic rate averaging designed to ensure low-cost residential, small-business, and rural service is no longer applicable. It might be argued that competition will reduce rates and make universal access to the network and to network services affordable. But competition and cost-based pricing could lead to increases in connection charges that some segments of the population cannot afford. Further, competitive networks have no incentive to serve low-cost customers and will gravitate to the high-density, high-volume customers where profits are greater. Residential users, small businesses, and rural areas may very well be left with no option but a poor public network as a carrier of last resort.

Internal subsidies within the same carrier such as those now provided by "Life-Line" and "Information Link-Up America" programs are not possible in a competitive environment. Carriers without these internal subsidies could cut prices for users whose costs would be higher with a competitor providing subsidies. Furthermore, because large users have more options, residential users may end up paying more for service.

There are other options for providing this necessary support. For example, in exchange for tax credits all carriers could be required to contribute to a universal service fund to subsidize access and a basic standard "information appliance" enabling low-income users to acquire information.[26] A value-added or excise tax on communications and information services to support the fund has also been proposed but is not likely to be popular.[27]

The present support program focuses on the elderly (who may also be needy) but who are unlikely to discontinue telephone service even if there is a modest increase in its cost. The target population for assistance should be low-income families for whom access is a lifeline. Those registered for welfare assistance should be candidates for subsidized telecommunication services. The existing welfare system might very well serve as the agent for providing this assistance, thereby reducing administrative costs.

Information assistance subsidies should be explicit and targeted toward those who need them—especially the poor. If public policy deems that access to information is as important as access to communications, the cost of terminals may need to be underwritten by an "Information Link-Up America" subsidy paid as part of monthly rental of telephone services, or in the cost of the information service package purchased.

The debate over universal access to the NII is becoming increasingly heated. The Consumer Federation of America and the NAACP, along with other civil rights and consumer groups, claim that the regional telephone companies are bypassing most poor and minority neighborhoods in a form of "communications redlining," concentrating their initial construction and services in more affluent neighborhoods. There are, of course, valid economic reasons for doing so: The infrastructure is very capital intensive, and early revenues are needed to offset these high installation costs. But a policy must be stated, now and unequivocally, that the lines will be extended everywhere with specific target dates set to ensure that services will reach all neighborhoods.[28]

AN OPEN MARKETPLACE FOR IDEAS

Equitable access to restricted or censored information is of little value. For access to be meaningful, it requires free, open, uncensored information from diverse sources, representing a wide range of opinions, some of which may very well be distasteful to the carrier. Anything less will not meet the promise of information abundance. Interactive switched-digital communications systems offer the prospect for electronic media with the diversity of information associated heretofore with print media.

In 1980, the chairman of the FCC raised the question of whether a newspaper delivered electronically is an extension of print and therefore free of regulation or whether it is a broadcast and consequently under the control of government.[29] Thus, the policy consequences of the convergence of print and broadcast communications were raised. Today, we must deal with the convergence of three communications systems—print, broadcast, and telecommunications—to which must be added the strange case of cable television.

Until these recent developments, the nation had been well served by three media policies offering three interpretations of the First Amendment. For print, the First Amendment governs. For broadcasting, a complex scheme of politically managed regulations was created, based upon the assumption of spectrum or channel scarcity. For telecommunications, policies were designed to provide equitable access as defined by common carriage. Cable television has found itself in the uncomfortable position of acting like a broadcaster but resembling a telephone carrier.

Cable television can provide interactive services, including the delivery of teletext and data, and has an almost unlimited number of transmission channels.[30] Cable operators vigorously opposes common-carrier status and broadcast regulation, claiming they should be granted full First Amendment rights, as are print media. Similar definitional difficulties will be encountered in efforts to regulate the "information superhighway."

In the past, issues of content have not been a regulatory concern; carriers provided transport alone. Now, however, the telephone companies are moving closer to providing video services and other forms of content, while cable companies are becoming increasingly interested in providing telecommunications services. Each is trying to move into the other's business; this is what convergence is about. As the distinctions between the mass media and telecommunications disappear, the print media model of free expression becomes possible—but only if some form of common carriage remains the cornerstone of policy for the information highway.

With the end of channel scarcity, more varied sources of news and opinion, as well as education and entertainment, may emerge. Interactive media holds great potential—for example, it can provide a forum for electronic public discourse, helping to restore public confidence in government. While the notion of an electronic "direct democracy" is found wanting by some, there is no disagreement that more informed public discourse is necessary for a vibrant democracy. However, this will not occur unless common-carriage responsibilities are developed within the new media environment. Absent this, we are likely to have (in the words of Les Brown) "more channels, less discourse."[31]

Local franchises require the cable operator to carry local stations. Cable operators have claimed that this infringes on their First Amendment rights. In the late 1970s, the FCC required cable operators to offer the so-called public benefit channels: public access, government access, and educational access. Cable operators successfully claimed that this, too, infringed on their First Amendment rights. Cable operators can deny access to content with which they may not agree and can promote programs that serve their political or religious views. Reports of mergers and alliances of cable operators, telephone carriers, and program producers creating vertical monopolies are in the news daily.

Despite the growth of cable and the aspirations of the cable industry, it is the nation's telephone companies that will be the major providers of the information superhighway. And regardless of the fact that they are, by law, common carriers, they insist on being information providers as well. Both the development of new technologies and the evolution of traditional technologies pose regulatory challenges. There are excellent grounds for guarding against monopoly in all markets—and in an information society, threats to the health of democracy add an additional layer of concern.

Government alone will not build the information superhighway, nor would we want it to. That could lead to government intervention in or supervision of content, a clear infringement of the First Amendment. We also cannot expect industry to provide highways without profitable content. A common-carriage policy must be crafted that allows a transport provider to live in both worlds, as a transporter of content and as a content provider. If a carrier guarantees access to information providers, it can also provide its own information services. With the unlimited channel capacity of digital networks and with future developments in switching capacity, there should be few if any limits to access by providers and consumers of information and other network services. A large number of channels for consumers and producers could be an antidote to monopolization of information sources and distribution systems.

PRIVACY

Privacy has always loomed as large in our system of values as freedom of speech and religion. Yet each of us reacts differently when confronted with situations that impinge on our privacy. The bank card, credit card, and telephone calling card can open individuals and businesses to unlawful probing. Yet we use them daily. We surrender our Social Security number easily when asked and give our address and telephone number when buying even simple items. We use information 800-numbers to inquire about rail schedules, sports results, weather, the price of items advertised in the newspaper, news, and customer services, often knowing that our telephone number is being recorded at the receiving end and that we shall probably be added to yet another mailing list. We rage over the possibility that a potential employer will inquire into our credit rating or attempt to examine our health history. Yet employers have the right to use drug, psychological, genetic, and honesty tests to find not just competent, qualified, and safe workers but to find the ideal worker. As the information economy unfolds, electronic communications and computing are becoming increasingly personal. Our conversations and transactions have increasing value for marketers because our conversations and our transactions can be interpreted as behavior.

In Chapter 10 in this volume, Joel Reidenberg notes that, in the United States, the "regulation of the treatment of personal information by the private sector has been narrowly targeted and extremely complex." Distrust of and the desire to restrain government leads to dependence on state and federal legislation addressing particular problems such as credit reporting and cable viewing patterns. Common law in the states provides "some protection against outrageously intrusive information-gathering techniques or false and misleading disclosures of information." Our tradition of free expression and individualism leads to reliance on private rather than public action for enforcement of any privacy laws that are in place.

Personal information has become increasingly valuable in our market-oriented society, just as today's information technology has made it relatively easy to gather such information surreptitiously. The absence of a unified body of regulations concerning personal privacy is a problem in both the international arena and domestically.

THE "INFORMATION PANOPTICAN" IN THE WORKPLACE

The computer in the workplace provides "techniques of control . . . for monitoring, surveillance, detection, and record keeping," according to Shoshanna Zuboff.[32] Interactive information access leaves a trail at the receiving end. Unlike telephone messages, which are ephemeral, computers create a textual record of our interactive behavior. "Information systems that translate, record, and display human behavior can provide the computer age version of universal transparency that would have exceeded even [Jeremy] Bentham's most outlandish fantasies."[33] Zuboff compares the exercise of power this trail can bestow with Bentham's panoptican and calls this "the information panoptican."[34]

This power to control by breaking into the "zone of personal privacy" is in conflict with current management theories and practices. Empowering workers is touted today in the office and factory. Management theories call for creating "knowledge nodes" or teams in order to allow workers' intelligence freer rein and thereby improve productivity. The use of electronic bulletin boards and electronic mail is encouraged to facilitate the exchange of ideas. Midlevel management is reduced, the hierarchy of the firm is flattened, and the individual team "cultures" generate creativity and improve morale.

Nevertheless, managers are insecure. Eavesdropping on these bulletin boards and into electronic mail is quite common, reducing employee loyalty and thereby limiting creativity and productivity. Surveillance of worker behavior is easy to do when so much of the communications in the office or factory is by computer transactions, which leave textual messages. A continuous record of keystrokes per hour on the word processor can be used to improve a worker's performance or to condemn him or her for perceived inadequacy. Monitoring telemarketers, airline reservation clerks, or workers on the automated production line, or the threat of such monitoring, converts the workplace to a prison instead of improving performance. Yet, despite the evidence, managers cling to this power in pursuit of higher productivity.

This "information panoptican" is not limited to the workplace. Information about patterns of purchasing behavior gained by recording transactions on bank cards and in the computers that monitor checkout counters and television viewing habits are of immense value to advertisers. Using information technology to match viewing of advertising with purchasing behavior, made eminently feasible by interactive cable transactions, and the computerized checkout counter are seen as instances of smart marketing rather than an invasion of personal privacy.

Just as there is a fine line between marketing information and individual privacy, there is a line between the degree of management control and the employee's right to privacy. Government has made laws to regulate relations between employer and employee covering issues like the minimum wage, hours of work, arbitration, piecework at home, and so forth. It is appropriate for government to protect workers' privacy rights as well as management's pre-rogatives to ensure productivity.

Privacy is considered by some "part of the bundle of rights that universal service ought to comprise."[35] But the concept of universal service will expand as the nation becomes more involved in and dependent on constant access to information resources. And this leads to significant new challenges to individual privacy. Reconciling universal access and privacy is a difficult task because universality carries with it a strong presumption of affordability. Achieving privacy by, for example, encryption is expensive; other means of providing for privacy could raise the cost of access too high for universality. Indeed, ensuring privacy may impose a cost on all users of the system, but people do not value privacy equally and may not be willing to pay for it.

There is a "zone of privacy" of the individual that must be defined and respected. However, there is no agreement among different states about the need for privacy laws, let alone any agreement as to what those laws should be. Technological developments run far ahead of concerns about how they impinge on individual privacy. As a first step, periodic reviews delineating essential personal privacy in the information context should be mandated by government. Such reviews could be performed by an independent national privacy commission with authority to harmonize state and federal privacy laws.

UNEMPLOYMENT, JOB DE-SKILLING, AND WORKER INSECURITY

After decades of promise, new information technologies and modern tele-communications are finally exerting their full force in both the manufacturing and services sectors. This is not unexpected. Innovations may require as long as forty years to seep through organizations and restructure work and jobs.[36] In the face of increasing global competition, firms are rethinking the way work can be performed in order to reduce costs and increase productivity, a process known as reengineering. Hierarchical structures are giving way to more flexible models in which teams of workers assume more responsibility for decision making. Corporate alliances, outsourcing work, and the use of consultants rather than full-time employees provide organizations with the ability to expand their markets and respond rapidly to market changes. Nowhere is this more evident than in the telecommunications industry, which has always been in the technological forefront and has successfully integrated the information technologies. For example, more than 300,000 midlevel managers were displaced between January and June of 1993 as organizations have been flattened and hierarchies eliminated. In the Regional Bell Operating Companies (RBOCs), the number of access lines per employee went from 66 employees per 10,000 lines in 1984 to 44.4 employees per 10,000 lines in 1991.[37] Between 1984 and 1990, AT&T reduced its staff by 25 percent, or more than 91,000 workers, through attrition and layoffs. In the first year alone after divestiture, AT&T furloughed more than 28,000 workers. The RBOCs also reduced their staffs by 25 percent between 1984 and 1992, for a total of 142,223 workers furloughed.[38]

THE COMING ERA OF DISPOSABLE JOBS

Since the notion of information workers became well enough defined to measure, there has been a steady rise in their number, which has doubled from 1960 to 1993. The increase was about 4 percent a year between 1960 and 1980, but during the 1980–85 period, the number of information workers grew at only 1.4 percent a year. From 1990 to 1993, the number of information workers in the workforce actually declined by three million.[39] Job categories that were decimated included professional-technical, clerical, and managers and proprietors. Service sector firms such as brokerage houses, consulting firms, and banks took advantage of the productivity gains made possible, in large measure, by information technology and laid off large numbers of employees.

Two out of every five jobs today are part-time jobs. Many of these part-time workers are displaced "information workers"—data-entry clerks, telemarketing sales agents, bank tellers, warehouse supervisors. Part-time employment accounts for two million more jobs than are available in high-wage factories.[40] These part-time, often skilled unemployed are the very information workers for whom the information economy was to be a boon.

The manufacturing sector has also felt the impact of information technology and automation as well as the global recession. In 1980, *Business Week* warned that the U.S. economy had ceased to grow. It cautioned that manufacturing jobs were disappearing as Detroit automobile plants closed and prepared to move south and as the U.S. Steel Corporation announced it was permanently closing down fourteen steel mills, laying off thirteen thousand workers, and going into the oil business.[41] Barry Bluestone and Bennett Harrison noted in 1982 that newscasts reported a steady stream of stories about plant shutdowns and another thousand jobs disappearing and of workers unable to find full-time jobs that would use their skills and provide enough to support their families.[42]

Bluestone and Harrison rarely mention the impact of computers and information technology in the manufacturing sector, concentrating instead on the effect of competition in steel from Korea, automobiles from Japan, and the rash of buyouts by conglomerates that generally led to downsizing as the firms consolidated. However, the effects of information technology can be seen in intelligent manufacturing, which has as its core the processing of orders sooner, faster, and without pausing for retooling, even for lots of one.[43] The key words that lend meaning to the term intelligent manufacturing are *lean*, which means efficient, unwasteful, less costly manufacturing; *agile*, which describes a manufacturing system's speed in reconfiguring itself to meet changing demands; and *flexible*, which describes the system's ability to adjust to customer's preferences.

Ramchandran Jaikumar notes that manufacturing technology has moved ever closer to these goals for more than two hundred years and, in doing so, has altered significantly a host of parameters, one of which is the ratio of people to machines.[44] The latest stage in the evolution of manufacturing is computer-integrated manufacturing made feasible by the telecommunications and information technologies. Today, the ratio of people to machine is 1 to 30. Ten years ago, in the era of numerical control, this ratio was 1 to 100, and at the end of 1970s it was 1 to 300. Taken together, these developments have transformed the nature of work itself, creating enormous insecurities for workers who suddenly find their skills inadequate. Adding to this burden is global competition in the midst of a worldwide recession that is almost ten years old. Unemployment among skilled workers, especially among information workers whose jobs were supposed to be safe and highly valued in the information society, has risen to unparalleled levels. Midlevel managers are clogging the unemployment lines and trying to shift to industries that are more service based, believing that these industries have not yet felt the impact of the information and telecommunications technologies. However, productivity and efficiency gains as well as process redesign and redeployment are shifting more of the transaction burden to the customer, eliminating jobs in the service sector as well.

There have been wage declines during the past ten years for both blue- and white-collar men, for both high school and college graduates. The fall in wages has been most precipitous among workers without college educations. While the top and bottom wage levels of the labor force have grown, the center has been hollowed out. Disposable jobs are being produced with little or no health care or pension coverage, with hours often altered by the employer at will, and with no assurances that the job will still be around next week.

A SOCIAL SAFETY NET AND/OR AN INDUSTRIAL POLICY

The jobs that have been lost will not be found again. The skills that were valuable in the past—toolmaker, warehouse foreman, midlevel manager—have been replaced by computer-integrated manufacturing requiring fewer workers with higher skills. Technological innovation in the workplace should lead to increasing job value, to upgrading of workers' skills, and to higher productivity. However, productivity is being achieved at workers' expense, rather than with the creative utilization of advanced manufacturing and office technologies. Indeed, the key to higher productivity seems to be downsizing the company, requiring workers to work longer hours, and farming work out in order to save overhead costs. As the *New York Times* put it, "For all but the elite in the developed countries of the world, work holds less promise, less purpose, less security, and less dignity than it did a generation ago."[45] Observers have noted that in other recessions workers believed that a solution would be found and that their pain would soon disappear. Today, there seems to be greater hopelessness and the fear that no one knows how to climb out of the hole many workers find themselves in. Yet in the United States there is an elite core of 500,000 "supernovas" earning vastly more than their peers in Europe and Japan.[46]

Social cohesion is in danger when people see executives earning one hundred to two hundred times more than they are paid on the shop floor, and when those who have achieved middle-class standing are now uncertain about finding a job that pays well enough to support a family. Unions with significantly reduced memberships in firms that have been in the forefront of new technology—communications, machine tools, instruments and electronics, chemicals and drugs, among others—have little power to negotiate issues such as the rate of adoption of information technology and automation. Conflicts over these issues in the office and the factory can only reduce U.S. competitiveness.

Short-term solutions are necessary, but at best they are Band-Aids. One such solution may be shorter work weeks and job sharing during periods of high unemployment. This would at least minimize the creation of disposable jobs with no health care or retirement benefits and no job security. Nevertheless, there will still be large numbers of part-time workers without health benefits. A national health program could ease this dilemma. A broad-based social safety net may be required in the future. Indeed, an unemployment rate of 10 percent is considered reasonable in many industrialized nations undergoing rapid technological change in the global information economy. These nations have long since discovered that a social safety net is a political necessity. It is time for the United States to recognize that we may soon find ourselves in a similar situation.

A possible midrange approach focuses on small business as the major developer of jobs in the nation. A national information infrastructure offers the potential for the development of many marketplaces on many networks and for the creation of many small and medium-sized enterprises on these networks.[47] Producers and repackagers of information for specific applications, such as insurance, brokering, real estate, consulting, education and training, marketing, and so on are candidates for businesses on a network suitable for small enterprises. They require relatively small capital investment. However, small entrepreneurs often do not have the know-how needed to make the most of information technology, nor have they the skills to navigate the complexities of tomorrow's information highways.

This is reminiscent of the early days of agriculture in the United States when the Agriculture Extension Service in the land grant universities was formed to assist farmers in applying the latest techniques and equipment. The result was an industry that continues to have an extremely high rate of productivity growth. A "Technology Extension Service" is required to assist small businesses to utilize information technology effectively.

Even if economic growth resumes, the nature of work has changed so radically that without significant investments in retraining and education it is unlikely that workers with today's skills will find high-paying jobs. Clearly retraining is of utmost importance. However, this raises the question: Training for what—for jobs that may not appear? There is no substitute for an industrial policy that includes retraining to provide skills that will be needed to achieve the goals of that policy. Secretary of Labor Robert Reich often points to the German apprenticeship system as a model for bridging the gap between training and a job. Tax incentives for firms offering such programs as well as providing retraining for soon-to-be-displaced workers may be necessary. Unions should be encouraged to use their resources to retrain members who have lost jobs as a result of restructuring of firms and tasks. Serious consideration should be given to encouraging apprenticeship programs to prepare non-college-bound high school graduates for meaningful jobs in industry. Regulation of worker-employer relations is often unpopular among executives the United States. The minimum wage, hours worked, child labor laws, equality of job opportunities for minorities and women, labor arbitration, and so on have at times been seen as inappropriate in a capitalist society in which the market and the profit motive are the driving forces behind success. Resolution of these issues, even through greater regulation, has strengthened industry, reduced confrontations, and enhanced productivity and economic growth. In the global information economy, firms continue to downsize, merge, and reengineer, resulting in continuing unemployment. Government may find it desirable to take action to soften the blow on workers when firms adopt these strategies. When firms do not accept some responsibility for their laid-off workers, government must bear a heavier burden. There is a relationship between the responsibility of the firm and the cost of the social safety net the government may have to create.

Firms also have the responsibility to humanize their employment policies. For example, technology choices and implementation policies that enhance workers' jobs, that permit the creation of new jobs requiring higher-level skills, and that lead to a higher standard of living should be given preference over technologies that merely reduce the workforce or downgrade skills. New technologies can and should be designed to create higher-level jobs, not merely replace people. People without jobs do not purchase goods or services. Whenever reengineering takes place, the well-being of the community overall should be considered.

POLICY RECOMMENDATIONS

1. *Universal access to information networks must be guaranteed.* Recognizing that there are important information services that should be available to all citizens regardless of their ability to pay, an information safety net should be established that includes programs enabling qualified households to purchase screen-based terminals, underwritten by an "Information Link-Up America" subsidy.

    Information services to be included in the safety net will emerge from experience in the marketplace and/or through state-federal experimentation with various levels and mixes of information services. It is unrealistic, even perhaps naive, to expect that competition among network providers will drive costs down and thereby make access affordable for low-income households. Funding options for providing universal access include the following:

    ▼ All carriers should be required to contribute to a universal access fund in exchange for tax credits to subsidize access and a basic and standard "information appliance," enabling low-income users to acquire information.

    ▼ A value-added or excise tax on communication services, although un-popular at present, may need to be devised to support such a fund.

    ▼ Information assistance subsidies should be explicit and targeted to the poor.

2. *In the best of all possible worlds, ensuring the availability of free and uncensored sources of information requires that conduit providers should not be content providers.* Anything less will not meet the promise of information abundance. However, in the real world, a new common-carrier model needs to be crafted, one that allows a carrier to be both transporter and provider of content, but only if the carrier guarantees access to all other information providers.

3. *Network interconnectivity and interoperability are necessary prerequisites for achieving universal information services.* Many common-carrier and quasi-common-carrier networks will operate in a competitive environment and utilize novel technologies that could be incompatible with established standards. It may be uneconomical for these carriers to interconnect, and

if it is required by regulation, who is to bear the cost? A significant hurdle to be surmounted in achieving this interconnectivity will be the selection of some agency to oversee network standards and interconnectivity.

Standards for network interconnectivity and interoperability must be established by the appropriate government agency, overseen by a strong FCC.

4. *Because technological developments run far ahead of protection of personal privacy, periodic reviews of these protections in the information context should be mandated.* This should be carried out by an independent national privacy commission with authority to harmonize state and federal privacy laws.

Consideration of the costs and benefits of privacy should be recognized in the making of communications policy. Further, consumers must be offered options regarding how much privacy they wish to buy. Individuals must be given the opportunity to deny access to information gained from monitoring and keeping records of their purchases and other transactions and television viewing behavior. Serious consideration must be given to encryption as a means to protect privacy, but at reasonable costs.

Government must protect workers' privacy rights through regulation of employer-employee relations.

5. *Training and retraining are necessary to develop a workforce for the twenty-first century, one that is capable of performing highly valued jobs.* To ensure that workers are trained for jobs that will be available, there is no substitute for an industrial policy that encourages training in the skills that will be needed to achieve the goals of that policy.

Disposable jobs are very likely to increase. A social safety net, of which the national health care initiative is one component, should be crafted and implemented.

Tax incentives or other incentives should be offered to encourage firms to engage in on-the-job retraining and apprenticeship programs.

Small business could be the main beneficiary of the global information economy and of a national information infrastructure. A Technology Extension Service modeled on the Agriculture Extension Service should be established to enable these businesses to navigate the complexities of information networks and create information products and services.

CONCLUSION

It is difficult to argue that the public has benefited yet from the advancements in technology that have led to the global information economy. Indeed, citizens are overwhelmed by the images of globalism and high technology they face everyday. Global firms are in the news; there is the world car, the world drink, the world sport, a world newspaper, and a world television. Is there a world religion on the horizon and that bogey of all worlds, a world government? People fear that a relatively few very large firms will provide many of the products and services they need. They fear that their consumer interests and information choices will be limited rather than expanded. They fear that national interests will become subservient to corporate plans as countries search for an economic niche in the global economy. Fears for national sovereignty cannot be far behind.

The vast majority of U.S. citizens are not yet participants in the information economy. They are not equipped with screen-based terminals and fear getting lost on the information highway. Yet newspapers and television trumpet the arrival of the national information infrastructure and multimedia as a panacea for high unemployment, inadequate education, poor health care, and more. Once again, the consumer and small business person must wait for this information infrastructure to "trickle down" to them. Meanwhile the gap between the information haves and have-nots continues to widen.

The battle lines are clearly drawn. Two models of the nation's communication future can be identified. On one side there is the Internet model, which is open, nonhierarchical, not centrally controlled, and without heavy governance— providing, indeed, the sort of public access that was dreamed of in the early days of cable television. On the other side there are the dreams of large media conglomerates combining the features of yesterday's AT&T with the tightly controlled access of today's broadcasting. It is not the size of the enterprises that is of concern but how they might control access to information and services through pricing. In the face of massive information conglomerates, citizens have little choice but to look to federal and state governments to ensure that the marketplace of ideas remains free and accessible to all.

Some hold to the naive view that we should allow these conglomerates to make the investments necessary to pave the nation with data highways. Then, once this has been achieved, we should examine how best to use these highways in the public interest. The danger is that, as has happened so frequently in the past, public interest goals will be overwhelmed and soon forgotten.

Public participation in decision making is necessary to ensure that the public interest is met. This is why encouraging and providing for public participation in the new information technologies are the most important tasks now facing federal and state governments.

PART III

POLICIES FOR THE GLOBAL INFORMATION INFRASTRUCTURE

7

BUILDING THE GLOBAL INFORMATION HIGHWAY: TOLL BOOTHS, CONSTRUCTION CONTRACTS, AND RULES OF THE ROAD[1]

PETER COWHEY

Will there be a global information highway? If so, how will it be built, provisioned, and used? The development of this new infrastructure creates massive technological opportunities for global society but also raises the question of who will profit from it and how. The roads built during the Roman Empire raised similar questions about the division of construction profits and tolls. Developing a common technological backbone for the fragmented global village raises far more difficult issues.

Among the most powerful policy tools available to the U.S. government for influencing the shape of the global highway are the bilateral trade and regulatory rules that govern the telecommunications equipment and services markets of the industrial countries. U.S. information diplomacy concerning these bilateral rules has its roots in the distinctive American approach to information technology and regulation. Over the past decade, domestic innovations have prompted the United States to nurture a revolution in international market regulations. Nonetheless, a significant gap remains between the latest American innovations and global market rules, partly because the American approach to information technology has itself evolved: Over the past few years, the configuration of technology, technology leaders, and regulatory issues has shifted from the "oligopoly revolution" to the "distributed information revolution."

The oligopoly revolution can be thought of as the shift from a telephone monopoly and three national television networks to a world of competition among long-distance carriers, independent computing networks anchored on IBM mainframes, cable television networks, and a continuing monopoly by the Baby Bells in local telephone services. In this environment, oligopoly suppliers of equipment and services confronted large corporations with vast buying power.

The distributed information revolution involves the emergence of desktop computing networks; the scramble by telephone, cable, and wireless companies for control of the revenues from local communications traffic (including video services); and the rapid rise on the network of providers of content (such as movies, records, and magazines) as important economic and political forces. In this digital world, the ranks of suppliers have multiplied and fragmented, while smaller users have become a potential bonanza.

Despite these new developments, U.S. international trade and regulatory policy remains focused on the challenges posed by the oligopoly revolution. The key players in the distributed information revolution—including holdovers from the oligopoly era—lack a coherent agenda for international policy, and the U.S. government is not far ahead of them. U.S. policy can adapt by redefining market segments and regulatory objectives for equipment and services, combining trade and technology strategies, changing the policymaking processes to encourage new participants, and reconciling bilateral and multilateral trade and regulatory approaches.

TWO REVOLUTIONS:
FROM OLIGOPOLY TO DISTRIBUTED INFORMATION

Like all revolutions, those in global communications and information infrastructure have no neat chronology. Technology spawned the transformations and, depending on their politics and economics, nations responded differently to the new technology. But the birthplace of the transformations was the United States.

The oligopoly revolution introduced shared data processing and communications over long distances. These developments began in the 1960s but did not mature fully until the late 1980s, when communications and data processing became central to redefining the core processes of corporations. Corporate management information systems, computer-integrated manufacturing and logistics, and extensive telephone and computer support services for customers are only a few outgrowths of the oligopoly revolution.[2]

At the outset of this transformation, it became clear that conventional communications networks could not easily meet the price and performance demands of U.S. business. Large users insisted that telephone companies accept specialized new networks that they themselves ran or value-added networks for data.[3] These new networks refuted the myth that telephone companies had to own and supply all terminal equipment and that only telephone companies could specify reliable network designs. Still, these new information networks continued the tradition that each communications medium (for example, telephone, telex, and television) would have its own specialized equipment, standards, and networks.

Computing and communications had relatively fixed parameters for optimum performance; this made them inflexible and slow to meet emerging user needs, such as a new format for data communication. The product was frequently compromised because of network limitations (for example, limited television broadcast technology meant a low quality of film for television shows). Moreover, information remained embedded in inflexible media—stacks of old magazines yielded computer data only through slow, costly efforts.

These rigidities were partly a holdover of analog technology, especially for transmission, which was slow, inflexible, and error prone. Moreover, memory and central processing capabilities (in both mainframes and central office switches) were expensive and thus were treated as a scarce network resource. Even with all these limitations, the oligopoly revolution had two profound implications.

First, computerization put the giants of computing and telephones on a collision course. AT&T concluded that higher growth rates would exist on the digital computing frontier for equipment and services, while competitive entry by Japan would squeeze margins on traditional telecommunications equipment. AT&T's decision in the mid-1980s to venture further into the realm of providing computer equipment and services meant inevitable conflict with powerful computer firms like IBM.

Second, data networking within and between corporations sparked an explosion in faxing and long-distance telephony that turned firms into advocates of cost-based prices for all communications services. Businesses wanted the freedom to create private networks tying together their global operations and linking up with their major suppliers and customers. Because these large customers constituted the telephone companies' most profitable markets, their efforts threatened the cross-subsidies to households built into every telephone company's pricing structure.

Yet for all the drama of the oligopoly revolution—especially the birth of telephone competition in the United States, Japan, and Great Britain—another revolution arrived in the 1990s. This is the distributed information revolution, symbolized by the decline of IBM.

IBM's plunge occurred because mainframe computers, compared to desktop systems, became too expensive for their processing "bang," too inflexible in their format and use, and too demanding of specialized networking arrangements.[4] The development of digital technology, vastly improved price and performance of processing and memory, and the looming market for the mass application of advanced information networks triggered efforts to create new multimedia technologies and networks: The race was on to replace the television network of old with interactive video networks, create computing networks where many users could work simultaneously on a common document and interconnect everything from copying machines through coffee makers to computers. (Table 7.1 compares the oligopoly revolution and distributed information revolution.)

TABLE 7.1

COMPARING THE OLIGOPOLY REVOLUTION AND DISTRIBUTED
INFORMATION REVOLUTION

OLIGOPOLY	DISTRIBUTED INFORMATION
1. *Segregation*: Information and communications applications segregated.	1. *Integration*: Information and communications systems integrated.
2. *High Cost, Hierarchical Network*: Computing and communications expensive, but computing cost/performance improving faster than communications. Users and value-added networks seek control over their terminal equipment and standards to loosen control of networks with hierarchic structures.	2. *Low Cost, Shared Network*: Intelligence and transmission capacity abundant and cheap. Control of network shared. All forms of network equipment subject to mix and match.
3. *Fixed Parameters*: Computing and communications networks have fixed parameters. Optimize network and application jointly to get economies of scale and interconnections.	3. *Individual Tailoring*: Network design and application may be optimized individually, but greater commingling of service and equipment design standards for joint computing and telecoms applications.
4. *Focus on Standards Planned by Suppliers*: Network architecture of the network of the future planned through the standards process, but a clash between computing and communications companies over which plan and technical standards to follow. Many closed proprietary standards clash with standards set by governmental committees.	4. *Experimentation and Shared Innovation*: Difficult to plan such a network. Big public networks emphasize overlay networks (ad hoc additions of functionality). Emphasis is on experimentation and dissemination of best practices. Proprietary standards are licensed on attractive terms, but demonstration is key. Users often design own networks while suppliers act as subcontractors.
5. *Inflexible Media*: Information captured in inflexible media.	5. *Flexible Media*: Information can be transformed flexibly across media.

The digital age is multimedia precisely because technology has erased previous distinctions between equipment and applications. Computers incorporate faxes and telephones. Television sets will compute. Digital information appliances (like Apple's Newton) will be multifunctional while offering a variety of screen size, portability, and special features. This commingling also implies rivalry over which technologies provide what capabilities for users. For example, Microsoft and Novell argue that inexpensive intelligence and transmission may enable desktop computer networks to substitute for rigid hierarchical networks relying on central office switching.

Digital systems also segregate network and content design problems; digital broadcasting can carry any content, and content designers can choose many network delivery options. Moreover, it will be possible to disaggregate an integrated technical package (for example, a word processing package or tele-phone switching system) into mix-and-match components (with, for example, desktop computers sharing the functions of the network switch but mixing features of different software). It also means that content will be independent of delivery medium: Magazines can be published on computer or on paper; spreadsheets can have voice annotations.

Resource constraints still exist. New functions require huge amounts of memory, which remains relatively more expensive than other computer com-ponents. Because of this, some functions may remain on central data servers (such as massively parallel supercomputers) tied to distributed networks; but there will be a greater mixing of computing and telecommunications standards to provide novel applications (as in Microsoft's provision of the operating system for Sega games on interactive networks).[5] Controlling standards for these network applications will create competitive advantages in both equipment and services businesses. Many standards will change too rapidly for government standards committees to dominate the process. Moreover, there will inevitably be clashes between the telecommunications and computing companies over the terms and conditions for managing the sharing of technology through the licensing process. However, in the end, all technologies will become more easily interoperable, and the terms for licensing will emphasize accessibility. Moreover, users will become important innovators in network design and applications.

In order to understand the significance of the distributed information revolution for policy, one must first understand how it challenges the policy response to the oligopoly revolution—including accommodations to that revo-lution made as recently as the end of the 1980s.

WINNERS AND LOSERS IN THE OLIGOPOLY REVOLUTION

The oligopoly revolution rebalanced who won and who lost in the communica-tions and information industries. The oligopoly revolution came fastest and went farthest in the United States because its political economy traditionally has been the most open to periodic industrial reorganization. In contrast, the governments of Japan and Europe slowed the pace of the oligopoly revolution to limit the losses of established beneficiaries.

THE OLIGOPOLY REVOLUTION AND DOMESTIC MARKETS

The oligopoly revolution in the United States affected both producer and consumer welfare. First, it transferred rents from monopoly telephone companies and their workforces to large users with massive buying power and middle-class households (who vote heavily and use long-distance services intensively). Second, it transferred rents from traditional suppliers of telecommunications equipment (such as AT&T) to other electronics firms. (It also transferred rents from the telephone companies' equipment suppliers because the cost of equipment plummeted once competition emerged.) Third, it transferred rents from telephone companies to specialized service suppliers, particularly those developing mainframe computer networks and their service applications.

The oligopoly revolution in Japan and Europe did not go nearly so far. Japan introduced competition in telephone networks and specialized services in 1984, but restrictive regulations on pricing, entry, and the deployment of network capacity still favored traditional equipment suppliers over users of communications services. The reorganization allowed only a modestly larger pool of equipment suppliers and limited competition with new network providers. Japan blunted change further by limiting the entry of foreign suppliers.

Japan's regulatory restraints discouraged use and efficiency. Even after adjusting for the number of telephone subscribers, the U.S. telecommunications networks in 1992 generated almost 3.3 times more minutes of local use and over 1.5 times the level of long-distance minutes as did Japan's. Japanese carriers charged almost four times more per minute for most uses and required almost three times the level of net plant investment per telephone call—an indicator of significant inefficiencies in network design, use, and pricing.[6] While Japanese carriers spent heavily (and often inefficiently) on network modernization, their pricing discouraged use and thus retarded learning about information systems necessary for the distributed information revolution. The same restricted competitive environment permeated computers where NEC's proprietary operating system for desktop computers allowed it to dominate the Japanese market at prices far above its American counterparts and discouraged the networking of business computers.

The problems of belatedly harmonizing Europe's widely divergent communications infrastructures and commercial practices limited the European Union (EU) to cautious reforms in the 1980s. EU policy liberalized only such new services as advanced computer networking and wireless communications. It also slowly liberalized competition in equipment while backing a massive common research and development program for telecommunications to boost EU suppliers. Like Japan, networking restrictions slowed the interpenetration of computing and networking; for example, in 1993, a data circuit cost on average three to ten times more than in the United States, and restrictions on interconnecting leased circuits greatly hindered efficient use.[7] Unlike Japan, however, foreign products significantly penetrated the EU equipment markets.

DIPLOMACY AND THE OLIGOPOLY REVOLUTION: LINKING SERVICE AND EQUIPMENT MARKETS

The oligopoly revolution spurred competition in what was until then a protectionist world information industry. The computer industry had traditionally enjoyed significant protection. Telecommunications was worse yet—a bastion of mercantilism in a world of free trade. For the most part, governments owned the telephone networks, and trade rules exempted government procurement of equipment from trade obligations from the General Agreement on Tariffs and Trade (GATT).[8] Telephone companies bought network equipment from one or two local suppliers. The monopoly network even provided household telephones. Telephone companies were national champions of the electronics industry when possible, or local subsidiaries of a few multinational firms when not. (U.S. antitrust policy prevented AT&T from becoming a global supplier. ITT was the principal U.S. firm operating overseas, and its holdings were absorbed in 1987 by France's Alcatel.)

The rules of the International Telecommunications Union (ITU) treated international telephony as a jointly provided service: In theory, two national telephone companies invested collectively in the facilities that connected their individual networks and provided their own domestic connections. (Each country had absolute control over who provided services in its territory and most relied on a monopoly.) Thus, an international telephone call was considered a joint undertaking, with the two companies dividing revenues according to an agreed-upon accounting rate (usually a 50–50 split). Each company charged what it wanted for the call but reimbursed the other company according to the accounting rate, with the side originating more calls owing money to the other. Periodically, the two countries settled accounts.

The oligopoly revolution in the United States was mainly a response to domestic conditions; the subsequent regulatory changes thus largely neglected the realm of international trade. This meant that the domestic telecommunications equipment market was opened unilaterally to international competitors without U.S. firms gaining comparable access abroad. As a result, the trade balance in telecommunications equipment moved from a surplus in 1982 to a deficit of over $2 billion in 1986.

The largest payoffs from the oligopoly revolution for producers and consumers of equipment were in computing and terminal equipment (for example, faxes) because the smaller and slower-growing telecommunications equipment market was still only imperfectly open to new competitors. Table 7.2 shows the market in the United States in 1992, at the dawn of the distributed information revolution. Communications services were still the largest item in the U.S. information market, but about half of these were local exchange services that were just becoming competitive. Similarly, while private networking and value-added networks were vital for innovative financial and manufacturing service users, the bigger payoffs went to producers of computer and software services and equipment—far larger global markets than telecommunications equipment and international communications services.[9]

In short, the oligopoly revolution helped U.S. consumers and suppliers primarily by leveraging American innovations in the broader computing market.

TABLE 7.2

THE U.S. INFORMATION MARKET IN 1992 (IN BILLIONS OF US$)

1.	DATA PROCESSING EQUIPMENT	57.0 (world total=176)
2.	TELECOMMUNICATIONS EQUIPMENT	35.4 (world total=110)*
	▾ Network equipment	17.6
	Customer premise	4.8
	▾ Radio and television equipment	17.8
3.	DOMESTIC TELECOMMUNICATIONS SERVICES	160.5 (world total=420)
	▾ Long-distance toll	59.4
4.	INTERNATIONAL TELECOMMUNICATIONS SERVICES	8.7 (world total=42)
5.	PACKAGED COMPUTER SOFTWARE	28.5 (world total=72)
6.	ELECTRONIC INFORMATION, DATA PROCESSING, AND NETWORKING SERVICES	52.4
7.	COMPUTER PROFESSIONAL SERVICES	55.4
8.	ENTERTAINMENT SERVICES	52.4
	▾ Movie box office	4.9
	▾ Music recordings	9.0
	▾ Videocassettes	14.5
	▾ Cable television	24.0
	TOTAL	450.3

* World total excludes broadcasting equipment.

Source: Cowhey, "The Global Information Industry: Liberalization and Competitive Challenges," in Van Whiting (New York: Oxford University Press, forthcoming).

But this left U.S. producers of telecommunications equipment angry over market losses and both users and suppliers of computing technology impatient over delays in opening foreign markets. These frustrations converged by the mid-1980s in an attack on foreign telecommunications monopolies. Makers of network equipment (especially AT&T and Motorola) became determined to penetrate foreign markets and prevent competitors from using their protected home markets to finance expansion abroad.[10] Major users wanted global networks liberalized to match innovations in the United States. Since the 1960s, large users and pioneering global value-added networks (especially those of General Electric and Control Data) had won government assistance in keeping restrictive ITU and national regulations ambiguous enough to permit expanding value-added networks, but regulatory restrictions remained onerous.

U.S. trade negotiators shrewdly identified an opportunity for good trade policy and good politics by using bilateral and GATT trade negotiations to force foreign network and equipment liberalization. Fortunately for the United States, it had great clout in the world marketplace because it anchored five of the seven largest international communication routes and represented the largest equipment market (35 percent of the world total). The price set by the United States for access to its market was the transformation of the rules governing global telecommunications.[11] Nonetheless, the bilateral talks remained in a legal limbo throughout the decade because there was no framework provided by GATT rules. Resentment grew overseas because, whatever the rationale for bilateral negotiations, such talks implied that the United States might invoke sanctions—penalties that could be considered illegal under the GATT. The Omnibus Trade Act of 1988 further required the U.S. trade representative (USTR) to create a special list of countries with objectionable telecommunications policies, and then mandated bilateral negotiations on a strict time schedule, with sanctions threatened if the talks failed.[12] The question is how much these talks achieved.

THE IMPACT ON SERVICES AND THE GLOBAL RBOC MODEL

The bilateral negotiations on services undermined the most restrictive of global regulations. However, the United States still accepted a global framework resembling the Regional Bell Operating Company (RBOC), or Baby Bell, model of local services in the United States—a monopoly national carrier for public switched voice services positioned atop a market riddled with competitive nonvoice services and limited private voice networks. (Unlike the U.S. case, the local carriers in other countries also controlled long-distance services.) Oligopolistic entry for selected new providers of computer networking services and transmission facilities (for example, communications satellites allowed to compete on the margin of the INTELSAT monopoly) would accommodate large users. Only the content on the networks might be largely competitive.

Although the United States accepted monopolies in voice service, its promotion of global private networks created the conditions for major competitive change as technology advanced. For example, the United States advocated the freedom of the customer to choose and own terminal equipment as long as it did not harm the network. This opened the way to computer equipment vying with traditional telecommunications equipment for control of the network. (The Internet is a dramatic example of how computing technology can usurp traditional telecommunications equipment in the creation of a network.) Furthermore, value-added network providers slowly won permission to establish their own private networks in other countries and invest to provide support personnel and programming. This was the opening wedge for the privatization of networks and the introduction of competition. Most important, the United States promoted cost-based and nondiscriminatory pricing for telecommunications services, especially on transmission circuits rented to competitive value-added networks. It also advocated an end to restrictions on the shared use or resale of extra circuit capacity among several customers in order to permit more efficient use of circuits. Once some networks could acquire circuits at a discount and resell their use, arbitrage against accounting rates for individual calls became easier and inflated prices came under pressure.

Foreign carriers feared rightly that even limited competition could hurt them badly unless delayed until after they had undergone restructuring. First, data transmission grows much faster than voice, and the traffic of sophisticated users is the most profitable market.[13] Second, barriers to international competition are falling faster than for local services, yet international traffic generates bigger profits. The margins on accounting rates between the United States and Europe and Asia sometimes exceed 400 percent. Yet international leased circuits that can avoid inflated accounting rates already account for 10 to 20 percent of the market; their share will grow even faster if they can be interconnected to the public network at one or both ends of the international circuit.

New service entrants took little comfort from the fears of incumbent carriers, as regulatory details often blunted the potential gains from new trade principles. For example, during negotiations over the new Japanese tele-communications legislation in 1985, the United States fought hard to win rules permitting significant foreign equity in new telephone companies and streamlined registration procedures for value-added networks. Yet the implementing regulations usually worked against foreign entry. As a result, the United States had to negotiate such issues as the number of new inter-national telecommunications carriers (benefiting Great Britain's Cable and Wireless); the territories assigned to new cellular companies in Japan (assisting Motorola's Japanese partner outside the Tokyo region); and the speed at which Japanese carriers introduced network technology capable of supporting equipment (concerning the use of Motorola equipment in IDO, a cellular network backed by Toyota and the Japanese Highway Corporation).[14] In short, the United States learned that securing access often required plunging into the complex details of domestic regulations.[15] The 1994 impasse between the United States and Japan over the legitimacy of mandatory targets for foreign market access (the "managed trade" question) is only one variation on disputes over what constitutes a legitimate system for communications regulations.[16]

THE SURPRISE IN VOICE SERVICES

Conventional wisdom in the mid-1980s still deemed monopolies in basic telephone service to be unbreakable, especially the extraordinarily profitable international voice market. As a result, the United States did not challenge the monopoly on international voice services, with the exception of the U.S. side of the connection (for example, Sprint competing with MCI for traffic originating in the United States). Thus, in 1984, when the United States allowed new competitors to INTELSAT for satellite services, the new entrants (such as PANAMSAT) were not permitted to provide traditional telephone services.

At the same time, the United States encouraged other countries to privatize their telephone systems and permit foreign investors to purchase them. The RBOCs, chafing under domestic restrictions, invested overseas to leverage their money and expertise in ways not permitted at home. As a result, they became collectively the most important global owners of foreign telephone, cellular, and cable systems. But U.S. antitrust policy limited how the RBOCs could interconnect between their foreign and domestic networks, thus reducing their incentives to push for competition in international telephone services.

It was not until the 1990s that the United States became serious about securing competition in international voice services. By then, the economics of one-sided competition in international telephone services were seriously distorting the market. For example, if one country lowered its international telephone rates due to domestic competition while the other country remained a monopoly, traffic flows became distorted. The low-priced country would send more messages than it received because lower prices stimulate demand. If the other country retained inflated accounting rates, it could reap enormous profits and growing surpluses. Settlements on accounting rates, which do not reflect costs accurately, represent a net transfer payment from U.S. customers to foreign carriers; indeed, intra-European accounting rates are significantly lower than those offered to U.S. carriers, although there is no economic justification for the practice. In 1992, for example, the United States had almost 3.5 million more minutes of outgoing telephone calls than it did incoming telephone calls. At an average of about $1 per minute in revenue, this represented about a $3.5 billion deficit on the U.S. balance of payments once the United States settled accounts with other countries.

One-sided competition also creates a problem for the individual competitive carrier. For instance, if AT&T sends 75 percent of all calls from the United States to France, it expects France Telecom to return the favor. However, if for some reason France Telecom wishes to punish AT&T, it can switch discretionary traffic, including nontelephone services, away from AT&T and effectively drop AT&T to a 50 percent share of return traffic.[17] As traffic in leased circuits and other new services grows, the question of who gets what share of the traffic becomes more important, yet regulatory protections against discrimination remain patchy.

The U.S. response as of 1992 was twofold. First, the Federal Communications Commission (FCC) instructed U.S. carriers to negotiate accounting rates that corresponded more closely to costs, especially in Europe and Asia. This would reduce the rate distortions that fueled the payments imbalance.[18] Second, the United States openly supported a move toward global competition in voice services. The question was how to achieve it.

A particularly difficult problem was the U.S. refusal to drop its own restrictions on foreign ownership (called "310[b]" after the legislation creating them). Most importantly, these rules limit foreign ownership of broadcasters and common carriers using radio licenses to no more than 25 percent of corporate stock. But the rules left some "wiggle room" for major foreign investment. For example, they did not prevent foreign companies like Cable and Wireless from establishing telephone companies using all wire-line facilities.

The new U.S. agenda meant that voice services would be as critical to the agenda for the distributed information revolution as value-added services were to the oligopoly revolution.

PARADOXICAL PROGRESS IN THE EQUIPMENT MARKET

The RBOC model had two consequences for world equipment markets. First, the United States advocated free trade in terminal equipment, including the right of customers to connect their own equipment freely to the public network. As a result, terminal equipment accounted for most changes in telecommunications equipment trade balances, especially because of the rapid entry of major Japanese firms into the American and European markets. Fax machines, key telephone sets, and cellular telephones accounted for the large Japanese trade surplus for equipment.[19] Analysts wondered if this loss of the mass consumer market to Japan would soon tip the network equipment market, where U.S. firms had retreated, to the Japanese advantage. Second, continuing network monopolies reinforced the stickiness of entry and change in network equipment markets. No one expected trade negotiators to open the network equipment market completely, but the United States demanded that government procurement policies for network equipment allow foreign bidding subject to reasonable rules governing local content.

Secondary or tertiary sourcing of network equipment from new foreign firms via local subsidiaries became more common.[20] But the new entrants usually held less than a quarter of the market, and foreign sales meant foreign investment to produce end systems while sourcing components from the home company.[21] Weaker firms disappeared and the consolidation left only six "first-tier" suppliers of traditional network equipment: AT&T, Northern Telecom, Ericsson, Alcatel, Siemens, and the Nippon Telephone and Telegraph (NTT) supply family, plus a few specialized suppliers of cellular networks (especially Motorola and Nokia). This number will shrink further.

As the center of the global market slowly shifted from North America and Europe, U.S. entrants had to catch up with entrenched suppliers in countries like India, China, Indonesia, and Mexico. U.S. diplomacy in support of this belated entry turned a few U.S. companies—such as AT&T and Motorola—into de facto American champions. The industry's economies of scale and scope, including learning by doing, justified this special treatment. (The strategy appears to be working; in 1992, $1 billion of AT&T's $10.8 billion sales of network equipment came from Asia.) But this preferred treatment also created a problem. The U.S. champions do not represent the full range of companies leading the distributed information revolution.

THE IMPLICATIONS OF THE DISTRIBUTED INFORMATION REVOLUTION

The distributed information revolution is redefining the payoffs from technological change. In the equipment market, it is blurring the lines between computing and telecommunications equipment; the highest growth rates are in equipment to support high-speed communications networks. The distributed information revolution also will drive up growth rates for services toward convergence with computer equipment by tapping other previously separate markets. Publishing and media products will become actively networked services subject to competition; computing software and applications will become much of the basis for networks serving mass markets and small business; cellular and wireless services markets will explode when interconnected to private corporate networking for data and voice; and competitively provided private networks will become interconnected independently of the public telephone networks, thereby making it much easier to exit from traditional telephone networks. Thus, just as the microprocessor and cheap memory revolutionized the computer industry in the 1980s, the networking of all kinds of services is transforming old definitions of market segments and changing the basis for competitive advantage.

More specifically, the "unbundling" and specialization of equipment and software applications redistributes rents from all-purpose hardware with lots of bundled software (such as the central office switch) to specialized equipment and software packages, and leads to rivalry among different types of specialized switches (for example, cellular network equipment).[22] Moreover, there is growing rivalry between software and equipment as market boundaries blur. New products, such as the global $8.5 billion industry in local area and enterprise-wide computing networks (markets that were tiny ten years ago), involve an intricate mix of software, hardware, and networking.

The revolution also will shift competitive advantages among communications networks. The distinction between specialized value-added networks and general telecommunications networks will often be a function of market positioning and regulation rather than any inherent technical distinctions. The largest networks with the highest levels of general functionality may not win out, even for many voice services. The winners will make money on small margins and constantly juggle products to enter changing market niches where profits may be a bit higher (as we see in mass software applications). This formula favors networks with higher labor productivity, faster response to market demands, and better capacity to provide sophisticated support services to customers (such as customized billing information). Winners will also leverage revenues off successful network features by getting other networks to pay fees for their use. (Indeed, like the airline industry, these features may be more profitable than most network services.) Because the mixture of desktop and traditional telecommunications networking will be volatile and innovative, the highest margins will go to those whose proprietary solutions to networking define the market. These firms will license their know-how, but they will also benefit from being the first to move in subsequent rounds of innovations. This is gloomy news for non-U.S. carriers who delayed liberalization while gambling that an "all-purpose" public network with wide scope and sophistication would fend off narrow specialists.

A rivalry over delivery systems will also extend to battles over content and pose new risks for carriers. A major struggle is developing among alternative delivery network technologies (such as cable and radio) for the delivery of services. Therefore, network providers want to increase their margins (and guarantee traffic flows) by integrating the production of content into their activities, as shown by the dizzying deals among carriers, film studios, and cable firms. These deals also transfer risk from content providers to carriers when large sums are at stake over finding markets for content. The inter-penetration of content and delivery systems also creates new conflicts over what is proprietary information about how to design and deliver content (as in the Macintosh computer interface) and what should be common knowledge shared by all carriers in order to make multimedia networks interoperable.

REVISITING DOMESTIC POLICIES

The advent of the distributed information revolution has forced the major in-dustrial countries to revisit their prior policy choices. The debate in the United States focused on three questions about competition and network development. Had network investment accelerated rapidly enough for broadband networks? Had the United States stimulated enough technical cooperation among suppliers and customers to develop the broadband network? Had the United States done enough to make the emerging information highway accessible to a mass consumer audience?

The policy response of the Clinton administration to date has been to use competition to drive down costs and create new infrastructure; to accelerate competition by opening up cross-entry in all segments of the communications network (for example, AT&T into cellular services and the RBOCs into information services); to create a several-billion-dollar program of "demand pull" stimulus through the supercomputing network and demonstration projects designed to build common applications (especially for quasi-public sector users like schools) and interoperable networking standards that would open new markets, thereby justifying further infrastructure investment; and to shift subsidies for an expanded definition of universal service more directly to users rather than to the carriers.

Even as they supported major new programs to increase spending on advanced networks, Japan and the European Union also acknowledged problems created by extensive regulation. For example, Japan's sluggish network environment had led Japanese computer firms to follow IBM's flawed strategies for the information future. By 1994, NTT began partnerships with U.S. firms leading in distributed information technologies (such as Silicon Graphics) to restructure its network capabilities. The Japanese government was still contemplating a breakup of NTT to further stimulate competition. Meanwhile, the Commission of the European Community concluded that monopoly telephone environments provided inappropriate incentives for the development of equipment and service. In 1994, the European Union backed competition in long-distance services by 1998, including competition in providing network infrastructure. This new policy convergence in support of competition, however, does not resolve the question of how to make global competition work while stimulating the development of the global information infrastructure.

COMPETITIVE IMPLICATIONS OF THE DISTRIBUTED INFORMATION REVOLUTION

The distributed information revolution raises three fundamental problems. First, will the IBM mainframe story be revisited in telecom services and network equipment? In retrospect, U.S. progress in liberalizing terminal equipment was even more important than originally recognized. While Japan reaped the oligopoly revolution's benefits from competition in products with slowly changing standards, such as fax machines, U.S. producers have dominated the distributed information revolution's markets for solutions created by fast-changing technologies employing proprietary standards, such as bridgers and hubs for corporate networking. As freedom of terminal equipment and the distributed information revolution expand, this "crossover equipment" market (such as superservers for video networks) will take market share away from the traditional network equipment market, which will remain more protectionist. Novell, a supplier of computer networking systems, may one day face off against Alcatel, a supplier of telephone network switches. Specialized electronics and computer suppliers think that they will control the interface linking television sets to interactive networks. While the United States

needs to compete strongly in the market for telecommunications network equipment, the bigger payoffs may come in this new crossover market, much as
success in the market for personal computers and software was more vital than
winning in the mainframe computer market.

Second, as raised above, are traditional telecommunications networks likely
to dominate growth in the new global network environment? The new prizes may be
in the software used to design networks, as in the Microsoft software for interactive
networking, or in the specialized application networks, such as America Online or
electronic data interchange systems for commerce. Can traditional telecommunications networks compete against specialized networks with less expensive
equipment and fewer employees per revenue dollar? The U.S. restructuring showed
just how much rationalization of telephone companies even the limited oligopoly
revolution could force. Most fundamentally, traditional carriers may find that large
parts of their physical plant are obsolete due to new content and technology
packages. This applies both to terrestrial and radio carriers. Therefore, networks
may encounter financial problems due to speculation, surplus capacity, or low
margins because of their failure to adapt to the market or inadequate modernization
(if the carrier cannot afford to write off old plant fast enough). Moreover, new
network entrants may doom the RBOC model for global services.

Third, is the problem of market access timing even more critical in the
distributed information revolution? The architecture for future information
technology, including the entire mix of equipment and services, is in transition. Will
what emerges resemble the U.S. approach of decentralized computing with flexible
standards on custom-tailored networks? One important determinant will be how
fast "learning by doing" (or "hands-on" applications) about specific products and
network standards can take place across a variety of national environments at an
early date. The Clinton administration's emphasis on government-sponsored
consortia to advance such learning makes access to foreign consortia for such
purposes critical. So, too, is the timing of market access—a technology must be
available at the time of transition if it is to influence the path of change.

THE NEW GLOBAL NETWORK

The problem of timing is especially important for innovative global networks.
Competition in facilities means that a new service provider may be able to put
together the lowest-cost package for delivering complex applications. The
network provider does not even have to own all the transmission facilities
because leasing and resale of circuits can substitute for ownership of facilities.
This is changing the basic economics of the global market.[23]

Suppose that Ford Motor Company (one of the two thousand multinational
corporations targeted by all international carriers) contracts with an international
carrier for integrated global communication services called "virtual private
networks." Ford buys a certain level of global network capacity each month for
service between itself and its major suppliers, and between itself and other

selected organizations, such as its law firms. (This qualifies as a "closed user group" that may legally bypass conventional telephone services in many countries.) The carrier in the United States runs dedicated lines directly to the major Ford operating centers, bypassing completely the local telephone company. It then carries the Ford traffic overseas on its long-distance transmission network. But that traffic is traveling overseas by means of a leased circuit (or its own fiber capacity)—not by way of a jointly provided telephone call. Moreover, the carrier takes the international circuit to a point of presence—a telephone switch and transmission termination point—as close as possible physically to the major Ford affiliates, thus minimizing the use of local telephone services. In some cases, the carrier still needs to lease a circuit from the local telephone company, but it does so using a flat leased rate instead of call by call. In this way, Ford would deal with only one telephone company carrier, enjoy a predictable bill (except for the cost of local telephone services), and rely on a network whose software and services are configured precisely to its needs. On the negative side, Ford may have "lock-in" costs created by optimizing around a carrier's particular offerings.

Which firm can best serve a company like Ford? The candidates are betting on the creation of common operating vehicles that can provide one-stop shopping for major customers, integrate technology to provide innovative quick responses, and create a powerful marketing organization. The $4.3 billion purchase in June 1993 of 20 percent of MCI by British Telecom and its creation of a commonly owned company, Concert, to provide international services to large users is the boldest example to date. The British Telecom investment in MCI helps the two companies align their pricing, technologies, and service approaches.[24] Sprint announced plans in June 1994 for a similar arrangement in which France Telecom and Deutsche Bundespost Telekom would pay $4.3 billion for 20 percent of Sprint, if regulatory authorities approved. In response, AT&T, KDD of Japan, Unisource (a common corporation owned by the Dutch, Spanish, Swedish, and Swiss telephone companies), and Singapore Telecoms have formed a joint venture for "WorldSource" virtual private network services that has a common holding company, WorldPartners, in which they each hold equity. Unlike the MCI and Sprint deals, the WorldSource partners do not hold equity investments in one another.

For all their publicity, these ventures may fail. AT&T ultimately chose to buy all of McCaw rather than only 20 percent because it concluded that integrating the two companies' networks and services effectively with only 20 percent ownership was not feasible. If this was thought to be unworkable within one national market, why should it succeed across national borders? International strategic alliances are especially prone to failure, and the Sprint and AT&T arrangements seem to be even less tightly integrated than Concert.[25] Moreover, except for its private networking component, these alliances still operate under the rigidities of accounting rates and other international regulations for voice services.

An alternative to these vehicles involving equity investments is franchising, the method through which McDonald's and Sheraton Hotels have become global market leaders. These two companies own only a small percentage of the restaurants and hotels that bear their names. Franchises succeed because the parent company creates an idea for a service product, develops and tests a successful model for implementation, builds a strong reputation for its service and methods, carefully selects local franchisees capable of upholding the standards of the company, and then invests in creating a global infrastructure of support services (ranging from a global reservation system to the creation of "hamburger universities" to train managers). They also spend heavily on marketing and monitoring to adapt the product to the local market and assure that the franchisees uphold the firm's reputation.

Hotels and hamburger franchises may seem an odd parallel to the technological wonders of modern networks. But technology often requires a rethinking of basic business models before it revolutionizes markets. This reconceptualization of the telecommunications network is as much about pursuing mass markets as it is about serving giant customers.

The franchising model has surfaced in commercial arrangements between the United States and Canada, which only recently introduced competition in long-distance services. MCI has licensed its proprietary network software to Stentor, Canada's leading long-distance carrier, for a $150 million fee. This included, for example, the MCI software for extremely customized billing and highly targeted provision of 800-service numbers. The agreement also included arrangements to facilitate coordination of pricing on certain services and to advertise jointly for cross-border services. AT&T responded by making a similar arrangement with Stentor's new Canadian competitor.[26] In essence, MCI and AT&T were franchising their approach to complex advanced services and their brand-name reputation to their Canadian partners (Stentor would advertise that it offered MCI's service packages). Stentor is not going to become MCI Canada, but it is featuring the service concept and delivery approach of MCI, just as a hotel in Tokyo might feature a franchise of Maxim's of Paris. And MCI announced in 1994 that it would take on a major Mexican bank as a partner to offer private network services in Mexico and apply for a long-distance license in the MCI name (even though MCI will be the minority equity owner). Similarly, Worldsource essentially franchises AT&T's name brand and capacities for advanced corporate networks.

Franchising requires a strong brand name attached to a product trusted by customers. It may be a particularly desirable option as long as international regulations restrict competition on jointly provided services (by requiring proportional sharing of traffic and revenue splits) because it allows innovative carriers to leverage revenues off software and marketing assets while reducing bills for overseas facilities. It also may be attractive for software firms seeking to address global multimedia markets for small businesses and households, such as Microsoft's deals with NTT to experiment with using Microsoft software on the NTT network.

Still, franchising may never deliver on the need for quickly responsive, cost-competitive innovations and pricing on a global basis. It is conceivable that no international consortium of telephone companies acting as equal partners for international services will be able to achieve the distinctive cachet or flexible performance required for a strong franchise. As a result, the ultimate winners may be those firms gambling on becoming "global carriers."

Global carriers aim to establish end-to-end control over delivery of services to business centers globally and to contract with national carriers only for local service deliveries. Think of Federal Express as a model. Or think of the national network developing into something like a "virtual shopping mall" hosting a variety of department stores provided by the global carriers.

Unisource has elements of being a global carrier, as does Concert. The extension of this approach would require the most sweeping changes in global regulations and competitive strategies. It would abolish jointly provided services for switched telephone traffic except as a voluntary contractual option for individual carriers. Access charges for connecting to national networks might replace international accounting rates. With their extensive overseas holdings, the RBOCs, Cable and Wireless of the United Kingdom, and Telefonica of Spain are best positioned to explore this strategy—albeit selectively. For example, as a first step in this direction, digital radio services could challenge traditional networking economics because such services can skip international settlements procedures. For example, cellular carriers may lease circuits for their major international calling routes and then load them onto the network of a foreign carrier as a local call (thereby circumventing the accounting rate procedure), as one company in Europe with several European cellular franchises is planning to do.[27]

In short, the framework for regulating international services needs serious revision because it hinders new alternatives better suited for the distributed information revolution. U.S. policy has already evolved in response to the MCI deal. To simplify the story, BT-MCI sought approval of its investment after a U.S. government review of its 310(b) and antitrust rules. It also filed with the FCC to offer its own virtual private network and to establish international simple resale (ISR) of leased circuits connected to the public network between the United States and Great Britain. It did *not* ask to end the traditional system of accounting rates and jointly provided services for basic inter-national telephone services.

In response, AT&T acknowledged that British law allowed easy competitive entry into its domestic telecommunications market. But BT's continued dominance of the market let BT hamper the entry of new rivals, especially because there were few regulatory safeguards to restrain BT. Moreover, the United Kingdom still allowed only two competitors (a duopoly) for international telephone facilities—BT and Cable and Wireless. Thus, AT&T argued, practical entry and competition in Great Britain and between Great Britain and the United States were not assured.

The U.S. government's antitrust and regulatory reviews (including sidebar consultations with the United Kingdom) prompted the British government to create additional regulatory safeguards to protect new competitors. While the duopoly policy for international facilities remained, AT&T understood that it would receive a license to operate a telecommunications network in the domestic

British market. The British government also granted ISR rights to U.S. carriers (the next best thing to facilities-based competition), with the expectation that the United States would later reciprocate. For its part, the FCC granted a waiver on 310(b) restrictions because it concluded that the BT-MCI deal would increase competitive efficiency in the market. At the same time, the United States imposed numerous competitive safeguards on the venture in order to assure that BT did not discriminate against other U.S. carriers.[28]

To summarize, the U.S. government believed that British policy generally favored competition in all market segments except ownership of international facilities. It also knew that many U.S. companies were establishing themselves successfully in the United Kingdom. Thus, the BT-MCI deal was a relatively easy case. The question was what to do in markets where competition was less well established. AT&T argued strongly that the United States faced a "do or die" choice about achieving global competition. It claimed that U.S. approval of the BT-MCI deal had gutted the 310(b) limits on foreign ownership of U.S. telephone carriers. If the Sprint deal also was approved, foreign carriers would have great influence over two major U.S. international carriers, while the United States failed to win reciprocal foreign entry for U.S. competitors.

PROCUREMENT CODES: A RECIPE FOR THE EQUIPMENT MARKET?

U.S. diplomacy involving equipment issues faced difficulties comparable to those for services. Foreign firms have significant shares of every part of the U.S. home market. American companies run a trade surplus with Europe in tele-communications equipment but are weak in the network equipment markets of France and Germany. Network sales have increased significantly in Japan but remain small. The United States criticizes both trade partners, but contradicts itself in doing so. It stresses Japanese failure to buy more even though it is subject to elaborate procedural safeguards, then criticizes the European Union for lack of safeguards even though the United States runs a surplus with Europe. The United States still does not know what it wants.

The frustrations regarding Japan reveal the shortcomings of one of the strategies of the past fifteen years—forcing liberalization by ever-more minute codes of conduct. In 1981, Washington won the first procurement agreement governing conduct by NTT, a code that has remained in place despite NTT's partial privatization.[29] By 1986, NTT purchased about $250 million of foreign equipment. This amount rose to $1 billion by 1992, with the United States accounting for over 90 percent of the total (including Northern Telecom in switching, Siecor in fiber cable, and AT&T in transmission and switching). Nonetheless, NTT continues to reserve about 60 percent of key equipment markets for the NTT family; foreign suppliers provide less than 6 percent of sourcing of NTT investment (this figure includes significant purchases of paper imports for telephone books as investment). In the case of KDD, the former Japanese monopolist for international long-distance services, less than 3 percent of its network is provided by foreign suppliers, and it is not subject to special procurement rules.[30]

The Clinton administration tried to tighten the procurement code when it used the Motorola negotiations with IDO as a model for designing new trade agreements based on quantifiable measures of progress, a process that Japan denounced as managed trade incompatible with the GATT. Japan marshaled considerable international support for its position; other countries feared there would be no restraint on the United States if its demands on others implied no obligations on itself. Costless ambition (even in the global public interest) is a dangerous thing in the eyes of cautious diplomats.

Similar problems plague reciprocity proposals for government procurement regulations. For example, the European Union placed all major carriers under its procurement authority, set rules mirroring the "Buy America" act of the United States, and then requested reciprocal treatment from the United States.[31] The EU argued that the issue was more than who owned a carrier; the carrier's market dominance should also count. The EU claimed that dominant carriers like the Baby Bells and AT&T should be subject to the GATT procurement code.

The United States rejected the European position. During the GATT talks, the United States and the European Union traded EU access to U.S. state and local government procurement for U.S. access to European telecommunications procurement, but neither side found the other's specific offer satisfactory. They will continue to negotiate until 1996. Ironically, the RBOCs could pass any reasonable procurement test: EU companies (led by Siemens) have 18 percent of the U.S. switching market, Japan does well in transmission plant, and Alcatel recently won a big contract for transmission equipment from AT&T.[32]

In short, the United States claims correctly that equipment markets require further liberalization. Specialized codes and agreements going beyond broad GATT frameworks on procurement and other issues may be necessary. But what alternative organizing principle can work? Ironically, the most important action may be in achieving effective implementation of rules on liberalizing terminal equipment markets where agreement on the principles of liberalization were reached years ago. It is in the advanced equipment and software interconnecting to the traditional communications market where the United States enjoys great competitive advantages and where the market is growing most quickly. This is where the distributed information revolution is exploding.

ASSESSING INTERNATIONAL STRATEGIES

What are the United States' global interests in the distributed information revolution? There are different objectives for producers of equipment and services, investors in foreign telecommunications franchises, and customers. The challenge is to recognize the long-term priorities the principal stakeholders have in common—propagating the U.S. approach to the distributed information revolution. The shared goals are threefold:

1. Establish the viability of the American distributed information revolution as a global competitive strategy involving customized, price-driven, distributed computing and communications capabilities with maximum ease of market entry and exit.

2. Assure interconnectivity of evolving global communications and information networks while protecting intellectual property rights. Leverage American demonstration projects in applications and network management/control into models for global networking. Emphasize that successful applications of the technology require appropriate, procompetitive regulations.

3. Assure flexible routes for foreign market access for U.S. firms. In a digital world there must be choices between access by direct sales of software or equipment, deploying a network, or creating a joint venture.

U.S. strategy deserves good marks to date in advancing these goals. But the distributed information revolution will require further reevaluation of some key policies.

A BENCHMARK FOR MARKET ACCESS

While there is no perfect answer to what constitutes adequate market access, the U.S. government needs a better benchmark. Under classic GATT rules, as long as the process was adequate (in, for example, honoring tariff commitments and non-discrimination), one simply raised complaints on an ad hoc basis. In fact, many markets had significant trade barriers, and trade partners made rough estimation of their tolerability. Frequently, quiet accommodation satisfied both parties while everyone continued to believe that general tariff reductions would fuel steady progress toward world market integration. As border barriers, such as tariffs and quotas, become less important, it becomes harder to judge good-faith compliance with particular trade obligations and assess general progress toward integration. Accordingly, we need clearer benchmarks for measuring how market segments fit together.

Effective market access (or contestability) is the U.S. objective. This goal permits each country to pursue reasonable social welfare goals and limited industrial policies to develop national comparative advantage. Within this framework, the United States has three concerns. First, it should judge both equipment and services in computing and communications contexts. Services should include major networked applications. (For example, will U.S. movies and interactive software management systems have access to new European interactive television networks?) It also means that the United States has to consider whether firms have flexible routes of entry into the market. (If individual customers have freedom to choose and buy their own equipment, it is less vital for U.S. firms to be able to sell terminal equipment to cellular networks.) Second, U.S. firms need to win commercial access to development opportunities for emerging technology processes and applications. All major industrial regions are experimenting with mixed public-private initiatives to develop technologies and key applications that will stimulate markets. The United States needs access to these experiments on nondiscriminatory terms. Third, timing is critical for global competition. The most serious complaint against Japan is that the country retards effective access to foreign firms until major opportunities for a generation of technology have passed.

Market access is not the same as a demand for "mirror-image" reciprocity between national markets. Two examples show why such an approach could harm U.S. interests. France sold its smallest network equipment supplier in 1987 to Ericsson because U.S. and German government initiatives on behalf of purchase bids by AT&T and Siemens, respectively, had created a diplomatic deadlock. Germany had argued that Alcatel's subsidiary had a substantial share of its market, and reciprocity would be fair play. The lesson? Narrow demands for reciprocity may harm the United States in regional markets where it is not dominant (and the United States remains a small player in most high growth markets). Similarly, the United States has restrictions that could harm its claims for foreign access. The United States' archaic limits on foreign ownership—the 310(b) provisions—exceed those of the United Kingdom and could have been used to deny access to U.S. firms under strict reciprocity. In short, reciprocity is often a classic case of the best being the enemy of the good.

A Constitution for Bilateral Diplomacy

The three criteria for market access suggest that the United States should address particular problems in the European Union but that the problems with Japan must take precedence. Foreign penetration of the Japanese information market as a whole is far smaller than in the rest of the world.

At the same time, the United States must recognize that other countries object to the U.S. tendency to set international standards unilaterally. Even when they agree with U.S. complaints, other countries fear that American wrath may be turned unpredictably against them later. Once begun, the bilateral process invites others to play the same game. Even if the United States acts reasonably, the same may not be true of others. Bilateral crusades also weaken the ability to manage global interests coherently. While the United States has global interests, bilateral remedies often focus on selective problems, and the sum of the remedies does not necessarily serve the global interest. Indeed, they may create a kind of political "double jeopardy": Bilateral agreements may fix enough specific problems to make every special interest less willing to sacrifice on behalf of a general political settlement through the GATT.[33]

Therefore, the United States needs to make sure that bilateral agreements serve multilateral interests, both to allay diplomatic objections and to simplify its own task. Generally, an earnest attempt is made to explain how bilateral pacts can assist multilateral progress. But the United States needs some new device to further reassure its trading partners. To this end, the United States should endorse "multilateral impact statements" on bilateral pacts that would articulate how the bilateral agreement advances multilateral principles. Parties to bilateral agreements would need to make them conform to GATT obligations, as was the case with the U.S.-Japan semiconductor agreement setting a target of a 20 percent foreign share of the Japanese market. Such parties would also have to state how innovative arrangements fit their general international trade and regulatory obligations. In short, concessions asked from others could become the basis for claims made against one's own country, thereby converting bilateral pacts into something akin to common law precedents for general commercial diplomacy.

The impact statements would also provide structure for the growing links between domestic policies and international commercial obligations, such as international accountability for the setting of technical standards. The information industry needs faster decisions than those provided by harmonization (common international rules governing domestic regulations) but less sweeping ones than simple mutual recognition of national regulations as practiced in the EU.[34]

"Trade-related oversight" is the best solution. Countries can pursue their own preferred form and mix of regulations as long as these do not interfere with existing international commercial obligations. When a regulation is challenged, a country must show that its choice is not intentionally discriminatory and does not impose unfair damage on foreign interests. If the damage is unacceptable, the country may still follow the general policy but must introduce modifications to mitigate damage to foreign interests. One way to evaluate a contested domestic policy would be to examine the precedents claimed in the nation's impact statements.[35]

The final element in the constitution of commercial diplomacy is achieving strong industrywide codes under the GATT. The Uruguay Round could not resolve all differences over the extension of telecommunications service agreements to voice telephony nor end the discord over procurement decisions. In the end, the governments adopted something like conditional reciprocity: There are tiers of agreement where larger concessions will be exchanged only by those willing to take on special rights and duties. While adopted in part to avoid deadlock, this approach facilitates the creation of general rules for specific industries under the umbrella of the GATT. The deadline for these negotiations is April 1996. The negotiations demand the strongest attention of the U.S. government. But, even assuming that they succeed, they still provide only a framework for the global market. The question is what the United States wants to achieve substantively.

THE APPROACH TO EQUIPMENT ISSUES

The United States should have three guidelines for organizing commerce in the equipment market. It should first reaffirm its commitment to promoting entry into networks and facilities markets around the world in order to create networks that do not involve long-standing commitments to local national champions. New entrants can profit from the crossover equipment in which the United States excels.

This leads to a related, second position. The degree of competition in service networks plus private ownership of the networks should be the two criteria that determine the necessity of special procurement codes. This standard monitors the worst perverse incentives for equipment procurement— government entities that do not respond to commercial incentives and very restricted competition that makes it easier for even private firms to subsidize local suppliers.[36] The merit of this standard comes out in the case of IDO in Japan. IDO is partly owned by a state corporation (the Japanese National Highway Corporation), its sole competitor is NTT (a predominantly state firm), and Japan denied competitive entry to a carrier that would have supported the standard used in much of the rest of the national market. Ironically, stumbling on procurement talks in the Uruguay Round has also changed the situation facing the RBOCs. The U.S. position at GATT had ignored the fact that AT&T was not only private but was in a fully competitive market. In contrast, the RBOCs were private but had a quasimonopoly. With their strong record of foreign purchasing and growing competition in local services, the RBOCs now could win an exemption from procurement rules. In contrast, Alcatel could not buy France Telecom and win an exemption from the procurement code if there were still substantial elements of local service monopolies.

Third, the distributed information revolution means that the United States has to give as much attention to terminal equipment and the new networking equipment (such as the bridgers for private networking) as it does to traditional applications like central office switching. It should lower trade barriers to terminal and new networking equipment to levels no higher than those for desktop computers while advocating users' freedom of choice about how to interconnect to networks. In particular, the United States has to involve the smaller and newer suppliers early in the process of reexamining issues concerning local content (such as, how much value added has to occur in Europe in order for a product to be considered European), spectrum allocation, intellectual property, and standards setting.

TRADE DIPLOMACY AND THE NEXT GENERATION OF SERVICES

The controversy over moving toward competitive entry in voice services requires applying basic priorities judiciously. The United States wants more flexible competition in the distributed information revolution, not a balancing of the fates of individual carriers to every letter of the regulatory writ. U.S. policy should be encouraging facilities competition, creating a framework for more complete liberalization, and emphasizing participation of a new generation of users and producers in decisions about global network policies.

To begin, the United States should reaffirm its respect for regulatory diversity as long as it does not create harmful asymmetries in commercial relations. The global standard is still adherence to the RBOC model. But countries following the RBOC model should face a much tougher regulatory scrutiny of their communications and information service exports to the United States. Countries claiming to adopt a more competitive model (as the European Union will by 1998) should be made to prove it. The United States also has no obligation to cross-subsidize other countries' strategies by means of international accounting rates.

Second, the United States should continually promote liberalization of facilities. As alternative facilities grow, the United States can relax its minute oversight of monopoly bottlenecks. Instead, it should push to reduce restrictions on interconnection of new national and international facilities. Moreover, because one can measure the degree of effective facilities alternatives, the United States should accept fewer regulatory safeguards in countries with comparable indices of facilities alternatives to the United States.

Third, regulatory review of alliances like those of Sprint with France Telecom and Deutsche Telekom ideally should prompt negotiation on a comprehensive agreement on liberalization. The three countries (and perhaps the EC) should agree on what they minimally want under full liberalization. They could then take temporary derogations on specific measures and could agree to speedy arbitration on questions of compliance under a preestablished dispute resolution mechanism. The parties would also develop indicators for measuring and comparing such regulatory features as access charges between the two countries. The purpose is to develop common baselines for evaluation, much as was done in arms control agreements. Equally important, the United States should insist on strong mechanisms for the representation of U.S. users and producers in administrative rulemaking in other countries.

The agreement should have a strict time frame (perhaps two or three years). Failure to complete liberalization by the end of the pact would lead to automatic reversion to the status quo prevailing before the pact. The objective would be to tackle the end game of liberalization up front rather than by ad hoc advances. Once the two sides have formed the framework, investment by the interested suppliers will create specialized capabilities that will be at risk if the governments renege (because of the automatic cancellation provision). Moreover, customers will provide significant incentives to comply. Customers will be less likely to sign on with the Sprint group if they worry that it could face penalties within two years because of a failure to achieve the promised liberalization in France or Germany.

This ideal strategy lays out the logic of what should be done. But negotiation may be impractical, as it would be lengthy and could complicate the GATT talks on voice services. Also, U.S. law gives primary jurisdiction in these matters to the Department of Justice (due to antitrust issues) and the FCC, not to trade authorities. As for the European Commission, it is preoccupied with internal market reform. As a result, the actual process of establishing an international framework for competition is likely to resemble the one for the BT-MCI deal.

France, Germany, and the EU may change their policies unilaterally in order to ease U.S. concerns about competition, just as the United Kingdom did. For its part, the U.S. government will use regulatory and antitrust proceedings to set the ground rules. However obliquely stated, those rules will include terms that other countries' policies must meet before the United States will accept a deal. Later on, the United States might agree to tinker with its rules as part of a GATT agreement on voice services.

How the rules are set is less important than what they are trying to achieve. The goal, quite simply, is to secure a competitive global market for all forms of communications and information services. The Sprint and MCI deals are only way stations en route to this goal.

BRINGING NEW PLAYERS INTO THE POLICY PROCESS

The bilateral trade talks illustrate the problem of relying on trade policy for promoting American global interests in informatics. Policy responses are too slow and the follow-up on trade talks is sporadic. The U.S. trade system is especially prone to the "too little, too late" syndrome: The trade system is geared to complaints, not to anticipating the competitive problems of U.S. companies. As long as the system relies largely on the USTR as firefighter for those complaining loudest, the United States will remain one step behind. Worse yet, being late makes it harder to resolve issues quietly and the charged atmosphere often impedes the ability to reach the best package. Worst of all, policy may become the tool of those companies that play the complaining game the best. This is especially worrisome now that the distributed information revolution is greatly expanding the numbers and types of firms involved in the world market. Trade policy can no longer be the realm of traditional producers, like IBM and AT&T, and traditional users, like the big banks, who do not represent the full promise of the distributed information revolution.

The United States must reexamine its own regulatory and trade advisory processes to give new weight to companies now relatively absent from the process, such as many software firms, content firms, and new equipment providers that lie at the core of the distributed information revolution. It is not so much that they are discriminated against by existing procedures as that they are not particularly attuned to the consultative maze of international telecommunications policy. However, the government cannot carry out an effective global policy unless these firms are active at home and in administrative processes abroad.

Such participation is vital because the information revolution has created a new generation of regulatory challenges: How regulation at home unbundles network services, how it treats control over numbering, and how it controls information about the calling patterns of users will set a benchmark for reciprocity arrangements globally. Many important network innovations will involve novel forms of networking like interactive gaming and computing. Here the real test may be less over foreign interconnect charges than over choices about intellectual property protection, competition policy governing network franchising, and open standards. Moreover, questions may arise that are tantamount to antidumping and government subsidy trade questions—for example, how to treat the tax relief and public lending needed to encourage network modernization or how to relieve major carriers who run into financial trouble and need to write off large parts of their older network plant rapidly. In this arena, domestic policy is international policy. This places a great burden on a country prone to making domestic policy with minimum attention to global consequences. It is even more difficult if the key players in the domestic market are not part of international policy discussions, and firms like Microsoft and Time Warner Cable have not usually been involved in international telecommunications negotiations.

DEMONSTRATION EFFECTS AND TECHNOLOGY DEVELOPMENT

U.S. trade policy should be only one part of international competition strategy. U.S. diplomacy also has to persuade the world of the virtues of the American version of the distributed information revolution. This will take more than trade initiatives. It will take leadership in showing how the new system can benefit everyone, especially developing nations.

The success of trade diplomacy in the oligopoly revolution depended partly on a demonstration effect. In the 1980s, the United States showed that the technology of computer networking and private voice networks could be unleashed without dire consequences. Today, demonstration projects and research on new applications could develop new political clienteles in support of the changes brought about by the American approach to the distributed information revolution. Thus, a broader strategy for embedding trade within the development of a global information highway is necessary. The Clinton administration gets high marks for endorsing this goal but the bulk of its practical attention had remained largely fixed on domestic aspects of the information highway.

The serious work on how to make the new networking succeed will be done in the industrialized world. The United States should invite the United Kingdom (and perhaps other highly liberalized countries) to create joint exercises in developing prototype applications for information networks, emphasizing "openness, heterogeneity, interoperability, scalability, and ease of use," and to develop principles on how to make the creation of technical standards more market driven.[37] There is, for example, a need to find new ways to cope with the challenges created by innovative competition. Diverse entry and network experimentation raises the risks of networks crashing. Finding ways to assure safety by assessing and managing risks, not by banning competition, should be a major goal of collaborative international projects.

An activist technology policy also must support desired rules of international trade. For example, the United States needs consistent domestic and international policies regarding the terms for foreign firms that belong to government-sponsored consortia for research and development; much of the proposed legislation on the subject clashes with standards that the United States wants other countries to maintain.

Finally, the Clinton administration has endorsed experiments on how to extend the information infrastructure to developing countries. But global exercises are often slower than well-designed bilateral approaches. One hybrid might be to create "showcases" by inviting selected countries and U.S. companies to propose special prototype projects on new applications of the distributed information revolution designed for their markets. The agreement might include, for example, package deals about intellectual property and regulatory reform as part of a project that uses wireless technology to distribute data to rural hospitals. The U.S. government would provide technical assistance for the policy reforms and perhaps financial guarantees to make it easier to obtain project financing. In the end, the global information highway must cross the borders of all nations. Neither traditional regulation nor economic assistance alone will suffice to realize this goal.

POLICY RECOMMENDATIONS

The distributed information revolution forces invention in the halls of government, not just in the digital paths from one computing frontier to the next. These innovations should:

▼ Establish the promotion of the U.S. approach to the distributed information revolution as the goal of U.S. information diplomacy. This entails a mix of trade, regulatory, and technology promotion policies.

▼ Endorse market access as the chief trade policy goal. Such a policy recognizes the interdependence of rules governing networks and equipment, the importance of international rules governing research and development, and the critical question of timing for competition in digital technology. Avoid attempts to impose strict reciprocity for market access while emphasizing market access for all countries as a goal of bilateral diplomacy.

▼ Adopt innovations, such as multilateral impact statements and industry-specific codes, to reconcile bilateral diplomacy with multilateral rule building.

▼ Judge equipment procurement obligations for telephone companies according to the type of ownership and the degree of competition in the services market. Give greater attention to terminal equipment and the new networking equipment and software.

▼   Promote further regulatory reforms for global services. The next generation
    of global networking may not fit the regulatory framework of jointly provided
    services, and there will be many different forms of networking with different
    commercial realities in each segment. The U.S. strategy should encourage
    competition in international facilities and a new framework for more
    complete liberalization of all services and the use of time schedules for
    obligations to liberalize.

▼   Reform U.S. policymaking processes for international markets to induce
    much greater participation by the new generation of suppliers and users
    who play a critical role in the distributed information revolution. Otherwise,
    a crippling disjuncture between domestic and international regulatory
    priorities may arise.

▼   Embed trade diplomacy in a complementary technology cooperation policy
    to create a positive "demonstration effect" based on the U.S. approach to
    information technology. Such a technology cooperation program requires
    separate (but complementary) components for projects among industrial
    nations, undertakings with developing countries, and rule making to
    reconcile the obligations of technology projects with market access rules.

8

WHY THE GLOBAL VILLAGE CANNOT AFFORD INFORMATION SLUMS

BRUNO LANVIN

If we truly believe in a global economy, then we must ensure that all regions of the world have the basic technology required to participate fully in that economy.
—Robert E. Allen, Chairman of the Board, AT&T (1991)[1]

A few years ago, to policymakers in most of the Second and Third Worlds, the notion of a "global information economy" was little more than a trendy vision of a coterie of Western academics. Today, with the collapse of the Berlin Wall and the rapid spread of market-based approaches to the economies of the East and South, most decisionmakers of developing countries and the former Soviet bloc have changed their perception of the importance of participating in the global information economy. By and large, however, they are not optimistic.

Meanwhile, in the industrialized countries, the discussion of information highways has moved from being an issue only in the United States (with the Clinton administration's strategy for a national information infrastructure, or NII), and has expanded quickly to other developed countries, especially those of Western Europe.[2] Yet the United States is still significantly more advanced than its partners in terms of both the conceptualization and the policy implications of information infrastructure issues. This is why the United States is presently (but not for long) in a unique position to offer innovative ideas and proposals on how and why global information infrastructures should be promoted. The elements presented by President Clinton at the Group of Seven meeting in Naples, Italy, provide a sound basis for these discussions, but need to be broadened beyond a strictly Group of Seven context. This is the goal of this chapter.

As information and telecommunications become the pivotal elements of international economic competition, the relative endowments of the 190-some countries of this planet remain strikingly uneven. About 30 percent of the world's population, roughly 1.3 billion people, live below the "absolute poverty threshold," according to the World Bank. Most of these live in sub-Saharan Africa and in the heavily populated parts of the Asian continent. One easy-to-remember set of numbers is this triplet: 77 percent of the world's population owns just 7 percent of the total wealth of the planet and 0.7 percent of its telephones. The similarity between the distribution of income per capita and the density of telephone lines is striking. One should, of course, refrain from judgments about causality: The similarity in proportions does not mean that a higher density of telephone lines automatically entails a higher standard of living. The correlation also works the other way: Those countries that can afford the technology and investment necessary for a viable national telecommunications system have the highest densities of telecommunications equipment. Causal questions notwithstanding, once one considers the economic benefits forgone in the absence of adequate telecommunications, it is clear that this correlation demands immediate attention and urgent action if the vicious cycle of underdevelopment is to be broken.

Moreover, the correlations described above are only part of the uneven reality of the "global" information economy. First, since the data represent national aggregates, they obscure disparities within national populations, such as the total absence of telecommunications facilities in many rural areas. Second, it requires much more than the existence of a telephone line to achieve "connectivity" in the global information economy: The quality of the service provided (particularly in terms of speed, reliability, and integrity) is more important to potential investors and trading partners than the mere number of operable sets.

If present disparities in the distribution of telecommunications facilities were to persist, the global information economy would be global in name only. It would be plagued by economic conflicts, political tensions, and endless negotiations that would produce only halfhearted compromises. Much of the potential worldwide benefits for international trade, employment, and socioeconomic development would be sacrificed, and there would be further delay in reaping the full benefits of a new industrial revolution. The information age will be global, or it will not be.

It is not as if these issues have gone unnoticed. In the 1980s, the Maitland Commission was assigned by the International Telecommunications Union (ITU) to investigate the status of telecommunications development worldwide.[3] The commission represented one of the best combinations of talent and experience available. Its work was remarkable for its quality and for the relevance of its conclusions and recommendations. It was not idealistic and it did not moralize. Instead, it pointed precisely toward the ways and means to achieve those objectives that the international community had long considered its priorities. Yet the Maitland recommendations (in particular those regarding the necessary mobilization of international funding for setting up basic telecommunications infrastructures in the Third World) remain unfulfilled. If the finest of blue-ribbon committees failed to mobilize international interest in integrating less advanced countries into the global information economy, what are the chances now?

To answer this question, we cannot ignore the facts of life in the emerging global information economy: Capital, technology, and information are heavily concentrated in a handful of countries, all of them in the developed world. So the question translates into a different one: Why should the advanced countries (the North) help developing countries (the South) and economies in transition (the East) enter the global information economy? There are at least three reasons why the North of the 1990s, as opposed to the North of the 1980s, is about to find that it is in its own interest to help the countries of the East and South participate actively in the global information economy.

First, the industrial countries have not completed their technological transition to a sustainable global information economy. The employment-reducing effects of the information revolution have yet to be offset by its employment-creating effects. Many of the marvels of the "wired society," including home banking, working from home, and other "tele-activities," have yet to be fully accepted. Meanwhile, automation takes its toll of unskilled and semiskilled jobs. If confined to the territory of domestic competition, the productivity gains resulting from the information revolution will result more in a reshuffling of domestic wealth between social and economic categories than in a net increase in total welfare. But if the productivity gains can be translated into improved international competitiveness, total domestic income will increase (notwithstanding the probably uneven fashion in which the additional wealth will be distributed among domestic players including carriers, industries, and consumers). This, however, will require that advances in telecommunications be reflected in new trade practices and new international rules of the game for information-intensive trade transactions. Involving as many countries as possible in such an exercise therefore becomes advantageous for the more advanced countries, including the United States.

Second, telecommunications is an innovation-intensive industry. As in any such industry, a major concern of producers of equipment and services is to achieve as early as possible a sales volume that will allow them to recoup their initial, often massive, investments. Information and telecommunication services resemble a "public good," in that the cost of delivering the service to one additional customer is often negligible compared with the initial cost of the delivery infrastructure. Considering the producers' will to broaden their markets and the relatively small cost of doing so, we must conclude that the main obstacle to the globalization desired by such producers[4] is neither economic nor technological; it is political.[5] The question for the more advanced countries and enterprises then becomes: How can the less advanced countries be persuaded that it is also in their interest to open their borders to the goods and services provided by the pioneers of the emerging global information economy? Only when this question has been answered will it be possible to reap the full economies of scale and scope[6] that global firms now see as within reach.[7]

Third, the advanced democracies of the North have an important stake in contributing to the credibility and sustainability of the reforms under way in both the South and the East. The choice made by political leaders of those nations to rely more on market forces and less on centralized, government-driven approaches was often a courageous one, since it took place against a long tradition of public intervention in economic and social affairs. In other cases (especially in the former socialist countries), the choice was made because the leaders had no alternative. In both situations, enthusiasm has been less than universal for the reforms. In many developing countries, income per capita has not increased significantly over the past decade.[8] In fact, in the former Eastern bloc, standards of living have declined markedly since the end of the Gorbachev era. The situation is clearly unstable. Partisans of reform face increasing difficulties if they cannot demonstrate tangible results. In the absence of adequate international support, progress toward democracy and more liberal economies may produce too little too late. If that happens, the backlash could be very costly to the international community as a whole and to Western democracies in particular.

THE COST OF NOT DOING IT: DANGERS AHEAD

Most developing nations and economies in transition are now prevented from reaping the benefits of their economic and political reform efforts by their inability to become a part of the growing global networked economy. If more advanced countries do not act to overcome this exclusion, bilaterally or through multilateral institutions, three major types of performance disparity would be worsened: North-South and North-East disparities, disparities among developing nations, and disparities within the economies of developing nations and the former Soviet bloc nations. Each of these disparities would have its own array of harmful consequences for all nations, including those of the North.

Less advanced countries that cannot upgrade their infrastructures and practices to the levels required by a global information economy will remain trapped in the traditional dilemma of "commodity economies." More of their energy will be spent exporting natural resources (including labor) at depreciating prices and servicing their external debts. Little or no resources will be left for any longer-term social or economic investment. Their national economies will not be able to escape the vicious cycle of poverty, and a large share of the world's population will remain at the periphery of the global information economy. Understandably, these countries would then be tempted to regard the global information economy as a new instrument of exploitation of the poor by the rich. Hostile North-South rhetoric would flare anew, as it did in the 1970s with discussions of a new world information order and a new international economic order, and opportunities for mutual benefits would be lost. Tension would become endemic between the "telecommunications rich" and the "telecommunications poor" (the haves and have-nots of the global information economy), further jeopardizing the promise of joint wealth creation offered by the global information economy.[9]

The mere continuation of present trends would drastically widen economic disparities among developing countries. Over the past ten years, the African continent as a whole has experienced negative growth rates year after year. At the same time, some Southeast Asian countries like Thailand, Malaysia, Hong Kong, and Singapore have enjoyed growth rates significantly higher than those of the rest of the world. This growing disparity among developing economies has been one of the most striking features of the past decade.[10]

Institutions like the World Bank have been quick to attribute the divergences among countries' growth rates to the different policy choices made by these countries: Those that opted for open trade were generally better off than those that followed inward-looking policies. In the emerging global information economy, however, such policy choices will hardly be possible in the absence of a minimal ability to connect to international networks. Failure to make such connections feasible for all could conceivably result in a dangerous situation in which only a critical mass of developing countries would upgrade to the global information economy; as soon as enough poorer countries had done so to allow the North to generate the economies of scale and scope it expects, the rest of the developing world might be left to fend for itself, possibly worsening further the political climate in those countries. Entire regions and subcontinents (including most of Africa) would be excluded from the benefits of the global information economy. This would do immeasurable harm to the standards of living, health, and environments of these regions.[11] Abject poverty, coupled with heightened isolation, may also exacerbate underground political movements and corruption; illegal traffic of all kinds flourishes when legal activities cannot provide the means for survival. For the North, further performance divergence among poorer countries would thus translate into additional threats to free trade, health, the global environment, and governance.

The third major cost of inaction would be widened disparities among different population groups within the less advanced countries. For example, if the telecommunications sector were left entirely to the private sector, profit imperatives would lead to the rapid satisfaction of the needs of highly populated and economically active areas, typically the large cities. Most rural areas would remain unconnected. This is why privatization and liberalization schemes should be pursued in line with underlying socioeconomic master plans. Experience shows that gross internal economic disparity poses a dangerous challenge to the credibility and political stability of local government. It is often this type of "next-door disparity" that spurs the emergence of fundamentalist or traditionalist movements portraying outward-oriented policies as a betrayal of the true values of their respective countries and cultures. In such a context, religions and cultures cease to be sources of creative diversity and become obstacles to international integration.

FRAGMENTED GLOBALIZATION?

Continued inaction regarding the disparity in national incomes and telecommunications infrastructures could lead to the formation of telecommunications blocs, replicating the trading blocs that loom under the current combination of regional trading arrangements and protectionist tendencies. If regional telecommunications standards-setting bodies were to flourish, some of them might be tempted to attract additional countries and enterprises in order to build the critical mass needed to make nonglobal standards viable. Economies in transition are already a target for such alliances. As the president of Deutsche Telekom stated recently, "The next step will be to open up European bodies such as the European Telecommunications Standards Institute and the European Telecommunications Network Operating Association to all Eastern European nations."[12] Should the United States decide to follow a similar strategy with Latin America and Canada through an enlarged version of the North American Free Trade Agreement (NAFTA), the high-definition television (HDTV) syndrome of competing norms would become the model for a fragmented globalization. The direct economic costs would be enormous.

Indirect costs would be even more significant. For one, international trade would be hindered at a time when its revitalization is most needed. Global trade is becoming essentially paperless and more information intensive. Unless global agreement can be reached on the legal and technical bases for electronic commerce, the most dynamic sector of international trade will be inhibited in its expansion. Telecommunications blocs would not only replicate trade blocs, they would reinforce them, with the distinct risk of making fragmented globalization an irreversible phenomenon.[13]

If the world is to avoid the serious consequences of a fragmented global information economy, it must formulate norms and standards that will establish a "global commons." To do so, a series of difficult questions will have to be answered: Which international bodies are able to formulate and enforce such norms and standards? Should the international community rely on such active sources of standards setting as individual industries or regional institutions and then consolidate their results into globally acceptable rules of the game? Should more resources be allocated to existing global institutions such as the ITU to allow them to perform better than they have so far? Or should other, more flexible structures such as the Internet be given part of the task?

Two courses of action are needed. The first should be multilateral, pursued through existing multilateral institutions like the United Nations agencies and the ITU. Those institutions, however, must be considerably revamped if they are to meet the challenges of the global information economy. The second line of action should allow developing countries and economies of the former Soviet bloc to identify and pursue their own policy objectives through more active participation in the global information economy.

How to Do It: Aid, Investment, and Trade

The developing countries and economies in transition are facing a complex array of opportunities and challenges resulting from technological changes and modified international competition. Yet the most advanced countries and international organizations have not offered real help; indeed, they have delivered a clear message that developing countries can expect little but lip service unless they privatize their telecommunications firms and open their markets for equipment and services to international competition. Although this prescription is generally sound, experience shows that it needs to be customized to the specific needs and constraints of different countries. The same experience suggests that reform will not be fully effective without appropriate action from the governments and firms of the more advanced countries, and without significant adaptation in the mechanisms of international cooperation.

Those developing countries and economies in transition that have perceived the importance of an efficient telecommunications sector for their own economies, as well as for foreign partners, have adopted measures to reform their telecommunications sectors (through privatization, in particular). In some cases, such reforms have been strongly suggested by international institutions such as the World Bank. After some trial and error, these efforts have produced important results, in particular in terms of improved quality/price ratios. The array of tools available to reform telecommunications is now richer and more adaptable to the specific needs and requirements of those developing countries interested in reform. However, more funding is needed if these efforts are to bear fruit in all the interested countries. This is where governments and the private sector have a role to play, with the support of upgraded international mechanisms.

New Roles for Governments and Business in the North

In the past, the governments of the more advanced countries have not been very active in providing assistance to the development of telecommunications in the Second and Third Worlds. In many instances, assistance was granted more on the basis of political ties than because of the intrinsic merits of projects. In other instances, donor countries provided subsidies to their domestic companies, which then equipped beneficiary countries with systems that were not always the most appropriate for their specific needs or ability to use them. In some cases, what was installed was what the companies of the North could supply rather than what the beneficiary countries needed. Since a major objective of part of this assistance was to sell telecommunications equipment, little or no funds were allocated to the maintenance or upgrading of such equipment. Developing regions—especially Africa—are littered with out-dated telecommunications devices.

In the next few years, significant amounts of additional bilateral and multilateral aid will be required to allow Second and Third World nations to up-grade their telecommunications systems. Their national development agencies will have a pivotal role to play in this process, since they can, through appropriate funding of national and regional projects, send signals to attract foreign investment. It will be necessary for the government authorities responsible for these agencies to establish adequate criteria to help them meet the require-ments of the global information economy.

By and large, the private sectors of industrialized countries have performed slightly better than their governments in furthering telecommunications development in Second and Third World nations. This somewhat surprising result stems from the fact that some of the largest providers of telecommun-ications equipment and services have a more coherent vision of the global information economy than many governments. Private telecommunications companies have chosen to invest in developing countries on essentially economic grounds, guided by business interests instead of politics, which has produced better returns on investment as well as better coordination of projects. For example, network nodes have been located on a regional, rather than national, basis and intraregional cooperative arrangements have been implemented. The greater ability of private telecommunications companies to assess the needs of local users (including domestic and foreign business communities) has also resulted in a more rational and better-targeted selection of investments.

In high-risk environments (such as the telecommunications sectors of a number of countries in Eastern and Central Europe), private companies generally have reacted faster than governments, which explains why private investment to modernize the telecommunications systems of Hungary and Poland came long before public funds were available. Other countries like Belarus or Ukraine are still waiting. It is likely that technological advances will increase the interest of private companies in the development of telecommunications infrastructures in less advanced countries. For example, wireless networks require less time to install and, therefore, can become profitable faster than traditional cable networks. Mobile telephony and the new possibilities offered by low earth orbiting satellites (LEOS) should stimulate greater participation in the near future. This new dimension of the relationship between development and telecommunications can greatly enhance the efficiency of international trade.

REVAMPING INTERNATIONAL INSTITUTIONS

The emergence of a global information economy poses new challenges to the multilateral trade machinery created over the past fifty years. With the (notable) exception of the ITU, this machinery—including the World Bank, the International

Monetary Fund, and later the General Agreement on Trade and Tariffs (GATT)—was part of the "new order" that was created following World War II. In the 1950s and early 1960s, the emergence of developing countries as a definable group triggered some additions to this machinery, such as the United Nations Conference on Trade and Development (UNCTAD). The perceived convergence between democracy and the liberal values of market economies led to other creations, such as the Organization for Economic Cooperation and Development (OECD). However, thirty years later, the global information economy carries many of the unmistakable characteristics of another new order: The sources of international competitiveness and the production and distribution of wealth are being reshuffled in unprecedented (and sometimes unanticipated) fashion.[14]

The machinery of multilateral cooperation is in urgent need of updating. Both its purpose and its operating methods need to be examined and changed to adapt to today's needs. As far as telecommunications is concerned, three kinds of organizations emerge as top candidates for such an update.

First, the organizations specializing in telecommunications—mainly the ITU—should refocus their activities in two directions: increasing international awareness of the opportunities and challenges of the global information economy, and mobilizing international attention, support, and finance to help the global information economy develop on fair and sustainable bases.[15] These changes would require the ITU to take an active part in the mobilization of private and public funds to finance telecommunications infrastructures in the less advanced countries. The ITU should also play the role of technical adviser to other institutions (such as GATT) that are beginning to become involved in telecommunications issues. Standards-setting activities also now require a more flexible approach than that offered until recently by the International Consultative Committee on Telegraph and Telephone (traditionally designated by its French acronym, CCITT),[16] and the ITU should function as a repository of such standards, leaving it to the dynamics of various sectors and regions to propose the standards required by the global information economy. In such a process, there may be a role for broader structures like the Internet. In any case, frequency and spectrum allocations should remain the responsibility of the ITU.

Second, international bodies with financial clout, like the World Bank and the United Nations Development Program (once it overcomes its present difficulties), should consider reordering their priorities to reflect the increasing importance of telecommunications for the economic and social development of the less advanced countries. An additional challenge for these organizations will be the competition between East and South for development assistance. For example, the investments required to build modern telecommunications infrastructures in Eastern and Central Europe are sizable. In 1991, it was estimated that to achieve the standard Western penetration of twenty-seven to thirty operational mainlines per one hundred inhabitants in Romania, Poland, Hungary, Czechoslovakia, Yugoslavia, and Bulgaria (not considering Russia), the total investment needed would be somewhere between $38 billion and $52 billion.[17]

Third, international organizations with a mandate in social development (such as the International Labor Office and the World Health Organization) or in trade (UNCTAD, GATT, and the new World Trade Organization, or WTO) should examine how the emergence of a global information economy affects their respective areas of competence, and what kinds of consequences this is likely to have on the development and transition processes of the less advanced countries. Increased engagement should make such organizations more relevant and efficient in pursuing the goals for which they were created.

The redefinition of the roles of multilateral institutions needs to be accompanied by profound changes in their operational methods. In particular, these organizations will need to work more closely with the private sector, especially those enterprises that have already developed a global vision.[18] This cooperation will become more necessary because of the need to take into account—in the area of international trade, for example—strategic alliances and networked strategies in order to address issues such as regulatory convergence and competition policies. In developing countries and economies in transition, small and medium-sized enterprises represent one of the most important sources of employment creation and external competitiveness. Allowing such firms access to the technology and the know-how required to take an active part in the global information economy is a major challenge in which international cooperation must play a leading role.[19] The way in which this challenge has begun to be addressed offers a striking example of how political will and existing multilateral mechanisms can be combined into an agenda for action.

AN AGENDA FOR ACTION

THE TRADE DIMENSION OF TELECOMMUNICATIONS: A NEW ENGINE FOR DEVELOPMENT

Clearly, an adequate telecommunications system is an important prerequisite for the domestic socioeconomic development of all countries, including developing countries and former socialist countries. This point requires little more emphasis than it has received over the past decade from the Maitland Commission and the abundant body of "universal service" literature. But the rapid changes that result from the adoption of open economic policies bring with them the same kinds of social disruptions and economic suffering that accompany any reforms. Domestic support for reform thus requires visible results in the short term, which makes it particularly important that before changes are made, those areas of economic activity in which telecommunications investments are likely to yield significant, rapid benefits be identified. International trade is such an area.

Back in 1982, when the United States proposed including services in the agenda for a new round of multilateral trade negotiations, the developing nations expressed little interest. Only a few reacted, and those with suspicion and sometimes opposition. However, after four years of strenuous effort, a delicate compromise was achieved at Punta del Este, and a new GATT round (the Uruguay Round) was launched.[20] At the time, developing countries were thinking mainly of those services that they could readily export, such as labor-intensive services, tourism, or shipping. For these countries, telecommunications was not an area of major interest, at least from an export point of view. Even those in developing countries who regarded telecommunications as important for the development process were thinking more in terms of financing and infrastructure than in terms of international trade.

Unfortunately, in spite of the powerful analogies drawn by Juan Rada[21] and others, comparing, for instance, the invention of refrigerated ships (which allowed Latin America to export beef to Europe) with that of worldwide telecommunications (which allowed many services to become internationally tradable), many developing countries have not yet fully realized the magnitude of the potential impact of better telecommunications on their own development process, and in particular on their export potential. That potential, however, is substantial.[22] The strategies formulated by the companies and governments that have taken a quick lead in the global information economy emphasized international transactions. Their experience makes it clear that international trade is the area in which investments in integration of the global information economy are likely to be recouped most rapidly.

THE TRADE EFFICIENCY INITIATIVE

A decade later, the contracting parties to the GATT finally concluded the delicate negotiations involved in the Uruguay Round. The macroeconomic package agreed to on December 15, 1993, in Geneva will allow reductions in two kinds of obstacles to international trade: tariffs and nontariff barriers (NTBs). Due mainly to successful previous GATT rounds, tariffs are now less than 5 percent of the total value of international trade flows. NTBs however, are much higher: Although they are generally of a qualitative nature, and therefore more difficult to measure, they are estimated to amount to the equivalent of 15 to 25 percent of the value of trade. Nobody knows how many of these barriers will actually be dismantled in the foreseeable future. One of the difficulties of lowering tariffs and NTBs is that contracting parties will agree to do so only on the basis of reciprocity—and reciprocity is basically a bilateral concept, often difficult to transpose to multilateral agreements.[23]

There is, however, a third type of obstacle to trade, much less subject to reciprocity controversies, since its elimination benefits all partners immediately. These can be described as "procedural" obstacles and consist of all the paperwork, procedures, licenses, authorizations, and certificates that any potential exporter must obtain before entering the international trade arena. According to conservative estimates,[24] such obstacles (procedural costs) represent at least 10 percent of the total value of international trade. Unless such obstacles are reduced in the short run, many countries and enterprises will be excluded from the additional trade flows that the GATT's macroeconomic framework will generate. This simple consideration leads to the following practical conclusion: The international trading community is in urgent need of a *microeconomic GATT*. This is what the Trade Efficiency Initiative—launched officially by the approximately 180 member countries of UNCTAD in February 1992—seeks to accomplish.[25]

By allowing a broader use of information technologies and a more coherent use of telecommunications, this initiative aims at curtailing the procedural costs of international trade by 25 percent before the year 2000. Based on the conservative estimates quoted above, this would mean savings of some $100 billion per year, which would go a long way toward financing telecommunications infrastructures and other integrative tools in developing countries and economies in transition.

The core objective of the Trade Efficiency Initiative is to open international trade to new participants, especially small and medium-sized companies, by simplifying and harmonizing trade procedures worldwide and giving traders access to advanced technologies and information networks. This will be achieved principally through the establishment and interconnection of trade points,[26] which will offer traders practical tools to increase the efficiency of their operations through a better and more systematic use of information technologies. The United Nations International Symposium on Trade Efficiency (UNISTE), held in Columbus, Ohio, October 17–21, 1994, offered a remarkable showcase for the Trade Point Program. In the presence of trade ministers from the 187 member-countries of UNCTAD, as well as of several heads of government and heads of state, this trade summit drew upon individual experiences in an effort to develop a model trade point to be reproduced throughout the world. Embedded in the Columbus Ministerial Declaration, the Trade Point Global Network was officially launched on that occasion and is now expanding exponentially.

The Trade Efficiency Initiative will contribute to increasing predictability and sustainability in the emerging global information economy by closing the performance gap between the haves and have-nots of information technology; promoting a consensual approach to the adoption of common rules of the game, including norms and standards; relieving pressure on governments of less advanced countries by allowing them simultaneously to proceed with reforms, create employment, alleviate poverty, and restore the financial equilibrium of their respective national economies; and generating entrepreneurial attitudes throughout their economies through higher visibility and success of smaller firms, thus highlighting profitable alternatives to illegal or underground activities such as drug trafficking or corruption.

This process could be described as "telecoms with a purpose." It will be developed in three distinct phases. In the first, consensus will be built among business, governments, and international bodies to combine the fundamentals of the emerging global information economy and the objectives of trade and development. A broader dissemination of information technologies and telecommunications know-how will generate some of the "trust and security" mechanisms essential to greater participation and efficiency in international trade. Beneficiary Second and Third World countries will be in a position to pursue long-term social objectives (including universal service, but also health and education-related goals), while being able to attain visible and rapid results in trade. If, moreover, such an effort is targeted toward small and medium-sized enterprises, effects on employment creation will be significant.

In the second phase of the Trade Efficiency Initiative, with the support of local business, a greater number of countries of the Second and Third Worlds will become interested in promoting the adoption of global rules of the game for trade, development, and telecommunications. Such rules will include norms and standards for electronic commerce (for example, electronic data interchange, or EDI) as well as information equipment and services more broadly. The outcome of the second phase could be defined as the establishment of a "global commons" for an information-intensive economy. This would include the legal and technical bases on which competition and free trade will be able to contribute to lessening the North-South and North-East development gaps. In this way, the less advanced countries should be in a position to benefit from new developments such as those already occurring with LEOS.[27]

In its third phase, the Trade Efficiency Initiative will contribute to accelerated employment creation and poverty alleviation in less advanced countries, thus increasing popular support for an open global market economy and securing the practical bases for the joint wealth-creation mechanisms that the global information economy theoretically generates. The objective of this third phase could be labeled "generating the global information economy commonwealth."

POLICY IMPLICATIONS

Until now, efforts toward changing the telecommunications reality of the Second and Third Worlds have been made principally by the developing countries and economies in transition themselves. But in the absence of external support, these efforts will remain limited in scope, depth, and results. The possible sources for the external support that is so necessary for success include the governments and enterprises of the North. In the new international order that underlies the global information economy, the United States has the most prominent role to play.

In addressing the challenge of integrating nations of the East and South into the global information economy, the public agencies of the United States have an irreplaceable role to play domestically, bilaterally, regionally, and in the broad multilateral context. The main reasons for assuming this role are as follows:

▼   As a pioneer provider of advanced telecommunications technology, the United States has immediate economic reasons for encouraging the integration of a larger number of players into the game.

▼   As a promoter of a "new world order," the United States has medium- and long-term interests in building worldwide support for globally accepted norms and standards.

▼   As the sole remaining superpower, it is in the interest of the United States that developing nations and economies in transition take part in the information revolution to create employment, alleviate poverty, and become active participants in and supporters of an open and liberal global information economy.

AVENUES FOR GOVERNMENT ACTION

At all four levels of action (domestic, bilateral, regional, and multilateral), U.S. government authorities have the power to play a critical role. If pursued together and backed by a true global vision, such actions can produce important benefits for U.S. business as well as for the international community as a whole.

Domestically, efforts should focus on increasing awareness by the public and private sectors of the challenges of the emerging global information economy, and of the risks and lost opportunities that would result from a fragmented globalization. There must also be heightened awareness of the business opportunities that the markets of these countries represent, both for the providers of telecommunications equipment and services and for producers of information-intensive services such as banking, insurance, and transport-related services. In the United States, the current NII debate offers an ideal opportunity to achieve this goal through the injection of international concerns into some of the ongoing discussions. Priority should be given to the stimulation of business partnerships involving providers of telecommunication services and equipment; U.S. companies (especially small and medium-sized enterprises) with a potential for exports or a desire to import on better terms; and companies from developing countries and economies in transition, again, preferably small and medium sized. The purpose of such matchmaking exercises would be, first, to stimulate business relationships between partners of comparable size and interests, and second, to allow the industries of less advanced countries to identify and formulate their own telecommunications needs and contribute to guiding their respective governments toward the adoption of efficient telecommunications policies.

Bilaterally, the U.S. government has an important role to play as the promoter of fair telecommunications practices. For most developing countries and economies in transition, telecommunication accounting rates can distort significantly the economic viability of some infrastructure investments. The basic elements of the problem of accounting rates are spelled out elsewhere in this volume.[28] It is clear that these asymmetries in international accounting rates should be addressed in the bilateral context, where they can best be settled. At the same time, they should not be addressed within an exclusively commercial context, since, in less advanced countries, they constitute a publicly visible element of telecommunications policy, and one that has a high symbolic value.

In bilateral relations, official U.S. support should be offered to those countries that have undertaken to reform their telecommunications sectors. In particular, distribution of U.S. Agency for International Development (AID) funding should shift from political criteria to depend more systematically on the intrinsic value of projects. Such value should be assessed in terms of the projects' ability to foster growth, employment, and entrepreneurship in the beneficiary nations, and their ability to promote the commercial interest of U.S. companies. In their bilateral relations with developing countries and economies in transition, U.S. government authorities should also work more closely with the U.S. Chambers of Commerce and other business associations active in these countries whenever telecommunications issues need to be addressed.

Regionally (that is, mainly in the context of NAFTA), the U.S. government also has an important role to play in shaping what could very well become a model for future international agreements in telecommunications. As trade expert Robert Lawrence has pointed out, regional trading blocs have the potential to be either stumbling blocks or building blocks for an open trading system. However, it should be clear that, given the increasing information intensity of international trade, the emergence of telecommunications blocs (with competing norms and standards and large gaps between the various categories of haves and have-nots of telecommunications) would tilt the scales toward a highly fragmented trading system in which regional blocs would indeed stand in the way of efforts to create a global open economy. The United States must guard against such a development. Considering the active policy followed by Mexico in reforming its telecommunications sector, as well as the remaining telecommunications disparities among NAFTA partners, there will be great interest in seeing what practical arrangements are worked out in information-intensive sectors. Many developing countries and economies in transition are closely monitoring NAFTA's provisions for telecommunications and information services, either because similar provisions could soon become part of their own trade relations with the United States (as in several Latin American countries) or because they could have an influence on their relations with other advanced countries. Regional arrangements offer a testing ground for specific provisions or even for new legal or regulatory instruments.

Multilaterally, the U.S. government has played a central role in reshaping existing institutions over the past few years. Because of its financial weight (the United States generally contributes more than 20 percent of the total budgets of multilateral institutions), the United States will continue to be heard when it advocates changes in the priorities and working methods of these institutions. Because it has more experience than any other country in dealing with the different dimensions of the global information economy, the United States is in a unique position to help multilateral bodies identify and address the important issues. One of the paradoxes of the emerging global information economy, which is largely a business-driven phenomenon, is that it will require more, rather than less, multilateralism. One simple reason for this is that, as other chapters of this book show, many of the problems raised by the information revolution are inherently global. Internationally accepted norms, standards, agreements, and rules of the game will be more indispensable than ever. The possibility that elements of the "global commons" can first be formulated and implemented in a limited geographical or sectoral context does not diminish the need to eventually promote them internationally. This is a task for multilateral bodies.

At the same time, existing multilateral institutions will need to undergo significant reforms in order to be able to address the new issues with some degree of effectiveness. The ability of developing countries and economies in transition to rely on a supportive multilateral environment will be essential to the success of reform in the area of telecommunications. Financial help will remain a prominent issue, as long as there is a "missing link" (as the Maitland Commission termed the developing nations). Washington will have a critical role to play in the World Bank, the ITU, and in the United Nations system to ensure that priority and support are provided to programs and activities that, through better telecommunications policies and uses, are likely to enhance employment creation, poverty alleviation, and trade competitiveness in the Second and Third Worlds.

AVAILABLE TOOLS, FORESEEABLE OBSTACLES, AND EXPECTED REWARDS

The tools to be used should be adapted to the targets and terrain of the actions pursued. Domestically, awareness can be enhanced through information and sensitization campaigns, especially those aimed at the business community. Congress will also have a specific role to play in adapting U.S. policies (trade policy in particular) to the specific needs of the global information economy. But much will remain in the hands of the executive branch for at least two reasons: First, relations with developing countries and economies in transition have traditionally been handled by the State Department, and second, what is most needed at this stage is the expression of a global vision—one that provides a foundation for a U.S. policy that promotes the integration of East and South into the emerging global information economy.

The obstacles are many—and more will arise as practical measures are taken. First, resistance is likely to be expressed within government itself whenever cross-sectoral measures affect agency turfs and territories. Second, the business community will not unanimously recognize that telecommunications should be a priority in U.S. relations with the Second and Third Worlds; sectoral lobbies will plead for their own narrow interests and others will question policies that increase foreign competition abroad and possibly at home. Finally, other nations will criticize a more active U.S. policy (especially within multilateral institutions) as an attempt to pursue U.S. commercial interests in the guise of humanitarian and idealistic goals.

Such obstacles should not be underestimated. Governmental action will overcome them only if it shows determination and consistency in promoting a truly global vision of international relations and integration into the emerging global information economy. But the main instrument through which the resistance can be progressively diminished is the tangible benefits the United States economy will derive from such policies.

Short-term results will include higher activity levels for several sectors of the U.S. economy. Allowing the world as a whole to benefit from better telecommunications infrastructures will promote the activity of information-intensive global companies, many of which are U.S. companies. Another short-term result of such action will be the creation of substantial business opportunities for U.S. manufacturers of telecommunications equipment and providers of telecommunications services.

Medium-term results will include an improvement of the international environment for U.S. business. Allowing local firms (especially the smaller ones) to benefit from better telecommunications infrastructures and move to higher levels of efficiency in production and trade will bring support for standards setting, acceptance of uniform rules of the game, and respect for international guidelines regarding intellectual property, confidentiality, and security of networks. Enhancing the capacity of local firms to use telecommunications to create employment and participate in international trade will increase the support of the populations of developing countries and economies in transition for reform, including privatization and liberalization. This should, in turn, result in a better climate for multilateral discussions and negotiations, with rewarding results in terms of international cooperation.

In the longer run, appropriate action from the U.S. government will contribute to strengthening international support for the creation of a dynamic, fair, and predictable international environment—one in which all countries will be able to derive the highest possible benefits from the tremendous productivity gains allowed by advances in information technologies and telecommunications. If done well, the result will be an open global market economy with enough dynamism for sustained joint wealth creation, and with sufficient safeguard mechanisms to guarantee a fair distribution of this common wealth.

CONCLUSION

As the global information economy gathers momentum, it continues to be plagued with serious imbalances and unresolved problems. In many of the more advanced countries, high levels of unemployment fuel a never-ending debate on the pros and cons of technological innovation, with protectionist tendencies gaining support. In the rest of the world, large and heavily populated areas remain at the outskirts of some of the most significant changes brought by the information revolution. This situation is feeding two unhealthy tendencies: First, disparities are widening between the respective economic performances and standards of living of the information and telecommunications haves and the have-nots; second, the emerging economic order appears to be unable to stave off fragmenting tendencies, which bear a striking and ominous resemblance to those that characterized international economic relations from the crash of 1929 to the outbreak of World War II.

The emerging global information economy offers the potential for a new path for growth and improved welfare, but it is akin to a runner still in the starting blocks, unaware that his untied shoelaces may cause a fall in the near future. As the unrivaled leader of the global information economy pack, the United States has the biggest stake and a unique responsibility for solving the challenges that the global information economy raises for international relations between North, East, and South.

9

MULTILATERAL COOPERATION IN TELECOMMUNICATIONS: IMPLICATIONS OF THE GREAT TRANSFORMATION

ANTHONY M. RUTKOWSKI

Multilateral cooperation in the telecommunications field dates back to 1850, when increasing use of the electric telegraph for generating international communications traffic made it impractical and inefficient to physically transfer messages between border telegraph stations. Rather remarkably, the models and practices that were followed in 1850 for multilateral cooperation in telecommunications remained relatively unchanged for most of the next 135 years. Then, in the short space of a decade beginning in the mid-1980s, twin forces—the transformation of telecommunications into a commercial industry and the spread of digital computer technologies—produced fundamental and irreversible changes in the nature and models of multilateral cooperation.

For 135 years, international telecommunications were provided entirely through state-owned or sanctioned telecommunications monopolies acting as an international cartel under the aegis of intergovernmental organizations. This arrangement proceeded under a nominal norm of "universal communications" that served as its ultimate goal. While some of that old environment still persists, the established international order for telecommunications is today dramatically different—a complex mixture of largely private sector providers that both compete and cooperate in a global marketplace offering a wide variety of international, regional, and local services.

Intergovernmental roles in this new environment are being transformed as well as diminished. (A few sets of arrangements remain basically unchanged, such as those coordinating global radio spectrum management.) As for international norms, they have been transformed by the location of telecommunications under the GATT Agreement on Trade in Services (GATS) and the emergence of a World Trade Organization (WTO); here, competitive trade and antitrust norms reign supreme and national trade authorities negotiating with their peers determine the conditions for the provision of telecommunications services.

In general, however, it is private telecommunications providers themselves that are most responsible for shaping the direction and laying the groundwork for the provision of such services. In doing so, these providers are inventing new forms and forums for international cooperation that are more agile, far faster, and more focused on immediate needs than those of the past.

It is not possible in these pages to portray everything occurring today in the realm of multilateral telecommunications activities, much less convey a history of how this came to be and where it is going. Instead, I have chosen to describe a fundamental transition taking place between the old and new telecommunications worlds and to examine the fundamental differences between those worlds and the "multilateral-like" needs that have arisen or are now appearing. The seemingly inescapable conclusion of this analysis is that a new kind of dispersed, autonomous, and heterogeneous "multilateralism" is emerging, where an array of new entities and processes—including market economies—are performing the same roles once reserved for nation-states and kingdoms.

MULTILATERALISM IN THE AGE OF HIERARCHICAL TELECOMMUNICATIONS MONOPOLIES: 1850–1988

From a contemporary vantage point, the history of international telecommunications cooperation brings to mind the opening of Stanley Kubrick's film *2001: A Space Odyssey*—a slow-motion scene in which prehistoric apes first encounter tools. While today we are used to thinking of rapid technological changes to which governments and corporations must swiftly respond, this was hardly the mind-set during the first 135 years of telecommunications multilateralism. Instead, the long era was remarkable for its sameness. Major new technologies like the telephone, radio, and data communications emerged only infrequently and, once they did, it took decades for governments incrementally to develop the technical standards, operating procedures, and other rules necessary to incorporate them into the international system. Moreover, the nature of the issues, the identities of the players, the decision-making procedures employed, and the character of the agreements reached rarely changed to any significant degree. Every element of the policy framework was engineered as conservatively as possible for the ultimate in institutional durability and immutability, down to the selection of Switzerland as the site for the headquarters of the International Telecommunication Union (ITU).

This near-glacial pace of change was due first and foremost to the identities and interests of the major participants in the multilateral process. The ITU was designed by and for a coalition of European governmental entities known as Ministries of Posts, Telegraphs, and Telephones (PTTs). Within their respective countries, these PTTs served as monopoly providers of telecommunications networks and services and as the makers of national policies on regulation, technical standardization, and so on. As both umpire and sole player on the field, the PTTs were in a very comfortable position, and one which they had no interest in seeing disrupted by outside forces. In consequence, the multilateral agreements they devised reflected, buttressed, and extended to the international sphere their own power. Moreover, as the ITU expanded in the twentieth century to encompass almost all the world's nations and colonies, the vast majority of members were represented by governmental PTTs designed along the old European model. For the handful of countries that had regulated private telecommunications carriers—such as the United States, parts of Canada, and (for a time) Latin America—establishing and expanding international communications required participation in a game originally defined by the European PTTs. This generated some unwelcome disagreements regarding such matters as tariffs and the treatment of corporate customers. However, since the private carriers were often monopolists or near monopolists within their own markets, on major issues like the undesirability of competition with or among national carriers, there was essentially universal agreement to preserve the institutional status quo above all else.

In short, the overarching challenge for governments was to preserve their national monopolies while coordinating their international relations. This they did from 1865 to 1933 in the International Telegraph Union. In 1934, the union expanded in functional scope to cover telephone and radio matters, and was relaunched as the International Telecommunication Union. Over the next sixty years, the ITU underwent several internal reorganizations, the details of which have been described elsewhere and need not be recounted here.[1] The most recent reshuffling was in 1992; it consisted largely of renaming and regrouping functions rather than redefining the functions themselves in light of new market realities. Hence, while the current structure briefly summarized below represents some improvement in organizational efficiency, on the whole the ITU remains fundamentally the same rigidly formalized intergovernmental bureaucracy it has always been.

At the top of the organizational hierarchy is the Plenipotentiary Conference, which comprises high-level government representatives and is held every four years to revise the union's governing documents, the Constitution and the Convention. Below it are the Telecommunications Standardization Sector, the Radiocommunications Sector, and the Development Sector. Each of these bodies comprises numerous specialized study groups and working parties that meet several times per year to undertake studies and, in the case of technical standardization, issue recommendations that have historically been adopted by national governments. All three bodies also hold world conferences at regular intervals of two to four years to adopt various measures including, in the case of radio, a binding international treaty called the International Radio Regulations. Alongside these meetings lies the World Conference on International Telecommunications, which is held as needed to revise a parallel treaty, the International Telecommunications Regulations. Finally, an elected council of forty or so member countries meets annually to provide administrative guidance, and a General Secretariat performs various other policy and housekeeping functions.[2]

The main products produced by these bodies and their predecessors can be summarized as follows: First, there is an international telecommunications regime covering the management, technical standardization, and economic organization of international networks and services. This regime is negotiated in the Plenipotentiary Conference, the World Conference on International Telecommunications (prior to 1992, called the World Administrative Telegraph and Telephone Conference, WATTC), and the Telecommunications Standardization Sector (previously, the International Consultative Committee on Telegraph and Telephone, CCITT). The regime's prescriptions and proscriptions are codified in the instruments generated by these three bodies—the Convention and Constitution, the Regulations, and the Recommendations, respectively.

Second, there is an international radio regime governing the organization and utilization of international radio frequency spectrum. This regime is negotiated in the Plenipotentiary Conference, the World Radiocommunication Conference (prior to 1992, the World Administrative Radio Conference, WARC), and the Radiocommunications Sector (previously, the International Consultative Committee on Radio, CCIR).[3] And third, in addition to providing fora in which members negotiate these two regimes, the ITU also performs a number of operational and information functions for member governments. For example, its General Secretariat conducts studies of telecommunications issues and publishes statistics, and the new Development Sector provides some technical assistance to developing countries. But from the standpoint of understanding the global telecommunications marketplace and the changing role of intergovernmental rules of the game, it is the two regimes that are our main concern here.

THE "ANCIEN" INTERNATIONAL TELECOMMUNICATIONS REGIME

As William Drake has argued, the fundamental objectives of the *ancien* regime were threefold: to maintain national sovereignty, which was generally interpreted as meaning monopoly control over national networks; to facilitate the interconnection and interoperability of such networks through the adoption of voluntary technical standards; and to organize the joint, noncompetitive provisioning of cross-border services.[4] What was both remarkable and somewhat unfortunate about this regime was its sheer longevity and its stubborn resistance to significant change during more than a century of progress in international communications.

The earliest treaty of record to link telegraph systems of two states was established in 1849 between Prussia and Austria. Several similar bilateral arrangements followed the same year. These bilateral agreements were then superseded by the 1850 Treaty of Dresden among Austria, Prussia, Bavaria, and Saxony concerning the establishment of the German-Austrian Telegraphic Union—the first multilateral agreement for international telecommunications. Fifteen years later, twenty countries signed the Treaty of Paris, launching the International Telegraph Union. Over the 130 years that followed, many marginal treaty revisions followed, as the rechristened International Telecommunication Union expanded both its functional scope to cover new technologies, and its membership to encompass over 180 nations today. But even as the regime grew in these directions, many of its key provisions remained unaltered. In fact, if you set the 1850 Treaty of Dresden next to the 1982 International Telecommunication Convention, for example, strikingly similar language is evident in a number of important areas.

This continuity existed because of a lack of significant change in the central players and in their visions of how technology and markets should be organized. The 1850 Treaty of Dresden borrowed liberally from the international postal agreements that preceded it, in part because the electrical telegraph was regarded simply as a faster means of delivering postal service—referred to then as "telegraphic correspondence." Moreover, two of the four governments attending the treaty conference were represented by the heads of their postal departments, which over time came to control telecommunications in most member states through integrated PTTs. With the Treaty of Berlin in 1885, ITU members began the long process of incorporating the new telephone technology into the existing conceptual model and regime framework. In 1903, it was radio's turn, and some sixty years later, computer communication's. In each case, the initial tendency was to regard these new technologies as threats to prior network investments and thus to force them to conform to the same rigid mold. Hence, well into the 1980s, the international policy framework for telecommunications remained grounded in the sleepy world of the post office, even as it began to metamorphose into one of the most dynamic and technologically complex industries in the world economy. This disjuncture between a static regime, on the one hand, and an increasingly market-driven technological environment, on the other, would lead to a change in the regime beginning in the late 1980s, and to its growing irrelevance in the mid-1990s.

How did the PTT approach shape regime elements? Regarding the regime's first principle of national sovereignty, all of the ITU's main instruments reaffirmed the notion of sovereign control. The ITU's jurisdiction was limited specifically to international connections, with each state free in principle to adopt whatever framework it desired at the national level. In practice, however, most chose government monopolies; the United Kingdom was not admitted to ITU membership until it nationalized its telegraph system. Only national repre-sentatives could vote in ITU bodies and those representatives were from the

PTTs. Not surprisingly, then, a wide variety of additional measures were added to the Conventions, the Regulations, and the Recommendations over the years in the name of sovereignty that were actually designed and understood to protect the power of monopoly carriers. On the supply side of the market, the competitive provision of international services was never endorsed, and indeed was rarely mentioned as a conceivable possibility. Instead, the rules explicitly banned competition by, for example, precluding arbitrage and routing patterns designed to take advantage of tariff differentials. On the demand side of the market, a broader and more explicit set of provisions was placed in the Recommendations limiting how corporate customers could configure and use their internal leased circuits, customer premise equipment, and so on.

The second regime principle was international interconnectivity. As the use of the new electric telegraph spread in the 1840s, governments and companies alike quickly recognized its potential to increase vastly the speed of international communications for diplomatic, commercial, and personal messages. However, the ability to reap these benefits was limited by the lack of a shared telegraphic language and set of technical standards for the interconnection of incompatible national networks. Consider this representative situation at the border of France and the Grand Duchy of Baden in 1850:

> A common station was established at Strasbourg with two employees, one from the French Telegraph Administration, and the other from Baden. The French employee received, for example, a telegram from Paris. . . . This message he wrote out by hand onto a special form and handed it across the table to his German colleague. He translated it into German, and then sent it again on its way [via Baden's separate national network].[5]

This bilateral procedure involved substantial transaction costs that were compounded in the international aggregate—each country had to go through a similar procedure with every other country with which it wished to correspond. Clearly, the efficiency of the new technology would be greatly enhanced if multiple national systems could pass messages directly among themselves in accordance with compatible internetwork connections.

In the nineteenth century, ITU members responded to this challenge by having specialists attached to the diplomatic and administrative conferences set some basic standards, such as the adoption of the Morse code for telegraphy, for inclusion in the treaties. As networks became progressively more complex, achieving the interconnection of national systems—physically, logically, and operationally—required that more and more issues like different national languages, operating practices, customs, and electrical equipment be reconciled, and the term *harmonization* become sanctified as the expression of this common aim. This activity ranged from the specification of the digital codes, to line electrical interface characteristics, to levels of message priority, to hours of operation. The task became even more difficult when telephone systems appeared on a large scale near the end of the last century, not only because of the technical problems associated with a new technology, but also because these systems were perceived by the national administrations as a threat to their prior investments in telegraphy. In response, the telephone was simply folded into the existing telegraph system model, with largely the same monopoly operators and the same multilateral activities and institutions leading the way. One result was that extensive efforts to promote international standardization of the telephone—thereby facilitating its expansion—was not begun until the 1920s, fifty years after its invention.

A second potential challenge to the existing order was the invention in 1896 of the radio, which was initially used internationally for wireless telegraphy between ships at sea and coastal stations. But it was not the existence of this technology that resulted in the first international wireless telegraphy agreement. It took an irate German prince, who could not announce his arrival in New York at the turn of the century because his equipment was not manufactured by the same company as that of the coastal station, to call for a meeting at Berlin in 1903. The Marconi Company (whose head was the inventor of the radio) had restrictive licensing agreements associated with its equipment, thus remarkably diminishing connectivity. The Preliminary Conference in 1903 drafted a protocol, followed by a full agreement three years later, that put an end to this practice. Thereafter, wireless telegraphy systems were operated as extensions to the existing networks, once again largely subjected to the same national and international institutions and procedures.

This basic pattern was repeated in somewhat different form with the advent of data communications in the 1950s. The monopolies were initially unable to provide the requisite capabilities for data communications through their national public networks, so most activity was initiated by transnational corporations who were users, rather than providers, of telecommunications services. Banks, airlines, and large industrial enterprises led the way by purchasing computers, modems, private branch exchange switches, and other new equipment, and integrated these systems with circuits leased from the monopolies to create private corporate data networks. Within the CCITT (the predecessor of today's Telecommunications Standardization Sector), the monopolies responded by setting standards that imposed strict rules on how such private circuits could be configured and used so as to meet basic customer requirements while precluding the rise of stealth competition. By the early 1970s, monopolists in the industrialized world were finally ready to offer public switched data networks of their own, but the hoped-for mass migration of corporate users away from private networks and to these new and frequently inferior offerings did not materialize.

In response, the carriers launched in the mid-1970s a massive long-term effort to reign in the explosive growth of computer communications under their own centralized systems. The official term was integrated services digital network, or ISDN, but suspicious corporate users referred to ISDN as "innovations subscribers don't need."[6] And no wonder:

> From a technical viewpoint, integrated digital networks made sense. However, the connotation that "integration" meant not only interoperability and interconnection, but also PTT provision of all future services, was obviously controversial. . . . [A] unified system could benefit small business and residential users, who were unlikely to invest in advanced private systems. The ISDN would also be good for trade unionists working for national carriers, and for protected manufacturers seeking exclusive, long-term contracts for a new generation of systems. Above all, it was desirable for the carriers, who could defend their extant monopolies while expanding their roles in both new communication and information markets, and in industrial policies for "high-tech" goods. But was it in the interest of large corporate users and new suppliers seeking competitive entry and control?[7]

Most users believed not; but, as luck would have it, it took the monopolists over a decade to agree on sufficient CCITT standards and begin building up their national ISDNs, by which time the spread of deregulation and liberalization rendered ISDN just another competitive offering, and one for which corporate demand remained soft. As such, this generalized connectivity platform has been only partially successful—generally at the lowest layers of connectivity—and its direction has been significantly bounded and redirected by the dramatic changes in the global telecommunications industry that began to unfold in the mid-1980s. Both the evolution of information systems technology and the emergence of global information and telecommunication systems competition have profoundly affected these efforts both substantively and institutionally.

The slow pace of standardization in telephony and, later, data communications was a result of the organizational structures and procedures employed. As noted above, nineteenth-century standards were generated by specialists attached to the diplomatic and administrative conferences. But as networks become more complicated over the years, it became desirable to move much of the technical detail to specialized fora and publications that became recognized in their own right as standards-making activities and bodies. Those for telegraphy, telephony, and radio were all created as independent committees in the 1920s, but they developed a close working relationship with the ITU and formally became a part of it in the late 1940s.[8] Their workloads expanded steadily over time, they came to involve thousands of people meeting in specialized Study Groups and Working Parties several times yearly, and they produced massive amounts of technical Recommendations on many aspects of international interconnectivity. For example, the 1988 CCITT Blue Book contained a full eighteen thousand pages of Recommendations. Yet, despite these indicators of activity, the reality was that the standardization process was too slow and too tightly controlled by the national monopolists to support the needs of the private sector. This would become the major factor in the subsequent breakdown of the old standards order in the late 1980s.

The third major objective of the ancien regime was to organize the provision of cross-border services by national monopolists. Competition was not allowed, meaning that a carrier in one country could not provide services directly to customers in another country. Instead, the first country's network would carry a message to an imaginary halfway point where it would be handed off to the recipient's network, often with transit routing by intermediary countries; revenues would be divided evenly among the participants according to a complex formula of accounting rates and settlements.[9] In essence, this system amounted to a carefully controlled global cartel. The ITU became the OPEC of the telecommunications world, with membership limited and pricing and other decisions shielded from any public scrutiny. Admission—even of private telecommunication providers—was contingent upon signing an agreement to abide by the rules and decisions of the cartel. All this was justified by the assertion that only such a cartel could assure "universal service." Price fixing, defining allowed services, establishing routing tables, and settlement of accounts were a fundamental part of this regime. The nature and price of every service to every destination, the basis and timing of account settlement for initiating or handling transit or terminating traffic, the currency of exchange, and so on, were all delineated in excruciating detail. International meetings under ITU auspices were held every few years to review and adjust provisions. Even today, the ITU continues to publish many of these details through formal plans, tables, and bulletins, although they are rarely followed anymore.

The maintenance of an international telecommunications cartel was as much a fundamental prerequisite for maintaining the architecture of the old provisioning regime as were the technical requirements of connectivity. If even one participant in the global regime were allowed to deviate by offering rates that were lower than the rest, by competing for transit traffic, or by selling capacity to third parties, the entire regime would collapse and be replaced by a global marketplace environment. In effect, this is exactly what is now unfolding. The genie of the global marketplace has emerged from the bottle. Diverse global networks operated by consortia or transnational corporations, and cooperative networks of networks like the Internet are emerging as models of the new paradigm. What remains for further investigation is why the global cartel arrangement persisted for so long. Why, in a world where planned economies were not the norm and, moreover, were generally seen as abysmal failures, was a similar economic model allowed to prevail as the single model for the world of public telecommunications? Perhaps the answer lies in the relatively encapsulated nature of hardware-dominated, single-application telecommunications systems like telegraphy and telephony, which lend themselves to highly standardized practices and known scales of economy. Monopolies under such circumstances can be effective deployment tools. Global information systems, however, seem to require exactly the opposite conditions to be deployed successfully and used effectively. Their appearance has brought the old regime to an abrupt halt.

It should be noted that during virtually this entire period, the role of the U.S. government in this sector of multilateral activity was very limited. The regulated U.S. telecom monopolies—AT&T and the international record carriers like Western Union—performed most of the multilateral activities on behalf of the United States. The U.S. government was not involved in these issues until the Federal Communications Commission (FCC) was created in the 1930s. The United States did not sign any of the ITU's regulatory treaty instruments until 1973.[10] And well into the 1980s, only the most cursory of U.S. oversight existed. It was not until the entire international telecommunication provisioning regime began to change fundamentally that a corresponding change in the role of the U.S. government became necessary. Indeed, the struggle to define and effect a U.S. government role independent from the residual effects of these long-standing AT&T/record carrier relationships is still being worked out. In light of the GATT accord on services, described in Chapter 11 in this volume, it would appear that this role increasingly will be played by the U.S. trade representative.

THE INTERNATIONAL RADIO REGIME

The management of the radio spectrum fell into multilateral hands rather quickly after the application of radio technology in the form of wireless telegraphy for ship-to-shore communication.[11] Although, as noted above, the impetus for the original multilateral meeting related to connectivity, the principles and tools devised were quickly implemented and came to constitute the regime that persists with some market-oriented modifications today. Like the telecommunications regime, the radio regime rests on the notion that nation-states have sovereignty over the use of spectrum in their territories, but that the realities of an open medium for propagating radio signals necessitates international cooperation. The fundamental principles laid down in 1906 and still with us today were twofold: First, certain radio spectrum bands should be devoted to specific "radio services." This has not changed over the past ninety years. Government representatives convene periodically at formal meetings to define radio services and decide which services can use various portions of the radio spectrum. The results are contained in a Table of Allocations published in the International Radio Regulations, an excessively formalized and rigid treaty negotiated in laborious meetings.[12] Over time, new technologies, new applications, and new interested parties produced expansions and shifts in radio spectrum allocations. However, activity at the international and domestic level has always been slow and cumbersome, and has often been manipulated by special interests in search of spectrum advantages. Indeed, in the current context, the application of new digital technologies to radio as well as the dynamics of information systems and global competitive provisioning have made this allocations process ineffective and unnecessary.

The second principle was that any nation-state could secure the right for a radio station under its jurisdiction to use portions of the radio spectrum free from significant interference from the stations of other states. This was achieved by coordinating state activity through the allotment of usage rights, for which two different approaches were typically employed. One relies on a state registering the use of particular frequencies with an international bureau at the ITU. The other involves the pre-allotment of certain frequencies to particular states, a process referred to as "planning." The registrations are contained in a master register; the planning exercises produce plans published in international treaties. One of the most interesting innovations was the attempt in the late 1940s to develop a plan for the entire radio spectrum that would be continually administered by a kind of court of spectrum justice called the International Frequency Registration Board. The scheme was doomed from the outset, however, and it took until 1992 to scale down the board's functions and fold it into the new Radiocommunications Sector.

At different points during the past ninety years, highly politicized debates ensued over the bases for proceeding with these allotment processes. In the early part of the century, these conflicts often pitted industrialized countries against each other, particularly along the East-West axis. Since the 1970s, the conflict has shifted to the North-South axis, as developing countries demanded a priori allotments of spectrum as their sovereign right, even when they were not yet prepared to make use of the spectrum involved. These battles over the zero-sum division of a scarce resource were seen in the context of the new international economic order debate in which developing countries demanded preferential concessions in trade and other matters, and were waged in huge world and regional administrative conferences held every five to ten years.[13] In the current context, however, any notion of allotment or planning of radio spectrum use by a formal intergovernmental body is sheer folly. Radio technology and uses are simply changing too quickly: Radio transmission techniques like spread spectrum now allow dynamic sharing, and the telecom delivery environments have become increasingly competitive.

The ITU's radio activities also involved some cooperation on international broadcasting matters. International broadcasting first became important during the 1920s, and the first activity was primarily spectrum related—namely, efforts to prevent interference. In the 1950s, with the growing East-West shortwave radio broadcasting battles of the Cold War, national broadcasters began to coordinate their activities. During these decades, nearly all multilateral activity revolved around spectrum issues that produced allocation plans. (The only exception was a rump effort in the late 1930s organized by the Soviet

Union that sought under the remnants of the League of Nations to affect a treaty regarding broadcasting in the cause of peace.) No new areas of multilateral activity emerged until the 1950s, when television technology was mature enough for a mass market and significant multilateral standards-related activities began to unfold in the CCIR. The world was effectively carved up into trade zones as a result of the divergent and incompatible television standards chosen by different nations.

In sharp contrast to the telecommunications regime, the U.S. government from the outset took a highly activist approach to multilateral radio matters. As was the case with most countries, representatives of the U.S. Navy and intelligence services attended the conferences, as both national sovereignty and security interests were involved. Over the decades, the roles and policies of the U.S. government in the radio regime have evolved as the functions of government agencies and the interests of affected parties have also evolved. With the growing commercial use of radio in the 1920s, these roles and policies became divided between governmental and nongovernmental sectors. The Department of Commerce and its secretariat activities on behalf of the Inter-Department Radio Advisory Committee (IRAC) have served as home base for government interests, while the Federal Radio Commission and later the Federal Communications Commission served as the focal point for nongovernment activities. The State Department has typically played a passive role in participation in the ITU.

In parallel, the U.S. government played a direct and significant role in multilateral broadcasting activity. The shortwave broadcasting allocation and coordination activities were brought about primarily by the U.S. Information Agency and its predecessors, along with the Board for International Broadcasting with some liaison with the IRAC and the FCC Broadcast Bureau. In standards-making activity, the FCC took the lead role through its National Television Standards Committee (NTSC).

Typically, the FCC has devised its international radio policies through a fairly formal "notice and comment" process in which all interested parties are assumed to be pursuing their own interests or those of the industry group with which they are identified. The role of the FCC has been limited to that of a facilitator of common ground among the parties. The IRAC has played a similar role among U.S. government agencies. In case of a continuing dispute between the FCC and IRAC, the State Department on occasion has acted as a neutral broker. Such a concatenation of highly bureaucratic processes has operated perennially almost by rote and has rarely been known for its speed or enlightenment. The fact that the international process has not changed significantly in the past ninety years says something about the dynamics of this environment. It is fair to say, however, that the United States has generally been a strong voice for minimizing unnecessary international provisions and specifications and urging flexible allocations and allotment processes.

THE INTERNATIONAL SATELLITE REGIME

While the primary focus of this chapter is on multilateral cooperation in the ITU, it should be noted that there is a third broad international regime in the telecommunications field. This is the regime for the provision of satellite services, which is based in another treaty organization, the International Telecommunications Satellite Organization (INTELSAT). Launched in 1964 at the instigation of the U.S. government, INTELSAT was set up as a "carrier's carrier" to provide satellite uplinks and downlinks to the national carriers that controlled it. Moreover, it was established as a monopoly, a sort of meta-PTT in the sky, by ITU members. No significant competition from separate satellite systems was allowed. Under Article 14D of INTELSAT's governing instrument, no system—such as the regional satellite networks established by some PTTs in the 1970s and 1980s—could take away more than 3 percent of INTELSAT's potential market in a given set of relations, and any such system was compelled to coordinate with INTELSAT on technical, operational, and financial matters. Over time, the U.S. government began to regret its involvement: Because of the U.S. stake in INTELSAT, it had to intervene to help INTELSAT retain its monopoly position, even as INTELSAT began to face increasing competition from more desirable submarine cable facilities and others seeking competitive entry to its market. Moreover, INTELSAT's 3 percent rule became a problem in the 1980s when the Reagan administration began to authorize separate private systems like PANAMSAT to provide certain services.[14] Ultimately, however, the spread of fiber-optic cables and of private satellite systems in the era of global liberalization would undermine INTELSAT's monopoly power and throw into question the U.S. government's continuing commitment to this bastion of monopoly power.

MULTILATERALISM IN THE AGE OF DISTRIBUTED INFORMATION NETWORKS: 1985–1995

For over a century, the global telecommunications industry was controlled by national monopolies that carefully designed complex systems of rules intended to buttress their market power and political authority. As we have seen, this process played out not only at the national level, but also at the international level within the telecommunications, radio, and satellite regimes. Happily, this self-contained world of closed organizations imposing closed technological and economic architectures on the industry began to break apart after the 1984 divestiture of AT&T. As many of the contributions to this volume indicate, telecommunications has shifted on a global scale from the stagnant world of the nineteenth-century post office to become the most dynamic and central sector in a market-driven global information economy. Accompanying this shift are dramatic mutations in technologies, concepts, regulations, markets, provisioning approaches, and applications. It is plainly a time of great innovation, as the expanding nexus of telecommunications, computers, and microelectronics heads into uncharted territory. How did this happen, and what does it mean for the future of multilateral cooperation and U.S. foreign policy?

The two most powerful of the driving forces of change are, first, microelectronic and computer technologies, both of which have commoditized information networks and transformed telecommunication transmission into transparent "bit pipes," and, second, the long overdue consigning of the telecommunications monopolies to the trash heap of history.

The first of these forces is captured by the motto of one of the leaders of the revolution, Sun Microsystems: "The computer is the network." As Richard Solomon discusses in the appendix to Part I, the new technologies have centripetally dispersed much of the software-based intelligence required to operate systems and services away from the centralized networks of dominant carriers and toward the edges—to customer's equipment, such as personal computers and workstations. Moreover, entrepreneurs have been able to take advantage of these powerful new information processors to upgrade and customize circuits leased from those carriers or constructed de novo to launch competitive services and private enterprise networks. Although it is unlikely to happen anytime soon, the advent of advanced software packages for desktop computers (for example, Microsoft's expected Windows Applications Interface for Signalling System No. 7) will allow users to interact with intelligent networks more effectively. For those who deal with technologies and their use, change itself is a critical factor that is now expressed in a "time to market" and is measured in months. The significance of the current dynamics of change is impressing itself on the consciousness of every company active in a competitive marketplace. Technologies and markets today literally are evolving by the week.

Hence, from a technological standpoint, we are not at the end of a process of change, but rather on the cusp of a new one. Every three years, we see a fourfold factor of improvement in semiconductor density. One-gigabit memory chips will be here by the end of the decade, with minisupercomputers ("Crayettes") on people's desks. More than 100 million personal computers have already been deployed worldwide; coupled with local-area networks and router technologies that provide ubiquitous application connectivity, they have destroyed the single solution megafantasies of the 1970s like the ISDN and the bureaucratically designed open systems interconnection (OSI) model for computer communications. Moreover, this transformation in the technological foundations of the information economy is affecting the voice as well as the data market. Some of the most rapidly growing new sectors in telephony encompass the nearly endless opportunities to pursue services built around the dynamics of today's transmission networks, a modicum of network intelligence, user preferences, and rate arbitrage. These applications include calling cards, call home, resale, refile, and special transit arrangements. All these and other services waiting in the wings will be essential components of the national and global information infrastructures of the twenty-first century.

In parallel with the technological transformation, the second driving force has been the institutional change associated with global liberalization. In the postdivestiture environment, the cracking of the international telecommunications cartel combined with the disappearance of national monopolies has very quickly catalyzed the globalization of firms and markets, as Linda Garcia explains in Chapter 3 in this volume. Through a variety of arrangements including outright buyouts, new national licenses, overlay networks, or global joint ventures, transnational networks of networks are emerging around the world. Given this trend toward alternative and interconnected transborder systems, it is not too hyperbolic to suggest that by the end of the decade, much of the industry may look architecturally remarkably like the Internet—a vast global agglomeration of heterogeneous and autonomous networks with a small number of global backbones operated by megacarrier consortia. In this environment—which offers business opportunities in markets with seemingly endless demand elasticity—there is a surprising willingness among carriers to cooperate through diverse kinds of new international mechanisms.

What does this worldwide technological, economic, and political transformation mean for the shape of multilateral activity? Above all, it shifts control into the hands of those actually using information networks—individual and organizational consumers—who require from telecommunications only dumb pipes capable of carrying the information forms they wish to send or share. In such a user-oriented environment, the old multilateral institutions and activities become irrelevant, and perhaps even liabilities. Quite simply, multilateral activities that fail to accommodate these changes will be bypassed.

THE NEW INTERNATIONAL TELECOMMUNICATIONS REGIME

The global spread of liberalization around the world proceeded during the 1980s in essentially three waves, with the United States, the United Kingdom, and Japan leading the way, followed by the other industrialized countries and later the developing world. As national institutions and markets began to change, pressures emerged from below for a redefinition of the international telecommunications regime. The national monopolies of old were shifting toward more commercial postures; new market entrants were seeking to provide competitive services (particularly computerized value-added services); and corporate users were demanding greater freedom to configure, control, and interconnect their internal networks. Moreover, other players within governments, such as ministries of trade and industry, were demanding a more procompetitive stance within international arrangements. Over time, these factors forced governments to begin a painful redefinition of both the ITU's policymaking apparatus and the regime it had produced.

In terms of the policymaking process, the ITU has attempted to reform itself in order to respond more effectively to technological imperatives and market demands. Plenipotentiary conferences in 1989 and 1992 adopted a series of measures that enhanced somewhat the transparency, flexibility, and speed of its programs, particularly in the field of technical standardization, and that made it easier for private firms to participate on more equal footing in a variety of decision-making bodies. Paralleling these internal reforms, the ITU has attempted to define a better working relationship with the many external organizations that have greatly increased their roles in international telecommunications policy over the past five years. These include, for example, the GATT, which has become central to the architecture of service provisioning, and a variety of regional and system-specific technical standardization bodies.

In terms of the regime product, ITU members began to relax some of the more onerous of their regulatory agreements at a watershed conference, the 1988 WATTC. For the first time, the International Telecommunications Regulations specifically endorsed the ability of nonmonopoly providers to enter into special arrangements for the cross-border provision of services and applications.[15] In the following years, ITU members loosened the many Recommendations that had restricted competitive provisioning and the customer usage of private leased circuits and networks in the name of national sovereignty. Similarly, they adopted new Recommendations that improved somewhat (but did not replace) the old system of joint service provisioning or cartel management, notably by encouraging cost-based and transparent accounting rates.[16] Without delving further into the details of the provisions involved, it is safe to say that

> the international regime is undergoing transformation. Although sovereignty as a constitutional concept remains, the assumption that it must be operationalized via monopolies has been jettisoned. There is now a broad consensus that varying mixes of public and private control are viable means to economic and social ends. Joint provisioning by administrations is no longer viewed as the singular solution for service provision, as end-to-end carriers have proliferated in advanced services and are seeking entry into basic telephony. And . . . [the] principle of interconnection via standardization has also been reconstituted. Liberalization and private control have altered the substantive nature of the standards in demand and the process by which they are supplied.[17]

Laudable as they may be, these efforts to revise the regime first laid down in 1850 are a case of too little, too late. The entire world of telecommunications has changed too much for a still PTT-dominated organization and system of rules to preserve their historical places in the industry, even if they have become a bit more market friendly. As noted above, the genie is out of the bottle and the center of activity is migrating elsewhere. In a world of commoditized information networks, the nature and substance of multilateral activity becomes quite different and generally much more complex. Indeed, most of the complexity simply cannot be dealt with in the context of traditional multilateral activity and needs to be left to the marketplace, just as complex national economies cannot be planned by central government authorities.

In broad terms, the new world of heterogeneous networked information systems is characterized by the following goals:

▼ Providing open access transport architectures, including specified technical and operational requirements designed for competition

▼ Devising norms and practices that allow and even encourage cost-based, competitive provisioning of telecommunications services and discourage or prevent the emergence of monopolies or cartels

▼ Accommodating global constructs for provisioning and use of information network resources that have little or no relationship to national boundaries

To appreciate the difficulty of these challenges, let us reconsider in more depth two of the fundamental objectives of the telecommunications regime: technical standardization and the organization of services markets. With regard to standardization, in the 1950s and 1960s, activity relating to information systems networks began to occur in the International Organization for Standardization (ISO), as well as in the ITU. In the 1970s, the Internet Activities Board became the site of still more activity relating to internetworking technologies, and, in the early 1980s, standards for local-area networks came to be addressed within the Institute of Electrical and Electronics Engineers (IEEE). For the most part, this work constituted mixed private sector-governmental activity on an international scale. Although this standards-making activity was not extensive prior to the mid-1980s, it provided the basis for some of the dramatic changes that later began to unfold as part of the global information networking revolution.

Because standards-making activities are so sensitive to the factors transforming the global information environment, they have been among the first multilateral activities to be affected. Between 1984 and 1993, the following quite remarkable events unfolded:

▼ New standards organizations form to take on some of the functions once performed within the ITU. At the national and regional levels, activities formerly dominated by monopoly carriers become the purview of comparatively open and market-oriented bodies characterized by extensive and diverse private sector participation. In the United States, the Exchange

Carriers Standards Association's Committee T1 is launched in 1984; in Japan, the Telecommunications Technology Committee is established in 1985; and in Europe, the European Telecommunications Standards Institute is created in 1988.[18]

▼ These organizations constitute a new architecture for telecom standards making. Beginning with the first InterRegional Telecommunications Standards Conference in February 1990, they begin a process of interacting directly among themselves rather than dealing with the prevailing international standards body, the CCITT.

▼ The new telecom bodies fail to move fast enough to meet the needs of the marketplace and are bypassed by newer, ad hoc standards organizations (including the Frame Relay Forum, ATM Forum, SMDS Forum, and so on) that focus on specific important market sectors.

▼ Traditional information standards bodies oriented around OSI abstraction expand in scope and spawn numerous new regional and national bodies (such as ANSI X3, EWOS, and so on). ISO allies itself with CCITT. To deal with implementation and testing standards, still more bodies and organizations are formed.

▼ The internetworking community creates its own international standards organization under the Internet Activities Board (now known as the Internet Architecture Board). This community proceeds to develop within a very short time frame complete, tested, and implementable standards to meet specific user needs and distributes these standards electronically.

▼ As "time to market" becomes ever more critical, ad hoc industry consortia become the norm for developing nearly all computer-related standards. Even individual software vendors like Microsoft or Sun Microsystems become promulgators of international standards by attracting large cross-sections of their industry around open specifications.

▼ The old model of standards making collapses as the marketplace shifts toward the standards of new fast, agile organizations.

Although some of these efforts were much more successful than others, they all represent an extensive new class of "multilateral" information infrastructure activities devoted to producing much more open networks. Thus, during the 1980s, a number of factors combined to make common open access transport environments a shared pursuit worldwide.[19] These factors included large-scale implementation of common digital transport, switching, and network management systems by carriers and carrier equipment manufacturers. They also included the implementation of voice and data networks on these systems. Other important factors were lower procurement and maintenance costs, the ability of equipment vendors to pursue global markets, increasing demand for private leased lines for enterprise and public overlay networks, and pressures arising from new competition-oriented national and regional regulatory requirements such as Open Network Architectures, Open Network Provisioning, the European Union (formerly the Commission of the European Community) Green Paper, the Japan Ministry of Posts and Telecommunications White Paper, and so on.[20] Considerable multilateral activity will continue to be directed toward securing efficient and flexible open access transport. It will take the form of standards activities in new bodies such as the ATM Forum, in contractual or joint venture relationships, and in potential new GATT-related actions that continue the process already under way of harmonizing different national Open Network regulatory requirements.

Today, for all practical purposes, intergovernmental standards-making activities—although they continue to exist—are becoming increasingly irrelevant. Even after the ITU's reforms, with development times for even initial standards measured in years, there are few new standards of any significance now being developed within the ITU. Similar considerations apply to the ISO, which although it is not exclusively an intergovernmental organization, has many of the same liabilities. This is not an indictment of the ITU or ISO. Rather, it is a recognition that time to "market" and consensus among significant players on an implementable standard are the factors of greatest importance in today's global networking world—not the adoption or recognition of standards by an intergovernmental body. Slow-moving international standards bodies that cannot even initiate standards activity in less than a year, much less develop a standard that meets immediate marketplace needs, clearly are not going to be relied on heavily.

The world of standards making, both international and domestic, has become much more diverse. An important feature is the mixture of cooperation and competition. Even strong competitors are cooperating in these bodies because of their common incentive to create a new market. The new environment has also transformed the meaning of the term *multilateral*, with major transnational corporations and international consortia playing roles once reserved for governments. The resulting "multilateral activities" seem much better suited to the times. Potential problems remain, however, which may provide some peripheral new intergovernmental roles. Although the internetworking standards world has been highly successful because of its fully open processes and widespread dissemination of standards, most other standards bodies remain relatively closed. In the GATT Uruguay Round negotiations, considerable discussion occurred regarding the need for easy, timely, and open access to standards and standards-making procedures, lest the standards themselves become nontariff trade barriers. Already, the ITU has begun to play a potentially valuable role as a clearinghouse for standards information via the Internet. In the future, it is possible that the intergovernmental role in the standards arena will be one not of standards making, but of the dissemination of information about standards.[21]

Turning from the standards function to service provisioning, we find even more interesting new multilateral activities that render irrelevant the old ways of doing business in the ITU. Because information transport is destined to become a low-cost commodity subject to intense competition, it seems likely that the settlement and accounting practices that have been bedrock of international provisioning for the past 140 years are about to change. The inappropriateness of existing practices has been given considerable publicity in publications such as the *Financial Times*, in the Organization for Economic Cooperation and Development, in a current FCC proceeding, and most recently, in the ITU itself. In an environment of complex autonomous networks, the overhead necessary to support settlement and accounting practices is often much more costly than the transport service itself. The global Internet, which currently consists of fifty thousand (as of December 1994) interoperating networks in more than ninety countries, already maintains successfully a "sender keeps all" accounting and settlement regime, which is the opposite of the revenue division approach practiced by national carriers under ITU rules. Virtually all enterprise networks follow the same practice. The Internet accounting model (if not the Internet architecture itself) could be a model for all information networks. Under this model, everyone would buy bandwidth from providers at highly competitive rates. Providers would attract customers and earn their primary revenue by offering an assortment of differentiating network management and information services—not by selling transport. Notable exceptions would probably include broadcast/multicast services and transport to environments where bandwidth may not be a commodity.

International service rules face an equally interesting future. The ITU's treaty instruments—the Constitution, Convention, and Regulations—remain, despite recent reforms, fundamentally divorced from reality. As such, they seem destined increasingly to be ignored to the point where they must be completely rewritten to reflect a world of private sector provisioning. In such a world, the focus of intergovernmental activities would be in the GATT or, now, the World Trade Organization (WTO). In this context, it is interesting to contemplate the evolution of procompetitive international provisioning norms—and potentially even antitrust provisions and enforcement procedures. Might it be possible to have an international equivalent of Harold Greene, the judge who presided over the AT&T divestiture? Are global agreements on antitrust rules possible?

In any event, the shape of multilateral requirements has already been affected profoundly by the transition from telecommunications to computer networking. Perhaps foremost, this transition has been marked by a shift of intergovernmental responsibility for market organization from the ITU to the WTO.[22] The former has been left with almost no apparent role in the domain of telecommunication services. (Indeed, its most recent activity has been devoted to studying what, if any role, would remain in a transformed provisioning world.) In this emerging multilateral world, governing arrangements are made by diverse competing private companies collaborating and competing through consortia or private-sector-driven international organizations, and the old distinctions between providers and users disappear. How the ITU fits into the new game is thus far from clear; privatization of the organization might need to be considered if it is to play any effective role in the future.[23]

THE INTERNATIONAL RADIO REGIME

Multilateral management of the radio spectrum remains today a wholly intergovernmental activity. Ten years after calls for deregulation of the Radio Regulations, the international radio environment continues to be the subject of detailed regulation in international treaty instruments. Yet some cracks are beginning to appear in these massive regulatory walls. Global radio systems like Motorola's iridium project, radio-based universal personal communications, digital signal processing, and spread spectrum technology will put increasing pressure on global spectrum management bureaucracies to change their practices. Indeed, the ITU's recent WARC-92 conference on global spectrum management was for the first time heavily influenced by the demands of private competitive suppliers of new wireless services not only from the United States, but also from Europe and beyond.[24]

Still, it is notable that, although the telecommunications regime has been transformed, the radio regime remains unaltered in its fundamental assumptions and principles. After almost ninety years, we still rely on an intergovernmental agreement for the distribution of spectrum through ponderously slow decision-making procedures and rigid treaty agreements. Although a dialogue on the subject of radio regulatory practices was attempted—and rebuffed—during the course of the GATT Uruguay Round negotiations, one hopes that the issue will reappear in that context, leading to global deregulation. For its part, the ITU has recently attempted to streamline its means for achieving global management of the radio spectrum through some restructuring of its forums and secretariats. However, it seems clear that much more fundamental changes in the regime will need to occur in order to increase its responsiveness to the new environment.

THE INTERNATIONAL SATELLITE REGIME

In the new global information environment, the old intergovernmental provisioning organizations and relationships may eventually just disappear. Perhaps recognizing this as inevitable, INTELSAT members have agreed to loosen substantially the Article 14D provision that had long protected the organization from competition, thereby opening the way slightly for the further development of private competitive systems. Moreover, INTELSAT members are understood to be attempting to attract private sector investors and to be seriously considering privatization of the organization. This would be a logical step and probably the only way for the body to preserve some of its competitive position in a multivendor future. Indeed, most other international facilities arrangements are being privatized quickly and blended into the world of competing global carriers. The INMARSAT maritime organization, too, is aggressively pursuing the global mobile communications market. In general, however, while both INTELSAT and INMARSAT have made significant changes in adapting to an increasingly competitive market environment, it is not clear whether in the long run they can continue to exist as intergovernmental organizations.

POLICY IMPLICATIONS
OF THE GREAT TRANSFORMATION

Success in a new globally competitive information technology (IT) universe could be enhanced through a strategic vision coupled with an effective means of implementing that vision. An all-encompassing government industrial policy in the IT sector is not appropriate; in fact, history seems to demonstrate that such efforts are likely to be highly detrimental to implementing information infrastructure and achieving a globally competitive position. On the other hand, there are some cohesive policies and actions that can be taken to further U.S. strategic needs and objectives within multilateral fora.

First, there is a pressing need to restructure the U.S. policymaking process for multilateral activity, although not necessarily through the sort of administrative consolidation advocated by Henry Geller and Joel Reidenberg in this volume. The U.S. institutions responsible for multilateral activity are themselves presently in the midst of major evolution. The old FCC-State Department-National Telecommunications and Information Administration (NTIA) triad has diminished in importance—an inevitable trend in light of the shrinking need for intrusive government involvement in global information networking. Perhaps the least needed and most ineffectual of these is the Department of State, which expanded in the 1980s far beyond its original role, and which is the only "foreign ministry" in the world that remains involved in telecommunications matters—a subject area greatly removed from its sphere of competence.

An entirely new "triad" for dealing with multilateral matters has been emerging slowly in recent years and should be encouraged by U.S. government policy. This consists of strategic science and technology (S&T); norms for global trade; and a national competitiveness policy for telecom transport.

STRATEGIC S&T

A rather disjointed strategic science and technology community has existed behind the Washington telecommunications policy scene for many decades. The key player consistently over the past thirty years has been the Department of Defense Advanced Research Projects Agency (DARPA), which has served as the de facto core of a loose and highly decentralized community of people and functions within the intelligence community, the National Research Council, the White House's Office of Science and Technology Policy (OSTP), the National Science Foundation, congressional S&T committees, science and technology offices within independent agencies, and the academic and research communities.

Parts of this community can be traced back as far as 1914 to the emergence of the Naval Research Lab and its focus on new applications of radio technology, and later on signals intelligence. For many years, this community had an exclusive focus on radio technologies, as most of the innovations in telecommunications (particularly those with a strong national security component) were occurring in the radio field. This focus began to change with the emergence of early computing machines, advanced cryptology techniques, and finally digital and microelectronic technologies.

For the past two decades, the strategic federal S&T community has provided a foundation for industrial development and policymaking that has significantly shaped the entire IT realm. An extraordinarily large number of new networking and computer technologies can be traced to DARPA-related activities and its legendary leader for many years, Robert Kahn. Indeed, virtually the entire new computer and computer-networking marketplace—now dominated by U.S. industry—emerged from strategic federal S&T programs. DARPA had the vision and skill to know what kinds of technologies to develop; moreover, it was able to encourage the right innovative generic developments without being overly intrusive in picking winners and losers among technologies or market sectors.

Until the 1992 presidential election, the U.S. strategic S&T community operated in the background in a decentralized fashion, largely disconnected from the more prominent federal agencies dealing with information and telecommunication policies like the FCC and the NTIA. These "foreground" agencies typically have used traditional politically oriented public policy processes that have little or no strategic S&T component, seeking mainly to maximize the collective benefits among competing industry constituents.

This sub rosa approach to S&T policy has frequently become acutely disconnected from U.S. multilateral activities during the past decade. The most prominent examples include the U.S. State Department becoming the advocate for Japan HDTV standards or support for European Community OSI networking industrial policies in multilateral fora, even against the interests of the U.S. industrial base.

In the Clinton-Gore administration, the strategic S&T communities have come to play the lead role in shaping U.S. multilateral activities in the IT sector—coordinating the other two legs of a new triad that deals with international trade norms and competitive transport policy. The OSTP appears to be central to this activity. This reorientation is well suited to the new global information networking environment where most developments are driven by technology, and where heavy-handed technology-oriented industrial policy programs and policies in other regions and nations are endemic.[25]

NORMS FOR GLOBAL TRADE

The strongly procompetitive policies that emerged in the late 1970s and early 1980s from the FCC, the NTIA, and the Modified Final Judgment (MFJ) that brought about the AT&T divestiture set the stage in the public policy arena for the unraveling of the international telecommunications cartel in the years that followed. The first shot across the cartel's bow was the FCC's celebrated resale and shared-use proceeding in 1981 that brought the threat of instant retribution by the former director of the CCITT. Thereafter, actions like forcing competition in the U.S. international telecommunication market, establishing competition between and among satellite and submarine cable systems, requiring the competitive provisioning of telecommunications terminal equipment, allowing the interconnection of international private lines to build global value-added networks (VANs) and private networks and transiting traffic across the United States piece by piece began to crack the international cartel.

The stage was being set for the next step—the development of inter-national norms for participating in a global information and telecommunications market. Not surprisingly, with the effective commoditization of information networks, the international model and institutional forum shifted from the ITU to the GATT. Just as the ITU was the chief international mechanism for main-taining a two-level monopoly world, the GATT was designed as the instrument for the new global competitive commodity environment.

In the United States, the U.S. trade representative's office took an early lead in recognizing this transition, developing a set of norms for global trade in telecommunications, and bringing these norms within the Uruguay Round of the GATT negotiations. The USTR approach was innovative and was tailored to an emerging world of global information networks where the keys to success were access to national markets and underlying transport facilities.

In pursuing these efforts, the USTR fostered its own international mechanisms, including a well-qualified domestic and international organization staff and contacts in all major trading nations. An entirely new international regime was under construction. In pursuing this initiative, the USTR worked with a few specialists from the FCC and the Department of Commerce. From overseas, the USTR was seen as operating independently of the Department of State, which largely ignored, if not opposed, GATT-centered developments by continuing to adhere to the ITU as a favored institution. During the detailed GATT negotiation sessions on the Telecommunications Annex, it was USTR and FCC staff that negotiated with European Community, Japanese, and Korean representatives to develop a new regime. In effect, the negotiators were seeking to harmonize their own national and regional policies pertaining to competitive provisioning as well as open up their respective standards-making activities.

Even prior to the recent successful conclusion of the GATT services negotiations, the compelling need for a trade-based regime already gained it de facto acceptance by many parties. It seems likely that the USTR will continue to take the lead among U.S. agencies in developing and administering this regime in close coordination with OSTP and the FCC.

NATIONAL COMPETITIVENESS POLICY FOR TELECOM TRANSPORT

The third leg of the new U.S. triad is an aggregation of agencies that focus on regulation of the traditional telecom transport marketplace—the FCC, the NTIA, and the Department of State. The relevant State Department bureaucracy, however, has metamorphosed back to its prior existence as a very small administrative staff located in the Economic Bureau and responsible only for handling formal correspondence with the ITU. This transition is appropriate and should proceed to the complete removal of the State Department from any major involvement in global information networking matters, as had been the case prior to 1982. This may seem like harsh treatment; however, a branch of government that exists mainly for dealing with intergovernmental politics is unlikely to make a positive contribution in the field of information networking. State Department participation encourages politicization of the negotiating process not only by virtue of its institutional role, but also because of the political orientation of the foreign service personnel who staff it. Indeed, the involvement of the U.S. "foreign ministry" in the global telecommunications business is without parallel in the world and sends the wrong message to other countries.

By far the most serious mischief has occurred in relation to the State Department's involvement in the activities of the ITU. These activities can be more effectively handled by other federal agencies or by private sector bodies. Because of its foreign affairs functions, the State Department is exempt from many due process and open government requirements normally required of federal agencies. At the same time, its activities provide blanket antitrust immunity for the companies involved. And to exacerbate an already bad situation, the State Department has perennially had virtually no staff with substantive knowledge of the telecommunications field. This situation has created an open invitation for companies, lobbyists, and foreign agents to manipulate U.S. policies, positions, and representations in matters before the ITU, its subsidiary standards bodies, and other multilateral and bilateral fora.

In the radio field, the legal "loophole" offered by the State Department has always provided a convenient mechanism for savvy players to alter what was decided in the FCC's public processes and to further their own special interests. However, a relatively knowledgeable engineering staff in other federal establishments provided a kind of safeguard to wholesale exploitation. Prior to the 1980s, this loophole was not significant for international telecommunications policymaking because it took place within a monopoly environment, and because AT&T and the record carriers nominally represented U.S. interests anyway. As this environment began to change and become highly competitive during the 1980s, the loophole began to be exploited far more extensively pertaining to telecom than for radio. Additionally, the needless bureaucratic step of funneling all private sector contributions to ITU standards bodies through the State Department proved to be a meaningless brake on the robustness and innovation of the private sector. On all too many occasions, the loser was U.S. national competitiveness as well as specific industry sectors or players.

In sum, eliminating the involvement of the State Department in telecommunication and information matters and transferring these functions to the private sector or to other government agencies would be a significant step toward improving U.S. competitiveness and its participation in multilateral fora.

The GATT services negotiations in the telecommunications sector have already provided a significant role for the FCC in promulgating and harmonizing what amounts to a global open network architecture policy. In the coming years, as complex and dynamic interconnection arrangements arise among diverse national information transport systems, the FCC will surely be called upon to insist on open competitive opportunities before allowing entry into comparable U.S. markets. A potential quasijudicial process within the GATT's General Negotiation for Services (GNS) for resolving some of these disputes would also require FCC activity. All in all, the FCC can be expected to play a significant role in this area of intergovernmental multilateral activity.

The NTIA's role in recent years has been less clear and has focused largely on radio spectrum management issues, particularly for the federal government. The Clinton-Gore administration has recently provided NTIA with an ambitious mandate to assist the White House OSTP and USTR in furthering their policies and agenda. It is presumed that INTELSAT and INMARSAT will transform themselves quickly into competitive global carrier consortia. The United States could encourage this by altering its relationship with COMSAT— the U.S. public company that serves both as the monopoly reseller of INTELSAT services and as U.S. representative in INTELSAT bodies—and by selling shares in INTELSAT and INMARSAT on the open market. This would alleviate the necessity of U.S. government agencies being involved in the governance of these telecommunications facilities organizations.

Beyond restructuring the domestic policy apparatus, there is a pressing need to rethink fundamentally the role of intergovernmental organizations in a dynamic and market-driven global information infrastructure. Surprisingly, some of the questions asked least frequently during many years of public policy debate are those with a global perspective: What are the strategic assets of the United States? What are its strategic interests? What strategies would best further those interests? In large part, the absence of such a perspective is due to the reliance on the marketplace characteristics of U.S. thinking. The answers to the questions are simply those collectively divined in the marketplace. This is a perfectly acceptable approach; however, in the extreme, it fails to recognize the reality that government and intergovernmental activity inevitably exists and can be channeled in a highly beneficial direction. Indeed, many of the most significant developments in microelectronics, information systems, and telecommunications would not have evolved as fast as they did without some government influence. There are many lessons to be learned from the experience of the past twenty years about what works and what does not. The DARPA model of government intervention has demonstrated its success well beyond what was even intended. It has encouraged and produced national information infra-structure of great value to the nation and the world. The MFJ and FCC models that forcefully disaggregated the old monopoly structure have been similarly successful on a global scale. Conversely, attempts by the governments to become involved in the details—like attempting to champion particular kinds of standards like OSI or technologies like ISDN—have been abysmal and costly failures.

The new vision of a broad "information infrastructure" involves much more than just the underlying digital pipes. Even at the transport level, such a vision encompasses both network-based and non-networked-based mechanisms (like CD-ROM and other potential mass-memory devices) and all the enabling microelectronic, processor, mass storage, display, and operating systems technologies that go along with them. At a higher level, information infra-structure encompasses those tools, applications, and skills that allow people in business, government, education, health care, or any other economically or societally significant field to rapidly and effectively create, discover, filter, process, understand, distribute, communicate, receive, or store information. These activities provide means for collaborating, for improving job performance, for rethinking missions, and for otherwise enhancing the ability to lead productive and creative lives.

If we accept that the pursuit of such a broad, comprehensive information infrastructure constitutes a strategic vision for the nation, the following questions pertaining to the United States' multilateral governmental activities must be answered:

▼   What are the strategic assets of the United States? One of the most important is our exceptional ability to create, develop, adapt, produce, market, and apply new information infrastructure efficiently and within short time periods. This ability is driven by the great diversity of the nation itself and constitutes an important underlying strategic asset. As other nations develop these same abilities, the United States may find a "meta" role in facilitating global information commerce to the mutual benefit of many nations.

▼   What are the strategic interests of the United States in the global in-formation economy? Above all, the United States must seek to use effectively its strategic assets in a global marketplace that produces significant economic growth for the nation and the world—and also results in ancillary benefits like greater national security, global stability, and human rights.

▼   Which multilateral strategies should be pursued to further these interests? In general, the best policies encourage the emergence of an open, competitive, global information marketplace with minimal governmental— especially intergovernmental—intrusions or barriers. Key to pursuing this strategy is a recognition that the concept of multilateralism in the global information economy encompasses many new kinds of activities and institutions and has come to involve parties that for the most part are not governments.

10

INFORMATION FLOWS ON THE GLOBAL *INFOBAHN*: TOWARD NEW U.S. POLICIES

JOEL R. REIDENBERG

*I*f there is to be a vibrant global information economy, data will have to flow among nations over seamless, interconnected networks; at the same time, if the end result is to be an open, entrepreneurial, competitive global market, the personal information and intellectual property entrusted to those networks will have to be governed by rules that will inspire confidence. Without such fair ground rules, people and corporations will lack the requisite confidence in the integrity of global networks. Unfortunately, in the United States, confidence in network information practice is already eroding; citizens believe they have lost control of their personal information, and businesses, out of a belief that they face the same danger, are attacking the U.S. government's effort to displace proprietary security standards through the "Clipper Chip."[1]

In two critical areas, privacy and intellectual property, the United States is presently embarked on a counterproductive path both for robust development of information flows on the emerging national information infrastructure (NII) and for American competitiveness within the global information infrastructure (GII). The United States lacks the consistent norms and coherent policymaking mechanisms that are a prerequisite for leadership in the global information economy. Narrowly drawn policies have often produced incongruous results in these areas at both the domestic and international levels. For example, transaction records in the United States of video sales and rentals are protected against nonconsensual disclosure, but transaction records of credit card purchases reflecting attendance at movie theaters showing the same films are not. At the international level, the U.S. government has argued against requiring legal standards for privacy protection, while maintaining that U.S. privacy protection is comprehensive. Similarly, in the intellectual property area, a copyright is available in the United States for computer programming standards but not for factual works.[2] Meanwhile, in international circles, the United States argued to increase protection of intellectual property around the world yet had great difficulty adopting the Berne Convention for the protection of copyrights. In each of these two key policy areas, government decision making is diffused across a confusing maze of agencies, including the Federal Communications Commission (FCC), the National Telecommunications and Information Administration (NTIA), the State Department, and the U.S. Trade Representative (USTR). The results of such fragmented decision making are often conflicting international positions, such as the White House push for open systems on the NII and the simultaneous criticism at the international level of open standards for connection to the global information infrastructure.[3]

In these two key areas, the NII and global *infobahn* both challenge our traditional legal, cultural, and political principles. In response, domestic policy has sought too little protection for privacy and too much protection for intellectual property. International policy remains confused by the short-term interests of large corporations, particularly financial companies, telecommunications companies, and equipment manufacturers. The interests of individuals and American society are rarely represented despite their enormous stakes in the issues.

To ensure privacy protection, the United States must adopt a set of clear and consistent standards for the fair treatment of personal information that reconciles the positions of all the interested parties (commercial enterprises, individuals, and government). Privacy policy must be rebalanced to promote the participation of all people on an equal footing in an information society. Furthermore, if the competitive position of U.S. business is to be maintained on the global information infrastructure, these new domestic standards must be compatible with worldwide trends in data privacy. To safeguard intellectual property rights, the United States must create domestic standards that emphasize open, dynamic information markets with low barriers to entry, and it must support these goals with consistent policies at the international level.

This chapter examines information flows and the key challenges they pose to existing U.S. domestic and international policies. The first section explores privacy issues. It analyzes the impact of information technologies on fair information practices in the United States, assesses the compatibility of U.S. policies with foreign norms, and argues for new standards in the United States to promote compatibility with international networks. The second section addresses the ownership of information and intellectual property. It argues for restructuring policies to promote open, competitive information highways. The final section makes specific recommendations for U.S. government action.

INFORMATION FLOWS AND PRIVACY

American society is being transformed economically and politically by the global information infrastructure. On the domestic side, the NII promises an astounding array of multimedia services. Already, at the international level, networks allow real-time access to data and information services across long and short distances. A company executive, for example, can access inventory data in a store in Milwaukee and use this information to redirect production flows at the manufacturing plant in Italy. From a notebook computer in California or Istanbul, a person can access bank account information in New York, execute a fund transfer, or order goods and services from a shopping network.

The proliferation of interactive communications creates a massive volume of transaction records and increases the possibility of hidden surveillance of private citizens. The linking of transaction records to individuals and the combining of separate records provide the information for detailed profiles of a person's likely habits, tastes, clothing, wealth, and health. A credit card telephone call, for example, leaves a trace of the details of the transaction (calling party, day, time and duration of call, and the number called) and the payment arrangements. In processing this transaction, the telecommunications service provider, the card-authorizing agent, any party processing the transaction, and the card issuer all obtain some of the transaction information and maintain transaction records. Americans are generally unaware of the extent of transaction record keeping. These transaction details have important uses in many contexts. Traces of isolated activities can and are combined to establish detailed profiles of individuals. For example, the AT&T Universal Card links telephone call patterns with credit card transaction records, such as restaurant preferences and itemized purchases, and the MCI Friends and Family discount program tracks call patterns associated with particular relationships. Because many of the uses of personal information relate to the collection of information in one context and the use for marketing purposes in another context, transaction information offers an economic benefit to commercial enterprises exploiting the data. The benefit, however, is widely viewed as a short-term benefit;[4] once consumers become aware of the uses, they become angry and react negatively toward the offending company.[5]

Real-time interactivity, pervasive data collection, and the secondary use of personal information have critical implications for national policies in the global information economy. Although U.S. policy decisions tend to emphasize short-term commercial values, the penetration of information technology in society has shifted political power so profoundly that it has thus far escaped policy consideration. The NII and global information infrastructure heighten the need to understand these shifts and articulate appropriate standards for privacy policy.

SHIFTING "BIG BROTHER" AND THE STAGNANT U.S. POLICY

In the 1960s and early 1970s, control of computing and telecommunications was generally centralized in the hands of government and large corporations.[6] Fear of "Big Brother" surveillance focused on government abuses of information about individuals or on unwanted public sector information practices.[7] During this period, Americans viewed computer technology from a civil liberties perspective and perceived problems in terms of government action.

Beginning in the 1970s, private-sector use of information technology began to raise isolated concerns. In the United States, specific problems arose in a few contexts, like credit reporting practices and bank record confidentiality, stimulating a recognition of private abuse of personal information. The private sector was not, however, perceived as the potential Big Brother.[8] Most court and legislative decisions were concentrated on limiting Big Brother powers of government only. The U.S. legal system neither comprehensively nor consistently addressed issues involving the private collection, accuracy, use, or storage of personal information outside the government. Standards for fair information practices in the private sector were allowed to develop haphazardly, as industry argued—often successfully—for self-regulation. Cases of specific abuse led to narrowly targeted regulation constraining credit reporting disclosures, strengthening telecommunications confidentiality, and limiting disclosures of cable entertainment viewing patterns.[9]

By contrast, in Europe at the same time, the distribution of computer technology in society was raising significant fears about both government and private-sector surveillance.[10] Indeed, by the late 1970s, several European and Scandinavian countries including France, Germany, Denmark, and Sweden had adopted computer privacy laws that sought to restrain both government and private-sector Big Brothers. The European legislative approach was to enact broad, omnibus laws comprehensively regulating the collection and use of personal information in both the public and private sectors, a clear rejection of the U.S. preference for industry self-regulation.

In the absence of comprehensive or consistent legal standards for the U.S. private sector, the emergence of personal computers and networking in the mid-1980s radically expanded Big Brother in the commercial sector. Smaller private-sector organizations gained access to sophisticated information-processing capabilities through inexpensive equipment and local-area networks (LANs). Individuals obtained new access to vast information resources through modems and gateways to services such as Prodigy, CompuServe, and America Online. Individuals and smaller businesses found globalized access to information through the Internet and private networks. At the beginning of the 1990s, information processing was decentralizing even within large corporations as networks replaced mainframe computers.

In essence, the old single-track path of information flows had been opened up in the 1990s to multiple paths of access by innumerable private organizations through an exponential growth in electronic transaction records and cross-sectoral information sharing. Technology, in effect, shifted information resources into the hands of private-sector organizations. In today's decentralized environment, interactive communications enable significant amounts of transaction information or "information about information" to be generated in one context and used in another. For example, caller identification technology, combined with data capture equipment and information service offerings, allows even small companies to build profiles of individuals in previously unimaginable detail.

Big Brother was usually conceived of as an omnipotent monolithic organization engaged in surveillance and assembling a massive database; today, the decentralization of information processing has made possible omnipresent surveillance by organizations and even individuals through access to multiple sources of data. With more participants in a network, there are more points of data capture and larger volumes of transaction-generated information. Decentralization of information processing in fact results in the capability for any network participant to centralize data. Bits of information may be scattered throughout many isolated parts of the network, yet may be accessible from any place on the network. These possibilities are just in their infancy. For example, sophisticated information providers and intelligent networks already enable combinations of audiovisual images and sounds with other interactive services. Any private organization participating in the global information economy or traveling the global information infrastructure can now be part of Big Brother.

In spite of this major transformation from public to private surveillance of information, U.S. policymakers continue to address issues of private-sector surveillance in a reactive, ad hoc style. Because of our strong traditions of free expression and individualism, Americans have sought historically to restrain the exercise of government rather than private-sector power. As a result, regulation of the treatment of personal information by the private sector has been narrowly targeted and extremely complex. Federal and state laws tend to address particular problems such as credit reporting and cable communications viewing patterns. State common law rights can also provide some protection against outrageously intrusive information-gathering techniques or false and misleading disclosures of information.[12] Traditionally, the United States relies on private action for enforcement; there is no government agency at the federal or state level responsible generally for fair information practices in the private sector.

Even as the decentralization of information processing in the United States dramatically broadened the role of private-sector data processing, American business lobbying succeeded in maintaining the legacy of narrow privacy protection rights for individuals. American political discourse militates any suggestion of impediments to the free flow of information. While U.S. industry recognizes the importance of fair standards for information practices, proposals for new rules on the treatment of personal information in the private sector have been strenuously opposed by the business community. That community has insisted on self-regulation instead of legal standards; indeed, public standards for privacy tend to come about only as a reaction to a notorious scandal or incident, such as the protection of video rental records in response to the disclosure of records for a nominee to the U.S. Supreme Court.

Overall, individuals have few legal protections in the United States against private-sector use of their personal information by the private sector, particularly secondary use.[12] For example, data from transaction records are routinely compiled into such lists as those of incontinent women, arthritis sufferers, impotent men, and compulsive gamblers. While the legal protections are haphazard and scanty, reputable businesses do adhere to fair practices. Credit card companies, for example, may monitor cardholder purchasing patterns, but are unlikely to disclose specific card purchases to third parties. Unfortunately, these laudable practices, where they exist, are usually invisible; companies decline to make their standards public or disclose them to individuals. Private citizens have few effective ways to learn about or participate in decisions about the use of their personal information. Despite industry trade group statements calling for transparency in how business handles personal information, companies do not readily or widely disclose their information practices.[13]

Today, private organizations control decisions about the standards of fair information practices based on commercial interests, despite the important public stake in the issue. Only 25 percent of U.S. businesses are reported to be willing to initiate privacy policies, and even fewer address fair practice issues in a thorough manner. There has historically been no mechanism for individual or public input. Individuals cannot even readily identify the sources behind the circulation of personal information, nor can they learn the criteria for circulating personal information.[14]

Companies themselves are often unsure of the appropriate treatment of personal information in the information age. For example, a customer relations department may view data confidentiality differently from the way the security or marketing division views it. Unsettled standards of treatment have resulted in costly and embarrassing experiences for companies. The abandoned Lotus/Equifax consumer marketing database and the AT&T attempt to reuse subscriber information a few years ago both reflect this growing problem. In 1990, Lotus and Equifax planned to release a jointly developed consumer database on CD-ROM. The database contained detailed personal information including marital status, income, and shopping preferences of 120 million Americans. Public opposition pushed Equifax to cancel the release of the product after it was developed.[15] Similarly, AT&T planned to offer subscribers a directory of toll-free numbers; the directory sent to each recipient would match the profile of the household's specific calling patterns. For example, a directory of toll-free numbers for airlines would be sent to households that frequently called airline numbers. AT&T business clients objected vehemently to providing consumers with information on competitors' toll-free numbers through the directories and their objections forced AT&T to abandon the project.

There is an urgent need for the United States to develop sensible policies on fair information practice. The reactive U.S. policy process may have served us well for many years, but as personal information processing has evolved over the past three decades, the justification for that process at both the government and business levels no longer holds. Information technology and usage are developing too fast and the cross-sectoral uses of personal information are too significant to be governed by the current narrow, reactive policies.

FOREIGN APPROACHES AND INTERNATIONAL COMPATIBILITY

Other countries, particularly in Europe, have approached the treatment of personal information more systematically and more prophylactically than the United States. Over the past two decades, social democratic and civil law traditions have led to broad legislation that seeks to balance free flows of information with individual human rights. These "data protection laws" usually apply to both the public and private sectors and set out principles for the fair collection, storage, use, and dissemination of personal information.[16] The European laws tend to give great weight to the role of individuals in determining if, when, and how personal information will be circulated. And, unlike in the United States, enforcement is usually delegated to independent government agencies that serve roles ranging from licensing authorities to ombudsmen. European data protection laws have had the important effect of preserving citizen participation in the use of personal information and imposing continual review of fair information practices during evolutionary developments in technology and networking.

In the mid-1970s, as these foreign countries began to worry about fair information practices, many focused on cross-border or transborder data flows. A significant number of European national laws have, in fact, adopted provisions that allow the government to restrict flows of personal information to countries that are perceived to lack sufficient levels of privacy protection.[17] Because ad hoc legal standards prevail in the United States, privacy commissions in other countries have begun to scrutinize the U.S. treatment of personal information, and the European Union has recently taken an active interest in U.S. privacy law and practice.[18] Despite the importance of these initiatives, there is no real U.S. government participation in ongoing multilateral discussions of standards among foreign privacy commissioners. Informally, many foreign privacy commissioners have sought guidance on U.S. legal rights from academics and interested parties.

In the late 1970s, well before the recent scrutiny of international data flows, two international organizations, the Organization for Economic Cooperation and Development (OECD) and the Council of Europe, had begun developing comprehensive codes of fair information practice to deal with clashing regulatory styles and content. At that time, the United States and other countries engaged in controversial negotiations over the harmonization of minimum standards through either mandatory rules or voluntary norms. To minimize obstacles to international data flows, the OECD emphasized free flows of information, while the Council of Europe favored stronger protection for human rights.

The United States participated only in the OECD effort and insisted that the final document be considered a set of objectives, rather than mandatory rules. U.S. companies, predominantly from the computer manufacturing and financial services areas, strenuously opposed any outside regulation of fair information practices and lobbied strongly, whenever possible, in favor of a free information market governed only by self-regulation. These companies sought to preserve the status quo of ad hoc, haphazard regulation for the private sector.

The U.S. position prevailed and the OECD effort resulted in a set of voluntary privacy guidelines. In contrast, the Council of Europe effort resulted in a treaty that imposed mandatory standards for enactment into the national laws of signatory countries.[19] Both instruments contain similar, comprehensive principles for fair data collection, legitimate use of personal information, restrictions on unlimited storage of personal information, and proper transmission and dissemination of personal information. Over the past decade, these general principles have been interpreted in particular fields. Various trade associations have developed voluntary guidelines in the hope of refining the principles for sectoral applications. The Council of Europe also has issued a number of recommendations for the application of the European Convention in specific fields such as financial services, employment, and direct marketing.

In the meantime, companies in the United States quickly made public statements in support of the voluntary OECD guidelines. However, the ad hoc nature of U.S. regulation and company practices assured that these guidelines would not be widely implemented in the United States.[20] Nations that adopted the mandatory standards have been better poised than the United States to address the cross-sectoral and social transformation issues.

The success of efforts at international harmonization has also been complicated by an underlying sensitivity to trade relations. Standards for fair information practice are seen by some as a form of trade protectionism. This trade approach leads to rather different perspectives on international data flows. Within the European Union, a proposed directive on data protection seeks to harmonize member-state laws in order to remove internal barriers to trade.[21] Yet the proposal will nevertheless erect barriers—either in the form of closer scrutiny or even prohibition—for data flows to countries with inadequate privacy protection. During the Uruguay Round of the General Agreement on Tariffs and Trade (GATT) and the negotiations of the North American Free Trade Agreement (NAFTA), privacy was also discussed as a possible barrier to trade in services. Proposals that envisioned a fair information practices code were rejected by the United States in summary fashion. U.S. business lobbies were opposed to any new rules that might impose obligations on the United States to treat fair information practices in a comprehensive manner or support the extension of foreign data protection laws. Instead, the Annex on Telecommunications for the GATT allows restraints on information flows only to protect security and confidentiality of communications, while NAFTA permits restrictions to protect the privacy of subscribers as well.[23] The texts of the trade agreements still provide that no restraints may be imposed as disguised or discriminatory restraints of trade.

For international information flows, the harmonization effort through the trade approach is inevitably elusive because of the need for context-based interpretations, such as the meaning of "fair" information collection.[23] In addition, information standards are closely linked to national governance ideals. For example, it would be politically undesirable and legally difficult for the United States to adopt the kind of intrusive mechanism for data protection enforcement that is found in some European countries. Harmonization of laws also ignores a distinctive feature of information practices in the private sector. Choices of technology, such as caller identification versus automatic number identification, or Clipper Chip encryption embed fair information practice standards directly in the infrastructures of information systems. Insistence on harmonized national laws ignores the pace of technological development. Implementation standards will necessarily vary according to the specific circumstances of information flows and cannot readily be harmonized.

DEFINING AND ACCEPTING KEY STANDARDS OF FAIR INFORMATION PRACTICE

In developing information standards, the United States cannot ignore the worldwide trend reflected in the proposed European Union data privacy directive.[24] The proposal, currently under active deliberation, restricts data transfers to countries perceived to lack sufficient privacy protection.[25] These restrictions can affect a broad range of U.S. corporate activities, including payroll processing, electronic mail, financial services, and travel reservations. Because U.S. business is global, standards of fair information practice compatible with those adopted internationally will be necessary to maintain U.S. competitiveness.

For the United States, a comprehensive set of standards also is essential to catch up with the transformation of society and stay competitive in the global information economy.[26] Fair information practices mean good business on the NII and global information infrastructure. An Equifax poll in 1990 showed that growing numbers of people refuse to disclose personal information in business transactions and refrain from economic participation in society to avoid loss of privacy—double the numbers of ten years earlier.[27] At the international level, the United States will only be able to interact efficiently with the rest of the world if it can convince trading partners of the fairness of U.S. information practices.

For U.S. standards to be fair, they must include the following principles for the treatment of personal information throughout the private sector:

1. Fair collection of personal information (including rights of notice and consent and limitations to prevent collection of unnecessary data)

2.   Accuracy of personal information (including rights of access and correction)

3.   Purpose limitations on the use of personal information

4.   Storage requirements for personal information (including duration limits and integrity protections)

5.   Effective enforcement of standards

The appropriate balance of commercial, individual, and public interests in information standards cannot, however, be determined generically, nor can it be determined by the private sector acting on its own. Any set of information standards must recognize that evolving information flows will require flexible guidance for implementation in particular contexts. The context of information processing is critical, and the evolution of information technology keeps any target in perpetual motion.

Politically, the NII is likely to force the acceptance of new legal standards by those business lobbies that previously opposed them. Companies will recognize that an absence of comprehensive private-sector standards harms the perception of the integrity of business. Some larger companies in the United States are already recognizing that fair information practices will define information services on the NII and global *infobahn*; corporate annual reports are even beginning to refer to the strategic importance of their privacy policies.[28] In addition, a continuing absence of legal standards will put U.S. companies on the defensive in satisfying foreign regulators and foreign citizens that personal information will receive fair treatment. At the same time, industry trade groups are having a great deal of difficulty in developing any consensus over their policies. The cross-industry and context-specific uses of personal information by companies cripple attempts to articulate a single industry view. For example, the Information Industry Association took several years to write a privacy code that was acceptable to its members; the resulting text merely "encourages" members to adopt policies containing the principles. Pressure from privacy advocates to establish new standards and from foreign regulators scrutinizing U.S. information practices will become more effective forces of change in the face of disintegrating business cohesion.

As the United States develops new information privacy standards, the style and content of its regulations are likely to differ from those of other countries. The pluralistic global marketplace can still cause an important clash in regulatory values. On the global information infrastructure, foreign rules and customs become "local" through network activity across great distances and traditional jurisdictional boundaries. In a diverse world, this closeness may often cause conflict. The United States must therefore articulate a workable international policy on transborder data flows. To this end, the United States should focus on the promotion of functionally similar results rather than the harmonization of specific information standards or the delivery of a polemic on trade barriers.

Under this approach, nations may adopt varying rules for the treatment of personal information.

In the context of global information flows, as long as the norms are satisfied abroad, the means do not need to be harmonized. Using this approach, legal as well as technological norms can offer effective and comparable data protection.[29] Company activities may also supplement fair information practice standards. By promoting the similarity of protection through each of these techniques, U.S. policy can advance a more flexible and more appropriate approach to international information flows. This is an important departure from existing policy, which has stressed U.S. opposition to any foreign discussion of international data flow rules. A revised policy can improve the vibrancy of the global information infrastructure.

INTELLECTUAL PROPERTY AND OWNERSHIP OF INFORMATION

Information flowing through global networks also presents a critical challenge to concepts of ownership. In the United States, a strong belief in private property led to the development of significant intellectual property rights—economic rights creating private ownership of information. Elsewhere, intellectual property protection may encompass broader rights, such as the personality or moral rights aspect of foreign copyright laws and may include particular views on the public interest, such as the compulsory licensing requirements of many foreign patent laws. Until recently, former communist countries and developing countries rejected the very concept of intellectual property protection.

Ownership of information has historically been found in four types of rights: patents, trademarks, copyrights, and trade secrets. Each of these rights was designed to protect the possession of different elements. Patents historically controlled the right to use novel inventions. Trademarks protected identifying marks or brand names. Copyrights protected the expression of ideas, though not the ideas themselves. Trade secrets preserved the confidentiality of commercially valuable information.

There is an inherent tension between these sets of intellectual property rights and an open global information infrastructure. Dynamic growth in the information economy depends on open markets and wide access to infrastructure technology. Open markets assume that barriers to entry will be low. Intellectual property rights, on the other hand, can pose a formidable barrier to market entry, particularly in cases where an industry's standards are proprietary. The tension is compounded by the increasing value placed on information "assets." For example, three years ago, the European Telecommunications Standards Institute (ETSI) proposed a rules change that would make licensing of intellectual property a condition of membership. Because ETSI sets interoperability standards for the European telecommunications sector and consists of both the national authorities and the major private-sector players, the rules change was particularly controversial. Many larger equipment manufacturers protested the proposal and filed complaints with the European Union.[30] This contentiousness reflects the conflict between proprietary rights and standardization for open access. In essence, the revolution in information technology challenges traditional concepts of intellectual property protection and requires a reexamination of U.S. policy toward proprietary rights for technological standards.

THE TECHNOLOGICAL CHALLENGE TO TRADITIONAL CONCEPTS

The traditional forms of protection adapt poorly to the global information economy. Patents can be used to lock up entire new spheres of the information economy.[31] Copyrights were not designed to deal with functional tools like computer software. In addition, attributing ownership can become a confusing process if multiple players or artificial intelligence contribute to the creation. Similarly, boundary lines between forms of intellectual property protection have blurred; the type of protection can be determined by an innovator's choice in packaging of information.[32] Digital technology and the convergence of tele-communications with computing challenge traditional concepts of ownership. The proprietary value of information is now malleable and transformable. For example, through digital sampling, audiovisual works can now be created using images and sounds that may never have been performed in real life. Computer software can be transformed from written code to circuitry to CD-ROM, defying classical notions of property.

Despite the conceptual problems, U.S. policy has sought to expand proprietary standards through the traditional forms of intellectual property. From the 1970s, software and database protection were sought under copyright law. In effect, this approach tries to bring new types of protection within old labels: Copyright claims for software sought to protect nonliteral elements, and claims for databases sought to develop some protection for facts. Because the technology and information flows are extremely dynamic, this policy presents a never-ending struggle over the scope of the traditional protections.

In the case of functional expressions like computer software, value resides in the function itself and the efficiency of the programming, rather than in the text of the code that produces the function. Traditional intellectual property rights were not generally designed to protect this kind of value. Copyright, which traditionally protects the expression of ideas in books and other written material, has, for example, been distorted to protect the "look and feel" of software rather than the true form of expression; patents, which traditionally have been applied to the protection of new inventions, have even been awarded for software.[33] The only case of an entirely new sui generis right was the enactment in 1984 of legislation protecting semiconductor chips.

The push for an expansion of the scope of existing proprietary standards is justified on grounds that it will encourage investment in research. Yet expanded protection is just as likely to discourage entrepreneurial technological advances. Software litigation and the open network architecture (ONA) telecommunications plans of the late 1980s all battled the scope of proprietary standards; look-and-feel cases were all about expanding proprietary rights, while ONA plans sought to decrease proprietary telecommunications systems. Proprietary standards that are widely accepted raise barriers to market entry for innovative products. Limiting protection of proprietary standards can promote a more diverse marketplace and encourage easier market entry.[34] The video games market illustrates this point. A popular game equipment maker, Sega Enterprises, sought to prevent developers of video game programming from reverse engineering the Sega game consoles in order to discover the interface protocols.[35] Developers could not write games for use on the popular Sega consoles without the interface protocol. The court found that, although copyright law prevents reverse engineering without permission, prohibiting the practice in this case would effectively extend protection to noncopyrightable ideas in the interface. One of the results was robust competition in the end market for video games.

For factual expressions like databases, a similar technological challenge has not been met. Valuable factual compilations, for example, do not fit within normal copyright protection. Facts themselves are not protectable, but there can be significant value in the process leading to the creation of a database of facts. "Sweat-of-the-brow" efforts, no matter how time-consuming, will not qualify the database for protection;[36] originality in the selection and arrangement of the facts is required to qualify for protection. To promote the creation and distribution of information services, protection of factual compilations is nevertheless desirable to some extent. The value added of factual compilations can easily be co-opted by rearrangement. A large investment in compiling data may benefit from protection due to selection and arrangement of data. But, if a user takes the data and inexpensively rearranges them or changes the selection, the original investor has subsidized the latecomer. Novel approaches to rights of fair use can be developed to define the protection in a way that does not impede information flows and undermine innovative compilers. For example, the European Union has proposed an original type of protection for factual compilations in the form of an "extraction right." The right allows protection for factual compilations to the extent that an unfair extraction is prohibited.[37] The proposal limits the reuse of data extracted from a protected compilation.

In general, U.S. policy has not focused on the technological challenge as a catalyst for thinking about new ownership concepts. The rapid pace of technological advances in international information flows suggests that innovation itself can be a key instrument of ownership. If intellectual property rules stress constant innovation rather than legally freezing market development, then competitive advantage will come through rapid product evolution. Fairness in the marketplace can be assured through competition policy. Agreements in restraint of trade and abuse of dominant positions by players can be sanctioned as anticompetitive actions.

POSITIONING FOR INTERNATIONAL TRADE

Important differences exist around the world in the scope, duration, and conditions of intellectual property protection. Many nations still do not have intellectual property rights at all, and others have only weakly enforceable rights. Although policymakers in the United States have recognized this, they have argued for a globalization of the traditional forms of intellectual property protection, ignoring the strain posed by international information flows on these rights. For example, the USTR expressed opposition to the ETSI position on intellectual property rights and telecommunications standardization, yet the ETSI movement away from traditional proprietary standards is the same direction that U.S. law has taken in the past few years.[38] In the 1970s, the United States opposed attempts by developing countries to limit intellectual property rights through technology transfer regimes.[39] The United States also opposed efforts in the early 1980s of the World Intellectual Property Organization (WIPO) to bring the protection of information technologies under a new sui generis international umbrella. The United States rejected, for example, a WIPO multilateral initiative on software protection in favor of the application of national copyright law.

By the mid-1980s, the United States became alarmed at the huge amount of pirated and counterfeit U.S. products available in countries without intellectual property protection. These actions cost U.S. business an estimated $43 billion to $61 billion in 1986 alone.[40] To counter continued losses, the United States led a successful effort to include traditional intellectual property protection on the world trade agenda during the Uruguay Round of GATT. International information flows were recognized to the extent that the GATT proposals and Agreement on Trade-Related Aspects of Intellectual Property, Including Trade in Counterfeit Goods (TRIPS) accord contained specific applications for information technologies: computer programs must be protected by copyright, and compilations must be protected to the extent that the selection, arrangement, or content reflects intellectual creations.[41] Similarly, the United States insisted that NAFTA include comparable provisions.[42]

While this trade approach to intellectual property protection does solve a number of first-generation problems, placing intellectual property in the trade framework has inadvertently raised a series of second generation issues.

One of the major first-generation issues is the adoption of traditional intellectual property rights in other parts of the world such as the Asia/Pacific region, which should reduce bootleg copying and counterfeiting of specific products in many countries. However, for international information flows, the second generation is ignored: the basic problems relating to scope of protection will remain, and national differences will not be resolved. Trade treaties, like the

TRIPS text of GATT and the NAFTA document, only set general obligations to have a regime of protection for intellectual property. The scope of protection for information technologies remains muddled. It is unlikely that international treaties will result in uniform interpretations on the scope of protection for international information flows. For example, while the United States was pushing for traditional protections in international organizations, the European Union began to address more fundamental issues of information flows and adopted a directive on computer software protection that carves out important limitations on proprietary standards.

Another key second-generation issue for the United States is the shrinking role of unilateral policy decisions. In some ways, TRIPS and NAFTA may even invite greater conflict as differences over the appropriate scope of protection are pushed to the respective treaty's dispute settlement process instead of national and international policy fora. For the past few years, the United States has relied on unilateral trade sanctions under Section 301 to force foreign protection of intellectual property and border enforcement under Section 337 to keep out foreign products alleged to infringe U.S. intellectual property rights. Within a trade treaty environment, the United States will no longer be able to act unilaterally. In fact, its power to act may already have been constrained. A GATT panel has ruled that Section 337 violates existing GATT obligations. The reduction in unilateral power will be difficult to support politically when controversies erupt over critical questions of scope of protection for vital elements of the infobahn.

Unless underlying U.S. intellectual property policies appropriately protect information flows, trade sanctions will be ineffective in safeguarding U.S. long-term interests in the information economy. When other countries, particularly those in the European Union, are moving ahead with far more progressive sui generis and hybrid intellectual property rights for information flows, the trade environment is likely to generate increased ownership friction.

POLICY IMPLICATIONS AND RECOMMENDATIONS

In thinking about the policy implications of the NII and global information infrastructure for information flows, policymakers must recognize the dynamic nature of technology. Today's state-of-the-art product is next week's dinosaur. Government policies regarding privacy and intellectual property cannot be wedded to particular technologies. Indeed, U.S. policy should strive to accommodate and encourage technological advances, which means that policy decisions should, at a minimum, build in flexibility for technological advances.

Flexibility is necessary because the boundary lines between fair information practices and ownership are converging. Fair information standards may have implications for the exercise of ownership rights to information infrastructure. If individuals have some control over the circulation of personal information, the "owner" of the information no longer has a pure intellectual property interest in the information. The ownership rights are limited by the privacy policy. In addition, technical rules for network security and interoperability will also determine some aspects of information practice and ownership possibilities.[43] Consistency across these areas is important, yet the groups working on these issues tend to have limited cross-sectoral input.

Jurisdictional boundary lines are also blurring. National boundaries matter, but so do network boundaries.[44] Legal regulation continues to rely on national lawmaking, while network security and interoperability require common protocols and interfaces at the borders of networks. These boundaries overlap one another; nations and networks cross one another's borders. As a result, there is a need to seek congruent regulatory results for each type of border.

The challenges to U.S. policy evolving from global information flows point to three sets of specific policy recommendations for the United States:

1. *Develop standards for fair information practice.*

    ▼   Enact at the federal level a set of principles of fair information practice with flexible mechanisms for interpretive guidance in varying contexts. Private citizens must have an effective way to participate in the use of their personal information; the business community needs a means to develop broad consensus on fair information practice standards; and the United States needs more efficient compatibility with international standards. Because the implementation of any standards will depend on particular contexts, appropriate practices will emerge through interpretation of general standards.

    ▼   Place responsibility for international policy and fair information practices in one high-level federal agency. To develop any new fair information practice policy, the United States is confronted with an institutional dilemma. As noted elsewhere in this volume, the policy process for information standards and intellectual property protection is diffused in agencies throughout the government. Bits and pieces of fair information practices are treated at the FCC, the NTIA, the USTR, the State Department, and the U.S. Office of Consumer Affairs. The lack of any agency with full responsibility for fair information practices cripples clear thinking on the overarching issues.

    ▼   In addition, because of the sparse legal protection, companies will be obliged to persuade foreign regulators that specific practices satisfy foreign standards. Industry groups will lose effectiveness as advocates for U.S. business because foreign regulators are likely to examine specific companies rather than industries as a whole. Without a high-level federal government agency to help promote U.S. interests, U.S. companies will face more skeptical foreign regulators and have a harder time achieving their goals.

▼ Promote policies that strive for similarity of results, rather than harmonization or substantive equality (that is, rather than seek uniform standards, the United States should seek ways to accommodate differing rules). By promoting a results-oriented analysis, U.S. policymakers can avoid intractable disputes over the appropriate legal rules for the treatment of personal information that threaten to impede international data flows. Results analysis does not challenge national philosophies of regulation or national views on the relationship between the government and the private sector.

2. *Promote ownership standards that encourage open, competitive markets. Limit protection for market-designated standards.*

▼ Once a proprietary standard becomes widely accepted in the marketplace, the principles of open access and competition in a dynamic information economy dictate that limits be placed on the proprietary protection available to the standard.

▼ Use competition principles to define ownership of technology. Competition principles may be used to limit the expansion of claims to proprietary protection for market standards, while still preserving incentives for research and investment in technological advances.

▼ Emphasize technological advance as an instrument of ownership. Diminished proprietary protection emphasizes technological progress as a key means to stay competitive and profitable.

▼ Remove the taboo on government-business partnerships and offer tax incentives for technology innovation. If private industry loses some degree of intellectual property protections, some substitute incentive to invest research and development money will become necessary. This can be accomplished in either one of two ways: The government can foster partnerships with business, or it can offer tax incentives for innovators.

▼ Create new protection for factual compilations. The value in factual compilations may not now be adequately protected in the United States. Some form of extraction right, as seen emerging in the European Union, can fill this important void.

▼ Redirect trade sanction efforts. Treaty obligations under GATT and NAFTA now make the use of unilateral trade sanctions for intellectual property problematic.

3. *Create a Presidential Council of Technology Advisers to advise on information technology issues on a continuing basis.*

The implementation of these policy recommendations will not be an easy task. Throughout this volume, authors have noted that the U.S. government needs to have a broad-thinking, technically skilled, and coordinated policymaking apparatus. For international information flows, the need is critical. The issue crossovers cannot be understood, let alone solved, without interdisciplinary analysis. A Council of Technology Advisers akin to the President's Council of Economic Advisers or a Presidential Advisory Council composed of experts from outside the government should be created to serve this important need. The mission of the Information Infrastructure Task Force.[45] illustrates that these issues will not be resolved overnight. The issuance of the task force's report will only begin the process of reworking U.S. policy. Continued thinking will be critical to the United States.

11

INTERNATIONAL TRADE IN INFORMATION-BASED SERVICES: THE URUGUAY ROUND AND BEYOND

KALYPSO NICOLAÏDIS[*]

On April 15, 1994, ministers from 121 countries gathered in Marrakesh, Morocco, to sign the declaration closing the Uruguay Round of multilateral trade negotiations. One of the most complex and controversial facets of these negotiations was a new set of principles and rules to govern international trade in services, the General Agreement on Trade in Services (GATS). These mark the first comprehensive attempt by the world community to deal with new patterns of international exchange fostered by the advent of a global information economy.

The information revolution has led to new modes of interaction between economic actors, operating through an increasingly dense web of public and private communication networks. For the past decade, policymakers and analysts from around the world had sought to adapt the traditional trade principles embodied in the General Agreement on Tariffs and Trade (GATT) to the radically new ways in which value is exchanged across borders. The GATS is a first step in this direction, although it is not the only institutional framework within which such issues are to be addressed (bilateral deals and specialized organizations also have a role, as other chapters in this volume suggest). But the GATS will now serve as the focal point for discussions about governance of the global information economy.

In assessing the current reach and future agenda of the GATS, it is important to keep in mind the major challenge faced by policymakers today: how to foster the worldwide dissemination, sharing, and exchange of information

*I would like to thank Julian Arkell, Arnaud Bordes, Geza Feketekuty, Jim Murray, and Raymond Vernon for their various contributions to this paper.

and information-based services while ensuring against new types of risks and network exclusions—and at the same time striving to improve the social welfare of people around the world.

In many ways the GATS is a more far reaching agreement than most of its participants first envisaged. As a constitutional framework, it covers the whole range of international service sectors—from finance to the professions, from telecommunications to transport—thereby initiating a process of liberalization for a $1 trillion world market.[1] In doing so, it forces a rethinking of the very notion of market access and brings under international scrutiny regulations that had previously been the sole purview of sovereign nations. Moreover, in 1995 the GATS is to come under the umbrella of a new World Trade Organization (WTO)—an institution with more political clout, resources, and enforcement authority than GATT could ever draw upon.[2]

Yet the GATS as it stands today is only a beginning. The broad principles contained in the general framework are vague and remain open to different interpretations. When negotiators reached the point of making more specific liberalization commitments, they simply sidestepped the most contentious issues, leaving areas like financial or audiovisual services or the disciplining of national monopolies for future negotiations. Most important for the long run, the GATS does not address the central obstacle to effective governance of the global information economy: the problem of regulatory fragmentation among national jurisdictions. Dealing with this will require a profound reconceptualization of the meaning of economic integration in a world of network-based transactions and a radical shift in traditional understanding of territorial sovereignty.

These limitations in the GATS should not be considered inherent flaws. They simply point to policy challenges that the United States and its trading partners will confront in the coming decade. But these challenges must be faced. The GATS, by allowing many market participants to make effective and fair use of new freedoms, creates a dangerous window of opportunity in which a few might abuse such freedoms at the expense of all.

This chapter provides an overview of the new multilateral services regime and its implications, focusing on the dynamics between the United States and Europe.[3] Among the issues that will be explored are the fact that the GATS must be seen as an *evolutionary* framework for governing international trade where much will depend on future interpretations and modes of enforcement. It is also important to remember that, particularly in the areas of telecommunications and audiovisual services that involve more conflict, the end of the round reflected a *transitory* state of play; disagreements here relate more to the pace and conditions of liberalized market access than to the principle itself, as parties seek to buy time for internal reform. In this realm, where the United States has taken the lead in promoting liberalization, progress is likely to be contingent on reassuring the Europeans that under increasingly market-led dynamics, local actors will remain central players in network provision; that public authorities will retain enough control over transnational networks to safeguard against potential threats to the public interest; and that some degree of reciprocity in competitive opportunities will be ensured. Finally, it is essential that the *incompleteness* of the GATS is recognized: the results of the give-and-take between Europe and the United States will need to be embedded in overarching regulatory bargains (involving, for example, multilateral recognition and competition policies) that address the need for compatibility between national or regional supervisory regimes. Here I will argue that the European Union may provide, if not a model to be reproduced, at least a valuable lesson for the future, from which the United States may need to take its clues.

DEFINITIONAL ISSUES

How do activities falling under the broad label of "international trade in information-intensive services" relate to the notions of a global information economy and global information infrastructure? This question can be addressed at several levels. At a general level, while information constitutes an increasingly important "factor of production" and is often the form in which value is transferred to the consumer, international trade agreements deal with the actual objects or categories of transactions, as defined by sectors of activity or professions. National measures affecting the international flows of data, information, and knowledge, as well as the eventual international agreements regulating such measures, are categorized by types of services rendered rather than by types of information transferred.

Still at the macro level, the international services debate has been informed by the infrastructure metaphor in two ways: The reference to international services, like transport and finance, providing "the infrastructure for the world economy" has been a popular selling pitch for advocates of a new regime. At the same time, most if not all such services depend at least in part on an effective global information infrastructure in order to be delivered across borders. Without the informatics revolution, many services would not be traded internationally (computer, consultancy, or financial services are examples) or would be traded much less intensively (twenty-four-hour trading on stock exchanges or computerized reservation systems for transport are examples). Some services that are thought of as requiring the movement of either the consumer or the provider across borders are bound to be traded increasingly through communication links (remote medical treatment, engineering design, and education, for example).

Communication and data services play key roles in both the production and delivery not only of services but of an increasing range of products. Global enterprises use information networks in dramatically new ways to make and carry out decisions, as well as to interact with consumers, suppliers, employees, and governments. In short, as Bruno Lanvin illustrates in a recent study, access to and mastery of telecommunications and data services is emerging as a requirement for international competitiveness even in such traditional services as transport and tourism.[4]

Thus, effective governance of the global information infrastructure is both an element in and a determinant of the emerging trade system. The expansion of information-based services depends on telecommunications policies. These policies, in turn, influence the tradability of other services by affecting the cost of transmitting information across borders (determining, for example, the ability of firms to incorporate innovative equipment and services into their intracorporate networks and to use their networks to establish advanced communication links with their suppliers, customers, and distributors). Trade officials thus have become involved in telecommunications regulatory issues "because restrictive regulations can effectively limit market access for internationally traded information-based services and can disadvantage global firms that intensively use computer and telecommunications technology to manage their activity or to distribute their services."[5]

In the context of the Uruguay Round, information-based services can be seen as falling into three concentric circles of definition. The innermost circle encompasses those services delivered through international telecommunications networks via cross-border sales of information, either directly (transborder data flows) or indirectly (computerized network management). The second circle encompasses all services that involve the processing and manipulation of information and knowledge—from financial to professional services—and that can be delivered either through the movement of people or the local establishment of firms or communication networks. The broadest circle includes all transnational services delivery, which nearly always involves the management of, or participation in, global data networks developed within, between, or outside corporate structures. This may involve simply the marketing or financing phase, or the broader need for cooperation with other players in the market. In this sense, transportation or construction services are also information based.

The definition above suggests that many issues are involved in implementing trade liberalization in the realm of services. These issues can be grouped into two categories, the first defined as network-based rights of access, including:

▼ *Rights of access for communication services operators or providers*—including the right to interconnect with domestic telecommunications networks (public or private), for both private networks and equipment (such as modems); the right to use one's own protocol for transmission software; the right to establish private networks by linking together leased lines, private intracorporate or local-area networks, and private computer switching systems.

▼ *Rights of access for information services providers*—including the right to use domestic networks on a nondiscriminatory basis as local infrastructures for service delivery; and the right of access to leased lines as a key to cost reduction.

▼ *Rights of access for exclusionary network operators*—for example, the right to restrict the use of transnational links to a closed user group such as the Society for World-wide Interbank Financial Telecommunications and the Society for Airlines Communications and Information Services, as well as other types of electronic data interchange networks dedicated to specific purposes.

These rights may conflict with another type of rights concerning access to the local or global generation of information through information networks, which may constitute a key input to the local provision of a given service and may be threatened by the growing exclusionary nature of the information networks.

The second category of issues raised by trade liberalization in information-intensive services concerns national regulatory measures. To understand why, it is necessary to backtrack for a moment. Discussions within the Organization for Economic Cooperation and Development (OECD) in the early 1980s, when information-based services first appeared on the international agenda, made clear that it would be impossible for governments to control or tax cross-border information flows on the basis of content or value. If governments could not control the information circulating "above" borders, they could—in their capacity as host and home country regulators—still set rules for the services providers operating both into and from within their jurisdiction. This meant that global regulatory regimes (in, for example, banking or the professions) had to reflect the traditional concerns of national regulators to safeguard the public interest, protect consumers, and ensure against negative externalities. In this light, one of the core challenges for the new services regime was to find effective principles for minimizing the trade-restrictive character of domestic regulations, while at the same time ensuring that the regulatory concerns of national governments would continue to be met.

The difficulty is that domestic regulations restrict trade in information-based services not only when they discriminate blatantly against foreigners, but also simply because of differences among national regulatory systems. To a much greater extent than for trade in goods, barriers created by national regulations have a double-edged effect on trade in information-intensive services: Not only do they create costs associated with adapting to local regulatory measures, but they also distort location patterns, thereby creating what can be called "constrained location costs." In other words, licensing, accreditation, registration, as well as ongoing supervision and enforcement of regulations in the host country, act not only as a costly stamp of entry, but also restrain the providers' choice of "mode of delivery." Since an economic actor needs to be present locally in order to be controlled locally, jurisdictional control by the host country may simply preclude certain types of international service transactions from being conducted at all, at least through the means of cross-border information delivery.

The fact that information and communication technologies have allowed service providers to implement network strategies based on remote delivery in turn allows them to reap increased economies of scale and scope: For example, Reuters' provision of information services to currency markets, a firm engaged in long-distance data processing services, or a bank offering portfolio management services, can operate technically entirely from their home bases. National requirements for some degree of local control and thus local presence for service providers who operate simultaneously under more than one jurisdiction preempt their freedom to choose to access neighboring markets through such modes of cross-border delivery, not only leading them to forgo economies of scale but potentially deterring them from entering a market entirely. Thus, counterintuitive notions such as a right of nonpresence become key to trade liberalization in this area.

The GATS centers on the potential trade-restricting effect of domestic regulations. Yet it barely addresses the more fundamental problem of regulatory fragmentation due to jurisdictional boundaries between home and host states. Nevertheless, the GATS is not a one-shot game, contrary to the perception of some in the U.S. Congress; rather, it is an evolutionary framework that can, and must, serve as the basis for addressing the need for regulatory integration.

THE GATS AS AN EVOLUTIONARY FRAMEWORK

The GATS is the combined result of forty years' experience with the implementation of the GATT, during a period in which government intervention in the economy grew tremendously, and ten years of learning by negotiation by national representatives involved in the Group of Negotiations on Services (GNS). These negotiators were faced with the challenge of crafting an entirely new trade regime for services—a category of international transactions that a decade ago was not even accepted as "trade." Indeed, during the first four years of negotiations (which lasted until a ministerial meeting convened in Brussels in December 1990), national negotiators, and the broader community of analysts and scholars surrounding them, debated the extent to which traditional trade principles would need to be adapted (and the type of new concepts and principles that would need to be introduced) in order to fit the special characteristics of services.[6] This led to the so-called Dunkel draft for an overall framework agreement in December 1990. By 1991, the negotiators were engaged in efforts to exchange specific liberalization commitments; not surprisingly, this proved to be a contentious process. By the end of the round, there had been only small progress on financial services, telecommunications, shipping, and audiovisual services; more concessions had been exchanged in the areas of tourism, construction, professional services, consultancy, and the movement of persons.

Ultimately, the most important achievement of the Uruguay Round negotiations was not in the details; rather, it was in the collective scrutiny over restrictive practices agreed upon by all the signatories of the GATS. In spite of the lack of an explicit "standstill" provision, whereby governments would commit not to introduce new measures, this meant that governments would now find it much harder to use changes in domestic regulatory structures to reduce market access. Beyond this, most concrete progress toward liberalization lies in the future.

The GATS in its final form is made up of three main elements. First, the framework agreement contains general obligations and sets out a mechanism for negotiated commitments. Second, sectoral annexes are included when deemed necessary to clarify the broad concepts in the framework agreement. Finally, national schedules of commitments—two thousand pages of them—are attached to the agreement and are an integral part of it. The overall agreement is to be supervised by a Council for Trade in Services (CTS), with a chair elected by member states.[7] The structure of the agreement is presented in Table 11.1.

TABLE 11.1

THE GENERAL AGREEMENT ON TRADE IN SERVICES (GATS)

PART I SCOPE AND DEFINITION

Article I	Scope and Definition

PART II GENERAL OBLIGATIONS AND DISCIPLINES

Article II	Most-Favored-Nation Treatment
Article III	Transparency
Article IIIbis	Disclosure of Confidential Information
Article IV	Increasing Participation of Developing Countries
Article V	Economic Integration
Article Vbis	Labor Markets Integration Agreements
Article VI	Domestic Regulation
Article VII	Recognition
Article VIII	Monopolies and Exclusive Service Suppliers
Article IX	Business Practices
Article X	Emergency Safeguard Measures
Article XI	Payments and Transfers
Article XII	Restrictions to Safeguard the Balance of Payments
Article XIII	Government Procurement
Article XIV	General Exceptions
Article XIVbis	Security Exceptions
Article XV	Subsidies

PART III SPECIFIC COMMITMENTS

Article XVI	Market Access
Article XVII	National Treatment
Article XVIII	Additional Commitments

PART IV PROGRESSIVE LIBERATION

Article XIX	Negotiation of Specific Commitments
Article XX	Schedules of Specific Commitments
Article XXI	Modification of Schedules

PART V INSTITUTIONAL PROVISIONS

Article XXII	Consultation
Article XXIII	Dispute Settlement and Enforcement
Article XXIV	Council for Trade in Services
Article XXV	Technical Cooperation
Article XXVI	Relationship with Other International Organizations

PART VI FINAL PROVISIONS

Article XXVII	Denial of Benefits
Article XXVIII	Definitions
Article XXIX	Annexes: Article II Exemptions
	on Movement of Natural Persons Supplying Services Under the Agreement
	on Financial Services
	on Telecommunications
	on Air Transport Services
	on Negotiations on Basic Telecommunications
	Attached national schedules of commitments

The general framework of the GATS is based on four sets of principles: the definition and scope of "trade in services" and of the relevant national measures pertaining to such trade; the most-favored-nation (MFN) principle and its limits, exceptions, and reservations; general commitments to address the trade-hindering character of nondiscriminatory domestic regulations; and the mechanisms of progressive liberalization of trade in services, to be implemented by means of negotiated commitments.

DEFINITION AND SCOPE OF TRADE IN SERVICES

The new services regime is based on the presumption of "universal coverage" as spelled out in Article I of the agreement. This implies that, in the absence of provisions to the contrary, all service sectors, including financial and audiovisual services, are included under the general framework agreement. More specifically, "services" include any service in any sector, except "services supplied in the exercise of governmental authority." In order to restrict the exception to a minimum, the United States insisted that a government service would qualify for the exception only if it were supplied on a noncommercial, noncompetitive basis. This narrow exception implies that nearly all information, communication, and entertainment service providers fall within the purview of the GATS. Moreover, given that the agreement applies to all "measures by member states affecting trade in services," the GATS is universal not only in its sectoral but also in its regulatory scope. The kinds of government measures affected are defined very broadly in the agreement— "law, regulation, procedure, decision, administrative action, or any other form" (Article XXVIII) taken by central, regional, or local governments and authorities, as well as private bodies that have been delegated government power. The latter clause implies that bodies such as professional associations, audiovisual boards, or securities exchanges are directly bound by the agreement.[8]

Of course, a transnational activity is covered only insofar as it is considered "trade in services." Early in the negotiations, negotiators devoted considerable attention to this definitional issue.[9] They came to agree that a categorization into modes of delivery should be the basis for defining trade in services. Accordingly, trade in services is defined in the GATS as the supply of a service through four modes of delivery: from the territory of one nation into the territory of another, in the territory of one nation to a consumer in another nation, by a service supplier of one nation through commercial presence in the territory of another nation, and by a service supplier of one nation through the presence of natural persons of a nation in the territory of another nation.

This four-part categorization is one of the keys to the evolutionary nature of the GATS: it achieves two seemingly contradictory purposes by casting the widest net possible while allowing nations to carve out areas to exempt from liberalization. Under a narrow definition of trade, where products rather than factors of production move across a border, only the first category would apply. This category is especially relevant for information-intensive services, since it encompasses across-the-border transmissions by any technical means—ranging from data via computer links to audiovisual programs via cable or satellite—as well as services embodied in a physical medium, such as videos or tapes. The three other categories broaden considerably the traditional definition of trade. They are specific to services in that they reflect the frequent need for some degree of direct interaction between suppliers and buyers to complement or substitute for network-based delivery. Most important is the innovative notion of "commercial presence," which refers to the extent of local presence that is both necessary and sufficient to enable the sale of a given service, and thus may be either broader or narrower than the notion of "right of establishment," which refers to the legal status of such presence.

But the division into four separate, clearly identifiable modes of delivery not only provides comprehensiveness and definitional elegance; it also serves as the basis for disaggregating specific commitments, thereby excluding certain modes of delivery from the scope of liberalization. Thus, governments can choose to ban network-based delivery by including only delivery through local presence in their requirements. Rights of commercial presence may stop short of a right of investment—through majority shareholding, for instance—or may be narrowed to the right to open an office in a given country. Similarly, the presence of a person, which often complements commercial presence, has been narrowed in practice by the reservations introduced in the schedules to high-skill intra-corporate "transferrers."

THE MOST FAVORED NATION PRINCIPLE

The MFN principle that any trade concession accorded to one nation be unconditionally and immediately extended to all others was the core norm that underlay the rapid liberalization of trade after World War II and is the defining notion of multilateralism. Article II of the GATS provides that each member shall immediately and unconditionally accord to services and service suppliers from another member nation no less favorable treatment than it accords to like services and service suppliers from any other country. This is a general obligation, which applies to all services, regardless of whether they are included in the national schedules of commitments. Some nations, particularly the United States, were uneasy with such a requirement, not least because it would deprive them of the bargaining power needed to force the opening of foreign markets. But, while the MFN principle was slowly eroded under GATT by the implementation of so-called gray area measures (such as Voluntary Export Restraints [VERs]) that did not fall under the regulatory discipline of GATT, the GATS seeks to make MFN exemptions legal, provided they are the object of its surveillance.

Article II allows nations to exempt certain trading partners from MFN and give them preferential status simply by registering exemptions in a special annex to that effect.[10] According to the annex, the procedure is supposed to be transitional, for a maximum of ten years, and be justified by conditions to be reexamined every

five years by the Council for Trade in Services. The council will determine if the exemptions continue to be justified, with a view to progressively phasing them out after
ten years.

A second set of exemptions is covered by Article V of the agreement, which
indefinitely waives the nondiscrimination obligation for subsets of countries
bound by an economic integration agreement, provided that such agreement has
substantial sectoral coverage as in GATT Article XXIV. The fine-tuning here is
twofold. First, the notion of substantial coverage implies that all four modes of
supply are included in the regional liberalization process; this clause clearly
exempts the European Union from extending its recent services liberalization to
other GATS members. As a quid pro quo, however, the article is careful to
include as beneficiaries of regional privileges juridical persons "engaged in
substantive business operations" in the region in question and constituted
under the laws of one of its countries (read, U.S. firms in Europe).

Finally, and most fundamentally, a last type of MFN exemption relates to the
adoption of recognition agreements, which will be discussed later.

Defining Nondiscriminatory Domestic Regulations

Much of the difficulty of the services negotiations came from the need to
engage in an exercise that had stumped even the European Union (EU) until
recently: defining criteria for determining whether a domestic measure applied
to a foreigner could be considered legitimate regulation. The preamble of the
GATS recognizes

> the right of Members to regulate, and introduce new regulations, on
> the supply of services within their territories in order to meet national
> policy objectives and, given asymmetries existing with respect to the
> degree of development of services regulations in different countries,
> the particular need of developing countries to exercise this right.

This general premise of the sovereign right of host states to regulate all
transactions entered into within their territorial jurisdiction raises the question of
how nations are to agree that qualification requirements, technical standards, and
licensing requirements "do not constitute unnecessary barriers to trade." The
agreement provides only very general guidelines. Regulations applied to foreigners
must be based on "objective and transparent criteria" such as competence and
ability to supply a service. They must respect the principle of proportionality—
measures must not be "more burdensome than necessary" to ensure the quality of
the services. In addition, Article VI provides that domestic regulations applied in a
sector that a member has agreed to include under specific liberalization commitments
must be administered in a "reasonable, objective, and impartial manner." The
agreement also includes procedural guidelines requiring that decisions in cases
where the supply of a service needs authorization in the host country be issued

"within a reasonable period of time," and that signatories establish tribunals and procedures to process potential complaints by foreign service suppliers.

Discrimination against foreigners, however, is not ruled out across the board. The agreement allows states to maintain measures that may be discriminatory if the goal is to protect public morals, public order, or health, provided that they are not a means of "arbitrary or unjustifiable discrimination between countries where like conditions prevail, or a disguised restriction on trade in services" (Article XIV). Legitimate reasons for enforcing domestic regulations also include the need to prevent fraudulent practices, to deal with the effects of a default on services contracts, to protect individual privacy, to ensure safety of the consumer, and to collect taxes in an equitable manner. Finally, exceptions may also be grounded in security concerns, such as the requirement to serve the military establishment or to take action in pursuance of a state's obligation under the United Nations Charter for the maintenance of international peace and security.

Given such limitations and the likelihood of varying interpretations of the criteria allowing discrimination, in the short term the transparency requirements (Article III) may produce more significant changes in the regulatory environment faced by service exporters. Members are asked to publish promptly, except in emergency situations, all relevant measures that may affect foreign service suppliers. The Council for Trade in Services is to be informed of any changes in laws, regulations, or administrative guidelines that significantly affect its commitments in services. For transparency purposes, members are to establish points of enquiry to serve as regulatory hubs—one-stop shops for foreigners seeking information on the domestic regulatory landscape (although they "need not be depositories of laws and regulations" and members are not required to disclose "confidential information, the disclosure of which would impede law enforcement, or otherwise be contrary to the public interest, or which would prejudice legitimate commercial interests of particular enterprises, public or private"). Furthermore, developed countries are required to establish contact points to help developing country exporters.

MECHANISMS FOR PROGRESSIVE LIBERALIZATION

Where the line is drawn between general obligations and negotiated commitments is one of the chief ways in which GATS differs from GATT. While both are frameworks for negotiating smaller deals, GATT made discrimination illegal (in theory) and tariffs negotiable, while GATS makes almost everything negotiable (as is well known, services—unlike goods—carry no tariffs to protect them in any other way). In theory, any national measure that affects the transnational supply of a service is potentially under the scrutiny of the new regime if the measure cannot be justified by acceptable considerations. In practice, the general obligations embedded in the agreement, including MFN, do not in themselves constitute steps toward liberalization. The extent to which the general language constrains member states in the way they apply regulations to foreigners will have to be tested through dispute resolution. But the elimination of restrictive measures in place within member states takes effect only through negotiated commitments included in national schedules. In this context, a nation has two options: It may choose to maintain measures aimed at restricting trade in a given sector simply by not including the sector in its schedule of commitments; or it may choose to include a given sector in its liberalization commitments, making an explicit reservation in its schedule to protect any trade-restrictive measures it wants to keep for the moment. In the first case—which is what the Europeans did for the audiovisual sector—the sector will be subject only to the general obligations of MFN transparency and the like described above. (In order to avoid complete free riding, each country must include at least one sector in its schedule of commitment in order to become a member of GATS and, subsequently, of WTO.) Thus, the procedure for registering commitments in national schedules combines positive and negative undertakings: There are no liberalization obligations unless a sector or subsector is positively included in the schedule; but once it is, a member cannot maintain or introduce measures in that sector that are inconsistent with Articles XVI and XVII, which define so-called market access and national treatment obligations—other than those already included in its schedule.

Market access commitments (Article XVI) concern the abolition of measures that discriminate in some quantitative way against foreign suppliers (by limiting, for example, the number of service suppliers, the total value of service transactions, or the number of people who may be employed in a sector). Such measures invariably favor incumbents and, therefore, nations. Commitments regarding market access address existing or potential numerical quotas, monopolies, exclusive suppliers, or economic needs tests. They also concern requirements for foreigners to operate locally through specified types of legal entities or joint ventures or percentage limits on foreign shareholding. A commitment to do away with such requirements implies giving exporters the right to choose among modes of commercial presence, including nonestablishment at one end of the spectrum, and full acquisition of a domestic firm at the other end.

The second category of commitments included in country schedules pertains to the granting of national treatment (Article XVII), defined as the obligation for a nation to accord foreign service suppliers treatment no less favorable than it accords its own suppliers of like services. The decision that national treatment should not be a general principle (as it is in GATT), but a concession to be bargained for, was one of the major innovations and negotiating breakthroughs of the regime. A national treatment obligation is meant to affect qualitative, discriminatory measures against foreign suppliers, but it is a de facto rather than de jure standard; this implies that the treatment of foreigners and nationals must be equivalent in substance, not just in form. The idea of providing "equivalent competitive opportunities" to foreign suppliers gave rise to heated conflicts of interpretation during the negotiations. If deemed to constitute de facto discrimination, a given domestic measure is subject to national treatment requirements if the sector has been listed and unless the signatory asks for an exemption. On the other hand, measures that may have a restrictive effect on trade but are not deemed discriminatory, even de facto, need not be scheduled. In the latter case, the measure will be considered legal and could only be questioned if subject to commitments beyond national treatment. The GATS does provide for possible negotiation of such additional commitments by subsets of countries through the drafting of recognition agreements at some future stage. The Uruguay Round itself did not include such recognition agreements among parties but, as will be discussed below, they are certain to constitute a core element of the post-Uruguay Round agenda.

Finally, although the object of special provisions, several types of national measures have not yet been brought within the GATS discipline and will therefore require further negotiations. These include subsidies (Article XV simply calls for future negotiations); measures pertaining to the public procurement of services, although the Government Procurement Code was extended to cover services (Article XIII calls for negotiations within two years); restrictive business practices (Article IX says that members must "enter into consultation" if requested by another member); and national monopolies competing outside the scope of their monopoly rights (under Article VIII, the only requirement is to ensure that there is no abuse of dominant position).

In sum, the GATS provides an evolutionary framework for governing international trade in services, within which a number of future scenarios can take place. While drawing on many of the features of the GATT, it also incorporates some features of the European Union's treaties. For example, language on acceptable regulation, while vague, can provide the basis for dispute-settlement procedures that can be progressively fine-tuned to create a collective understanding of what constitutes acceptable domestic measures applied to foreign service suppliers (such a set of procedures could become the embryo of a global version of the European Court of Justice). In this sense, the GATS can be seen as a hybrid form of treaty, which, like the GATT, will be made operative only through further rounds of implementing negotiations but, like the Treaty of Rome, can be broadly interpreted by injured parties as constituting a binding constraint on national policies.

Yet the GATS leaves much to be done. First, even setting aside the often disappointing reach of initial obligations undertaken by member countries, there is the so-called unfinished business of the round itself—areas where the contracting parties agreed to disagree in 1994 because they did not want to hold the whole round hostage to agreements in these areas.[11] Second, there are issues that were never considered reasonable goals for agreement by the round's end, including the still-to-be-negotiated provisions mentioned above, as well as commitments to negotiate in previously out-of-bounds areas such as basic telecommunications. Third, there are issues that were not part of the Uruguay Round but that are now beginning to be seen as part of the agenda for the next round. These generally are cross-cutting issues, concerning new types of macrotrade-offs—for example, the linkage between trade and other domestic policy areas such as environmental or competition policies, or the linkage between regional and global liberalization processes.

THE ROAD AHEAD FOR COMMUNICATION SERVICES

The GATS established in 1994 represented a transitory state of affairs. Nations that had reached different stages of regulatory reform found that the requirements and concerns corresponding to their various situations might continue to be difficult to reconcile for a while, although they were likely to converge in time. A number of service sectors or subsectors were ultimately left out of most national schedules of commitments, making them subject only to the general obligations of the GATS.

Among the unresolved conflicts were those in the area of telecommunications and audiovisual services. In both cases, the most relevant fault line lay between the United States and Europe. In 1994, many European Union nations still preferred to move incrementally as they sought to assess and influence the extent to which national or regional information infrastructures would actually be vulnerable to foreign competitors. Faced with the opening up of both basic and value-added telecommunications, along with issues of access to Europe's "television without frontier," Europeans have been buying time in order to turn their fragmented infrastructure of communication and distribution networks into a more integrated regional one before radically opening their markets. The stakes are high, as both telecommunications sectors are in the midst of unprecedented technological and regulatory transformations that are likely to greatly affect their growth in the near future.[12]

The Europeans' cautious response to U.S. demands in the GATS negotiations reflected two interrelated strategies: to open from a position of strength and to give political priority to European integration. It is significant that eight years after the publication of the White Paper that launched the so-called Europe 1992 process of completing the internal market, the Commission of the European Community published a new White Paper arguing that for the sake of growth, competitiveness, and employment in Europe, the European Union was to become more than a "common commercial area"—it was to become a "common information area."[13] One of the most publicized aspects of the policy paper was a long-term plan to integrate Europe's telecommunications networks, along with its transport and energy networks. Jacques Delors' main argument in pushing for adoption of the program was that trans-European networks were needed because the single market would remain incomplete if the European Union's infrastructures remained fragmented along national lines.[14] As the White Paper states, "The objective of developing trans-European networks is to enable citizens, economic operators, and regional and local communities to derive full benefits from the setting up of an area without internal frontiers and to link peripheral regions with the center."[15] The proposal can be viewed as the European equivalent of the Clinton administration's program to speed up the introduction of new high-speed communications networks throughout the United States. In part, it may be this convergence on consolidating their respective information infrastructures that underlay the temporary equilibrium reached at the end of the Uruguay Round. But beyond this convergence, it is important for the U.S. public to understand Europe's intentions in order to assess the likelihood that the American lead on liberalization will be followed in the coming years.

Initiatives to develop truly integrated regional communication networks within the European Union long preceded the 1993 White Paper, but the latter served to frame the broader political vision that underlay these efforts. While its policy implications are controversial, the new blueprint for European integration at the end of the millennium, which was adopted by European heads of state in December 1993, reflects the preoccupations of European governments at the close of the Uruguay Round. It states:

> The development of an "information society" will be a global phenom-
> enon, led first of all by the Triad, but gradually extended to cover the
> entire planet. In pursuing its strategy, Europe should aim to achieve
> three objectives: (i) placing its approach on a worldwide perspective . .
> . ; (ii) ensuring, at the same time, that the system developed takes due
> account of European characteristics: multilingualism, cultural diversity,
> economic divergence and more generally the preservation of its social
> model; (iii) creating the conditions whereby, in an open and competitive
> international system, Europe still has an adequate take-up of basic
> technologies and an efficient and competitive industry.[16]

In a context of progressive global liberalization, European authorities were seen as having two primary responsibilities. The first was to address the societal implications of liberalization. Under the European model, new forms of social protection must be put in place because "despite the undeniable progress that has been made, the penetration of ICTs [information and communication technologies] is not an unmitigated success story. The changeover toward an information society has placed severe demands on the adaptability of those concerned."[17] The White Paper warned of the risk of exclusion as a result of inadequate skills or qualifications and, more generally, the emergence of a two-tier society, separating the connected from the unconnected. Accordingly, "Europe must prepare itself for this changeover in order to capitalize upon the economic and social advantages while analyzing and mitigating any adverse consequences: an increase in the isolation of individuals, intrusions into private life, and moral and ethical problems."[18] Along the same lines, the White Paper also stressed the need to focus on the job-creating potential of the information sector.

Second, European governments must also create conditions whereby "European companies develop their strategies in an open internal and international competitive environment, and can continue to ensure that crucial technologies are mastered and developed in Europe."[19] In particular, for its grand plan to

THE NEW INFORMATION INFRASTRUCTURE

develop trans-European networks, the commission proposed to invest ECU 150 billion (about $180 billion) in telecommunications by the year 1999, through new types of partnerships with private investors and users. (Less ambitious but similarly oriented approaches were to be taken in the audiovisual sector.) An intended side benefit of such investments at the continental level is to promote European integration as an end in itself. In addition to investment in communication networks at the European level, the European Union is planning to become increasingly involved in promoting the regional integration of telematic applications—including teleworking, distance learning, and specific applications in the fields of telemedicine and transport management—that would help offset the trend toward the centralization of industrial development in Europe. In the process, European service providers may well acquire a comparative advantage that could eventually be transferred to the global field.

The fulfillment of these two objectives—social and strategic—entails both a rethinking of the role of state intervention in this field and the integration of such intervention at a pan-European level. Accordingly, the European agenda for the 1990s includes both the acceleration of liberalization of communication services and a commitment to temper the deregulatory bent associated with such liberalization in the 1980s with a neo-Keynesian "New Deal" to provide for the integration of communication infrastructures and also the incorporation of citizens into such infrastructures. European policymakers and observers no doubt disagree on the optimal mix between public and private roles in developing Europe's information economy. But lying somewhere between French centralism and British antistatism, the German social democratic model may become the basis for the European version of regional governance of the information infrastructure. At the same time, the European Union is committed to a competition-based approach in the long run, which is clearly compatible with an opening of borders. In this respect, one could say that completion of the round of GATS negotiations was jeopardized by a simple question of timing. This question, however, raises a deeper one: How do nations or groups of nations prepare for the advent of radical opening to global competition?

THE NEW MULTILATERAL DEAL IN TELECOMMUNICATIONS

Beyond the general GATS rules described above, the deal reached on telecommunications during the Uruguay Round includes an annex that took effect in January 1995, and an agreement between parties to negotiate basic telecommunications services at a later date.[20] This deal reflects the temporary equilibrium reached in the mid-1990s between radical and evolutionary proponents of liberalization. As such, it strikes a subtle balance between freedom of access to telecommunications infrastructures across national boundaries and the diverging national views of what "governance" of such infrastructures implies about conditions for such access. Drafting a realistic U.S. strategy for the future requires the maintenance of this equilibrium.

This deal reflects above all the different starting conditions of the United States and European Union in the field of telecommunications, where internal competition among private carriers prevailed in the former, while public national monopolies persisted in the latter. The very existence of the deal on tele-communications signals an overall victory for the United States, the initial and constant proponent of speedy liberalization. But the content of the two-way compromise reflects rather faithfully developments occurring within the European Union at the same time. To be sure, the European telecommunications landscape itself is in part a function of U.S. actions. In this sense, the intervening changes between March 1990, when U.S. negotiators first introduced a draft proposal for a telecommunications annex, and the final agreement of December 1993 can be analyzed as a process of mutual accommodation between internal reform within the European Union and multilateral liberalization, a process that will continue beyond the Uruguay Round itself. On one hand, with the support of the great majority of developing nations as well as Japan, to some extent, the European Union's counterproposals insisted on strengthening conditions for access to networks (both with regard to privacy issues as analyzed by Joel Reidenberg in this volume and broader regulatory imperatives) and resisted American demands for liberalizing basic telecommunications. Generally, Europeans—and to an even greater extent most developing countries—have always been more concerned about access and use of networks for the provision of services generally than by the provision of telecommunications services specifically (Mexico took a similar position in the NAFTA negotiations). Reflecting such an emphasis, the annex emphasizes the dual role of telecommunications "as a distinct sector of economic activity and as the underlying transport means for other economic activities."

On the other hand, the combined pressure of global technological change and regulatory change in the United States, leading to threats of bypass, played a critical role in accelerating change within the European Union. In 1990, Europeans (following guidelines contained in their 1987 Green Paper on telecommunications) issued both a services directive maintaining the possibility of national monopoly rights for basic services, and an open network provision directive defining the essential requirements legitimizing limits to access. By 1993, the European Union market for telecommunications was open for value-added services and data communications; packet or circuit-switched data services had been liberalized by the end of 1992. Also, under pressure from the European Commission and Great Britain, member states had finally agreed to begin a progressive liberalization of "reserved" services.[21] Europe's program is to culminate in 1998 with the introduction of competition for basic voice telephony over public networks. Thus, by 1993 the major problem for European negotiators was one of timing, due to different stages of liberalization in individual member states, "not of a real impossibility of the European Community ever to liberalize the basic telecommunications markets."[22] In this sense, although the telecommunications deal may reflect a transitory equilibrium, it is adaptable in response to both the strategic game between the three sides of the

Triad and the speed at which the European Union will be able to develop mechanisms to compensate losers in its internal bargains.

From the point of view of the United States, the achievements embodied in the telecommunications annex should not be undervalued. At the most general level, the commitment not to introduce new regulations that could have a restrictive impact on trade is significant because, by the late 1980s, government regulators had generally given up on controlling methods of transferring services across borders. This commitment effectively ensured (at least on the books) that telecommunications networks would remain open. More specifically, the GATS annex guarantees nondiscriminatory "access and use" of telecommunications transport networks and services and access to leased lines (Article V.2). The annex also ensures a right of interconnection of private leased or owned circuits with the public network (Article V.2.2) and gives suppliers the right to use their own protocols (Article V.2.3). Not only have governments committed themselves not to interfere with the flow of information within and across borders, they have agreed that foreign service providers cannot be forbidden to use their communication networks for such purposes as corporate communications and access to local databases (Article V.3). In addition, the agreement commits all parties to the introduction of an arm's-length relationship between providing basic and value-added services, in order to ensure that network operators do not favor themselves in charges levied.[23] Transnational communication becomes the most securely guaranteed and available mode of delivery for any service provider.

Remaining constraints reflect the hand of European regulators. The annex allows for limitations of access to include "measures necessary to ensure the security and confidentiality of messages"; restrictions on resale or shared use; requirements to use specified technical interfaces for interconnection; requirements for the interoperability of telecommunications services; approval by type of terminals attached to the network; restrictions on interconnection of private leased or owned circuits; and, last but not least, the notification, registration, and licensing of foreign service providers. These conditions and requirements resemble closely those embodied in the open network scheme developed in Europe. Thus, a first problem in the implementation of the annex will be to ensure that the rights retained by host states, legitimate but extensive, will not be used abusively.

The problem may be amplified by the fact that the annex remains vague on the issue of standards and does not contain any obligation of mutual recognition of such standards (see discussion below). The only relevant provision is that members "recognize the importance of international standards for global compatibility and interoperability of telecommunications networks and services as carried out by ITU [International Telecommunications Union] and ISO [International Organization for Standardization]" (Article VII.1), and are encouraged to "make appropriate arrangements" for consultations with such bodies. Not surprisingly, the annex grants a general exemption to developing countries, recognizing their need to develop an advanced and efficient telecommunications infrastructure as a precondition for the expansion of their trade in services. To this end, technical cooperation is encouraged; developing countries are even allowed to introduce additional conditions to increase their participation in international trade in telecommunications services.[24]

The telecommunications agreement did fall short of U.S. ambitions in a number of areas, including rights of uplink and downlink with satellites, resale of leased lines, and commitments to cost-based pricing. In this last case, neither European PTTs nor developing nations' operators were prepared to give up their revenue base by 1995. Even in the area of value-added services, the United States did not win the unbundling of network services that it had sought (this would have allowed for targeted liberalization of specific activities—such as switching, billing, or consumer database services—that could be provided by someone other than the operators).[25]

Future negotiations on basic telecommunications services are to a great extent linked to all these issues. The agreement to proceed with further negotiations on basic telecommunications in 1995 and 1996, through the setting up of a Group of Negotiation on Basic Telecommunications ("telecommunications transport networks and services"), represents a spectacular achievement for the United States. Although the ultimate results will not be known for some time, few would have foreseen that the prospect of liberalizing basic telecommunications would be on the table before the end of the millennium. While the initial U.S. proposal included the liberalization of basic voice services, omitting only local infrastructure monopoly, the Europeans had long resisted such inclusion. But aggressive U.S. tactics between 1990 and 1993 (combined with internal developments in Europe) bore fruit. In fall 1990, the United States threatened to exempt telecommunications from the GATS MFN obligation, thereby seeking to give itself the option of negotiating bilateral deals without having to open its huge market to all. In early 1992, the United States replaced the stick with a carrot, proposing to phase out its MFN exemption if its major trading partners (mainly the European Union and Japan) liberalized their basic telecommunications markets within three years after the GATS took effect. The United States' partners have repeatedly condemned such tactics as "high-tech diplomacy," at odds with the stated U.S. commitment to world leadership in sustaining multilateral norms. But they realize that, given U.S. bargaining power, an approach based on bilateral negotiations would definitely stack the cards in favor of the United States. Therefore, they have agreed to launch negotiations on basic telecommunications with an April 1996 deadline.

As a quid pro quo, the United States has agreed that "no participant shall apply any measure affecting trade in basic telecommunications in such a manner as would improve its negotiating position or leverage." This bargain—concocted by the USTR against the wishes of the interagency groups—means that for two years the United States has given up the right to negotiate bilaterally, wielding the MFN club. Although the negotiations are to be entered into on a voluntary basis, this U.S. concession was clearly conditioned on European Union participation. The

MFN club can be picked up again if after two years the United States is not satisfied by the outcome.

There are three reasons U.S. negotiators may need to limit their ambition for these initial negotiations on basic services. For one, the announced negotiations are to be comprehensive in scope with no basic telecommunications excluded a priori. Thus, the negotiations are supposed to involve local, satellite, and mobile telephone services, and not just the long-distance and international basic services that the United States has argued for since 1990. This broadening of the agenda was introduced by European negotiators, prompted by the relative competitiveness of European mobile telephone operators and the potential gains to be made if U.S. markets are opened. The Americans have a competitive advantage in long-distance basic services, and European negotiators can use access to the European market in long distance as a bargaining chip for greater access to the U.S. mobile and satellite markets. There is a question, however, about whether these negotiations—essentially a disguised result-oriented bargain on mutual market access—might not be more fruitfully replaced by a systematic transatlantic debate on criteria for desirable degrees of competition in voice telephony, including optimal size for infrastructure monopoly.

Second, it is not clear that the Europeans have bought enough time to ensure the necessary coordination between internal reform and external concessions. The acceptance by European telecommunications ministers in June 1993 of a 1998 deadline for liberalization clearly depended on reaching consensus on universal service obligations in order to calm the public's fears of the effects of competition. A few weeks before the closing of the round, the European Commission issued guidelines to help national companies address the issue, although it left member states to decide exactly how to fund a universal service under a competitive regime. Since profits from international calls would quickly erode in global competition, European companies were called upon to progressively increase the cost of local calls. At the same time, Europeans backed India's refusal to commit immediately to cost-based pricing in Geneva— evidence that multilateral commitments on the part of the Europeans are entered into only after internal change is solidified and generalized across member states. Although Europeans agreed that rival companies would need to be charged for access to existing public networks to pay for basic minimum service for remote-area customers, they still concluded that peripheral regions in Europe would need additional direct subsidies through European Union funding to sustain the change. The "trans-European networks" project articulated in the White Paper and the completion of the European integrated services digital networks may well be a medium for such regional integration. But until integration of the periphery is secured it seems unlikely that Europeans will allow basic service competition, short of prohibitive tickets for entry.

Finally, further liberalization in the telecommunications field will most likely imply a growing degree of mutual scrutiny of the design and implementation of competition law. It is not clear whether U.S. agencies and corporations will be ready to have such fundamental domestic measures brought under international scrutiny so quickly. At the same time, the structure of the European telecommunications industry is likely to change radically in the next few years. The June 1993 alliance between MCI and British Telecom, and the alliance— partly in reaction—between France Telecom and Deutsche Telekom in December 1993, are symptomatic.[26] The former is seen by continental operators as a Trojan horse for U.S. competitors, but all sides may ultimately have an interest in introducing foreign competition in basic services through this route. The Franco-German alliance between the world's second- and third-largest carriers was not only a reaction to the unavoidable erosion of their respective monopolies, but also a response to growth of an international market for telecommunications outsourcing developed by operators such as MCI. For the moment, the new alliance is aimed at offering one-stop communication services to multinationals in Europe. But while this early, cautious initiative may flounder if such companies do not overwhelmingly decide to contract out their telecom requirements; France and Germany may seek to merge some or all of their basic voice service before 1998. In this case, will competition law apply differently to transatlantic and intra-European mergers? As the new wave of multimedia alliances that began in the United States reaches Europe, and as the global rivalry between giant telecommunications alliances intensifies, the international cooperation agenda is likely to shift from trade to competition policy, as is discussed below. This might prove as challenging as the eight years of the GATS negotiations.

"TELEVISION WITHOUT FRONTIERS": GOAL OR PREREQUISITE?

Another issue that reflects the transitory nature of the GATT bargain is the question of "cultural exclusion" for broadcasting services. Few recent controversies on the international economic scene have had such high public visibility. To an even greater extent than for telecommunications, the issue pitted two very different conceptions of state regulation against each other. Whether and how audiovisual services ought to be included under the GATS became a point of discord late in the game when Hollywood producers started to lobby the U.S. government to seek to redress the protectionist bent of the so-called television without frontiers directive adopted by the European Union in 1989. As part of the overall requirement to complete an "internal market without frontier" by the end of 1992, and in sharp contrast to a situation where most member states prohibited the broadcast of foreign channels within their territories, the directive allowed all residents in the European Union to have access to all broadcasts originating from any member state, via either satellite or cable, by October 1991.[27]

With the growing possibility of combining satellite and cable transmission for simultaneous broadcasts, the European communication industry was bent on reaping the scale benefits from a "Europe-wide broadcasting space," hoping this would stall the competitive challenge from the other side of the Atlantic. Such a goal, however, provoked sharp controversy within Europe itself, as member states sought ways to reconcile their different levels of regulation. One controversy centered on the need to transform national programming production quotas into European quotas. Ultimately, a compromise was struck between French dirigisme and Britain's liberal approach, as the directive required that member states reserve 50 percent of their broadcast time for European "work," including 20 percent for independent European producers—but only "whenever applicable."[28]

U.S. negotiators strongly objected to the market allocation schemes, particularly the 50 percent minimum European content contained in the 1989 broadcasting directive. In addition, they denounced the high level of state subsidies granted to European filmmakers (such as the French *avance sur recettes*) as a source of unfair competition. Why should politicians restrict the entertainment choices of consumers, U.S. negotiators asked, especially given the basic democratic commitment to free flow of information? Quotas aimed at protecting a culture on which citizens did not choose to spend their free time were clearly illegitimate; the worldwide popularity of American products was simply a reflection of the fact that the U.S. market was a multicultural microcosm in and of itself. On this front, however, U.S. negotiators have realistically held little hope of reaching compromise. Another, perhaps more important, goal for the United States was obtaining a European commitment to renounce any future restrictions on new technologies in the audiovisual sector. If current quotas could not be abolished in the short run, at least the new interactive and multimedia technologies would open up the rapidly growing European market to alternative entries.[29]

The Europeans had two answers to the American arguments. To begin with, they believed that it was wrong to assume that the European Union had been protectionist in this area, since nearly 80 percent of the films shown in European movie theaters were of U.S. origin, in contrast with the meager 1.5 percent European share of the American market. In addition, U.S. sales of audiovisual programming in Europe increased from $330 million in 1984 to $3.6 billion in 1992. The European market was clearly of great importance to U.S. exporters, representing 77 percent of their audiovisual sales abroad in 1991 and their second biggest export item after aircraft. In contrast, the European Union's annual deficit with the United States in audiovisual sales amounted to $3.5 billion.

Second, the European Union was prepared to defend the legitimacy of its measures even if they were considered protectionist. Like Canadians during their free trade area negotiations with the United States, Europeans argued that cultural products should not be treated as mere merchandise because they bear directly on national and regional identities that must be preserved at all costs. Communication is not just an industry but a value, as indicated by the fanatic attachment of peoples to the survival of their languages. Moreover, there is no level playing field in an area where products must be amortized in large domestic markets in order to be competitive worldwide; here, structural economic factors grant an incomparable advantage to the United States with its unified market generating 50 percent of worldwide audiovisual revenues. In contrast, the European film industry is hopelessly fragmented and underfunded, split among a thousand different operators and national distributors. As a European filmmaker put it, U.S.-European competition in this area is "like going into the home-made lemonade business and wondering why you are not adequately competing with Coca-Cola."[30]

Such differences in economies of scale in production and distribution have two consequences. For one, U.S. producers can budget much more money for individual features ($20 million versus $3.5 million on average in Europe), which in turn attracts a greater market of viewers. Moreover, contrary to the U.S. assumption that the dominance of U.S. products is due to consumer choice, broadcasters are not entirely driven by a market logic; they weigh what viewers want to see against profitability. Thus, although locally produced television dramas have higher ratings in general, European broadcasters have been ready to lose a marginal share of their viewers in order to buy U.S.-made television dramas at one-fifteenth of the cost. Hence, if Europe is not to become a passive consumer of other countries' audiovisual products, which would require the advent of Europe-wide producers and distributors, traditional trade concepts cannot be applied to governance of the audiovisual sector.

This was the line taken by France, backed by Spain and Belgium, in urging the European Union to obtain special cultural status for the audiovisual sector that would exclude it from all current and future GATS negotiations to "guard against further American invasion." Although the British and German governments were reluctant to follow the extreme French approach, their trade ministries were eventually overwhelmed by the cultural ministries and lobbies galvanized by the abrasiveness of the Motion Picture Association of America (which I am told recognized afterward that its negotiating tactics had backfired). But the United States did not bow to the European Union's demands for explicit recognition of special status. In the end, the dispute went unresolved and the parties "agreed to disagree" in order not to derail the whole round of negotiations. This is why we can speak today of a "cultural exclusion" rather than a "cultural exception" that would have put audiovisual services outside the GATS purview altogether. The notion of "exclusion" signifies that certain parties, mainly the European Union, have decided to exclude this sector from most of the new disciplines introduced by the GATS; they will not include the sector in specific liberalization commitments under Articles XVI and XVII and will exempt it from MFN treatment.

The result of this "deal by default" certainly appears lopsided. The only immediate discipline for Europe is the obligation of transparency in its regulatory framework. At the same time, the United States has agreed to extensive market access commitment without MFN exemptions, reserving only the right to require radio and television transmission licenses for foreigners. To be sure, U.S. commitments do not cost much in practice given the extent of foreign penetration of its audiovisual markets. By placing its audiovisual services under the GATS disciplines, and given the lack of commitment on Europe's part, the United States has effectively given up its right to use unilateral measures to pressure its partners into opening their markets or decreasing their subsidies. Finally, the GATS parties are not legally bound to enter any further negotiations in this sector. Little wonder that European Union negotiators consider the results a success: They gained time and flexibility under multilateral rules to put in place an effective audiovisual strategy at the European Union level, while at the same time securing legal protection against unilateral retaliation.

But, as mentioned above, issues at the core of European-U.S. disagreement (subsidies and domestic regulations, for example) will undoubtedly be reexamined after implementation of the GATS framework. Moreover, the first review of MFN exemptions and a new round of liberalization negotiations are to take place within five years. There is little question that the United States will raise the issue again. One can predict that, in the same way as in telecommunications, the positions of the United States and the European Union will converge within the next few years if the structures of their industries themselves converge. To this end, the Americans need to watch cooperative developments within the European Union and may have an interest in supporting them.

A first piece of evidence for such convergence is a Green Paper by the Commission of the European Communities, unveiled in April 1994 after the close of the GATS negotiations so as not to add to their complexity. It sets out suggestions for refining existing policy instruments in order to contribute to "guaranteeing not only the survival but also the growth of a viable audiovisual software industry in Europe into the year 2000."[31] The paper warns that the European film and television industry is in a financial crisis and will decline steadily in the face of U.S. competition unless it is radically overhauled.[32] Brussels called above all for more effective incentives on the part of European governments to promote transnational cooperation. Yet, in the aftermath of the Uruguay Round, there exists a deep division in Europe on how far to endorse such an evolutionary protectionist approach. Reflecting this unease, although the paper was pitched as a cornerstone of the commission's manifesto for developing Europe's information highways, neither the commission nor European governments have backed it up with a specific timetable.

European producers and directors have responded to what they see as governmental inertia with proposals of their own: the creation of two or three significant Europe-wide film and television distribution organizations chosen through competitive tenders, each capitalized at around $1 billion and benefiting from "soft loans"; the levying of a tax on the entire audiovisual industry to help fund new commercially oriented production; the training of future film and television makers to understand the marketplace, in an effort to move away from a supply-led to a demand-led industry; and cooperative efforts in multimedia technology. While it is still too early to tell, institutions like the European Parliament are likely to echo these proposals; by linking individual citizens with a great continental project, they fit well with the new agenda of a political Europe. But at a time of low economic growth, progress toward reducing fragmentation is uncertain.

Under these conditions, it may be wise for U.S. trade policymakers to adopt a wait-and-see attitude. During the run-up to Marrakesh, the U.S. government had already taken a more conciliatory stance, stressing that its first priority was to avoid further European restrictions, not to abolish existing ones.[33] In the information field, we have seen over and over how changing technologies render agreements, even agreements to disagree, obsolete. The Europeans know they are in a race against time—one that will not be won on legal grounds.

This is illustrated by the issue of entertainment material distribution in a future of broadband global information highways. In the near future, American firms will be able to distribute films nationally on demand through fiber-optic telecommunications networks. Instead of going to video stores, viewers will dial up and watch a film of their choosing. This is one of those potential new technologies for which U.S. negotiators sought rights of access to European markets. Despite the European exemption for the audiovisual sector, a shrewd defender of U.S. interests might argue that the Europeans committed themselves to admit such services under the telecommunications annex. Of course, the Europeans made sure that the annex explicitly excluded "measures affecting the cable or broadcast distribution of radio or television programming." But under Article V.3, parties to the GATS agreed to let foreign service suppliers use the public telecom network for, among other things, "access to information contained in data bases or otherwise stored in machine-readable form" in some other state. The dial-up service described above allows for customized programming in a time-independent fashion through access to "information stored in machine readable form," and may thus be included after all. European officials, of course, strongly deny such an interpretation.[34] In any event, this is not likely to become a significant market for a few years. Until then, defining the border between television programming and the distribution of entertainment through telecommunications networks may not be a central issue. But ultimately, if European service providers do not make such services available, European consumers will use transatlantic dialing, whatever the scope of the telecommunications annex. In a broadband future for the global information infrastructure, cross-border delivery of audiovisual services will elude the sectoral boundaries of national or global regulations.

More generally, everyone is becoming aware that demand-side growth will fundamentally alter the strategic calculations in this sector. Distribution techniques will multiply to include, for example, satellite, pay-per-view, video on demand, and interactive television. The number of television channels in Europe is expected to increase from 117 in 1993 to 500 in the year 2000. Encrypted programming hours are predicted to increase by a factor of 30. In this context, it is clear that no amount of protection can keep programmers from seeking ways to fill their time slots.

Trade pressures will not stop Europe's officials and its audiovisual industry from hoping to develop a "European audiovisual infrastructure" that could be used by American competitors but not elbowed aside by them. The U.S. government needs to continue to serve as a stimulus for improving the efficiency of the audiovisual sector in Europe, if only because European competitors may be better at identifying or creating new forms of demand on the part of the European viewer. In doing so, the United States' best bet may be to foster an industry-to-industry dialogue that will help alleviate the tensions of recent times. Indeed, as with telecommunications, each side has an interest in accommodating the other's structural adaptation. As this happens, however, public and private actors involved in reshaping the global economic environment will need to address the new "trade" agenda of regulatory integration.

PURSUING REGULATORY INTEGRATION: THE TRADE AGENDA ON THE WAY TO THE TWENTY-FIRST CENTURY

The pace and conditions for mutual concessions on market access in the near future may well be driven primarily by the type of strategic considerations sketched above. Yet, whatever mutually beneficial deals are reached between governments to allow for the activity of their nationals in each other's territory, they will need to address this key fact: Short of a world government, the increasingly global activities of economic actors operating in a networked environment will continue to be supervised under separate regulatory jurisdictions. Jurisdictional conflicts between two authorities that may both have a claim over the activities of a given economic actor may lead either to illegitimate extraterritorial application of laws or to regulatory bypass on the part of powerful network actors who seek to escape the constraints of the domestic regulations protecting their clients. As globalization increases, the commercial significance of regulatory fragmentation could become the hallmark of the next decade.

Governing the global information economy and its infrastructure would require embedding the types of arrangements suggested earlier in an overarching regulatory regime, requiring the reconceptualization of current domestic and transnational regulatory regimes. Indeed, one of the core challenges for developing the new services regime was finding effective principles for minimizing the trade-restrictive character of domestic regulations while ensuring that the regulatory concerns of host state governments would continue to be met. The first phase of this agenda is being implemented under the GATS: scrutiny of domestic rules of entry to ensure that their restrictive effect is proportional to their ends—for example, to protect the public interest, not special interests.

But, as discussed in the first section of this chapter, genuine freedom of mode of delivery for information-based services should ultimately imply transfer to the home authorities of whatever regulatory oversight is deemed necessary. Thus, if national commitments under the progressive liberalization scheme are to be truly effective, the home countries of services exporters must not only insist that host countries respect their negative commitment not to engage in regulatory discrimination—home countries must also, as a quid pro quo, engage in a positive commitment to regulate their citizens' activities abroad adequately. This might even mean accepting some of the host country's values and rules. In this scheme, worldwide regulatory integration does not mean the harmonization of legal systems across borders but, rather, ongoing institutional cooperation to ensure the enforcement of regulatory issues important to one party in part by another, and in part collectively. In short, the pursuit of worldwide regulatory integration need not mean adding an additional layer of supranational regulations.

Trade liberalization since World War II has involved shifts from the dismantling of quantitative border restrictions to those that are qualitative; from addressing border protection to outlawing internal domestic policies that explicitly discriminate against foreign firms; from considering discriminatory domestic measures as impediments to trade to considering those that are nondiscriminatory; and from seeking to dismantle impediments to trade stemming from government actions to addressing impediments due to private restrictive practices. The last two shifts are particularly relevant to the governance of the global information infrastructure: The third points to the need for combined harmonization and recognition of national laws and regulations, and the fourth to the need for coordination of competition policies across national borders.

The GATS treats these last two shifts as topics for future agreements. Regulatory integration will be at the core of the GATS agenda in the coming decade, but the institutional makeup of the trade regime will need to adapt if multilateral institutions are to serve as a hub for horizontal regulatory cooperation among public and private actors from different countries. The broadening of perspective under the new WTO might help achieve this. A new trade agenda for "beyond the Uruguay Round" is already emerging; its goal will be to forge criteria for linking trade liberalization or sanctions with regulatory developments within exporting states, from environmental to labor laws. The OECD is studying this set of interconnected issues intensively.[35] The challenge is to find a mode of collective governance that can stem the dangerous tendency toward seeing asymmetry in regulation between countries as evidence of trade distortion and, in the name of leveling the playing field, using trade leverage to engage in "regulatory imperialism," whereby those countries with the greatest market power impose their domestic rules on vulnerable exporters.

TOWARD MULTILATERAL MANAGED RECOGNITION?

As the GATS negotiations progressed, it became clear to those involved that for liberalization to be effective, commitments on national treatment or non-discrimination—even when defined broadly—would not be sufficient in the long run to address problems of jurisdictional fragmentation. Article VII of the GATS encourages nations to accept the "education or experience obtained, requirements met, or licenses or certification obtained in a particular country"; this could be negotiated on a reciprocal basis between two or more countries or be granted unilaterally. It may or may not be achieved through prior harmonization of the content of the relevant measures. Agreements under this clause will be the object of the next round of negotiations. What are the questions that must be kept in mind in this new exercise?

First, when is mutual recognition necessary or at least desirable from the point of view of economic actors? In addressing this question, policymakers will need to distinguish more explicitly between two types of recognition: the recognition of the content of foreign regulation—assessing when a license or criteria for professional authorization or financial soundness can be considered as broadly equivalent to one's own; and the recognition of the control or supervision exercised by the foreign authorities. With this distinction in place, one type of recognition may be granted without the other. Thus, while recognition of home supervision is a prerequisite to network-based service delivery (recognition is then the backbone of the right of nonestablishment discussed in the first section), such recognition need not be accompanied by the recognition of the content of the rules themselves, which may be totally harmonized. Often, supervisory functions can be performed only on the home country's territory where a company's assets and headquarters are located, or where a professional conducts her main center of activity. If there is a market for delivering services through communication networks, the demand for mutual recognition of all regulatory functions, including initial authorization and enforced rules of conduct, will increase accordingly.

Turning to the diverging preoccupation of governments and regulators when they are asked to recognize the legitimacy of foreign laws, regulations, and traditions of governance, the question is: What conditions make it acceptable for governments to give up their formal authority to control transactions within their territorial jurisdiction? Clearly, the preference for domestic over foreign regulation is based not only on cultural integrity (as discussed above) but also on differences in cultural perceptions of risks, degrees of consumer sophistication in assessing product quality, thresholds of financial security demanded, and so on. To what extent should such differences be overlooked?

In an attempt to address this issue, the European Union has fine-tuned over the past decade an approach—referred to here as "managed mutual recognition"—that has been applied to a great share of trade in information-based services.[36] One lesson from the European experience is that mutual recognition cannot usually be an open-ended concession, whereby regulation of the activities of an information service provider is transferred to its home base unconditionally. Managed mutual recognition includes allowance for wide-ranging host country safeguards, increased rights of regulatory oversight among member states, and the development of cooperative networks among national regulators to collectively "manage" the implementation of mutual recognition. The core idea is that it may be possible to keep the best of all worlds—free movement of information services and continued regulatory control—if regulatory authorities are able to develop mutual trust as well as mutual surveillance mechanisms.

To what extent is prior harmonization a necessary prerequisite for the centralization of jurisdictional authority in a single country? The European Union experience suggests the following ordering: First, negative externalities internationally (including the potential costs of substandard services that would not be borne by the suppliers, such as harm to the network) usually demand a high degree of regulatory convergence. Second, gaps in consumer protection or citizen protection can often be dealt with by developing a market for "information about information services" to increase users' awareness of the regulatory bundle and therefore the risk they incur in using a foreign-based service provider. (Alternatively, recognition of the foreign regulation can be customized so that the host state reduces its regulatory intervention, focusing it on the specific feature that it considers important.) Third, arguments denouncing "reverse discrimination" against domestic providers or calling for a level playing field for competition have not generally justified harmonization, since for most of the services concerned, regulatory obligations are not major determinants of competitiveness or locational choice.

Finally, how can this norm of mutual recognition be reconciled with the prevailing norms of multilateralism? Multilateralism is based on the twin notions of nondiscrimination—embodied in the principle of unconditional MFN and diffuse reciprocity—implying that broadly equivalent concessions are expected of all beneficiaries of nondiscrimination, but not on a quid pro quo basis. The MFN norm has come to be challenged in various ways, including through the negotiation under GATT of code-specific concessions, making it increasingly a conditional benefit. One can argue that mutual recognition represents a further challenge to the unconditional nature of MFN, but does not necessarily imply forgoing the broader notion of nondiscrimination. To be sure, negotiating mutual recognition arrangements will involve both the broad balance of concessions and the detailed equivalence of practices. Bilateral or plurilateral mutual recognition deals cannot be "multilateralized" automatically, as provided by the MFN clause, simply because concessions based on assessing current and future equivalence of regulations are not fungible. Hence, under multilateral mutual recognition, MFN treatment is indeed conditional, not on some symmetrical lowering of trade barriers, but on actual compatibility of rules.

In practice, customized rights of access obtained through recognition should not become a means of discrimination between countries. The GATS provides three types of guarantees to reconcile recognition with multilateralism if not with MFN:

▼   *Openness.* Members interested in negotiating their accession to existing or future recognition agreements must be offered "adequate opportunity" to do so; in particular, the council must be informed "as far in advance as possible" of recognition negotiations before they enter a substantive phase.

▼   *Equitable treatment.* When recognition is granted unilaterally, other members must also be given the chance to demonstrate that education, experience, licenses, or certification obtained in their territories should also be recognized.

▼   *Transparency.* The criteria for recognition should be multilaterally agreed upon and based on cooperation with relevant intergovernmental and nongovernmental organizations.

Beyond these commendable provisions, the contracting parties might need to take a more active approach to ensuring the multilateral character of recognition. This might involve supporting the development of mechanisms (such as field visits) to increase mutual adaptation and trust among national regulators, and supporting "regulatory upgrading" in developing countries in order to increase their potential acceptability as members of mutual recognition regimes.

In sum, the European Union experience suggests that the adoption of managed mutual recognition requires a degree of sustained regulatory cooperation within regulatory networks that may not easily be obtained at the multilateral level. It also suggests a drastic strengthening of the dispute-resolution process to adjudicate ambiguities and provisions for safeguard clauses associated with mutual recognition agreements. In order to minimize future conflicts arising from managed multilateral recognition, traditional patterns of trade diplomacy will need to be profoundly revised.

COOPERATIVE COMPETITION POLICIES FOR "FAIR" NETWORK ACCESS

Another item on the new trade agenda is what is sometimes called "global antitrust"—the need to increase the synergies between trade and competition policies, or at least render them compatible.[37] The traditional view is that trade rules under GATT regulate competition across national boundaries and discipline government practices, while competition policies are designed by national governments to regulate competition within their boundaries and discipline private practices. This view is already obsolete. As noted by Geza Feketekuty,[38] while only one form of private behavior—dumping by foreign suppliers—is specifically covered by GATT, it can be argued that GATT implicitly obligates governments to limit other private practices; failure to do so could be construed as nullifying trade benefits otherwise conceded through trade negotiations. Yet, although nations' obligations to take into account foreigners' interests in implementing their domestic policies might be a first step in the right direction, there is need for a more global "world antitrust" regime, especially for network-based activities.

A way to clarify this complex question is to isolate two separate dimensions of the new interconnection between competition and trade policies. One may be termed "constitutionalizing protection" and the other "perfecting liberalization." Constitutionalizing protection against unfair competition implies replacing the power of a host country to use unilateral countervailing measures with collective oversight of actions in the nation that is the home of the allegedly unfair competition. This is what the European Union has done in the Treaty of Rome, which outlawed antidumping measures between members while subjecting domestic monopolies, subsidies, and restrictive business practices to a common competition policy administered by the commission. As for the rest of the world, as well as for the external dealings of the European Union, many have denounced antidumping policies as bureaucratic fights against low prices in disregard of the general interest (consumers and taxpayers).[39] The use and abuse of antidumping and countervailing measures to justify targeted protection could fruitfully be replaced by international agreements on what constitutes "fair prices" and the like.

In another realm, countries have increasingly sought to protect themselves against what they see as the detrimental effect of mergers abroad through the extraterritorial application of their competition laws. Such an approach is ineffective and conflict prone. Instead, policymakers in the area of domestic competition must be systematically encouraged to seek cooperation by taking their reciprocal national interests into account. Such a comity approach was pioneered in the 1991 EC-U.S. agreement on competition policy and needs to be broadened to include joint proceedings.

The second dimension, perfecting liberalization, would use cooperation on competition policy not as a substitute for, but as a means to realize fully, the effects of trade policies. The argument that restrictive agreements between companies or the existence of state-sanctioned monopolies can be as protectionist as governmental measures and partly offset liberalization agreements has been at the core of the recent development of competition policies in the European Union.[40] For one thing, domestic competition policy enforcement must acquire a "trade flavor," which requires that trade considerations be included when cases are adjudicated. For example, the so-called rule of reason used to assess whether a particular practice—including mergers—is anticompetitive must be revised. Traditionally, the rule of reason weighs consumer welfare gains (such as those achieved by reduced costs) against welfare losses (such as losses in choice). The private action is legitimate if the former outweighs the latter. Adding trade considerations would imply weighing this trade-off against the loss to the foreign producer due to the barrier thus created. This would suggest, in turn, that the concern for income distribution among countries that lies at the heart of trade bargains be adapted to competition policy doctrines and reconciled with considerations regarding competitiveness.

Concurrently or alternatively, trade rules need to reach beyond governmental measures to discipline private business practices that directly affect access to domestic markets by foreign suppliers. In the European Union, for instance, while mutual recognition constituted a new guarantee of access de jure, it did not necessarily ensure equality of access de facto; private firms continue to require adherence to local rules by prospective employees or suppliers. Legitimate self-regulation must not amount to market cooptation. Thus, additional EU-level competition rules have been necessary to impose obligations of non-discrimination upon public and private agents alike. Competition policy also served as the means for completing the single market in services with regard to state monopolies and exclusive rights in sectors ranging from telecommunications to energy provision.

The current debate under way in the European Union as to whether such issues ought to be addressed under the aegis of "trade" or "competition" is not merely legalistic; it reflects changing concepts about institutional prerogatives that may inform multilateral debates. In the late 1980s, the European Commission and the Court of Justice increasingly used competition provisions in connection with the deregulation of certain service sectors. This led to the directive on telecommunications terminal equipment and the decision of March 1991 in which the Court ruled that the commission was empowered to ban exclusive rights relating to the importation, marketing, connection, bringing into service, and maintenance of terminal equipment under the free trade obligations of the treaty. The Court's most recent case law is now serving as a guide for the commission in opening communication services, including postal services, telecommunications, and audiovisual services.

Finally, as this combined application of internal trade and competition policy opens sectors previously excluded from competition, EU institutions are mobilized to ensure that these new freedoms are not abused by firms through restrictive arrangements. This applies particularly in areas such as trans-European payment systems, insurance, value-added telecommunications services, and air transport.

But it is clear that such developments have been contingent on the progressive increase in the investigative powers and resources of a supranational institution (the commission) and the constitutional power of a judicial body (the European Court), as well as the incorporation of EU law into national law. These developments may be hard to replicate at the global level. In this field more than in most others, progress will be conditioned on multilateral institution building.

REGIONAL VERSUS GLOBAL RULES OF THE GAME

Many analysts argue that the type of "deeper integration" warranted by the current evolution of economic interdependence can be addressed, at least in a first phase, only at the regional level.[41] There are, of course, obvious advantages of efficiency. Like-minded nations with similar values can more easily agree on minimal standards, and their regulators are more prone to develop the ties required by managed recognition or comity in competition law enforcement. There also are reasons of political economy for the emphasis on regional integration. Accountability is easier regionally and regional groupings are better suited to put in place the type of compensation across borders that will ease regulatory reform.

It is often remarked that regional arrangements resemble building blocks more than stumbling blocks for the advancement of multilateralism. But there are many empirical, legal, and strategic challenges to that diagnosis. Is trade diversion greater than trade creation? Do less efficient partners replace natural partners in the process of regional integration? Is regional liberalization substantial enough so as not to be targeted toward vulnerable sectors? Does it raise barriers against outsiders as those for insiders are decreased? Is the increased leverage gained through regional integration used to press for global liberalization or as a shield against retaliation? Does a two-step approach to liberalization ease the burden of adjustment, or does it simply solidify opposition to openness?

Whatever the diagnosis, regional groupings, as well as looser arrangements, are here to stay. The powerful factors underlying globalization do not necessarily help sustain multilateral cooperation.[42] Yet multilateralism has been one of the essential (albeit imperfect) supports of "economic peace" since World War II.[43] In the post-Cold War period, as the balance of power is determined more by economic alliances than by military alliances, the temptation of exclusion will arise and multilateral cooperation will become even more essential. A new form of regional multilateralism must therefore be developed— one in which the effects of bilateral, plurilateral, or regional arrangements on outsiders are systematically overseen by the world community.

Such regional multilateralism should be based on three normative pillars:

▼ Openness would require that rules for access to markets or accession to public or private groupings be made explicit and transparent, thereby strengthening the expansionary logic of limited agreements.

▼ Customized diplomacy would allow for the fact that an optimal regulatory area may not be the same for all economic sectors.

▼ The search for interregional compatibility would help guard against the asymmetric extraterritorial application of regional laws but stop short of full harmonization of laws and regulations.

IMPLICATIONS FOR POLICY

In light of the above analysis, a number of guidelines for future policymaking can be suggested. First, the U.S. government must continue to take the lead in promoting the liberalization of information-based services under the GATS. In dealing with the European Union in particular, however, aggressive tactics may be less effective than strategies that influence internal European Union developments and promote regional integration of information infrastructures. This is likely to improve both the negotiating environment and the economic environment for U.S.-based services operators. The United States will need to adapt to a new WTO where dispute resolution will be strengthened and where targeted unilateral pressures will most likely be formally condemned. Moreover, even if they become legal, retaliation measures against goods exports as a response to restrictions on services imports should be avoided as much as possible in order to retain a climate conducive to progressive liberalization.

Notwithstanding the need for respecting differences in the national pace of reform, work should begin immediately on applying mutual recognition and competition policy discipline to international information-based service transactions, avoiding the pitfall of first "testing" the policy on traditional merchandise activities. Most important, a mechanism must be put in place to monitor the rules of access to domestic information infrastructures in cases where networks also serve as markets. The monitoring should include both formal and informal rules designed by private actors. In this context, the United States should insist on a model of decentralized enforcement of commonly agreed upon rules. It is likely to find support for this model from Europeans who have been eager to enforce the principle of subsidiarity (such as designing or enforcing rules at the lowest level possible). Effective governance of the world information economy does not need a new regulatory superstructure; instead, regulators must develop mechanisms to avoid the bypassing of regulations by powerful network players. When standards do not need to be harmonized for pure interoperability purposes, more emphasis should be put on ex ante coordination.

Finally, although the GATS pays lip service to the need for cooperation with other international organizations, no formal mechanism has been created to promote such cooperation. The development of national contact points that would help exporters familiarize themselves with host country rules would be most useful if linked together to provide "just-in-time" updated information on the degree of compatibility between domestic regulations. The creation of a loose and flexible structure with a secretariat and a centralized database—a World Interconnection Forum sponsored by the WTO, for instance—could help fill this dual gap. Ultimately, governing the global information highways should not just be about opening markets. We must keep in mind that such governance will be considered legitimate by people around the world only if access to information fosters individual and collective empowerment, not dependence, and if exchange of information is a means of enhancing mutual knowledge, not a tool for colluding against others. At this turning point in the post-Uruguay Round period, the most important step that can be taken to ensure that the new GATS helps create the conditions necessary to enhance empowerment and mutual knowledge on a world scale is to give priority to building new institutions to govern the global information highway that is rapidly becoming a reality.

PART IV

OUTLOOK AND CONCLUSION

12

THE NATIONAL INFORMATION INFRASTRUCTURE DEBATE: ISSUES, INTERESTS, AND THE CONGRESSIONAL PROCESS

WILLIAM J. DRAKE

As *Business Week* has noted, the world is undergoing three simultaneous and historic upheavals.[1] The collapse of communism has relaxed the geostrategic pressures that dominated and distorted American politics, economics, and culture for almost fifty years. Almost all nations have shifted toward market capitalism, and many are pursuing aggressive economic liberalization that will change their societies for better and for worse in the years to come. And the spread of the information revolution is rapidly bringing about a global information economy in which computerized networks and information resources are central sources of wealth and power. Given the interplay of these three transformations, it is no exaggeration to suggest that we are entering not only a new millennium, but also a new era—one in which networked firms and markets increasingly will transcend boundaries, integrate national economies, and present new challenges to territorially based nation-states.[2] The liberalization and globalization of information-intensive industries is accelerating the mobility of assets and jobs, thereby pressuring governments to increase their attractiveness to footloose investors. At the same time, these forces threaten to leave behind less skilled individuals and groups, aggravating further the many social pathologies of class-divided societies.

While clearly not a panacea, the new information infrastructure could be useful in tackling such challenges. As François Bar notes in Chapter 2, many (but by no means all) large corporations have successfully used private information infrastructures to rationalize their operations; increase competitiveness; and improve their relationships with partners, suppliers, and customers. A broadly accessible and affordable public national information infrastructure (NII) could provide small- and medium-sized businesses with similar opportunities, helping in turn to revitalize local communities and stimulate innovation and job creation. A seamlessly interconnected global information infrastructure (GII) would extend these possibilities further by making such businesses' products and services visible—and in some cases, instantly deliverable—to customers around the world. And the potential benefits are not confined to the economic sphere: the NII also can be used to foster a democratic public sphere of ideas, build virtual and real life communities, enhance participation in civic and religious affairs, and improve the delivery of governmental and noncommercial services. But for these things to happen, the NII must be properly configured and governed.

The question is whether we are heading in the right direction: Is the federal government acting decisively to adopt a national strategy that balances increased incentives for private investment with measures to make advanced capabilities accessible to the broadest possible cross section of American society? This chapter describes the main contours of the NII policy process as it unfolded between 1993 and early 1995, and suggests that we are not. The first section presents an overview of the Clinton administration's NII initiative, while the second and third outline some of the key issues and interests involved in the corporate and public interest community debates. The fourth section lays out the principal features of the resulting NII legislation and the dynamics of the 103d and 104th Congresses. The author's views on alternative approaches to the issues raised here are presented in the concluding chapter in the context of a broader synthesis of the contributors' main policy recommendations.

THE CLINTON ADMINISTRATION'S NII INITIATIVE

To the casual observer, the NII may seem to have just landed on the national agenda. After all, press coverage did not really begin until the popularization of the Internet and the "information superhighway." Many of the key technological and economic forces driving today's debate, however, were gathering steam and generating discussion in industry and government circles throughout the 1980s. What was missing, as Henry Geller notes in Chapter 4, was a vision of the future broadband NII and a coherent national strategy to lay the groundwork for its development. Neither the Reagan nor Bush administrations gave priority to rethinking the fundamentals of electronic media in light of emerging technological capabilities and the broader shift to an information economy. About the only leadership they provided was endorsing deregulation and competition within the existing parameters of telecommunications, cable television, and broadcasting. And while Congress added a new cable title to the Communications Act in 1984, it failed to pass broader telecommunications legislation that could have helped lay the groundwork for a digital future.

The main action was in the courts, where the 1982 Modification of Final Judgment (MFJ) breaking up AT&T was being implemented, and at the Federal Communications Commission (FCC). During the Reagan era, the FCC undertook some initiatives important to the current debate, such as the 1986 Computer III inquiry that sought to impose open network and interconnection requirements on the Regional Bell Operating Companies (RBOCs). More often, though, the administration's hard-line crusade against government involvement in the economy limited the FCC's ability to fulfill its statutory mandate to guide the telecommunications industry's development. In contrast, the Bush administration's FCC adopted a more pragmatic stance that coupled incremental liberalization and cartel management with some policy support for new technologies such as personal communications services (PCS) and high definition television (HDTV). Particularly important from today's perspective was the FCC's adoption of video dial tone (VDT) rules in 1992, which cleared the way for the RBOCs to experiment with common carrier video platforms, albeit with inadequate public interest provisions.[3] In general, however, the absence of high-level government leadership and disagreements within the industry combined to slow the development of a forward-looking national strategy for the eventual deployment of broadband networks and interactive, multimedia services. Many people were talking about how the emerging technologies would soon revolutionize electronic media and along with it, the economy and society, but the outmoded federal policy framework impeded significant movement down that path.

It was in this context that the 1992 presidential campaign generated substantial interest within the world of communications and information. Bill Clinton ran as a "new Democrat" and a policy wonk who understood that the global economic transformation under way posed unprecedented challenges for the United States and who was eager to use the tools of government to address them. Moreover, some of his key economic advisors, such as Laura D' Andrea Tyson and Robert Reich, were prominent advocates of an activist government effort, in partnership with business, to increase national competitiveness, in part through the utilization of advanced communication and information technologies.[4]

But the strongest signal that Clinton would push the NII up the national agenda was the presence on the ticket of Al Gore. Senator Gore had been talking about an information superhighway for years and had established a record of congressional leadership on telecommunications issues, most recently by winning passage of the National Research and Education Network (NREN) program.[5] Gore undoubtedly would be the most technology-literate person ever to hold high national office; that he actually used the Internet in itself distinguished him from most top policymakers at the time, both here and abroad, who were making decisions about communication and information issues. Hence, it seemed that Gore's personal interest and involvement, combined with the broader economic vision of the Clinton team, would ensure the adoption of a strategy to advance the new information infrastructure. In part for this reason the ticket won the support of many otherwise Republican executives from communications and information companies, especially in Silicon Valley.

Once elected, the new administration set out to make good on its promise to get things moving. After adopting a series of initiatives on particular issues, in September 1993 the Clinton administration proposed a broad national strategy, embodied in a vision statement entitled *The National Information Infrastructure: Agenda for Action*. Widely circulated in the United States and abroad via the Internet, the agenda quickly became a central reference point for the escalating NII debate. The document laid out nine principles that would guide the administration's efforts: [6]

1.   Promote private sector investment, through tax and regulatory policies that encourage long-term investment, as well as wise procurement of services.

2.   Extend the "universal service" concept to ensure that information resources are available to all at affordable prices. Because information means empowerment, the government has a duty to ensure that all Americans have access to the resources of the Information Age.

3.   Act as a catalyst to promote technological innovation and new applications. Commit important government research programs and grants to help the private sector develop and demonstrate technologies needed for the NII.

4.   Promote seamless, interactive, user-driven operation of the NII. As the NII evolves into a "network of networks," government will ensure that users can transfer information across networks easily and efficiently.

5.   Ensure information security and network reliability. The NII must be trustworthy and secure, protecting the privacy of its users. Government action will also aim to ensure that the overall system remains reliable, quickly repairable in the event of a failure and, perhaps most importantly, easy to use.

6.   Improve management of the radio frequency spectrum, an increasingly critical resource.

7.   Protect intellectual property rights. The Administration will investigate how to strengthen domestic copyright laws and international intellectual property treaties to prevent piracy and to protect the integrity of intellectual property.

8.   Coordinate with other levels of government and with other nations. Because information crosses state, regional, and national boundaries, coordination

is important to avoid unnecessary obstacles and to prevent unfair policies that handicap U.S. industry.

9.   Provide access to government information and improve government procurement.

The agenda was thoroughly dissected and debated on the Internet and in scores of publications and conferences, and was taken by many as an encouraging sign that the federal government was going to get serious about the NII. There were, of course, complaints in various quarters that the vision statement was short on specifics and glossed over the more difficult and potentially divisive issues. And, predictably, corporate spokespersons and public interest advocates alike expressed concern that their favorite issues were not addressed fully.[7] Nevertheless, the agenda did map out the terrain of the administration's program for the coming years and help focus the emerging policy debate. Five aspects of the agenda in particular distinguish the administration's approach from that of its predecessors.

First, the agenda makes clear that the administration favors expanding competition in all segments of the digital marketplace in order to increase innovation and investment while lowering prices for consumers. But, at the same time, it recognizes that the promotion of market entry does not in itself amount to the sort of coherent national strategy required to get the maximum economic and social benefits from the new infrastructure's capabilities. For example, encouraging firms to build local broadband networks does not take one very far if access to these networks by consumers and content suppliers is limited; if users lack confidence that the privacy of their communications is protected or that their digital cash transactions are secure; or if the technical ability to use new tools is confined to a small segment of society. Hence, building a vital NII that people can use productively requires moving on multiple fronts simultaneously, from information policy to technology policy to labor policy and so on.

Second, while supporting liberalization, the agenda also proposed the establishment of public interest safeguards. Safeguards are necessary, among other things, to prevent abuses of dominant market positions by the major players; to promote universal service; and to ensure that broadband networks are configured in an open, flexible manner that allows all those interested to access, create, and disseminate information. In those specific instances where markets alone will fail to fulfill important national objectives, the administration argues that government has a responsibility to step in. In some cases, this may mean simply setting broad requirements (such as that networks and technical standards must be open) and letting the private sector figure out how best to realize these goals. In others, it may mean adopting targeted regulations to prevent abuse or pursuing policies designed to shape incentive structures so that firms will find it in their interests to make socially desirable decisions. In still others, it may mean participating in dialogues with companies on questions of network security and technical standardization, or providing direct financial support (usually, small amounts of seed money) for basic R&D and applications. In short, the administration is pursuing what might be called liberalization with a human face—not as a matter of charity or middle-class entitlement, but rather as a means to maximize the NII's contributions to the economy and society.

Third, and relatedly, the agenda coupled its call for competitive supply with attention to the demand side of the market—how individuals and organizations actually can use the new technologies. As it noted, the NII "is not an end in itself; it is a means by which the United States can achieve a broad range of economic and social goals" in areas like rural development; worker retraining; and the delivery of health, educational, and governmental services.[8] Accordingly, the administration has devoted time and resources to fostering the development of specific types of applications, including noncommercial applications at the grassroots level. This is one of the most innovative parts of the program.

Fourth, the administration is working to strengthen the telecommunications policymaking process. At the level of individual agencies, management has been improved and streamlined. For example, the FCC has created strong new bureaus responsible for wireless communications and international issues, both of which will be increasingly important in the years ahead. Similarly, at the State Department, the once separate (and controversial) Bureau of Communications and Information Policy has been folded into another bureau. Organizational changes have been enacted in a number of other agencies as well, in accordance with both the NII initiative and Vice President Gore's "Reinventing Government" program.

At the interagency level, the administration launched a parallel effort to improve the policymaking process. There are over twenty executive branch agencies with some role in telecommunications and information policy. Over the years, many observers have argued that substantive differences in perspective and bureaucratic turf battles among them have combined to impede effective policy development. Hence, to maintain consensus and benefit from specialized expertise, successive administrations have created interagency coordination groups focusing on particular domestic and international issues. Some of these are standing organizations, such as the Interdepartment Radio Advisory Committee, while others have been convened on an ad hoc basis. The Clinton administration decided to build on this approach by creating a "meta" interagency mechanism to oversee the full range of NII programs: the Information Infrastructure Task Force (IITF). The organization of the IITF is presented in Table 12.1

The IITF comprises over forty high-level representatives of all the federal agencies with stakes in the NII, ranging from those with a direct policy role such as the Departments of Commerce, State, and Justice, to those concerned with specific applications, such as the Environmental Protection Agency and the Departments of Education and Health and Human Services.[9] This blend of functional responsibilities and perspectives is intended to help the administration examine any given NII issue—whether a matter of regulatory, technology, or information policy—in an integrated fashion, rather than through the prism of a single agency's mandate. The IITF is chaired by Commerce Secretary Ron Brown and most of the coordination and staff work is done by his department's National Telecommunications and Information Administration (NTIA). The IITF operates under the aegis of the Executive Office of the President's Office of Science and Technology Policy (OSTP) and National Economic Council and has had the active participation of Vice President Gore and other senior White House officials. By integrating agency perspectives and engaging the highest levels of government, the IITF represents an important step toward alleviating some of the institutional and policy deficiencies decried by Henry Geller in Chapter 4.

Fifth, the NII initiative is noteworthy for the attention it gives to bringing diverse stakeholders into the policy process. On the same day the agenda was released, the president signed an executive order establishing the United States Advisory Council on the National Information Infrastructure. Commerce Secretary Ron Brown appointed twenty-seven people (later increased to thirty-seven) to the council for two-year terms. About two-thirds of the members are from the business community, with the rest drawn from the nonprofit sector, organized labor,

TABLE 12.1
ORGANIZATION OF THE INFORMATION
INFRASTRUCTURE TASK FORCE

APPLICATIONS AND TECHNOLOGY COMMITTEE

▼ Government Information Technology Services Working Group
▼ Technology Policy Working Group
▼ Health Information and Applications Working Group

TELECOMMUNICATIONS POLICY COMMITTEE

▼ University Service Working Group
▼ Reliability and Vulnerability Working Group
▼ International Telecommunications Policy Working Group
▼ Legislative Drafting Task Force

INFORMATION POLICY COMMITTEE

▼ Intellectual Property Rights Working Group
▼ Privacy Working Group
▼ Government Information Working Groups

NII SECURITY ISSUES FORUM

and state and local governments. The council's role is to examine the progress of the initiative and related NII issues and provide policy input to the administration, which sends representatives to its meetings. The council has launched so-called mega-projects to make recommendations in the following areas:

▼   *Visions and Goals for the NII*, focusing on applications in the education, health care, electronic commerce, and public safety arenas;

▼   *Access to the NII*, including how to define which services should be universally accessible and how to fund such access; and

▼   *Privacy, Security, and Intellectual Property*, covering such information policy problems as personal privacy, property rights, and First Amendment protections in electronic media, as well as national security questions of network reliability and vulnerability.

The administration's effort to open the policy process to public input is not limited, however, to appointing nominal representatives of various constituencies to the council. It also has adopted a number of unprecedented measures to make the policy process more transparent and accessible to the average citizen. For example, the FCC and other agencies have opened their doors to representatives of public interest groups and the nonprofit sector. The NTIA and IITF have convened numerous public conferences around the country and on the Internet (in most of which the vice president has participated) to solicit opinions on issues such as public interest safeguards, the promotion of universal service, barriers to NII development, the roles of state and local governments, and so on. Similarly, the council has held public meetings around the country.

The administration also has made good use of the Internet. The White House has established a multimedia home page on the World-Wide Web, where citizens can tour the building, hear a recording of Socks the cat, and access a range of more useful resources on government functions and policy. Similarly, federal agencies have established computer servers containing thousands of files on a huge array of topics. For example, the FCC produces a daily digest with dozens of items on various aspects of telecommunications regulation; even the State Department, which congressional budgeting has otherwise left in the dark ages of 1970s-era word processors and telex machines, has gotten into the act. Information on the activities of the IITF and the Advisory Council is also readily available through dozens of reports, minutes of meetings, and requests for public comment on various policy proposals. Finally, the administration is establishing a Government Information Locator System to give citizens one-stop Internet access to all federal agencies' documents.[10]

In sum, the agenda laid out the broad contours of an administration-wide NII initiative that differs sharply, both substantively and procedurally, from the narrow deregulatory approach to electronic media of the 1980s. Since its release, the administration has fleshed out the details by adopting regulatory decisions, policy programs, and legislative positions on a wide range of issues. Among other things, it supported (with some modifications) the principal reform bills pushed by the Democratic majority in the 1993–94 Congress; auctioned off radio frequency spectrum worth billions of dollars for new Personal Communications Services (PCS); launched an investigation of new information policies concerning issues such as personal privacy and intellectual property; redirected and expanded the federal government's advanced technology policy efforts; introduced an important program for the development of innovative applications in the nonprofit sector; strengthened the utilization of systems and services within federal agencies in the name of organizational efficiency and government transparency; and established mechanisms to help workers and small businesses adapt to the new economic environment.[11]

THE MOBILIZATION OF CORPORATE STAKEHOLDERS

The new administration's initiative added momentum to a growing bipartisan consensus that Congress should finally overhaul the Communications Act of 1934. Moreover, the act's approaching sixtieth anniversary provided a suitably symbolic target date for legislators who for years had grappled with telecommunications issues. The prospect of sweeping legislative reform added urgency to market trends already under way and a flurry of activity took place in 1993–94 as major firms jockeyed for position in preparation for media liberalization and convergence.[12] On a weekly or even daily basis, the business press brought news of corporate alliances between telcos, cable companies, wireless service providers, manufacturers, information service suppliers, software companies, and others across the spectrum of communications and information industries. Some of these alliances represented a good match of complementary skills that would result in real synergies, while others (like the ill-fated Bell Atlantic–TCI deal) looked like unhappy marriages of incompatible corporate cultures and financial conditions. Some clearly would enhance competition, while others promised little more than concentrated market power antithetical to an open and pluralistic NII. Some were purely domestic affairs, while others (like MCI's deal with British Telecom) reached across national borders to foreign partners. But all were driven by the same kinds of objectives: to acquire positions in markets outside traditional areas of operation, gain access to capital and expertise, spread investment risks, accelerate R&D, pursue economies of scope and scale, and develop competitively strong common platforms and products.[13]

In parallel with these strategic alignments, the business community accelerated its public relations and lobbying efforts. Companies churned out position papers and studies for public consumption and used the Internet to disseminate their views on the issues. Corporate executives talked up the information superhighway in the mass media and on the conference circuit, professing how much they favored open competition. A few were even pronounced visionaries by television and print journalists outside the business press.[14] Some firms began to run advertisements for products and services they were not remotely close to releasing, either to preemptively reinforce brand name identification among consumers or to derail their competitors' planning. More revealing than the hype, though, was the action away from the public eye. Some of the largest players, particularly the telcos and cable operators, were filing lawsuits under existing regulations to block competitors' alliances and market entry plans. They were also flooding Capitol Hill with high-priced lobbyists arguing that their opponents would have unfair competitive advantages in an open market and that legislative reform would have to redress any resulting imbalance.

Even while soliciting its support, some corporate executives found that simultaneously attacking the government was a useful tactic. For example, when the FCC rolled back some cable rates in accordance with the 1992 Cable Act, cable industry spokespersons argued that the FCC was undermining their ability to build the superhighway and was responsible for the collapse of the proposed TCI/Bell Atlantic and Cox Cable/Southwestern Bell alliances.[15] Some of the RBOCs pursued a similar strategy, sending representatives to the Hill to warn that legislation that failed to give them everything they wanted might result in their refusal to invest in broadband network development. The press took the bait and stories appeared implying that either through incompetence, bureaucratic rigidity, or an unspecified antibusiness impulse, the federal government was somehow responsible for "erecting roadblocks on the information superhighway."[16] These tactics were clever, in at least two senses. First, the firms involved recognized that the general enthusiasm and expectations about the NII presented a golden opportunity to redress their grievances about existing laws and regulations and to secure more favorable treatment in the future should reform legislation actually pass. The implicit message to politicians was: "Give us more incentives and revenue opportunities or the highway will not get built and you will get the blame." Second, the posturing established a presumption that public interest protections could be viewed as misguided obstructions to be limited or even eliminated, rather than legitimate tools for the development of a pluralistic and citizen-empowering NII.

As the congressional process gathered steam in 1993 and 1994, the corporate war of words and position—directed at each other and toward government restrictions (except those placed on their opponents)—became the dominant focus of press coverage and political calculations. The overriding question, then as now, was how to replace the old models for telecommunications, cable television, and, to some extent, broadcasting, with a new policy architecture that would spur the deployment of broadband networks and a new generation of services. In particular, this means deciding under what specific terms to eliminate the line of business restrictions embodied in the Communications Act, the MFJ, and a number of FCC regulations and other rules.

Some observers have argued that, given the need for huge capital investments and the uncertain nature of consumer demand for new services, the best way to accelerate NII development would be simply to eliminate all restrictions on companies' market entry, profits, and scope of operations.[17] But this seemingly elegant solution clearly was not in the cards; neither the major corporations involved, nor the administration or Congress, were prepared to throw the doors open and let the chips fall where they may. The legislative debate and drafting process of the 103d Congress therefore plunged deeply into the details of each market segment and prospects for competition within them. The inevitable result was complex legislation that many stakeholders and observers decried as micromanagement, albeit for varying reasons.

CONVERGING MARKETS, DIVERGING INTERESTS

LOCAL DISTRIBUTION

The major bottlenecks in the pursuit of enhanced competition and the development of open, accessible, and seamlessly interconnected public broadband networks are encountered at the level of local distribution. In telecommunications, local exchange carriers such as the seven RBOCs and their members, the General Telephone Company (GTE), and the small independents control the facilities through which customers can access other service providers—such as long distance telephone companies, cellular telephone companies, Internet access providers, commercial computer services such as Prodigy and CompuServe, and database vendors. While a handful of states recently have introduced a measure of competition, the local carriers generally retain monopoly control, which gives them a great deal of power over potential newcomers with regard to interconnection, access to network functions like signaling and switching, service tariffs, technical standards, number portability, and a host of other issues. Hence, while a few dozen Competitive Access Providers (CAPs) have managed to work around local restrictions and provide specialized services to large corporate customers, significant entry by firms serving the wider public has thus far been impossible.

Similarly, cable television companies control a major access point between independent video suppliers and consumers. Cable systems fit awkwardly in the transition to an open NII: they comprise analog networks with closed, proprietary architectures and have no common carrier obligations to interconnect with other networks or to give video suppliers access on a nondiscriminatory basis. Moreover, they wed control of the carriage or transport vehicle to control of the content. Cable executives are free to act as gatekeepers, deciding whose programming will be presented and where on the dial they will be positioned; some have used this power to give favored political groups a forum while barring others from speech. In short, cable represents what public interest advocates characterize as a "monster model"—one entity controlling both the pipes and the content that goes over them, even owning some of that content—that should be avoided in a future NII.

LOCAL AND LONG DISTANCE TELECOMMUNICATIONS

One of the most hotly contested dividing lines in the industry is the MFJ's separation between the markets of the RBOCs and AT&T. The RBOCs are eager to move into the lucrative long-distance business where their familiarity to local consumers could be a big plus in competing with AT&T, MCI, Sprint, and the 400-plus smaller service providers. In turn, AT&T is positioning itself to "go local" selectively in the short term through wireless services; to that end, AT&T has purchased the nation's largest cellular operator, McCaw Cellular Communications. MCI and Sprint are also buying into wireless. In addition, MCI plans to spend $2 billion on an integrated local/long-distance network to "cherry pick" large corporate customers in twenty major markets, while Sprint and GTE already have positions in some local markets. But despite such moves, the major long-distance operators are adamantly opposed to RBOC entry into their markets until there is demonstrable competition in the local loop. In congressional testimony, the chairmen of AT&T, MCI, Sprint, and of the Competitive Telecommunications Association (CompTel) and America's Carriers Telecommunications Association (ACTA)—both representing the small independent carriers—have cautioned that the RBOCs would abuse their local monopolies to gain unfair advantage in long distance. The chairman of MCI even went so far as to predict that "premature [RBOC] entry into long distance—prior to the development of effective local competition—would reduce real GDP by $24.4 billion and decrease employment by 322,000 by the year 2000."[18] The RBOCs have returned fire by arguing that there already is competition in the local loop from CAPs, cable, and cellular, but nobody appears convinced.[19]

TELECOMMUNICATIONS AND VIDEO ENTERTAINMENT

A second key boundary line divides the worlds of the RBOCs and cable television operators under the FCC's cross-ownership rules and the 1984 Cable Act. This gulf is already being bridged in places, as some telcos have launched video platforms under the FCC's 1992 VDT rules; the courts have recently ruled unconstitutional the restrictions on cable entry as they apply to certain RBOCs; and players on both sides of the line are pursuing alliances outside their regions as well as buying into wireless services. But to encourage the construction of broadband "information superdriveways" to the home, Congress needs to establish clear and consistent rules of the road for everyone. Here, too, the players have been divided.

With regard to cable's entry into telecommunications, some telcos argue that cable companies have an unfair advantage because they are not encumbered by common carrier obligations and related safeguards, and that there should be regulatory parity between the industries. For their part, the cable companies would like to avoid such requirements. While they currently lack switched, two-way wired networks and deep customer good will, and are dwarfed in size by the RBOCs, cable operators may become effective competitors in telecommunications services. A number of them are already experimenting with providing Internet access via special modems and their coaxial cables.[20] Moreover, the telcos may have additional competition from public utilities such as electric power companies, which have thousands of miles of fiber optic cable that could be reconfigured for certain telecommunications markets if Congress lifts the restrictions of the Public Utility Holding Company Act of 1935.

The terms of RBOC entry into the world of video program production and delivery is more controversial.[21] Members of the National Cable Television Association (NCTA) are concerned that telcos could present a serious challenge and have argued that entry should be delayed until there is open competition, interconnection, and access in the Baby Bell's local loops; moreover, some maintain that the RBOCs should be subject to the same local cable franchise requirements as they are.[22] Like the long-distance carriers, cable companies charge that the RBOCs will be tempted to unfairly cross-subsidize new service offerings with monies derived from captive ratepayers and that separate subsidiaries and books should be mandated. Moreover, the Clinton administration and others fear that the RBOCs might simply gobble up cable providers if given the opportunity, thereby limiting facilities-based competition and leaving the nation with only one broadband wire to the home. (Of course, direct broadcast satellite systems would still provide some competition for video delivery.) As such, they want to retain limits on full cross-ownership within service regions, except for rural and other areas where two-wire competition may not be viable.

Many stakeholders also worry that the RBOCs, which are seeking positions in video entertainment production through corporate alliances, could give preference to their own shows, games, and home shopping services within their cable television and VDT platforms (in a parallel to what the major airlines operating computer reservation systems have done). In response, the administration and others would like Congress to require that platform capacity be made readily available to unaffiliated video suppliers on a common carrier basis. Indeed, the Association of Independent Television Stations (AITS) and some other content providers have called for free access to the RBOC's video platforms.[23] The RBOCs reject this proposal as an unjustified constraint on their revenues and ability to build local broadband networks. The thousand-plus member U.S. Telephone Association (USTA), which includes GTE and the small independent local carriers, support the RBOCs' position.[24]

INFORMATION SERVICES

Another boundary controversy concerns information services and electronic publishing. The MFJ had restricted RBOC entry into this business, but in 1991 the courts eased the rules and the FCC lifted its separate subsidiary requirement.[25] The RBOCs did not make a major move in this direction in the years that followed, but that is changing and some stakeholders want Congress to lay down guidelines and safeguards. Members of the Newspaper Association of America (NAA) have in recent years launched over six hundred on-line publishing services and other traditional print publishers are doing the same. Many of these offerings are not very exciting, in that they usually involve simple reformatting of newspapers or other texts for viewing on a personal computer, but in time the addition of interactive multimedia capabilities combined with personal agent software could change that.[26] The RBOCs' deep pockets could provide serious competition for electronic publishers and their control of the local loop could be manipulated to give their own services preferential treatment. As such, the NAA asked the 103d Congress to prohibit the RBOCs from engaging directly in electronic publishing within their service areas over their monopoly facilities and to require that publishing in other regions take place through separate subsidiaries.[27] Similar concerns have been voiced by other on-line service supplies, including small Internet access providers.

MANUFACTURING AND EQUIPMENT

Also contentious are some matters concerning network and customer premise equipment. Two issues merit particular mention. First, there is the question of removing the MFJ's prohibition against the RBOCs manufacture of equipment. The prohibition served to foster a diverse and competitive industry that includes many small- and medium-sized suppliers, but it also forced the RBOCs out of a market where they could have much to contribute and into overseas production. There is now a broad consensus that this injunction should be lifted but, again, stakeholders disagree on how and when. For example, the Telecommunications Industry Association (TIA), which represents over 570 manufacturers, has argued that RBOC entry must be phased in over a period of years to prevent abuses of market power. Other industry associations and AT&T concur, arguing that the RBOCs' monopoly control over the local loop could result in discriminatory procurement, interconnection, and access to technical standards and other information, as well as hidden cross-subsidies derived from ratepayers.[28]

Second, there is the question of the computerized set-top boxes that will link television sets to broadband pipes. The cable converter boxes of today are generally proprietary and are designed to fit the narrow parameters of individual carriers' networks. As a result, diverse suppliers cannot produce them, nor can customers go to Radio Shack or a similar outlet and buy an interoperable model off the shelf; they must rent it from the carrier. Whether this is the right approach for the new set-top boxes, which will perform a vastly expanded range of functions, is a divisive issue. As one protagonist summarized the situation, "Everyone sees the set-top box as a way of controlling what the viewer experiences, so everyone wants to control the set-top."[29]

Influenced perhaps by its experience in the world of the UNIX operating system, Sun Microsystems—one of the more progressive forces in the computer industry—has argued that the interface between the network and the box should be open and that the FCC should establish a committee of representatives of consumer groups, government agencies, industry, and academia to set the broad requirements.[30] Moreover, while acknowledging that actual box implementations may be proprietary, Sun has warned against excessive license fees and intellectual property restrictions and has joined consumer groups and several other enterprises in encouraging Congress and the FCC to study the problems involved.[31] In contrast, General Instruments, which produces many of the cable converter boxes of today, has argued against standardization requirements.[32]

But the main force in this equation may be Microsoft. The software behemoth already controls about 80 percent of the market for personal computer operating systems and is preparing to roll out its long-awaited Windows95 system. Windows95 reportedly will instruct consumers to log onto the new Microsoft Network to register their purchase, and thereupon will be encouraged to join the Network (allowing them, for example, to peruse Microsoft founder Bill Gates' collection of digitized art and other services). Because the Network is gatewayed to the Internet, the impact on the multiprovider Internet access market could be significant. Beyond this, Microsoft is also reportedly positioning itself, with the support of some telcos and cable operators, for a parallel effort to establish *the* operating system for the set-top box on a proprietary basis. As Microsoft's representative explained in testimony before Congress, "We are going to try and license that software in a nondiscriminatory fashion to any network operator who wants to deploy it, whether that is on a trial basis or later on. So we do want to see you people use our software."[33] Undoubtedly.

BROADCASTING

A final struggle over the terms of convergence in the NII concerns the role of the broadcasting industry. There have been widespread suggestions in the press and industry circles that broadcasters could become "roadkill on the information superhighway." Quite apart from the expected squeeze on advertising revenues, analysts ask, where does over-the-air transmission of analog signals fit in an age of broadband digital pipes, five hundred channels, video on demand, interactive advertisements, and so on? Some observers even believe that, "once programmes are stored on servers, channels disappear."[34] That is, with the spread of client-server architectures akin to the Internet, consumers could simply dial up programming whenever they wanted; it would no longer be necessary to send out *Baywatch* or *Oprah* signals at a fixed time and the UHF spectrum could be reallocated to scores of new wireless services.[35] Of course, while the technology could make this feasible in principle, stakeholder interests and industry economics are unlikely to allow it in practice. More generally, these dire predictions overlook broadcasters' strength in programming and, CBS notwithstanding, their increasingly healthy advertising revenues and earnings from global markets. But the net effect of such talk has been to give broadcasters the same sort of pleading rights in Congress as everyone else.

On Capitol Hill and elsewhere, broadcasters have used their newfound vulnerability to make three major claims.[36] First, carriers like the RBOCs must be obliged to comply with "must carry" obligations and related rules protecting broadcasters' programming. Second, broadcasters need relief from FCC rules limiting their ownership of television and radio stations and preventing their cross-ownership of cable systems and newspapers in a given local market. And third, broadcasters need "spectrum flexibility." The FCC has designated spectrum for the broadcasters to develop high definition television (HDTV), but the investments required are large and high resolution pictures may not bring more advertising revenue. The industry would like to reallocate a large chunk of this spectrum to provide a new generation of digital services in competition with other wireless providers. Among the new services contemplated are scrambled pay television and broadcasting data to personal computers, personal digital assistants, and other information appliances. But the cable industry and other competitors have challenged these proposals.[37]

*   *   *

In sum, these are a few of the major issues that have dominated the NII debate on and off Capitol Hill. Schematic as the above overview may be, it underscores two main points. First, major firms are hoping to compete on favorable terms in a variety of new markets and are seeking a leg up through the political process. The legislative discussion has therefore been consumed with trying to balance the interests of these powerful contestants, which has complicated efforts to develop a far-sighted and impartial assessment of what policies are really in the national interest. Second, while it is the private sector's investments and innovations that make a broadband NII feasible, focusing on profit maximization alone may lead to a narrow definition of what is possible and desirable.

Undoubtedly, the business community will develop a wide variety of products that will help make peoples' lives easier, enhance organizational efficiency, and contribute to the national economy. But many firms have worked hard on the Hill to weaken or eliminate public interest safeguards. And when it comes to broadband to the home, the fundamental vision of the telcos, cable companies, and many other powerful firms seems to be about entertainment—pay-per-view movies on demand, video games, and home shopping. To people who are active in the Internet environment, this represents a limited conception of what to do with the bandwidth explosion and a missed opportunity to promote individual empowerment and sociocultural enrichment. As Anthony Rutkowski has said, "the National/Global Information Infrastructure is not about bringing more *Beavis and Butthead* to Joe Sixpack. It's about providing intuitive, powerful network-based capabilities to people for business, research, professional, and governmental kinds of needs."[38]

THE MOBILIZATION OF NONCOMMERCIAL STAKEHOLDERS

The view that the NII can and should be about providing such capabilities to the broadest range of citizens possible has not been without its ardent champions. For while powerful corporations were gearing up to slug it out in the markets and on the Hill, a parallel mobilization of forces was occurring within what I called the distributed sector in the Introduction to this volume. That this phenomenon has received little attention in the mainstream press is ironic in an era when pundits are decrying the breakdown of civil society's collective institutions and community groups. The rapid spread of personal computers, Internet access, and technical expertise has given many people in diverse occupational and social settings reasons to be concerned about how the NII is supplied, used, and governed. To be sure, quite a few of them have fairly libertarian attitudes; they believe the market will take care of most everything and are often sharply derisive of "digital do-gooders"[39] who want to see the government play an active role in maximizing the NII's benefits to society. But many others have reached the opposite conclusion and have organized to try and influence the policy debate. They have joined forces with individuals and organizations from outside the Internet community who also believe that the NII should not be defined by commercial values alone. For the sake of shorthand, we will refer to this community as the public interest coalition.

Broadly speaking, the coalition encompasses three kinds of people. The first are members of organizations with specialized expertise on electronic media issues, like the Alliance for Community Media, the Alliance for Public Technology, Computer Professionals for Social Responsibility, the Consumer Federation of America, the Electronic Frontier Foundation, the Benton Foundation, the Center for Civic Networking, the Center for Media Education, and the Taxpayer Assets Project. The second are people who belong to organizations that traditionally have focused on other social concerns, but who have come to recognize the NII's importance to their objectives. Such organizations include, among many others, the American Civil Liberties Union, the American Library Association, the National Association for the Deaf, the National Coalition for Black Voter Participation, People for the American Way, the United Cerebral Palsy Associations, and the United Church of Christ. And third are people who are not necessarily members or employees of any particular organization or interest group, but who nonetheless participate in the debate and/or support the coalition's general orientation; these include writers, artists, K-12 teachers, academics, Internet personalities, entrepreneurs, and so on. Some participants have years of experience in public interest media issues, while others are new to the field. Some are active at the grassroots level, while others work as beltway insiders. Some represent broad constituencies with varying levels of awareness of NII issues, while others represent only themselves.

When the Clinton administration came to office and progress on NII policies appeared imminent, public interest proponents felt the need to coordinate more extensively than they had in the past. In July 1993, about forty organizations met in Washington to discuss creating a peak association of like-minded groups and, by October, the Telecommunications Policy Roundtable (TPR) had been launched. The TPR, which has grown to over two hundred member organizations, holds open public meetings on a monthly basis that often have been attended by representatives of the Clinton administration, organized labor, and unaffiliated citizens groups. The minutes of these sessions and other materials are available over the Internet, where the TPR also hosts an often raucous discussion group. Dozens of public interest-oriented organizations both within and outside of the TPR make similar uses of the Internet. Issues are debated in on-line discussion groups and thousands of documents analyzing policy developments at the federal, state, and local levels are circulated on the Internet. Indeed, by using the Internet to get the word out, TPR members and other coalition supporters have on several occasions mobilized instant electronic letter writing campaigns that actually affected the policy process.

The cumulative result of all this activity, of which the TPR is just one important part, has been to foster a democratic dialogue outside the corridors of corporate and governmental power and to build consensus among a hetero-geneous array of stakeholders about how the NII should be governed. Not since the unsuccessful broadcast reform movement of the late 1920s and early 1930s has the communications policy process witnessed this sort of involvement by citizens' groups committed to the public interest. It would of course be foolish to expect the coalition to have as much impact on federal policy as, say, Bell Atlantic or Microsoft. And the coalition has not attracted enough involvement from the distributed sector's thousands of small- and medium-sized businesses, many of which are also concerned about the possibility of the larger firms accumulating too much market power and erecting anticompetitive bottlenecks. Nevertheless, coalition members have influenced the policy process on some key issues, and represent an important new force on the scene.

What do they want? In October 1993, the TPR put forward design principles for the NII that were endorsed by close to a hundred organizations and that accord with numerous vision statements produced by unaffiliated but like-minded organizations.[40] In a subsequent letter to Congress, these principles were expanded on as follows:

▼ *Universal Access.* Fundamental to life, liberty, and the pursuit of happiness is access to video, audio, and data networks that provide a broad range of news, public affairs, education, health and government information and services. Such services should be provided in a user-friendly format, and widely available to everyone, including persons with disabilities. Information that is essential to the functioning of citizens in a democracy should be free.

▼ *Freedom to Communicate.* Freedom of speech should be protected and fostered by the new information infrastructure, guaranteeing the right of every person to communicate easily, affordably, and effectively. The design of the infrastructure should facilitate two-way, audio and video communications from anyone to any individual, group, or network. The rights of creators must be protected, while accommodating the needs of users and libraries. Telecommunications carriers should not be permitted to constrain the free flow of information protected by the First Amendment.

▼ *Vital Civic Sector.* For our democracy to flourish in the twenty-first Century, there must be a vital civic sector which enables the meaningful participation of all segments of our pluralistic society. Just as we have established public libraries and public highways, we must create public arenas or "electronic commons" in the media landscape. This will require the active involvement of a broad range of civic institutions—schools, universities, libraries, not-for-profit groups, and governmental organizations. It will also require vibrant telecommunications networks at the national, regional, and state level.

▼ *Diverse and Competitive Marketplace.* The information infrastructure must be designed to foster a healthy marketplace of ideas, where a full range of viewpoints is expressed and robust debate is stimulated. Individuals, nonprofits, and for-profit information providers need ready access to this marketplace if it is to thrive. To ensure competition among information providers, policies should be developed to lower barriers to entry (particularly for small and independent services); telecommunications carriers should not be permitted to control programming; and antitrust policies should be vigorously enforced to prevent market dominance by vertically-integrated monopolies.

▼ *Equitable Workplace.* Because the information infrastructure will transform the content and conduct of work, policies should be developed to ensure that electronic technologies are utilized to improve the work environment rather than dehumanize it. Workers should share the benefits of the increased productivity that these technologies make possible. The rights and protections that workers now enjoy should be preserved and enhanced. To encourage nondiscriminatory practices throughout the information marketplace, public policy should promote greater representation of women, people of color, and persons with disabilities at all levels of management.

▼ *Privacy Protection.* A comprehensive set of policies should be developed to ensure that privacy of all people is adequately protected. The collection of personal data should be strictly limited to the minimum necessary to provide specific services. Sharing data collected from individuals should only be permitted with their informed consent, freely given without coercion. Individuals should have the right to inspect and correct data files about them. Innovative billing practices should be developed that increase individual privacy.

▼ *Democratic Policymaking.* The public must be fully involved in all stages of the development and ongoing regulation of the information infrastructure. The issues are not narrow technical matters which will only affect us as consumers; they are fundamental questions that will have profound effects on us as citizens and could reshape our democracy. Extensive efforts should be made to fully inform the public about what is at stake, and to encourage broad discussion and debate. The policy process should be conducted in an open manner with full press scrutiny. Effective mechanisms should be established to ensure continued public participation in telecommunications policymaking.

The last three principles, while crucially important, are fairly straightforward and do not require explanation here. However, some of the issues addressed under the first four principles merit elaboration, as they speak to fundamental questions of NII organization and governance.

First, regarding the universal access principle, coalition members agree with the administration, Congress, and the industry that the old system of hidden cross-subsidies administered by vertically integrated monopolists is untenable in a competitive environment. They have therefore supported proposals to establish a competitively neutral fund that would pool payments from all service suppliers to provide direct support to the disadvantaged.[41] Some groups have advocated well-monitored and equitable rules on cost allocations and other matters that will affect the size of firms' payments and have argued against the administration's proposal for in-kind contributions by suppliers on the grounds that these could be abused. Most have maintained further that the major network operators' tariffs should remain regulated, at least until there is substantial competition and consumer choice; that NII legislation must specifically prohibit electronic redlining, so that new offerings like VDT are not deployed only in wealthy communities; and that telcos should be obliged at a minimum to wire K-12 schools, libraries, and other public institutions and to offer them services for free or at low, preferential rates. Many also argue that any new definition of the services that are to be made universally available must not be too narrow, but rather should include full broadband capabilities—in short, a transition from "plain old telephone service" (POTS) to "plain old digital service" (PODS).[42]

The second principle, freedom to communicate, underscores the extent to which coalition members' thinking about the NII is influenced by the contrast between the Internet and traditional electronic media. In addition to its decentralized model of interconnection and service provisioning, the Internet is attractive because it allows citizens to have access to, create, and disseminate. on a switched basis different forms of information.[43] It also facilitates experimental forms of speech; for example, during the past year, several otherwise obscure local rock bands multicast performances over the net's MBONE and viewers around the world were able to send real-time sound and video commentaries back to the concert sites. Providing comparable capabilities in the broader NII would move the country toward an age of participatory electronic publishing, enhanced freedom of expression, and increased diversity of viewpoints in the electronic public sphere. For coalition members, advancing this kind of citizen empowerment, rather than delivering more television channels to the couch, is a fundamental purpose of NII development.

As a first step in this direction, the Electronic Frontier Foundation and other groups have been lobbying for "open platform" requirements for currently available narrowband Integrated Services Digital Networks (ISDNs), which are capable of delivering some advanced services, but not full video. Open platform obligations would include nondiscriminatory access, switched digital connections, and affordable prices. In a future broadband environment, these could be expanded to include sufficient upstream capacity to handle video and multimedia communications.[44] More ambitiously, the Alliance for Public Technology and other organizations want telcos to deploy systems like fiber to the curb (FTTC) networks that provide enough upstream digital capacity to support switched, two-way video communications and other advanced services.[45] Beyond promoting speech, open access to advanced networks could be a boon to small- and medium-sized businesses and would support the development of socially useful applications like telemedicine, distance education, special services for the disabled, and so on. However, while everyone in the coalition would like to see this happen, groups like the Consumer Federation of America are concerned that carriers would allocate the cost of upgrades in such a manner as to force ratepayers to fund the deployment of capabilities they might not all want or need.

Further, building networks like FTTC is expensive and carriers worry that consumer demand for real interactivity may be too soft and too sensitive to price to recover the investments required.[46] Indeed, skeptical industry analysts believe that grand schemes for broadband development will crash and burn, just as videotex services did years ago. Hence, many telco and cable companies are opting to deploy less expensive hybrid fiber coaxial (HFC) networks for their VDT platforms. (HFC networks are largely analog with some digital signals, are not switched, and provide what is often characterized as a superhighway downstream and a dirt path upstream. That is, they have enough bandwidth leading from the customer's home or office to support simple interactive functions like home shopping and movies on demand, but not enough for more intensive interactivity, like two-way video.) This model of VDT is not much of an improvement over the cable television of today, except insofar as independent video suppliers will be able to gain common carriage access to the pipes. Instead, it is the embodiment of the limited entertainment vision of the NII as an essentially one-way mechanism to deliver more amusements to the consumer for a price.[47]

The third principle, promoting a vital civic sector, is particularly high on the coalition's agenda. Members want to nurture robust noncommercial spaces in the NII where citizens can share ideas, have access to public services, and participate in democratic governance outside the limitations of market relationships. The pursuit of profits in the early days of broadcast radio and television squeezed out all other uses of the scarce spectrum, and that is precisely what this group wants to avoid. The public interest coalition therefore advocates a mixed model that accommodates both commercial and noncommercial objectives within the abundant bandwidth of broadband networks. Two current uses of electronic media provide foundations on which to build in pursuit of this vision.

In the realm of computer communications, there is a large civic networking movement whose goal is to provide low-cost or free access to community discussion groups; information on local events, public libraries, educational and governmental services; and so forth via personal computers and public kiosks.[48] Organizations like the Center for Civic Networking and Computer Professionals for Social Responsibility are advising people at the grassroots level how to set up such systems, and a few dozen community networks have joined together to create a National Public Telecomputing Network. The Clinton administration has been very supportive of these efforts within the limitations of the federal budget. For example, the NTIA has established a Telecommunications and Information Infrastructure Assistance Program (TIIAP) to award small matching grants of seed money to state and local governments, nonprofit health care providers, schools, libraries, and other entities developing noncommercial applications in their communities.[49] The TIAP allocated $26 million through a competitive selection process in 1994 and was to provide $64 million in 1995; however, the new Republican majority in Congress wants to cut the funding significantly. Administration staffers also have launched a volunteer group called Americans Communicating Electronically to work with civic networkers at the local level.

Local civic networks provide hints of what could be done in a nationwide broadband NII. For example, Frederick Williams has suggested that access to a wide range of multimedia public service information be made part of the basic universal service package and included at a flat rate in our phone bills. At the same time, customers might choose from a range of optional commercial services, which could be paid for either through a higher flat rate or on a pay-per-view basis.[50] And it is possible to imagine a much broader range of information services—in sound, video, text and/or graphic formats—that could be made available via personal information appliances or public kiosks in libraries, government offices, shopping centers, and the like. For example, the NII could provide inexpensive access to multimedia databases in the nation's 8,000 museums and 35,000 libraries—a possibility being explored by the National Initiative for Humanities and Arts on the Information Highways.[51] Interesting work is already under way in this area; one example is the Global Jukebox Project, supported by the National Science Foundation (NSF), which provides multimedia databases containing audio, video, and textual information on international music, dance, and cultural traditions.

Public access television provides another foundation on which to build. Some local governments require that cable operators set aside channels for public, educational, and governmental (PEG) services and use a portion of the local franchise fee to fund the facilities, equipment, and training citizens need to produce such programming.[52] The availability of public access channels and related support has spurred the development of a robust noncommercial video sector (the Alliance for Community Media has a membership of over 950 PEG organizations nationwide). PEG programs vary widely in quality and viewership, from inane drivel that only the producers' friends and family could be watching to local C-SPAN-style services; and in ideological orientation, from hate shows on the far right to Paper Tiger Television on the democratic left. PEG services are significant because they constitute the only direct and unfiltered opportunity in television for citizens to share such diverse views, as well as to have access to a wide range of educational materials and witness government at all levels in action.

The point is that there is enough capacity in the new information infrastructure to support both commercial and noncommercial uses. What public interest coalition members want is an NII that supports the expansion of the sort of noncommercial spaces currently represented by civic networking and public access television. This means requiring that the telcos build broadband networks that are easily accessible by independent content suppliers (including nonprofit organizations and individuals) on favorable terms. Hence, the Alliance for Community Media has campaigned against regulating new video services solely under the FCC's VDT rules and Title II of the Communications Act of America (as the administration and Congress propose) on the grounds that these measures do not protect local property rights or support PEG requirements. Alliance members therefore advocate a new approach combining Title II common carrier and Title VI local cable franchising obligations.[53]

Perhaps the most controversial coalition proposal concerns the possibility of a tradeoff for private carriers' access to public right of ways. When the Communications Act of 1934 was under consideration, public interest advocates tried and failed to secure an amendment setting aside a portion of the scarce frequency spectrum for noncommercial radio broadcasting.[54] Sixty years later, many TPR members were making the same argument for a vastly different medium. In a true broadband environment of infinite bandwidth and switched communications, it would be nonsensical to attempt to legislate a "channel" set-aside, no matter how public-spirited the motivation. But at present, some telcos and cable companies appear to favor a more limited approach, which has been labeled "near video on demand," but is not much different from conventional cable TV. Hence, the Center for Media Education's Jeff Chester testified before the Congress that, "industry programmers are projecting that as much as 90 percent of capacity will be taken up with movies repeated at five-minute or half-hour intervals throughout the day. Therefore, until there is a fully-switched system available in a service area that provides unlimited capacity, we recommend that a significant portion of bandwidth, at least 20 percent, be reserved for public use."[55] Network operators were not pleased with this proposal.

Finally, on the fourth principle of maintaining a diverse and competitive marketplace, there is probably greater agreement between coalition members and policymakers, such as the Clinton administration and key congressional Democrats, than anywhere else. In general, coalition members have supported eliminating the line of business restrictions as long as procompetitive and proconsumer safeguards are established to prevent abuses of market power. They favor such protections as separate subsidiaries, prohibitions on in-region cable-telco mergers, common carriage, open interconnection, rate regulation (where market power exists), firm antitrust laws, and so forth. There are, however, two notable exceptions to this meeting of minds. In contrast to the administration and a majority of Congress, some public interest advocates like Ralph Nader have opposed even certain out-of-region cable-telco mergers as threatening market concentration and a reduction in consumer choice. Similarly, many public interest groups oppose telco ownership of information content, arguing that carriers will inevitably give their own content preferential treatment. These groups simply do not believe that safeguards can be enforced effectively— a claim that has not been adequately debated.

These are some of the arguments that coalition members have put forward over the past few years. Naturally, agreement is more uniform on broad principles than it is on specific issues. And there have been some battles within the coalition over competing substantive positions, simple turf questions, and allegations about some groups' connections to the industry. But, on the whole, this diverse movement has been pushing in the same direction and has cultivated effective working relationships with administration officials and key members of Congress. As a result, public interest protections figured more prominently in the legislative debate of the 103d Congress of 1993–94 than they had in decades. The story, however, in the current, 104th Congress is different.

THE CONGRESSIONAL PROCESS

The highly mobilized forces from the oligopoly and distributed sectors converged on Capitol Hill as the 103d Congress began to take up NII issues. At the outset of the debate, legislative prospects were decidedly mixed. Over the past decade, Congress had tried and failed on several occasions to reform the Communications Act of 1934; there was no reason to believe that the mere importance of doing so now would be enough to override industry and partisan political differences. But with so many stakeholders clamoring for action and the Clinton administration raising expectations, the leadership of the relevant House and

Senate subcommittees moved aggressively to take charge of the policy debate on their own terms. As they did so, the balance of influence between the executive and legislative branches shifted demonstrably.

The vice president continued to make the rounds and promote the information superhighway, while the administration pursued the other major elements of its agenda in such areas as technology and applications policies. But when it came to the fundamental issue of legislative reform, the administration adopted an essentially reactive posture, supporting the work of congressional Democrats and suggesting minor changes to their proposals, but not coming forward with a bill of its own.[56] When the administration did provide bits of legislative language, like its proposed Title VII for the Communications Act, these sometime failed to attract congressional support, even from Democrats.[57] The main action was firmly in the hands of powerful committee and subcommittee chairmen and the lobbyists swarming around them, rather than in the administration. As things progressed, the debate about the future of the NII would be dragged into the murky waters of industry rivalries in each market segment and of partisan political rivalries in the period just before the 1994 congressional elections.

LEGISLATION IN THE 103D CONGRESS

A wide range of bills were introduced in the 103d Congress that bore directly on different elements of the administration's agenda. Probably the most significant one to actually pass concerned the management of radio frequency spectrum. Historically, the FCC had allocated frequencies and licenses through either comparative hearings or lotteries. By allocating spectrum to new market entrants, compelling wired networks to interconnect wireless suppliers on fair terms, and enforcing line of business and separate subsidiary requirements on RBOC mobile operations, the FCC had succeeded in promoting varying degrees of competition for services like cellular telephony and paging, even before the AT&T divestiture. However, by the mid-1980s, the lottery process was beginning to buckle under a deluge of cellular license applications—a situation that would no doubt worsen with the impending development of a new generation of wireless services. Economists were therefore getting a receptive hearing for their longstanding argument that it would be more efficient in some cases to auction off licenses to the highest bidders. Two of the world's most pro-liberalization governments, New Zealand and the United Kingdom, went ahead and launched such auctions in 1989 and 1990, respectively. The question was whether the United States should follow suit.

Some opponents of auctions argued that it would be inappropriate and would set a potentially onerous precedent for the government to raffle off public property to the highest bidder. Further, it was suggested that the government would be shortchanged by clever corporations and their game theorist advisors, who would manipulate the process to limit their outlays.[58] Some opponents thought the administration's prediction of a $10 billion windfall to the Treasury was inflated and that the budget-minded Congress would simply apply the money to general deficit reduction, thereby missing a golden opportunity to fund important NII programs. Another objection was that auctions would inevitably reward those with the deepest pockets, rather than those with the most innovative ideas. (Many of the most dynamic innovations in recent years have come from small- and medium-sized firms that could not afford to compete with the major telcos and cable companies for spectrum real estate.) Relatedly, opponents maintained that the FCC proposals to allow incumbent telephone, cable, and cellular companies to provide PCS within their existing service areas and aggregate their licenses into large blocks would lead to anticompetitive behavior.

Finally, others argued that it is simply shortsighted to divide up PCS spectrum at all. Several companies are developing new digital systems that could make it unnecessary to set aside fixed portions of the spectrum for specific services in order to avoid interference. As George Gilder has argued, these technologies

> can survey any existing swath of spectrum in real time and determine almost instantly which channels are in use and which are free. . . . Making channel sizes a variable rather than a fixed function of radios, [they] offer the possibility of bandwidth on demand. They could open up the entire spectrum as one gigantic broadband pipe into which we would be able to insert [digital] packets in any empty space—dark fiber in the air.[59]

Hence, instead of the FCC giving powerful firms the cyber-equivalent of prime beachfront property, we should be erecting "a model not of a beach but of an ocean . . . the FCC should not give exclusive rights to anyone."[60] But despite these and other objections, the Clinton administration and Congress decided to give it a try. In the summer of 1993, Congress passed a budget bill that authorized the FCC to conduct auctions. As part of a larger restructuring of spectrum usage, the FCC set aside 120 megahertz for PCS auctions and by the following summer was selling exclusive ten-year licenses to the highest bidders. The auctions set off a wave of corporate alliances and many large players gained key positions that they expect to translate into the rapid development of PCS in the years ahead. The administration also set aside space for minority- and women-owned small businesses, although it is not clear how financially viable these operators may be in the larger environment. In any event, at the time of writing, companies have promised over $7 billion for PCS licenses.

Another law to pass in the 103d Congress was the so-called digital telephony bill championed by the Federal Bureau of Investigation (FBI). In 1992, the FBI began a push for sweeping legislation that would force network operators to install equipment that would facilitate wiretapping in all electronic media because, it claimed, technological advances were increasingly frustrating law enforcement efforts.[61] When congressional sympathy for the FBI's position made adoption of a bill seem imminent, Representative Don Edwards and Senator Patrick Leahy, two longtime congressional champions of civil liberties, stepped in to try and craft a more narrowly targeted bill that contained some privacy protections. The resulting bill combining S. 2375 and H.R. 4922 was passed and signed by the president in October 1994. The new law authorizes the FBI to spend $500 million over the next four years to reimburse telcos for the cost of installing systems that facilitate wiretaps, which must be approved by a court order rather than a subpoena. Although computer services were exempted from the requirements and other safeguards were established, the majority of civil liberties groups condemned the legislation as unnecessary and intrusive.[62]

This furor was heightened by a concurrent controversy over a Clinton administration initiative launched in spring 1993. Designed by the National Security Agency, the Clipper Chip is a microcircuit employing a classified algorithm that can be used to encrypt and decrypt voice transmissions. Its relative, the Capstone Chip, can perform the same functions for data and video transmission. At the urging of law enforcement and intelligence agencies, the administration planned to have these chips incorporated into government telecommunications and information systems and to use the power of procurement to set a "voluntary" standard for private companies—particularly those doing business with the government. The objective was said to be the surveillance of criminal activity, but civil libertarians and much of the Internet population saw ample opportunities for abuse and violently opposed the initiative. As one participant in the debate put it, "Relying on the government to protect your privacy is like asking a Peeping Tom to install your window blinds."[63] Manufacturers and software companies also were distressed because they thought customers would not trust their products and because inclusion of the chips could harm their efforts to export overseas. Faced with a tidal wave of opposition, the administration decided in the fall of 1994 to rework its plan and develop a more widely supported national encryption strategy.

Beyond the digital telephony law, a number of other bills introduced in the 103d Congress could have affected personal privacy. The most promising of these was S. 1735, "The Privacy Protection Act of 1993." Introduced by Senator Paul Simon, the legislation would have created a small independent agency to oversee compliance with the Privacy Act of 1974, coordinate disparate federal privacy laws, develop coherent privacy guidelines, and provide a mechanism to assist citizens with complaints. Another potentially significant bill was H.R. 3627, "Legislation to Amend the Export Administration Act of 1979," which would have liberalized export controls on encryption tools—an objective backed by industry and public interest groups alike. Neither these nor any other pro-privacy bill passed the Congress.

The bills that would have offered technology policy support for information infrastructure for the benefit of nonprofit institutions and small- and medium-sized businesses also failed to pass. The National Competitiveness Act of 1993 would have, among other things, reconfigured Gore's NREN program and authorized appropriations for information technology applications and network access in such areas as libraries and education, research and training, manufacturing, health care, and energy management. However, business groups opposed language setting eligibility requirements for foreign countries seeking access for their companies to U.S. research and development grants, while some Republicans saw the measure as a form of industrial policy, which they oppose. The legislation passed the Senate and House as S. 4 and H.R. 820, respectively, but failed in conference during the fall of 1994.

By far the most important NII item to die on the Hill was the effort to devise a new policy model for industry organization in an age of convergence. This became the central focus of struggle among legislators and the subject of intensive lobbying campaigns by corporate and noncommercial stakeholders. In the 102nd Congress and early in the 103d, several bills had been introduced that addressed pieces of the puzzle, but none succeeded. By late 1993, there was new momentum in the reform process and three major bills drawing on previous proposals were introduced. In November 1993, Representative Jack Brooks, Chairman of the House Judiciary Committee, and Representative John Dingell, Chairman of the House Energy and Commerce Committee, introduced H.R. 3626, "The Antitrust Reform Act of 1993."[64] On the same day, Representative Edward Markey, Chairman of the House Subcommittee on Tele-communications and Finance, and Representative Jack Fields, ranking minority member of the subcommittee, introduced a companion bill, H.R. 3636, "The National Communications Competition and Information Infrastructure Act of 1993." Two months later, Senator Ernest Hollings, Chairman of the Senate Committee on Commerce, Science and Transportation, introduced his version of reform, "The Communications Act of 1994," with Republican Senator John Danforth as a principal cosponsor.[65] All three bills contained scores of provisions on a wide variety of issues, many of which were amended as they worked their way through the committees. While a full accounting of their details is not possible here, the main provisions of the bills reflect the dynamics discussed above and should be addressed.

The Brooks-Dingell Bill. H.R. 3626 was designed to release the Bell Operating Companies from the restrictions of the MFJ and court supervision. The bill as introduced split long-distance into three segments and allowed the Bells to apply to the FCC and the Department of Justice to attain entry. They could apply immediately to provide interstate services within their operating regions and interstate service incidental to other services like wireless, video, and information services; within eighteen months to provide interstate resale of capacity leased from carriers like AT&T; and within five years to provide the full range of long-distance services over their own facilities. In each case, the FCC was to make a public interest determination on the impact of market entry on customer rates and other conditions, while the Department of Justice would make an antitrust determination on whether there was a substantial possibility that a company or its affiliates could use market power to prevent competition.

The bill also allowed the Bells to begin manufacturing telecommunications equipment within one year of enactment. In return, they were to create separate subsidiaries, eschew cross-subsidization by rate payers, file information on technical specifications with the FCC, agree to sell equipment to unaffiliated carriers at the same prices and on similar terms, and manufacture the equipment within the United States whenever possible. On electronic publishing, the Bells again had to establish separate subsidiaries, could not provide services through their basic telephone packages, could not own more than 50 percent of the equity in any joint ventures with non-Bell companies or affiliates, and were obliged to provide independent publishers with nondiscriminatory access to their local networks. These restrictions were to end in the year 2000. In the case of burglar alarm services, the Bells could enter the market five-and-one-half years after enactment.

While the RBOCs could live with the provisions on manufacturing and electronic publishing, the requirement of staged entry into long-distance services was a major setback on their top priority. As such, they launched an intensive lobbying effort to win acceleration of the letting-out process. The campaign bore fruit, and the final bill allowed the Bells to seek authorization to provide all interexchange services upon the date of its enactment. Still, that the FCC and Justice Department would both have to give authorization calmed the incumbent carriers' fears somewhat that the Bells would enter long-distance before there was significant local competition. This compromise allowed the bill to go forward with broad industry and bipartisan political support.

The Markey-Fields Bill. In contrast, H.R. 3636 was much more ambitious in scope; because it touched on a wider range of issues, it unleashed heavy lobbying from a broader range of constituencies. Representative Markey's goal was to lay ground rules that would help usher in a new electronic medium. For example, the bill amended the Communications Act by stating that it is the government's mission "to make available, so far as possible, to all people of the United States, regardless of location or disability, a switched, broadband telecommunications network capable of enabling users to originate and receive affordable high quality voice, data, graphics, and video telecommunications services."[66] Markey worked closely with the Clinton administration (which modeled much of its legislative program on the bill), the private sector, and public interest groups in an effort to craft a progressive bill that would open markets to competition while spreading the NII's benefits across a wide range of social constituencies. To solicit diverse input, Markey even held the first congressional hearing to be multicast over the Internet. Balancing all the views of competing stakeholders was a difficult task and the bill underwent many revisions. But in the end most players came away feeling they had attained at least some of their key objectives, which for the noncommmercial stakeholders was a novel and heady experience. Among the many important provisions of H.R. 3636, ten are noteworthy:

1.   Telcos were required to allow competition in the local loop in exchange for being let out into long-distance and other markets. Local carriers were

required to provide competitors with, among other things, nondiscriminatory interconnection, unbundled access to network functions like signalling and switching, customer network information and other operational data, and the ability to resell leased capacity. Moreover, the charges were to be cost-based and to remain regulated until the FCC determined that the telco faces substantial competition.

2. Telcos were allowed to supply video services on a common carrier basis, including within their telephone service regions through separate subsidiaries. They were to offer access to independent programmers under nondiscriminatory rates and conditions; provide PEG programmers with preferential rates and the necessary capacity, facilities, and equipment; eschew electronic redlining in VDT deployments; and be prohibited from buying out existing cable companies in many instances.[67]

3. The bill as introduced required the telcos to establish open platforms, as advocated by the Electronic Frontier Foundation. These would have entailed nondiscriminatory access to switched, two-way digital services, presumably over existing ISDNs. Consumers would then have had ready high-speed access to the Internet and other multimedia services. However, since this proposal did not involve full broadband, it was opposed by Corning Glass, which makes fiber optic cables. The RBOCs did not like the requirement either, so the final bill simply asked the FCC to conduct an inquiry on the feasibility of requiring open platforms.

4. State jurisdiction over entry into local telecommunications markets was preempted over the heated objections of state regulators. (This feature of the bill also troubled public interest groups.) In parallel, telcos providing VDT services were not required to obtain a local franchise, as the incumbent cable companies are, although they were to pay an unspecified fee. Further, local governments could not extend franchise requirements to any nonvideo services provided by cable companies. Such provisions led the National League of Cities to oppose the deal.

5. The FCC was asked to examine the possible modification of broadcast ownership rules, and to establish regulations giving broadcasters spectrum flexibility in accordance with public interest criteria.

6. The FCC was obliged to ensure that advanced telecommunications services be provided to K-12 schools and health care institutions and public libraries at preferential rates and the NTIA was to conduct annual surveys on the availability of such services. The FCC was also to study the possibility of extending the obligation to cover post-secondary educational institutions. The bill called for most advanced services to be made available to tax-exempt

and government institutions at rates recovering only the added cost so they could be both users and providers of information to the general public. Implementation of this principle could have greatly stimulated the development of robust, noncommercial spaces in the NII.

7. The bill as introduced required that set-top box interfaces be open and called for greater government involvement in establishing broad requirements for certain types of technical standards. However, Microsoft and the box manufacturers strongly opposed the language, and in a compromise this issue also was turned over to the FCC for an inquiry.

8. The bill set up a Joint Federal-State Board to preserve universal service and expand its scope in light of technological changes. The board was to require nondiscriminatory contributions by all service suppliers, promote open platform services, and ensure the usability of advanced services by the disabled.

9. The FCC was to take steps to promote the participation of small businesses and minorities in the information marketplace.

10. The FCC was also to undertake an inquiry on how to advance civic participation via the Internet and to issue a request for comment on whether common carriers should be obliged to provide Internet access at reasonable rates. This provision was advocated by Ralph Nader's Taxpayer Assets Project as a way to promote citizen involvement in the policymaking process and ensure that the entry of large corporations into the Internet access market would not result in a widespread shift to metered, usage-sensitive pricing. However, many people in the Internet community, including Richard Solomon in the Appendix to Part I, criticized the provision as misguidedly opening the door to FCC involvement in the Internet.

The above list underscores a few key points. H.R. 3636 was crafted to lay the groundwork for the deployment of open digital broadband networks that would offer industry ample opportunity to generate new revenues from commercial services, while providing the noncommercial sector with the ability to carve out civic spaces for public information. In defining this balance, the public interest coalition had an unprecedented degree of influence on the policy process. As the bill worked its way through committee, however, strong pressure from corporate lobbyists watered down many of the relevant provisions, turning them into calls for FCC studies rather than immediate requirements. Still, these issues would remain on the policy agenda, unlike what happened with broadcast radio sixty years ago. Of course, this compromise approach implied a substantial increase in the FCC's responsibilities, which many observers felt it would have trouble discharging fully.

After the final revisions, the major corporate stakeholders all were able to accept the bill's compromises, albeit with varying misgivings. Under these conditions, the bill also enjoyed broad bipartisan support. H.R. 3636 and H.R. 3626 sailed through committee on unanimous votes in the spring of 1994, and in the summer were combined as H.R. 3626 and passed by the full House on a remarkable 420 to 4 vote. How many members had actually read and understood the legislation was subject to debate and some observers viewed the vote as a punt to the Senate where, it was expected, more restrictive language on RBOC entry would be introduced and fought out. Still, the bill's passage was taken as a sign that Congress might finally revise the Communications Act, lift the MFJ restrictions, and set the stage for broadband deployment and media convergence.

The Hollings-Danforth Bill. When the debate shifted to the Senate, the struggle rapidly evolved into intractable trench warfare. The Hollings-Danforth bill covered much of the same ground as the two House bills.[68] But there were three major differences. First, as it went through committee, S. 1822 incorporated as an amendment Senator Daniel Inouye's bill, S. 2195, "The National Public Telecommunications Infrastructure Act of 1994." Strongly supported by much of the public interest coalition, it called for up to 20 percent of network capacity to be set aside for noncommercial information suppliers, in return for carriers' use of public right of ways. Eligible entities were to include state, local, and tribal governments, educational institutions, public broadcasting stations, libraries, and other nonprofit organizations. This was a modern version of the failed Wagner-Hatfield amendment to the Communications Act of 1934, which called for 25 percent of the radio spectrum to be set aside for noncommercial broadcasters. Unfortunately, precisely which networks would be subject to the set-aside was unclear, which led to strenuous criticism from the carriers, academics, and other observers. By the end of the committee process, strong industry lobbying resulted in the set-aside being scaled back to up to 5 percent, with the range of eligible entities narrowed. Even so, the public interest movement regarded the amendment as an important victory for noncommercial uses.

Second, in the hours before mark-up, S. 1822 incorporated an amendment proposed by Senator James Exon to extend FCC censorship to the Internet. The provision made liable to criminal prosecution anyone who makes or transmits "lewd, filthy, indecent, or obscene" material, which could include both the originator of a message and the network operators who transmit it. Not surprisingly, the amendment was met by a huge uproar among civil liberties groups and on the Internet, where some adult (and even obscene) material is available if one knows where to look. Quite apart from its unconstitutionally expansive definition of prohibited speech, the amendment completely ignored the regulatory and operational differences between the Internet, which is a switched medium, and one-to-many media systems like television. Nonetheless, the amendment was included in the bill.

The third and, in the end, most important difference from the House bill was that S. 1822 established stronger prerequisites for RBOC entry into competitive markets. To enter long-distance markets, a Bell company was to petition the FCC, which would consult with the Attorney General and consider information provided by the relevant state regulators. The commission was to grant an in-region petition only if it found that there was "actual and demonstrable" competition in the Bell's local exchange from at least one unaffiliated provider, which was offered predominantly over facilities not owned or controlled by the company (that is, not mere resale); and an out-of-region petition if there was no substantial possibility that the Bell could use market power to impede long-distance competition. Moreover, a Bell had to establish a separate subsidiary that would fulfill any requests from other firms for exchange access services at nondiscriminatory rates and provide a quality of service equal to that which it provided to itself or its affiliates.

To provide information services, a Bell was to establish a separate subsidiary and not provide such services through its basic telephone package. Any facilities, services, or information provided to the subsidiary were to be available to unaffiliated entities on the same terms. A Bell could not own more than 50 percent of the equity or gross revenues of any joint venture. Further, a Bell gateway to information services would have to offer all suppliers of such services access on nondiscriminatory terms. The bill also barred Bells from alarm monitoring service markets for five and one-half years.

The RBOCs could manufacture equipment upon enactment of the bill, but only through a separate subsidiary. Production generally had to take place within the United States, and the manufacturing affiliate had to share technical information with competitors and the FCC. And on the telecommunications-cable television axis, the bill established a regime of regulatory parity between telephone and cable companies. Telcos and cable companies with market power would have to eschew cross-subsidization and would be barred from purchasing more than 5 percent of the other within their respective service areas. Telcos also had to establish separate subsidiaries for video services.

All these provisions were designed to ensure that the Bells would not use their control over the local telephone market to compete unfairly in other markets; as a result, the bill enjoyed the support of virtually everyone else, particularly the long-distance carriers. But the RBOCs were incensed. Hollings had long been a champion of the RBOC; as he himself put it, "I have been their boy . . . and they had me coached pretty good."[69] Now their boy was promoting entry tests they might not meet any time soon. "Actual and demonstrable" facilities-based competition in the local loop will take some time to materialize no matter what Congress does. Building local networks is expensive and providing basic service to residential customers may not generate enough short-term revenues to recoup the costs. What many potential entrants like the long-distance carriers have in mind is cherry picking lucrative business from corporate customers, particularly in big cities. Hence, the RBOCs advocated the simultaneous removal of all local and long-distance barriers to entry at a specified date, regardless of actual competitive conditions. To that end, they swung their support to Senator John Breaux's alternative bill, S. 2111, "The Telecommunications Services Enhancement Act of 1994," which was introduced in

May 1994. S. 2111 called for the lifting of all restrictions one year after enactment, a proposal strongly rejected by the Clinton administration and public interest groups.

The RBOCs began to play hardball, pressuring Senators and reportedly threatening to make large campaign contributions to opponents in the November 1994 election. And, as the *Wall Street Journal* noted, "The Bells don't just work Washington. With a presence in nearly every major community—and some $95 million to bestow upon 'grass-roots' causes in 1992 alone, according to FCC records—they have wired the system from top to bottom."[70] In parallel, they launched a massive public relations campaign trumpeting their affection for open competition, if the government would just get out of the way. Hollings' reaction to the pressure tactics was to dig in his heels and work his committee; in August, S. 1822 was reported out on an eighteen-to-two vote, with all eleven Democrats and seven of nine Republicans supporting the measure.

But things changed as the fall election approached. As the Republicans began to smell victory, they began to block virtually all legislation in order to deprive the Democrats of victories. On September 22, minority leader Robert Dole produced a list of "nonnegotiable" demands to eliminate key provisions that committee Republicans had previously supported. According to Dole, S. 1822's "major problems included its approach to universal service, its excessive regulation, its protectionist domestic content provisions, and its outlandish, if not unconstitutional, 5 percent set-aside requirements."[71] Lacking the votes for passage, on the next day Hollings decided not to carry the fight to the Senate floor and declared the bill dead. In a statement, he argued that

> we will not be held hostage at the last minute to ultimatums and to the desires of certain parties to substantially rewrite a bill that passed the committee by an overwhelming and bi-partisan vote. . . . Supporters of the bill include consumer groups, the burglar alarm industry, the long distance industry, the cable industry, the newspaper industry, the satellite industry, the competitors to the telephone industry, the broadcast industry, public interest groups, the electric utilities, the computer industry, the telemessaging industry, the payphone industry, and the directory publishing industry. Only one sector of the industry continues to oppose the bill—the telephone companies, and especially, the RBOCs.[72]

Over a year of painstaking negotiations among scores of stakeholders, staffers, and committee members in both houses had gone down the tubes.

LEGISLATION IN THE 104TH CONGRESS

The Republican landslide in the November 1994 congressional elections completely redefined the game. On the Senate side, Larry Pressler became chairman of the Commerce Committee and declared his intention to introduce new legislation that would promote more rapid and thorough deregulation than S. 1822. Soon after the 104th session began, closed door meetings were held with the industry chieftains whose firms had lavished campaign contributions on committee members (and, in the case of cable companies, free air time for the GOP's National Empowerment Television network). Democrats and public interest groups were not invited.[73] On the House side, Representative Thomas Bliley became Chairman of the Commerce Committee and indicated that he would push for legislation that was even more sweepingly deregulatory. The mood in the House was far more feisty due to the scores of "citizen politicians" who had been elected on a radical right platform and felt a personal allegiance to the new Speaker, Newt Gingrich.

Gingrich's views on information infrastructure have therefore become a central part of the congressional debate. These are heavily influenced by the writings of George Gilder, the futurologists Alvin and Heidi Toffler, and other members of an organization tied to the Speaker called the Progress and Freedom Foundation. The Tofflers argue that socioeconomic systems have progressed through three major waves, moving from the agricultural to the manufacturing and now the information age.[74] In broad terms, this three-stage narrative accords with the scholarly literature on the transition to an information economy, but the Tofflers add a political dimension that Gingrich has spun to his advantage. In his formulation, regulation is an artifact of the second wave and people who defend it must be either old guard dinosaurs or self-interested "bureaucratic elites" trying to stifle the dynamism of the third wave at the expense of "ordinary Americans."

In widely reported testimony before the House, Gingrich offered a concrete recommendation: "Maybe we need a tax credit for the poorest Americans to buy a laptop. Now, maybe that's wrong, maybe it's expensive, maybe we can't do it. But I'll tell you, any signal we can send to the poorest Americans that says, 'We're going into a twenty-first-century, third-wave information age, and so are you, and we want to carry you with us,' begins to change the game."[75] Any signal, that is, except such antiquated second wave notions as legislative provisions on rate and entry regulation, anti-redlining, PEG access, non-commercial spaces, and so on. The networks Gingrich has spoken of so approvingly may be inaccessibly priced, but at least the poor will have laptops and, presumably, forty acres.

It is in this intellectual and political environment that Congress again took up the challenge of crafting a new policy model for the NII. In January 1995, Representatives Dingell, Markey, and Conyors introduced H.R. 411, "The Antitrust and Communications Reform Act of 1995." The bill was essentially identical to H.R. 3626, which passed overwhelmingly in 1994. Similarly, in February, Senator Hollings circulated a draft "Universal Service Telecommunications Act of 1995" that covered some of the same ground as S. 1822, albeit with softened entry tests for the RBOCs and fewer public interest provisions. Both proposals were declared dead on arrival, although some of their language—particularly Hollings' universal service provisions—would remain on the table. The main focus was on a draft bill put forward by Chairman Pressler that was moving rapidly through the process. The lobbyists descended again, but even their supporters were tiring of their corporate pitches and wanted to see a bill passed. As one Republican member put it, "Everybody in this town who has a pulse has been hired by either the long-distance companies or the Bell operating companies." Pressler concurred, saying, "We've heard these arguments for years now."[76] Brief hearings with minimal public interest group input were held and in March the committee reported the bill out on a vote of seventeen-to-two.

The Pressler Bill. Among the key features of S. 652, The Telecommunications Competition and Deregulation Act of 1995, is Title I, the oddly named "Transition to Competition" provision. While requiring a Bell company to establish separate subsidiaries for manufacturing and for information and in-region long-distance services, S. 652's other competitive safeguards are lax. The RBOCs are not required to provide all competitors with network interconnection, non-discriminatory access to rights of way, and so on. There is no need to show "actual and demonstrable" competition before a RBOC is let out into long-distance markets. Instead, a RBOC merely needs to have entered into a local interconnection agreement that fulfills a "competitive checklist" of contract conditions like those mentioned above. This requirement could be met by a deal between a RBOC and a single weak competitor.

Moreover, government oversight is weakened in the legislation. State regulators can reject an agreement only under fairly narrow conditions. In principle, the FCC could deny a RBOC petition to enter into long-distance markets, but is constrained in doing so and cannot expand the checklist in light of changing technological and market conditions. And once the FCC has approved its long-distance petition, a Bell company can begin immediately to manufacture equipment and can enter alarm services markets in three years. Finally, the Department of Justice's Antitrust Division is relegated to a minor, consultative role in assessing conditions in the local loop before the RBOCs are allowed to enter into long-distance services. The RBOCs are pleased with the bill, which should help them preserve their market power in the local loop for years to come.

S. 652 eliminates the cable-telco cross-ownership restrictions, but goes further. A RBOC is not required to establish a common carrier VDT platform; it may choose to set up a conventional cable system subsidiary under Title VI of the Communications Act, thereby negating the promise of open broadband video markets. If it does construct a VDT platform, a local franchise agreement is not required. And if it offers all program providers nondiscriminatory access on the same terms (which are unspecified) and does not cross-subsidize (which would be difficult to verify), it need not establish a separate subsidiary. Most alarmingly, the committee bill contains no prohibition or limitation whatsoever on telco-cable buyouts within their service areas. One-wire consolidation is thereby promoted, eliminating facilities-based competition. For good measure, the bill allows the FCC to deem a basic cable rate unreasonable only if it exceeds substantially the national average for comparable services, which seems like a good reason for the large corporations that dominate the industry to coordinate their increases. Public utility holding companies may also provide telecommunications and information services through separate subsidiaries, and states can decide if other utilities must do the same.

If the RBOCs, cable, and utility companies got relief, so did the broadcasters. If the FCC allows broadcasters to use spectrum flexibly, they need only pay a fee not to exceed those paid by competitors like PCS firms, and they must provide only one free over-the-air advanced TV service. The bill also weakens concentration of ownership rules so that a single broadcaster can have 35 percent of the national audience, as opposed to 25 percent today, and it eliminates the broadcast-cable cross-ownership ban. And while weakening these safeguards on industry structure and behavior, the bill also moves to impose onerous guidelines on content. S. 652 includes a modified version of the Exon amendment to last year's Hollings bill. Common carriers, online services, and other companies transmitting messages now can avoid liability if they do not exercise editorial control over the messages they carry or if they make a good faith effort to comply with the statute. However, users of telecommunications facilities remain subject to criminal prosecution for engaging in constitutionally protected speech.

The bill makes four nods toward public interest concerns. First, universal service is defined in a relatively flexible manner, as "an evolving level of intrastate and interstate telecommunications services that . . . should be provided at just, reasonable, and affordable rates to all americans."[77] All telecommunications carriers are to contribute on an equitable and competitively neutral basis to preserving universal service; other service providers may be included if the public interest requires. However, no provision is made for consumer representation on the new Federal-State Joint Board, and the board is to limit universal services to those that already have been subscribed to by a substantial majority of residential customers.

Second, an important amendment was inserted on a close vote by Senators Olympia Snowe and John Rockefeller with support from the National School Boards Association, the National Education Association, and similar groups. The provision requires designated "essential carriers" in underserved rural areas to provide service to medical schools, community health centers, and nonprofit hospitals at rates comparable to those charged in urban areas. Further, it requires that all telecommunications carriers shall provide service to elementary and secondary schools and libraries at rates not higher than the incremental cost involved, and that the FCC is to establish rules enhancing their access to advanced services. This is a thin list of public institutions deserving support, but a reasonable step in the current climate.

Third, Senator John Kerry pushed through an amendment during mark-up that is critical for groups like the Alliance for Community Media and the Association of Independent Television Stations, as well as the viewing public.

It requires that providers of common carrier video platform services ensure that local broadcast and PEG stations have access to VDT platforms in their market at rates no higher than the incremental cost of providing such access. Relatedly, an amendment by Senator Kay Bailey Hutchinson allows communities to require that VDT providers pay a competitively neutral fee in lieu of a franchise fee. Fourth, thanks to lobbying by a number of organizations representing the disabled, service suppliers and manufacturers are to ensure that their offerings are accessible to and usable by persons with disabilities, "if readily achievable."

Clearly, the Senate legislation represents a sharp change in direction from the one charted by the Democrats in the previous Congress. There is greater freedom for large corporations to pursue revenues and industry consolidation, fewer safeguards for a diverse and competitive marketplace, and less public interest protection. As this volume goes to press, the Clinton administration has yet to respond in detail to the bill, although Vice President Gore has expressed strong reservations, particularly with regard to the prospect for cable rate increases. Further, the RBOCs are lobbying hard to scale back some of the public interest provisions, in particular the Kerry amendment on PEG access to VDT platforms. And the House is preparing to release its own version of reform, which is expected to be even more friendly to big business. The ball is still very much in play. Nevertheless, given the respective roles of the Senate and House in finalizing legislation and the unity and discipline that the Republicans on the Hill have displayed thus far, it is reasonable to think that something akin to S. 652 will be sent to the president as the new policy architecture for industry organization and behavior.

Finally, this approach should be viewed in the context of the majority's approach to other NII issues. While most of these proposals are still pending, Republicans have advocated radically downsizing or defunding the sort of technology and applications policies discussed by Lee McKnight and Russell Neuman in Chapter 5, some of which were launched under the Bush administration with Republican support. Among the many proposals now under discussion are the elimination of the High Performance Computing and Communications program; the elimination of the National Institute on Standards and Technology's (NIST) Advanced Technology Program, and perhaps of the NIST itself; and the elimination of the Office of Technology Assessment. Similarly, major cuts have been proposed for the National Science Foundation; the Defense Department's defense conversion, dual use technologies, and flat panel display programs; the National Center for Manufacturing Sciences and the Institute for Advanced Flexible Manufacturing; and the NTIA's Telecommunications and Information Infrastructure Assistance Program for noncommercial technologies and applications. Beyond the realm of technology and applications policies, there are the well publicized efforts to eliminate public broadcasting, the National Endowment for the Arts, and the National Endowment for the Humanities. There are even proposals to eliminate the FCC and Commerce Department.

CONCLUSION

The Democrats had an opportunity during 1993 and 1994 to establish a new policy architecture balancing corporate and noncommercial interests, but they lost it. The Clinton administration set forth a promising vision of the NII, assembled a good team, improved the policymaking process, reached out to diverse stakeholders, and launched a number of important programs in areas like technology and applications policies. But beyond Vice President Gore's occasional conference appearances around the country and on C-SPAN, the White House did not use its bully pulpit to move the issues to the top of the evening news and generate widespread public support for its approach. Hence, while the 103d Congress was working to craft a new legislative framework that would have had significant implications for most Americans, the overwhelming majority of the population was disengaged entirely from the debate. Compounding the problem, the administration adopted a reactive posture and did not try to provide the sort of leadership on the Hill that it had demonstrated with its crime bill and other measures. The process was thus dominated by a heated contest between powerful corporations and their lobbyists on the one hand and a hardworking but heavily outgunned public interest movement on the other. And once pre-election partisan politics entered the mix, all deals were off.

Now there is a new congressional majority calling the shots and the game has changed dramatically. The ideology of the day is that governing is a bad thing done by bad people—the "bureaucratic elite"—at the expense of "ordinary Americans." Regulation and antitrust rules are particularly bad, even if they are designed to promote open competition and media diversity. Instead, the largest corporations in the business are to be allowed to configure the public NII however they please, while the bothersome public interest protections proposed by out-of-touch "second wave" dinosaurs are to be avoided wherever possible. Further, programs that provide citizens with access to noncommercial information systems and services are to be eliminated under the guise of balancing the federal budget at all costs. And to make sure that this bold vision of the future is carried out without undue distractions, closed meetings with major corporate campaign contributors and rushed, unbalanced hearings are being held. The multiple parallels with the struggle sixty years ago over the emerging medium of radio broadcasting are striking: once again, power and money appear to be the preeminent forces shaping the selection of a policy model for a new mode of electronic communications and information. But the cost—of embracing an oligopoly policy in a potentially distributed era—may be even greater this time around.

POSTSCRIPT

While this volume was in production, the 104th Congress rushed down the path described above. Less than three months after the bill was introduced, the Senate passed S. 652 in mid-June of 1995 on an overwhelming 81 to 18 vote, with public-interest-oriented Democrats comprising most of the minority. In general, the major provisions described previously remained intact. The most notable changes from the committee version are: the insertion of a telco-cable buyout limitation (they can acquire up to 10 percent of one another within their service areas, and also may buy each other out in rural areas and places with less than 50,000 residents); a scaling back of the special tariffs for schools and libraries (rather than affordable rates not higher than the incremental cost involved, such institutions now are to be charged rates less than those paid by other parties for similar services); a prohibition on electronic redlining in VDT deployments; the elimination of all FCC-imposed ownership restrictions on radio stations; and an amendment requiring television manufacturers to build in microchips that would allow parents to block access to violent or sexually oriented programming. The White House released a statement applauding the few public interest improvements but decrying the main thrust of the bill and hinting at the possibility of a veto.

Events moved equally fast in the House. In early May, Republicans intro-duced H.R. 1555, the Communications Act of 1995, in the Subcommittee on Communications and Finance. Less than three weeks later, it passed the committee on a vote of 24 to 5, again with public interest-oriented Democrats comprising the minority. The legislation covered much the same ground as S. 652, but generally in an even more sweepingly deregulatory, proconsolidation, and anticonsumer manner.[78] Perhaps the biggest exception was that it required the presence of a facilities-based competitor in the local loop before the RBOCs would let out into long-distance markets. The Bells stridently opposed this re-striction, launched a multimillion dollar lobbying and public relations campaign, and succeeded in winning over the House leadership. In late July, a lengthy Managers' Amendment containing forty-two major changes to the committee's provisions was pushed through the House, which deleted this entry safeguard and swung the RBOCs into support for and the incumbent long-distance carriers into opposition to the bill. In the first few days of August, an extremely rushed floor debate was held as Members prepared for the summer recess, and the bill passed the full House on a vote of 305 to 117.

Just prior to the vote, President Clinton released a statement on H.R. 1555 noting that, "Instead of promoting investment and competition, it promotes mergers and concentration of power. Instead of promoting open access and diversity of content and viewpoints, it would allow fewer people to control greater numbers of television, radio and newspaper outlets in every community . . . if H.R. 1555 with the managers' amendment is sent to me without deletion or revision . . . I will be compelled to veto it. . . . " But that is precisely what he will get, and the margins of victory indicate that the President may lack the congressional votes needed to sustain a veto. In a separate statement, Vice President Gore was more direct, arguing that the bill is "abhorrent to the public interest and our national economic well-being. . . . This bill has been sold to the highest bidder. . . . The losers are the American people."[79]

CONCLUSION

POLICIES FOR THE NATIONAL AND GLOBAL INFORMATION INFRASTRUCTURES

WILLIAM J. DRAKE

*T*his volume has covered a good deal of ground, from telecommunications liberalization and globalization to U.S. domestic and foreign policies on information infrastructure. In examining these issues, the authors have argued that new approaches are required if the United States is to develop an optimally configured National Information Infrastructure (NII) and Global Information Infrastructure (GII). How do the pieces of the policy puzzle fit together and what kind of picture do they create? This conclusion addresses these questions by drawing together the project participants' major suggestions, which present the broad contours of a progressive approach toward some of the most pressing issues facing policymakers today.

The first group of recommendations covers the NII, including telecommunications and cable television, broadcasting, information policy, technology policy, human resources, and the policymaking process. Building directly on the legislative overview presented in Chapter 12, many of these take issue with the direction being set by the 104th Congress.[1] Among the most central recommendations are:

▼ The federal government should take into account the needs of both commercial and noncommercial stakeholders in setting policy for the new information infrastructure.

▼ The government should actively promote diversity in, rather than concentration of media ownership.

▼ The Regional Bell Operating Companies (RBOCs) should not be allowed to enter new lines of business until barriers to competition in their local markets have been removed.

▼ Common carriers must be required to establish open platforms that allow all customers to have access to all providers of content, such as video programming and computerized information services.

▼ Broadcasters should be allowed flexibility in the use of frequency spectrum, but only in exchange for meeting public interest obligations.

▼ Freedom of speech in cyberspace should be preserved by employing available blocking technologies rather than censorship to prevent minors from gaining access to inappropriate material on the Internet.

▼ A strong and coherent policy framework is needed to protect the privacy of citizens from abuses by government and private industry.

▼ A single, high-level organization within the executive branch should be given the lead in charting national strategy for the NII.

The second group of recommendations covers the GII, including the traditional international regimes for telecommunications, spectrum management, and satellite services; the new international trade in services regime; international privacy protection and technical assistance to developing countries; and the need to improve the institutional framework of multilateral cooperation on the GII. Among the most central recommendations are:

▼ Market liberalization at the global level, as at the national level, should be balanced with the promotion of media diversity, localism, and noncommercial uses.

▼ Alternatives to the telecommunications regime's accounting and settlements mechanism should be pursued.

▼ The World Trade Organization (WTO) should adopt multilateral competition policies and rules on restrictive business practices.

▼ Governments should remove artificial barriers to the development of the global Internet.

                                    *   *   *

What follows are the "top forty" recommendations. This list not only presents the recommendations, including the central recommendations presented above, but it elaborates on each of them.

THE NATIONAL INFORMATION INFRASTRUCTURE

I. GENERAL APPROACH

1. The NII must be configured so as to promote evolution toward competitively supplied, seamlessly interconnected, open broadband networks. The goal should be to offer fully interactive multimedia capabilities at reasonable prices to all Americans. The transition to a new information infrastructure offers an unparalleled opportunity to create a fundamentally new type of electronic media—one that empowers all segments of society to access, create, and disseminate information in all its forms. The provision of broadband capacity and digital capabilities that can be flexibly drawn on by users to develop whatever services and applications they need could represent a tremendous boon to the United States across the board: to the diversity and productivity of its economy, the education and training of its workers, and the vitality of its popular culture and public sphere of ideas.

In considering what might be possible, the participants in this project clearly are influenced by what is happening in the increasingly convergent computer and Internet environments where individuals and organizations from all walks of life are acquiring the desktop capacity to manage personalized information resources as never before.[2] It is here that the real creativity, dynamism, and promise of the information age resides—not in the entertainment-industrial complex of mass media conglomerates, broadcasters, cable companies, and telcos.

Nevertheless, it is the entertainment-industrial complex that has dominated the press coverage and congressional debate about the NII. Faced with an unparalleled opportunity to lay the groundwork for the "new civilization" of information-empowered citizens extolled by House Speaker Newt Gingrich and others, entertainment and communications firms have argued that what Americans really need is the chance to watch more television, play more video games, do more shopping from the couch, or get telephone service from another supplier.

What has gripped Capitol Hill over the past few years is the fight over who will control this brave new world—not a balanced inquiry into how advanced information resources can be configured for the greatest benefit to society. The fight has been entirely about money and it has been waged with money: millions of dollars in campaign contributions to friendly legislators, scores of high-priced lobbyists and well-endowed conservative think-tanks arguing that technological abundance tomorrow requires the gutting of regulations and safeguards today.

The Clinton administration supports an NII that promotes real competition between multiple providers in all key market segments and is architecturally open, flexible, interoperable, and easily upgraded—an NII that will evolve toward universally accessible, reasonably priced, switched, two-way broadband networks offering fully interactive multimedia capabilities. The participants in this project share that broad vision (although we sometimes differ on particulars of how to bring it about). But the Republican legislation of the 104th Congress does not lead us down that path; rather, it establishes an oligopoly-oriented framework favoring the largest firms for an era in which distributed information resources and true competition are essential. As such, the legislation poses a difficult choice for the president: veto it and be blamed by big business for erecting a "roadblock on the information super-highway," or sign it and be blamed by other stakeholders for walking away from the true promise of the NII.

   2. Diversity in, rather than the concentration of media ownership, should be promoted by the federal government. This is a first principle against which all policies for the NII—and indeed, for the GII—should be measured. As a previous Twentieth Century Fund study concluded, the public interest "must lie in the provision of a diversity of information from a diversity of sources—and therefore in the limiting of concentration of ownership."[3] Anthony Smith wrote these words about traditional mass media, but they are just as applicable to the new information infrastructure. This is not "just another industry"; concentrated ownership in the apparel or sporting goods business would be unfortunate, but concentrated ownership in the NII would be a disaster for the public's right to open and diverse information resources. Yet while extolling the virtues of free competition and multiple providers, the pending legislation contains provisions that cut sharply in the opposite direction. For example, it allows the RBOCs to acquire cable companies within their own regions in too wide a range of cases; raises the ceiling on how much of the national audience a single broadcast entity can serve to 35 percent; extends the term of broad-cast licenses; loosens foreign ownership restrictions on mass media;[4] and, in the House bill, eliminates cross-ownership restrictions on electronic media. The net effect of these measures will be to weaken government oversight, increase the power of the largest conglomerates, and reduce the diversity of voices available in the public sphere of ideas.

   There may be times when some consolidation is necessary (as in small markets that have financially troubled broadcasters or can't support competitive services), but a blanket legislative invitation to industry concentration is simply a giveaway to powerful interests. Indeed, quite apart from the legislation, there is already troubling evidence of anticompetitive practices that require antitrust scrutiny; for example, Microsoft's plan to bundle Internet access into its Windows95 operating system could force smaller suppliers out of a market where competition is particularly important. The FCC and the Department of Justice should evaluate all proposed mergers, acquisitions, and other activities that could stifle the development of a multiprovider NII, and congressional legislation should not bind their hands in performing this important task. Moreover, the government should take steps to ensure that media ownership reflects to some degree the diversity of American society, to the extent that congressional and Supreme Court attacks on affirmative action allow.

3. The NII should be governed by a mixed policy model that accommodates both commercial and noncommercial stakeholders and uses. Noncommercial information and stakeholders have been consistently marginalized in the evolution of American communications. In the early days of radio broadcasting, the universities, religious organizations, labor unions, and civic groups that were setting up stations were pushed aside to give business near-total control over the new electronic public sphere. Noncommercial radio and television subsisted on a starvation diet made up mainly of foundation grants until the Public Broadcasting System (PBS) was created in 1967, and its still-thin financial base is under attack in Congress. And while there are many civic networks, nonprofit computer bulletin boards, and public, educational, and governmental (PEG) cable television channels, these too exist on shoestring budgets and are accessible only to a small percentage of the public.

The popularization of the Internet indicates that many Americans value the opportunity to access, create, and disseminate information that is not defined by the market. Moreover, a number of opinion polls have shown that a broad cross-section of the public strongly supports public broadcasting. In the future, there will be increasing demand for services like high-quality PEG video or multimedia access to libraries, museums, educational institutions, and government agencies via home terminals, personal digital assistants (PDAs), or public kiosks. Steps need to be taken now to ensure that the abundant bandwidth of the NII will be configured so that it accommodates such possibilities from the outset, rather than as an afterthought.

4. Public property should be used to promote public interest objectives. While congressional Republicans and right-wing think-tanks seek to expand private property rights, there has been little discussion of how to defend the collective property of the American public. Network operators and broadcasters use this property under highly favorable terms to make billions of dollars each year. The public has a right to be compensated adequately for the use of its property, be it physical rights-of-way or radio spectrum. The funds generated thereby should be ploughed back into the NII to promote public interest objectives, rather than going toward general deficit reduction. Many developing countries historically have treated their telecommunications systems as cash cows to be plundered in order to finance unrelated activities—a practice that resulted in inadequate investment in network modernization and expansion. The United States should not follow this "third world" approach.

Beyond gaining fair compensation for taxpayers' assets, there is another way public property can be used to promote a pluralistic NII. In May 1995, Apple Computer Inc. petitioned the FCC to declare a portion of the public's frequency spectrum off limits to corporate acquisition, and instead to set it aside for free and open usage.[5] More specifically, Apple requested that 300 megahertz of underused spectrum be devoted to unlicensed use by all comers for video, voice, and data services, subject only to technical standards to prevent interference. This chunk of spectrum, which Apple has dubbed the "NII band," would provide citizens with high-speed access to advanced services without their having to pay established carriers expensive connection or airtime charges (although users would need the proper equipment). As the company points out, the NII band could become a dynamic domain in which small- and medium-sized firms create customized systems and services, thereby enriching and diversifying communications markets. It could also be used to promote a variety of public interest-oriented applications like civic networking and the interconnection of schools, libraries, and other public institutions. Apple's proposal is currently under consideration at the FCC; if it is found to be technically feasible, the commission should implement it quickly.

II. TELECOMMUNICATIONS AND CABLE TELEVISION POLICY

5. The MFJ restrictions should be lifted only when barriers to competition in local markets have been removed. Deregulation and liberalization are not always the same thing.* Simply removing government rules may not foster a diverse and competitive marketplace; this is particularly the case in arenas like the local loop, or local telephone exchange area, where the control of facilities constitutes a major bottleneck. The pending legislation allows the RBOCs to enter new lines of business before fully implementing such procompetitive safeguards as network interconnection, unbundling, resale, number portability, and dialing parity.

For example, provisions in the Senate bill allow a Bell company to fulfill the FCC's "competitive checklist" by negotiating a deal with a single weak competitor. The legislation could thus unduly preserve concentrated market power, retard the evolution toward open networks, and decrease price competition and consumer choice. Moreover, the legislation does not allow the FCC to expand the checklist in light of changing conditions and it confines the Department of Justice—the driving force in the break-up of AT&T, which ushered in long-distance competition—to a marginal role. These provisions are simply a giveaway to the RBOCs and are completely contrary to the Clinton administration's vision of the NII. Hence, the restrictions placed on the Bell companies by the Modification of Final Judgment (MFJ) that broke up AT&T should not be lifted until these competitive conditions are met in the local loop. Moreover, it is imperative that the FCC and the Department of Justice's Antitrust Division retain the full authority to ensure such competition.

6. Network operators with market power should enter new lines of business through fully separate subsidiaries. Network operators with captive ratepayers in their existing lines of business (such as telcos and cable operators) will inevitably be tempted to shift costs in order to finance their ventures into new competitive markets. The ability of regulatory agencies to monitor these operators' finances and prevent such abuses will be limited unless carriers enter new lines of business

---

* Eli Noam elaborates on this point in Chapter 1.

through fully separate subsidiaries that maintain separate financial records. However, the pending legislation contains inadequate safeguards on this score.[6]

More generally, the FCC must carefully monitor Bell company finances to ensure that customers requiring only basic telephone service are not forced to subsidize the deployment of advanced telecommunications services. It would be highly inappropriate for lower-income customers to pay for offerings that, at least initially, are likely to appeal primarily to upper-income customers.

7. Common carriers should be required to develop open platforms. The RBOCs control a key connection point between business and residential customers, on the one hand, and independent suppliers of information on the other. Should the long-distance carriers enter the local market in a serious way, they will be in a similar pivotal position. In the short term, customers and independent information suppliers must be ensured easy, nondiscriminatory access to each other at reasonable rates. And in the medium term, customers should have the ability to originate all forms of information (video, text, graphics, sound) on a switched basis—becoming, in effect, information suppliers themselves—if the NII is to reach its full potential. It is not clear how far the pending legislation moves us in this direction.

With regard to video markets, both the Senate and House bills contain provisions for the establishment of video dial tone (VDT) platforms that are comparable to the current FCC rules, but they also give telcos the option of constructing conventional cable television systems regulated under Title VI of the Communications Act. The Bells may find this approach tempting, since they could deliver entertainment with a bit of interactivity thrown in without having to undertake the costs and common carrier obligations of VDT. This would offer some competition in entertainment like that provided by direct broadcast satellite systems, but little more. Telcos should be required to enter video markets by offering platforms open to all content suppliers. Moreover, while the Senate bill does ensure that PEG programmers have access to any VDT platforms at incremental-cost-based rates, it says nothing about the charges for other independent suppliers. In contrast, the House bill calls for FCC regulation to ensure just and reasonable rates.

With regard to access to carriers' platforms by non-video information suppliers and electronic publishers, both the Senate and House bills are inadequate. Many members of the public interest coalition are concerned about the telcos owning content and possibly giving preference to their own services in customer interfaces.[7] Provisions in legislation of the 103d Congress, such as the safeguards on RBOC entry and rates, and the original language on open platform services, represented useful steps toward tackling these issues. The current legislation does comparatively little to set guidelines for the establishment of universally available open multimedia services and interfaces.[8]

8. Rate regulation of carriers with market power should be preserved. The FCC and the state public utility commissions (PUCs) have the expertise to establish proper rates for RBOC services and their hands should not be too tightly bound in this regard by Congress. The pending legislation properly allows these agencies to regulate local telephony and other offerings that will be included in an expanded definition of universal service. This will be important as traditional cross-subsidies are phased out and until there is substantial price competition in the local loop; unless the right regulations are adopted, many observers worry that residential users may end up paying more for the same service.* However, the legislation makes the mistake of curtailing the use of rate-of-return regulation in many instances. While price caps are sometimes superior, there are cases when rate-of-return regulation may be needed.

Moreover, cable television rates should not be substantially deregulated, as called for in the legislation. Some relief for small systems may be warranted, but for the major companies this giveaway is premature. Direct broadcast satellites systems provide only marginal competition to cable today, and it may be several years before the Bells provide serious alternatives in many markets. The short-term result will be significant and unnecessary rate increases for cable customers. Until there is substantial competition, any rate relief should be targeted only toward small cable operators, and it should be the province of the FCC to decide the merits of each case.

9. Government oversight is needed to ensure openness and interoperability at key interfaces. Technical standardization is an important determinant of whether we will have the seamlessly interconnected NII envisioned by the Clinton administration or a patchwork of closed and architecturally rigid networks and equipment that stifle competition and limit consumer choice. The dilemma is that while private firms may not always succeed in agreeing on truly open standards, government efforts to actually set standards and choose technologies generally yield abysmal results.† The question then is what role, if any, the government should play in this crucial arena.

Some participants in the project worry that increased government involvement could distort the market's selection of standards. Others believe it is appropriate for the government to set broad requirements for certain key interfaces, which industry would then decide how to implement. During the 103d Congress, Sun Microsystems proposed that the FCC create a broad-based committee of representatives from government agencies, consumer groups, industry, and academia to identify such requirements; this approach merits serious consideration. More generally, as a National Research Council report argues, federal agencies "should support and participate in the ongoing standards-setting processes more effectively, bringing to those processes an advocacy for the public interest and for realization of an open and evolvable NII."[9] Unfortunately, it is not clear that existing bodies like the National Science and Technology Council (NTSC) are up to this task. Hence, what is needed is "a body that will effectively blend the technical competence of the NTSC with the

---

* Herbert Dordick articulates this concern in Chapter 6.
† This point is emphasized by Lee McKnight and Russell Neuman in Chapter 5,
  Richard Solomon in the Appendix to Part 1, and Anthony Rutkowski in Chapter 9.

policy capabilities of the Clinton administration's Information Infrastructure Task Force (IITF) and be able to function for the extended period of time required to develop and deploy an NII with an [open] architecture."[10]

One case where broad government guidelines would be particularly important is the new generation of television set-top boxes. Liberalization and the MFJ threw open the telecommunications equipment market to competitive suppliers, which led to reduced prices and greatly increased consumer choice.* Long gone are the days when consumers were forced to rent a telephone from AT&T. Nevertheless, this remains the case for cable television set-top boxes. Major network operators and their preferred suppliers want to extend this outpost of monopoly power to the new generation of intelligent set-top boxes. There are legitimate concerns about the possibility of signal theft and potential difficulties when technology upgrades are needed, but many analysts believe that there are workable technical solutions to such issues. Congress should require that the new set-top boxes be interoperable and competitively provided so that diverse vendors can compete to create the best product.[11] Consumers will then be able to go to any retail outlet and purchase their set-top box, just as they would a telephone, fm machine, personal computer, or modem.

10. Universal service must be well funded and expanded in scope and domain. Three issues merit consideration here. First, how should universal service be funded? Although there is reason to wonder when real competition for residential customers will develop in the local loop, there is widespread consensus that the old system of hidden cross-subsidies within local monopolies must be replaced. Among the alternatives are to replace the present invisible taxes with a visible charge, drawing on either general government revenue or specialized communications fees.† Congress is pursuing the politically easier of these options by calling on the FCC and state PUCs to levy competitively neutral charges on carriers and, as necessary, other service providers. But some argue that carriers will just pass these charges on to consumers and that this form of indirect taxation may suppress network usage, penalize new entrants, and encourage bypass by corporate customers with private networks.‡ On the other hand, while using general government revenues would be more economically efficient, this would require new on-budget taxation and make the funds vulnerable to political attacks and cuts. Perhaps this political/economic trade-off could be balanced better by establishing a self-sustaining trust fund with a mixture of both types of revenues, supplemented by spectrum auction fees.‡‡

Second, which services are to be made universally available at affordable, regulated rates? The pending legislation leaves this question to the new federal-state joint board and the FCC for periodic reassessment in light of changing

---

* Noam demonstrates this in Chapter 1.

† See Noam, Chapter 1.

‡ Henry Geller makes this argument in Chapter 4.

‡‡ Geller suggests the use of spectrum fees in Chapter 4.

technological and market trends. However, some stakeholders argue that there is no need to wait for this process to begin before making advanced services available at affordable rates. Instead, Congress could require telcos to offer Integrated Services Digital Network (ISDN) services for the price of a standard voice grade line plus the incremental upgrade cost, at least until there are significant competitive alternatives in the local loop.[12] ISDN services would provide access to the Internet and commercial on-line services over existing copper wires at much higher speeds than those available over the typical modem. The technology is here today, but the Bells are shortsightedly pricing ISDN well above both their costs and the ability of most consumers to pay. Affordable ISDN would be a boon to customers, both individuals and small- and medium-sized businesses, and could stimulate the demand for more advanced services as these become available. Congress is unlikely to act on this proposal, but the FCC could still reconsider its approach to ISDN subscriber line charges as a first step in the right direction. (Down the road, modems being developed by the cable industry will provide far greater capacity, although the cost is likely to be prohibitive for many consumers.)

Third, who should receive universal service subsidies? Regarding residential customers, it is important to ensure that support is targeted to those most in need.* Regarding institutional customers, the Senate legislation gives K-12 schools, libraries, and nonprofit public health facilities access to universal services at incremental cost-based rates (and requires the FCC to establish rules to ensure that other advanced services will be available to such institutions). The House bill, in contrast, says only that common carriers should provide them with access. Further, it may be some time before many advanced services are brought under the universal service umbrella in accordance with the market-based definition in both bills (that is, services already subscribed to by a substantial majority of residential customers). Thus, it may be desirable to require now that certain advanced services be made available to designated nonprofit entities at incremental cost-based rates.

11. Noncommercial video and information services should be treated favorably. The NII must accommodate the dissemination of noncommercial ideas and information. While less than perfect, provisions in the legislation of the 103d Congress (like S. 1822's capacity set-aside requirement) would have established this as an important national objective and provided the basis for ongoing dialogue to that end. In comparison, the current Republican legislation charts a much more limited course. To be sure, PEG video programmers won reasonably favorable access to VDT platforms. But the provisions on non-commercial information services and electronic publishing within broadband networks are rather weak. S. 652 limits preferential access rates to K-12 schools, public libraries, and nonprofit health facilities, while H.R. 1555 merely mentions schools and says nothing about rates. A broader range of public institutions and community voices should be supported if there is to be a vital civic sector, as was specified in last year's bills.[13]

---

* See Geller, Chapter 4, and Dordick, Chapter 6.

III. BROADCASTING POLICY

12. Spectrum "flexibility" should be granted in exchange for public interest obligations. If the FCC allows broadcasters to use spectrum originally designated for HDTV for other purposes, the public should receive adequate compensation for the use of its property. Unfortunately, the proposed Senate bill asks very little from broadcasters—only that they provide one free advanced television service subject to traditional public interest criteria and pay fees comparable to those charged for less valuable spectrum. In return, broadcasters could launch a variety of potentially lucrative pay services on multiple channels derived through digital data compression from both their existing and new spectrum. This amounts to little more than a new entitlement for longstanding recipients of corporate welfare. In contrast, the House bill requires broadcasters to give up their old spectrum, but states explicitly that any fees levied be designated for the U.S. Treasury rather than for public interest purposes. Neither of these approaches is optimal.

The FCC should be free to set fees that reflect the true value of the spectrum and the funds collected should be ploughed back into the communications sector to support, for example, PEG services, public broadcasting, and/or universal service. Moreover, since close to 40 percent of U.S. households do not subscribe to cable services and only a small percentage of these offer PEG services anyway, Congress should require broadcasters to set aside a channel for free video and data PEG services. Another possibility would be to designate channels for leased access by unaffiliated program suppliers. Finally, there is the question of what sort of obligations should apply to the free advanced television service. In line with the traditional public trustee treatment of broadcasting, FCC Chairman Reed Hundt has considered requiring that time be provided for children's programming or to political candidates in the context of campaign finance reform. Whether this is the right approach depends on decisions made about the future of the public trustee concept.

13. The broadcast model should be reexamined in the NII context. The 103d and 104th Congresses have concentrated on reforming Titles II and VI of the Communications Act, which cover telecommunications and cable television. Beyond spectrum flexibility and ownership issues, they have not attempted to rethink Title III treatment of broadcasting in the new environment. But as Henry Geller has argued, "drastic reform is required now because the public trustee model has been and is a failure. It does little or nothing to ensure public service, and it has become a mere charade."[14] Program content guidelines vary from weak to nonexistent; the fairness doctrine has been abandoned; incumbents always retain their licenses in the comparative renewal process; and, with the termination of the FCC's anti-trafficking rule, "public trusts have been sold like 'hog bellies.'"[15] Since Congress consistently has refused to strengthen the public trustee approach, it might be worth considering its elimination. In exchange, broadcasters could be asked to contribute a spectrum usage fee of, Geller suggests, 1 percent of gross revenues for radio and 3 percent for television. These funds could be used to support robust noncommercial services alongside the standard commercial fare, as well as provide seed money for minority ownership of broadcast stations. While broadcasters initially might oppose such changes, long-term licenses and reduced administrative hassles ought to be sufficient inducement for them to reconsider their interests. In any event, the current system promotes neither the public interest nor economic efficiency and it will make even less sense in the future.

14. Public broadcasting should be supported, restructured, and insulated from the political process. The conservative crusade against public broadcasting rests on a series of distortions. The argument that it is a "budget buster" is belied by the fact that in 1992, the United States spent only $1.06 per capita on public broadcasting, as compared to $17.71 in Japan, $32.15 in Canada, and $38.56 in the United Kingdom.[16] The argument that public television is redundant because some Americans receive the Discovery Channel or Arts & Entertainment on their cable systems ignores the tens of millions who do not, as well as the substantial differences in program content across these services. And the argument that public broadcasting is ideologically slanted toward the views of "liberal elites" as opposed to those of "ordinary Americans" is based on a small number of shows that, in cities like San Diego, generally air at midnight or not at all. Moreover, every major opinion poll on the matter has shown that an overwhelming majority of Americans do not want public broadcasting to disappear.

Nevertheless, structural changes are needed if public broadcasting is to adapt to the new media and political environments. For example, a widely noted Twentieth Century Fund Task Force report points out that there are 351 public television stations in the country, many of them with overlapping signals and duplicative schedules, and that these consume about 75 percent of total funding. The report argues for a dramatic shift in resources toward national programming.[17] Individual station operations would have to rely more on the communities they serve for support, but this ought to be easier to attract if there is better programming. The Task Force also recommended that educational programming be expanded and commercialization resisted, and that federal funding be increased, ideally through revenues from spectrum auctions and usage fees. However the initial capitalization is attained, moving from annual congressional appropriations to a self-sustaining trust fund makes sense. As long as public broadcasting is dependent on the kindness of congressional strangers, it will be subject to political manipulation and demagoguery.

IV. INFORMATION POLICY

15. Freedom of speech in cyberspace must be preserved. Sensationalist stories in the mass media depicting the Internet as a seething cesspool of smut have distorted much of the general public's conception of the medium.[18] Already there are press reports of parents denying their children access to the educational riches of the Internet out of a computer-illiterate fear—exaggerated by yet another expertly orchestrated campaign by the far right—that logging on is the virtual equivalent of being shoved into an adult bookstore. With few senators willing to risk being depicted as "defenders of pornography" in the 1996 election, the passage of the "Communications Decency" amendment that became part of the Senate bill was foreordained.[19]

The censorship amendment is plainly unconstitutional. It attempts to criminalize speech that is "lewd, filthy or indecent" (as opposed to obscene), thus violating the First Amendment. Anyone who knowingly posts such material anywhere on the Internet where a minor could conceivably find it could be subject to a heavy fine or even a prison term. Nor is it clear by what standard such material would be judged; something as innocuous as the spicier passages of Newt Gingrich's forthcoming novel might qualify. To avoid the risks, the tens of millions of adults using the Internet would be forced to "dumb down" their speech to a level deemed acceptable for children and Internet access providers would be forced to cease carrying dozens of Usenet newsgroups.

Moreover, the amendment ignores the legal and operational differences between the Internet and other electronic media, and in fact relegates the Internet to a lesser constitutional status than print or movies. These and the many other problems involved are all well-known.[20] Also well known is that a number of companies are developing software filters that block access to designated network locations, which put the responsibility for controlling underage curiosity where it belongs—on parents and schools.

The White House is on record as opposing the amendment, House Speaker Gingrich has denounced it as a shallow political game, and the House bill currently contains no similar provision. As such, there is reason to hope that clear thinking might prevail in conference committee away from C-SPAN's cameras. If not, and if the president chooses to sign a bill that is later ruled unconstitutional, the Internet community could encounter problems until the courts finally rule. It would be far better to return to a proposal made by Senator Patrick Leahy for a Justice Department study of the problem's actual scope and the effectiveness of technological solutions.

16. Coherent privacy protections should be adopted, and an institutional apparatus for their implementation should be created. Privacy protections in the United States today range from anemic to nonexistent. This is ironic in a country that prides itself on protecting individual liberties, and that has strong paranoid elements in its civic culture. The Privacy Act of 1974 set down rules for the gathering and use of information by government agencies, but there is a widespread fear that the Clinton administration's digital telephony law and encryption strategy have too many loopholes that invite abuse by law enforcement and intelligence agencies. The administration should address these legitimate concerns in as open a manner as possible.

Moreover, the great taboo subject must finally be tackled: the private sector's gathering and use of information about citizens. While their strength and effectiveness varies, most industrialized countries have adopted omnibus laws laying down fair use principles for corporate behavior and have established mechanisms through which people can seek to limit intrusions or redress grievances.[21] In contrast, the U.S. approach to business violations of privacy is ad hoc and reactive—a patchwork of uncoordinated federal and state statutes covering sector-specific issues that offer little real protection.* In this legal void, corporations are largely free to monitor workers on the job, track purchasing patterns and other consumer behavior through transactional information, and make decisions about employees and consumers on the basis of their "digital personas."[22] Moreover, personal information has become a commodity to be bought and sold without restraint.[23] Increasing reliance on information infrastructure will only compound the problem. Every time anyone logs onto an on-line service, selects a movie on demand, uses a digital cash card, or passes through a toll gate on a "smart highway," networked computers will record these actions and corporations may then use and sell the information without consent.

The NII bills require that competing service providers get nondiscriminatory access to customer proprietary network information, but they place little restraint on the gathering, use, and marketing of citizens' information in the first place. For its part, the IITF is attempting to develop fair use principles applicable to the public and private sectors, but these are not intended to be comprehensive.[24] A European-style omnibus law that covers all players and issues might seem like an obvious solution, but this probably would not work because of the pace of technological change, the diversity of privacy-impinging activities across economic sectors, and the strong opposition of both data suppliers and users in the private sector. But it would be reasonable to begin by enacting broad federal principles for fair use, with flexible mechanisms for guidance about interpretation in various contexts.†

Furthermore, federal privacy policy needs an institutional home.‡ Congress could not keep abreast of the issues even if it were to try, and there is no executive branch agency with a statutory mandate to develop and enforce flexible and up-to-date regulations or handle citizen complaints. Senator Paul Simon's privacy bill in the 103d Congress, Vice President Gore's National Performance Review, and a recent study by the National Research Council have all recommended the creation of some sort of oversight body for government information. An entity with jurisdiction over private sector practices as well is needed. This need not be a huge, expensive, or intrusive bureaucracy; the privacy protection bodies found in other industrialized countries are not. With a comparatively small staff and a clearly delineated mission, a federal privacy commission could make a major contribution to citizen trust in the NII. It would also help the United States coordinate with foreign governments on problems raised by transborder flows of personal information (see recommendation 35).

---

* Joel Reidenberg makes this suggestion in Chapter 10.
† See Reidenberg, Chapter 10.
‡ See Dordick, Chapter 6, and Reidenberg, Chapter 10.

17. Intellectual property protections must balance the rights of producers and users. Intellectual property should be protected if people are to have adequate incentives to create and disseminate their work. But there are often significant tensions between the promotion of an open information infrastructure and the aggressive protection of property rights.* Whether the government continues to try to adapt traditional forms of protection to the changing technological environment or instead pursues new approaches, it is necessary to strike an equitable balance between the interests of information producers, their competitors, and users. In pursuit of such a balance, the IITF's Working Group on Intellectual Property Rights has been holding public meetings around the country and soliciting input from diverse stakeholders. Nonetheless, there is concern in some circles that the group may be leaning disproportionately toward property owners on a number of key issues.

For example, the group is considering proposals to change the Copyright Act by expanding significantly owners' control over network transmissions of their works; eliminating the "first sale" doctrine (which allows a purchaser to dispose of a copy of a work without infringing copyright—that is, by reselling or lending it) for computer networks; and prohibiting the importation, manufacture, and distribution of any devices that could be used to circumvent property protections.[25] Particularly troubling is the group's seemingly narrow interpretation of the fair use principle (which allows writers, teachers, librarians, and others to use protected materials in limited ways without violating copyright) as it applies to information infrastructure. If the vast, fluid realm of cyberspace is chopped into a series of exclusive domains with toll booths at their gates, the social and economic potential of the NII could be greatly diminished. Whether it concerns multimedia interfaces, network protocols, electronic publications, or something else, a consensual median point must be found between a cyber-enclosure movement and the hacker's credo that "information wants to be free." This applies to intellectual property in the GII context as well.

18. Government information should be easily available to the public under reasonable terms. Taxpayers' access to government information has absorbed a number of blows in recent years. The Reagan and Bush administrations privatized the ownership, control, and dissemination of a great deal of public information, handing out exclusive contracts to powerful publishers who charged high prices for the material. Under strong pressure from the public interest coalition, the Clinton administration has taken some steps to improve the situation, most notably by launching the free Government Printing Office (GPO) Access program on the Internet. Similarly, the new House Republican leadership made an important contribution by establishing a centralized Internet access point to congressional records under the auspices of the Library of Congress. However, librarians and others remain disappointed with the administration's continuing privatization of many types of materials, its lack of an equitable pricing policy for the vast array of

---

* See Reidenberg, Chapter 10.

items not on the Internet, its attack on the GPO's "monopoly" (much of the GPO's work is, in fact, outsourced to the private sector), and its related proposals to move toward a decentralized and less transparent document production system. Government information should be available to the public for free where possible and at cost where necessary. Networks should be used to provide citizens and businesses with one-stop access to information ranging from environmental or health and safety regulations to "how to" manuals and health tips. At the same time, it is important to ensure the availability of paper materials for citizens who do not have network access. Moreover, devising a coherent approach to the dissemination of government information might require the energies of an executive branch organization devoted entirely to the task, rather than having it in the OMB's Office of Information and Regulatory Affairs, as it is today. Finally, government policy should be formulated with extensive input from the library community and other relevant groups.

V. TECHNOLOGY AND APPLICATIONS POLICIES

19. Federal technology policies for information infrastructure can be streamlined, but they remain an important strategic investment. Over the years, Democratic and Republican administrations alike have pursued mission-oriented technology policies to meet government objectives, in particular in the military, space, and energy fields. Using targeted research and development grants, large-scale procurement contracts, and other instruments, the federal government has played a decisive role in stimulating and sustaining the development of telecommunications, computer, microelectronics, and internetworking technologies at times when commercial markets alone would not have supported them. As Anthony Rutkowski summarizes the situation, "the strategic federal S&T community has provided a foundation for industrial development and policymaking that has significantly shaped the entire [information technology] realm."[*] In part as a consequence, the United States has established a commanding lead in most of the technologies that serve as the building blocks of the global information economy.

Understanding their centrality at this transitional moment in economic history, the Clinton administration has expanded technology policy programs significantly. In parallel, it has broadened their focus from supporting specific agency missions to enhancing U.S. commercial competitiveness in a variety of industries.[26] And the administration is pursuing its agenda through a decentralized and agile institutional apparatus that is better suited to the dynamism of information infrastructure than are the more top-down policies employed by our major trading partners.[†] These activities and investments already have yielded important dividends, but, like the decisions to support computer

---

[*] See Rutkowski, Chapter 9.
[†] McKnight and Neuman make this argument in Chapter 5.

research in the early 1940s and internetworking in the late 1960s, their real value may only become clear down the road.

Nevertheless, congressional Republicans have proposed massive cuts in a number of important technology policy initiatives. A careful and nonideological analysis is needed. Any unnecessary corporate welfare should be removed with a scalpel (the Advanced Technology Program's grants to multibillion dollar corporations are an obvious place to start). But to cut indiscriminately programs that have helped small- and medium-sized businesses undertake R&D and attract venture capital is extremely shortsighted, since these funds are likely to yield long-term, multiplier benefits throughout the economy. Further, while retaining the flexible architecture that characterizes U.S. programs, the government should strive for enhanced coordination among agencies, companies, universities, and national laboratories.[27]

20. Policy support for new applications of technology should be strengthened for both noncommercial users and small- and medium-sized business. Noncommercial organizations in the fields of education, the arts, social services, and elsewhere play important roles in their communities but often lack resources.[28] Hence, in parallel with supporting supply side technology development, the Clinton administration has launched new applications policies for the demand side of the equation.[29] This is one of the most innovative achievements of the NII initiative. For example, the NTIA's Telecommunications and Information Infrastructure Assistance Program (TIIAP) provides these groups, on the basis of competitive and thoroughly reviewed bids, with seed money to develop the technological tools they need. Beyond helping to promote the enrichment of community life, such programs give nonprofits the ability to develop customized solutions that further the development of networking and information resources, thereby opening up new commercial and employment opportunities as well. Other programs geared toward small- and medium-sized businesses—such as the Manufacturing Extension Partnership—fulfill a similar dual function and are essential to the promotion of a pluralistic and dynamic NII.*

Nevertheless, congressional Republicans have attacked these small, effective programs with budget cuts and threats of elimination. Such cuts contribute little to deficit reduction and undermine Speaker Gingrich's vision of a grassroots-empowering, "third wave" economy and society. It would be infinitely better to point the ax at the approximately $50 billion in aid to dependent corporations contained in the 1994 budget and at other areas of real waste than to destroy those few programs that help people apply and advance the development of technological tools.

21. The congressional Office of Technology Assessment (OTA) should not be abolished. Now more than ever, Congress needs access to high-quality assessments of advanced technology issues. There is no way for all of its 535 members to devote the time needed to become experts in complex areas like information infrastructure; the OTA bridges the gap by providing them, on request, with dozens of first-rate reports every year.[30] OTA studies are also

---

* See Bar, Chapter 2, and Dordick, Chapter 6.

extremely valuable to thousands of people outside the beltway in the educational, research, and business communities. Weighing its diverse benefits against the modest cost of a $22 million budget, the OTA is clearly an excellent strategic investment and the congressional effort to abolish it is pennywise and pound foolish. Moreover, the OTA is not beholden to powerful special interests and does not push any particular agenda that favors some stakeholders over others. As such, its reports are a needed complement to those of the conservative think-tanks that dominate beltway debates. The federal government—and particularly Congress—will continue to need independent, expert analysis as it struggles to define strategies for a rapidly changing, technology-intensive global information economy.

VI. HUMAN RESOURCES POLICY

22. The promotion of education and training should be a central objective of NII policy. The employment-reducing effects of the information revolution have not yet been offset by its employment-creating effects.* And these employment-reducing effects are visible not only among less skilled workers, but also among professionals and managers.† Nevertheless, education and training remain the best hope for a future in an information economy where many tasks are being automated or performed with fewer workers. Those who have fungible skills—particularly technological skills—may have a shot at a decent career, but those who do not will be left behind. Since the latter category includes tens of millions of Americans, the prospects are for deepening inequality of opportunity. The Clinton administration is therefore right to emphasize that NII policy must be coordinated with education and training policies. The Vice President's challenge to the private sector to wire every school and library by the year 2000 is useful, but substantial progress cannot be attained on the cheap.‡ A shift in budgetary priorities and a coherent national strategy are needed.

As a first step, the Department of Education should provide more funding to help schools obtain adequate classroom technology (even a coordinated computer recycling program would be a good start). Moreover, better teacher training is required to overcome resistance to the introduction of technology by teachers who do not understand how to use it and who may fear it will undermine their authority.[31] These and other initiatives should be targeted at K-12 schools, community colleges, and vocational schools in disadvantaged areas. In parallel, state and local governments should establish networked job centers and aggressively promote adult education and retraining. Further,

---

* See Lanvin, Chapter 8.
† See Dordick, Chapter 6.
‡ Geller makes this point in Chapter 4.

tax incentives should be offered to encourage firms to engage in on-the-job retraining and apprenticeship programs.* The private sector must do much more to carry its share of the load if it wants a workforce that can help it compete internationally.

23. The right of employees to an equitable information-intensive workplace should be protected. Labor Secretary Robert Reich has noted on several occasions that, while German and Japanese corporations view their workers as assets to be invested in, U.S. corporations seem to see them primarily as costs to be reduced. Some of the many consequences of this approach are massive layoffs, declining wages, a shift to part-time employment without pensions and benefits, and widespread job insecurity.† These trends are as much a part of the information economy as the computer-wielding entrepreneurs lionized in "third wave" rhetoric.[32] But there is another problem: for many people who still are employed, the quality of the workplace is deteriorating. For example, corporate managers often deploy information technologies in ways that effectively de-skill workers or subject them to new, dehumanizing pressures like electronic surveillance.[33] It is not clear what, if any, role government can play in affecting internal corporate practices beyond enforcing health and safety standards, but the issues merit Labor Department consideration and wider public debate.

VII. THE POLICYMAKING PROCESS

24. A single, high-level organization within the executive branch should be given the lead in charting national strategy. Congress and analysts have argued for years about how to fix such executive branch problems as the absence of top-level leadership and the fragmentation of authority across more than twenty federal agencies. A variety of proposals have been put forth to create a single, coordinating agency within the executive branch.[34] Some reorganizations have even been tried: the Nixon administration established a White House Office of Telecommunications Policy (OTP) in 1970, but so badly misused it to harass the president's perceived enemies in the mass media that President Carter transferred its functions into the Commerce Department, creating the National Telecommunications and Information Administration (NTIA) in 1978. Similarly, President Reagan established a Bureau of International Communications and Information Policy within the State Department in 1985 to coordinate agency programs on international issues, but it suffered from a variety of problems and was downgraded by the Clinton administration in 1993. Given this long and fruitless debate, new proposals to consolidate and upgrade responsibility may be greeted with weary sighs. Nevertheless, the costs of

---

* See Dordick, Chapter 6.
† See Dordick, Chapter 6.

inaction are high today and "will continue to increase as the global information economy accelerates in the multimedia, highly mobile world of tomorrow."* The Clinton administration has taken important steps in the right direction, but there is no guarantee that future administrations will follow its lead. Institutionalizing reforms now could help head off problems down the road.

Some argue that a full fledged Cabinet-level agency absorbing the FCC and NTIA would be the strongest solution, but impossible to get through Congress. Similarly, the idea of a smaller EPA-style agency to exist alongside the FCC is reasonable, but probably also would die on the Hill. On the other hand, the "path of least resistance" option of a presidential assistant with a tiny staff might not mark a huge improvement over today's arrangements.† The Clinton administration has already given a prominent role to the White House Office of Science and Technology Policy, but information infrastructure policy requires more staff support than this allows. Two alternatives suggest themselves: a White House Office of Information Infrastructure Policy (OIIP)—without the power for Nixonian OTP-style abuses—could be created simply by moving the NTIA back where it came from. This would be a particularly attractive possibility if Republicans on the Hill go forward with their recent, misguided proposal to abolish the Department of Commerce. Alternatively, on a smaller scale, a Council of Communications Advisors (CCA) could be established.[35] Like the Council of Economic Advisors or the Office of the Special Trade Representative, the CCA could be located within the Executive Office of the President but outside the White House. Either a carefully defined OIIP or a CCA, created by shifting existing positions and responsibilities, would be a budget-friendly way to make much needed improvements in the policymaking process.

25. The policymaking process should be opened further to democratic participation by a diverse cross-section of stakeholders. To its credit, the Clinton administration has adopted what is unquestionably the most open and pluralistic approach in the history of U.S. communications policy. Nevertheless, there is room for improvement in three important respects. First, state and local governments should be treated as active partners in NII development. The legislation of both the 103d and 104th Congress has reflected a bipartisan consensus to preempt state regulatory authority over market entry and other important issues, and has denied local governments the right to require telcos to obtain franchises for their VDT platforms. Large carriers have pushed hard for preemption and a uniform set of rules for all markets and many independent analysts concur, arguing that some state and local governments lack the tools for effective policymaking. However, allowing authorities who are familiar with local conditions to have a say on key issues might encourage experimentation and yield results of potential interest to the nation.[36] Mechanisms like joint boards or even the Internet could be used to

---

* See Geller, Chapter 4.
† The above options are explored by Geller in Chapter 4.

enhance coordination among policymakers at different levels of government and facilitate the sharing of information and experiences. This is one policy arena where carefully defined "devolution" might actually make sense.

Second, the Clinton administration's expansion of the advisory process does not go far enough. For example, the composition of the NII Advisory Committee is still heavily slanted toward large corporations, includes only one representative from higher education (where much of the interesting work on advanced networking and applications is being done), and has no participation from civic networkers and PEG service providers. There is also inadequate consumer representation on the proposed universal service board. Moreover, the more specialized advisory committees, like the one working on International Telecommunication Union (ITU) issues, lack adequate participation by small- and medium-sized businesses.* Such firms are essential sources of innovation in information infrastructure, and their interests should be more actively reflected in both domestic and foreign policy. Finally, the general public must be made more aware of its stake in the NII policymaking process. The administration has succeeded only partially in using the mass media to raise public awareness of the issues associated with the NII and what it is trying to achieve in this area.

The Global Information Infrastructure

I. General Approach

26. Market liberalization at the global level, as at the national level, should be balanced with the promotion of media diversity, localism, and noncommercial uses. Fifteen years ago, the United Nations' International Commission for the Study of Communication Problems released a high-profile report surveying the global scene entitled, "Many Voices, One World."[37] Were the UN to create such a commission today, its final report would probably have to be called, "Many Markets, One World." The terms of discourse about global communications policy have changed radically since the early 1980s. The notion that communication is a uniquely important activity—one that is central to social development, cultural enrichment, and the public sphere of ideas—has been pushed aside by a narrow view of information as a commodity to be sold, bought, and consumed. The driving force in this transformation of perspective has been strong and consistent pressure from the United States. In the past, the U.S. government held up the "free flow of information" as a guiding principle of its foreign policy in communications; this phrase, while admittedly masking commercial interests, also reflected a libertarian, Jeffersonian impulse. Now, our guiding principle is simply "free trade," and we question the legitimacy of all policy measures adopted abroad if they in any way limit market access by U.S.-based transnational corporations (TNCs).

---

* Peter Cowhey and Anthony Rutkowski make this point in Chapters 7 and 9, respectively.

But while this broad U.S. vision increasingly shapes policy debates within intergovernmental fora and industry circles, it is often hotly contested abroad when applied to specific issues. The basic premise that liberalization can be beneficial is now widely accepted. In many countries, however, there are those who believe that free trade is not the only legitimate criteria for assessing carriage and (especially) content issues and who stress that other values—such as media diversity, responsiveness to local community concerns, and noncommercialism—should take priority in certain cases. These conflicts over values often translate into heated arguments and mutual disaffection between the United States and its partners abroad that can affect our larger relationships.* Hence, adopting an aggressive and narrow trade approach to every issue may actually impede movement toward the open and pluralistic GII envisioned by the Clinton administration.[38]

27. U.S. policy needs a better balance between efforts to secure market access for corporations and to promote international cooperation on applications of new technology. Announcing the GII initiative at the ITU's March 1994 development conference, Vice President Gore stated that the administration's agenda for the world was based on five principles drawn from its domestic NII initiative: private investment, competition, open access, regulatory flexibility, and universal service. At the same time, he noted that the GII could be used to tackle challenges like improving the environment, education, and health care. This blending of market opening principles with cooperative, problem-solving applications was reiterated in the administration's vision statement, *Global Information Infrastructure: Agenda for Cooperation.*[39]

This apparent broadening of focus is a welcome development; however, it is not clear how substantial the broadening really is. On the one hand, the administration does not have the necessary resources to pursue aggressively the applications side of its program; members of the noncommercial sector with the requisite expertise have not been mobilized to help out; and the United States has argued against some proposals by other governments that it deemed too "interventionist." On the other hand, when the IITF's International Telecommunications Working Group held a hearing in July 1994 to solicit input on the GII initiative, virtually all of the invited nongovernmental speakers represented large corporations seeking market access and freedom from regulation in foreign countries.[40] The administration has worked hard to advance the interests of these corporations in its international negotiations. In part as a consequence of this imbalance, the GII initiative has been met with a measure of cynicism by some people abroad who view it as simply the usual U.S. demands parading under a fancy new banner. The popular joke on the Internet that GII really stands for Global Information Invasion captures this sensibility.

It is therefore essential that the United States pursue cooperative international applications that demonstrate clearly the benefits of moving toward

---

* See Linda Garcia, Chapter 3.

a high-capacity GII. At the February 1995 Group of Seven (G-7) Ministerial Conference on the Information Society, the administration and its counterparts discussed joint projects in areas such as training and education, networked libraries and museums, telemedicine, environmental and natural resource management, and electronic commerce. These and other applications deserve adequate funding and the active participation of people in the noncommercial sector, both here and abroad. Moreover, international collaboration should not be limited to the G-7 countries if widespread support for the GII initiative is desired. Unfortunately, the principal GII-related multilateral institutions in which the United States participates—the ITU and the World Trade Organization (WTO)—are not the right places to pursue more inclusive projects. One alternative is for the United States to rejoin the United Nations Educational, Scientific and Cultural Organization (UNESCO). With some modernization, UNESCO could serve as an appropriate host for some of these activities. Another alternative is discussed in recommendation 39 below.

   28. Bilateral and plurilateral agreements should not undermine multi-lateralism. The United States has succeeded over the past decade in promoting global telecommunications liberalization. The most intensive efforts have been devoted to securing market access agreements with key countries, such as Canada, Japan, and the members of the European Union.* The Clinton administration has expanded this approach substantially, striking numerous bilateral agreements with countries in both the industrialized and developing world. In parallel, the administration is pursuing plurilateral agreements with the European Union and the North American Free Trade Agreement (NAFTA) countries, as well as in the G-7, the Organization for Economic Cooperation and Development (OECD), the Organization for American States, the Asian Pacific Economic Cooperation, and the Asia-Pacific Telecommunity.

   Yet, while these efforts could yield important gains for U.S.-based firms, the emergence of competing telecommunications blocs could bring about a highly fragmented trading system.† Furthermore, bilateral and plurilateral crusades "weaken the ability to manage global interests coherently . . . [such deals] often focus on selective problems, and the sum of the remedies does not necessarily serve the global interest. . . . Therefore, the United States needs to make sure that bilateral [and plurilateral] agreements serve multilateral interests, both to allay diplomatic objections and to simplify its own task."‡ Hence, some argue that exclusive membership pacts should include "multilateral impact statements" detailing their compliance with international regimes like the

---

* For a detailed discussion, see Cowhey, Chapter 7.
† See Lanvin, Chapter 8.
‡ See Cowhey, Chapter 7.

General Agreement on Trade in Services (GATS).* Moreover, it often would be appropriate to ensure that such agreements are transparent and even that they provide mechanisms for accession by like-minded, qualifying parties. The United States should promote a seamlessly interconnected and open GII, not a patchwork of exclusionary information blocs.

II. THE TRADITIONAL TRIAD OF INTERNATIONAL COMMUNICATIONS REGIMES

29. A flexible global standards-making process and open standards products are essential for the development of the GII. One of the most remarkable aspects of the international telecommunications regime's transformation has been the restructuring of the technical standardization process. From the 1920s to the late 1980s, multilateral standardization was generally carried out within the ITU, where national monopolies controlled decisionmaking. But in the context of global liberalization, many corporations grew frustrated with the ITU's slow-moving bureaucratic procedures and anticompetitive standards products. In response, the ITU has reformed substantially its institutional mechanisms in order to speed things up and become more market-friendly. Nevertheless, much standards-making activity has migrated out of the ITU and into a variety of specialized industry fora and regional organizations.[41] In consequence, some claim that, for all practical purposes, intergovernmental standards-making activities are becoming irrelevant.† One can argue about the degree of change, but clearly the role of governments and the ITU in the global standards architecture is being redefined.

Greater cooperation among the various bodies involved in standards-making is essential if the GII is to be open and seamlessly interconnected. The new Global Standards Coordination mechanism and the use of electronic networking among organizations are positive developments. But the United States has not always helped the cause. For example, it has slowed efforts to integrate wired and wireless standardization activities within the ITU; impeded cooperation between the ITU and the Internet Society; sometimes put regional deals before multilateralism; and in some cases been too aggressive in defending U.S.-based TNCs' closed, proprietary standards and intellectual property claims. The United States should consistently support open and flexible global standardization, preferably along the lines of the Internet model.

30. Alternatives to the telecommunications regime's accounting and settlements mechanism should be pursued. The international accounting and settlements mechanism negotiated within the ITU is deeply flawed.‡ The system created in 1968 worked well enough in the era of national monopolies and

---

* See Cowhey, Chapter 7.
† Rutkowski makes this assertion in Chapter 9.
‡ See Cowhey, Chapter 7; Lanvin, Chapter 8; and Rutkowski, Chapter 9.

comparable collection charges, but in the context of global liberalization it has become the source of substantial market distortions. Asymmetric deregulation across countries and variations in the tariffs levied on customers have produced huge imbalances in traffic flows and, because the United States has among the lowest tariffs in the world and must pay foreign carriers to terminate calls, U.S. carriers now hand out billions of dollars per year more than they receive. U.S. consumers in effect are subsidizing national monopolies in certain countries, particularly in the developing world. Moreover, the accounting and settlements system, combined with the high collection charges imposed by foreign carriers on their citizens, suppresses the use of public telecommunications facilities and encourages various forms of bypass, such as call-back services.* Rather than fixing the problem by lowering their rates and charges, many national administrations have sought instead to impose new national and multilateral regulations on bypass providers.

The United States led a successful reform effort in the ITU, which resulted in a 1992 agreement to adopt accounting rates that are more cost-oriented, transparent, and nondiscriminatory. Bilateral pressure has also led some countries to lower their accounting rates. Still, a case can be made that the system is fundamentally flawed and needs overhauling if not replacement.[42] It is hard to imagine that many customers will want to use regular public switched networks for transborder multimedia services at the exorbitant international tariffs encouraged by the accounting and settlement process. If the system is not changed, the Internet may well remain the sole means for the general public to browse the GII.

Some alternatives are raised in this volume, including the emergence of integrated global carriers† or the use of the Internet accounting model as a model for all information networks (this model is based on a sender-keeps-all method, and is vastly simpler and more efficient than what we have today).‡ Substantial reform of the accounting and settlements system is needed, but it is unlikely to be achieved solely within the ITU. The United States should push for its examination in the WTO. As one contributor to this volume concludes, the United States "has no obligation to cross-subsidize other countries' strategies by means of international accounting rates . . . the framework for regulating international services needs serious revision because it hinders new alternatives better suited for the distributed information revolution."††

31. The international radio and satellite regimes should be reexamined in the GII context. While the international telecommunications regime has been transformed in response to global liberalization, the international radio regime remains essentially unchanged. (There has been change *within* the regime, in its many detailed technical rules and decisionmaking procedures, but no change *of*

---

* See Cowhey, Chapter 7.
† See Cowhey, Chapter 7.
‡ See Rutkowski, Chapter 9.
†† See Cowhey, Chapter 7.

the regime—that is, of its overarching purposes and principles.) One can argue that this continuity is necessary because the distribution and management of a scarce global resource still requires extensive state involvement and a heavy reliance on intergovernmental agreements. Moreover, in recent years, the ITU has improved key elements of the regime like the frequency registration system in order to enhance its efficiency. But on the whole, the regime remains one of the most rigid and bureaucratic parts of the global communications order, as is exemplified by its phone book-sized treaty instruments and laborious technical standardization process. One participant in the project suggests that some cracks are beginning to appear in these walls, as global radio systems like Motorola's Iridium project, radio-based universal personal communications, digital signal processing, and spread spectrum technology put pressure on bureaucracies to change their practices.* How well the regime fits with an increasingly market-driven global wireless environment; whether it is possible to make some of its instruments less formal and open up the decisionmaking process; and how spectrum can best be managed to promote the development of a GII are questions that merit full international consideration.

Similar questions must be asked about the international satellite regime. With the spread of private satellites and fiber optic cables, what is the proper role for an intergovernmental organization like INTELSAT in a commercialized market? INTELSAT has recently taken steps to allow a measure of competition, but it retains an overwhelming advantage over private firms like PanAmSat because of its treaty status. Many in business and government circles (particularly in the United States) thus argue that fundamental change is required. Indeed, INTELSAT's own management has proposed privatizing the organization and relinquishing its role as a "carrier's carrier" so that it can compete directly for end users. However, privatization might not increase efficiency, and would raise problems in relation to INTELSAT signatories. Others have suggested decentralizing the organization into more flexible and market-friendly regional units. These and other proposals merit serous international debate, and not just within INTELSAT. Further, any reform must promote global connectivity and affordable prices for developing countries.

III. THE NEW INTERNATIONAL TRADE IN SERVICES REGIME

32. Regulatory convergence should be pursued by like-minded states on the basis of mutual recognition. The completion of the GATS and the institutionalization of ongoing services negotiations in the WTO are the most important development in the global telecommunications policy order since the creation of the ITU in 1865.[43] But the GATS does not address the central obstacle to effective governance of the GII: the problem of regulatory fragmentation among national jurisdictions.† When transnational networks are themselves markets for

---

* See Rutkowski, Chapter 9.
† Kalypso Nicolaïdis makes this argument in Chapter 11.

financial, professional, audiovisual, and many other services, domestic regulatory structures can cause significant distortions even if they were not formulated with trade barriers in mind. Seamless transborder digital commerce requires a framework to bridge the gaps between such structures, and the OECD and the WTO are thinking though the options.

Kalypso Nicolaïdis argues that "regulatory integration will be at the core of the GATS agenda in the coming decade, but the institutional makeup of the trade regime will need to adapt if multilateral institutions are to serve as a hub for horizontal regulatory cooperation among public and private actors from different countries. . . . The challenge is to find a mode of collective governance that can stem the dangerous tendency toward seeing asymmetry in regulation between countries as evidence of trade distortion and, in the name of leveling the playing field, using trade leverage to engage in 'regulatory imperialism,' whereby those countries with the greatest market power impose their domestic rules on vulnerable exporters." The United States must resist that temptation. Full harmonization of national regulations would be too demanding and divisive, would inevitably invite power plays, and could undermine legitimate domestic policies that are not fully compatible with narrow trade criteria. Instead, the best way forward may be to expand on the mutual recognition model pioneered by the European Union, while striving to ensure that this does not undermine nondiscrimination.*

33. Multilateral competition policies and rules on restrictive business practices are needed. A closely interrelated piece of "unfinished business" on the GATS agenda is the international coordination of competition policies or what, in the United States, would be called antitrust policies. Global telecommunications liberalization has moved both private and publicly-owned operators into an integrated environment where market power can easily be abused, both at home and abroad. As such, the traditional line between trade and competition policy issues is evaporating, and agreements will be needed about the management of concentrations of power and their abuse. To that end, some have called for the international equivalent of Judge Harold Greene's court, which broke up AT&T.† The rub is that even the normally procompetitive United States may not be ready to subject its domestic market structures to international scrutiny. But while major corporations would be sure to resist, it would be a mistake for the U.S. government to give in to such pressure. Multilateral cooperation on antitrust policies could provide a mechanism to address problems like national monopolies abroad and international accounting and settlements; moreover, it could open up vast opportunities not only for TNCs, but also for small- and medium-sized firms. "Trade rules need to reach beyond governmental measures to discipline private business practices that directly affect access

---

* See Nicolaïdis, Chapter 11.
† See Rutkowski, Chapter 9.

to domestic markets by foreign suppliers."* Mergers and acquisitions, restrictive business practices, and so on should be subject to fair competition rules, whether the entities involved are private or publicly-owned.

34. Cultural and linguistic diversity should be promoted in the GII. This is an issue on which project participants may be divided. Some believe that U.S. policy on international trade in audiovisual services is overly aggressive, hypocritical, and counterproductive.† It is overly aggressive because it seeks to impose on foreign countries a narrow U.S. conception of cultural content as a commodity to be bought and sold. It is hypocritical because U.S.-made television shows and movies already dominate the world's screens, yet the domestic United States market is one of the most closed in the world.[44] And it is counterproductive because it aggravates—needlessly, given the already huge U.S. market shares—important relationships with our trading partners and generates suspicions about U.S. intentions for the GII. By placing its audiovisual services under the GATS disciplines, the United States has limited its ability to use unilateral measures to pressure its trading partners, but continued conflict remains in the cards.

Looking to the future, trade in culture may raise new, difficult-to-resolve problems in the GII. For example, if and when the public can access transnational multimedia services other than on the Internet, what rules should apply? Some U.S. analysts believe that the GATS agreement on advanced telecommunications services would automatically be invoked, insofar as interactive audiovisual involves customization and could thus be considered just a value-added service.‡ While European governments have rejected this interpretation, France's efforts at the G-7 conference to win its neighbors' support for an expansion of the cultural exception to future broadband networks went nowhere. Assuming that there will someday be sufficient capacity for a multiplicity of information sources, domestic and foreign, the rationale for "cultural protectionism" will need to be reexamined in light of differences between the new information infrastructure and traditional mass media.

IV. OTHER ISSUE-AREAS

35. The United States should support multilateral coordination on effective privacy protections in the GII. The United States has posed the single greatest obstacle to multilateral cooperation on privacy protection. As with trade in culture, U.S. policymakers consistently have advanced a narrow view that other countries' privacy policies on transborder data flows (TDF) are motivated only by naked protectionism.[45] They argue that any measures limiting the movement of personal data files across borders must be intended to hamper

---

* See Nicolaïdis, Chapter 11.

† This is the editor's view.

‡ For discussion, see Nicolaïdis, Chapter 11.

U.S.-based corporations and stimulate local data processing industries. Accordingly, the United States fought to prevent the establishment of multilateral rules in the late 1970s, and instead pushed successfully for the adoption of voluntary guidelines within the OECD.* These guidelines have proven to be ineffectual and routinely ignored, but the Clinton administration continues to hold up voluntary guidelines as the solution to the next generation of privacy issues associated with the GII.

Nevertheless, the United States may soon find it in its interest to adopt adequate privacy protections. The European Union is going ahead with a plan to establish a strong and coherent regional framework, which could be used in some instances to prevent the corporate transmission of personal data into the American privacy-free zone. The United States should therefore articulate a workable international policy on TDF; its efforts should focus on achieving functionally similar results rather than harmonizing specific information standards.[†] If the administration adopted reasonably firm guidelines, a mutual recognition deal might then be struck with the European Union to avoid future problems.[46]

36. Multilateral development programs need greater support and coordination and should give greater attention to applications. In 1984, the ITU-sponsored Maitland Commission reported that two-thirds of the world's population had no local access to telephone services.[47] There has been some progress since then, particularly in the wealthier parts of Asia, but on the whole the quantitative disparities between rich and poor nations have persisted and the qualitative disparities appear to be growing.[48] The fragmented globalization of technologies and markets in which the "second" and "third" worlds' major cities and elite populations are connected to the global grid while the majority of their people are not is a cause for concern.[‡] Given the cross-sectoral importance of communications, the preservation of "information slums" stunts and distorts socioeconomic development and raises problems that bear directly on the "first" world's self-interest, normative considerations aside. But in response, "the most advanced countries and international organizations . . . have delivered a clear message that developing countries can expect little but lip service unless they privatize their telecommunications firms and open their markets for equipment and services to international competition."[††] Even when developing countries have privatized and liberalized, the mood in most industrialized countries— especially the United States—generally has precluded increased financial support. Hence, although the Clinton administration's GII initiative lists the promotion of universal service as one of its five guiding principles, the rhetoric is not backed up by resources.

---

* See Reidenberg, Chapter 10.
† See Reidenberg, Chapter 10.
‡ See Garcia, Chapter 3, and Lanvin, Chapter 8.
†† See Lanvin, Chapter 8.

Recognizing the rich countries' budgetary constraints and the poor countries' own responsibility for institutional reform, a number of pragmatic changes can be made in intergovernmental assistance programs. Four are highlighted here.* First, multilateral organizations with specialized expertise in this area—principally, the ITU, the World Bank, and the various regional telecommunications bodies—should focus on "increasing international awareness of the opportunities and challenges of the global information economy."† International institutions could play a more vital role in providing access to information about technology and markets, the costs and benefits of alternative institutional structures, model contracts with corporations, and so on, in addition to offering "big picture" ideas about the importance of telecommunications in an information economy. Staffing policies might need to be reevaluated in this light.

Second, specialized organizations should play a more active role in mobilizing both private and public funds. On the private side of the equation, the ITU has had difficulty over the years convincing corporations to contribute their share to its technical assistance and other programs. Changing direction, the ITU is now helping to launch a private sector multilateral organization called WorldTel, which will direct billions of dollars in private investment to the very poorest countries for infrastructure development—particularly rapidly deployable wireless networks—under build-operate-transfer agreements. With the right contractual terms, this new approach could be beneficial for corporations and developing countries alike. On the public side, existing resources need to be reallocated, since multilateral lending institutions such as the World Bank dedicate only 0.5 percent to 3 percent of their annual lending to telecommunications.[49] Additional funds will inevitably be needed, perhaps from sources other than the average taxpayer. For example, Nobel Prize-winning economist James Tobin has proposed financing information infrastructure modernization in the developing world through a tax on speculative international currency transactions. Proposals like this merit serious consideration.

Third, multilateral institutions in other areas—such as the International Labor Organization, the World Health Organization, WTO, and UNCTAD—should incorporate a focus on information infrastructure into their programs and coordinate more closely with specialized bodies like the ITU to that end. Finally, greater attention should be given to applications of new technology. Pumping hardware into developing countries is not enough; technical assistance programs must also focus on how to configure user-friendly systems that can help solve pressing problems in health, education, the environment, and so forth. UNCTAD's trade efficiency initiative provides an excellent example of such "telecoms with a purpose"—an approach other organizations should seek to replicate.‡ The

---

* These suggestions build on Lanvin, Chapter 8.
† See Lanvin, Chapter 8.
‡ Lanvin is the driving force in this initiative, described in Chapter 8.

proposal at the G-7 Summit for a new World Bank fund called InfoDev may be a step in this direction.

37. Governments should remove artificial barriers to the development of the global Internet. Essentially the same types of advanced technology are now being deployed around the world. However, the specific technical standards adopted for these systems often vary across countries and regional blocs, as does the institutional and economic organization of communications industries more generally.* Disparate governmental and corporate interests will continue to mean uneven progress toward the seamlessly interconnected and universally accessible global network of broadband networks envisioned by Vice President Gore and others. The private networks of transnational corporate users in industries like banking and automobile manufacturing will incorporate the latest advanced capabilities available, but offerings to the general public will, as always, lag well behind. As such, it will be a long time before consumers around the world can download foreign television programs or send multimedia messages across national borders via public switched networks. In the near term, the principal publicly accessible part of the GII will be the one we already have: the global Internet. Indeed, in a real sense, the Internet *is* the public GII.

In light of this fact and the ringing endorsements of a GII issued at the February 1995 G-7 summit and other international meetings, one might expect that governments around the world would be doing everything they could to facilitate the Internet's expansion. Unfortunately, this is not always the case. While the Internet was experiencing explosive growth in the United States during the early 1990s, many governments abroad impeded its development within their countries through high tariffs, restrictive licensing requirements, and other measures. In part, this was due to a "not invented here" mentality, but more fundamentally it was a matter of organizational control. Many national telecommunications monopolies saw the Internet's comparatively anarchic structure and user-driven patterns of standardization and development as a threat to their control over telecommunications.[50] Further, they viewed the Internet solely as a form of bypass, in that users can send messages anywhere for the cost of a local call, rather than rely on overpriced long-distance and international telephone, fax, and data services. The situation has improved in recent years and the Internet now comprises over fifty thousand interoperating networks in more than ninety countries. Nevertheless, in many cases access remains the exclusive province of national monopolies and is largely available to people working in large organizations or universities. Moreover, some authoritarian states still restrict the Internet in an effort to control the flow of information to and from their citizens. Governments professing enthusiasm for a GII should ensure that the general public has affordable access, preferably from a number of independent, competing providers.

---

* See Garcia, Chapter 3.

V. REINVENTING MULTILATERAL INSTITUTIONS

38. A comprehensive review and modernization of multilateral institutions and activities relevant to the GII is needed. If multilateral institutions and activities did not already exist, what would we have to invent in order to promote and govern the GII? Is the existing mix of organizations and regimes adequate to handle all the issues involved, or are there important cases that would fall between the jurisdictional cracks? Conversely, which existing organizations and functions would we no longer need? Questions such as these merit further investigation and broad debate within the international community. On the 50th anniversary of the Bretton Woods agreement, member governments and independent analysts analyzed the International Monetary Fund and the World Bank to determine what worked, what did not, and what was needed for the future. The same sort of assessment might be useful in thinking about the GII and the larger transformation to a global information economy. In addition, the major international institutions should conduct their own internal analyses and undertake modernization programs as appropriate. The United States should encourage such initiatives rather than impede them, as has happened with the ITU's reform program.

39. A World Interconnection Forum (WIF) should be created to serve as a focal point for cooperation on applications. One participant in this project suggests that a WIF be created under the auspices of the WTO to provide networked access to information on domestic regulations and other rules and procedures pertaining to trade.* The WTO and other international organizations should certainly take steps to facilitate networked access to their information by the public, but there may be a better use for the acronym: the promotion of international cooperation on applications. A WIF with both public and private sector participation and a small secretariat staffed by networking, software, and applications experts could, with a modest budget, perform a number of useful functions. It could provide national governments and other international organizations with assistance on projects over the Internet or in person as appropriate. It could serve as a focal point for collaboration between national agencies, international organizations, and other entities on programs that cut across their individual missions. It could host fora for discussion among stakeholders from around the world—from librarians to human rights activists to multimedia entrepreneurs and beyond. And it could serve as an integrated global library of applications projects and provide people in the public, private, and noncommercial sectors with networked one-stop shopping when looking for information about what has been done and ideas about what could be. Such an organization would fill an important gap in the multilateral matrix and could help to accelerate the deployment and public utilization of the GII.

---

* See Nicolaïdis, Chapter 11.

40. Intergovernmental institutions should be opened to democratic input by diverse stakeholders, and should encourage networked access to their information by the public. Most of the international organizations involved in GII-related activities are off limits to the world's publics. Citizens cannot attend meetings or obtain the documents needed to understand what is going on within various agencies, yet they are being encouraged to embrace the GII enthusiastically. This was demonstrated clearly at the G-7 conference, where public interest groups were relegated to holding an alternative meeting at another venue while government bureaucrats and corporate executives gathered to extol the GII's potential contributions to democracy and civic culture. This sort of exclusion is a mistake on more than normative grounds. In the age of distributed information resources, there are thousands of small- and medium-sized firms, nonprofit organizations, and individuals that could contribute much to international institutions' programs if given the opportunity. Curiously enough, the ITU—an institution that in the past was completely closed to public scrutiny—offers a good model to build upon. Over the past few years, the ITU has changed its rules to facilitate participation by a wider range of companies, has allowed some members of the public to attend certain meetings, and has established free Internet access to thousands of documents. Recognizing that actual negotiations do need to be closed in certain cases, international organizations nevertheless should strive to increase their transparency—if nothing else by setting up World-Wide Web sites stocked with non-sensitive materials. As the Clinton administration has found in the United States, it is important and beneficial to allow a wide variety of stakeholders to contribute their views and expertise on how the new information infrastructure should be governed. This is a lesson that foreign governments and international organizations should take to heart.

*   *   *

This volume began with the observation that we have reached a turning point in the history of communications and information. Public and private sector decisions made over the next few years will contribute to a new national policy model that will shape industry structure and behavior for years to come, as happened during the early years of telecommunications, broadcasting, and cable television. Arguably, the stakes are even higher this time around because of the different historical context: the information revolution and transition to a (global) information economy mean that every industry is increasingly dependent on networks and information resources, as are individuals and organizations within the noncommercial sector. As such, the ripple effects of NII policy choices will reach far beyond the boundaries of the communications and information business to affect everything from education, popular culture, and the public sphere of ideas to health care, banking, manufacturing, and so on. In light of these cross-sectoral effects, it is essential to ensure that the kinds of issues raised by the participants in this project are thought through in a systematic and farsighted manner that accommodates the range of stakeholders and variety of uses of the new information infrastructure. As Vice President Gore said at last year's public interest summit, "We need to insure that the NII, just like the personal computer, is open and accessible to everyone . . . [if so,] the future will look and work like the Internet today."[51] Unfortunately, it is not clear that we are on the road to such a future.

‖ NOTES

INTRODUCTION

1. Congressman Edward Markey, former chairman of the House Subcommittee on Telecommunications and Finance, quoted in Jonathan D. Blake and Lee J. Tiedrich, "The National Information Infrastructure Initiative and the Emergence of the Electronic Superhighway," *Federal Communications Law Journal* 46, no. 3 (1994): 398.

2. Figure cited in "Prepared Statement of Reed E. Hundt," in *S.1822, The Communications Act of 1994*, Hearings before the Committee on Commerce, Science, and Transportation, United States Senate, 103d Congress, 2d sess., February 23, March 2 and 17, and May 4, 11, 12, 18, 24, and 25, 1994 (Washington, D.C.: U.S. Government Printing Office, 1994), p. 58. Hundt is the chairman of the Federal Communications Commission.

3. Digital cash refers to techniques being developed for charging for economic transactions over the Internet.

4. Distance education involves the provision of educational instruction and learning through telecommunications technologies; for example, a lecture can be delivered to a remote location via a television monitor.

5. For example, as the Commerce Department's Thomas Sugrue recalls, ". . . even the best analogies can be taken to extremes. Within the government, many of us were so taken with the superhighway analogy, that we began to rack our brains for ways to extend the image. Certain kinds of communications were compared to off-ramps or different styles of roads. But then I began to receive memos explaining how one element of the communications system was the concrete in the highway, and another was the lane markers. Then, diagrams appeared with median strips and clover leafs. Opponents began to use the metaphor against us, saying, for example, there was no need to build six-lane expressways to everyone's driveway. Finally, the use of the highway analogy engendered considerable confusion about the role of government in this process. In short, things were getting entirely out of hand. The metaphor was overtaking reality. So, although we still use 'information superhighway' as a metaphor, we have tried in recent months not to overextend the analogy." See Sugrue, "The Government's Role in the National Information Infrastructure," *Media Law and Policy* 3 (Winter 1994): 18.

6. As Vice President Gore noted later, "The idea of the federal government constructing, owning, and operating a nationwide fiber-optic network to the home is a straw man. . . . It is a phony choice that some people see between a federal public network and no federal involvement at all." Quoted in Mitchell Kapor, "Where Is the Digital Highway Really Heading? The Case for a Jeffersonian Information Policy," *Wired*, July/August 1993, pp. 53–59, 94.

7. For more detailed discussion of systems integrators, see Chapter 1 in this volume.

8. National Telecommunications and Information Agency, Information Infrastructure Task Force, *The National Information Infrastructure: An Agenda for Action* (Washington, D.C.: U.S. Department of Commerce, September 15, 1993), pp. 5–6.

9. The same point is made in Jane Griffith Bortnick and Marcia S. Smith, *The Information Superhighway and the National Information Infrastructure*, CRS Report for Congress 94-112 SPR (Washington D.C.: Congressional Research Service, March 22, 1994), p. 1.

10. Brian Kahin, "Information Technology and Information Infrastructure," in Lewis M. Branscomb, ed., *Empowering Technology: Implementing a U.S. Strategy* (Cambridge, Mass.: MIT Press, 1993), p. 138.

11. For a highly accessible overview of some of the coming technologies, services, and applications, albeit from a narrowly business-oriented standpoint, see the articles in "The Information Revolution," Special Bonus Issue, *Business Week* (1994).

12. For a popular introduction to life on the net, see Howard Rheinghold, *The Virtual Community: Homesteading on the Electronic Frontier* (Reading, Mass.: Addison-Wesley, 1993).

13. An exception is the occasional and roundly denounced "spamming" by people who violate community norms and mass mail unwanted ads via the Internet. Spamming was much debated last year after two people sent unwanted advertisements electronically, despite thousands of requests to stop. Adding insult to injury, they then wrote a book explaining how to do it, the title of which will not be advertised here.

14. Lewis M. Branscomb, "Balancing the Commercial and Public-Interest Visions of the NII," in *20/20 Vision: The Development of a National Information Infrastructure* (Washington, D.C.: National Telecommunications and Information Administration, March 1994), p. 7.

15. George Gilder, *Life after Television: The Coming Transformation of Media and American Life*, rev. ed. (New York: Norton, 1994), pp. 60–61.

16. For a good illustration of how the same advanced network technology can be configured in distinctly different ways in accordance with varying organizational interests and institutional frameworks, see Robin Mansell, *The New Telecommunications: A Political Economy of Network Evolution* (Newbury Park, Cal.: Sage, 1993).

17. For a pro-AT&T interpretation of this history, see Alan Stone, *Public Service Liberalism: Telecommunications and Transitions in Public Policy* (Princeton: Princeton University Press, 1991). For an assessment that is sharply critical of AT&T, see Gerald Brock, *The Telecommunications Industry: The Dynamics of Market Structure* (Cambridge, Mass.: Harvard University Press, 1981).

18. For a fascinating account of this struggle, which has some direct parallels with the NII debate of today, see Robert W. McChesney, *Telecommunications, Mass Media, and Democracy: The Battle for the Control of U.S. Broadcasting, 1928–1935* (New York: Oxford University Press, 1993).

19. Ithiel de Sola Pool, *Technologies of Freedom* (Cambridge, Mass.: Harvard University Press, 1983).

20. Quoted in John Carey and Mark Lewyn, "Yield Signs on the Info Interstate," *Business Week*, January 24, 1994, p. 89.

21. Quoted in Ken Auletta, "Under the Wire," *New Yorker*, January 17, 1994, p. 49.

22. On the critical role of the federal government in launching the computer industry, see Kenneth Flamm, *Creating the Computer: Government, Industry, and High Technology* (Washington, D.C.: Brookings Institution, 1988).

23. See the Appendix to Part I by Solomon in this volume.

24. This is only one aspect of a complex argument about the historical evolution of control techniques and technologies. For the rest of the story, see James R. Beniger, *The Control Revolution: Technological and Economic Origins of the Information Society* (Cambridge, Mass.: Harvard University Press, 1986).

25. These corporate pressures were not the only factors at work, but they were certainly among the most important and are frequently underemphasized in standard accounts of telecommunications liberalization. For treatments of their domestic and international

effects, respectively, see Dan Schiller, *Telematics and Government* (Norwood, N.J.: Ablex, 1982); and William J. Drake, "Asymmetric Deregulation and the Transformation of the International Telecommunications Regime," in *Asymmetric Deregulation: The Dynamics of Telecommunications Policies in Europe and the United States*, Eli M. Noam and Gerard Pogorel, eds. (Norwood, N.J.: Ablex, 1994), pp. 137–203.

26. See Chapter 7 by Cowhey in this volume.

27. Some of the issues introduced in this brief section are explored at greater length in the conclusion to this volume.

28. For fairly representative samples of corporate opinion on broad principles, see *Vision for a 21st Century Information Infrastructure* (Washington D.C.: Council on Competitiveness, May 1993); and *Competition Policy: Unlocking the National Information Infrastructure* (Washington D.C.: Council on Competitiveness, December 1993). The council also has some members from labor unions and academia.

29. It should be noted that opinions are not uniform on such issues. While many providers of information services, Internet access, and so on worry about the entry of the major carriers into their lines of business, others believe that the resulting competition will have a positive, market-expanding effect. One recent survey of 300 information service providers found that 72 percent favored RBOC provision of in-region services. See Arlen Research, *1993 Information Industry Opinion Survey* (Wellesley, Mass.: Marx Group, November 1993), p. 5.

30. For two excellent discussions of the Internet's implications for the broader NII, see *Computer Professionals for Social Responsibility, Serving the Community: A Public Interest Vision of the National Information Infrastructure* (Palo Alto: CPSR, October 1993); and National Research Council, NRenaissance Committee, *Realizing the Information Infrastructure: The Internet and Beyond* (Washington, D.C.: National Academy Press, 1994).

31. For further elaboration of François Bar's views, see Chapter 2 in this volume and his "Network Flexibility: A New Challenge for Telecom Policy," *Communications & Strategies*, no. 2 (Montpellier, 1991): 113–23.

32. The term is from Esther Dyson, George Gilder, Jay Keyworth, and Alvin Toffler, "A Magna Carta for the Knowledge Age," *New Perspectives Quarterly* (Fall 1994): 26–37.

33. In the 103d Congress, the bills were *H.R. 3626, Antitrust Reform Act of 1993*, 103d Congress, 1st sess., November 22, 1993; *H.R. 3636., National Communications Competition and Information Infrastructure Act of 1993*, 103d Congress, 1st sess., November 22, 1993; and *S. 1822, Communications Act of 1994*, 103d Congress, 2nd sess., February 3, 1994. In the 104th Congress, the bills were *S. 652, Telecommunications Competition and Deregulation Act of 1995*, 104th Congress, 1st sess., March 30, 1995; and *H.R. 1555, Communications Act of 1995*, 104th Congress, 1st sess., May 3, 1995.

34. For example, the Senate Commerce Committee, the home of the Hollings bill, reportedly received $2,046,886 in contributions from the communications industry during the previous election cycle. Joe Abernathy, "Highway Robbery: Selling the Net," *PC World*, May 1994, p. 61.

CHAPTER 1

1. Gerald W. Brock, *The Telecommunications Industry* (Cambridge, Mass.: Harvard University Press, 1981), p. 112.

2. Alan Stone, *Public Service Liberalism* (Princeton, N.J.: Princeton University Press, 1991), p. 138, referring to J. J. Nate, "Texas and Telephones," *Telephony* (1904): 332–34; E. J. Mock, "Story of the States—Illinois," *Telephony* (January 1907): 1–8; B. G. Hubbell,

"Independent Telephony in the Empire State," *Telephony* 6 (1903): 210, 211; and A. B. Cass, "Independent Telephony in Southern California," *Telephony* (November 6, 1909): 459.

3. Richard Wiley, "Competition and Deregulation in Telecommunications," *Telecommunications in the United States: Trends and Policies* (Dedham, Mass.: Artech House, 1981), pp. 53–54.

4. FCC Industry Analysis Division, *Trends in Telephone Service* (Washington, D.C., 1991), p. 3, Table 1.

5. Gene Kimmelman and Mark N. Cooper, "Telephone Penetration," in *After the Breakup: Assessing the New Post-AT&T Divestiture Era*, ed. Barry G. Cole (New York: Columbia University Press, 1991), p. 384, Figure 9.10.

6. FCC Industry Analysis Division, Monitoring Report, CC Docket no. 87-339, July 1991, p. 39.

7. The official poverty line for a household of four was $11,012 in 1987.

8. FCC, Monitoring Report, Table 1.4, pp. 30–39. Statistics for low-income blacks and Hispanics seem particularly subject to substantial swings from one reporting period to the next.

9. Ibid., and FCC, *Monitoring Report*, 1995.

10. Ibid.

11. Robert Crandall, *After the Breakup: U.S. Telecommunications in a More Competitive Era* (Washington, D.C.: Brookings Institution, 1991), p. 61.

12. FCC, *Trends in Telephone Service*, p. 14, Table 10.

13. Crandall, *After the Breakup*, pp. 112–15.

14. See Jonathan M. Kraushaar, "Service Quality," in *After the Breakup: Assessing the New Post-AT&T Divestiture Era*, ed. Barry G. Cole, p. 256. The FCC has adopted this method on the premise that the magnitude of change in service quality as it is reported may be affected by extraneous factors, while the important variable is the nature or direction of the change.

15. Ibid., based on FCC, Common Carrier Bureau, "Update on Quality of Service for the Bell Operating Companies," June 1990.

16. Walter G. Bolter and James W. McConnaughey, "Innovation and New Services," in *After the Breakup: Assessing the New Post-AT&T Divestiture Era*, p. 295.

17. Marianne G. Bye, *Telecommunications Services Industry Follow-up: Regional Holding Companies Third-Quarter 1991 Results; 1984–91 Quarterly Data Sheets* (New York: Shearson Lehman Brothers, November 19, 1991).

18. Robert W. Crandall and Jonathan Galst, "Productivity Growth in the U.S. Tele-communications Sector: The Impact of the AT&T Divestiture" (Unpublished paper, Brookings Institution, Washington, D.C., 1991), Table 1.

19. Daniel P. Reingold, "Max Headroom: The Baby Bells Are Not All Alike" (New York: Morgan Stanley Investment Research, 1990), p. 15.

20. Michael A. Noll, "The Effects of Divestiture on Telecommunications Research," *Journal of Communications* 37, no. 1 (1987): 73–80.

21. Kenneth Labich, "Was Breaking up AT&T a Good Idea," *Fortune*, January 2, 1989, pp. 82–87.

22. FCC, Monitoring Report, p. 154. The FCC's regulatory changes reduced long-distance carriers' access charge payments in part by instituting an end-user line charge and by cost shifting from inter- to intrastate service; these figures account for this saving.

23. FCC, *Trends in Telephone Service*, Table 25 ("AT&T's Share of Interstate Minutes").

24. Ibid., p. 29.

25. William E. Taylor and Lester D. Taylor, "Postdivestiture Long Distance Competition in the United States," *American Economic Review* 83, no. 2 (May 1993): 186.

26. Northern Business Information, 1991.

27. U.S. Department of Commerce, U.S. Industrial Outlook, 1993, p. 29–1.

28. Ibid.

29. Bye, *Telecommunications Services Industry Follow-up.*

30. Danish Ministry of Communications, *Political Agreement on Telecommunications Structure*, press release, June 22, 1990.

31. Oftel, Annual Report, London, Her Majesty's Stationery Office, 1991.

32. Richard Kramer, *A Faith That Divides: Competition Policy in European Telecommunications* (Philadelphia: University of Pennsylvania, Annenberg School for Communication, 1991).

33. Eli M. Noam and Richard Kramer, "Telecommunications Strategies in the Developed World: A Hundred Flowers Blooming or Old Wine in New Bottles," in *Telecommunications in Transition: Policies Services and Technology in the European Community*, ed. Charles Steinfield (Newbury Park, Calif.: Sage, 1994).

34. Eli M. Noam, "Beyond Liberalization: From the Network of Networks to the System of Systems," *Telecommunications Policy* 18, no. 4 (May/June 1994): 286–94.

35. Eli Noam, "Beyond Liberalization: Reforming Universal Service," *Telecommunications Policy* (1994), vol. 18, no. 9 (November 1994): 687–704.

36. Eli Noam, "Beyond Liberalization: The Impending Doom of Common Carriage?" *Telecommunications Policy* 18, no. 6 (August 1994): 435–52.

37. Ibid.

38. Eli Noam, *Interconnecting the Networks of Networks*, (Washington, D.C.: American Enterprise Institute, forthcoming).

CHAPTER 2

1. Daniel Bell, *The Coming of Post-Industrial Society: A Venture in Social Forecasting* (New York: Basic Books, 1976).

2. Stephen Cohen and John Zysman, *Manufacturing Matters: The Myth of the Post-Industrial Economy* (New York: Basic Books, 1987).

3. Ramchandran Jaikumar, "From Filing and Fitting to Flexible Manufacturing," HBS Working Paper, no. 88-045 (Boston, Mass.: Harvard Business School, 1988).

4. For opposite views of these developments, see, for example, Michael Piore and Charles Sabel, *The Second Industrial Divide* (New York: Basic Books, 1984), and Martin Kenney and Richard Florida, *Beyond Mass Production: The Japanese System and Its Transfer to the U.S.* (New York: Oxford University Press, 1993).

5. See, for example, Michael Burawoy, *Manufacturing Consent: Changes in the Labor Process Under Monopoly Capitalism* (Chicago: University of Chicago Press, 1979), and Larry Hirschhorn, *Beyond Mechanization: Work and Technology in a Post-Industrial Age* (Cambridge, Mass.: MIT Press, 1984).

6. For two contrasted points of view, see Robert Reich, "Who Is Us?" *Harvard Business Review* (January–February 1990): 53ff, and Laura Tyson, "They Are Not US," *The American Prospect* (Winter 1991): 37ff.

7. James Womack et al., *The Machine that Changed the World* (New York: Rawson Associates, 1990).

8. Alfred D. Chandler, *The Visible Hand: The Managerial Revolution in American Business*, (Cambridge, Mass.: Belknap Press, 1977), p. 207.

9. For more on the meanings and measures of globalization, see Chapter 3 in this volume.

10. Stephen Cohen makes this argument in *Corporate Nationality Can Matter a Lot*, Berkeley Roundtable on the International Economy (BRIE) Working Paper no. 44 (University of California, Berkeley, BRIE, 1990); and BRIE, *Globalization and Production*, BRIE Working Paper no. 45 (University of California, Berkeley, BRIE, 1991).

11. These points are explored in greater detail in François Bar and Michael Barrus, with Benjamin Coriat, *Networks and Business Strategies: Issues for Competitiveness and*

Telecommunications Policy, Proceedings of an OECD-BRIE conference presenting the results of the OECD-BRIE Telecommunications User Group Project (Paris, OECD; Bruxelles, CEE: October 19 and 20, 1989).

12. Static flexibility is "the ability of a firm to adjust its operations at any moment to shifting conditions in the market," while dynamic flexibility is "the ability to increase productivity steadily through improvements in production processes and innovation in product." See Cohen and Zysman, *Manufacturing Matters*, pp. 131–34.

13. Benjamin Coriat, "Globalization," in *Variety and Mass Production: The Metamorphosis of Mass Production in the New Competitive Age* (Paris: CREI, Université Paris XIII, 1993).

14. For descriptions of related cases in other manufacturing industries, see "Manufacturing à la Carte," *IEEE Spectrum*, special issue (September 1993), pp. 24–85.

15. For detailed analyses of the Toyota case, see Yasuhiro Monden, *Toyota Production System: Practical Approach to Production Management* (Norcross, Ga.: Industrial Engineering and Management Press, Institute of Industrial Engineers, 1983), and Benjamin Coriat, *Penser à l'envers* (Paris: Christian Bourgeois, 1991).

16. This description of the C4 Program is based on interviews in Detroit with GM and EDS personnel, as well as trade press articles.

17. François Bar and Michael Borrus, *The Future of Networking in the U.S.* (Brussels: Commission of the European Communities, RACE, 1992).

18. François Bar and Michael Borrus, *From Public Access to Private Connections: Network Policy and National Advantage*, BRIE Working Paper no. 28 (University of California, Berkeley, BRIE, 1987).

19. François Bar, "Network Flexibility: A New Challenge for Telecom Policy," *Communications & Strategies*, no. 2 (1991).

20. François Bar, "Configuring the Telecommunications Infrastructure for the Computer Age: The Economics of Network Control" (Ph.D. diss., University of California, Berkeley, 1990) (available as BRIE Working Paper no. 43).

21. The distinction between the two forms of learning is from Nathan Rosenberg, *Inside the Black Box: Technology and Economics* (Cambridge: Cambridge university Press, 1982).

22. Kenney and Florida have referred to the resulting process as "innovation-mediated production" in *Beyond Mass Production*.

23. These policy recommendations are developed in Bar and Borrus, *Future of Networking in the U.S.*

CHAPTER 3

1. Information Infrastructure Task Force, "The National Information Infrastructure: Agenda for Action," *Telephony* (March 28, 1994): 10–11.

2. Steven Tisch, "Gore Urges Ambition for Global Telecom," *Telephony* (March 28, 1994): 10–11.

3. As cited in Daniel Czitrom, *Media and the American Mind: From Morse to McLuhan* (Chapel Hill: University of North Carolina Press, 1982), pp. 11–12.

4. As Ruggie describes, "Perhaps the best way to put it is that the globe itself has become a region in the international system albeit a nonterritorial one. Thus, global does not mean universal. Instead the concept refers to a subset of social interactions that take place on the globe. This subset constitutes an inclusive level of social interaction that is distinct from the international level, in that it comprises a multiplicity of integrated functional systems, operating in real time, which span the globe." John Ruggie, "International Structure and International Transformation: Time and Method," in *Global Changes and Theoretical*

Challenges: Approaches to World Politics for the 1990s, ed. Ernst-Otto Czempiel and James N. Rosenau (Lexington, Mass.: Lexington Books, 1989), p. 31.

5. See for one discussion, Eli M. Noam, "A Theory for the Instability of Public Tele-communications System," in *The Economics of Information Networks*, ed. Cristano Antonelli (Amsterdam, The Netherlands: North-Holland, 1990), pp. 107–29.

6. For a discussion of market failures in networked technologies, see Joseph Farrell and Garth Saloner, "Horses, Penguins, and Lemmings," in *Product Standardization and Competitive Strategy*, ed. H. Landis Gable (Amsterdam, The Netherlands: North-Holland, 1991).

7. Lucian W. Pye, ed., *Communications and Political Development* (Princeton, N.J.: Princeton University Press, 1993), p. 4.

8. For a discussion of how communications systems affect political, economic, and cultural opportunities, see *Critical Connections: Communications for the Future* (Washington, D.C.: U.S. Government Printing Office, 1990).

9. As described by McClelland, "Perhaps for the first time communications are being recognized as a strategic underpinning of civilization, as important perhaps as the provision of clean water. The implicit fear for many countries must be that an inadequate communication infrastructure will forever keep a national economy out of the world economic structure that is shaping up for the 21st century, in addition to the fear that government relinquishes an important political tool. It is into this cauldron that telecom is being pushed. . . ." Stephen McClelland, "The International Dimension: PTTs," *Telecommunications* (June 1992): 31. See also, for a comparison of the U.S. and European approaches in this regard, Loretta Anania, "The Protean Complex: Are Open Networks Common Markets?" in *The Economics of Information Networks*, ed. Cristano Antonelli (Amsterdam, The Netherlands: North-Holland, Elsevier Science 1990), pp. 367–95.

10. See for discussions of how markets tend to collapse social values, Roger Friedland and A. F. Robertson, *Beyond the Marketplace: Rethinking Economy and Society* (New York: Aldine de Gruyter, 1990); and Thomas Michael Power, *The Economic Pursuit of Quality* (Armonk, NY: E. E. Sharpe, 1988).

11. See for a history and an overview, John H. Davis, Neil F. Dinn, and Warren E. Falconer "Technologies for Global Communications," *IEEE Communications Magazine* (October 1992): 35–43.

12. As described by Davis, Dinn, and Falconer, "Due to technology, the costs of transport for transatlantic cable systems has been going down dramatically ever since TAT-1 was installed in 1958. In today's equivalent dollars, each circuit in TAT-1 cost about $6 million. By 1993, each circuit in a new fiber-optic cable will cost as little as $4,000. In 35 years, the equivalent cost of a transatlantic cable circuit has been reduced by a factor of 1500. . . . Stimulated by lower costs and higher quality, demand has grown dramatically, leading to rapid increase in capacity being deployed." Ibid., p. 38.

13. David Prince, "What Are the Implications for Your Business of the Global Telecom Revolution," *Management Accounting* (June 1992): 31.

14. Still to be completed in the area of Asia are the HAW-5 cable, linking the U.S. mainland to Hawaii; the ACRIM EAST, connecting Hawaii and New Zealand; the PACRIM WEST, joining Australia and Guam; the ASPAC system linking Singapore, Malaysia, the Philippines, and Guam. In addition, by 1997, the PC-5 loop, providing two fiber-optic cables with alternative routes between Japan and the United States, going through Guam and Hawaii, is scheduled for completion (Gary C. Staple, *The Global Telecommunications Traffic Report—1991* [London: International Institute of Communications, 1991], p. 5).

15. Patrick Flanigan, "VSAT: A Market and Technology Overview," *Telecommunications*, (March 1993): 19–24.

16. George Lawton, "Russia: Satellites Offer Users Hope," *Communications Week International*, October 5, 1992.

17. The Organization of American States has been asked to coordinate the frequencies and other requirements of three new satellites that will provide regional service and are scheduled to begin operations in 1995. However, a recent proposal to develop a Latin American satellite system, which was introduced at the first American Regional Telecommunications Development Conference, failed for lack of support. See Karen Lynch, "Americas Set Telecom Goals," *Communications Week International*, April 20, 1992, p. 33.

18. Bruce Wiley, "Business Networks in Latin America," *Telecommunications* (January 1993): 32; see also Bruce Wiley, "A Latin American Telecommunications Primer," *Telecommunications* (January 1993): 31–33.

19. Ellen Hoff, "The Race Is On: Asian Carriers Increasingly Must Adjust to Regional Competition," *Communications Week International*, January 18, 1993.

20. Ibid.

21. Anton Lensen, "Concentration in the Media Industry: The European Community and Mass Media Regulation" (Washington, D.C.: The Annenberg Washington Program, 1992), p. 8.

22. Dawn Hayes, "Space Segment Still Out of Reach," *Communications Week International*, December 1991, p. 12; and Dawn Hayes, "Satcom Protest," *Communications Week International*, December 16, 1991, p. 4.

23. Andreas Evagora, "VSAT Advances Pitched in Europe," *Communications Week International* , April 5, 1993, p. 23.

24. For a discussion of this technology, see Office of Technology Assessment, *The 1992 World Administrative Radio Conference: Technology and Policy Implications* (Washington, D.C.: U.S. Government Printing Office, May 1993), chap. 2.

25. Planning is presently under way for approximately twelve LEOS, one of which is intended to serve Latin America, another the Soviet Union. All together these twelve LEOS systems would require the use of about three hundred satellites and cost approximately $7.3 billion. Evagora, "VSAT Advances Pitched in Europe."

26. Joseph Pelton, "Will Small Sat Markets Be Large?" *Satellite Communications*, February 1993, pp. 39–42; See also Andreas Evagora, "Doubts Shadow LEO Gains," *Communications Week International*, December 14, 1992, p. 6; and John Yeoman, "Getting Mobile Off the Ground, *Communications Week International* , August 10, 1992, p. 18.

27. OTA, *1992 World Administrative Radio Conference*, p. 124.

28. C. Bruce Page, "Microwave Vendors Gear Up for New Growth," Re: Transmission, April 6, 1992, pp. 10–11.

29. Cellular technology is a non-wire-line radio technology that transmits information via the public spectrum. The technology is evolving rapidly, promising even greater efficiency and system capacity.

30. Jennifer Shenker, "Interconnect Revisited," *Communications Week International* , July 6, 1992, p. 3.

31. In 1992, growth in the Asia Pacific region outstripped that in Europe and the United States, with the number of subscribers up from 2.7 million to 4 million. Paging and telepoint technologies are similarly advancing at an amazing rate. "The Coming of Seamless Networks—Part II," *Telecom Highlights International* 15, no. 14 (November 3, 1993): 17.

32. The U.S. Cellular Telecommunications Industry Association originally came out in support of time division multiple access (TDMA). However, six of the Bell Regional Operating Companies are now conducting trials using code division multiple access (CDMA), a technology that was first developed in the military but that is now being adapted for civilian use by Qualcomm. See Andreas Evagora, "Common Mobile Components Sought," *Communications Week International*. March 2, 1992, pp. 1, 6; Tom Crawford, "Why CDMA Should Be the Choice for Digital Cellular Carriers," *Telecommunications* (March 1993): 49–51; and John Williamson, "Bids for Global Recognition in a Crowded Cellular World," *Telephony* (April 6, 1992): 37–40.

33. Karen Lynch, "U.S. Seen Losing Cellular Advantage," *Telecommunications* (March 22, 1993): 44.

34. Ibid. Such an agreement would initially harmonize components for mobile terminals and later be extended to a wider range of terminal and customer premises equipment. Terminal prices reflect the fact that, until now, terminal companies have had to develop proprietary interfaces between different manufacturers' products. U.S. chip manufacturers have not been involved in these negotiations.

35. Still in the concept phase, FPLMTS is seen by the Europeans to be the successor to GMS. As presently conceived, it would consist of a terrestrially based system (perhaps supplemented by satellite technology) using large towers located throughout a region to provide an array of voice, data, and video services to mobile users. The United States has remained somewhat skeptical of this technology, on the grounds that clear service definitions and specifications have yet to be developed. Instead, the United States has concentrated on the development of personal communication systems. See OTA, *1992 World Administrative Radio Conference*, p. 77.

36. Ibid. Although the United States and the Europeans disagreed at the World Administrative Radio Conference (WARC-92) about bandwidth allocation for FPLMTS, the Federal Communications Commission (FCC) has recently proposed to allocate PCS bandwidth that falls, to a considerable degree, in the same range of spectrum as that allocated at WARC to FPLMTS. Thus, even if the United States and Europe pursue different technologies, an FCC decision such as this would still allow for a viable, worldwide mobile communication system.

37. One key player was Advanced Network Services (ANS), a nonprofit joint venture between IBM, CMI, and Merit Networks, which had been established in 1990 to operate the National Science Foundation backbone network. In May 1991, ANS spun off a for-profit subsidiary—ANS CO+RE—to develop a T1 Internet backbone, the excess capacity of which it was then free to sell to commercial users. Equally important, in 1991, Performance Systems International (SPA), BARRNET, CERFNET, and UUNET Technologies (later followed by U.S. Sprint) joined together to form the Commercial Internet Exchange Association (CIX) with the aim of providing interconnection between their commercially owned services. See Gary H. Anthese, "Commercial Users Move onto Internet," *Computerworld*, November 25, 1991, p. 50; Alton Hoover, "Scenarios for Internet Commercialization," *Telecommunications* (February 1992): 190; and Karen Lynch and Donne Pinsky, "IP Means Business," *Communications Week International* , September 15, 1992, p. 62.

38. rs.internic, nis.nsf,sri.com (Lottor), Landweber as of April 1993.

39. Usage of IP networks breaks down as follows: 50 percent commercial, 29 percent research, 9 percent government, 7 percent defense, and 4 percent educational. For the Internet, the corresponding figures are 29 percent commercial, 48 percent research, 7 percent government, 9 percent defense, and 6 percent educational. rs.internic, nis.nsf, sri.com (Lottor), Landweber as of April 1993.

40. In Europe, networks based on the IP protocol have been developed in conjunction with E-bone, a consortium of thirty-five groups including regional networks, universities, and laboratories dedicated to creating an open, value-added multiple protocol network. Now commercial IP networks are also under way in Europe.

41. Ibid.

42. EDI is a computer-based method whereby companies order, invoice, and bill their products and services. Such common transaction functions as invoices, shipping notices, and bills, which have traditionally entailed the transfer and processing of paper documents, are replaced by electronic transfers between the businesses' computers.

43. The European EDI service market generated $100 million in revenue in 1991 and is predicted to reach $500 million in 1996. The North American EDI market, which suffers from

less fragmentation, is expected to reach $1.5 billion by 1998. See Donne Pinsky, "AT&T, BT, and IBM Connect Euro EDI," *Communications Week International* , October 19, 1992, p. 48.

44. Alice LaPlante, "Handling Standards That Aren't Standard," *Computerworld*, April 13, 1990, p. 80.

45. As described by the European telecom manager for Westinghouse Communication System. "It is not always easy to match up ISDN in the United States with ISDN in Europe. And in countries where we need it most, like Spain, ISDN is just not available." Cited in Terry Sweeney, "Mix and Match Networks," *Communications Week International* , April 5, 1993.

46. Frame relay technology has experienced a similar fate. Many multinational corporations would use frame relay as a networking technology if it were available in more than a few major cities. In February 1993, Finland was the only country in Europe where a public frame relay service was available. Although customized services are available from public network providers, the costs are prohibitive for most companies. Frame relay also suffers from interoperability problems, since unlike x.25, frame relay networks use different trunking protocols. See David Yuen and Bob Reinhold, "Frame Relay Faces National Boundary," *Network World*, April 13, 1992, pp. 17–18; and Donne Pinsky, "So Close Yet So Far," *Communications Week International* , January 18, 1993, p. 3.

47. Virat Patel, "Pan-European High-Speed Networks: Fact or Fiction," *Telecommunications* (April 1992): 5–7.

48. See Staple, *Global Telecommunications Traffic Report*, p. 17

49. A subsequent and more modest effort was undertaken in 1990 with the establishment of the General European Network. It will provide eight channels of two megabits per second each between nodes in Frankfurt, London, Madrid, Spain, Paris, and Rome. The European Telecommunications Standards Institute (ETSI) is also presently involved in developing a standard for a connectionless broadband data service that would be based on the IEEE 802.6 standard. Jennifer Schenker, "European Carriers Set Plan for Broadband Network," *Communications Week International*, August 10, 1992, p. 35.

50. Donne Pinsky, "Euro-Infrastructure Group Proposed," *Communications Week International* , May 11, 1992, p. 6.

51. Gary C. Staple, ed., *TeleGeography 1992: Global Telecommunications Traffic Statistics and Commentary* (Washington, D.C.: International Institute of Communications, 1992), p. 61.

52. Ibid., p. 62.

53. Colin D. Long, "Interconnection in Europe: The Legal and Regulatory Dimension," *Telecommunications Policy* (July 1991): 95–98.

54. McClelland, "International Dimension," pp. 31–37; and Bruce Wiley, "Latin American Telecommunications Primer."

55. Graham Finnie, "Interconnect in Europe: The Legal and Regulatory Dimension," *Telecommunications Policy* (July 1991): 95–98.

56. Thus, depending on the particular case, it might be best for a firm to disperse many of its production facilities—such as design modification, fabrication, and assembly—to foreign countries, and to focus its own domestic production on the fabrication of key components. Alternatively, a firm might decide to manufacture a product domestically, but transfer abroad such downstream activities as distribution, sales, marketing, and service. See Michael Proter, ed., *Competition in Global Industries* (Boston: Harvard Business School Press, 1986).

57. See Peter Cowhey and Jonathan Aronson, *Managing the World Economy: The Consequences of Corporate Alliances* (New York: Council on Foreign Relations, 1993); see also, David Lei and John W. Slocum, Jr., "Global Strategy, Competence-Building and Strategic Alliances," *California Management Review* (Fall 1992): 81–97. Once generally associated with U.S. industries, multinationals are, themselves, becoming increasingly global in nature. For example, globally networked Japanese and European firms, while differing somewhat

in style from U.S. firms, have grown significantly in number in the course of the past decade. See Bruce Kogut, Weijian Shan, and Gordon Walker, "Knowledge in the Network and the Network as Knowledge," in Gernot Grabher, *The Embedded Firm: On the Socioeconomics of Industry Networks* (London: Routledge, 1993), p. 90.

58. Karen Lynch, "Global Services Showdown: Communications and Computer Companies Jockey to Redefine Themselves as International Service Providers," *Communications Week International*, May 11, 1992, p. 22.

59. Bruno Lanvin, "Information Technology and International Trade," in *Trading in a New World Order: The Impact of Telecommunications and Data Services on International Trade in Services*, ed. Bruno Lanvin (Boulder, Colo.: Westview Press, 1992), p. 4; See also OTA, *U.S. Telecommunications Services in European Markets* (Washington, D.C.: U.S. Government Printing Office, August 1993).

60. Meheroo Jussawalla, "Introduction," in *Global Communication Policies: The Challenge of Change*, ed. Meheroo Jussawalla (Boulder, Colo.: Westview Press, 1992), p. 4.

61. See "Soros Makes Investment in Viatel," *Telecom Highlights International* 15, no. 41 (October 13, 1993): 5.

62. Rita Das, Kenneth E. Ferrere, and Douglas P. Macbeth, "Global Networks—The Easy Way," *AT&T Technology: Products, Systems and Services* 8, no. 4 (1993): 10.

63. OTA, *U.S. Telecommunications Services in European Markets.*

64. "Telecommunications Is the Measure of Economic Growth," *Telecom Highlights International* 15, no. 49 (October 6, 1992): 2.

65. Staple, *Telegeography*, 1992,

66. An FCC report, *Preliminary 1992 Section 43.61 International Telecommunication Data*, reported that U.S. customers spent about $10.8 billion for international services in 1992, an increase over the previous year of $1.0 billion. In 1992, U.S. customers made 1.7 billion calls and received 1.1 billion. According to the FCC report, U.S. carriers supplied 13,013 private line circuits between the United States and international points in 1992. See "FCC Releases International Traffic Data," *Telecom Highlights International* 15, no. 39 (September 29, 1993): 13.

67. *Information Technology Outlook 1992* (Paris: Organization for Economic Cooperation and Development, 1992), pp. 6–7.

68. Karen Lynch, "Global Service Showdown: Communications and Computer Companies Jockey to Redefine Themselves as International Service Providers," *Communications Week International*, May 11, 1992, p. 22.

69. OTA, *U.S. Telecommunications Services in European Markets.*

70. Ibid.

71. The positive effect that increased information exchange had on trade was clearly exhibited, for example, with the development of the first transatlantic cable in 1866. Before the completion of the Atlantic telegraph, New York financiers were unwilling to trade in London markets, unless prices were very attractive, because it took six weeks to clear prices and have their orders executed there. The completion of the undersea cable radically changed the situation, bringing about an immediate convergence of prices on both sides of the Atlantic. Kenneth D. Garbade and William L. Silber, "Technology, Communication, and the Performance of Financial Markets in 1840–1975," *Journal of Finance* 33 (June 1978): 819–32.

72. A tariff describes the services available, the conditions under which they will be provided, the cost structure, and the price of service. For a discussion of tariffing and the general factors on which it is based, see Phyllis Bernt and Martin Weiss, *International Telecommunications* (Carmel, In.: Sams Publishing, 1993), pp. 37–53.

73. Ibid. See also Robin Mansell, "Tariffs: Who Should Pay for the Telecommunications Network?" *Telecommunications* (July 1993): 41–45.

74. Bernt and Weiss, *International Telecommunications*.

75. Mansell, "Tariffs," p. 41.

76. Bernt and Weiss, *International Telecommunications*, pp. 83–97.

77. OTA, *U.S. Telecommunications Services in European Markets*.

78. Ibid. See also, "Study Says EC Firms Favor Opening Telecommunications," *Telecom Highlights International* 15, no. 39 (September 29, 1993): 7.

79. "The Countries of Europe React to Spur of Global Competition," *INTUG News*, October 1993, p. 4.

80. See for one discussion, G. John Ikenberry, "The International Spread of Privatization Policies: Inducement, Learning and Policy Bandwagoning," in *The Political Economy of Public Sector Reform and Privatization*, ed. Ezra N. Suleiman and John Waterbury (Boulder, Colo.: Westview Press, 1990), pp. 99–106; see also, Bjorn Wellenius, Peter A. Stern, Timothy E. Nulty, and Richard D. Stern, eds., *Restructuring and Managing the Telecommunications Sector* (Washington, D.C.: World Bank, 1989).

81. According to one estimate, by 1995, 70 percent of the world's access lines will be privately managed, as opposed to 45 percent in 1992. See "What Are the Implications for Your Business of the Global Telecom Revolution," *Management Accounting*, June 1992, p. 46; See also, McClelland, "International Dimension," p. 31.

82. In its Green Paper on telecommunications, the Commission of the European Communities called for a competitive community-wide telecommunications market by 1992. In June 1993, the Council of Ministers decided to postpone until 1998 (and in the case of some member states even longer) the mandatory liberalization of communication service. See Commission of the European Communities, *Towards a Competitive Community-Wide Telecommunications Market in 1992: Implementing the Green Paper on the Development of the Common Market for Telecommunications Service and Equipment* (Brussels: Commission of the European Communities, 1988).

83. The Dutch and the Danish state-owned telecommunications and postal companies are scheduled for privatization later this year. Spain and Portugal have decided recently to open up their networks to private investors.

84. As described by McClelland, "Internationalization has become the day, with a first strike at someone else's territory as the preferred method of defense." McClelland, "International Dimension," p. 31.

85. "The Countries of Europe React to Spur of Global Competition," *INTUG News*, October 1993, p. 305; and "Deutsche Telekom Plan Approved," *Telecom Highlights International* 15 (July 7, 1993): 27.

86. See "Singapore Starts Telecom Sell-Off," *Telecom Highlights International* 15, no. 34 (August 25, 1993): 5.

87. "World Bank Urges Telecom Liberalization," *Telecom Highlights International* 16, no. 8 (February 23, 1994); and "More Notes on the S.E. Asia Market Potential," *Telecom Highlights International* 16, no. 11 (March 16, 1994): p. 3. Taking advantage of Western capital and expertise, Malaysia aims to increase telephone subscribers from 2.3 million today to 7.8 million by the year 2000.

88. Restructuring usually takes place by selling companies privately. In some cases, however, they are first sold to a consortium, the stock of which is later sold publicly. Sometimes the U.S. portion of the consortium and the stock is later sold to institutional investors. See Margaret Price and Marlene Givant Star, "Privatization Brings Global Opportunities," *Pensions and Investments*, July 26, 1993, p. 3; for a comparison of the approaches being followed in Latin America, see Randa Zadra, "The Telecommunication Revolution in Latin America," *Telecommunications* (July 1993): 33–36.

89. For example, Matav, the state telephone company of Hungary, recently sold 30 percent of its holdings to an American-German consortium made up of Ameritech

Corporation and Deutsche Bundespost Telekom, for $850 million. This deal is the largest to date in Eastern Europe. The consortium will have exclusive rights to provide local service in 299 regions for the next eight years. See "Western Ventures Helping Eastern Europe," *Telecom Highlights International* 16, no. 2 (January 12, 1994): 1.

90. "World Bank Sets Telecom Aid Rules," *Telecom Highlights International* 16, no. 11 (March 16, 1994): 4.

91. Ibid.

92. Patricia Kranz and William Glassgall, "Bells Are Ringing All Over the World," *Business Week*, December 27, 1993, pp. 96–97.

93. Price and Givant Star, "Privatization Brings Global Opportunities," p. 3.

94. OTA, *U.S. Telecommunications Services in European Markets*. The Modified Final Judgment (MFJ), which broke up the Bell system in 1984, prohibited the Regional Bell Operating Companies from engaging in a number of manufacturing, long distance, information, and video services. This restructuring led to the Regional Bell Operating Companies to invest in these activities. Legislation presently before Congress would repeal, or at least weaken, many of these restrictions.

95. "Notes on the Possible Privatization of Inmarsat," *Telecom Highlights International* 15, no. 49 (December 8, 1993): 15.

96. Ibid.

97. Peter Heywood, "Fresh Air for Cross Border Networking," *Data Communications International*, April 1993, p. 83.

98. Klaus Grewlich, "Agenda for the 1990's," in *Global Communication Policies: The Challenge of Change*, ed. Meheroo Jussawalla (Boulder, Colo.: Westview Press, 1992), pp. 233–34.

99. Paul Strauss, "The Struggle for Global Networks," *Datamation* 39, no. 8 (September 15, 1993): 26.

100. See Stephen McClelland, "Global Chess," *Telecommunications,* international edition (July 1993).

101. Richard House, "A Global Mating Game," *Institutional Investor*, September 1993, p. 65.

102. "Global Telephone Networks Expand," *Corporate Growth Report*, June 14, 1993, p. 6685.

103. AT&T has a 50 percent holding in WorldPartners, which will have its headquarters in New York. KDD will have a 30 percent share, and Singapore Telecom a 20 percent share. Associate members include the Australian long distance carrier, Telestar, Korean Telecom, and Unitel. See Dan O'Shea, "AT&T Details Global Plan," *Telephony* (May 31, 1993): 7.

104. "More Notes on the Franco-German Talks," *Telecom Highlights International* 15, no. 47 (November 24, 1993): 1.

105. "Three's a Crowd," The *Economist*, November 13, 1993, pp. 72–73.

106. "Spanish PTT to Link with Unisource," *Telecom Highlights International* 15, no. 49 (December 8, 1993): 7.

107. Jonathan Levine, "A Counter Coup in Telecom," *Business Week*, November 15, 1993, pp. 51–52.

108. "More Notes on the Franco-German Talks," *Telecom Highlights International* 15, no. 47 (November 24, 1993): 1.

109. See, for one discussion, Ikenberry, "International Spread of Privatization Policies."

110. For a discussion of culture as an increasing source of cultural conflict, see Samuel P. Huntington, "The Clash of Civilizations," *Foreign Affairs* 72, no. 3 (Summer 1993): 22–50; For a discussion of culture as it is related to trade and the global economy, see Benjamin R. Barber, "Jihad vs. McWorld," *Atlantic Monthly*, March 1992, pp. 261–69; see also, Diana Quintero, "American Television and Cinema in France and Europe," *The Fletcher Forum of World Politics* 18 (Summer–Fall 1994): 115–28.

APPENDIX TO PART I

1. An order of magnitude is ten times, best expressed as a logarithm.

2. For example, H.R. 3636 required various levels of regulation of the Internet, which is simply a large number of computers and computer systems internetworking through common protocols and bypassing the public switched network to some extent. The bill also required new, common-carrier-like regulation of digital uses of the airwaves formerly restricted only to analog broadcasting uses. Defining services, applications, costs, and who is the user and who the carrier will be a continual, fruitless definitional nightmare— as has been the case in the FCC's Computer I, II, and III Inquiries, dating back to the mid-1960s. Happily, these provisions were not retained in subsequent legislation.

3. Possibly the only network element with a future is the conduits for fiber optics and some of the more modern fibers themselves. The fiber is not a major cost, but the underground installation, being labor intensive, is—and interface optoelectronics follow the same product cycle lifetime as other electronic equipment. Hence, carriers are installing as much "dark" fiber as they can afford, on the theory that installation costs will rise and the future fiber will be no better than present designs. This, too, is a gamble: that the fibers and their conduits are going to be useful despite continual technological change, and that no other technology (such as computer-controlled radio spectrum) may come along to displace current investments—or, more importantly, that the demand for fiber and conduits will continue to grow. There is a great deal of dark fiber being installed in the United States, some in the most unlikely places; competition alone will keep prices close to commodity cost levels.

4. The time frame for this development is probably no more than ten years; chips are on the market that today perform 400 million instructions per second.

5. "Recursiveness" in computerese.

6. The essence of a "von Neumann" machine.

7. Converting analog waveforms into digital code that computers can read is not the same as computerization, but it is an essential first step toward computer manipulation. (All human inputs and outputs are essentially analog, although some digital processing takes place in the brain and ear.) Not only human information can be digitized; physical objects, telemetry, and so on can be represented digitally for machine processing. Hence, sculptures can be "imaged" with laser beams in three-dimensional and high-resolution, and the information captured and translated into codes that can then replicate the sculpture by carving a duplicate physical object.

8. For example, analog information, such as a sound wave, is "sampled" at specific intervals as specified by a mathematical theory of information. The theory, developed by Claude Shannon during World War II as part of a cryptographic exercise, demonstrates that it is possible to reconstruct a waveform if certain sampling parameters are met. Modern electronics and optical technology have made digitization very cheap and easy to control. Speech, music, and still images are commonly stored and transmitted using this technique (most telephone calls in the United States today are digitized before being transmitted, some even at the telephone receiver; compact disks are an example of very high quality digitization). Television and video are just entering the digital era, and high-resolution digital imaging promises to revolutionize both motion pictures and scientific photography, since digitization lends itself readily to digital signal processing as well as simple transmission and storage.

9. Theory indicates that with proper electronic interfaces, ordinary telephone wires, depending on distance from the central switching office, deterioration of the insulation, and power applied to the wires, can carry about one thousand times the capacity of an unmodified wire pair—or about ten million bits per second versus about ten thousand for the unmodified

pair. Simple, unshielded wire pairs used in Ethernet local-area networks carry about ten Megabits/second today, but the distances are much shorter than the average three thousand feet of a telephone "loop" from the customer to the central switching office. The telephone companies are experimenting with a technology called asymmetric digital subscriber loop (ADSL), which can be added to existing wire pairs to yield six Megabits/second in one direction (more than sufficient for several VHS-quality television signals), and sixty-four Kilobits/second in the other direction, for signaling and two or more voice or low-speed data connections. There is a growing family of such technologies to enhance the existing copper wire plant, all coming under the rubric of digital "pair-gain" carrier, ranging from the so-called T-1 carrier, which dates back to the early 1960s and permits bidirectional 1.5 Megabits/second on two wire pairs (sometimes termed "four-wire"), to integrated service digital networks (ISDNs) offerings, which permit two sixty-four-Kilobit voice circuits plus sixteen Kilobits/second signaling on one wire pair, or a 1.5 Megabit, twenty-three-voice channel circuit on four-wire circuits.

10. Termed "orthogonal frequency division multiplexing" (OFDM).

11. Richard J. Solomon, "Computers and the Concept of Intellectual Property," in *Electronic Publishing Plus,* ed. Martin Greenberger (White Plains, N.Y.: Knowledge Industry, 1985); and Richard J. Solomon, *Intellectual Property and the New Computer-Based Media* (U.S. Congress, Office of Technology Assessment, Washington, D.C., August 1984). A solution to the problem is offered in Branko Gerovac and Richard J. Solomon, "Protect Revenues Not Bits—Identify Your Intellectual Property," in *Proceedings of the June 1993 MIT-Harvard Conference on Protection of Intellectual Property in a Digital World* (Cambridge, Mass.: Interactive Multimedia Association, March 1994). This author first identified these problems for a digital world in "Transborder Data Flows: Requirements for International Cooperation," Policy Implications of Data Network Developments in the OECD Area (with Ithiel Pool), *ICCP* vol. 3 (Paris: OECD, 1980); Pool and Solomon, "Intellectual Property and Transborder Data Flows," *Stanford Journal of International Law* (Summer 1980); and Solomon and Pool, "The Regulation of Transborder Data Flows," *Telecommunications Policy* (September 1979).

12. Stored-program machines are designed to hand over control to other machines ("interrupts"), depending on complex "states" of their programs.

13. It is also different from the control concepts found in early resource-sharing networks where the mainframe had a master-slave relationship to the terminal, even going so far as to use a protocol to lock the keyboard of the remote device when data could not be accepted by the communications link.

14. The Internet is a network of networks, interconnecting (or more precisely "internetworking") more than ten thousand networks worldwide, comprising today about thirty million users—and growing. Connectivity is achieved through a suite of data protocols for virtual networking, creating a form of virtual cyberspace for data and information flows. A host of mixed physical connections on public switched and private tandem circuits carry the actual transmissions, but these are completely invisible to the users. Most of the investment in and processing for the Internet takes place on customer-owned and operated local networks and appliances. Not only is the network user-controlled and mostly user-owned, but the user community, through the Internet Engineering Task Force (IETF), devises the protocols, applications software, and administrative devices for operations, maintenance, and interworking. For more information, see the Chapter by McKnight and Neuman in this volume.

15. For a discussion of how this evolved into so-called high-level data controls, see Richard J. Solomon, "New Paradigms for Future Standards," in *The Economic Dimension of Standards in Information Technology,* Report no. DSTI/ICCP/EIIT/90.4 (Paris: OECD, August 1990). Portion published in *Communications & Strategies,* no. 2 (Montpellier, France, 1991).

16. An analogy could be made to a conductor assigned to one railroad car on a long train of cars. The conductor knows who is in her car, and even knows where each passenger is

to get off. This is the level "below" the conductor. The conductor can walk from one end of the car to the other, but not to the next car; she "knows" her car is connected to a train (which is the level "above" her car), and she knows when the train stops and who gets off where, but she knows nor cares little about the rest of the train (that is not part of her job). The information about the passengers is self-contained within the car, although the car is part of a train that is taking the passengers to their destination. Replacing the train metaphor with a data packet, we have an inverse pyramid where the lowest layer connects to the actual circuit, and only the data in the center of that layer are important to the circuit, and to the data in the layer immediately above it. All the rest of the data in the layer are baggage; the packet train only knows it is to deliver the baggage-data somewhere, but cares little about how the data are packed or arranged. Indeed, if the data do not get there intact, it is not the problem of this layer. Some other layer has the responsibility to reorder, discard, or change them. If every part of the railroad had to worry about every other part all the time, the overhead would cause so much congestion that nothing would move; this is the basic philosophy behind designing a network model that determines reference points in a total system architecture for different network functions.

17. W. Stallings, *Handbook of Computer-Communications Standards: The Open Systems Interconnection Model*, vol. 1 (New York: Macmillan, 1987), p. 2 (emphasis added).

18. The layer function need not be a hardware box, but can be computer software embedded either in an application program or a microchip, or some permutation of these.

19. J. McQuillan and V. Cerf, "A Practical View of Computer Communications Protocols," IEEE Document no. 137-0, 1978.

20. One of the key problems is that optimal routing algorithms often have an adverse impact on what otherwise would seem to be optimum flow control or congestion protocols for a link. Cerf notes that a routing algorithm that causes loops to be formed can lead to network congestion. Inefficient routing algorithms that require substantial network resources for their implementation and operation can render the network useless for carrying any "paying" traffic. If there is a message here, it may be that the old "divide-and-conquer" adage is misapplied in network design if one tries to design and build independent techniques for flow and congestion control and routing which do not take their interrelation into account. Despite this caveat about separating network components, Cerf points out that decomposition permits the creation of a network model composed of "horizontally partitioned layering of functions which must be performed to realize any particular application running on a computer attached to the network."

21. Steven Minzer, "Preliminary Special Report on Broadband ISDN Access," Document no. SR-TSY-000857, Issue 1, December 1987, Bell Communications Research, Livingston, N.J. Also see Zahir Ebrahim, "A Brief Tutorial on ATM [Asynchronous Transfer Mode]," March 5, 1992, available on the Internet via the World Wide Web gopher at farnsworth.mit.edu.

22. Steven Minzer in *IEEE Communications Magazine* (March 1989).

23. Richard J. Solomon, "Shifting the Locus of Control: Computers and Communications in the '90s," in *Annual Review of Communications and Society* (Queenstown, Md.: Institute for Information Studies/Aspen Institute, September 1989); Solomon, "Transborder Data Flows."

24. See L. Bertalanffy, "Der Organismus als physikalisches System betrachtet," *Die Naturwissenshaften* 28 (1940): 521–31; A. C. Burton, "The Properties of the Steady State Compared to Those of Equilibrium as Shown in Characteristic Biological Behavior," *Journal of Cellular Composition and Physiology* 14 (1939): 327–49; and Bertalanffy, *General System Theory* (New York: Braziller, 1968).

25. Bertalanffy, *General System*, p. 143.

26. Ibid., pp. 142–43.

27. Based on Samuel S. Snyder, "Computer Advances Pioneered by Cryptologic Organizations" (reprint of sanitized NSA documents; it should be noted that there are several versions of this document in circulation, with some differences among them). *Annals of the History of Computing* 2 (January 1980): 60–70; Vannevar Bush papers, Library of Congress; Bush, *Pieces of the Action* (New York: Morrow, 1970). On ERA, see Erwin Tomash and Arnold A. Cohen, "The Birth of an ERA: Engineering Research Associates, Inc. 1946–1955," *Annals of the History of Computing* 1 (October 1979): 83–99.

28. NSA funds produced a new generation of computation devices roughly every three years, and as a side effect, yielded the first computer games. Also during that decade, billions were spent by the U.S. Air Force for air defense computer-controlled radar, which spun off computer display and graphics terminals and multiprocessing machines, as well as put IBM, Digital Equipment Corporation, and the forerunner of Control Data and Cray in the forefront of global computer manufacturing. (Another side effect of the second wave was the stimulation of AT&T's microwave network and direct-distance dialing, eventually permitting low-cost transcontinental telephone calling.)

29. For example, ten pages in ten seconds using a 14.4-Kilobit/second modem instead of ten minutes on a Group 3, 9,600-bit/second fax.

30. It is not necessary for a human being to control the signaling; it can be built into the software applications, as is the case on the Internet with "gopher" and similar applications.

31. The FCC's study "Changing Channels: Voluntary Reallocation of UHF Spectrum," Working Paper no. 27 (November 1992), estimated that a six-Megahertz UHF station in the Los Angeles area would be worth $1 billion. For the nation as a whole, if hundreds of megahertz are released for new services applying new technologies, then the total value of the television spectrum would be worth far more. If we estimate that each box would cost no more than $300 if, say, 200 million were manufactured, then the value of the released spectrum is easily within the order of magnitude of the cost of the boxes. The devil, of course, would be in the details of such a transition.

32. George Taylor and Irene D. Neu, *The American Railroad Network, 1861–1890* (Cambridge, Mass.: Harvard University Press, 1959). Some exceptions were made for certain mountain, narrow-gauge western railroads.

CHAPTER 4

1. See the appendix to Part I by Solomon and Chapter 7 by Cowhey on distributive processing, both in this volume.

2. See Chapter 9 by Rutkowski in this volume.

3. See Chapter 1 by Noam in this volume.

4. See *U.S. v. Western Electric Co.*, 552 F. Supp. 131 (D.D.C. 1982), aff'd *Maryland v. U.S.*, 460 U.S. 1001 (1983); see Chapter 1 by Noam in this volume.

5. See Communications Act of 1934, Sections 309(j), 332, 47 U.S.C. 309(j), 332 (1993).

6. The FCC thus long hesitated to turn to spectrum auctions or, even today, to greater flexibility to use the allocated spectrum (such as in large blocks like television broadcasting) because of this fear of congressional retaliation. For the same reason, the agency hangs back from declaring that Section 310(b)(4) of the Communications Act allows foreign entities to own radio licenses under the public interest standard so long as U.S. companies are afforded similar opportunity in the foreign country.

7. James M. Landis, *Report on Regulatory Agencies to the President-Elect*, p. 6 (1960).

8. W. Cary, *Politics and the Regulatory Agencies* (New York: McGraw-Hill, 1967), p. 11.

9. R. Noll, ed., *Reforming Regulation* (Washington, D.C.: Brookings Institution, 1971), p. 42.

10. See, for example, *Thill Securities Corp. v. New York Stock Exchange*, 433 F2d 264, 273 (". . . the regulatory agency usually becomes dominated by the industry which it was created to regulate").

11. See F. Friendly, "Politicizing TV," *Columbia Journalism Review*, March–April 1973.

12. See Chapter 7 by Cowhey in this volume.

13. See U.S. Department of Commerce, *NTIA Telecomm 2000* (October 1988): 179.

14. See H. Geller, "The Federal Structure for Telecommunications Policy," Benton Foundation, 1989, p. 13.

15. OTA Report Brief, September 1993, p. 2. The report further concluded that "Congressional action may also be needed to strengthen the policymaking structure for international telecommunications, if this is not done by the Administration, either by taking steps to enhance the ability of the State Department's CIP, or by legislation eliminating CIP and lodging the coordination function in the Executive Office." But see p. 1, supra, for downgrading of CIP. See also discussion in the fall report, U.S. Congress, OTA, *U.S. Telecommunications Services in European Markets*, OTA-7CP-548 (Washington, D.C.: U.S. Government Printing Office, August 1993), chap. 8 of the full report.

16. Remarks of Assistant Attorney General Charles Rule to the Brookings Institute, October 5, 1988, p. 2.

17. See, for example, *MCI v. FCC*, 561 F2d 365 (D.C. Cir. 1977), cert. denied, 434 U.S. 1040 (1978) (allowing new carrier entrants to engage in toll operations on an unrestricted basis).

18. See, for example, *Schurz Communications v. FCC*, 982 F.2d 10A3 (7th Cir. 1992).

19. Rate of return regulation gives the telco a fair return on an established rate base (and is thus a cost-plus approach). Because it has been criticized as not promoting the most efficient operation (since a telco gains nothing from efficiencies if it is earning at the top of its allowed return), many states and the FCC have turned to incentive regulation that focus on the price of basic services and "freezes" then for some specified period (e.g., four years), subject to adjustments for inflation and productivity. This spurs the telco to be as efficient as possible since it keeps the ensuing financial reward (or shares it with ratepayers).

20. *Capital Cities Cable, Inc. v. Crisp*, 467 U.S. 691, 694 (1984); emphasis supplied.

21. *Louisiana Pub. Service Com. v. FCC*, 476 U.S. 355 (Louisiana), at 364, n.3, 370, 375.

22. *California v. FCC*, 798 F.2d 1515, 1518 (D.C. Cir. 1986).

23. For an excellent discussion of this subject, see Haring and Levitz, "The Law and Economics of Federalism in Telecommunications," *Federal Communications Law Journal* 41 (1989): 261.

24. See Section 332(c)(3), 47 U.S.C. 332(c)(3) (1993).

25. For example, this has been accomplished in Maryland by the state commission delineating what constitutes an evolving basic service and then allowing persons on welfare to obtain such service from any carrier, which in turn deducts the cost of such service (also set by the state) from the carrier's gross receipt tax imposed annually by the state.

26. See *MCI Telecommunications, Inc. v. AT&T*, Case No. 93-356, issued June 17, 1994.

27. Administration White Paper on Communications Act Reforms, p. 1. See also the National Information Infrastructure Agenda for Action, U.S. Department of Commerce (NTIA), September 15, 1993; Remarks of Vice President Gore at UCLA, Los Angeles, January 11, 1993.

28. See *Telecommunications Reports*, June 20, 1994, pp. 24–25.

29. H.R. 3626 and H.R. 3636, 103d Cong., 1st sess.; H.R. 103–560, 103d Cong., 2d sess.; H.R. 103–559, pts. 1 and 2, 103d Cong., 2d sess.; S. 1822 and S. 2111, 103d

Cong., 2d sess. The legislation passed in the House by an overwhelming margin, but failed in the Senate when it was not brought to the floor in the closing days of the 103d Congress.

30. The FCC 1990 Cable Report (FCC 90-276), at pars. 121–23, points up the dire consequences to the First Amendment if, rather than open, nondiscriminatory access, the cable model is adopted. In 1985, NBC sought to enter the general cable news market as a competitor to CNN. TCI, the largest cable operator, declined to let NBC compete with CNN, and NBC was forced to offer a different service, CNBC, a consumer news and business channel. At a news conference this year, Rupert Murdoch, the chairman of the News Corporation, stated that he and at least four other companies "would like to start a 24-hour news channel" but have been rejected by TCI and Time-Warner. See *Broadcasting & Cable Magazine*, January 17, 1994, p. 8; January 24, 1994, p. 22. The underlying premise of the First Amendment is that the American people receive information from as diverse sources as possible—yet in cable, the rising video force, the American people are allowed to receive only one twenty-four-hour news channel because of the cable model.

31. See H. Geller, *Fiber Optics: An Opportunity for a New Policy* (The Annenberg Washington Program of Northwestern University, October 1992), pp. 12–23.

32. *Washington Post*, July 8, 1994, p. F2.

33. "G-7 to Hold Telecommunications Parley in the Fall at the Suggestion of Clinton," *Wall Street Journal*, July 7, 1994, p. A14.

34. See U.S. Department of Commerce, *NTIA Telecomm 2000*, 1988, pp. 183–84.

35. The Executive Branch should not be allowed to make or implement policy, licensing, or adjudications directly in the electronic mass media field (unless and until there is complete deregulation of that field). The Watergate experience establishes the need for this exception. See n. 11, supra. Further, an independent collegial system is better suited to the promulgation and implementation of policy in this sensitive mass media field. It has the advantage of reflecting the viewpoints of several members, so that if the majority is embarked upon a course that raises serious constitutional or similar public interest questions, dissents can highlight the matter, bringing increased congressional or judicial scrutiny. This is not to say that the administrator could not take policy actions affecting the electronic mass media. To use an analogy, the government can and does include the mass media in general taxation schemes. So also in this field, the administrator's rules or policies of general applicability should be permissible.

36. See discussion of page 120.

37. See n.35.

38. To address mass media matters, an independent agency (like the Federal Energy Regulatory Commission, FERC, in the Department of Energy) would be housed in the FTIA and would deal with licensing, network, and multiple ownership rules, political broadcasting rules, etc.

39. See 42 U.S.C. 7173.

40. See U.S. Department of Commerce, *NTIA Telecomm 2000*, 1988, pp. 179, 184.

41. See *Multichannel News*, December 14, 1992, p. 5.

42. See "Introduction" by Drake, in this volume; M. Porter, *The Competitive Advantage of Nations and Their Business* (Boston: Free Press, 1990).

CHAPTER 5

1. We define technology policy as a set of policies intended to support the development of new technologies. More specifically, technology policy consists of government support for precompetitive research and the development of generic technologies.

2. W. Russell Neuman, Lee McKnight, and Richard J. Solomon, *The Gordian Knot: Political Gridlock on the Information Highway* (Cambridge, Mass.: MIT Press, 1995).

3. Cynthia A. Beltz, *High Tech Maneuvers: The Policy Lessons of HDTV* (Washington, D.C.: American Enterprise Institute, 1991).

4. Nathan Rosenberg and L. E. Birdzell Jr., *How the West Grew Rich: The Economic Transformation of the Industrial Revolution* (New York: Basic Books, 1986); Louis Hartz, *The Liberal Tradition in America* (New York: Harcourt Brace, 1955); and Alexis de Tocqueville, *Democracy in America* (New York: Schocken Books, 1961 [originally published in 1856]).

5. Compatibility is sometimes also called interoperability, interworking, interconnectivity, and/or interconnection, depending on the context.

6. SMPTE Header/Descriptor Task Force, "SMPTE Header/Descriptor Task Force: Final Report," *SMPTE Journal* (June 1992): 411–29; SMPTE Task Force on Digital Image Architecture, "Report of the Task Force on Digital Image Architecture, *SMPTE Journal* (December 1992): 855–91.

7. Thomas W. Malone and John F. Rockart, "Computers, Networks, and the Corporation," *Scientific American* 265, no. 3 (September 1991): 128–37.

8. Lee McKnight, "HDTV and the Technopolitics of Standardization," *Project Prométhée Perspectives*, no. 10 (June 1989): 15–20.

9. Jeffrey A. Hart, Rival Capitalists: International Competition in the United States, Japan and Western Europe (Ithaca, NY: Cornell University Press, 1992).

10. Lee McKnight, "The Making of Industrial Policy" (Ph.D. diss., MIT, 1989).

11. Lee McKnight, *Ad Hoc Corporatism and Expert Commissions* (Washington, D.C.: American Political Science Association Annual Meeting, September 1989).

12. Daniel I. Okimoto, *Between MITI and the Market, Japanese Industrial Policy for High Technology* (Stanford: Stanford University Press, 1989).

13. Jonah D. Levy and Richard J. Samuels, *Institutions and Innovation: Research Collaboration as Technology Strategy in Japan* (Cambridge, Mass.: MIT Japan Program, 1989).

14. Lee McKnight, "European and Japanese Research Networks: Cooperating to Compete," in *Building Information Infrastructure*, ed. Brian Kahin (New York: McGraw-Hill, 1992), pp. 46–58.

15. Izumi Aizu, "New Information Infrastructures in Japan: A Critical View," *Project Promethee Perspectives*, no. 23 (April 16, 1993): 33–38.

16. Ministry of Posts and Telecommunications, *Toward the Creation of a New Info-Communications Industry* (Tokyo, January 1994).

17. This use of a foreign threat is a characteristic rationale for U.S., European, and Japanese technology policy initiatives. However, although the specter of an exaggerated foreign threat may have a solid political grounding, it may not represent a sound basis for technology policy.

18. Alain Minc and Simon Nora, *The Computerization of Society: A Report to the President of France* (Cambridge, Mass.: MIT Press, 1980).

19. Clark Johnson, Richard J. Solomon, Lee McKnight, W. Russell Neuman, and Suzanne Neil, *America's Approach to HDTV: A Government-Industry Success Story* (Cambridge, Mass.: MIT Research Program on Communications Policy, 1993).

20. See Chapter 4 by Geller in this volume.

21. We have developed a model of Open Communications Infrastructure as a self-conscious technique to address the gridlock problem. See W. Russell Neuman, Lee McKnight, and Richard J. Solomon., "The Politics of a Paradigm Shift: Telecommunications Regulation and the Communications Revolution," *Political Communication* 10, no. 1 (January–March 1993): 77–94.

22. White House, *Technology for America's Economic Growth: A New Direction to Build Economic Strength* (Washington, D.C.: U.S. Government Printing Office, February 22, 1993).

23. Robert Reich, *The Work of Nations: Preparing Ourselves for 21st-Century Capitalism* (New York: Knopf, 1991).

24. The authors write as both participants and observers in the HDTV process. They participated in research related to HDTV while affiliated with the MIT Advanced Television Research Program and the MIT Media Laboratory in the 1980s. Neither is currently associated with the MIT-HDTV partnership with industry known as the "Grand Alliance." They both continue to contribute in a variety of ways to industry and government HDTV, advanced digital video, and networked multimedia standards-setting and policy fora. Opinions expressed in this Chapter are solely those of the authors.

25. Branko Gerovac and Richard J. Solomon, "Protect Revenues, Not Bits: Identify Your Intellectual Property," in Brian Kahin, ed., *Technological Strategies for Protecting Intellectual Property in the Networked Multimedia Environment*, IMA Intellectual Property Project Proceedings 1, no. 1 (January 1994): 49–62.

26. W. Russell Neuman, *The Mass Audience Looks at HDTV: An Early Experiment* (Las Vegas: National Association of Broadcasters Annual Conference, 1988).

27. Gerald F. Seib and David Wessel, "Three Free-Marketeers Shape Bush's Domestic and Economic Policy," *Wall Street Journal*, April 27, 1990, p. 1.

28. Patrick Choate, *Agents of Influence* (New York: Knopf, 1990).

29. NRenaissance Committee, National Research Council, *Realizing the Information Future: The Internet and Beyond* (Washington, D.C.: National Academy Press, 1994).

30. Jeffrey A. Hart, Robert R. Reed, and François Bar, "The Building of the Internet: Implications for the Future of Broadband Networks," *Telecommunications Policy* 16, no. 4 (November 1992): 666–89.

31. New industries that do business on the Internet are beginning to emerge; for example, "network publishing" will provide ample information at low cost, all in digital format. Much of the cost of information comes not in the creation of content, but in storage and efficient delivery—in essence, the cost of paper, printing, trucks, warehouses, and other physical distribution mechanisms, plus the cost of personnel. The Internet demonstrates that electronic networks can reduce transaction costs by orders of magnitude.

CHAPTER 6

1. While the purchase of TCI, the nation's largest cable television company, by Bell Atlantic Inc., the second largest of the Regional Bell Operating or Holding Companies, has been abandoned, other partnerships are going strong. USWest is acquiring a 25 percent stake in Time-Warner Communications, Southwestern Bell has announced plans to purchase two cable systems from Hauser Communications, Bell South is buying 22.5 percent of Prime Management Co., a cable system operator, and NYNEX is investing in Viacom and owns Liberty Cable.

2. While AT&T's monopoly practices under Theodore Vail in the early years of the century went a long way toward creating an environment that lent itself to this social policy, it was the Communications Act of 1934 that embodied the requirement for universal service at affordable cost in law.

3. For example, General Electric was not allowed to offer CNBC in a news format channel because Time-Warner and TCI, two of the nation's largest cable operators, were shareholders in Turner Broadcasting, the owner of CNN.

4. U.S. Constitution, Article 1, Sec. 8, Par. 7

5. Alexis de Tocqueville, *Democracy in America* (New York: New American Library, 1956 original printing), pp. 198–202.

6. See, for example, Barry Wellman, Peter J. Carrington, and Alan Hall, "Networks as Personal Communities," in *Social Structures: A Network Approach*, ed. Barry Wellman and S. D. Berkowitz (Cambridge: Cambridge University Press, 1988), pp. 130–84, and Mark

Granovetter, "The Strength of Weak Ties; A Network Theory Revisited," in *Social Structure and Network Analysis*, ed. Peter Marsden and Nan Lin (Beverly Hills, Calif.: Sage Publications, 1982), pp. 105–30. Audiotex services, information services available by telephone (the 800-number services), were accessed by 87 percent of households surveyed in a recent study by H. S. Dordick and R. LaRose, *The Telephone in Daily Life*, (Annenberg School, University of South Carolina, 1992.

   7. As an example of a permissive technology, the telephone has no peer. Recent research, for example, has shown that it and the new information technologies permit families to regain control of their communications environment in a way that may begin to reconstitute the healthy separation between the domestic sphere and the public sphere. See Dordick and LaRose, *Telephone in Daily Life*.

   8. Theodore Vail, *1910 AT&T Annual Report*. Historians of the telephone industry point out that an outcome of Vail's strategy of interconnecting independent telephone operators led to the acquisition of many of these companies in the early years of the twentieth century and, consequently, went a long way toward achieving his 1910 goal as well as establishing AT&T as the nation's telecommunications monopoly.

   9. Over the years the phrase "to all people of the United States a rapid efficient nation-wide and world-wide wire and radio communication service with adequate facilities at reasonable charges" has evolved into "universal service at affordable costs." The Communications Act of 1934, P.L. 416, Title 1, Sec. 1.

   10. Networks may be interconnected but if the rules of the road or protocols by which they operate do not provide for the exchange of information; that is, they are not interoperable, interconnection is of little value.

   11. For an additional discussion, see Chapter 1 by Noam in this volume.

   12. The number of households in the United States increased by 10.4 percent between November 1983 and November 1990. During this same period the percentage of households with telephones increased by 12.7 percent and the number of households without telephones decreased by 14.9 percent (Monitoring Report, CC Docket No. 87–379, January, 1991. Prepared by the staff of the Federal-State Joint Board in CC Docket no. 80-280, p. 13).

   13. Robert Crandall, *After the Breakup: U.S. Telecommunications in a More Competitive Era* (Washington, D.C.: Brookings Institution, 1991), p. 61.

   14. Herbert S. Dordick, "Toward a Universal Definition of Universal Service," in *Universal Telephone Service: Ready for the 21st Century, Annual Review* (Queenstown, Md.: Institute for Information Studies/Aspen Institute, 1991), pp. 119–22.

   15. Despite the FCC's attempts to remedy this situation, dual federal and state regulations often make this difficult. For discussion of this issue, see Chapter 4 by Geller in this volume.

   16. See, for example, Chapters 7 and 8, by Cowhey and Lanvin respectively.

   17. See Dordick and LaRose, *Telephone in Daily Life*, pp. 28–33.

   18. National Telecommunications and Information Agency, Information Infrastructure Task Force, *National Information Infrastructure: An Agenda for Action* (Washington, D.C.: U.S. Department of Commerce, September 15, 1993).

   19. Internet is the child of the ARPANET, the U.S. Defense Department experimental network designed to support military research that was born about twenty years ago. This network had proven to be of considerable value to the university and research communities, so much so that the National Science Foundation then built its network, NSFNET. The NSF promoted universal educational access by funding campus connections if the universities and colleges provided universal access on their campuses. This led to a large number of networks being constructed throughout the nation and, indeed, around the world. Today, these networks are interconnected as the Internet—a network of networks with more than fifteen million users throughout the world, growing by about 8 percent per year. It is

noncommercial and nonhierarchical, and it offers access to all who wish to pay the small telephone access charges to a node. Free-access nodes to the Internet are also growing. There is no governance of the system and no overseers, and its uses are as varied as are its users. Internet is often touted as the model for the national information infrastructure.

20. U.S. District Court, District of Columbia, Modified Final Judgement, *United States v. Western Electric Co. Inc.*, and American Telephone and Telegraph Co. Civil Action no. 82-01982, August 24, 1987.

21. Private networks installed by large corporations are often called "virtual networks" because they are created for a particular purpose and may utilize only portions of the public network.

22. Personal communications networks and systems (PCN/PCS) are small hand-held telephones that can fit into one's pocket and may eventually resemble Dick Tracy's wristwatch radio. With the rearrangement of spectrum allocations now under way, these telephone are very likely to be as ubiquitous as the telephone in the household early in the next century.

23. For example, a community of physicians may choose to operate a network for the exchange of information in their specialty. It would be available only to practitioners of that specialty. A network of school teachers, principals, and administrators can be established to discuss local educational policies. Can the physicians control access to this network and deny access to others who may have an interest in the specialty but not be formally associated with that specialty? Can the school network control access to their network denying, for example, access to parents and others who wish to participate in the policy planning?

24. For a more detailed description of the nature of tomorrow's networks and services see the appendix to Part I and Chapter 1.

25. These are the "Life-Line" and "Information Link-Up America" programs designed to serve low income households that otherwise would not be able to afford telephone service. For a discussion of these services see Dordick, "Toward a Universal Definition of Universal Service," pp. 109–40.

26. Providers of interstate telephone relay services now contribute a percentage of their revenues to a universal services fund (FCC, 47 CFR 64.604 C43 within Title 4 of the Disabilities Act, 47 USC 225B, 1d and 3b.). This is, in effect, a tax on revenue for which tax credit is given.

27. For one alternative, see *Local Competition: Options for Action Forum Report of the Eighth Annual Aspen Conference on Telecommunications Policy*, Robert M. Entman, rapporteur, Washington, D.C., 1993. See also Chapter 4 in this volume.

28. This issue of "redlining" was faced by the municipalities franchising cable television. In most cases line extension rules were written into the agreements with specific construction target dates to ensure the cabling of all areas of the franchise area in a reasonable time.

29. Charles D. Ferris quoted in Ithiel de Sola Pool, *Technologies of Freedom* (Cambridge, Mass.: Harvard University Press, 1983), p. 1.

30. Cable television developed as a nonswitched system, but is nevertheless capable of providing signals "upstream"—that is, from the home to the "head-end" or retransmission site. Teletext is a method by which text information can be inserted into the television signal without disturbing the video; it can be used, for example, to deliver electronic newspapers to the home.

31. Les Brown, "The Paradox of Democracy: More Channels, Less Discourse," *Media Studies Journal* (Fall 1992): 113–23.

32. Shoshana Zuboff, *In the Age of the Smart Machine: The Future of Work and Power* (New York: Basic Books, 1989), p. 113.

33. Ibid., p. 322

34. Ibid., pp. 322–24.

35. Daniel Brenner, "What about Privacy in Universal Telephone Service?" in *Universal Telephone Service: Ready for the 21st Century,* Annual Review (Queenstown, Md.: Institute for Information Studies/Aspen Institute, 1991), pp. 29–52.

36. Paul A. David, *Computer and Dynamo: The Modern Productivity Paradox in a Not-Too-Distant Mirror,* CEPR publication no. 172 (Palo Alto, Calif.: Stanford University, 1989).

37. Marianne G. Bye, *Telecommunications Services Industry Follow-up: Regional Holding Companies Third-Quarter 1991 Results*; 1984–91 Quarterly Data Sheets (New York: Shearson Lehman Brothers, November 19, 1991). Also, see Chapter 1 by Noam in this volume.

38. In 1991, AT&T increased staff by about forty-three thousand workers as a result of several acquisitions. See *Hoover's Handbook of World Business, 1992* (Austin, Tex.: Reference Press, 1992).

39. Bureau of Labor Statistics, Handbook of Labor Statistics, 1992 and *Monthly Labor Review,* March 1993.

40. Of the first quarter of 1994 job surge, almost one-half are part-time jobs.

41. "The Reindustrialization of America," *Business Week* (special issue), June 30, 1980.

42. Barry Bluestone and Bennett Harrison, *The Deindustrialization of America* (New York: Basic Books, 1982), pp. 3–6.

43. For a discussion of intelligent manufacturing, see Chapter 2 by Bar in this volume.

44. Ramchandran Jaikumar, "200 Years to CIM," Harvard Business School in the *IEEE Spectrum* Special Issue (September 1993): 26–27.

45. Peter T. Kilborn, in *New York Times,* September 5, 1993, section 4, p. 1.

46. Ibid.

47. Buyers and sellers can transact business on a network; hence, the network can be seen as a marketplace. These marketplaces can facilitate the purchase of goods and services including insurance, securities trading, travel services, accounting, financial management services, and many others. These industries offer opportunities for small and medium-sized enterprises to develop on an electronic network. The concept of marketplaces on electronic networks was explored in H. S. Dordick et al., *The Emerging Network Marketplace* (Norwood, N.J.: Ablex, 1980).

CHAPTER 7

1. This paper was written before September 1994. It reflects the personal views of its author and not those of the U.S. government.

2. Stephen P. Bradley, Jerry A. Hausman, and Richard L. Nolan, eds., *Globalization, Technology, and Competition: The Fusion of Computers and Telecommunications in the 1990s* (Boston: Harvard Business School Press, 1993).

3. Value-added networks for data change, store, manipulate, or otherwise act upon information from the sender before it reaches the receiver.

4. Charles H. Ferguson and Charles R. Morris, *Computer Wars* (New York: Times Books, 1993).

5. Michiyo Nakamoto and Alan Cane, "Microsoft in Video Game Link with Sega," *Financial Times,* January 18, 1994, p. 1. Don Clark, "Microsoft's Tiger Video Server Blazes New Trail," *Wall Street Journal,* February 18, 1994, p. B1.

6. Calculated from data in Roger Noll and Frances Rosenbluth, "Telecommunications Policy: Structure, Process, and Outcome," in Peter F. Cowhey and Matthew McCubbins, eds., *Structure and Policy in Japan and the United States* (New York: Cambridge University Press, 1995). About 56 percent of U.S. business personal computers are on local area networks versus about 13.5 percent in Japan. Andrew Pollack, "Now It's Japan's Turn to Play Catch-Up," *New York Times,* November 21, 1993, p. F1.

7. The higher estimate is from Reuters, as reported in *Telecom Markets*, April 1, 1993, p. 8. OTA, *U.S. Telecommunications Services in European Markets* (Washington, D.C.: U.S. Government Printing Office, 1993), p. 60.

8. Even when GATT finally began to govern government procurement, it specifically exempted telecommunications procurement decisions.

9. According to the Yankee Group, half of the VAN market is in the United States. For example, the European market for VANs (and the information services on them) was just over $1 billion per year; in contrast, the less contestable markets for leased communications circuits used in corporate networks (still largely a monopoly of the telephone company outside the United States) was much larger, about a $10 billion business, and data communications over public voice connections (a monopoly service) were about $13 billion. OTA, *U.S. Telecommunications Services in European Markets*, pp. 54–55. John J. Keller, "Ameritech, GE Plan $472 Million Data Venture," *Wall Street Journal*, December 21, 1993, p. A3.

10. Richard H. Vietor and David B. Yoffie, "Telecommunications: Deregulation and Globalization," in *Beyond Free Trade: Firms, Governments and Global Competition*, ed. David B. Yoffie (Boston: Harvard Business School Press, 1993).

11. Foreign political leaders had their own reasons for using U.S. trade demands as a focal point for national discussions on reform. The stagflation crisis of the 1970s caused political leaders to view privatization and competition as a dramatic (and profitable for government treasuries) effort to revive sluggish progress in high technology.

12. In 1974, Congress authorized the president in Section 301 of the trade bill to invoke sanctions against countries whose markets were closed in violation of GATT rules and against "unreasonable" practices, including those in services. The "Super 301" legislation of 1988 required the USTR to identify countries with particularly egregious patters of import barriers and market restrictions and enter into negotiations to correct them. Unless the president ruled otherwise, retaliations had to follow failed negotiations. Sections 1374 and 1375 of the 1988 act required special negotiations to open foreign telecommunications equipment markets and impose penalties ranging from higher tariffs through exclusion from government procurement contracts if negotiations failed. This authority lapsed until revived by executive order of President Clinton in 1994.

13. Half of AT&T's traffic will be data in the near future, and faxing constitutes half of the traffic on AT&T's Pacific network. Conventional statistics miss the change because many data messages are handled over conventional voice connections. See William Marx, Jr., "Building the Broadband Society," in *Globalization, Technology, and Competition: The Fusion of Computers and Telecommunications in the 1990s*, ed. Stephen P. Bradley, Jerry A. Hausman, and Richard L. Nolan (Boston: Harvard Business School Press, 1993), p. 361. Furthermore, business generates between 40 and 50 percent of European communications traffic. From 1986 to 1992, international telecommunication traffic expanded from about $16 billion to $42 billion (of $420 billion in total communications services) as globalizing companies integrated their far-flung operations. Gregory C. Staple, ed., *TeleGeography* 1993 (Washington, D.C.: International Institute of Communications, 1993). John Haring, Jeffrey H. Rohlfs, and Harry M. Shooshan III, *The U.S. Stake in Competitive Global Telecommunications Services: The Economic Case for Tough Bargaining* (Bethesda, Md.: Strategic Policy Research, December 1993).

14. The most successful new carrier, DDI, uses switches from DSC of Texas, partnered with Motorola for cellular outside of the Tokyo-Nagoya market and in 1993 led a consortium of Japanese firms in financing 15 percent of Motorola's proposed Iridium satellite network.

15. In 1985, Japan agreed to license new carriers committed to buying less expensive American communications satellites. The United States had to revisit this issue under Super

301. See Michael Mastanduno, "Do Relative Gains Matter? America's Response to Japanese Industrial Policy," *International Security* 16 (Summer 1991).

16. The test case for initial retaliation, Motorola's access to IDO's market, involved U.S. deadlines for installation of network equipment capable of supporting Motorola phones. Although Tokyo protested that this was something new, in reality it simply extended a key development in the global trade regime—finding ways of monitoring conduct when confronted by nontariff barriers.

17. When MCI or Sprint establishes direct telephone service with other countries, the national telephone operator contracts to return traffic in proportion to what it receives. France Telecom cannot demand better terms from AT&T for returning traffic to it. The FCC forbids U.S. companies from acquiescing to such "whipsawing." But the rules are ambiguous with regard to rapidly growing "private voice" networks.

18. A variety of innovations already had produced competition in the market for international voice services. "U.S.A. Direct" services permitted U.S. customers to contact an AT&T operator even in Paris, for example, and bill their calls as if originating from the United States. International resellers permit a customer in Rome calling Tokyo to call a number in the United States instead and have the call forwarded to the Japanese number. The U.S. rates are much cheaper than the direct call. Ironically, these devices lowered costs to consumers but worsened the U.S. deficit because they shifted traffic to the United States. Associated International Information Technology Group, Resale Report (London, 1993). The Strategic Policy Research Study for AT&T (see note 13) estimates that cost-based accounting rates would increase foreign calling to the United States by 300–400 percent while boosting U.S. demand by 60 percent. Removing pure (non-cost-related) transfer payments of $1 billion to $2 billion per year is common sense.

19. Peter F. Cowhey, "Telecommunications," in *Europe 1992: An American Perspective*, ed. Gary Hufbauer (Washington, D.C.: Brookings Institution, 1990), pp. 217–18.

20. The COS market generates revenues only in the range from $2 billion (NEC, Siemens, and Ericsson) to $4 billion per year (Alcatel, AT&T, and Northern Telecom) for the leaders, yet there are rising R&D costs (the next generation of COS could cost $1 billion in R&D) and increasing economies of scale. This forced many mergers. It also made each telephone company wary of subsidizing a national champion solely by its network purchases, thereby increasing costs just when large users were complaining. Therefore, national telephone companies liked more competition from foreign firms and adherence to global network standards in equipment to improve sourcing options.

21. Vietor and Yoffie, "Telecommunications"; Cowhey, "Telecommunications."

22. For example, data communications equipment now accounts for yearly sales of $7.4 billion in the United States, almost a third of the total for traditional telecommunications equipment. Estimate is from International Data Corporation as reported in *Business Week*, "The End of the End for 'Big Iron,'" January 10, 1994, p. 81.

23. Global networks serving the most sophisticated international customers, including European and Asian firms, disproportionately center on the United States. It is advantageous to route from the low-cost American market. There is active international competition to become a communications hub attracting the network management facilities and sophisticated traffic of many carriers.

24. U.S. and European regulatory approvals did not come until 1994. International telephone calls will still be a jointly provided service and "return traffic" shares will still be based on traditional criteria. But the new venture will move customers toward formats that bypass jointly provided services when possible.

25. Peter F. Cowhey and Jonathan David Aronson, *Managing the World Economy: The Consequences of Corporate Alliances* (New York: Council on Foreign Relations Press, 1993).

26. AT&T explicitly referred to franchising when suggesting that Telstra of Australia and Korea Telecom might market WorldSource services. *Telecom Markets* (May 27, 1993): 9–10.

27. It should also be noted that AT&T is spending $100 million on new facilities in Asia-Pacific markets and $350 million in Europe. Cowhey and Aronson, *Managing the World Economy*, chap. 7.

28. BT agreed to classification as a dominant carrier. Great Britain had already granted ISR to Canada, Sweden, and Australia. *Telecom Markets* no. 219 (March 18, 1993): 6–8; no. 240 (February 17, 1994): 2–3.

29. NTT could continue inviting firms to enter into long-term development projects designed to produce products that met NTT performance goals as long as the process was transparent and open to foreign firms.

30. The new carriers have also been subject to occasional administrative guidance in procurement and they remain minnows compared to NTT and KDD. New common carriers accounted for less than 20 percent of Japanese network investment in 1992. Ministry of Posts and Telecommunications, "An Outline of the Telecommunications Business," Tokyo, 1993, p. 18.

31. Except for applying to private phone carriers, the European Union codes mirror those of the United States.

32. According to Ambassador Mickey Kantor in *Telecommunications Reports*, April 5, 1993, p. 16.

33. Bilateral trade negotiations do not invariably disadvantage foreign countries. It depends on how they are structured. Cowhey and Aronson, *Managing the World Economy*, chaps. 8–10.

34. Miles Kahler, *Trade and Domestic Issues*, IRPS Research Report 06-93, Graduate School of International Relations and Pacific Studies, University of California, San Diego, June 1993.

35. The international VAN agreements are a precedent because they are solely an exchange of official views of the two governments, not a formal treaty, yet both governments treat them as authoritative declarations guiding their individual regulatory decisions.

36. In 1993, the U.S. telecommunications equipment industry called for a bilateral initiative to address procurement by Canada's dominant carriers, Bell Canada (BCE) and Stentor, from Northern Telecom (which is 52 percent owned by BCE). The U.S. position on European Union procurement policy implied that there was no basis for trade coverage, so the U.S. government had to use the subterfuge of refusing to represent Northern Telecom as a U.S. company until Bell Canada ended Northern's right of first refusal on sourcing. My approach would have provided conventional trade jurisdiction. *Telecommunications Reports*, February 22, 1993, pp. 11–12.

37. The quotation is from the Cross-Industry Working Team, a group representing twenty-eight U.S. corporations. "Multi-Industry Group to Focus on NII Technical Issues," *Telecommunications Reports*, November 29, 1993, p. 21.

CHAPTER 8

1. R. E. Allen, "Bringing Information to the Doorstep of the World: The Resources Needed and the Strategy to Be Followed" (paper presented at the Sixth World Telecommunications Forum, 1991). Reproduced in Forum 91, Policy Symposium, "Towards a Global Networked Society," Geneva, October 7–10, 1991, ITU, Geneva.

2. Elements of the European debate over information highways include the "Barre Report" (1992), Jacques Delors' "White Book" (1993), and the "Bangemann Report"

(1994). See, respectively, Foundation IDATE, *Trading Telecommunications: Contribution to a European Doctrine*, report published under the authority of Raymond Barre, Paris, 1992; *Growth, Competitiveness, Employment: The Challenges and Ways Forward into the 21st Century*, (White Paper), European Union, Brussels, 1993; *Europe and the Global Information Society: Recommendations to the European Council* (Brussels: European Union, 1994).

3. On January 22, 1985, Sir Donald Maitland, former ambassador of the United Kingdom to the United Nations, transmitted to the secretary-general of the International Telecommunications Union (ITU) the Report of the Independent Commission for Worldwide Telecommunications Development. This report, often referred to as the Maitland Report, or by its final title, *The Missing Link*, had been requested by the ITU Plenipotentiary of 1982. See *The Missing Link, Report of the Independent Commission for Worldwide Telecommunications Development* (Geneva: ITU, 1984).

4. As reflected in the quotation by R. E. Allen subtitling this Chapter.

5. It can be argued that for any type of good or service produced in one particular country and potentially exportable, trade will take place only if the following three conditions have been met: if the good or service is technically tradable, if it is economically tradable, and if it is legally tradable. Recent advances in information technologies and telecommunications have improved radically the technical tradability of many services (including banking, accounting, computer maintenance, and even education and health care). At the same time, dramatic reductions in the cost/performance ratio of international telecommunications have rendered such trade economically viable, meaning that the cost of sending massive amounts of information across international networks is now low enough to justify both the initial investments (such as cables, satellites, transponders, earth stations, and so on) and the usage and maintenance costs of such networks. It is thus not surprising that, in the early 1980s, some of the more technically advanced countries such as the United States began to press the international community to address the issue of international trade in services. See Bruno Lanvin, ed., *Trading in a New World Order, Atwater Series on the Information Economy* (Boulder, Colo.: Westview Press, 1993).

6. Economies of scale are realized when the cost of producing "a" unit of product X is less than "a" times the cost of producing 1 unit of X: $C(a.X) < a.C(X)$. Economies of scope appear when the cost of producing jointly product X and product Y is less than the cost of producing them separately: $C(X \text{ and } Y) < C(X) + C(Y)$.

7. For a well-documented analysis on how corporate alliances and strategies have reshaped some key economic sectors such as automobiles, semiconductors, and telecommunications, see Jonathan D. Aronson and Peter F. Cowhey, *Managing the World Economy* (New York: Council on Foreign Relations Press, 1993).

8. United Nations figures show that from 1982 to 1991, industrialized countries enjoyed real growth of gross domestic product per capita of 2 percent per year, far less than the 3.6 percent rate achieved by the "dragons" of South and East Asia, and the vigorous 7.5 percent of China. By contrast, in the same period, all other regions of the world registered a net decrease in income per capita: -0.4 percent in Eastern Europe and the former Soviet Union, -0.6 percent in Latin America, -0.7 per cent in Africa, and -3.3 percent in the Middle East and Western Asia. See *World Economic Survey 1992* (New York: United Nations, 1992), Table A.1.

9. This point was emphasized eloquently by Vice President Al Gore in his keynote address to the ITU Conference on Telecommunications and Development (Buenos Aires, March 22, 1994).

10. See the United Nations figures quoted in note 8.

11. According to the World Health Organization (WHO), Africa has seen the most rapid increase in cases of AIDS over the past eight years: WHO also points to a renewed

expansion of malaria in many regions of the world, especially those where poverty, with its attendant negative effects on sanitation and basic health care, has been spreading. Numerous studies suggest that poverty also leads to irreversible environmental damage. A famous example is that of desertification in Sahelian Africa largely because wood is the only fuel that is available to and affordable for local populations. See *Human Development Report 1993* (New York: United Nations Development Program, 1993).

12. H. Ricke, "Management of Change, in Particular in East-West Relations" (Paper presented at the Sixth World Telecommunications Forum, 1991). Reproduced in Forum 91, Policy Symposium, "Towards a Global Networked Society," Geneva, October 7–10, 1991, ITU, Geneva.

13. Recently, Robert Z. Lawrence has argued that, under certain conditions, emerging trade blocs could very well become the "building blocks" of new, open trading systems. Should telecommunications blocs become a reality, the "Lawrence conditions" would become extremely difficult to satisfy.

14. For American, European, and Japanese views on this issue, see Bruno Lanvin, ed., *Global Trade: The Revolution Beyond the Communication Revolution* (Montpelier/Paris: IDATE, 1989).

15. As the ITU was preparing for its first telecommunications and development conference (Buenos Aires, April 1994), some fresh thinking seemed to begin making its way through the arcane idiosyncrasies of this venerable institution: There is a growing awareness that a widening gap exists between the information rich and the information poor, i.e. between the developed, industrialized, high telecommunications penetration countries and the developing, low telecommunications availability countries. As this wide gap is detrimental not only to the underdeveloped areas, but also to the developed countries, new and innovative ways need to be found by all members of the ITU and their governments to hasten the growth of the telecommunications capacity and capability in underdeveloped areas of the world. From *Telecommunications Visions of the Future: A Perspective of the World Telecommunications Advisory Council* (Geneva: ITU, 1993), p. 13. See also *Tomorrow's ITU: the Challenges of Change*, Report of the High Level Committee to review the structure and functioning of the ITU (Geneva: ITU, 1991).

16. On March 1, 1993, CCITT was replaced by the Telecommunications Standardization Bureau (TSB).

17. These figures were quoted by Helmut Ricke, president of Deutsche Telekom. See Ricke, "Management of Change." OECD calculations show that the needs of the former Soviet Union would be roughly equivalent to twice the total needs of the six countries quoted above. See T. Kelly, "Telecommunications in the Rebirth of Eastern Europe," *OECD Observer* (Paris: OECD, December 1990/January 1991). The total investment needs for Eastern and Central Europe therefore amount to some $140 billion. The resources that Germany expects to spend in order to bring its eastern part (the former DDR) up to the level of its western telecommunications network is about $7 billion.

18. In this respect, also, the likely evolution of the ITU may very well lead the way for other international institutions. As the High Level Committee on the Future of the ITU found: A major challenge here is that individual governments are not likely to be in a position to have a considered global vision. National sovereignty will remain an inhibitor in achieving a global plan and in general there will tend to be a vacuum in global policy setting. The industry members themselves have the opportunity to take a lead in guiding such global policy, with the ITU as a facilitating structure (*Telecommunications Visions of the Future*, p. 13).

19. This challenge is not limited to less advanced economies. For example, in the United States and in Europe, it is estimated that over 80 percent of smaller firms have

no access to electronic data interchange (EDI) techniques and know-how. See T. McCusker, "How to Get from 80 to 100% EDI," *Datamation*, February 1993.

20. For a detailed record of the efforts made from the United States side, see G. Feketekuty, *International Trade in Services* (Cambridge, Mass.: American Enterprise Institute/Ballinger, 1988). The telecommunications aspects of the Uruguay Round negotiations are discussed in Chapter 11 by Nikolaîdis in this volume.

21. For example in Juan Rada, "Information Technology and Services," in *The Emerging Service Economy*, ed. O. Garini (Oxford: Services World Forum/Pergamon Press, 1987).

22. See Bruno Lanvin, "Telecommunications Essential for Development," *Transnational Data Report* 16, no. 1 (January/February 1993). For a detailed exploration of how information technology has affected several services sectors (banking, insurance, tourism, software, accounting, and management consultancy), see Lanvin, *Trading in a New World Order*. On the specific issue of Indian software exports, see also Lanvin, "Le Tiers-Monde regorge de matiere grise, et il a l'intention de s'en servir," *Le Temps Stratégique*, Geneva, September 1990.

23. See Chapter 11 by Nikolaîdis in this volume.

24. Such as those made by SWEDPRO and SITPRO, the trade facilitation bodies of Sweden and the United Kingdom, respectively.

25. As mentioned in the Columbus Ministerial Declaration of October 1994, trade efficiency tries to provide solutions to the "microeconomic issues in international trade"; this is why it is often referred to as the "microeconomic GATT."

26. A trade point combines three main functions: information, facilitation, and connection. It is a place (physical or virtual, depending on the technologies available) where importers and exporters can obtain information on products, prices, and markets; benefit from efficient trade-supporting services (for example, banking, transport, and insurance) and streamlined procedures (for example, customs); and connect to electronic highways for global trade. UNCTAD has established over forty trade points in all parts of the world, and its Trade Point Global Network is emerging as one of the major worldwide networks for trade-related information. For more detailed information on trade points, see E. Messmer, "UN Seeks Backers for Export Trade Centers," *Networld*, July 13, 1992, and "Trade on Better Terms," The *Economist*, March 21, 1993; F. Williams, "UNCTAD to Build Trade Information Network," *Financial Times*, November 18, 1992; or J. Zarocostas, "Technology May Facilitate Trade in Poorer Nations," *Journal of Commerce,* November 18, 1992.

27. LEOS projects such as Iridium or Globalstar have been described since the early 1990s as the global low-cost solutions for mobile telephony by the end of the decade. Officially presented by Motorola at WARC 1992, Iridium stirred some controversy among ITU members, in particular because of the broad frequency allocation it required (which would not allow competition from providers of similar services). Since then, Motorola has returned to a more traditional conception of its system of polar-orbit satellites: Their number, initially planned for seventy-seven (the atomic mass of iridium) was scaled down to sixty-six (the atomic mass of dysprosium, although the project has not been renamed). Globalstar, which is a multinational project combining satellite services and complementary ground networks (most of them already in existence) participated in the first session of UNCTAD's Ad Hoc Working Group on Trade Efficiency (November 1992). Even more recently, a new controversy arose between the sponsors of Iridium and Inmarsat, which plans to offer a similar service in the next few years. While Inmarsat claims that Iridium would have "line-of-sight" problems (compelling users to move around for proper reception), Iridium contends that Inmarsat, with its monopoly on maritime communications, would be an unfair competitor for global mobile telephony. See K. Lynch, "Sky-High Showdown: Inmarsat and Iridium Trying Different Market Approaches," *Communications Week*, August 16, 1993. For most developing countries, mobile telephony represents a major opportunity, since (especially for large countries such as China, India, or Brazil) it can alleviate

considerably the necessity for large-scale investments in cable (or even fiber) networks. Some authors have argued that the technological developments that took place in the past ten years have produced new possibilities for leap-frogging strategies in the less advanced countries. See, for example, C. Antonelli, *The Diffusion of Advanced Telecommunications in Developing Countries* (Paris: OECD Development Center Studies, 1991).

28. See Chapter 9 by Rutkowski in this volume.

CHAPTER 9

1. For an overview of the ITU up to the 1980s, see George A. Codding, Jr., and Anthony M. Rutkowski, *The International Telecommunication Union in a Changing World* (Dedham, Mass.: Artech House, 1982).

2. For more details on the ITU's organizational structure and division of responsibilities, see "The New ITU: Round-Up" (Geneva: Press and Public Relations Service of the International Telecommunication Union, January 1993).

3. While it is not particularly important here, it should be noted that the Radiocommunications Sector also holds regional conferences and world assemblies with specialized functions, as described in "The New ITU."

4. See William J. Drake, "Asymmetric Deregulation and the Transformation of the International Telecommunications Regime," in *Asymmetric Deregulation: The Dynamics of Telecommunications Policies in Europe and the United States*, ed. Eli M. Noam and Gerard Pogorel (Norwood, N.J.: Ablex, 1994), pp. 137–203.

5. *From Semaphore to Satellite* (Geneva: International Telecommunication Union, 1965), p. 45.

6. For a detailed discussion of this initiative, see Anthony M. Rutkowski, *Integrated Services Digital Networks* (Dedham, Mass.: Artech House, 1985).

7. See Drake, "Asymmetric Deregulation," p. 155.

8. The ITU historically had a fairly complex "federal" structure that granted specialized bodies that began outside the union, like the consultative committees on radio and telegraph and telephone, a good deal of autonomy once they were brought into it. This structure has changed somewhat in recent years. For a discussion, see George A. Codding, Jr., and Dan Gallegos, "The ITU's 'Federal' Structure," *Telecommunications Policy* 15 (August 1993): 351–63.

9. For a description and critique of the trade restrictive aspects of this arrangement, see Henry Ergas and Paul Paterson, "International Telecommunications Settlement Arrangements: An Unsustainable Inheritance?" *Telecommunications Policy* 15 (February 1991): 29–48.

10. On the role of the U.S. government in the old regime, see Anthony M. Rutkowski, "The USA and the ITU: Many Attitudes, Few Policies," *Intermedia* 10 (July/September 1982): 33–39; and Drake, "Asymmetric Deregulation."

11. For discussions of the historical evolution of the radio regime, see Codding and Rutkowski, *International Telecommunication Union in a Changing World*; and James G. Savage, *The Politics of International Telecommunications Regulation* (Boulder, Colo.: Westview Press, 1989).

12. For a discussion of the problems involved, see Anthony M. Rutkowski, "Deformalizing the International Radio Arrangements," *Telecommunications Policy* 7 (December 1983): 309–16.

13. For a discussion of WARC politics, see Savage, *Politics of International Telecommunications Regulation*. It should be noted that in addition to the ITU at the international level, there have also existed a broad number of secondary spectrum management-related global and regional organizations. These range from global bodies like the International Civil Aviation Organization that focus on particular radio application areas, to the North

Atlantic Treaty Organization and the Organization of American States, which deal with regional radio spectrum matters.

14. For discussions of INTELSAT and its responses to competitive pressures, see Lee McKnight, "The Deregulation of International Satellite Communications: U.S. Policy and the INTELSAT Response," *Space Communication and Broadcasting* 3 (1985): 39–59; Peter F. Cowhey and Jonathan D. Aronson, "The Great Satellite Shootout," *Regulation*, May/June 1985, pp. 27–36; and Marcellus S. Snow, *The International Telecommunications Satellite Organization—INTELSAT* (Baden-Baden: Nomos Verlagsgesellschaft, 1987).

15. For discussions of this crucial negotiation, see Anthony M. Rutkowski, "Regulation for Integrated Services Networks: WATTC-88," *Intermedia* 14 (May 1986): 10–19; and William J. Drake, "WATTC-88: Restructuring the International Telecommunication Regulations," *Telecommunications Policy* 12 (September 1988): 217–33.

16. For discussions of these changes in regime instruments and rules, see Peter F. Cowhey, "The International Telecommunications Regime: The Political Roots of Regimes for High Technology," *International Organization* 44 (Spring 1990): 169–99; and Drake, "Asymmetric Deregulation."

17. William J. Drake, "The Transformation of International Telecommunications Standardization: European and Global Dimensions," in *Telecommunications in Transition: Policies, Services, and Technologies in the European Economic Community*, ed. Charles Steinfield, Johannes Bauer, and Laurence Caby (Newbury Park, Cal.: Sage, 1994), p. 80.

18. For a discussion of these organizations and their relationship to the ITU, see Drake, "Asymmetric Deregulation and the Transformation of the International Telecommunications Regime."

19. See Richard J. Solomon, "New Paradigms for Future Standards," *Communications and Strategies*, no. 2 (1991): 51–90.

20. The shift toward and significance of open architectures is discussed in Anthony M. Rutkowski, "Open Network Architectures: An Introduction," *Telecommunications* (January 1987): 30–40.

21. For an early discussion of such possibilities, see Anthony M. Rutkowski, "Networking the Telecom Standards Bodies," *ConneXions* 5 (September 1991): 26–35.

22. For discussions of the shift of authority to the GATT, see Jonathan David Aronson and Peter F. Cowhey, *When Countries Talk: International Trade in Telecommunications Services* (Cambridge, Mass.: Ballinger, 1988); Peter F. Cowhey and Jonathan D. Aronson, *Managing the World Economy: The Consequences of Corporate Alliances* (New York: Council on Foreign Relations Press, 1993); Bruno Lanvin, ed., *Global Trade: The Revolution Beyond the Communication Revolution* (Montpellier: IDATE, 1989); William J. Drake and Kalypso Nicolaïdis, "Ideas, Interests, and Institutionalization: 'Trade in Services' and the Uruguay Round," in *International Organization* 46, no. 1 (Winter 1992): 37–100; and Chapter 11 by Nicolaïdis in this volume.

23. For more on the merits of ITU privatization, see Anthony M. Rutkowski, "Privatizing the ITU" (unpublished paper, Geneva, 1990).

24. See Liching Sung, "WARC-92: Setting the Agenda for the Future," *Telecommunications Policy* 16 (November 1992): 624–34.

25. See Chapter 5 by McKnight and Neuman in this volume.

CHAPTER 10

1. In April 1993, the National Institute of Standards and Technology of the U.S. Commerce Department announced the development of the "Clipper Chip." The microcircuit chip was developed by government engineers to scramble telecommunications transmissions

using a government encryption algorithm. The government, through a "key escrow" system, would hold the codes to unscramble all communications using the Clipper Chip. Under the government plan, telecommunications equipment would in effect become "wire-tap ready."

2. See *Computer Associates International v. Altai, Inc.*, 982 F.2d 693 (1992) (adopting rule that allows standards because of program market success to be copyrighted); *Feist Publications v. Rural Telephone Co.*, 499 U.S. 340 (1991) (rejecting copyright protection for "sweat of the brow" compilation of facts).

3. The White House called for universal access and open systems on the NII. See White House Background Paper on the Information Infrastructure (January 11, 1994). Yet, at the same time, the U.S. trade representative criticized the ETSI effort to create more open standards for communications within Europe.

4. See, for example, H. Jeff Smith, "Information Privacy Policies and Practices: Inside the Organization Maze," *Communications of the ACM*, (December 1993),

5. See H. Jeff Smith, *Managing Privacy: Information Technology and Corporate America* (Chapel Hill, N.C.: University of North Carolina Press, 1994).

6. See U.S. Privacy Protection Study Commission, *Personal Privacy in an Information Society: The Report of the Privacy Protection Study Commission* (Washington, D.C.: U.S. Government Printing Office, 1977).

7. The Privacy Act of 1974 addressed public sector information practices. The legislative history noted that the private sector did not pose the same fears as the public sector. See, for example, S. Rep. No. 1183, 93rd Cong., 2nd sess., 14 (1974).

8. In 1974, Congress created an independent commission to study privacy in the United States for both government-held information and privately held information.

9. See 18 U.S.C. 2510 et seq. (the Electronic Communications Privacy Act); 15 U.S.C. 1681 et seq. (the Fair Credit Reporting Act); 47 U.S.C. 609 (the Cable Communications Policy Act). See also *U.S. Privacy Protection Study Commission, Personal Privacy in an Information Society*.

10. See Alain Minc and Simon Nora, *L'informatisation de la société* (Paris: La doc. française, 1978).

11. There are essentially four common law privacy torts: (1) intrusion upon another's seclusion; (2) publication of private facts; (3) portraying another publicly in a false or misleading way; (4) misappropriating the name or likeness of an individual. See Restatement (Second) of Torts, § 652 (1979). These torts are hard to apply in the context of personal information and data processing. Joel R. Reidenberg, "Privacy in the Information Economy: A Fortress or Frontier for Individual Rights?" *Federal Communications Law Journal* 44 (1992): 195–243.

12. See Reidenberg, ibid., note 13.

13. See Paul Schwartz and Joel R. Reidenberg, *A Study of American Data Protection Law: Report to the Commission of the European Community* (forthcoming); Smith, *Managing Privacy*.

14. See, for example, letter, dated May 10, 1993, from Susan Coe Heitsch, vice president, First Card, to Joel R. Reidenberg ("your name was obtained from one of the mailing lists which we purchased. Both the source of this list and the credit criteria which qualified you . . . are proprietary in nature, and for this reason, I am unwilling to disclose this information").

15. See Lawrence M. Fisher, "New Database Ended by Lotus and Equifax," *New York Times*, January 24, 1991, p. D4.

16. See Joel R. Reidenberg, "The Privacy Obstacle Course: Hurdling Barriers to Transnational Financial Services," *Fordham Law Review* 60, no. 6 (1992): S137–S177.

17. Among others, the Danish, Dutch, French, German, and British laws all contain clauses on transborder data flow.

18. The European Union Commission has funded a major comparative law study of European and American privacy norms and a study of the types of personal information flowing between the European Union and the United States. At least one other study examining U.S. data privacy law has also been prepared in the past year for a Canadian government ministry through the University of Montreal.

19. The United States was not a member of the Council of Europe and did not participate in the negotiations.

20. One good example of this problem is the case of medical information. Despite the obvious sensitivity of medical records, the treatment of health data in the United States lacks the most basic protections of fairness to the patient. See Fair Health Information Practices Act, Hearings on H.R. 4077 before the Subcommittee on Information, Justice, Transportation, and Agriculture of the House Committee on Government Operations, 103d Cong., 2nd sess., (May, 1994) (statement of Paul Schwartz, associate professor, School of Law, University of Arkansas, Fayetteville).

21. See Amended Proposal for a Council Directive on the Protection of Individuals with Regard to the Processing of Personal Data and on the Free Movement of Such Data, European Commission Document COM (92) 422 (final SYN 287) (October 1992).

22. See GATT Annex on Telecommunications, Article 5.4; North American Free Trade Agreement, Article 1302(5).

23. See Joel R. Reidenberg, "Rules of the Road for Global Electronic Highways: Merging the Trade and Technical Paradigms," Harvard Journal of Law and Technology 6 (Spring 1993): 287–305.

24. See Amended Proposal.

25. For example, Denmark, France, Germany, the Netherlands, and the United Kingdom all have laws that allow the prohibition of the export of personal information.

26. Telecommunications Network Security, Hearings Before the Subcommittee on Telecommunications and Finance of the House Committee on Energy and Commerce, 103d Cong., 1st sess. (April 1993), statement of Joel R. Reidenberg.

27. See Louis Harris Associates and Alan Westin, The Equifax Report on Consumers in the Information Age, 14–15 (1990).

28. See, for example, Equifax Annual Report (1992); Dun & Bradstreet Annual Report (1993).

29. See Reidenberg, "Rules of the Road."

30. The Computers and Business Equipment Manufacturer's Association was one of the groups in vocal opposition to the proposal. The Commission of the European Union also issued a statement on telecommunications standardization and intellectual property. See Communication of the Commission on Intellectual Property and Standardization, COM (92) 445.

31. There has been significant controversy in the United States, for example, over the grant to Compton for multimedia applications. The U.S. Patent and Trademark Office held hearings during winter 1994 to solicit public comment on the granting of software patents.

32. For example, programming can be embedded on a chip and qualify for sui generis semiconductor chip protection, or stored on a disk and receive copyright protection, or incorporated in hardware and be patented.

33. See Whelan Associates v. Jaslow Dental Laboratories, 797 F.2d 1222 (3d Cir., 1986).

34. The business disincentive to make research investments without proprietary standards can be overcome by government and business partnerships to develop certain technology base standards and promote innovation.

35. See Sega Enterprises v. Accolade, 1993 U.S. App. LEXIS 78 (9th Cir.).

36. See Feist Publications v. Rural Telephone Service, 499 U.S. 340 (1991).

37. See Jean Hughes and Elizabeth Weightman, "EC Database Protection: Fine Tuning the Commission's Proposal," *European Intellectual Property Review* 14 (1992): 147.

38. See, for example, *Computer Associates International v. Altai*, 982 F.2d 693 (2nd Cir., 1992); *Lasercomb America v. Reynolds*, 911 F.2d 970 (4th Cir., 1990); *Feist Publications v. Rural Telephone Co.*, 499 U.S. 340 (1991).

39. The United States, along with other industrialized countries, were opposed to LDC efforts at the United Nations Conference on Trade and Development (UNCTAD) to draft a code for technology transfer.

40. See U.S. International Trade Commission, *Foreign Protection of Intellectual Property Rights and the Effect on U.S. Industry and Trade,* USITC. Pub. no. 2065, February, 1988.

41. GATT Agreement on Trade-Related Aspects of Intellectual Property Rights, Including Trade in Counterfeit Goods, Article 10.

42. North American Free Trade Agreement, Article 1705.

43. See, for example, Reidenberg, "Rules of the Road."

44. Ibid.

45. See National Telecommunications and Information Agency, Information Infrastructure Task Force*, National Information Infrastructure: Agenda for Action* (Washington, D.C.: U.S. Department of Commerce, September 1993).

CHAPTER 11

1. International Trade Statistics (Geneva: General Agreement on Tariffs and Trade, 1993), Table A5, p. 88

2. The World Trade Organization (WTO) will be composed of three pillars: the GATT and all the sectorial codes negotiated under it, the new GATS, and the new Trade Related Intellectual Property Agreement.

3. For discussion of the interests and strategies of Japan and developing countries, see Chapters 7 and 8 in this volume.

4. Bruno Lanvin, ed., *Trading in a New World Order: The Impact of Telecommunications and Data Services on International Trade in Services* (Boulder, Col.: Westview Press, 1993), p. 4.

5. Ibid., p. 24.

6. For a historical analysis of the services negotiations and an assessment of the role of new ideas in the crafting of the GATS, see William Drake and Kalypso Nicolaïdis, "Ideas, Interests, and Institutionalization: 'Trade in Services' and the Uruguay Round," *International Organization* 46, no. 1 (Winter 1992): 37–100.

7. Sectoral committees were also to be put in place that will report directly to the council on the application of the agreement in member states, examine proposals for amending annexes, provide assistance to developing countries, and develop cooperation with other international organizations. The GATS also includes a separate process for dispute settlement and the establishment of panels.

8. The inclusion of all levels of federal authorities was particularly intended for the United States, which was indeed vulnerable throughout the negotiations to accusations on the part of other negotiating parties that commitment on the part of the U.S. government did not guarantee nondiscriminatory practices on the part of state authorities.

9. For an early and most influential discussion, see Gary Sampson and Richard Snape, "Identifying the Issues in Trade in Services," *World Economy* 8 (June 1985): 171–82. See also Drake and Nicolaïdis, "Ideas, Interests and Institutionalization," and Nicolaïdis, "Defining Trade in Services," Working Paper (Geneva: UNCTAD, June 1987).

10. In addition, and in order to provide for special conditions in border areas, members are also allowed to accord advantages to adjacent countries "in order to facilitate exchanges limited to contiguous frontier zones of services that are both locally produced and consumed."

11. These areas of unfinished business included maritime transport, financial services, the movement of labor, and audiovisual services. Talks started again in early May 1994 in Geneva on maritime transport, the movement of labor, and basic telecommunications. Talks on the movement of labor and financial services are due to be concluded in 1995, while those on shipping and telecommunications will be extended until 1996. Negotiations on audiovisual services are open-ended for the moment.

12. Telecommunications and audiovisual services have an estimated global market value of ECU 285 billion and 257 billion, respectively—with the EU's share representing ECU 82 billion and ECU 23 billion. Source: OMSYC 1993 Report.

13. See *Growth, Competitiveness, Employment: The Challenges and Ways Forward into the 21st Century* (White Paper) Commission of the European Communities, Bulletin, 6/93 (Luxembourg: Office of Official Publications of the European Communities, 1993).

14. The framework for setting up trans-European networks is put forth in Title 12 of the Maastricht Treaty on European Union, 1991.

15. Ibid., p. 75.

16. Ibid., p. 95.

17. Ibid., p. 93.

18. The White Paper stressed that along with biotechnology and energy related to the environment, the entertainment industry was one of the three areas where a high number of new jobs could expectedly be created.

19. Ibid., p. 96.

20. The story of the negotiations themselves has been told elsewhere. See, for instance, the contributions by Brian Woodrow and Pierre Sauvé, as well as William Drake, in Charles Steinfield, Johannes M. Bauer, and Laurence Caby, eds., *Telecommunications in Transition: Policies, Services and Technologies in the European Community* (Newbury Park, Calif.: Sage, 1994). See also *Commerce International et Telecommunications*, IDATE Report (Montpellier, 1992).

21. The EU had avoided trying to draw strict definitions of basic and enhanced services, using instead the concepts of competitive and reserved services, the latter being limited to voice telephony.

22. Personal interview, Brussels, March 1994.

23. To be sure, the actual value of national offers put forth under the precepts of the annex depend to a great extent on the regulatory system of the country making the offer. If a country opens its market for value-added services but if it is not possible to connect a leased circuit to the public service for the provision of such services, the offer is to a great extent nullified.

24. Article V.7. To this end the text calls for full participation in the development programs of the International Telecommunication Union, the United Nations Development Program (UNDP), and the World Bank (Article VI.1). Developed countries are also called on to make available to developing countries information on telecommunications technology, although the clause is qualified by "where practicable" (Article VI.2). Private foreign suppliers in developing countries are also encouraged to assist in such transfers.

25. With greater accumulated experience, U.S. service providers may be more efficient in providing a portion of the overall communication service, which may be valued differentially by different consumers, such as guaranteed rerouting in case of system failure and other high security requirements.

26. See Andrew Adonis, "A Brief Encounter, Now Line Is Engaged," *Financial Times*, December 9, 1993. For a discussion of the role of global alliances in forcing new worldwide market access regimes, see Peter Cowhey and Jonathan Aronson, *Managing the World Economy: The Consequences of Corporate Alliances* (New York: Council on Foreign Relations Press, 1994).

27. Council Directive of October 3, 1989, on the coordination of certain provisions laid down by law, regulation, and administrative action in the member states concerning the pursuit of television broadcasting activities, 89/552/EEC *(Official Journal of the European Communities*, 50 [1989]: 298).

28. This excludes news, sports, game shows, advertising and teletex. "European work" is specifically defined according to production and content criteria. In addition, host states were allowed to fix language quotas for radio broadcasters. Individual states continue to be allowed to impose stricter rules upon their national broadcasters; France for instance has a 60 percent minimum European content.

29. The third contentious issue lay in U.S. questioning of the fairness of the tax on blank tapes levied in several European countries, because its proceeds—theoretically surrogates for copyrights on commercial records, often owned by Americans—were then divided among European artists, in contrast with the U.S. approach, where such proceeds are distributed among all creators as a function of their share of consumer expenditures.

30. David Putnam, interviewed in "Riding a Chariot of Fire on the Screen," *Financial Times*, April 11, 1994.

31. White Paper, p. 105.

32. See "Brussels Warns Audio-Visual Sector," *Financial Times*, April 7, 1994. The paper considers such controversial proposals as a European-wide tax on cinema tickets along the lines of the French system—a proposal opposed by some non-French quarters of the commission.

33. During the period, Brussels undertook a review of a five-year exemption from competition law of the leading Hollywood studios' European distribution arrangements. The United States pledged to accept its findings providing the case was given "a transparent, fair, due process hearing on its merits."

34. Personal interview with a member of the European Union Commission, Brussels, March 1994.

35. The OECD has traditionally played a discrete but important role in exploring topics that would in a later phase be included under international institutions with the power to turn its blueprints into binding commitments. In 1992, it set up six working committees on the linkage between trade policies and, respectively, environment, competition, high technology, labor standards, and the tension between regional and multilateral cooperation. For a preliminary summary of this work, see the paper by the chairman of this group, Geza Feketekuty, *The New Trade Agenda* (Washington, D.C.: Group of Thirty, 1992).

36. For a discussion of the emergence of managed mutual recognition in the European Community, see Kalypso Nicolaïdis, "Mutual Recognition among Nations: The European Community and Trade in Services" (Ph.D. diss., Harvard University, 1993).

37. For a recent very thorough overview of the debate see, Ernst Ulrich Petersmann, "International Competition Rules for the GATT-MTO World Trade and Legal System," *Journal of World Trade*, (Winter 1994): 35–83; see also Edward M. Graham's edited volume on competition policy (Washington, D.C.: Institute for International Economics, 1995).

38. Feketekuty, *The New Trade Agenda*, p. 10.

39. See Petersmann, "International Competition Rules for the GATT-MTO World Trade and Legal System," p. 82.

40. For a discussion, see C. D. Ehlermann, "The Contribution of EC Competition Policy to the Single Market," *Common Market Law Review* (1992).

41. See Robert Lawrence, *Regionalism, Multilateralism and Deeper Integration* (Washington, D.C.: Brookings Institution, 1994).

42. For a discussion relating globalization and multilateralism, see, for instance, Charles Oman, *Globalization and Regionalization: The Challenge for Developing Countries* (Paris: OECD, 1994).

43. For a discussion underlying the importance of multilateralism to the postwar system, see John Ruggie, "Multilateralism: The Anatomy of an Institution," in *Multilateralism Matters: The Theory and Praxis of an Institutional Form*, ed. John Ruggie (New York: Columbia University Press, 1993), pp. 3–48.

CHAPTER 12

1. Christopher Farrell, "The Triple Revolution," in *21st Century Capitalism*, Special 1994 Bonus Issue, *Business Week* (1994), pp. 16–25.

2. For a discussion of the tensions between transnationally networked firms and markets, on the one hand, and the capacities of the territorial nation-state, on the other, see William J. Drake, "Territoriality and Intangibility: Transborder Data Flows and National Sovereignty," in Kaarle Nodenstreng and Herbert I. Schiller, eds., *Beyond National Sovereignty: International Communications in the 1990s* (Norwood: Ablex, 1993), pp. 259–313.

3. See Federal Communications Commission, *Second Report and Order, Telephone Company-Cable Television Cross Ownership Rules,* Rec. 5781, 1992.

4. See, for example, Laura D'Andrea Tyson, *Who's Bashing Whom? Trade Conflicts in High-Technology Industries* (Washington, D.C.: Institute for International Economics, 1993); and Robert B. Reich, *The Work of Nations* (New York: Random House, 1991). For a solid, if somewhat acerbic, critique of the competitiveness debate and those involved in it, see Paul R. Krugman, *Peddling Prosperity: Economic Sense and Nonsense in the Age of Diminished Expectations* (New York: W.W. Norton & Co., 1994).

5. The "NREN" label is somewhat misleading since it does not refer to a specific new network, but rather to a broad program of support for high speed networking and super-computing in the Internet environment. See U.S. Congress, *High Performance Computing Act of 1991*, Public Law 12-94, December 9, 1991. For a good collection of essays on the NREN and related issues, see Brian Kahin, ed., *Building Information Infrastructure: Issues in the Development of the National Research and Education Network* (New York: McGraw Hill, 1992).

6. Information Infrastructure Task Force, *The National Information Infrastructure: Agenda for Action* (Washington, D.C.: U.S. Department of Commerce, September 15, 1993), pp. 6–7.

7. See, for example, James Love, "The Clinton Administration's 'Vision' Statement for the National Information Infrastructure," Taxpayer Assets Project Information Policy Note, Washington, D.C., September 24, 1993, in U.S. Congress, *National Communications Infrastructure, Part 3: Hearings before the Subcommittee on Telecommunications and Finance of the Committee on Energy and Commerce*, House of Representatives, 103d Congress, 2nd Session, February 8, 9, and 10, 1994 (Washington, D.C.: GPO, 1994), pp. 379–82.

8. Information Infrastructure Task Force, *The National Information Infrastructure: Agenda for Action*, p. 13.

9. As an independent agency outside the executive branch, the FCC is not formally represented in the IITF's leadership, although staff members do participate in task force activities.

10. On the World Wide Web, the White House is at http://www.whitehouse.gov. The State Department's Foreign Affairs Network (DOSFAN) is at http://dosfan.lib.uic.edu. The IITF's large archive of NII documents is at http://iitf.doc.gov. Congressional legislation and related materials can be found at both http://thomas.loc.gov and http://www.house.gov.

One of the best starting points for a plunge into NII documentation—including a vast array of hypertext linked files from business, government, and non-profit sources—is the home page maintained by Jeffrey Mackie-Mason at the University of Michigan, http://www.ipps.lsa.umich.edu.

11. For a detailed survey of federal agencies' various efforts to advance the NII and employ new technologies and services in their daily operations, see Information Infrastructure Task Force, "NII Principles and Actions: A Checklist of the Clinton Administration's Progress, 1993–94," September 1994.

12. Convergence refers to the elimination of boundaries between formerly distinct media systems, services, and industries.

13. The explosion of corporate alliances in the communications and information world is a recent enough phenomenon that there is not yet any published overview of the hundreds of deals. For assessments of the dynamics underlying the trend, see Robert W. Crandall, "The Economic Impetus for Convergence in Telecommunications," in Crossroads on the Information Highway: Convergence and Diversity in Communications Technologies (Queenstown: The Aspen Institute, 1994), pp. 1–18; OECD, Telecommunications and Broadcasting: Convergence or Collision? (Paris: OECD, 1992); and OECD, Convergence between Communications Technologies: Case Studies from North America and Western Europe (Paris: OECD, 1992). For a journalistic look at some of the corporate strategies and personalities involved in media convergence, see Kevin Maney, Megamedia Shakeout: The Inside Look at the Leaders and Losers (New York: John Wiley, 1995). The strategic alliance mania surrounding the NII is an extension of a pattern that has been taking hold in many industries for over a decade; for a broad discussion, see Peter F. Cowhey and Jonathan D. Aronson, Managing the World Economy: The Consequences of Corporate Alliances (New York: Council on Foreign Relations, 1993).

14. For one of the more spectacular pieces of hero worship, see Elise O'Shaughnessy, "The New Establishment: Power. Influence. Vision." Vanity Fair (February 1995), pp. 209–241.

15. The heads of TCI and Bell Atlantic later admitted that the charge was bogus and that the deal collapsed due to factors internal to their firms. See the interviews with John Malone and Ray Smith, respectively, in David Kline, "Infobahn Warrior," Wired 2 (July 1994): 86–90, 130–131; and David Kline, "Align and Conquer," Wired 3 (February 1995): 110–117, 164. In his interview, Malone joked that Reed Hundt, Chairman of the FCC, should be shot—an indication of the adversarial tone being set in some industry circles. For an administration view, see Larry Irving, "The Death of the National Information Infrastructure, or Don't Believe Everything You Read," presentation to the Association of Local Telecommunications Service Conference, Washington, D.C., May 4, 1994.

16. See, for example, Mark Robichaux and Mary Lu Carnevale, "Will the FCC's Cable Rate Cuts Slow Traffic on Information Superhighway?" Wall Street Journal, February 25, 1994, p. B1; Edmund L. Andrews, "Failed Partners Assert F.C.C. Ruling Killed Pact," New York Times, February 25, 1994, p. C4; and, "Taking the Scenic Route: Is the American Government Delaying the Information Superhighway?" The Economist, April 16, 1994, pp. 67–68, 71.

17. For a vigorous argument along these lines, see Bruce L. Egan, "Building Value Through Telecommunications: Roadblocks on the Information Superhighway," in, Colin Blackman and Hans Schoof, eds., Competition and Convergence, a special issue of Telecommunications Policy 18 (November 1994): 573–87. See also Egan, Information Superhighways: The Economics of Advanced Public Communication Networks (Boston: Artech House, 1991).

18. See the prepared statement of MCI's Bert Roberts Jr., in U.S. Congress, *S. 1822, The Communications Act of 1994: Hearings before the Committee on Commerce, Science, and Transportation*, United States Senate, 103d Congress, 2nd Session, February 23, March 2 and 17, and May 4, 11, 12, 18, 24, and 25, 1994 (Washington, D.C.: GPO, 1994), p. 431. See also the prepared statements of AT&T's Robert Allen, Sprint's William Esrey, CompTel's Bernard Ebbers, and ACTA's John Kane, at pp. 409–17, 444–49, 451–54, and 459–62, respectively, in the same volume. Similar testimony is also contained in U.S. Congress, *National Communications Infrastructure, Part 3*.

19. A detailed discussion of the issues is presented in William J. Baumol and J. Gregory Sidak, *Toward Competition in Local Telephony* (Cambridge, Mass. and Washington, D.C.: The MIT Press and the American Enterprise Institute for Public Policy Research, 1994).

20. For an upbeat assessment of the cable industry's prospects, see George Gilder, "Washington's Bogeyman," *Forbes ASAP*, June 6, 1994, pp. 115–24.

21. On the economic aspects of this issue, see Leland L. Johnson, *Toward Competition in Cable Television* (Cambridge, Mass. and Washington, D.C.: The MIT Press and the American Enterprise Institute, 1994); and Leland L. Johnson and David Reed, *Residential Broadband Services by Telephone Companies?* (Santa Monica: The RAND Corporation, June 1990).

22. For example, see the prepared statement of the NCTA's Decker Anstrom in U.S. Congress, *S. 1822, The Communications Act of 1994: Hearings before the Committee on Commerce, Science, and Transportation*, pp. 263–81.

23. See, for example, the prepared statement of the AITS' Al Devaney in U.S. Congress, *S. 1822, The Communications Act of 1994: Hearings before the Committee on Commerce, Science, and Transportation*, pp. 493–516. Devaney warns of a coming "national information tollroad."

24. See, for example, the statement by the USTA's Richard D'Antonio in U.S. Congress, *S. 1822, The Communications Act of 1994: Hearings before the Committee on Commerce, Science, and Transportation*, pp. 290–92.

25. The restriction involved some murky and badly resolved definitional issues that have continued to plague the current policy discussion. On the peculiar conceptual history of the RBOC ban, see Michael K. Kellog, John Thorne, and Peter W. Huber, *Federal Telecommunications Law* (Boston: Little, Brown, Inc., 1992), pp. 315–27. This 900-page volume also provides a solid overview of federal law on many other issues, circa 1991.

26. For an assessment of the problem, see Jon Katz, "Online or Not, Newspapers Suck," *Wired* 2 (September 1994): 50–58. For a more optimistic evaluation of the possibilities for electronic newspapers, see Roger Fidler, "Newspapers in the Electronic Age," in Frederick Williams and John V. Pavlik, eds., *The People's Right to Know: Media, Democracy, and the Information Highway* (Hillsdale: Lawrence Erlbaum, 1994), pp. 25–45.

27. For a discussion, see the prepared statement of the NAA's Frank Bennack Jr. in U.S. Congress, *S. 1822, The Communications Act of 1994: Hearings before the Committee on Commerce, Science, and Transportation*, pp. 117–21. Similar concerns about RBOC involvement in information services are contained in U.S. Congress, *National Communications Infrastructure, Part 2: Hearings before the Subcommittee on Telecommunications and Finance of the Committee on Energy and Commerce*, House of Representatives, 103d Congress, 2nd Session on H.R. 3626 and H.R. 3636, January 27, February 1, 2, and 3, 1994 (Washington, D.C.: GPO, 1994). In the end, the NAA and RBOCs managed to cut a deal on these safeguard issues.

28. See the prepared testimony of the TIA's John Major in U.S. Congress, *S. 1822, The Communications Act of 1994: Hearings before the Committee on Commerce, Science, and Transportation*, pp. 188–97; and in U.S. Congress, *National Communications Infrastructure, Part 3*, pp. 69–90.

29. Sun Microsystems' Wayne Rosing, quoted in, "Feeling for the Future: A Survey of Television," *The Economist,* February 12, 1994, p. 8.

30. See the prepared statement of Wayne Rosing in U.S. Congress, *National Communications Infrastructure, Part 2,* pp. 345–52.

31. See Taxpayers Assets Project, "Information Policy Note: 'Set-Top' Box Debate and Open Interfaces," Washington, D.C., July 20, 1994. Sun joined citizens groups like People for the American Way and the Media Access Project, firms like Amdahl Corporation and Oracle Corporation, and trade groups like the Software Industries Coalition and the Computer and Communications Industry Association in asking the Senate to support an FCC investigation into broad guidelines for essential interface standards.

32. See the prepared statement of General Instrument's Hal Krisbergh in U.S. Congress, *National Communications Infrastructure, Part 2,* pp. 301–310.

33. Testimony of Microsoft's Nathan Myhrvold, in U.S. Congress, *National Communications Infrastructure, Part 2,* pp. 376–77.

34. "Feeling for the Future: A Survey of Television," *The Economist,* p. 11.

35. One proponent of this kind of vision is Nicholas Negroponte of the MIT Media Lab. See his *Being Digital* (New York: Alfred Knopf, 1995).

36. See, for example, the prepared statement of the National Association of Broadcasters' Ron Loewen and the Association of Independent Television Stations' John Siegel in U.S. Congress, *S. 1822, The Communications Act of 1994: Hearings before the Committee on Commerce, Science, and Transportation,* pp. 220–30.

37. For example, some manufacturers in the so-called grand alliance that developed digital HDTV argue that broadcasters should be allowed to develop such services only if they are committed to pursuing HDTV aggressively and preserving free over-the-air transmission and if they pay the FCC a usage fee for the spectrum. (The grand alliance comprises General Instruments, AT&T, MIT, AT&T, Philips Electronics North America, the David Sarnoff Research Center, Thomson Consumer Electronics, and Zenith Electronics.) On the spectrum flexibility issue, see the prepared statement of Robert Rast in U.S. Congress, *S. 1822, The Communications Act of 1994: Hearings before the Committee on Commerce, Science, and Transportation,* pp. 244-48. For more on the politics of HDTV, see the Chapter by Lee McKnight and W. Russell Neuman in this volume.

38. Quoted in Michael Sullivan-Trainor, *Detour: The Truth about the Information Superhighway* (San Mateo: IDG Books, 1994), p. 178.

39. The term is from Michael Schrage, "Information Age Have-Nots? Let Them Read Books," *Los Angeles Times,* January 6, 1994, pp. D1, D9.

40. Telecommunications Policy Roundtable, "Renewing the Commitment to a Public Interest Telecommunications Policy," in U.S. Congress, *National Communications Infrastructure, Part 2,* pp. 486–88.

41. How contributions to the fund are to be calculated and administered has been the subject of extensive debate. For one of the most interesting proposals, see Eli M. Noam, "Reforming the Financial Support System for Universal Service in Telecommunications," in U.S. Congress, *National Communications Infrastructure, Part 2,* pp. 705–22.

42. For discussions and proposals on these and similar points, see Center for Media Education, "Press Release: 'Information Superhighway Could Bypass Low Income and Minority Communities," Washington, D.C., May 23, 1994; "National Press Foundation, "National Press Forum: Is There a Place for Have-Nots in Cyberspace?—Unofficial Transcript," Washington, D.C., May 24, 1994; Susan G. Hadden, "Technologies of Universal Service," in *Universal Telephone Service: Ready for the 21st Century?* (Queenstown, Md.: The Aspen Institute, 1991), pp. 53–92; and the prepared statement of the Consumer Federation of America's Mark N. Cooper, in U.S. Congress, *S. 1822, The*

Communications Act of 1994: Hearings before the Committee on Commerce, Science, and Transportation, pp. 551–559.

43. For a good discussion, see Computer Professionals for Social Responsibility, *Serving the Community: A Public Interest Vision of the National Information Infrastructure* (Palo Alto: CPSR, October, 1993).

44. See Electronic Frontier Foundation, "Open Platform Campaign: Public Policy for the Information Age," Washington, D.C., November 1, 1993, p. 5.

45. See Alliance for Public Technology, "Connecting Each to All: A Telecommunications Platform for the Information Age," Washington, D.C., 1993.

46. For a good discussion of how consumers may use interactive television-based services and related issues, see W. Russell Neuman, *The Future of the Mass Audience* (New York: Cambridge University Press, 1991).

47. On the relative merits of FTTC and HFC from a public interest perspective, see Mary Gardiner Jones, "NII Networks to the Home: The Impact of Video Dial Tone Networks on Consumer Interests," paper presented to the National Communications Forum, September 19, 1994.

48. For an excellent overview of the civic networking movement and its implications for the NII, see Center for Civic Networking, *A National Strategy for Civic Networking: A Vision of Change,* Washington D.C., October 6, 1993.

49. For an outline of the program, see National Telecommunications and Information Administration, *Telecommunications and Information Infrastructure Assistance Program* (Washington, D.C.: Department of Commerce, 1994). For more on the administration's efforts to develop applications, particularly noncommercial ones, see Information Infrastructure Task Force, *What it Takes to Make it Happen: Key Issues for Applications of the National Information Infrastructure* (Gaithersburg, Md.: National Institute of Standards and Technology, January, 1994); Information Infrastructure Task Force, *The Information Infrastructure: Reaching Society's Goals* (Washington, D.C.: Department of Commerce, 1994); and Office of Science and Technology, *Information Infrastructure Technology and Applications* (Washington, D.C.: The White House, February, 1994).

50. Williams' list of public services includes abortion rights and counselling, alcohol abuse, bilingual instruction, local transportation schedules and conditions, calendars of local events; city and county offices and services, consumer warnings, telephone and other network addresses, divorce laws and counseling, drug abuse, environmental hazards, insurance terms and tips, employment opportunities, adult education and training, library services, and local weather. Optional services include movie reviews, news headlines, recreational attractions, sports events and scores, horoscopes, and television program schedules. See Frederick Williams, "On Prospects for Citizens' Information Services," in Williams and John V. Pavlik, eds., *The People's Right to Know: Media, Democracy, and the Information Highway* (Hillsdale: Lawrence Erlbaum, 1994), pp. 15, 19.

51. See "National Initiative for Humanities and Arts on the Information Highways: A Profile, Final Report," sponsored by the Getty Art History Information Program, The American Council of Learned Societies, and the Coalition for Networked Information, September 1994.

52. For an overview of the laws, regulations, and issues involved in public access television, see Jason Roberts, "Public Access: Fortifying the Electronic Soapbox," *Federal Communications Law Journal* 47 (October 1994): 123–52.

53. For discussions of this crucial issue, see "VDT Rules Could Kill PEG Access," *Community Media Review* 18 (January, 1995): 14; and "Alliance for Community Media Lobbying Packet," Washington, D.C., January, 1995. It should be added that direct broadcast satellite operators also have no such requirements.

54. For a discussion of this struggle, see Robert W. McChesney, *Telecommunications, Mass Media, and Democracy: The Battle for the Control of U.S. Broadcasting, 1928–1935* (New York: Oxford University Press, 1993).

55. See the prepared statement of Jeffrey A. Chester in U.S. Congress, *S. 1822, The Communications Act of 1994: Hearings before the Committee on Commerce, Science, and Transportation*, pp. 297–98.

56. Indeed, a number of sources on Capitol Hill have been quoted as suggesting that a major motivation for action on the part of at least one key senator was to preempt the administration from presenting its own bill. See "Hollings Bill Comes, In Part, Out of Desire to Preempt Administration," *Washington Telecom Week* 3 (February 18, 1994): 4–5.

57. The Communications Act regulates telecommunications common carriers under Title II and cable companies under Title VI, which means that firms in the same markets are subject to different rules. The administration therefore proposed a new elective Title VII that provide a symmetrical framework for the deployment of switched broadband networks. See "Administration White Paper on Communications Act Reforms," in U.S. Congress, *National Communications Infrastructure, Part 2*, pp. 171–81. Critics charged that in an increasingly competitive environment, many firms would have little incentive to choose Title VII treatment. As Eli Noam argued, "the voluntary nature of this regulation makes this approach meaningless. Contract carriers are unlikely to voluntarily assume the obligations of open access, plus universal service, mandatory interconnection and local franchise fees . . . Title VII is not likely to accomplish an opting-in of these new services to common carriage, but to the contrary, it will legitimize an opting-out." See his "Beyond Liberalization II: The Impending Doom of Common Carriage," *Telecommunications Policy* 18 (August 1994): 435–52.

58. For a discussion of the role of game theorists in structuring the auction process and advising the players, see John McMillan, "Selling Spectrum Rights," *Journal of Economic Perspectives* 8 (Summer 1994): 145–62.

59. George Gilder, "Auctioning the Airwaves," *Forbes ASAP,* April 11, 1994, pp. 110–12.

60. Gilder, "Auctioning the Airwaves," p. 112.

61. For a discussion, see General Accounting Office, *Advanced Communications Technologies Pose Wiretapping Challenges*, Briefing Report to the Chairman, Subcommittee on Telecommunications and Finance, Committee on Energy and Commerce, House of Representatives, GAO/IMTEC-92-68BR, July 1992.

62. The decision of the Electronic Frontier Foundation to work with Edwards and Leahy to tighten protections caused a huge rift within the public interest movement. For an overview of and debate on the legislation, see "Special Issue on the Digital Telephony Bill," *Privacy Forum* 3 (October 7, 1994); and "EFF Statement on and Analysis of Digital Telephony Act," October 8, 1994.

63. John Perry Barlow of the Electronic Frontier Foundation, quoted in Peter H. Lewis, "Of Privacy and Security: The Clipper Chip Debate," *New York Times*, April 24, 1994, p. F5. For a broader critique of the initiative, see Barlow, "Jackboots on the Infobahn," *Wired* 2 (April 1994): 40, 44, 46–49.

64. H.R. 3626, "The Antitrust Reform Act of 1993" and H.R. 3636, "National Communications Competition and Information Infrastructure Act of 1993" in *National Communications Infrastructure, Part 2*, pp. 4–77 and 78–116, respectively.

65. *S. 1822, The Communications Act of 1994*, 103d Congress, 2nd Session, February 3, 1994.

66. *H.R. 3636, National Communications Competition and Information Infrastructure Act of 1994*, 103d Congress, 2nd Session, February 10, 1994. This language was added to the bill as reported by the Committee on Energy and Commerce.

67. While the public interest coalition generally supported the VDT provisions, these were not as strong as some members had hoped. For example, the original language required telcos to set aside 75 percent of their VDT capacity for independent programmers, but the final version simply required the RBOCs to have a margin of capacity able to meet the growth in demand. Similarly, PEG programmers would have liked firmer language obligating the RBOCs to abide by the type of commitments contained in many conventional cable franchise agreements. Finally, many consumer advocates maintained that the language on telco-cable buyouts was too permissive. Buyouts were allowed in rural regions, when the VDT system served less than 10 percent of the households in an RBOC telephone service area, or areas with no more than 35,000 inhabitants (or 50,000 inhabitants if the system was not affiliated with a cable system in a contiguous franchise area). Given the size of RBOC telephone service areas and the number of regions that fit the other descriptions, consumer advocates charged that telcos would be able to take over a substantial portion of the cable market in the national aggregate.

68. For example, the Senate bill endorsed the vision of switched, digital broadband services that would allow individuals and organizations to both access and disseminate information in all its forms; required the RBOCs to comply with procompetitive requirements in the local loop like open interconnection, nondiscriminatory access, and unrestricted resale; created a Joint Board on Universal service, and called on the FCC and the States to establish regulations obliging service providers to contribute to its preservation, as well as to promote access to advanced services by the disabled and to periodically revise the definition of universal service in light of technological change; required telcos to offer services at preferential rates to certain educational institutions, health care facilities, local and state governments, public broadcasting stations, public libraries, and other public entities; required that telcos provide either conventional cable or common carrier VDT platform services through separate subsidiaries; gave the FCC an explicit mandate to promote interconnection and interoperability, including to establish standards when industry participants failed to reach agreement; allowed public utility companies to provide telecommunications services; called on the FCC to modify broadcast ownership rules as necessary, and to grant spectrum flexibility for the provision of new services in exchange for a fee equivalent to those collected in the spectrum auctions; and preempted state and local regulatory authority over market entry in telecommunications and related issues.

69. Quoted in Rick Wartzman and John Harwood, "For the Baby Bells, Government Lobbying is Hardly Child's Play," *The Wall Street Journal,* March 15, 1994, p. A15.

70. Wartzman and Harwood, "For the Baby Bells, Government Lobbying is Hardly Child's Play."

71. Bob Dole, "Statement on Hollings-Danforth Telecommunications Bill (S. 1822)," September 23, 1994.

72. Ernest Hollings, "Statement on the Withdrawal of S. 1822," September 23, 1994.

73. On the monetary and other dynamics of the leadership transition, see Christopher Conte, "What's Going On with the National Information Infrastructure," The Benton Foundation, Washington, D.C., January, 1995. On February 7, 47 public interest organizations wrote a letter to the heads of the House Commerce Committee and Subcommittee on Telecommunications and Finance protesting the closed door meetings and asking that their views be heard.

74. Alvin Toffler, *The Third Wave* (New York: William Morrow, 1980).

75. Quoted in Michael Kinsley, "Let Them Eat Laptops," *New Yorker,* January 1995, p. 5.

76. Representative Michael Oxley and Senator Larry Pressler quoted in Edmund L. Andrews, "Phone Bill Lobbyists Wear Out Welcome," *New York Times,* March 20, 1995, p. C9.

77. The bill reads: "Universal service is an evolving level of intrastate and interstate telecommunications services that the Commission, based on recommendations from the

public, congress, and [the newly created] Federal-State joint board periodically convened under [the act], and taking into account advances in telecommunications and information technologies and services, determines should be provided at just, reasonable, and affordable rates to all Americans, including those in rural and high-cost area and those with disabilities, to enable them to participate effectively in the economic, academic, medical, and democratic processes of the Nation . . . universal service shall include any telecommunications services that the Commission determines have, through the operation of market choices by customers, been subscribed to by a substantial majority of residential customers." U.S. Senate, *S.652 The Telecommunications Competition and Deregulation Act of 1995*, pp. 39–40.

78. Among other things, H.R. 1555 requires the FCC to establish regulation promoting movement toward open interconnection and access in the local loop (but does not delay RBOC entry into long-distance until this is achieved), and limits the Department of Justice to a consultative role on the latter score (*H.R. 1555* is somewhat stronger than S. 652 in this regard); preempts state and local regulations on entry and related matters; speeds RBOC entry into the manufacturing of equipment; allows telco-cable buyouts under a number of conditions (that is, in rural areas, where the cable system serves less than 10 percent of households in an RBOC telephone service area—these are often huge—and in areas of less than 35,000 inhabitants, or where the cable system is not in one of the top twenty-five markets); allows common carriers to establish cable systems; allows RBOCs to provide information services and electronic publishing through separate affiliates or joint ventures in which they do not have more than a 50 percent equity interest; establishes vague guidelines on universal service and access by public institutions that are generally weaker than those in S. 652; deregulates cable television rates and bars rate-of-return regulation in telephony; provides broadcasters with spectrum flexibility, but stipulates that they must give up their existing license when granted additional spectrum; raises the television broadcasting ownership ceiling to 35 percent of the national audience, and allows greater in-region consolidation within broadcasting and between broadcasting and other media; mandates television V chips for parental blocking; and sends a rather mixed message regarding Internet censorship (while one provision prohibits FCC censorship and protects operators and users from liability, another buried in the Managers' Amendment and passed without much acknowledgment imposes fines and jail terms on people who describe sexual or excretory actions and organs to minors, for example, an eighteen-year-old talking to a seventeen-year-old). The few clear public interest protections include the requirement that VDT platforms be offered in-region through a separate subsidiary, have enough capacity to meet the growth in demand, and do not discriminate among video programmers on the basis of content; the application of PEG access requirements to VDT platforms under conditions broadly comparable to those in cable franchise agreements; the FCC obligation to supervise certain aspects of network planning and adopt regulations ensuring the competitive availability of navigation devices and set-top boxes; the requirement that RBOCs provided network access and interconnection to independent electronic publishers at just and reasonable rates; and the establishment of a Telecommunications Development Fund using interest payments on spectrum auction deposits to provide seed money for small businesses.

79. See Office of the Press Secretary, The White House, "Administration Statement on Senate Passage of S. 652," June 15, 1995; Office of the Press Secretary, The White House, "Statement by the President on *H.R. 1555*," July 31, 1995; and Office of the Vice President, The White House, "Statement by Vice President Gore on *H.R. 1555*," August 3, 1995. For detailed administration critiques of the two bills, see "Administration Concerns Regarding S. 652: The Telecommunications Competition and Deregulation Act of 1995," April 19, 1995; and "Administration Comments on *H.R. 1555*: The Communications Act

of 1995, and Related Legislation Before the House of Representatives," May 15, 1995. All these documents are available on the World Wide Web at http://iitf.doc.gov.

CONCLUSION

1. The key bills at the time of publication were S. 652 and H.R. 1556, both discussed in Chapter 12 of this volume.

2. On the increasing convergence of the Internet and computing, see John W. Verity with Robert D. Hof, "Planet Internet: How the Center of the Computing Universe has Shifted," *Business Week*, April 3, 1995, pp. 118–124.

3. Anthony Smith, *The Age of Behemoths: The Globalization of Mass Media Firms* (New York: Priority Press Publications, 1991), p. 71.

4. One bill proposed in the House, H.R. 514, would lift the limitations on foreign ownership in broadcasting. This would represent yet another blow to the provision of diverse, locally-oriented content. Foreign ownership questions are better left to the executive branch to handle in the context of international trade negotiations.

5. Apple Computer Inc., "In the Matter of Allocation of Spectrum in the 5 GHz Band to Establish a Wireless Component of the Nation Information Infrastructure—Petition for Rulemaking, RM-8653," May 24, 1995.

6. The Senate bill requires that a RBOC establish a separate subsidiary to provide in-region long-distance, manufacturing, and information services, but it does not require this for the provision of common carrier VDT. Nor do cable companies and public utilities need separate subsidiaries when providing telecommunications services. The final House bill is better in this regard; as amended its separate subsidiary requirements for the RBOCs include video services.

7. As Herbert Dordick summarizes the situation, "In the best of all possible worlds, ensuring the availability of free and uncensored sources of information requires that conduit providers should not be content providers. Anything less will not meet the promise of information abundance. However, in the real world, a new common-carrier model needs to be crafted, one that allows a carrier to be both transporter and provider of content, but only if the carrier guarantees access to all other information providers," Chapter 6, p. 170.

8. The sole safeguards are the RBOC separate subsidiary requirements in both bills, and the House bill's call for just and reasonable rates for independent electronic publishers and information services.

9. National Research Council, *Realizing the Information Infrastructure: Report of the NRENAISSANCE Committee* (Washington, D.C.: National Academy Press, 1994), p. 13. The case for government involvement is elaborated further by Linda Garcia and colleagues in *Office of Technology Assessment, Global Standards: Building Blocks for the Future* (Washington, D.C.: OTA, March, 1992).

10. National Research Council, *Realizing the Information Infrastructure*, 1994, p. 14.

11. *H.R. 1555* addresses this issue by calling on the FCC to adopt regulations to ensure the competitive availability of navigational devices; however, efforts to insert parallel language in S. 652 were defeated.

12. See Taxpayer Assets Project/Ad Hoc Coalition for Low Cost ISDN, "Background Notes on ISDN (Integrated Services Digital Network) and Telephone Rates," May 15, 1995.

13. S. 1822 as introduced in the 103d Congress stated that "it shall be the duty of all telecommunications carriers that use public rights of way to permit educational institutions, health care institutions, local and state governments, public broadcast stations, public libraries, other public entities, community newspapers, and broadcasters in the

smallest markets to obtain access to intrastate and interstate services provided by such carriers at preferential rates." See U.S. Senate, *S. 1822, The Communications Act of 1994*, 103d Congress, 2nd Session, February 3, 1994, p. 13.

14. See Henry Geller, *1995–2005: Regulatory Reform for Principal Electronic Media— Position Paper* (Washington, DC: The Annenberg Washington Program, November 1994), p. 15. For additional discussion of proposed reform of the public trustee model, see Geller, "Broadcasting," in Paula Newberg, ed., *New Directions in Telecommunications Policy, Volume I—Regulatory Policy: Telephony and Mass Media* (Durham: Duke University Press, 1989), pp. 124–154.

15. Geller, *1995–2005*, p. 15.

16. Figure from the Corporation for Public Broadcasting, cited in *Quality Time? The Report of the Twentieth Century Fund Task Force on Public Television,* with Background Paper by Richard Somerset-Ward (New York: The Twentieth Century Fund Press, 1993), p. 152.

17. *Quality Time?* p. 4.

18. The feeding frenzy about dirty type and pictures is part of a larger phenomenon. After a year or so of enthusiastic coverage of the Internet, much of the general interest press has veered toward backlash stories about how the Internet is a threatening, seedy place populated by weirdos and/or an over-hyped disappointment that is no substitute for real life. The most elaborate exposition of the latter theme is, Clifford Stoll, *Silicon Snake Oil: Second Thoughts on the Information Highway* (New York: Doubleday, 1995).

19. What was difficult to anticipate was just how "Internet-unaware" the floor debate would be, and how summarily the 35,000 petitions from Internet users brought in by Senator Patrick Leahy would be dismissed as irrelevant. Senator Russell Feingold's brilliant critique of the amendment also fell on deaf ears, and the Senate passed the amendment on a 84 to 16 vote.

20. For one of many good overviews, see Electronic Frontier Foundation, "Constitutional Problems with the Communications Decency Amendment: A Legislative Analysis by the Electronic Frontier Foundation," in EFFector Online 8 (June 16, 1995): 1–8.

21. For cross-national comparisons that underscore the limited nature of privacy protection in the United States, see Colin J. Bennett, *Regulating Privacy: Data Protection and Public Policy in Europe and the United States* (Ithaca: Cornell University Press, 1992); and David. H. Flaherty, *Protecting Privacy in Surveillance Societies: The Federal Republic of Germany, Sweden, France, Canada & the United States* (Chapel Hill: University of North Carolina Press, 1989).

22. For a fine discussion of the digital persona in the age of pervasive computer tracking, see Philip E. Agre, "Surveillance and Capture: Two Models of Privacy," in, Agre, ed., *The Digital Individual*, a special issue of *The Information Society* 10, no. 2 (1994): 101–27.

23. For two strikingly different views on the commodification of personal information, see Anne Wells Branscomb, *Who Owns Information? From Privacy to Public Access* (New York: Basic Books, 1994); and Oscar H. Gandy, Jr., *The Panoptic Sort: A Political Economy of Personal Information* (Boulder: Westview Press, 1993).

24. IITF, Privacy Working Group, "Request for Comments on the Draft Principles for Providing and Using Personal Information and their Commentary," April 21, 1994. An interesting critique of the draft principles was presented in a letter from the Electronic Frontier Foundation, available on the World Wide Web at http://eff.org.

25. See IITF, "A Preliminary Draft Report of the Working Group on Intellectual Property Rights," July, 1994.

26. For an overview, see The White House, *Technology for Economic Growth: A New Direction to Build Economic Strength* (Washington, D.C.: U.S. Government Printing Office, February 22, 1993).

27. See Lewis M. Branscomb, ed., *Empowering Technology: Implementing a U.S. Strategy* (Cambridge: MIT Press, 1993).

28. Applications policies refer to the use of networks and information resources in different functional domains—for example, telemedicine, distance education, networked libraries, and so on.

29. The noncommercial sector that exists alongside the public and private sectors accounts for 6 percent of GNP and 9 percent of national employment; this figure is likely to grow in the coming years. See Jeremy Rifkin, *The End of Work: The Decline of the Global Labor Force and the Dawn of the Post-Market Era* (New York: G.P. Putnam's Sons, 1995), pp. 240–41.

30. Among notable recent OTA reports in this area are *Critical Connections: Communication for the Future* (Washington, D.C.: Government Printing Office, January 1990); *Global Standards: Building Blocks for the Future* (Washington, D.C.: Government Printing Office, March 1992); *U.S. Telecommunications Services in European Markets* (Washington, D.C.: Government Printing Office, August 1993); *Making Government Work: Electronic Delivery of Federal Services* (Washington, D.C.: Government Printing Office, September 1993); *Electronic Enterprises: Looking to the Future* (Washington, D.C.: Government Printing Office, May 1994); *Information Security and Privacy in Network Environments* (Washington, D.C.: Government Printing Office, September 1994); and *Teachers & Technology: Making the Connection* (Washington, D.C.: Government Printing Office, April 1995).

31. This point is made in Council on Competitiveness, *Breaking the Barriers to the National Information Infrastructure—A Conference Report* (Washington, D.C.: December 1994).

32. For a detailed if slightly imbalanced discussion, see Rifkin, *The End of Work*, 1995.

33. For detailed discussions of such practices, see Harley Shaiken, *Work Transformed: Automation and Labor in the Computer Age* (New York: Holt, Rinehart and Winston, 1984); and Shoshana Zuboff, *In the Age of the Smart Machine: The Future of Work and Power* (New York: Basic Books, 1988).

34. For various proposals, see Indu B. Singh and Ted Y. Joseph, "Restructuring Telecommunications and Information Policy Making: A Proposal for the Bush Administration," *Telematics and Informatics* 6 (January 1989): 27–35; Stuart N. Brotman, "The Council of Communications Advisors: The Right Place for Executive Branch Communications Policymaking, the Right Time for Change," (Washington, D.C.: The Annenberg Washington Program, 1989); Joan M. McGivern, "U.S. International Telecommunications and Information Policy: Congress Considers Reorganizing Policymaking," *Law and Policy in International Business* 15 (1983), pp. 1297–1332; *International Information Flow: Forging a New Framework, Thirty-Second Report by the Committee on Government Operations, Together with Additional Views,* 96th Congress, 2nd Session, House Report No. 96-1535, 1980; and National Telecommunications and Information Administration, *Long Range Goals in International Telecommunications and Information: An Outline for United States Policy,* printed for the Use of the Senate Committee on Commerce, Science and Transportation, 98th Congress, 1st Session, 1983.

35. Stuart N. Brotman, "The Council of Communications Advisors," 1989.

36. Many state and municipal governments have launched interesting programs for local information infrastructures. See Edwin B. Parker and Heather E. Hudson, with Don A. Dillman, Sharon Strover, and Frederick Williams, *Electronic Byways: State Policies for Rural Development Through Telecommunications* (Boulder: Westview Press, 1992); and The Center for Civic Networking, *A National Strategy for Civic Networking: A Vision of Change* (Washington, D.C.: CCN, October 1993). For one city's approach, see Mayor's Advisory Committee on the City of the Future, *San Diego: City of the Future—The Role of*

Telecommunications (San Diego State University: International Center for Communications, March 1994).

37. International Commission for the Study of Communication Problems, *Many Voices, One World: Towards a New More Just and More Efficient World Information and Communication Order* (New York: Unipub, 1980).

38. As a National Research Council report argues, "It is not appropriate for U.S. private or government groups to try to dictate national network approaches to other countries despite the fact that many U.S. companies are competing in foreign countries for intra- and international telecommunications business...[foreign networks] should be considered as peers to the U.S. networks, and it should be understood that the 'global NII' will likely not be a reflection of the U.S. NII." See National Research Council, *Realizing the Information Infrastructure*, pp. 275, 273.

39. Al Gore and Ron Brown, *Global Information Infrastructure: Agenda for Cooperation* (Washington, D.C.: Government Printing Office, February 1995).

40. See the transcript, "The Emerging Global Information Infrastructure: Department of Commerce International Telecommunications Hearing, July 27 and 28, 1994," available on the World Wide Web at http://iitf.doc.gov.

41. For a discussion, see William J. Drake, "The Transformation of International Telecommunications Standardization: European and Global Dimensions," in Charles Steinfield, Johannes Bauer, and Laurence Caby, eds., *Telecommunications in Transition: Policies, Services, and Technologies in the European Economic Community* (Newbury Park: Sage, 1994), pp. 71–96.

42. For an excellent overview of the problem and the options for change, see Henry Ergas and Paul Paterson, "International Telecommunications Settlement Arrangements: An Unsustainable Inheritance?" *Telecommunications Policy* 15 (February 1991), pp. 29–48. On the role of accounting and settlements in the broader regime context, see William J. Drake, "Asymmetric Deregulation and the Transformation of the International Telecommunications Regime," in Eli M. Noam and Gerard Pogorel, eds., *Asymmetric Deregulation: The Dynamics of Telecommunications Policies in Europe and the United States* (Norwood: Ablex, 1994), pp. 137–203.

43. For an assessment of the institutionalization process, see William J. Drake and Kalypso Nicolaïdis, "Ideas, Interests, and Institutionalization: 'Trade in Services' and the Uruguay Round," in Peter M. Haas, ed., *Knowledge, Power and International Policy Coordination, a special issue of International Organization* 45 (Winter 1992): 37-100.

44. Our distribution system for audiovisual services is no less protectionist than that of the Japanese automobile industry. When was the last time anyone saw a Belgian film at the local cineplex or watched an Italian soap opera on television? U.S. distributors claim that foreign products are not good enough, or that the public will not tolerate dubbed or subtitled programming, and yet we insist that the Japanese buy automobiles with the steering wheels on the wrong side.

45. Privacy was only one issue that divided governments in the TDF debate; for a broad overview, see William J. Drake, "Territoriality and Intangibility: Transborder Data Flows and National Sovereignty," in Kaarle Nordenstreng and Herbert I. Schiller, eds., *Beyond National Sovereignty: International Communications in the 1990s* (Norwood: Ablex, 1993), pp. 259–313.

46. For more on the privacy issue, see Joel Reidenberg, "A Commentary on Data Protection, Privacy and Regulatory Conflicts between the European Community and the United States," *Access Reports*, May 1, 1991, pp. 5–9.

47. Independent Commission for World Wide Telecommunications Development, *The Missing Link* (Geneva: International Telecommunication Union, December 1984), p. 13.

48. For a detailed assessment of the current situation, see *World Telecommunication Development Report* (Geneva: International Telecommunication Union, 1994).

49. Karen Lynch, "Telecoms Funding Body Set," *Communications Week International,* February 2, 1995, p. 3.

50. For discussions, see Carl Malamud, *Exploring the Internet: A Technical Travelogue* (Englewood Cliffs: Prentice Hall, 1992); and William J. Drake, "The Internet Religious War," *Telecommunications Policy* 17 (December 1993), pp. 643–49.

51. Quoted in David L. Wilson, "Vice President Gore Says National Data Highway Must be 'Open and Accessible to Everyone,'" *The Chronicle of Higher Education,* April 6, 1994, p. A.28.

‖ INDEX

▌ ABOUT THE AUTHORS

François Bar is an assistant professor of communication at the University of California, San Diego (UCSD). Before coming to UCSD, he served as program director for the Berkeley Roundtable on the International Economy (BRIE), at the University of California, Berkeley, in charge of BRIE's research programs on telecommunications policy and information networking. He remains associated with BRIE as a senior research fellow. Professor Bar is also a visiting professor at the THESEUS Institute in Sophia-Antipolis, France, where he teaches telecommunications economics, policy, and government-business relations.

Peter Cowhey is a professor of political science and international relations at the University of California, San Diego. Beginning in September 1994, he is on leave from UCSD for two years while serving as senior adviser in the International Bureau at the Federal Communications Commission. He has also served as a consultant for AT&T and other major communications companies. Professor Cowhey is the author (with Jonathan David Aronson) of *Managing the World Economy: The Consequences of Corporate Alliances* (Council on Foreign Relations Press, 1993) and numerous studies on the international communications industry.

Herbert S. Dordick is a visiting professor of communication at the University of California, San Diego. He has taught previously at the Annenberg School for Communications at the University of Southern California and at Temple University, from which he recently retired. Professor Dordick has written widely in the field of telecommunications and is the author of *Understanding Modern Telecommunications* (McGraw Hill, 1986); *The Information Society: A Retrospective View* (Sage, 1993); and *The Emerging Network Marketplace* (Ablex, 1981). In the early 1970s, he served as director of the Office of Telecommunications for the City of New York.

William J. Drake is an assistant professor of communication at the University of California, San Diego. His research, consulting, and teaching activities focus on the political economy of national and international telecommunications and information, particularly international regulations and standardization, trade in services, transborder data flows, the global information economy, and the changing role of multilateral institutions. He is currently working on a book on the historical evolution and contemporary transformation of the international telecommunications regime.

Linda Garcia is a project director and senior associate at the Office of Technology Assessment (OTA), a research arm of the U.S. Congress. As a member of the Telecommunications and Computer Technologies program, she focuses on information technology and education, human resources for information technology research and development, and information policy. In her eighteen years at OTA, she has served as project director for many OTA reports, including *Intellectual Property Rights in the Age of Electronics and Information*; *Critical Connections: Communication for the Future*; and *The Electronic Enterprise*. At present, she is heading a new study on Global Communications: Issues and Technology.

Henry Geller is a communications fellow with the Markle Foundation and a senior fellow with the Annenberg Washington Program of Northwestern University. He is also visiting professor of the practice of telecommunications policy at the Terry Sanford Institute of Public Policy at Duke University. From 1978 to 1981, Mr. Geller was assistant secretary for communications and information and administrator of the National Telecommunications and Information Administration (NTIA) in the U.S. Department of Commerce. From 1964 to 1970, he served as general counsel of the Federal Communications Commission. In all these capacities, he has focused on telecommunications policy issues and research.

Bruno Lanvin is head of the strategic planning unit of the Special Program for Trade Efficiency of the United Nations Conference on Trade and Development (UNCTAD) and deputy executive secretary of the United Nations International Symposium on Trade Efficiency (UNISTE). Through the Special Program, the United Nations is supporting the establishment and interconnection of several hundred "Trade Points," making extensive use of the Internet, in an effort to make trade practices more efficient. A United Nations specialist in international trade issues, Mr. Lanvin has been responsible for research, analyses, and negotiations related to technology and trade. Mr. Lanvin is the author of many publications on technology and international trade, including *Global Trade* (IDATE, 1989) and *Trading in a New World Order* (Westview Press, 1993).

Lee McKnight is a lecturer in the Massachusetts Institute of Technology's Technology and Policy Program. He is also associate director for research and management of the MIT Research Program on Communications Policy, a research program on interface technologies and their strategic and policy implications for high resolution systems and networked computing. He has consulted on national and international telecommunications and information technologies, markets, and policy for public and private organizations. He is a coauthor of *The Gordian Knot: Political Gridlock and the Communications Revolution* (MIT Press, forthcoming 1995).

W. Russell Neuman is the Edward R. Murrow Professor of International Communications and director of the Murrow Center at the Fletcher School of Law and Diplomacy at Tufts University. He is also a research fellow in the MIT Research Program on Communications Policy and the Media Lab. He has consulted for media, telecommunications, and publishing firms, and has testified before Congress on information infrastructure issues. His current research focuses on the economics, regulation, and social impact of new media technologies. His books include *The Gordian Knot* (MIT Press, forthcoming 1995); *Common Knowledge* (University of Chicago Press, 1992); *The Telecommunications Revolution* (Routledge, 1992); and *The Future of the Mass Audience* (Cambridge University Press, 1991).

Kalypso Nicolaïdis is assistant professor at the Kennedy School of Government of Harvard University. She also teaches at the Ecole Nationale d'Administration in Paris. Her current research concerns the post-Uruguay Round trade agenda, including world antitrust policies, standardization, and regulatory conflicts associated with the implementation of the new services regime. She has published on topics including the European Community, Eastern Europe, and the GATT and is the editor of *Strategic Trends in Services: An Enquiry into the World Services Economy* (Harper and Row, 1989). Professor Nicolaïdis is currently the chairman of Services World Forum, an international lobbying and research group.

Eli M. Noam is professor of finance and economics at the Columbia University Graduate School of Business and director of the Columbia Institute for Tele-Information (CITI)—an independent research center focusing on strategy, management, and policy issues in telecommunications, computing, and electronic mass media. Professor Noam has also served as public service commissioner engaged in the telecommunications and energy regulation of New York State. His publications include over a dozen books, including *Television in Europe* (Oxford University Press, 1992), and about 200 articles on domestic and international telecommunications, television, information, and regulation.

Joel R. Reidenberg is an associate professor of law at Fordham University in New York City. Prior to his faculty appointment in 1990, he practiced law in the international telecommunications group of Debevoise & Plimpton and served as an intellectual property fellow at Prométhée, a European policy studies center based in Paris. In 1994, the U.S. Congress Office of Technology Assessment appointed Professor Reidenberg to serve as a privacy expert on the advisory panel for a congressional study of information technology for control of money laundering. He has also testified on fair information practices before the House Subcommittee on Telecommunications and Finance of the U.S. Congress and before the President's Information Infrastructure Task Force.

Anthony M. Rutkowski is the executive director of The Internet Society—the global international organization that fosters the development of Internet technologies, networks, applications, and use. From 1992 to 1994, he was director of technology assessment in the Strategic Planning Group of Sprint International, and from 1987 to 1992, he was counselor to two different secretary-generals of the International Telecommunications Union (ITU) in Geneva. Mr. Rutkowski is also the former publisher and editor-in-chief of *Telecommunications* magazine and served as staff advisor to two chief scientists of the Federal Communications Commission.

Richard Jay Solomon is associate director for technology of the MIT Research Program on Communications Policy. He has consulted extensively for domestic and international firms on telecommunications and new technologies and has testified before Congress on these issues. He has prepared detailed research for the congressional Office of Technology Assessment and the Organization for Economic Cooperation and Development on intellectual property, database access, national infrastructure, and network security. He is the author of numerous articles and a coauthor of *The Gordian Knot* (MIT Press, forthcoming 1995).